Children: The Early Years

Dr. Celia A. Decker
Professor of Home Economics
Northwestern State University of Louisiana
Natchitoches, Louisiana

REBECCA LAWRENCE

JOHN SHAW

JOHN SHAW

The Goodheart-Willcox Company, Inc.
South Holland, Illinois

Library of Congress Catalog Card Number 89-30203
International Standard Book Number 0-87006-747-8

1234567890-90-9876543210

Library of Congress Cataloging in Publication Data

Decker, Celia Anita.
  Children—the early years.

  Includes index.
  1. Child development. 2. Child psychology.
  I. Title.
HQ767.9.D43 1990 155.4 89-30203
ISBN 0-87006-747-8

Introduction

JOHN SHAW

Children: The Early Years helps you understand how to work with and care for children as they grow. It explains how children change as they grow physically, mentally, socially, and emotionally. And it helps you apply what you've learned to meet children's needs in the best possible ways.

Children are different from adults. For this reason, you need to know how children grow and develop in order to work with children effectively. This text begins by explaining the basics of learning about children. It helps you understand why studying child development is important whether you become a parent, work in a child-related field, or just spend time with children occasionally. It also discusses the choices and preparation involved in becoming a parent.

This text takes you through each stage of development from prenatal through school-age. As you study each stage, the text presents the facts and theories involved in the child's development. Each part uses many examples to help you apply this information when working with children in each stage.

Children: The Early Years helps you explore how family situations affect children. The special needs and concerns of children with developmental differences are explored. And ways that you can care for children — through play activities, through keeping children healthy and safe, through group programs, and through careers — are presented.

Contents

JOHN SHAW

JOHN SHAW

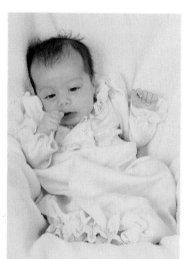

JOHN SHAW

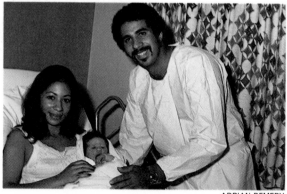

ADRIAN DEMERY

5

part three
Infants

JOHN SHAW

EVENFLO PRODUCTS CO., DIV. OF QUESTOR

6

part four
Toddlers

JOHN SHAW

part five
Preschoolers

JOHN SHAW

JOHN SHAW

part six
School-age children

JOHN SHAW

PHOTO COURTESY OF FUJI PHOTO FILM

part seven
Special considerations

JOHN SHAW

JOHN SHAW

10

part eight
Caring for children

JOHN SHAW

JOHN SHAW

Getting ready for the baby

COSCO PETERSON

Just enjoying each other

JOHN SHAW

After teaching so long, he's still learning

Grandma's pride and joy

part one

Children in today's world

Just swingin' in the hammock with Daddy

Children are an important part of society. By studying them, you can learn how to help children grow and develop into happy, healthy adults.

1

Learning about children

After studying this chapter, you will be able to:
- ☐ List some reasons for learning about children.
- ☐ Explain what is meant by the term child development.
- ☐ Describe three forces promoting growth and development.
- ☐ Explain and give examples of some of the major principles of development.

Everywhere you look, people are talking, writing, and reading about children. People are concerned about children themselves. They want to know how children grow and develop. They want to learn ways to foster "good" changes in children and prevent problems in the home, the school, and other settings. People are also concerned about children's surroundings. They want to know how care products, toys, schools, and other factors affect children. See 1-1.

Children are not only discussed over the phone or backyard fence, but in meetings and workshops for parents and for adults with careers in child-related fields. Mass media covers these topics, too—in news broadcast features, TV and radio talk shows, and public service broadcasts. Writing on children and their needs is found in books, pamphlets, magazines, and newspapers. We are a *child-centered society*—a society that sees children as important and that works for the good of children.

WHY STUDY CHILDREN?

Being an adult in a child-centered society is not easy. Helping children involves more than wanting to meet children's needs. It involves knowing how to meet their needs. And knowing how requires much effort. Before studying how adults can meet children's needs, you need to ask why you should study children.

To pass down culture

Both children and adults are part of a culture. *Culture* is the way of life for a group of people. It includes a group's language, attitudes, values, rituals, and skills. What a culture expects of its members is handed down from adult to child.

The process of handing down the culture is called *enculturation*. The only way for enculturation to happen is through children, 1-2. Thus, children make it possible for a culture to continue. Children of today determine the future of our society.

To protect children

Children are easily hurt because they are physically weaker than adults and they cannot reason as adults. Children have not learned how to relate to others as well as adults. Thus, children must be protected.

Over the years, the treatment of children has become more humane. The shift toward more humane treatment has come from both social policies and rights. *Social policies* are broad ways of thinking and working on behalf of others. Social policies for children have helped meet family needs such as children's health services, recreational programs, day care programs, schools, and juvenile courts. *Rights* usually come out of social policy. But unlike social policy, rights carry a claim and can thus be enforced by law.

The law protects children from the results of their own lack of judgement. For instance, children are not held responsible for their contracts. Neglected children are entitled to protective action of juvenile courts such as placement in foster care. More recently, children have been given the rights of due process and fair treatment in juvenile courts and schools. And, in many states, children may receive medical information without parental consent.

1-1 Many people are concerned about how new technology affects children.

1-2 Learning family rituals is part of a child's enculturation.

Parents have the rights of guardianship. Parents determine the upbringing of children. For instance, they control the level of financial support of children, religious and moral teachings, the kind and extent of their education, and choices concerning health care.

Society through government can set up regulations on behalf of children. School attendance laws, child labor laws, and laws against the sale of drugs to minors protect children and society as a whole. The state can intervene between a parent and child when the courts feel the child needs more care or protection. For instance, the state may require foster care. And, the state can also legislate for the development of various child welfare services. For instance, the state office checks on the quality of day care programs.

To be a better parent

A parent helps create a new person. A parent fosters all aspects of a child's growth and development. Thus, the quality of parenting is determined by an adult's knowledge and skills.

Parenting is a mind-boggling task to say the least. Parents are responsible for children's many needs:

- Physical needs. Parents must provide for the physical needs of children. Children need the right diet for a growing, active body. They need clothes that fit and that promote self-esteem. Shelter and physical protection are other needs, 1-3.
- Intellectual (mental) needs. Parents need to provide good experiences for their children, 1-4. Experiences can help children learn and develop skills they need to survive. Parents also should provide for the creative needs of children, 1-5.
- Social needs. Parents must provide opportunities for their children to be with other children. They need to help their children learn to respond to others. Part of a parent's responsibility for meeting social needs is helping a child develop character. *Character* is an inward force that guides a person's conduct. It helps people make choices that meet acceptable standards of right and wrong. Throughout this book, you will read about methods of guiding children's social development. These methods will help develop a child's character.
- Trust needs. Children need to feel that they can cope with demands of family, friends, and society. They gain confidence through trusting their parents. Trust begins early in life when parents meet their children's needs. It continues to grow when parents allow their children freedom to develop.

1-3 Infants and young children have many safety needs.

1-4 Adults need to provide the right learning experiences for a child's stage of development.

1-5 Children grow intellectually through creative experiences.

• Love/discipline needs. Parents and children need each other's love. In loving children, parents must learn to listen to their children, set limits, and share reasons for needed limits, 1-6. Through love and discipline, parents help children grow into self-directed adults.

By studying children, parents (and parents-to-be) know children's needs at each stage of growth and development. They know how to respond to those needs in the best ways. Studying children also helps parents have realistic expectations for their parenting abilities.

To work with children

Adults who have careers in child-related fields need to know about the growth and development of children. (See Chapter 27 to read about these careers.) Most careers focus on only some of the needs of children. For instance, a school cook is concerned with children's nutritional needs. A teacher is more

1-6 Setting limits is part of loving and disciplining children.

18

concerned with children's intellectual needs. But the child is a whole person. Anyone in a child-related field should know about all aspects of children's growth and development, 1-7.

To understand yourself

Studying children's growth and development helps adults grow. It can help you appreciate all that goes into taking those first steps or saying that first word. It feels good when you help a child overcome a fear or learn a skill. Adults often take delight in just being with a child, 1-8. You can join children's awe of beauty, their frankness, or their world of magic. Children can share gifts that adults often sadly outgrow.

Many times, adults are not aware of how their personal priorities affect their feelings and reactions to children. As you study children, you can gain insight into your own growth, development, and personal priorities. This self-knowledge can help you accept children and serve them in better ways.

1-8 Just being around children is a happy experience for many adults.

1-7 Classroom teachers are mainly prepared to meet the mental needs of children. But they must also be aware of children's other needs and how these affect mental growth.

WHAT IS CHILD DEVELOPMENT?

Development is the process that turns babies into adults. The process has many stages such as infancy, childhood, adolescence, and adulthood, 1-9. Development goes on from the time you are conceived until you die.

Adults have always observed, discussed, and written about children's development. But scientific studies were not begun until the late 1800s. Scientific study of children follows strict rules. The rules help to make sure that information is true. The scientific study of children from conception to adolescence is called *child development*.

Child development is concerned with changes that occur in children. It includes the way

REBECCA LAWRENCE

1-9 Between infancy and adulthood, children go through many stages of development.

children's bodies grow and develop. Child development is concerned with the way children think and learn, the way they feel about themselves, and the way they interact with others.

Many fields add knowledge to child development. Experts in medicine, education, sociology, and home economics may do research about children. They help build on what we know about children. People in those areas then use the information to learn more about children.

Child development is not just for the experts. Anyone who is around children can use knowledge about children. Child development helps to explain facts so that people know who children are and how to care for them.

FORCES PROMOTING GROWTH AND DEVELOPMENT

Each child is very different from all other children. Differences are due to the unique inborn traits and environment of each child, and from the way the inborn traits and environment affect each other. In spite of differences, all children follow similar patterns of growth and development. These likenesses can be described.

Growth and development are products of both *heredity* and *environment*. Heredity is all of the traits from blood relatives that are passed down to a child. Environment is all the conditions, objects, and situations that affect a child. Many studies have been done to understand the effects of heredity and environment on children. Much has been learned about how these forces promote growth and development, but there is still much more to be learned in the future.

Heredity

Heredity is passed on through genes. Genes carry the inborn instructions which help make a person what he or she is. Genes are found in a person's cells. Genes affect growth and development in many ways:

- The genes' instructions are lifelong. For example, the same genes determine hair color for life. A person may be born with dark hair that later turns blond, then brown, and finally gray. Although the hair color changes, the genes do not.
- Genes affect some parts of growth and development more than others. For instance, body features—like height, facial structure, and color of hair, eyes, and skin—are mostly determined by genes, 1-10. Mental ability and social-emotional traits are affected only partly by genes.
- Some genes determine whether or not a person has a trait. For instance, a person either is or is not an albino. An albino is a person with white skin, almost white hair, and pink eyes.

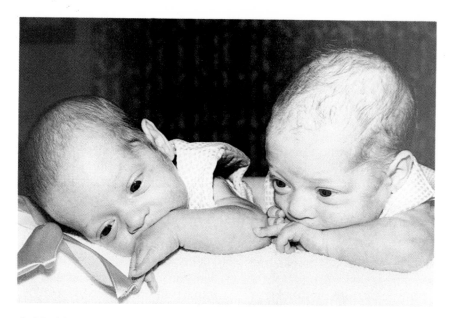

1-10 Identical twins look alike because they have the same genes. Their personalities may not be the same, though, because genes do not have such a strong effect on social-emotional traits.

- Other genes affect the range of a trait. Traits like height (very short to very tall) and athletic ability (almost no ability to greatness) come from these kinds of genes. These genes determine a trait's highest *potential*. Potential is the greatest amount or level possible. Whether a person will show or use that trait to its potential depends on the person's life. For instance, good diets will help children grow in height. But once they reach their potential, they cannot grow taller. On the other hand, children with poor diets may not achieve their full potential.

Environment

The environment also affects growth and development. The environment includes physical conditions such as food and rest. It includes the first-hand experiences from which children learn, 1-11. What others tell children through speech and writing is also part of their environment. So are children's relationships with others.

REBECCA LAWRENCE

1-11 Playing in the mud is one way children learn through first-hand experiences.

Learning about children 21

All of these factors affect the way a child grows and develops. Some affect physical traits. For instance, diet can affect height and health.

Most factors in the environment affect mental and social-emotional traits. Studies show that babies do not learn as quickly as other babies when no one holds or talks to them. Children who are given attention and the chance to read, hear music, and play games often learn easier than other children.

Heredity and environment combined

For years, people argued about whether heredity or environment had a bigger force on growth and development. Now, experts agree that heredity and environment work together.

For instance, genes control how quickly a baby's muscles and bones grow (heredity). A proper diet is needed for the baby to grow (environment). But a better diet does not make bones and muscles bigger than heredity allows (heredity and environment).

Going one step further, parents can exercise their baby to help muscles become stronger (environment). But the baby cannot walk until his or her muscles and bones are ready (heredity). When the baby's body is ready, parents can help the baby walk as soon as possible through exercise and encouragement (heredity and environment).

PRINCIPLES OF GROWTH AND DEVELOPMENT

Each person is unique. But people are more alike than different. Experts study the ways we are alike to find *principles of growth and development*. Growth and development take place in a pattern that these principles describe. They do not fit any person in an exact way, but they are true enough that we can use them as a guide in learning about children.

Growth and development are constant

There is much constancy (being the same) in the growth and development of a person. What a child is today is a good hint—but not proof—of what he or she will be tomorrow.

For example, tall two-year-olds tend to be tall adults. Children who are good students in the early school years are likely to be good students in high school. Happy, secure children tend to be cheerful, confident adults.

There are two reasons for constancy in growth and development. First, traits controlled by heredity do not change. Second, people often live in the same environment for years. For major changes to happen in growth and development, there must be major changes in the environment.

Growth and development are gradual and continuous

Growth and development are gradual and continuous because changes that take place happen in little, unbroken steps. A child does not grow or change overnight. For instance, a baby takes those first steps on a certain date. But on each day before walking, the baby grew, the body matured, and other motor skills (crawling, pulling up, etc.) were practiced. All of these led to those "first steps," 1-12.

In a positive way, the principle suggests that good development does not reverse overnight. A few mistakes or stresses do not often cause severe problems. For instance, a one-day junk food diet does not have very harmful results on a healthy person.

The principle also suggests that lags in growth and development can be helped at any later point in a person's life. For instance, if children are not taught to read at age five, they can learn a few years later without too many problems. (One exception is changes in the body. Once growth and change are complete in places such as the bones and brain, therapy cannot help.)

On the negative side, the principle suggests that poor growth and development is not easily reversed. For example, a child with poor health due to a long-term poor diet may need many months of a carefully planned diet to restore health. Thus, the principle can work to a person's advantage or disadvantage.

There are times when changes occur very fast or very slow and even when there appears to be a complete break in growth and develop-

1-12 All children must practice many motor skills before they take their first steps. Before walking, children pull themselves mainly by their arms (A), creep on all fours (B), pull themselves up onto their feet (C), stand without support (D), and try standing on one foot (E).

ment. This may happen for at least three reasons:

1. The child may have had a change in the environment. For instance, a toddler may be able to handle a baby-sized spoon with ease, but may find the adult-sized spoon clumsy for many weeks.
2. The child may be working on one skill and giving less effort to other skills. For instance, during summer vacation, children's reading skills often fall, but their skills in climbing, jumping, and running increase.
3. There are times when one change in a person triggers the need for many other changes. Because these times tend to occur as the child moves from one stage of growth and development to another

stage, they are often called *transition times,* 1-13. Changes seem to "pile up." Old patterns of doing things do not seem to work very well.

So many demands may result in the child's coming "unglued." Transition times are followed by "coming together" periods in which balance and calm are restored in the child. Changes are slower during these times and the child is better able to cope.

TRANSITION TIMES

TYPES OF CHANGES	EXAMPLE
Changes in physical development.	Rapid growth times such as the late childhood or early teen years.
Changes in status.	No longer the baby of a family after the birth of a new baby.
Changes in roles.	Going to preschool or school for the first time.

1-13 Changes that happen during transition times place many demands on children.

Growth and development happen in sequenced steps

For growth and development to be continuous, change must build on what is already learned. For instance, writing comes from making marks that are not letters. The steps in growth and development follow one another in a specific order called *sequenced steps.* Adults can think about the changes that happen in children in ranked stages—that is, one stage occurring before another stage.

One way to see the steps of growth and development is through Robert J. Havighurst's theory of *developmental tasks.* Havighurst is a well-known educator and behavioral scientist. He defines developmental tasks as tasks that should be mastered at a certain stage in a person's life. Achieving these tasks results in happiness and success with later tasks, 1-14. Failure to achieve tasks leads to unhappiness and problems with later tasks. Developmental tasks arise from three sources:

1. Physical growth. The baby comes into the world as a helpless being. As the body matures, the child is able to learn many new skills such as walking and reading.
2. Social pressures. Society (family, friends, teachers, etc.) pressures the child through rewards and penalties to master important

DILCON SCHOOL, BUREAU OF INDIAN AFFAIRS

1-14 Mastering school tasks is needed for success in later life.

tasks. Some developmental tasks differ from culture to culture, because different groups value different skills and learnings. For instance, playing in order to win has no value to Hopi Indian children. But most other American children feel that winning is of value. Tasks differ from region to region, too, 1-15. Over time, changes in a society also change the tasks. See 1-16.

3. Inner pressures. The actual push to achieve comes from within children. In the end, the child is responsible for mastery of each task. Children will work harder to learn tasks that they like.

When the body is ready, society requires, and the self is ready to master, the *teachable moment* has arrived. See 1-17. If a child has

1-16 Learning computer skills is a developmental task that is needed because of changes in technology.

1-15 Children in southern states may learn how to catch crawfish (crayfish).

Learning about children 25

SOURCES OF DEVELOPMENTAL TASKS	EXAMPLE
	Area: Motor Task.
	Task for Middle Childhood: Learning physical skills needed for common games.
	Example of task: Skill needed to play ball.
Physical growth.	Child needs bone and muscle growth; eyes and hands must work smoothly together.
Social pressures.	Other children reward skillful players (accept them as friends) and punish failures (tease or reject them as friends). Parents and school coaches may also expect children to master the skill.
Inner pressures.	Desire to be admired by other children and by parents and coaches.
Must see new possibilities for behavior.	Child sees older children playing ball.
Must form new concept of self.	Child thinks, "I can also be a player."
Must cope with conflicting demands.	Child thinks, "I can get hit with a ball and I can be teased for striking out. But if I do not play, the other kids will make fun of me and my parents and coaches will not consider me grown-up."
Wants to achieve the next step in development enough to work for it.	Child now spends hours in practice.

1-17 Children master developmental tasks when their bodies are ready, others require, and they want to learn a new skill.

not reached the teachable moment, trying to master a task or skill can cause stress. Waiting too long after the teachable moment has occurred may cause problems, too. For example, children who were ready to ride a bicycle in the late preschool years or early school years may have more trouble learning the skill as an adult.

Growth and development happen at different rates

Growth and development happen at different rates throughout life and for different people. Experts know when the fast and slow periods of growth and development happen. For instance, height and weight increases are fast in infancy, moderate in the preschool years, slow in the elementary school years, and fast in junior high and high school years.

Rates of growth and development vary from one child to another. Some children develop quickly and others slowly. Although the *sequence* of growth and development is about the same for all children, differing *rates* of change are the rule and not the exception. Children grow and develop at different rates because of heredity, environment, and motivation.

Heredity determines different growth rates. For instance, growth rates of boys and girls are different during childhood. At all ages, girls' bones and organs (heart, lungs, liver, etc.) are more mature than those of boys.

A good environment is needed for growth to occur at the best rate for each child. If the environment is lacking in some way, lags occur in growth and development. However, there is no reason to believe that trying to speed up development is good. Adults' attempts to hurry the child's growth and development may cause harmful stress.

Motivation, the child's own desire to achieve, also makes growth and development rates vary. Some children are eager to achieve and others are more weakly motivated.

Growth and development have interrelated parts

Different "threads" of growth and development form a complex weave. The physical, mental, and social-emotional aspects of growth and development are often discussed in separate sections or chapters in this book. This is so that you can better see each "thread." But in real children, all aspects interact with each other in complex ways. For instance, as children's bodies grow and mature, their motor skills become better. These motor skills, in turn, aid social skills, 1-18. As social skills improve, children talk to more people and learn about new ideas. This improves mental skills. And as mental skills improve, children can play in more complex sports, thus improving motor skills.

People who work with children must understand how different parts of growth and development affect each other. For instance, a teacher's job is to improve children's intellectual growth. But the way a teacher treats children also affects their social-emotional growth. Understanding these interrelationships improves the way that people work with children.

1-18 Becoming mature enough to ride bicycles brings hours of fun with friends.

SCHWINN BICYCLE CO.

Understanding needs

Maslow, a noted psychologist, felt that development comes from the meeting of one's needs. According to him, the needs which all humans work to fulfill are basic needs and higher-level needs.

Basic needs are both *physiological* (organic or body) and *psychological* (feelings). Maslow divides basic needs into four categories. One category includes all physiological needs. The other three categories are the psychological categories of safety, belonging and love, and exteem. Higher-level needs include the category Maslow labeled, "aesthetic and cognitive and self-actualization." See 1-19.

Maslow places basic needs and higher-level needs in a hierarchy of human needs, or a ranked order. In other words basic needs are lower-level needs and must be fulfilled to a reasonable extent before the higher-level needs can be met.

Understanding Maslow's hierarchy of human needs is important for all adults desiring to study and care for children. Maslow's work implies that the further up the hierarchy of needs a person can go, the more growth and fulfillment he or she seeks. Maslow sees humans as driven by the need to become.

Adults need to learn and practice ways of helping children meet their needs. The first step is to help children meet their basic needs. For instance, adults help children meet physiological needs by feeding them nutritious foods. Once basic needs are met, adults are then able to guide children in meeting their higher-level needs. For example, well-fed children can turn their attentions away from eating to feeling the fur of a soft kitten or to planning ways to share a toy.

MASLOW'S NEEDS

CATEGORIES	EXAMPLES
Basic Needs	
1. Physiological	1. Food, water, air, shelter, and clothing.
2. Safety	2. Avoidance of illness, danger, and disruption; security.
3. Belonging and love	3. Affiliation (belonging to groups such as family), acceptance, and love.
4. Esteem	4. Mastery, adequacy, achievement, competence, and recognition.
Higher-Level Needs	
5. Aesthetic and Cognitive and Self-actualization	5. Knowledge and appreciation of beauty, goodness, freedom, and a realistic view and acceptance of self and others.

1-19 Maslow sees two systems of needs in all humans: basic needs and metaneeds.

to Know

character . . . child-centered society . . .
child development . . . culture . . .
development . . . developmental tasks . . .
enculturation . . . environment . . . heredity . . .
principles of growth and development . . .
rights . . . sequenced steps . . . social policy . . .
teachable moment . . . transition times

to Review

Write your answers on a separate sheet of paper.

1. Give two examples that show we are a child-centered culture.

2. List five reasons why people study children.

3. Child development is concerned with _____ (a few, all) aspects of development.

4. What are the three forces that promote growth and development?

5. True or false. The genes affect the physical, mental, and social aspects of development to the same degree.

6. The environment _____ (does, does not) greatly affect growth and development.

7. True or false. Principles of growth and development apply in an exact way to every child.

8. Which of the following statements is most true about child growth and development?

   a. The order of the steps and the rate of change in growth and development are about the same for most children.

   b. The rate of change in growth and development is about the same for most children.

   c. The order of the steps in growth and development is about the same for most children.

9. During transition times, growth and development are _____ (faster, slower) than at other times.

10. Match each source of mastering developmental tasks with the correct example.

   _____ Physical growth.

   _____ Social pressures.

   _____ Inner pressures.

   a. The child's teacher says that learning math skills is important.

   b. The child's brain cells are developed.

   c. The child has read about careers in the space industry and feels that such a career would be fun.

11. Explain Maslow's hierarchy of human needs.

to Do

1. Make a display titled, "We Are a Child-Centered Society." In the display, use newspaper clippings, magazine articles, and other information on children and products for children.

2. Ask your school or local librarian to help you find information on child labor laws. Share with your class how the needs of children led to these laws.

3. Read all or some of the chapters from the Laura Ingalls Wilder series, *Little House in the Big Woods* or *Farmer Boy.* Share with your class some examples of the skills and personal priorities that parents handed down to children in the stories.

4. Interview a person over 60 years of age. Ask the person to describe some of the developmental tasks (chores, hobbies, games, etc.) that he or she mastered but that are seldom mastered by people today.

5. Read about the life of a famous person in any career. Write a paper that gives examples of constancy in the person's growth and development that led to fame in their career.

6. Invite a first-grade teacher or a reading supervisor to explain some of the skills that children must master before they are able to read. (Ask him or her to stress the order in which the skills should be learned.)

7. Divide into groups and discuss how aspects of development are interrelated. Each group should trace the effects of a different problem—such as poor nutrition or lack of affection—on all aspects of development. Share your group's results with the rest of the class.

Baby showers are often part of the preparation for a new baby.

30

2

Preparing for parenthood

After studying this chapter, you will be able to:
- ☐ Describe the differences between parenting and other tasks.
- ☐ Analyze some of the motivations for and against parenthood.
- ☐ Identify the choices that couples considering parenthood must make.

Parenting is a rewarding but difficult task. Many people see their children as the major investment of their lives in terms of money, time, and emotions. Most parents hope their children will have all their strengths and be spared all their weaknesses. They also hope their children will have opportunities they did not have.

A person must *become* a good parent, because parenting skills are not automatic. Being biologically able to parent does not equal good parenting any more than strong and agile fingers equal a concert pianist. And, becoming a good parent is perhaps more difficult than becoming a concert pianist for two reasons.

First, parenting involves relationships among people. Relationships are always difficult because they involve humans. All humans have their own strengths and weaknesses and their own goals. In a good relationship each person should seek the well-being of the other in all aspects of that person's life. He or she should support the other's unique worth as a person. The parent-child relationship is especially difficult because it is more one-sided than other relationships. For many years parents are the "givers" and children are the "takers," 2-1.

The second reason is that training to become

a parent is not nearly as specific as training to become a pianist. In the past, children could see their parents handling younger brothers and sisters. They may have helped with their care. But with family size becoming smaller, many children do not have this opportunity. Also, for years, most young parents turned to relatives for "answers" and even direct help. But in the United States today, there are not as many *multiple-generation families* (grandparents or other older relatives living with younger family members). In many cases, *mobility* (moving to another location) has placed many miles between young parents and any of their relatives.

Although good parenting is difficult, most parents do not have a deeper longing in life than to be worthy parents. Growing out of this desire is the need to be well-informed. The recent need for aid with parenting has given rise to new sources of help. More books are being written on parenting and child development. There have been some TV programs dealing with this subject. More courses are offered in high schools and colleges and by social agencies (for instance, American Red Cross) on these topics.

Of course all parents, even the best-intentioned and well-informed, make mistakes. Wanting to be good parents and having knowledge of sound child-rearing practices cushions the effects of mistakes. Perhaps the best success of parenthood is not "perfection" but rearing a child who can say as an adult, "Had I been able to choose my parents, I would have chosen you."

Like any other major undertaking, having a child requires serious consideration of all aspects of parenting. This chapter discusses some of the important decisions that must be made in order to prepare for parenting.

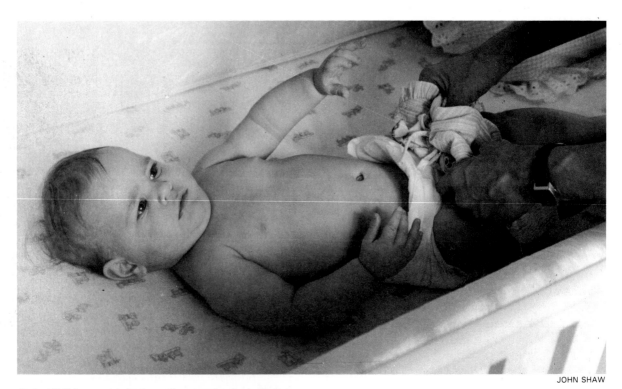

JOHN SHAW

2-1 Children require much care in their first years. They are not able to give much in return.

MOTIVATIONS FOR
AND AGAINST PARENTHOOD

Deciding whether to become parents is a personal choice. For the sake of the couple and the future child, the choice should be a mutual one—that is, the husband and wife should agree on the decision. Hopefully, the couple discussed their feelings about parenthood before marriage. The decision to parent is unlike many life decisions in two ways.

First, the decision to parent is a permanent choice. Once a child is conceived, it belongs to the parents for life. (There are some cases where parents give up their rights to raise a child, but they are not common.) A person may change careers several times, but once a parent—always a parent.

Second, a decision *not* to parent need not be a permanent choice. (Of course, it can be a permanent choice.) Many choices in life must be made within a limited amount of time. For example, if a person wants to have a career in ballet, study must begin at an early age and continue for years. The decision to parent can be made within a longer time-frame. Young couples have 15 or more safe childbearing years, and the possibility of adopting a child may extend this time by a few years. Thus, some couples may want to be parents, but they want to wait until a better time. Other couples may not be sure about parenthood and want to take more time before making a choice. Some couples may decide they never want children, but they can change their minds later.

Couples have different motivations for and against parenthood. Some of these are discussed below. In the end, each couple must make the choice in light of their own feelings and needs.

Motivations for parenthood

Couples give many reasons for wanting children. Perhaps the best reason is to share their love with a child. Couples may give other reasons that are good as long as they are coupled with the first reason. Still other reasons are not at all appropriate.

"We want to share our love with a child." Of all couples who have children, few find it easy to explain why they wanted to become parents. Perhaps this is because the most important reason for wanting a child is so simple. The desire to welcome a child into one's life and to share one's love and time is the best reason for parenthood. Parents should want a child with no strings attached. If a child is wanted to fulfill other needs or other goals, the parent-child relationship may not be good.

Parents may want to welcome a child into their lives because they enjoy caring for another person. An infant and young child is totally dependent on the parent's care. The child's need for guidance and economic support is present until adulthood. Caring means being responsible for the child on a 24-hour basis every day of the week.

Parents may want a child because they desire to teach another person, 2-2. Teaching one's child goes beyond instructing in facts and skills. It includes more difficult tasks like developing values and attitudes.

SCHLAGE LOCK CO., BJ STEWART ADVERTISING AND P.R.

2-2 Parenting involves much informal teaching. Some of life's most important facts, skills, and priorities are taught by parents.

Preparing for parenthood 33

JOHN SHAW

2-3 Parenting involves mutual sharing and growth for both the parent and the child.

Parents may see having a child as an opportunity for mutual growth. Parents who are "tuned-in" to children learn from them, 2-3. The German author Goethe once wrote, "You have to ask children and birds how cherries and strawberries taste." In turn, growing parents help their child grow.

"Wouldn't it be nice to have a 'cute, little' baby?" Some couples see others with babies, and they think about how nice it would be to have a "cute, little baby." Most babies are cute. And, it's good for couples to have a positive attitude toward babies. The problem is that babies aren't always cute. All babies are sick, fussy, and contrary at times. And, babies do grow up!

"Our parents want to be grandparents." Some couples want to grant their own parents' desires to be grandparents. It is nice for a child to have grandparents who wanted a grandchild. Grandparents can offer much love to a child. However, it is more important for a child to have the love of his or her parents.

"Our older child needs a brother or sister." In wanting a brother or sister for an older child, the couple is trying to fulfill someone else's needs—not their own. This reason is similar to wanting a baby so that their parents will be grandparents. Although a child might enjoy a brother or sister, there are other ways of meeting the only child's needs for playmates.

"A child can make us proud." Other couples see children as sources of pride. They want children to carry on the family name and customs, inherit the family business or money, or achieve certain goals for their parents. It is good for parents to be proud of their children and want them to achieve. But they must be careful that their hopes as parents do not stifle their children's goals. Parenthood is not a good choice if a child is wanted only to boost the parents' ego or to meet their unfulfilled goals.

The parent-child relationship suffers when children cannot "live up" to their parents' goals. Not meeting parents' goals can make children feel inadequate. The relationship also suffers when children can meet the parent's goals but feel that they can't be themselves. This often leads to resentment of their parents.

"Others will see me as a stable, reliable person." A few couples see having children as giving them the image of stable community members and reliable employees. Fortunately, such ideas are beginning to break down. People are judged more today on their own merits and not on family status. Parents should not want children simply to help parents fulfill their own goals.

"A child will be a comfort in our old age." Sometimes couples mention children as sources of help in their old age. It is natural for people to think about being helpless or lonely. However, an aging parent cannot count on a child's help. In fact, parents may outlive their children.

"A child will make us love each other." Some couples hope that a child will save a failing marriage. Children may enrich family life for stable couples. But unstable couples may find that children make their problems worse. Studies show that couples with children often argue about their viewpoints about childrearing practices—especially discipline. Children also add a financial burden. Usually, these problems add to the instability of marriages. Couples who stay together "because of the children" may always be unhappy. Sadly, their children often feel responsible for the home problems.

Motivations against parenthood

Some couples decide to postpone parenthood, and three to five percent of all couples plan permanent childlessness. These couples feel that parenthood is not wise for them—at least at the present time. Even couples who want children should think about motivations against parenthood. The arguments that couples who don't want children present are problems that must be faced and solved by many parents.

"We're not 'ready' for a child." When couples say that they're not "ready" yet, they usually mean that they need to mature. They may want more time to pursue their own interests (personal growth and maturing) before caring for a child. They may feel that they need more time as a couple for their marriage relationship to mature. And, they may need more time for educational or job maturity. Some jobs take many years of education or training, 2-4. Most people must spend some time establishing themselves in a career.

"A baby costs a lot." Babies do cost a lot. At one time, large families were economic aids, because the children helped with work. In today's economy, children cannot contribute a great deal, if anything, to family income. Later in this chapter, you will see more closely the cost of having a child.

JOHN SHAW

2-4 One of the problems of parenting is having enough time and energy to meet the demands of a career and parenthood.

"A child will tie us down." With children comes continuous responsibility. Unlike many other responsibilities, childrearing cannot be "put off until later" or ignored while "on vacation." Even with the best babysitters in charge, parents cannot completely forget their roles. They are always called if children are hurt or ill or for any other serious reason. However, many of the couple's needs for personal time can be met with a little planning.

"A child will interfere with our careers." Children and careers both take time. The most common problems of meeting career/parent demands are having enough time and energy for both and finding good childcare services.

Some careers seem more compatible with parenting than others. For example, school teachers have hours and vacation times similar to those of their children.

Some careers may require careful planning if they are to be combined with parenthood. They include careers with very long hours, night hours, or irregular hours. They also include jobs that require much travel, moving, or pressure. Other jobs require living in areas that are unsafe or that don't have schools.

Some employers are trying to ease some of the problems for their employees who are parents. They offer extras such as company child care and liberal leave for men and women after their children are born. Other extras may include summer camp programs for children and family recreation programs.

"Our child could be defective." There are no guarantees that a child will be born "perfect." And serious injury or illness can occur after birth. Good medical care before and after birth reduces, but doesn't eliminate, the risks. Defective, ill, or injured children do have special needs beyond the needs of "normal" children, but rearing such a child may be highly rewarding.

"Our marriage could fail, and I don't want to be a single parent." Couples whose marriages are not stable or who worry about divorce may give this reason for not wanting children. There is a growing number of divorced and single-parent families. Most married couples know the problems of working and meeting their families'

needs. They try to share the load. A single-parent family usually has fewer resources. Single parents may lack financial support, aid with household and child care tasks, and emotional support from a spouse. Without these resources, the single parent can't always take part in as many adult activities as singles without children or couples. This may make single parents feel lonely. Many single parents are able to work toward positive solutions to their problems. These solutions are discussed in Chapter 21.

TRANSITION TO PARENTHOOD

Parenthood is abrupt. With the birth or placement of a child, a person instantly takes on all the tasks of parenting. There are few, if any, other jobs in which a novice is given such responsibility. No wonder most people refer to their first child as the "experimental child."

You can discuss and think about parenthood, but no one can do more than make an educated guess about how they will feel as parents. Expert opinion should help you make up your own mind about parenting. It also should enhance your confidence in working with children. To prepare yourself for the abruptness of parenthood, you need to be aware of how children will change your life.

Considering family organization

People who consider having children need to look at their lives. Couples need to look at the strengths and weaknesses of their present relationships. And, they need to remember that for the healthy growth of children, the balance should be in strengths, 2-5. The couple also must think about how family organization may change with parenthood.

The couple. Couples should begin looking at their relationships by asking questions that have a direct bearing on parenting. They should think about their feelings for others. For starters, couples might ask these questions:

- Are we loving and sensitive to the needs of others?
- Are we careful in our judgments about people and ideas?

2-5 When couples have happy, sharing relationships and desire children, their children have the best chances for growth and development.

- Can we recognize and respect the rights of others?
- Are we self-disciplined?
- Do we relate well with others?
- Are we flexible enough to accept changes?
- Are we brave about challenges?
- Can we be honest about our feelings for others?

Next, the couple should think about how their relationship with each other could change if they were parents. These questions may help:

- Do we have the time and energy to give to children?
- Do we want to share some of our time together with children?
- Are we doing in our day to day lives what we would want our children to do? (Children model parents' behavior.)

Couples can't set up a "formula" for successful parenting. They need to realize that children bring extra work to marriage. Children do not often stabilize a weak marriage. But if a couple can answer most of these questions positively, their relationship is probably strong enough that parenthood would be off to a good start.

Relatives and friends. Couples need to look at their present relationships with others, too. Good relationships with others can be positive for the couple and for possible children. Couples might want to ask themselves these questions about their relationships with relatives and friends:

- Do our relatives and friends share our basic values? Can we ignore little differences in beliefs?

- Can we ask for advice but use our own judgment?
- Can we tell others of our needs and accept the help others offer?
- Can we recognize the needs of others and offer our help?
- Can we avoid abusing others' generosity—time and money?
- Can we share fun times with others?

If couples can answer most of these positively, having a child should not cause problems in relationships outside of the family. When couples enjoy their relationships with relatives and friends before parenthood, 2-6, these relationships often extend to include children.

Couples need to think about how their relationships with others can affect their children. There are at least three advantages: (1) Relatives and friends provide children with their first link to the outside world. (2) Grandparents and older relatives can teach children about the past. (3) When many relatives and friends care for children, they feel more rooted to their family. Each of a couple's relatives and friends will be unique. Children learn to accept the uniqueness of people and grow through seeing how people are different. Thus, children will find getting along with others easier as they grow older.

Sharing responsibilities

Couples should examine how they feel about responsibilities for home care. Some couples practice more traditional roles. In these roles, the husband brings home the paycheck and the wife is responsible for all or most of the housework. (The husband may take care of some chores on a regular basis—such as yard work or home repairs. Or he may help the wife with any chores during his free time.)

Today, many wives work for reasons of self-fulfillment and/or economics. When wives work outside the home, husbands may help with housework and child care tasks more than

JOHN SHAW

2-6 Couples who have fun with other adults may find that they will also enjoy children.

JOHN SHAW

2-7 Sharing household tasks can be fun. It also frees time for each member of a couple to spend alone, with each other, and with a child.

they would in traditional roles, 2-7. Many men enjoy this widened role. In a few cases, husbands and wives have reversed the traditional role. The wife works outside the home and the husband assumes major home care tasks. Couples need to ask themselves these questions:

- Are we happy now with the way responsibilities are shared?
- Do we appreciate each other's help?
- Do we feel equally important in efforts to reach our goals?

Then the couple needs to consider how children might affect the sharing of responsibilities. They might ask these questions:

- If we become parents, will there be major changes in the way we share responsibilities?
- Can we agree on whether or how home and child care tasks will be divided?

- If one of us is a full-time employee and other is a full-time homemaker, will we feel that we are both contributing to our goals such as providing a financially and emotionally secure home? How will the full-time employee develop a close relationship with the child?
- How can we make sure we will both be involved with our child in early years? (Relationships with both parents are often seen as an emotional insurance against the loss of one parent.)

Couples who want to share responsibilities should look for answers to these questions that meet both partners' needs. The distribution of tasks can vary a great deal depending on each person's needs. Only careful planning and trial-and-error attempts provide the right formula.

Learning child care skills

Couples who consider parenting should evaluate what they know about caring for children. They need to find out what resources they can use to learn more. Couples will find it helpful to look ahead and find resources that they can use for advice once they have a child.

Couples should realize that many other couples feel that they need help in learning child care skills. Adults, who can handle their jobs, are often embarrassed that they do not have very good child care skills. They forget that they have studied and trained much more for their careers than for parenting roles. Couples need to consider these questions:

- Are there professionals and/or successful parents who are available for advice?
- What literature (books, magazines, etc.) is accurate, practical, and available?
- Are there classes available in child care skills? (Community colleges and local American Red Cross chapters may offer such classes.)
- Can we spend more time with infants and young children? (Babysitting and doing volunteer work in schools, churches, and recreational projects are ways to spend more time with children, 2-8.)

New parents should not be afraid to turn to resources for help. Even child care professionals can need quick advice on some facts.

For instance, they may not know how long to boil tap water for a baby to drink. Nothing can make parents feel more helpless than a helpless infant!

New parents should also realize that there is no "one right way" of parenting. Some methods may be thought of as better than others, but many factors influence the parenting roles. The culture in which a child is raised affects how parents care for children. The personalities of each parent and the child also affect the parenting role. And how parents care for their children is affected by the ways they have seen others—such as their parents and friends—care for children. All of these factors are important when learning child care skills.

Learning to guide and discipline. One important child care skill needed by parents is the ability to guide and discipline children. Parents provide children *guidance* through all of their actions and words around children. For instance, when parents face frustrations, but react calmly, they are guiding their children. Children learn that they do not need to get upset when they cannot have everything their way.

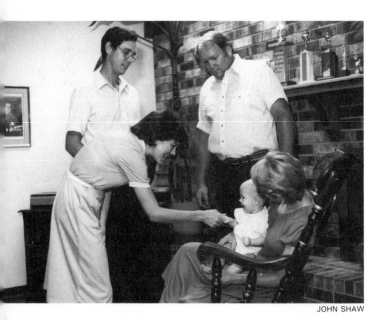

JOHN SHAW

2-8 A couple can learn more about children by babysitting for the child of a friend.

Learning to guide children in positive ways can be hard work. Parents need to think about all of their actions in terms of what they are teaching their children.

Discipline is a part of guidance. *Discipline* is using different methods and techniques to help teach children self-control. Through discipline, children learn to act in ways that society finds acceptable.

Many different techniques can be used to discipline children. Parents should explore and learn about these techniques before they have children. Different techniques seem to be more effective with different age groups. These techniques will be discussed in later chapters on meeting children's developmental needs.

Finding a parenting style. Most parents want to raise their children in a way that will help them become responsible, well-mannered adults. They realize that guidance and discipline are important. New parents need to give some thought to the style they will use to guide and discipline their children. Parenting styles can be grouped into three main categories: authoritarian, permissive, and democratic.

Some parents use an *authoritarian* parenting style. These parents think that obedience is the most important behavior their children should learn. They expect children to respect their authority with little or no explanation as to why children should obey. Such parents are likely to use physical punishment when children are not "good." They seldom reward good behavior.

Authoritarian parenting may teach children to obey their parents. But these children may not understand why they should act as their parents wish. They may not be able to develop self-control. They may also fear their parents and even rebel against them when they become older. Most parents do not practice this style of parenting any more.

Permissive parents give children almost no guidelines or rules. They feel that children should make their own decisions about right and wrong. They may think their children will feel unhappy or unloved if they set limits for their children. In fact, these children may feel lost without guidelines. Later in life, they may have trouble getting along with others because they have never needed to follow rules.

Most parents find a compromise between these two styles of parenting. They use a *democratic* style, setting some rules, but allowing some freedom. When they set rules, they explain to children why the rules are needed. Children may even be allowed to help set some rules and decide some punishments. These children learn self-discipline in a positive, encouraging setting.

Planning financial resources

Couples need to realize that children are expensive. The first year is expensive, and expenses grow as the child grows. Children eat more as they get older, but that's just the start. As needs and wants change, expenses often increase. Expenses for an infant dress may change to a prom or wedding dress. Other expenses may change from a simple ball to sporting equipment; from a toy xylophone to a quality musical instrument; or from a baby's first book to a college text. And, some child-related expenses only happen in later years. These include expenses for music or other lessons, cosmetics, club memberships, and spending money or allowance.

A few expenses may decrease as the child grows older. For example, if the child is healthy and is not a victim of an accident, health care expenses may decrease. Child care expenses are eliminated after a few years. However, the costs that decrease do not offset the costs that increase.

The first baby is often considered the most expensive. It is true that later children may be able to use some of the first born's supplies. But for the most part, each extra child multiplies the care costs. At some point, expenses go beyond another "mouth to feed." For example, a larger house or car, which costs more, may be necessary to meet the family's needs. Each child is unique in needs and wants, too. An item purchased for one child may not fit another child's needs or wants.

A couple should think about these questions:
- How do we earn and spend our money now? Are we happy with our budget?
- Do we have some regular savings that could be used to meet child-related expenses? If not, can we adjust our budget to meet such expenses?
- Can we expect more income over the next few years or lower expenses in some budget items (such as furniture payments) to offset increased child-related expenses?
- What type of savings goals for a child would be possible?
- What is the rough estimate of child-related expenses for the first and next several years?
- What are the *indirect costs* of having a child? Indirect costs are not actual expenses, but they represent resources that could have been used to meet goals other than child care.

Couples must think about many factors when they estimate the direct and indirect costs of parenting. Couples should realize that although estimates of direct costs are available, they are averages. Each family is different. These differences show in the way they spend their money. Couples' priorities should help shape their estimates of costs. For instance, one couple may want only the latest fashions for their child. Another couple may be happy with less costly brands or home-sewn clothing. Family resources other than money may also affect direct expenses. For instance, a parent in one family may have the time and skill to give his or her child piano lessons. Another family may have to hire a piano teacher.

Indirect costs also depend on the needs of each couple. Some couples may have relatives who will babysit free of charge. The time that they give up is an indirect cost for that couple. Other couples may give up earnings because one parent stays home to raise the child. This is called *foregone income,* 2-9. Foregone income is greater for the person who would earn a higher salary than for the person who would earn less. If the person is not employable, there is no foregone income. Also, foregone income is greater per child when a parent stays home with one child than with more than one child.

Another indirect cost is the impact on career opportunities due to time out of the labor force. This cost is the most difficult to calculate.

Carefully planning financial resources is important for everyone, 2-10. In some ways, financial planning becomes more important when couples begin to think about children. This is because children rely on their parents for financial support for many years. Parents are also models for their children of either good or poor consumers.

CALCULATING FOREGONE INCOME

STEP 1

Add costs of earning an income.

Taxes on earned income.	$_____
FICA.	$_____
Transportation to and from work.	$_____
Food away from home.	$_____
Costs to update skills (required seminars, courses, and conferences paid for by employee).	$_____
Clothing appropriate for job—including uniforms or safety equipment.	$_____
Professional or union dues.	$_____
Child-care costs while working or updating skills.	$_____
Incidental costs (gifts, office parties, or other).	$_____
TOTAL	$_____

STEP 2

Subtract costs of earning an income from gross income.

Gross income.	$_____
Costs of earning income.	$_____
Foregone income.	$_____

Foregone income is an estimate, because exact costs are impossible to calculate and fringe benefits may increase gross income.

2-9 Foregone income may be a high indirect cost when a parent stays home to raise a child.

Thinking about the family life cycle

Couples need to think about more than the diaper years as they think about having children. They need to realize they are entering a new family life cycle. The family life cycle can be divided into the following stages:

- Establishment stage: when the couple gets to know each other and begins thinking about having children.
- Childbearing stage: when the couple begins having children.
- School years stage: when the children begin entering school.
- Adolescent stage: when the children are teenagers.
- Launching stage: when children begin leaving home.
- Post-parental stage: when children have left home and the couple may become grandparents.

Just as children grow and develop through different stages, the family grows and develops through these stages. Couples should be pre-

JOHN SHAW

2-10 Parents need to carefully budget their income to meet the high costs of having a baby.

42

pared for the changes that take place at each new stage.

Most new parents give much thought to the childbearing stage. They understand their role in caring for and guiding children through their earliest years. But as parents enter later stages, they may not be prepared to meet their changing roles.

As children enter the school years, parents must leave much teaching and guiding of their children to others. Children begin to learn more from teachers and peers. Parents need to stay involved with their children's growth. But they also need to accept the fact that other people are becoming important to their children.

The adolescent years can be confusing for parents as well as children. Their children are striving to become more independent. But they are not always ready to handle as much responsibility as they want. Adolescents may want much more privacy, but they still need to know that they can talk to their parents. Parents need to begin treating their children as adults. But they also need to know when to step in to provide guidance and help.

The launching years bring new feelings to parents. As children leave home, parents may feel lonely or unwanted. They also need to acknowledge the fact that their children are adults. Parents may still be involved in their children's lives. But their relationships may be on more equal terms.

In the post-parental stage, parents may begin finding more time for themselves than they had when their children were at home. They may still keep in touch with their children. They may be very involved with their grandchildren. Post-parental stage parents may find new challenges. They may want to have more influence over how their children are raising the grand-children. Health problems may cause them to need help from their own children. These times can be big adjustments for all family members.

A new challenge for families has been children who return home after the launching stage. Economic troubles, divorce, or other situations may cause children to return home. Parents may have to learn new ways of relating to these children. They may have adjusted to the fact that their children are adults. But they may not know how to treat them as adults when they are all living in the same home. Likewise, children may not be clear on what is expected of them. Open communication is needed to make sure that family members continue to get along.

Making other decisions

Couples who plan to have children must make many other decisions. Three major decisions include deciding whether both parents will work; choosing child care services; and planning for future children.

Deciding whether to work. Couples must decide whether they will both work or whether one will stay home and care for children. Fathers have chosen to stay home and let mothers work, but this is not as common as the reverse situation. Women are usually the ones who must decide between staying home or working outside the home. Therefore, many studies focus on mothers and work. Findings show that most women today are employed and that their attitudes about work affect their children.

Over 50 percent of all mothers are employed and three-fourths of these women have full-time jobs, 2-11. A recent survey shows that pregnant women are more likely to stay on the job until just before the baby is born. And they return within three months of the birth, although many would prefer more time off. Most mothers do not stay off the job longer because of financial or career reasons.

If children have proper care during work hours, they are not harmed by separation from parents. But the mother's attitude toward work seems to be most important. Studies show that happiest children come from homes where the mother wanted to work and did, or where the mother wanted to stay home and could. Children were not as happy in homes where mothers wanted to work and could not or where they wanted to stay home but could not. In other words, if mother is happy in her situation, children benefit from this attitude. And, children tend to suffer if their mother's attitude toward her work situation is negative.

2-11 Working mothers often have dual pleasures and dual responsibilities.

Several problems seem to be common among working couples. Couples will need to answer these questions:

- Can we find good child care during working hours?
- Can we balance job demands and children's needs? For instance, will there be enough time left for children after work is completed? Can we give complete or only partial focus to our children's needs during the time set aside for them?
- Can we work out mutual responsibilities for childcare tasks, housework, etc.?
- Can we have enough time for ourselves as individuals and as a couple free of all other concerns?
- Can we be organized? Can we be flexible to meet some changes in our schedule? For instance, what will we do to meet the needs of a sick child? What will we do when job demands are heavy for a short time—such as the closing days of school for a teacher?
- If any of the above are answered negatively, what are other options for us?

Choosing special services for children. Children must have special services from the beginning of life. The two major services are medical and child care.

A couple considering parenting should think about medical care. Before conceiving a child, a couple should have thorough check-ups. Health problems are best solved before having children. As soon as a woman believes she is pregnant, she should find a family physician or an *obstetrician*. An obstetrician is a physician skilled in the medical care of a pregnant woman through the time she gives birth and for the six or more weeks of recovery from the birth.

Usually the family physician takes care of mother and baby. But obstetricians deal with a mother's care. Most obstetricians require that you select a *pediatrician* (physician skilled in the medical care of children) who will care for the baby after birth.

A couple will want to select a good physician who will answer their questions. The physician should be willing to follow their wishes about such points as type of delivery desired by the couple. (Of course, the wishes should be followed only if they are medically sound for the couple's case.)

Couples also need to think about child care services for their future child. Child care services are needed when the parents are working or absent for short periods of time. Parents must choose child care carefully, because children need to feel secure and happy when parents are not with them. Children learn values when they are away from home as well as in the home.

Couples can find out what types of child care services are available in their town or city. There are three basic options in child care services. These are *in-home care, family day care,* and *group day care.* The advantages and disadvantages of each are shown in 2-12.

TYPES OF CHILD-CARE SERVICES AND THEIR ADVANTAGES AND DISADVANTAGES

TYPE OF CARE	ADVANTAGES	DISADVANTAGES
In-home: A person is hired to come into the home and care for children. (The person may perform domestic duties, too.)	All attention is given to one's own child or children. Chances of having health and safety problems are small. Children can be cared for when ill. Children are not ''taken out'' in inclement weather or early hours. Children stay in a home atmosphere.	Quality care is a major problem. Backup arrangements must be made by parents if the hired person cannot work. Social security employer taxes must be paid.
Family day care: A small number of children are cared for in another person's home.	There may be a good selection of family day care services in a community. Usually all children can get the attention they need. This type of service is suitable for after-school care. Hours of operation are often flexible in an effort to meet each parent's needs. Children from the same family who are different ages may be cared for. Children stay in a home-like atmosphere.	Quality care may not be given in all family day care programs. (Most of these are not licensed.) Backup arrangements must be made by parents if the person cannot take children on a given day. Children must be ''taken out'' of their own home each day Many family day care services do not care for sick children.
Group day care: A fairly large number of children are enrolled in a center.	Cooperative play and social living are emphasized. Centers are often licensed so quality may be more or less insured. Backup arrangements are made by the center director. The center may provide special services such as an educational program. Facilities and equipment are designed for children.	Parents are often concerned about the health and safety of their children. The day may be too highly structured, especially for the young child. A home atmosphere is usually not present. Every child may not get the attention they need. Hours and days of operation are not often flexible. Often payment is expected in advance and even when the child is absent. Often ill or injured children cannot be cared for in the center. Children must be ''taken out'' of their own home each day. Some centers are very costly.

2-12 Each type of child-care service has its advantages and disadvantages.

Family planning. Most couples today practice some type of *family planning*. Family planning is deciding on the number and spacing of children. Family planning is more successful today than ever before because many *birth control methods* are available. Birth control methods are methods used to prevent conception. Couples who want to plan their families need to discuss the different methods with their physicians. Physicians can explain each method in terms of:

- How the method prevents pregnancy.
- How successful the method is in preventing unwanted pregnancies.
- The possible side effects and the persons more likely to have these effects.
- The cost of the method.

The physician will look at the couple's health history and give a complete check-up before giving medical advice. A couple can make an educated choice based on the physician's counsel. They also should think about their *personal preferences* (including religious beliefs or likes and dislikes for certain methods) before choosing a method.

Couples can think about the number of children they may want. But they should decide to have a second child only after having the first child. (A joint decision should be made each time a new baby is considered.)

Although the family planning process should take place over time, couples should look at the pros and cons of having more than one child. Other people always seem willing to give advice in this area. They might make statements that encourage having more children like "An only child is usually spoiled," "Two are as easy as one," "Get all the diapers behind you," and "An only child is lonely." Or they might make discouraging statements like "Don't add to the population explosion," and "It's not fair to the first child to have more."

With so much advice couples often wonder what to do. There are no hard and fast rules. Older couples may not be able to space births wide apart. If a woman gives multiple birth, the couple cannot control spacing. The number and spacing of children should be a personal choice for each couple.

There are some points that couples should keep in mind as they make family planning choices. First, for protection of the mother's health, a year or more between pregnancies is advised. After several pregnancies, more time may be needed. A woman needs to consult her physician about her health.

Another point to think about is that there is often less jealousy over the new baby if there are three-year differences between the ages of the children. That way, the "older" children can help with the new baby. Also, some research shows that children spaced three years apart have a better chance for the best development. The spacing gives parents time to work with each child alone before they have to divide their attention.

Not all couples feel that they can handle another child right away. Their feelings depend on their finances, emotional and physical energy, careers, ages, and life-styles. They should realize that only children are not always spoiled or lonely. Couples should not feel guilty if they want only one child. The most important reason for wanting more than one child is the same reason for wanting the first child. If a couple desires to welcome another child into their lives and to share their love and time with that child, they should.

to Know

birth control methods . . . discipline . . .
family day care . . . family planning . . .
foregone income . . . group day care . . .
guidance . . . indirect costs . . . in-home care . . .
mobility . . . multiple-generation families . . .
obstetrician . . . pediatrician

to Review

Write your answers on a separate sheet of paper.

1. True or false. For most couples, parenting is a natural, automatic response following the birth of a baby.

2. Parenting is a rather _____ (even, one-sided) giving relationship between the parent and child for the first few years.

3. True or false. The arguments of those who prefer to stay childless need not be considered by those wanting a child.

4. The most common problems of meeting career and parenthood demands are _____ and _____.

5. Which reason is the most important reason for having a baby?
    a. Our parents want to be grandparents.
    b. Babies are so cute.
    c. A son or daughter could carry on the family business.
    d. We want to share our lives and love with a child.
    e. A child will give us a reason to love each other again.

6. True or false. Good medical care reduces the risk of having a child with birth defects, but it offers no guarantees.

7. Describe three styles of parenting and their effects on children.

8. As a child grows, most expenses _____ (increase, decrease).

9. Most women keep their jobs after birth of children because of _____ and _____ reasons.

10. Three types of child care services are _____, _____, and _____.

11. True or false. Choices about family planning should be made by the woman.

to Do

1. Write a short paper giving your views on the kinds of maturity couples should have before becoming parents.

2. Have a panel discussion on changes that happen in family life because of children.

3. Construct a poster or collage showing the responsibilities of parenthood.

4. Interview several young couples about the parenting skills they had to learn after having their children. (Perhaps they can supply some amusing stories about things that happened when trying to care for their children.)

5. Invite a child care professional offering parenting classes to speak on parenting programs. Have them explain the importance of the programs, the topics covered, costs, number of sessions, and other points. Invite the person to give a demonstration lesson as well.

6. Collect some books, magazines, and pamphlets that are available on child care. Write the title of publication, name and address of publisher, topics covered, age of children discussed, and other important information on 5" x 8" index cards.

7. Interview parents in the post-parental stage of the family life cycle on how their roles as parents changed throughout different stages. Write a paper on your findings.

8. Invite a couple with a full-time homemaker and a couple who both work to discuss how they share home care and child care tasks.

9. Tour one or more local child care settings which fit each of the three types of child care services. Discuss the differences in these services.

JOHN SHAW

Making room for baby

ADRIAN DEMERY

Baby's first chance to see Mom

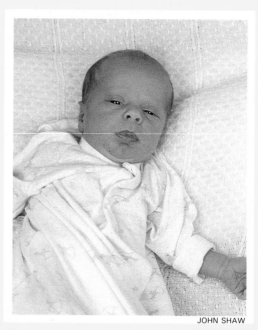

JOHN SHAW

The snug little newborn

48

part two

Prenatal development and the newborn

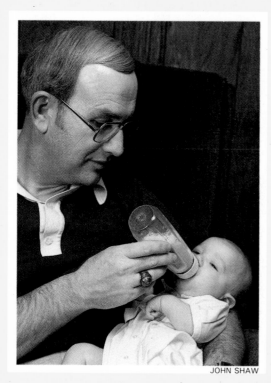

JOHN SHAW

Suppertime with Dad

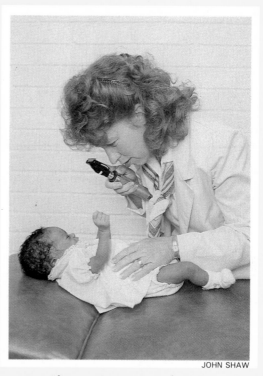

JOHN SHAW

The well-baby checkup

3-1 These children inherited traits from their parents. The younger boy looks like his mother in many ways.

3

Pregnancy

About nine months before the newborn comes into the world, genetic forces start the developmental process. The growth and development of a child begins with the union of an *ovum* (egg or female sex cell) and a *sperm* (male sex cell). Many complex changes take place throughout the nine months before birth. And they are only a preview of the changes that follow.

Much of a person's appearance, temperament, and growth potential are preset by the genes. Genes are given to each person from both the mother and the father, 3-1. These genes control how babies grow and develop before they are ever born.

THE BIOLOGY OF HEREDITY

All people begin life as a united ovum and sperm. At this beginning, called *conception*, every person is just one *cell*. (A cell is the smallest unit of life that is able to reproduce itself.) As the cell grows into a human being, it becomes different from any other person. The differences are caused by heredity. The biology of heredity is complex. You may understand it better by reading about Steve.

Steve is a five-year-old boy. Like many other children his age, Steve asks many questions, enjoys pretend games, and shows interest in letters and numbers. Although Steve shares many traits of other five-year-olds, he is uniquely Steve—not Kate, Peter, Susan, or even his older brother Chris. How did Steve change into a unique collection of billions of cells?

Steve began life as a single cell. The *nucleus*, or center, of any cell contains a hereditary blueprint. This blueprint is a set of instructions for building a living thing—a person, an animal, or a plant. It is written in what scientists call a genetic code.

The genetic code is made of chemical compounds. These rod-shaped chemicals are called *chromosomes*. They contain the information needed to make Steve a complex human. Normal humans have 46 chromosomes (or 23 pairs). Plants and other animals have fewer or more chromosomes.

Each chromosome contains *genes*. Genes are bead-like structures that are strung together to form the rod-shaped chromosomes. There are probably one million genes in a human cell or about 20,000 genes per chromosome. Sometimes, one gene determines one trait. Other times, a group of genes determines one trait.

Steve's genes have determined that he has blue eyes; light brown hair with a reddish tinge; and fair, freckled skin. Steve's genes give him Rh positive blood, type O. They also give him a better than average chance of getting high blood pressure. Because of his genes, Steve learns quickly and shows good recall. This is only part of Steve's genetic information. The sum of Steve's genes, along with his environment, makes him Steve and no one else.

The information in Steve's genes has been passed to him from many generations. His genes came from his parents, grandparents, great-grandparents, and so on. When Steve was conceived, he inherited an equal number of genes from his mother and father. Steve's parents each inherited an equal number of genes from their parents, and so on. That's why Steve may have traits that were passed on from as far back as his great-grandparents, or even further back.

Cell division

Steve's traits were passed on through germ cells. *Germ cells* are the sperm and ova. They are given that name because they are the basis for growth, like a germinating seed is the basis of growth for a flower. Germ cells are different from the *body cells*. Body cells make up bones, nerves, muscles, and organs.

Germ cells contain half the number of chromosomes found in the body cells. This is so that new people have the same number of chromosomes as their ancestors. It also insures that people inherit equally from the mother and father. When Steve was conceived he received 23 single chromosomes from his mother and 23 from his father to make 23 pair or 46 chromosomes. See 3-2.

Germ cells have half the chromosomes of body cells because they divide differently. When body cells duplicate themselves, the chromosomes double and then the cell divides. The two cells left after the division each have 46 chromosomes.

The number of chromosomes in the germ cells are halved through two cell divisions. First, the 46 chromosomes duplicate themselves and divide into two cells. Then, the two cells divide to make four cells with 23 chromosomes each. In the male, there are four sperm from the cell divisions. In the female, there is one ovum and three incomplete cells that do not survive.

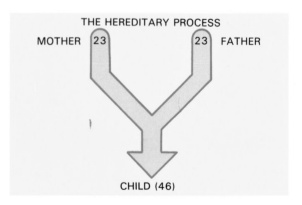

THE HEREDITARY PROCESS

MOTHER 23   23 FATHER

CHILD (46)

3-2 Every child inherits 23 chromosomes from his or her mother and 23 chromosomes from his or her father.

Inheriting unique traits

Steve doesn't look exactly like anyone in his family. But some of his features look like his father's and others look like his mother's. Some don't look like either of his parents'. For instance, Steve's hair is the same color as his mother's. His body build is like his father's. But Steve's eyes are blue, even though both of his parents have brown eyes.

Steve inherited so many different traits because of the way germ cells divide. If the chromosomes of the germ cells always divided in the same way, children of the same parents would probably be identical. But before germ cells divide, the genes in each chromosome change positions. Some genes change positions within the chromosome. Others may *cross over* to the chromosome with which they are paired.

When the germ cells finish dividing, their chromosomes contain very different information than the chromosomes from which they were made. Thus, no two ova or sperm carry the same inheritance.

When the sperm and ovum unite, even more new combinations are made. The chromosomes from the father's sperm join with similar chromosomes from the mother's ovum. When the chromosomes join, gene pairs form to determine different traits. Half of each pair is from the mother and half is from the father. The final combination determines which traits the baby may have.

The genes in a sperm or ovum can be arranged in trillions of different combinations. No two sperm or ova contain exactly the same inheritance. And out of all these germ cells only two unite to make each person. Thus, each person is not "one in a million," but one in trillions.

Dominant and recessive traits

You read before that Steve's eyes are blue and his parents both have brown eyes. You may wonder how Steve's parents could pass on this trait even though neither has blue eyes.

People can pass on traits that don't show up in them. This is because some traits are *dominant* and some are *recessive*. Dominant traits show in a person even if only one gene in a gene pair is for that trait. Recessive traits do not show if only one gene is present. Both genes in the pair must be the same for a recessive trait to show.

Genes for brown and blue eye color are examples of dominant and recessive genes. Brown eyes are dominant and blue are recessive. See 3-3.

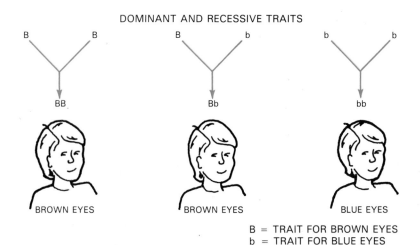

DOMINANT AND RECESSIVE TRAITS

B = TRAIT FOR BROWN EYES
b = TRAIT FOR BLUE EYES

3-3 A dominant trait shows whether both or one of the genes in the pair are for that trait. Recessive traits only show if both genes are for that trait.

Steve's mother has one gene for brown eyes and one for blue, so her eyes are brown. Steve's father also has one gene for brown eyes and one for blue. His eyes are brown. But when the chromosomes of each parent are split to make germ cells, some are left with a gene for blue eyes. Steve was conceived from an ovum with a gene for blue eyes and a sperm with a gene for blue eyes. Since both genes in the pair are the same, Steve's eyes are blue.

The sex of a child is another example of dominant and recessive traits. Sex is controlled by a whole chromosome called the *sex chromosome*. The X chromosome is for female traits and the Y chromosome is for male traits. The X chromosome is recessive, and the Y chromosome is dominant.

Because X is recessive, all normal females have two X chromosomes. Therefore, all ova contain an X chromosome.

Normal males have one X and one Y chromosome. This is because Y is dominant and because all males inherited one X chromosome from their mother. Therefore, a sperm may have an X or a Y chromosome.

Because the female only contributes X chromosomes and the father can contribute either, the sperm always determines the sex of a child. When a sperm with an X chromosome unites with an ovum, the child is female (XX). When a sperm with a Y chromosome unites with an ovum, the child is male (XY). See 3-4.

MULTIPLE PREGNANCY

Sometimes, two or more babies develop in the same pregnancy. This is called a *multiple pregnancy*. Multiple pregnancies are not as common as single pregnancies. Likewise, twins are more common than triplets, and triplets are more common than quadruplets.

In the United States, the frequency of having twins is one in 73 births of blacks and one in 93 births of whites. The likeliness of having triplets is one in 10,000. And only one in 620,000 births is of quadruplets. These statistics vary in different parts of the world.

In the future, multiple pregnancies may become more common. This is because more

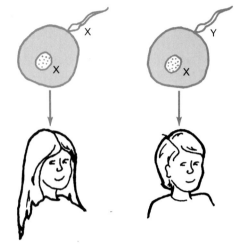

UNION OF SPERM AND OVUM

3-4 The father's sperm alone determines whether a child will be a boy or a girl.

women who have trouble conceiving are using drugs to help them become pregnant. Many of these drugs increase the chances of multiple pregnancy.

There are two main types of multiple pregnancies. They are *dizygotic pregnancy* and *monozygotic pregnancy*. Some multiple pregnancies are combinations of dizygotic and monozygotic pregnancy.

Dizygotic pregnancy

The most common multiple pregnancy is dizygotic pregnancy. ("Di" means two and "zygotic" refers to fertilized ovum.) In a dizygotic pregnancy, children develop from two or more ova. Each ova is joined with a different sperm, 3-5. Each child has different genetic messages, so they are as much alike and different as any other brothers and sisters, 3-6. These children are often called *fraternal* (brotherly) twins, triplets, etc.

Increased hormones seem to be related to dizygotic births. Women with high levels of hormones are more likely to produce two or more ova at one time.

Certain women are more likely to have dizygotic children than others. They include women who have a history of twins in their

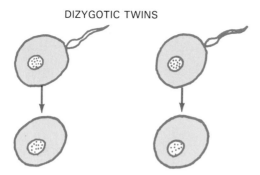

DIZYGOTIC TWINS

3-5 Fraternal twins grow from two separate zygotes. Each zygote carries different genetic codes from the same parents.

mothers' families. (This is because hormone levels may be genetically determined.) Women between the ages of 32 and 37 are also more likely to have twins. After age 38, twins are rare. Women who take artificial hormones to help them get pregnant are likely to have twins.

Fraternal children may or may not be the same sex. They look different at birth and show

greater differences as they mature. Children of dizygotic births each have their own *chorion*, 3-7. (The chorion is a membrane that surrounds the baby in the uterus.)

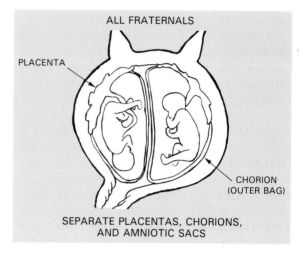

ALL FRATERNALS

PLACENTA

CHORION (OUTER BAG)

SEPARATE PLACENTAS, CHORIONS, AND AMNIOTIC SACS

3-7 All fraternal twins have separate chorions.

JOHN SHAW

3-6 One of these fraternal twins looks more like his older brother than his twin.

Monozygotic pregnancy

In a monozygotic pregnancy, children develop from a single ovum which was united with a single sperm. ("Mono" means one and "zygotic" refers to a fertilized ovum.) During the early days of the pregnancy, the ovum splits to produce two or more children, 3-8. The reason for the splitting is unknown.

If the ovum does not completely split, the babies will be *Siamese twins*. They are joined in one or more places. Some may even "share" internal organs such as a stomach.

Babies from a monozygotic pregnancy carry the same genetic background. This is because they came from one fertilized ovum. Thus, these babies are usually called *identical* twins, triplets, etc.

Identical children are very similar in appearance. They are often confused by family members, 3-9. But except for their genes, identical children are not exactly alike. Their fingerprints, palm prints, and foot prints are similar but not exactly the same. Also, environment

MONOZYGOTIC TWINS

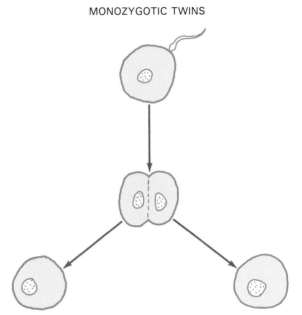

3-8 Identical twins grow from a single zygote that splits into two cells carrying the same genetic code.

3-9 Even in different outfits, these identical twins are often confused.

makes identical children different. For instance, one child may be larger because of better nourishment, even before birth.

Some identical twins are *mirror twins*. They look the way you and your mirror image would appear. For instance, one may have a birthmark on the right shoulder and the other may have one on the left shoulder. One may be right-handed and the other left-handed.

Sometimes it is difficult to tell whether children are identical. At the time of birth, a physician may be able to tell. Identical children must be of the same sex. Unlike dizygotic children, they usually share one chorion. See 3-10. However, identical children may each have their own chorions. Blood tests can be used for positive proof. Skin grafting can also be used as a test.

Mixed types

Multiple pregnancies may be both monozygotic and dizygotic if three or more children are born. In mixed types, two or more ova are fertilized by separate sperm (dizygotic). Then, one or more of the the fertilized ova may split (monozygotic).

In a mixed pregnancy of triplets, two children are identical and one is fraternal, 3-11.

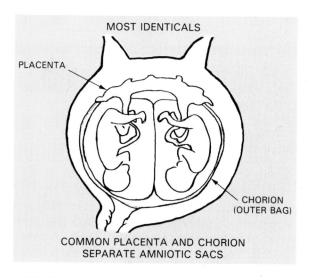

3-10 Twins who share a common chorion are identical.

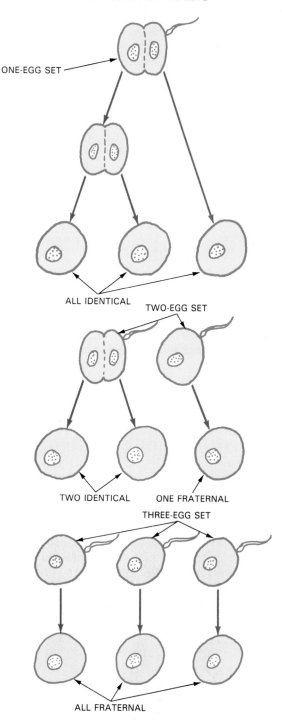

3-11 Depending on the number of zygotes, triplets may be all identical; two identical and one fraternal; or all fraternal.

With quadruplets, there could be three identical and one fraternal. Or two could be identical with two fraternal. There could even be two identical pairs, but as far as anyone knows there has never been such a case.

STAGES IN PRENATAL DEVELOPMENT

As you read earlier in the chapter, each person is produced by the union of one ovum with one sperm. Many changes happen between conception and birth. The development that takes place during that time is called *prenatal development*. Prenatal development is divided into the *germinal stage*, the *embryonic stage*, and the *fetal stage*.

Germinal stage

The first stage of prenatal development is called the germinal stage. The germinal stage covers about two weeks of the pregnancy.

Each ovum is stored in a small sac inside the ovary called a *follicle*. Hormones cause some follicles to grow and fill with fluid each month. Around the middle of the menstrual cycle, one ovum is released from the follicle, and the other follicles become inactive. (Sometimes more than one ovum is released—as in a dizygotic pregnancy.)

The *Fallopian tube* is a hollow tube connected to the uterus with fingerlike projections. It gathers up the ovum as it emerges from the ovary. Once inside the Fallopian tube, the ovum moves very slowly down the tube.

At the time the egg is released, hormones help the Fallopian tubes move to gather the egg. They also prepare the *uterus* for the arrival of the fertilized egg. The uterus is the organ in which the baby is developed and protected until birth.

Over 100 million sperm enter the woman's body during intercourse. These sperm begin a journey to the ovum that lasts around ten minutes. Many sperm do not survive. Only a few hundred reach the Fallopian tube.

Sperm may meet the ovum at any point. Conception usually happens when the ovum has moved no further than one-third of the way down the Fallopian tube. Conception after that point isn't likely because the ovum begins to die about 24 hours after ovulation.

About a dozen sperm approach the ovum and try to break through its surface. Only one sperm successfully enters, or fertilizes, the egg. Once one sperm is accepted, no other sperm can enter the ovum. This is the point of conception. It marks the beginning of the germinal stage of pregnancy.

The fertilized egg is called a *zygote*. It remains a single cell for about a day and a half. After that time, it begins to divide. On the third day, a 32-cell egg enters the uterus. Cell division continues at a rapid pace for about three days. See 3-12. Through this time, the egg floats freely in the uterus.

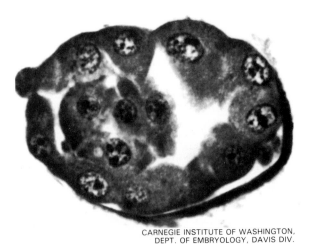

CARNEGIE INSTITUTE OF WASHINGTON, DEPT. OF EMBRYOLOGY, DAVIS DIV.

3-12 During the germinal stage, a four-day old zygote like the one pictured would enter the uterus.

About one week after conception, the ovum begins to embed in the wall of the uterus. The cells continue to divide. The chorion and *amnion* (a fluid filled sac) begin to form. They surround the cells and protect the baby until birth. The *placenta*, an organ filled with blood vessels, begins to develop against the wall of the uterus. The *umbilical cord* grows out from the placenta and connects with the baby at the navel. See 3-13. The umbilical cord is a group

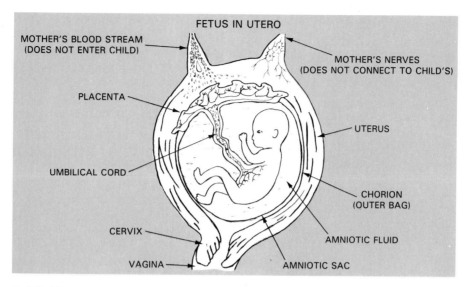

FETUS IN UTERO

MOTHER'S BLOOD STREAM
(DOES NOT ENTER CHILD)

MOTHER'S NERVES
(DOES NOT CONNECT TO CHILD'S)

PLACENTA

UTERUS

UMBILICAL CORD

CHORION
(OUTER BAG)

CERVIX

AMNIOTIC FLUID

VAGINA

AMNIOTIC SAC

3-13 The amnion, chorion, and placenta develop at the
end of the germinal stage. They protect and nourish
the baby until it is born.

PREPARATIONS HAPPENING IN THE GERMINAL STAGE

(Time frame: Conception through day 14)

Cell divisions occurring.
Fertilized egg embedding in uterine wall; amnion,
placenta, and umbilical cord beginning.

3-14 Cell division results in the beginnings
of a baby and in a life-support system
between the mother and baby.

BODY SYSTEMS DEVELOPING IN THE EMBRYONIC STAGE

(Time frame: Day 15 through 8 weeks)

Internal organs (heart, liver, digestive system,
brain, and lungs) developing.
Tissue segments (future vertebrae in a spinal
column) forming.
Limb buds (future arms and legs) appearing.
Ears and eyes beginning.

3-15 All major body systems are developed
during the embryonic stage.

of blood vessels that nourishes the baby,
removes its wastes, and provides it with needed
hormones. When the baby can receive nourishment from the mother, the germinal stage has
ended, 3-14.

Embryonic stage

The second stage of prenatal development is
the embryonic stage. This is thought of as the
most critical stage of pregnancy. At this time,
almost all body systems develop as shown in
3-15. The embryonic stage lasts about six
weeks.

During this time, changes happen so quickly
that by the end of the stage the embryo
resembles a small human being. See 3-16. The
embryo has tiny arms, legs, fingers, toes, and
a face. But it does not have solid bones.
Cartilege supports the body. Cartilege is soft
bone tissue like that found in the tip of your
nose. The embryo also has a beating heart, a
brain, lungs, and all the other major organs.

Because of the rapid development of all parts
of the body, problems during this stage can
affect the baby for life. Preventing problems
at this stage is the best insurance for a healthy,

Pregnancy 59

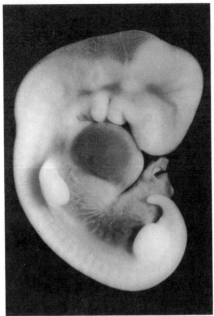

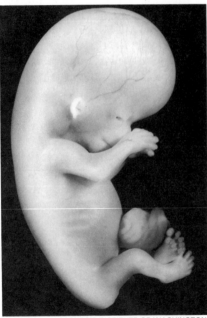

3-16 The baby changes quickly during the fetal stage. At four and one-half weeks, the brain, spinal cord, limb buds, and eyes can be seen (A). In just a little more than two months, the tiny embryo (1 1/2 inches) is well-developed (B).

normal baby. From this point, the baby receives both good and harmful substances from the mother through the umbilical cord. The mother's health habits become very important during this stage.

Fetal stage

When bone cells begin to replace cartilege, the baby enters the fetal stage of development. This stage begins about nine weeks after conception. From this point until birth, a baby is known medically as a *fetus*.

During the fetal stage, all parts of the body mature and overall size increases quickly, 3-17. Major changes in the fetus are listed in 3-18.

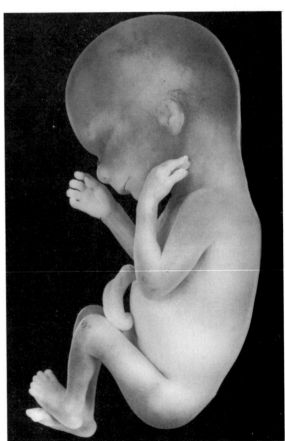

3-17 A three-month, four-inch fetus will continue to grow and mature until birth.

RAPID GROWTH OCCURRING IN THE FETAL STAGE

(Time frame: Beginning of third month until birth)

(9 weeks)
Facial features forming.
Limbs, hands, feet, fingers and toes developing.

(12 weeks)
3'' (7.5 cm) long; 1 oz. (28g).
Muscles forming.
Teeth and vocal cords developing.
Eyelids and nails appearing.

(16 weeks)
6-8''(15-20.5 cm) long; 5-6 oz. (140-168g).
Lanugo (cottony growth) appearing.
Heartbeat audible through a stethoscope.
Eyebrows and eyelashes growing.

(20 weeks)
10-12'' (25.5-30.5 cm) long; 1 lb. (1/2 kg).
Sweat glands forming.
Head hair appearing.
Vernix caseosa (cheesy material) covering body.
Skin developing.

(24 weeks)
14'' (35.5 cm) long; 2 lbs. (1 kg).
Eyes maturing.
Taste buds developing.

(28-38 weeks)
Rapid growth.
Lanugo disappearing.
Fatty tissue forming under skin.
Body organs maturing.

3-18 The baby grows and body systems mature during the longer fetal stage.

By the fourth month, the fetus has usually grown enough for the mother to look pregnant.

Two milestones happen during the fetal stage. Between the fourth and fifth months, a mother begins to feel her baby's movements. The baby can turn, swallow, and even suck its thumb. The baby also can move its head and push with the hands, feet, and limbs. The mother's feeling of movements is called *quickening*. The mother should report to her physician the date when she first feels these movements. This stage is often the first time when the baby's heartbeat can be heard with a stethoscope as well.

A second milestone is reached when the fetus is seven months, or 28 weeks, old. This is the age at which most babies could survive if they were born. By this time, the baby's brain has more control over the body systems than it ever had before. The seventh month after conception is called the *age of viability*. Most babies born at this time would need some intensive care in hospitals. A few babies born before seven months have survived with special care.

Even though a baby born at seven months can survive, it has a better chance of surviving the closer it gets to nine months. (This is true unless earlier delivery is needed for medical reasons.) In the last two months of pregnancy, the baby's lungs become stronger. The baby becomes larger.

In the ninth month of pregnancy, the fetus receives immunities from the mother. These help prevent the baby from catching some diseases after it is born. The baby also turns to a head-down position (in most cases) to prepare for birth.

to Know

to Review

Write your answers on a separate sheet of paper.

1. Germ cells have _____ (23, 46) chromosomes.

2. True or false. Because Susan looks just like her mother, she inherited more traits from her mother than her father.

3. Paul and Emily both have blue eyes. They are expecting a baby. Their baby's eyes will be:
    a. Brown, because both of Emily's parents and Paul's father have brown eyes.
    b. Blue, because neither Paul nor Emily carry traits for brown eyes.
    c. Blue or brown, because Emily inherited a trait for brown eyes from her mother.

4. Patty and Patrick—who look almost alike in size, coloring, and facial features—are _____ (identical, fraternal) twins.

5. True or false. In the germinal stage, the zygote receives nutrients through the placenta.

6. The stage in which the baby's body systems and organs start to appear is the:
    a. Fetal stage.
    b. Embryonic stage.
    c. Germinal stage.

7. True or false. The mother's nutrition doesn't matter during the embryonic stage because the baby has not developed enough.

8. During the fetal stage, the baby's limbs are supported by _____ (cartilage, bones).

9. By the fourth or fifth month of pregnancy, the baby begins to:
    a. Develop vital organs.
    b. Receive nutrients from the mother.
    c. Turn and kick.

10. True or false. A baby born at seven months has a better chance of surviving than a baby born at nine months.

to Do

1. You have heard it said that Jane has her mother's smile, her uncle's artistic ability, and so on. Because our blood relatives have common ancestors, family members share common traits. Make a list of some traits of someone you know. Include physical, mental, and personality traits as well as interests, and talents. Beside each trait, write the name(s) of a relative(s) with whom that person shares a trait.

2. Collect pictures of identical and fraternal twins, triplets, etc. and note how alike or different they are. Try to find pictures of the same people that have been taken over a period of several years.

3. On a bulletin board or poster, show how quadruplets can be all identical, three identical and one fraternal, two identical and two fraternal, two identical pairs, and all four fraternal.

4. Design a poster on the theme: "Be Good to Your Baby Before it is Born."

JOHN SHAW

Because of the way genes are combined in reproduction, brothers and sisters may have many differences as well as similarities.

The prenatal period is full of preparations for the new baby. Besides getting the house ready for the "new arrival," the mother's body is preparing for birth.

Prenatal care

After studying this chapter, you will be able to:
- ☐ Describe how health and care factors affect the unborn baby.
- ☐ List ways that family members can be involved in pregnancy and childbirth.
- ☐ Explain what happens during the three stages of labor.
- ☐ Describe the options available to parents for childbirth and care of the newborn.
- ☐ Explain the physical and emotional changes in the mother during the postnatal period.

At no other time are the lives of two people—mother and baby—closer than during the prenatal period. Even before the mother knows that she is pregnant, the baby affects the mother's life. The mother's body changes to prepare for nine months of growth. The baby continues to affect the mother's body through delivery. The mother, in turn, has a great affect on her baby's body. Mother provides the safe "home" for the baby. She eats, breathes, and eliminates wastes for both of them, and she helps bring the baby into the world.

All family members need to be close during the prenatal stage. Each family member should support other members in making adjustments to the new life of the baby. Closeness at this time can set the stage for better marriage relationships. It can insure better parenting through each stage in the child's development.

CARE FOR THE PREGNANT MOTHER

The National Foundation March of Dimes uses the slogan, "Be good to your baby before it is born." Parents-to-be should take this slogan seriously. Because more is known about pregnancy, childbirth, and care of the infant than ever before, there are many steps parents-to-be can take to safeguard the mother's and baby's health.

Prenatal care should start even before pregnancy. Good health habits through childhood and adolescence help prepare a person for childbearing. But prenatal care directed by a physician is needed as soon as a woman believes she may have conceived. Care is needed whether it is a first, second, or later pregnancy.

Signs of pregnancy

A woman cannot feel the union of sperm and egg in the Fallopian tube. She cannot feel the cell divisions as the baby begins to develop. But her body is immediately signaled to nourish and protect the new life. Hormones trigger changes in some of the woman's organs. These changes are recognized through certain signs.

The signs of pregnancy should not be thought of as symptoms of an illness. Pregnancy is a normal process. If a woman is in good health and is happy about having a child, she may even feel better than before pregnancy. The signs of pregnancy are given in 4-1. They are divided into *presumptive signs* and *positive signs*. The presumptive signs could be symptoms of something other than pregnancy. Physicians need to determine the cause. On the other hand, positive signs of pregnancy are signs which physicians identify as definitely caused by pregnancy.

SIGNS OF PREGNANCY

PRESUMPTIVE SIGNS	
Amenorrhea (cessation of menstruation). If the woman is usually regular in her menstrual cycle, a delay of 10 or more days is a sign.	**Swelling tenderness of the breasts.** Breast enlargement and tenderness is often the first sign noted by pregnant women.
Nausea. Nausea is present in about half to two-thirds of all pregnancies. Because it often occurs in the morning hours, it is called ''morning sickness.'' Nausea may happen at any time of the day or evening. Nausea occurring at the same time each day or evening through the fourth to twelfth weeks is a sign.	**Skin discoloration.** Red marks may be seen as the breasts and abdomen enlarge. Darkening of skin may be noted on face and nipples of some women.
	Internal changes. Physicians often note softening of the cervix (Goodell's sign). There also may be a softening of the lower part of the uterus (Hegar's sign) and a bluish tinge to the vagina and cervix due to circulatory congestion (Chadwick's sign). The uterus is also enlarged with irregular areas of firmness and softness (Piskacek's sign).
Sleepiness or tiredness. Many women feel tired or sleepy during the first few months of pregnancy.	
Frequency of urination. The growing uterus puts pressure on the bladder. Or hormones may cause more frequent urination.	**Other signs.** Other symptoms include backache, groin pains, faintness, abdominal swelling, leg cramps, varicose veins, and indigestion.
POSITIVE SIGNS	
HCG (Human Chorionic Gonadatrophin). HCG is a hormone found in the blood and urine of pregnant women. Lab tests may detect the hormone's presence as early as the first two weeks of pregnancy.	**Fetal image.** Fetal image may be seen on X-ray film or with ultrasound scanning (which uses sound waves to project the baby's outline on a screen).
Fetal heartbeat. Fetal heartbeat can be heard through a stethoscope at 16 weeks.	**Fetal shape.** The baby's shape may be felt through the abdominal wall.
Fetal movement. Spontaneous movement begins at 11 weeks but is not felt until 16 to 18 weeks.	**Uterine contractions.** These painless contractions may be noted by a physician.

4-1 Pregnancy is not an illness, but changes in the mother's body may be signs of pregnancy.

Medical care and supervision

Medical supervision is the best insurance for safe and successful childbearing. Prenatal care is given by private physicians and by physicians in hospital clinics, public health centers, and private health organizations.

Ideally, a woman should have a complete check-up before she becomes pregnant. Some health problems can be corrected before pregnancy. Once a woman believes she is pregnant, she should make an appointment. It is a good idea for the father-to-be to go along. The first appointment is the main one for preparing the soon-to-be parents for the pregnancy.

At the first appointment the physician usually gathers some general information (address, employment, age). He or she obtains the health history including background on the woman's menstrual cycle and other pregnancies. Next the woman is examined, 4-2. The check-up usually includes measures of height, weight, and blood pressure; urine analysis; and blood tests. Blood is tested for blood type, Rh factor, and for ruling out anemia and syphilis. Checks on eyes, ears, nose, throat, teeth, heart, and lungs are also made. The physician examines breasts and abdomen and conducts a pelvic (internal) examination possibly including measurements of the birth canal. Following the check-up, the physician will give an estimated due date for the baby's birth. He or she will discuss prenatal care such as diet and exercise.

The physician may explain options and procedures for the parents-to-be. These may include prenatal education, childbirth, and types of pain relief. Rules of the hospital (husband in labor/delivery and rooming in with newborn) and costs including insurance coverage also may be discussed. The date for the next appointment is chosen. Usually a physician sees the woman once a month during the first six months of pregnancy, twice a month during the seventh and eighth months, and once a week for the rest of the pregnancy.

The health of the newborn

An unborn baby depends on the mother for a healthy start. Mothers who have healthy babies often share certain characteristics. They also follow good health practices.

Maternal characteristics. Women with certain "ideal" characteristics may have a head start toward a problem-free pregnancy. Women who do not have these characteristics are often considered high risk mothers-to-be. Important factors are age, size, Rh factor, and emotional stability.

The ideal ages for childbearing are 21 through 28 years. Teens and women over 36 years of age are high risk cases. Because teenage mothers are still growing themselves, they cannot always meet the needs of their babies. Teens have more premature babies (babies born too soon or too small), still births (babies born dead), and malformed babies than do women in the ideal age group. Women over 36 years

JOHN SHAW

4-2 Checking weight is a routine part of a mother-to-be's check-ups.

of age have more babies with birth defects than women of ideal childbearing age. But normal, healthy babies born to these older women tend to be brighter than average. This is because older parents often spend more time with their children.

Proper weight for age, height, and body build is vital to a healthy pregnancy. A woman whose non-pregnant weight is below 85 percent or above 120 percent of her proper weight could endanger her health and her child's health. The mother's dietary needs are often met before those of her baby. An underweight woman's food intake will often be used first to correct her own deficiencies. In these situations, the baby may be undernourished. Underweight women often have low-birth weight infants.

Compared with an ideal-weight woman, an obese woman uses a greater proportion of her food intake for energy. High blood pressure, *diabetes* (excess sugar in the blood and urine), and delivery problems are more likely when a woman is overweight.

A mother should achieve her ideal weight before becoming pregnant. Most physicians do not try to make major changes in the mother's weight during pregnancy. If a pregnant woman eats less, she may not eat enough nutrients for proper growth of the baby. A pregnant woman should carefully follow her physician's recommendations on diet.

Rh factor affects the baby's health. The Rh factor is a protein substance found in the red blood cells of about 85 percent of the population. (The substance was discovered and first tested in the Rhesus monkey. This is why it is named Rh factor.) People who have the substance are called Rh positive (Rh +), and those who do not are called Rh negative (Rh −).

In 12 percent of all marriages, there is an Rh + man and an Rh − woman. The Rh + man and Rh − woman is the only combination that can cause the Rh disease. If their baby inherits the Rh + blood type from the father, he or she may be a victim of the disease. The Rh disease is a blood-destroying anemia of the baby. It is medically known as *erythroblastosis fetalis*.

The Rh disease does not affect the first Rh + unborn. But during any pregnancy, some of the baby's Rh + cells may enter the mother's bloodstream. The cells often enter during birth. This problem occurs in four percent of the cases. These cells are foreign to the mother's Rh − system. The mother's body fights these Rh + cells by making antibodies. The mother is then immunized against the blood cells of future Rh + babies. In the next pregnancy, these antibodies cross the placenta. If the baby has Rh + blood, the antibodies destroy the baby's red blood cells.

Once parents who had this problem had to limit their family size. This is because once the Rh problem begins the effects worsen with each pregnancy. But in 1968 a vaccine, *anti-Rh − immune globulin* was approved for use. The Rh − mother is given the vaccine within 72 hours after birth of each Rh + baby. The vaccine blocks the growth of antibodies. The vaccine must also be given after a miscarriage or abortion of a Rh + baby. If an Rh − female receives Rh + blood during a transfusion, she should receive the vaccine, also. The vaccine is almost 100 percent effective. But it does not work if the woman has already become sensitized to Rh + cells.

If an Rh − pregnant woman has already become sensitized, physicians can tell whether the fetus has this blood disease. They use a test called *amniocentesis* to detect the disease and its severity. Amniocentesis is a test in which a needle is inserted through the woman's abdomen into the amniotic sac and a sample of the fluid is removed for a cell study.

The physicians can combat the problem in one or more of several ways. They can deliver the baby, even if premature, in order to save its life. Immediately after birth, physicians can gradually replace the newborn's damaged blood with Rh − blood (exchange transfusion). Or they can use exchange transfusion(s) while the baby is still in the mother's uterus. These methods have saved many babies, but they are risky.

A woman's thoughts and feelings are also important to a healthy baby. Feelings stimulate the nervous system and the flow of *adrenaline*. (Adrenaline is a hormone which prepares the body to cope with stress. Adrenaline can make a person feel more energetic.) Both the nervous system and adrenaline control heart rate, breathing, and muscle tension. When a mother is happy and relaxed, her adrenaline level is low, her heartbeat and breathing are slow and steady, and her muscles are relaxed. See 4-3.

When the mother is under stress, adrenaline crosses the placenta to the baby carrying its silent stress signals. Thus, the mother's stress increases both her heartbeat and muscle tension and the baby's. Later in the pregnancy, the baby not only receives the adrenaline signal but also hears changes in the mother's heartbeat and breathing.

Of course mothers-to-be cannot avoid all stress. For this reason, one question often asked is, "Can stress harm the unborn baby?" There are some myths about stress, especially fright. A rather commonly held myth is that fright

ADRIAN DEMERY

4-3 Staying relaxed and content is important to the baby's health.

caused birthmarks on the baby. This is not true. Stress affects the unborn in much the same way as it does you.

Some stress can be handled by the unborn baby. If the stress is long-lasting, severe, or frequent, the mother may have a more difficult delivery. The baby may be smaller, fussy, or very active. Thus, emotional support during pregnancy is good for both mother and baby.

Maternal health habits. Maternal health habits are very similar to good health habits for all people. Good health habits are always important. But when a woman is pregnant health habits have an even greater bearing on her health and her baby's health.

There are some changes in health habits due to pregnancy. For instance, a pregnant woman may be advised to increase the intake of some foods. She may be advised to use diet supplements such as vitamins and iron preparations in order to support her own needs and those of her baby.

A few precautions are also added to regular health care. Some precautions are taken because of the changing nature and needs of the mother's body. For instance, during the last few weeks of pregnancy, the mother's size and shape and her lowered energy-level may require her to give up tennis.

Precautions must be taken for the baby, too. For instance, *rubella* (three-day measles) is not a serious disease for most children or adults. But serious, life-threatening birth defects may occur in the unborn if the mother has this disease during the early weeks of pregnancy.

Basic maternal health guidelines should be followed by every pregnant woman. Because every pregnancy is different, the mother-to-be should ask her physician for specific recommendations and follow the suggestions.

Nutrition. The old saying that mothers-to-be are "eating for two (or even more)" is correct. During the first week, the baby is fed entirely on the contents of the yolk sac of the ovum. But after embedding, the fertilized egg feeds on the mucous tissues that line the womb. By the twelfth week, the yolk sac is completely used, and the baby depends totally on the mother.

Prenatal care 69

"Eating for two" does not mean doubling or greatly increasing caloric intake. After all, the unborn baby is very small. But the mother does need more nutrients than normal to meet the baby's need for growth.

Scientists now feel that a woman needs to get essential nutrients throughout her life to prepare for motherhood. Providing for her

DAILY BASIC DIET FOR PREGNANT MOTHERS

Milk	(3 servings for the first three months [4 if mother is a teenager]; 4 servings for the next six months).
	Typical servings: 1 cup whole evaporated, skim, dry milk, buttermilk, or yogurt; two 1 inch cubes of hard cheese; part can be in cream soups, custards, or puddings.
Protein Foods	(3 servings for the first three months; 4 servings for the next six months.)
	Typical servings: 2 to 3 oz. of cooked lean solid meat, poultry, or fish. 3/4 cup cooked dry beans, peas, or lentils; 1/4 cup peanut butter; 1 oz. (30 g) nuts, and 2 eggs.
Leafy Green Vegetables	(2 servings)
	Typical servings: 1 cup raw or 3/4 cup cooked spinach, kale, dark leafy lettuces, broccoli, chard, collard and other greens, brussel sprouts, asparagus, cabbage, watercress.
Vitamin C Rich Fruits and Vegetables	(1 serving)
	Typical servings: 1 cup raw or 3/4 cup cooked oranges, grapefruit, papaya, tangerines, pineapple, tomatoes, cabbage, brussels sprouts, broccoli, cauliflower.
Other Fruits and Vegetables	(1 serving)
	Typical servings: 1 cup raw or 3/4 cup cooked carrots, potatoes, sweet potatoes, yams, squash, hominy, bean sprouts, mushrooms; fresh apricots, peaches, apples, bananas, persimmons, pears, plums, watermelon, figs, berries, grapes; dates, prunes, raisins. (Salads and raw fruit nibbles are good for snack.)
Grain Products, Whole or Enriched	(3 servings)
	Typical servings: 1 slice of bread; 1/2 cup rice, hot cereal, or cooked pasta; 2 corn tortillas; 1 large flour tortilla; 1 muffin, biscuit, dumpling, pancake, or waffle. 2 inch square of cornbread; 3/4 cup of ready-to-eat cereal (not sugared kind).

4-4 Pregnant women should consult their physicians about diets suited to their own special needs.
(Adapted from the National Foundation March of Dimes.)

own needs and those of her unborn baby puts a nutritional strain on the woman's body. Pregnant girls under 17 years of age have more nutritional problems because of their own growth demands. Good nutritional habits begun in pregnancy should be continued after the baby is born. Parents are responsible for shaping the eating patterns of their families. There is a direct link between what a pregnant woman eats and:

- Her weight gain.
- The unborn's weight gain.
- The infant's growth.
- The infant's mental capacity.
- The infant's physical performance.

Thus, a well-balanced diet is essential.

Normal cell growth calls for proteins, fats, carbohydrates, minerals, and vitamins. Diets from reputable sources, such as the one shown in 4-4, include all these nutrients. Diets for pregnant and nursing mothers provide more calcium, iron, folic acid, and protein than diets for non-pregnant women. But it is important for each pregnant woman to get advice from her physician about her own needs. Physicians sometimes prescribe vitamin and mineral supplements. These are not substitutes for good nutrition. They should be taken with a regular diet.

Mothers-to-be and their physicians are concerned about weight gain. People have advised weight gain from 10 pounds to no limit. Now experts suggest between 25 and 35 pounds depending on the woman's height and non-pregnant weight. To do this, mothers need to eat 200 to 300 extra calories per day. Weight gain during pregnancy is not all stored as fat. See 4-5.

Physicians monitor the weight gain of their patients throughout pregnancy. Weight gains depend on the stage of pregnancy. The following amounts are common:

- 1-3 months—about 5 lbs. total.
- 4-8 months—about 2-3 lbs. per month.
- 9 months—about 1 lb. per week.

Physicians are concerned about too much weight gain. Too much weight puts extra strain on the heart and makes the woman uncomfortable and clumsy. At one time, people thought that longer labor and *toxemia* (a metabolic disorder that affects blood) were related to weight gain. Research now shows that this is not necessarily true. But sudden, generalized swelling and weight gain are very serious. They require immediate medical attention.

Hygiene practices. Normal grooming and general body care is continued during pregnancy. Careful grooming (with a new hair style or make-up) may actually help the mother-to-be feel better during any physical discomforts or emotional stress of pregnancy, 4-6.

Many physicians may make these suggestions to their pregnant patients:

- Have a dental check-up.
- Avoid very cold or very hot baths.
- Replace tub baths with showers or sponge baths during the last 4 to 6 weeks of pregnancy to prevent internal infection and possible falls due to body shape and size.
- Wash any crust on the breast with a clean cloth and warm water. (A crust may be formed by the drying fluid which has oozed from the breast. Soap is not needed to remove this.)

Pregnant women should ask their physicians for advice about hygiene during pregnancy.

WEIGHT GAINED DURING PREGNANCY

Portion of added weight	Weight gain in pounds	Weight gain in kg
Baby	7.5	3.0
Uterus	2.0	1.0
Placenta	1.5	.5
Amniotic fluid	2.0	1.0
Increased maternal blood volume	3.5	1.5
Increased maternal breast mass	1.5	.5
Increased maternal stored fat and protein	4.0	2.0
Increased maternal fluid retention	4.0	2.0
Total weight gain =	26.0	11.5

4-5 Pregnancy adds to normal weight.

Rest and sleep. A mother-to-be needs much rest and sleep. Many physicians advise eight hours of sleep at night and at least one 15 to 30 minute rest with or without sleep during the day. Most women feel fatigued during the first few months and last few weeks of pregnancy. Exhaustion is never good, especially in pregnancy. But a sleepless night or two is not dangerous. If a woman has special sleep problems, she should always avoid "relaxing or sleeping" drugs until advised by her physician.

Physical activities and exercises. Unless advised by her physician to limit her physical activities, a pregnant woman can and should be active. Generally, exercise is important. It helps keep weight within normal limits, strengthens muscles used in delivery, aids oxygen use, increases energy, and relieves tensions.

Many physicians do advise that mothers-to-be avoid contact sports, sports which jolt the pelvic region, and sports that could result in falls. On the other hand, physicians often advise walking throughout pregnancy.

Special exercises are often taught in childbirth classes. These exercises are used to relieve back and leg strain of later pregnancy and prepare the muscles for delivery. Other special exercises have been designed for after delivery. They help the uterus contract and strengthen the stretched abdominal muscles.

Protection from drugs, diseases, and other agents. Many pregnant mothers fear that the children they carry may be born deformed or mentally retarded. One-fifth to one-third of all pregnancies end in *spontaneous abortions* (miscarriages). Many of these spontaneous abortions were caused by defects. Serious birth defects harm one in 50 newborns. Other newborns have birth defects that are not discovered until the child is older.

What many pregnant women don't know is that many birth defects can be prevented if the mother protects herself before and during pregnancy. Only about 20 per cent of all birth defects are strictly inherited. Most are caused by outside agents such as drugs or diseases.

Early prenatal care is most important. A mother can take many steps on her own to

JOHN SHAW

4-6 Wearing cheerful clothing and keeping hair and makeup attractive helps the mother keep a good attitude through pregnancy.

insure a healthy baby. She should eat a balanced diet and avoid alcohol and smoking. She should also be careful about taking prescribed and over-the-counter drugs. People in the United States tend to take a lot of drugs. One nationwide study showed that most women take at least four drugs during pregnancy, not including home remedies and vitamin supplements.

Many agents (drugs, diseases, and other substances) that enter the mother's body pass through the placenta to the unborn baby during the birth process. Many harmful agents are drugs. These include over-the-counter drugs, prescription drugs, and illegal drugs. One disaster connected with drugs and pregnancy dealt with a prescription drug called Thalidomide. Thalidomide is a tranquilizer that was used in Europe in the early 1960s to control morning sickness during pregnancy. More than 10,000 babies of mothers who took this drug were born with birth defects.

Some diseases the mother has during pregnancy cause problems for the unborn. Diabetes and anemia often cause serious problems for both mother and the unborn. *Sexually transmitted diseases (STDs)* are extremely dangerous for both the mother and the unborn. STDs are highly contagious diseases passed from one person to another mainly through sexual contact. Some STDs, such as syphillis, become dangerous about mid-way in the pregnancy if the mother has not been treated. Other STDs are transmitted during the birth process. There is about a 50 percent chance of transmitting *Acquired Immune Deficiency Syndrome (AIDS)* during the birth process when the umbilical cord separates from the placenta of a mother with AIDS. Chlamydia, gonorrhea, and genital herpes infect the baby in the birth canal. These diseases may also infect the baby if the amniotic sac breaks prior to delivery. Unlike many other diseases, rubella (German measles) is rarely dangerous to a mother. But it results in severe problems to the unborn if exposed early in the pregnancy.

Other agents, too, cause problems such as X-rays and inadequate maternal diet. Chart 4-7 gives agents known to be dangerous. Other agents may be added to the list as research finds them. Any agent may be harmful to an unborn child under certain circumstances.

Mothers should also know that in most cases the strength of the drug or disease is not as important as the timing. For instance, mothers who took one tablet of Thalidomide between the twenty-seventh and fortieth day of pregnancy were as likely to have defective babies as those who took many tablets during that time. Harmful agents cause birth defects more frequently from the second to the eighth week of pregnancy. On the other hand, smoking is more dangerous in the second half of pregnancy. Aspirin creates more problems during the last three months of pregnancy.

THE ROLE OF THE FAMILY

Pregnancy should be a family affair. Studies show that fathers-to-be who become involved with pregnancy and childbirth later become more involved in rearing their children. Children enjoy preparing for the new arrival. Even a two-year-old can place a toy in the nursery. And, children who help prepare for the new baby are not as jealous of a new sister or brother.

When mothers had their babies at home, some fathers became involved. However, women relatives and friends more often helped the new mother. When hospital deliveries became common, fathers were further detached from the birthing process. It was the father's duty to call the doctor and bring his wife to the hospital. Once in the hospital, he was sent to the "pacing room" to pace the floor, nap, compare notes with other fathers, and watch the clock. When the "ordeal" was over, the bleary-eyed father handed out cigars and smiled at his baby through the nursery window.

Many recent fathers-to-be are taking a more active role during the pregnancy and delivery of their babies. The husband's role changes throughout the pregnancy and birth. During the first few months, many mothers are concerned about their own health and their babies'. Husbands need to reassure their wives. Husbands can also help with the selection of a physician and other decisions concerning delivery.

The middle part of pregnancy is often the most pleasant for the entire family. Mothers-to-be often feel their best. Husbands and other family members are more aware of the growing child as they can see the growth and feel the baby's movement. In many families, this is the time of home preparations. Family members may decorate a nursery and gather many of the items needed for the baby. Young children are often told about the baby at this time. They should be included as much as possible in the preparations.

The final months are an exciting and trying period. Mothers-to-be are often concerned about their own health and safety in delivery. They may also feel more tired as the due date approaches. Husbands should support their wives. Couples often elect to become educated about childbirth by reading books and attending classes, 4-8.

EFFECTS OF HARMFUL AGENTS

NAME OF AGENT *Teratogen*	POSSIBLE EFFECTS ON FETUS OR NEWBORN
Drugs	
Hormones used for birth control or treatment of reproductive disorders	Limb malformations.
Aspirin	Prolonged labor. Bleeding in mother and baby.
Tranquilizers	Decreased activity. Cleft palate.
Narcotics	Delivery complications. Reduced growth rate. Respiration (breathing) problems. Withdrawal symptoms.
Drugs given for pain reduction in labor/delivery (especially a general anesthetic)	Respiration problems.
Steroids (such as Cortisone)	Cleft palate.
Nicotine (tobacco products)	Fetal distress (abnormally high and low heart rate). Low birth weight. Spontaneous abortion. Stillbirth. Death during first few weeks of life. Lasting effects such as smaller physical size, retarded reading skills, and poorer school adjustment.
Alcoholic beverages	Low birth weight. Heart, joint, and eye defects. Mild to moderate mental retardation. Very active (nervous). Stillbirth. Lasting effects such as smaller physical size and retarded development.
Tetracycline (antibiotic)	Teeth and bone problems.
Sulfa	Liver function problems.
Vitamins (excessive) K	Severe anemia with possible brain damage or death.
D	Circulatory damage.
B_6	Convulsions (repeated and prolonged).
Diseases	
Rubella (German measles)	Cataracts. Deafness. Heart problems. Dental deformities.

Continued.

4-7 These agents are considered harmful to the baby although any agent could be dangerous.

NAME OF AGENT _Teratogen_	POSSIBLE EFFECT ON FETUS OR NEWBORN
Diseases	
Diabetes	Increased chance of toxemia. Delivery complications due to large baby. Stillbirth. Spontaneous abortion.
Anemia	Anemia.
Toxoplasmosis (common infection caused by microscopic worms found in raw meat or in fecal matter including dust inhaled while dumping kitty litter)	Mental retardation. Deafness. Blindness.
Sexually Transmitted Diseases (STDs)	
AIDS (Acquired Immune Deficiency Syndrome)	Deficient or non-operative immune system with little or no protection from diseases. Death from a disease likely to occur before the child's third birthday.
Chlamydia	Eye infections. Pneumia. Death.
Genital Herpes (HSV-2)	Eye damage. Brain damage. Death.
Gonorrhea	Eye damage.
Syphillis	Eye damage. Ear damage. Bone damage. Brain damage. With latent syphillis, the baby appears healthy, but 5 to 15 years later, the child becomes blind, has damage to the nervous system, and has heart failure.
Other Agents	
Radiation (X-rays)	Retarded growth. Mental retardation. Sterility. Possible cancers in later life.
Inadequate maternal diet	Retarded physical development. Retarded mental development. Lowered resistance to infection.
Changes in maternal hormones due to stress (repeated or prolonged)	Spontaneous abortion. Delivery complications. Irritability.

4-7 Continued.

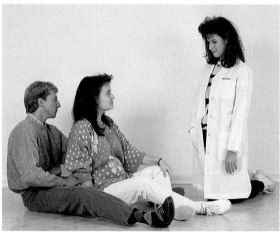

JOHN SHAW

4-8 Husbands can support their wives through pregnancy by attending childbirth classes.

Today more than 50 percent of fathers see their babies being born. When fathers are involved in childbirth, there are many benefits. Some research shows that mothers who have helpers during labor have shorter and more problem-free labors. This is because helpers have a calming effect on the mothers. Anxiety changes the blood chemistry which decreases contractions (longer labor) and flow of blood to the baby (possible damage to the baby). Husbands who assist with labor and delivery often have closer, warmer relationships with their children.

Some employers have *paternity leave* for fathers. Paternity leave is like a maternity leave for mothers but without sick pay. It is usually an unpaid, six-month leave after the birth of a child. At the end of six months, the father must be offered a job and salary comparable to the one he left. Some companies have longer paternity leave. A few companies pay for the leave.

There have been some problems with paternity leave. These include economic hardships during the leave and a few complaints that the companies did not give salary raises and promotions to men who chose the option. These problems may change if more men take paternity leave.

Even with the problems, the fathers who have taken paternity leave seem "sold" on the idea. They felt they had good relationships with their children. Their time off gave them better understanding of a day in the life of a housewife and parent. And it helped them remember what they're working for—a better total life for their families (not just material rewards).

The roles of the husband and children during pregnancy are basically supportive. But it would be unfair to view their roles as only supporting the mother. Fathers-to-be may be overwhelmed and concerned about additional costs. Fathers and children may feel that too much attention is on the baby. They may feel their needs are not being met. Mothers-to-be should be alert to their families' needs, too. Mutual support can help bring the family closer during pregnancy.

CHILDBIRTH AND POSTNATAL CARE

The months of waiting and excitement during pregnancy come to an end sooner than expected. Celebrations such as baby showers are often given. Parents may put the final touches on the nursery and arrange and rearrange baby items for the "umpteenth" time. Boy and girl names are often chosen. If hospital delivery is planned, a suitcase is packed. The house is cleaned. Arrangements with employers are made for the childbirth. Babysitters are secured for young children.

Final natural preparations are taking place, too. The mother's body is making hormone changes needed for labor to begin. The baby is moving into its final position for birth. The physician checks these preparations and keeps the parents informed.

The onset of labor takes most parents by surprise. Labor may begin any time and any place—even in the middle of sleep. The first contractions are usually so mild that many parents still wonder if the time has really come. Once begun labor and delivery are completed within hours. The baby is born! But following childbirth, there is a period of readjustment for the mother to a non-pregnant condition. The father (and other children) also must make changes brought on by the new baby.

This section describes the final phases of pregnancy. The section details what happens naturally. It also gives some of the choices and decisions that parents-to-be may make.

Stages of labor

Birth occurs about 270 days after conception. *Labor* is the process by which the baby is moved out of the mother's body. The baby is moved with a series of contractions in the uterine muscles. These contractions are *involuntary*. In other words, the mother cannot make these contractions happen. Their beginning, length, and strength are controlled by natural signals from the body. Contractions are separated by periods of time to allow the mother's muscles to relax.

The nature of contractions change throughout labor. In early labor, contractions may last about 30 seconds. But the length gradually increases to one minute. The strength of the contractions increases until the baby is born. The intervals of relaxation begin at 15 to 20 minutes and decrease to about two minutes.

During the last few weeks of pregnancy, especially for a first baby, the mother experiences *lightening*. Lightening is a change in the position of the unborn. The uterus settles downward and forward, and the baby descends lower into the pelvis. In most cases, the baby rotates its body so that its head is toward the birth canal. In about two percent of the cases, the baby gets into a buttocks first position. This is called *breech birth* position. When lightening happens the mother can breathe easier. But she may have leg cramps and may need to urinate more often due to the lower pressure.

Because the mother's body is preparing for labor during lightening, the mother may have a few irregular contractions. These irregular contractions are known as *false labor*. The contractions are real, but true labor has not begun. Some parents-to-be have gone to the hospital only to find out that the contractions were false labor. (Most physicians prefer that the mother goes to the hospital if she is not sure. They don't want the mother to end up having the baby at home.) Mothers should carefully time the intervals between several contractions to tell whether she is really in labor.

Besides regular contractions, there are several other signs of the coming labor. One sign is that the mother may feel a burst of energy due to increased adrenaline. Mothers shouldn't use the energy to scrub the house or do other strenuous tasks. They should save the energy for labor.

Another sign is that the mucous plug which is in the cervix will become loose. The small amount of blood in the mucous is called *the show*. It means labor should happen within 24 hours. A third sign is that part of the amniotic sac (sometimes called the "bag of waters") may break before labor begins. (Often the sac breaks after labor begins.) If the mucous plug becomes dislodged or the amniotic sac breaks, the mother should not bathe. Once contractions begin the mother should not eat food or drink liquids.

In medical terms, labor is divided into these three stages: (1) *dilation*, or opening, of the cervix; (2) *explusion,* or birth of the baby; and (3) expulsion of placenta. See 4-9.

Dilation of the cervix. In the early part of labor, contractions come every 15 or 20 minutes and last about 30 seconds. The uterus narrows. This straightens the baby's body and presses the baby's head (or buttocks) against the cervix. As the baby pushes against the cervix, the cervix flattens and opens (dilates).

If the amniotic sac has not broken, the physician will break it when the cervix has dilated four inches. The fluid in the sac lubricates the birth canal. When the cervix has opened four and one-half to five inches in width, the first stage of labor ends. The length of time varies a great deal, but the average length of labor in the first stage for first pregnancies is eight hours.

Expulsion of the baby. During the expulsion stage, the baby's head enters the birth canal. The mother's muscles push to move the baby down. The walls of the upper part of the birth canal are very elastic, but the arrangement of muscles in the lower part of the canal causes resistance. The resistance is painful for the mother. Many physicians use an injection to

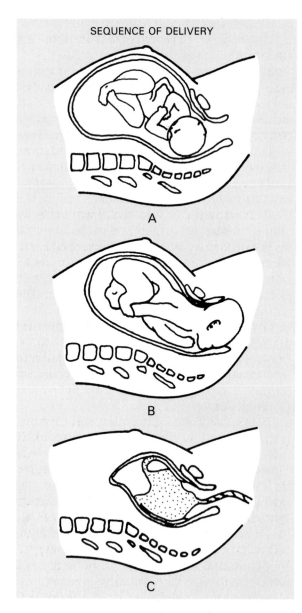

SEQUENCE OF DELIVERY

A

B

C

4-9 The three stages of labor are (A) the dilation of the cervix, (B) the birth of the baby, and (C) the expulsion of the placenta.

prevent pain in the lower part of the canal. Or they may have the mother use natural techniques such as breathing to reduce pain. They may also make an incision *(episiotomy)* from the vagina to the anus to prevent tearing. After delivery the incision is closed.

The baby changes position during birth. The baby faces downward as the head emerges. Then the head rotates to the side, and the shoulders, abdomen, and legs follow. The remaining fluid from the amniotic sac is expelled. The physician helps the baby by holding and turning the baby as needed. The physician uses instruments to suck out fluid from the baby's mouth and helps the baby take its first breath.

The second stage ends when the baby is free of the mother's body. The second stage usually lasts from 30 to 90 minutes. The umbilical cord is cut before the third stage begins.

Expulsion of the placenta. About 20 minutes after birth, the mother has a few irregular contractions. These cause the placenta to completely detach from the uterus and descend. This stage is often called the afterbirth. As the third stage ends, mothers feel physically a little cold and tired and emotionally relieved and overjoyed.

Giving birth

Parents make many choices before the baby is born. They choose a place to give birth such as hospital or home. They also choose a method of delivery such as natural childbirth or a C-section delivery. Arrangements for care of newborn such as a nursery or rooming-in arrangement are also made.

Parents should base their choices on their physician's advice as well as their own preferences. Availability of facilities or arrangements may affect plans. And the condition of mother and baby may limit options.

All parents need to learn about their options concerning giving birth. After thinking about these choices, they should discuss their feelings with a physician. This permits parents to make a choice with more understanding.

Each physician may prefer certain conditions for giving birth. He or she may like certain methods because of past experience. The physician will know what methods are best for the conditions of each pregnancy.

The physician is limited by the facilities in the hospital in which he or she is on staff. For instance, many hospitals do not have birthing rooms. Many do not allow the newborn to stay in the mother's room after birth. Parents who feel strongly about their birth settings need to keep this in mind as they choose a physician.

Physicians may have to make certain choices for the health and safety of the mother and/or child. For instance, natural childbirth may have been planned. But the position of the baby may require the physician to perform a C-section. Also, some babies require special care in nurseries. Placement in a rooming-in arrangement may not be possible for them.

Parents-to-be may choose between home and hospital deliveries. Home deliveries were the norm 50 years ago. Hospital delivery became more common because women wanted the relief from pain and safer conditions that hospitals provided.

The medical profession has taken a stand against home births. They cite the risks of emergency. Special medical help is needed for 10 to 15 percent of deliveries. Also, the infant death rate is higher for home births than for hospital births.

Those who favor home births believe parents should have more control over their children's births. To them, hospital deliveries tend to treat childbirth as an illness rather than a natural process. They think hospitals replace family warmth and support with medical objectivity. To make home births safer, some parents use *Certified Nurse Midwives* (CNM). These nurses have special training in delivering babies of normal pregnancies. CNMs do not handle high-risk pregnancies. Many CNMs work out of hospitals where they can call for help if an unexpected need arises.

More hospitals are offering parents the choice of a home-like *birthing room* rather than a standard delivery room. The birthing room is furnished like a bedroom. It is used for both labor and delivery. Family members and/or a few close friends stay with the mother-to-be throughout labor and delivery. In most hospitals, a nurse attends the labor. Then a physician is called just before delivery. The birthing room is an effort to offer the best of home and hospital births. It provides a home-like setting with family support and hospital safety.

Parents may choose between many methods of delivery. All methods try to make labor and delivery safer and more comfortable for the mother and her baby. Many methods include the father. Sometimes other family members are allowed to support the mother. These methods make the family an important part of the baby's life from the beginning. Three delivery methods are common. These are natural and educated childbirth methods; the Leboyer method; and instrument and C-section methods.

Natural and educated childbirth methods. Labor is hard work. Many muscles are used. Some of these muscles are seldom used except during labor. Pain is a part of labor, but if muscles are tense the mother has even more pain. Different types of delivery vary in the use of drugs to relieve pain.

Some mothers hope to be totally awake and alert through delivery. They cope with pain by using breathing and relaxation techniques. Other mothers prefer some drugs to help them cope with pain. A few mothers ask to be asleep through delivery.

Using drugs to relieve pain was common from the mid 1800s through the mid 1900s. Since then, physicians have moved away from using drugs. Most physicians like the mother to stay awake and alert through delivery. An awake mother can help bring the baby into the world. Also, any drugs used can cross the placenta and affect the baby. Drugs used to put the mother to sleep can make the baby sluggish.

One method of delivery without drugs is called *natural childbirth*. This method was developed in the 1930s by Dr. Grantly Dick-Read, an English physician. Dr. Dick-Read questioned the regular use of drugs when one of his patients chose not to use them. The woman felt very little pain during labor. The case made Dr. Dick-Read decide that part of the pain from labor was due to fear.

In natural childbirth, the woman has the birth process explained to her so that she knows what to expect. She also is trained to breathe and relax in a way that helps the birth process. With this training, the woman can deliver without drugs. The father is encouraged to play an active role in prenatal study and delivery with this method.

Another method similar to natural childbirth is called the *psychoprophylactic method* (PPM). It was developed in Russia, but it soon became popular in France. The method is called the *Lamaze method* in the United States. (It is named for Dr. Fernand Lamaze, the French physician who made the approach popular.)

The idea behind the Lamaze method is that women are conditioned to fear childbirth. In Lamaze training, the mother is taught to focus on something other than pain. The process is like an injured athlete thinking about the competition rather than the pain of the injury.

In this type of delivery, breathing patterns (such as deep breathing or panting) are used to keep the mother's mind off her discomfort. This is different from natural childbirth where breathing is used to help the birth process. Classes are held for the mother and her "coach" (usually the father). The classes help the mother prepare mentally and physically through instruction and practice. The Lamaze method has these features:

- The physician usually delivers the baby. But the father or another person learns the breathing patterns and assists the mother-to-be through labor.
- Medication is given when necessary. Not all women can deliver without drugs even when they are prepared (educated) for childbirth. The need for drugs often arises when there are complications. Drugs may also be used if the woman becomes too afraid.
- Training in childbirth is given in small classes. Usually no more than 10 women and their "coaches" are allowed. Classes are held weekly for eight to 12 weeks before the delivery date. The instructor provides factual information about childbirth. He or she teaches physical exercises to tone the body for delivery and breathing patterns to use in labor and delivery. The instructor also encourages discussions of feelings.

Many parents who used this approach said that childbirth was both comfortable and rewarding. Mothers were more alert and felt better without the excessive use of drugs. There was also no concern about the effects of drugs on the baby. And the mother and father shared the experience. Both parents were present and ready to welcome their newborn, 4-10.

Leboyer method. All methods of delivery are concerned with the safety of the baby as well as the safety and comfort of the mother. Frederick Leboyer, a French physician, developed the *Leboyer method* of delivery. This method is concerned with not only the safety but the comfort of the baby during delivery. The Leboyer method is based on the assumption that the delivery is painful for the baby as well as the mother. It discourages such delivery room techniques as using bright lights and placing the newborn on a hard, flat table for checking and measuring. These techniques are thought to add to the discomfort of the baby.

Of course, babies can't tell someone how they feel. But people know that the environment before and after birth is different. Some studies show that babies are less fussy when the Leboyer method is used compared to babies born using standard methods. The Leboyer method may also have a calming affect on the mother.

The Leboyer method calls for the lights in the delivery room to be cut to the minimum needed for delivery. Noise is also avoided by talking in quiet tones. The baby is supported by the physician after its head appears.

After birth the baby rests on the mother's body as she cuddles her newborn. The umbilical cord is cut after it stops functioning. Thus, the baby begins breathing on its own. A few minutes after birth the baby is lowered into water that has been heated to near body temperature. The supported baby can kick and move about in a way similar to that before birth. Finally, the baby is dressed and wrapped in a warm blanket.

Instrument and C-section methods. Sometimes the unborn baby appears to be in danger due to a prolonged labor, too much pressure on the head, or lack of oxygen. The physician may use *forceps* to speed up the birth. Forceps are used to grip the baby's head and very gently pull or turn the baby.

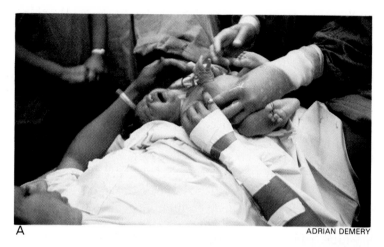

ADRIAN DEMERY

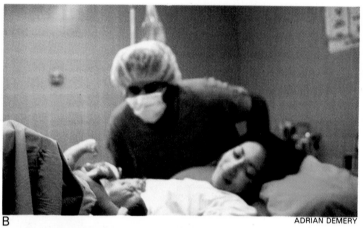

ADRIAN DEMERY

ADRIAN DEMERY

4-10 Childbirth is a shared experience for this family as the awake mother reaches for and cuddles her newborn (A), the father proudly shares his daughter's birth (B), and the baby gazes at her parents (C).

In other cases, the traditional methods of delivery would be unsafe or unwise. Six to seven percent of all children are born by the *Cesarean* or *C-section method*. In the C-section, the mother's abdomen and uterus are surgically opened and the baby is removed. The incisions are then closed as with any other surgery. The method was named for Emperor Julius Caesar who, it has been said, was born that way. There are several reasons for C-section deliveries:

- The mother's pelvis is small or not shaped correctly for an easy birth.
- The baby's head is very large.
- Contractions are weak or absent.
- The baby is in an incorrect position for birth.
- The physician feels that previous Cesarean scar(s) could rupture during labor. (But one Cesarean birth does not necessarily mean that all later births must be C-sections, too).

Some couples have planned for a Lamaze method delivery but found that a C-section was necessary. To help these couples share the childbirth experience, some hospitals use drugs that permit the mother to be awake but feel no pain during the surgery. They allow the father in the room. These couples are able to experience the same benefits and joys of couples who used the Lamaze method.

Besides choosing a place and method of birth, parents need to make arrangements for care of the newborn. Years ago, home was the place of birth and care for the newborn. When hospital births became common, babies were cared for in the hospital nursery.

Care in nurseries is given by nurses who are on duty at all times. The contact the mother is allowed to have with her baby varies in different hospitals. Some hospitals hire a person who is not a nurse to rock and help feed the babies in the nursery. Fathers (who are gowned) are often encouraged to be with the mother and baby in the mother's room. Other family members may only be allowed to see the baby through the nursery windows during certain hours. Brothers and sisters under 12 years of age may not be able to see the baby until the mother and baby are home. Jealousy over the new baby may be partly caused by not being a part of the baby's first days. For this reason, more hospitals are beginning to allow sibling visits, 4-11.

Some hospitals provide a rooming-in arrangement. If the baby is healthy, he or she is placed in a bassinet in the room with the mother. (Sometimes the father stays in the room, too.) Nurses help the parents learn to feed, change, clean, dress, and soothe the baby. Parents are encouraged to take over these responsibilities before leaving the hospital. (Of course, if mother needs extra rest, the nurse on duty cares for the baby.)

Rooming-in helps parents develop a warm feeling for their new baby. The rooming-in arrangement for the baby is an attempt to offer the best of both home and hospital care.

JOHN SHAW

4-11 Many hospitals now encourage the whole family to spend time together with the new baby.

Postnatal maternal care

Postnatal care is the care the mother receives in the six to eight weeks following the birth of her baby. (The medical term for postnatal care is *postpartum* care.) The six- to eight-week period is the time when the mother's body returns to its pre-pregnancy state. For nursing mothers, the complete return to the pre-pregnancy state requires more time.

Many physical changes happen quickly during the postnatal period. The mother's body which changed for nine months reverses itself in about two months. The first hour after birth is a critical time for restoring body stability. Vital signs (pulse, respiration, and other body functions) are measured every few minutes just as they are following surgery. Special attention is given to make sure the uterus contracts properly.

In order to regain their strength and avoid health problems, women are encouraged to get out of bed within 24 hours of delivery. Many women walk much sooner.

After a few days, certain exercises, done with the physician's approval, help tone the abdominal muscles. These exercises are done slowly and gradually for safety and best results. Most mothers also want to lose some of the extra weight from pregnancy. On the average, 11 pounds are lost during birth, and another seven pounds are lost during the couple of weeks after birth. The remaining weight must be lost through diet and/or exercise.

A woman should check with her physician about dieting. A well-balanced diet is essential to everyone and especially to a new mother as her body returns to normal. For nursing mothers, the final pounds are usually shed after weaning.

Rest is also important. For a couple of days after delivery, many mothers seem to need a great deal of sleep. A middle of the day nap and eight to 10 hours of sleep at night are often advised throughout postnatal care. New mothers can get some needed rest by planning ways to lessen their work load. A mother can take the following time-saving steps:

- Ask a friend to watch the baby so that the mother can take a nap.
- Put away knicknacks that add to housekeeping time.
- Prepare and freeze meals before baby comes to use after the baby is born.
- Buy disposable diapers, plates, and cups for a few days or weeks.

If the mother must return to work before the end of the postnatal period, she should get special guidance from nurses and physicians. The key to complete recovery, whether the mother is at home or on the job, is to go slow with activity. Too much activity slows the reversal process.

Closely linked to physical changes are emotional changes. Emotional changes may be due to changes in the hormones. Some women experience a down feeling within a few days after birth. This feeling is called *postpartum blues*. It is caused by hormone changes that began at conception. Hormone levels do not return to normal until three to 10 weeks after delivery and later for nursing mothers.

The blues may also happen because of the around-the-clock care a new baby requires. After birth, the mother fatigues quickly. She may feel overwhelmed with the work involved in caring for the baby.

The blues usually pass rapidly. Following these suggestions seem to help most new mothers:

- Get enough rest.
- Improve her appearance. She may try new cosmetics, a new cologne, get an easy-care hair style, or buy a new blouse or dress.
- Seek some non-mothering stimulation. She may develop some outside interest, plan an evening out, or buy a new record, book, or magazine.
- Talk to others who've had babies.

Physicians are concerned about the emotional well-being of their patients as well as their physical health. Mothers who have intense or prolonged postpartum blues should discuss the problem with their physician.

By the third month, most women are in good shape. But no two women are alike in their stamina. A new mother should be patient with her body and give it all the time needed after having the baby.

to Know

amniocentesis . . . adrenaline . . .
birthing room . . . breech birth . . .
Cesarean section . . . Certified Nurse Midwife . . .
dilation . . . episiotomy . . . expulsion . . .
false labor . . . forceps . . . labor . . .
Lamaze method . . . lightening . . .
Leboyer method . . . natural childbirth . . .
spontaneous abortion . . . paternity leave . . .
postpartum . . . postpartum blues . . .
Rh factor . . . rooming-in . . .
sexually transmitted diseases (STDs) . . .
the show . . . toxemia

to Review

Write your answers on a separate sheet of paper.
1. Which of the following is *not* a sign of pregnancy?
   a. Enlargement and soreness of the breasts.
   b. HCG in urine and blood.
   c. Craving for pickles and ice cream.
   d. Missed menstrual cycle.
   e. Morning sickness.
2. The best age for a woman to have a baby is between:
   a. 17 and 20 years.
   b. 21 and 28 years.
   c. 36 and 40 years.
3. True or false. The unborn baby is able to take whatever nutrients it needs for its own growth and development, even if the mother's diet is insufficient.
4. True or false. During pregnancy it is safer to take over-the-counter drugs like cough medicine and aspirin than to take prescription drugs.
5. True or false. Babies may be affected differently by an environment problem (such as rubella or a mother's smoking). No one knows how susceptible a baby will be to a problem.
6. Which of the following statements is most true about a normal pregnancy?
   a. Pregnant women should limit physical activities to prevent loss of the baby.
   b. Most women feel tired and uncomfortable during the entire pregnancy.
   c. Because of the need for extra calories, women cannot return to their original weight before pregnancy.
   d. Good health practices are almost the same during pregnancy as they are before pregnancy.
7. List two ways a father can take an active role during pregnancy and childbirth.
8. Place these steps of labor in proper order:
   a. Birth of baby.
   b. The "show."
   c. Dilation of cervix.
   d. Expelling placenta.
   e. Cutting of the umbilical cord.
9. True or false. "False labor pains" are not real pains. They are just imagined by the mother.
10. Which of the following is the most accurate statement concerning delivery?
   a. The delivery method should mainly depend upon the condition of the mother and her baby.
   b. Natural childbirth is best because drugs can be harmful to the baby.
   c. Cesarean sections are best because the mother and baby can avoid a long and uncomfortable labor.
   d. Being put to sleep is best, because fear of pain makes labor longer and more difficult.
   e. The method of delivery should be only the mother's choice, because it is her body.
11. True or false. The birthing room and the rooming-in arrangements are designed to provide the best of home and hospital delivery and care.
12. _____ care is essential for a healthy return to a non-pregnant state.

to Do

1. As a group project, make a fill-in booklet of information a pregnant woman would need to give her physician. Also list questions she needs to ask her physician. Some suggested topics for starters are:
   a. Information physician needs:
      (1) Family health history.

(2) History of menstrual cycle.

(3) History of any serious or chronic diseases or conditions.

(4) History of other pregnancies.

(5) Date of last menstrual period.

(6) Current use of drugs including over-the-counter drugs.

(Add your own.)

b. Information mother-to-be needs:

(1) Due date.

(2) Weight and weight gain.

(3) Recommended diet, exercise, rest/sleep.

(4) Treatment of any disease or condition.

(5) Information on giving birth (e.g., places, types of delivery, and arrangement for care of newborn).

(6) Fees and insurance.

(7) Appointment dates and how to contact physician in an emergency.

(Add your own.)

Placing the booklet in a folder with pockets is often helpful, because many physicians give their patients charts and pamphlets.

2. Role play a fictitious interview of two women who had their children two or three generations apart. The title of the interview could be "Pregnancy and Childbirth Yesterday and Today."

3. Invite a health care worker to speak to your class about childbirth classes for parents-to-be.

4. Make arrangements to visit a local hospital's facilities for giving birth and care of the newborn.

5. Invite a Certified Nurse Midwife to discuss the advantages of a home versus hospital delivery, the type of training required of a CNM, and the type of deliveries the CNM handles.

6. Make a bulletin board on the theme "Eating for Two Requires Careful Planning." The bulletin board might contain one week's sample menus for a pregnant woman. Pictures and/or a list of some potentially fattening, non-essential foods might be used on the bulletin board, too.

7. Give a class report on one birth defect. (The March of Dimes Foundation has excellent pamphlets on many birth defects.)

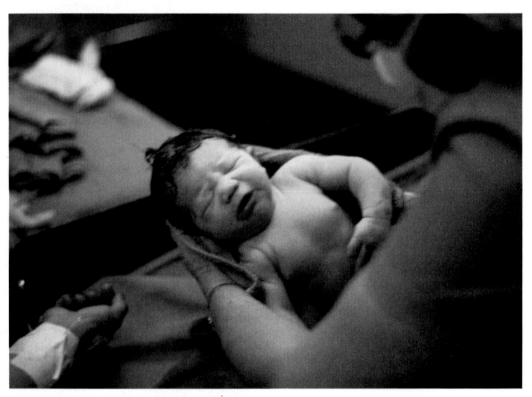

Newborns need special care as they begin
life without the safe environment their
mothers provided.

5

The Newborn

After studying this chapter, you will be able to:
☐ Describe the characteristics of a newborn.
☐ Meet a newborn's physical, intellectual, and social-emotional needs.
☐ Explain how parents of newborns can meet their own needs.

The end of the second stage of labor marks the beginning of a new life separate from that of the mother. The official time of birth is when the baby is clear of the mother's body. The baby may breathe or cry moments before or after birth. From birth to the age of one month, the baby is medically known as a *neonate*. (Neonate is from the Latin words *neo*, meaning new, and *natus*, meaning born.)

The newborn or neonatal period of growth and development is one of vast changes. Newborns come from a world that was dark and quiet. They had a home of warm, comfortable water. Their food and oxygen needs were supplied without effort or waiting. Their movements were cushioned from shock and made easier due to the water's support.

At the moment of birth, babies are thrust into a more exciting and stimulating world. But that world is very different and perhaps even frustrating. There is light and noise. The newborn's life support system—the placenta and umbilical cord—stops functioning within minutes after birth. The newborn's air passage must be drained of water, and the newborn's lungs must expand to accept the first breath of air. When hungry, the baby must now search for a nipple and suck. Even the newborn's body feels different because gravity restricts movement. Suddenly the head and trunk seem "heavy" to the baby.

Newborns can adjust to their new world easily because their bodies are marvelously equipped at birth. Babies continue to grow and develop in order to meet their ever-changing needs.

The time of birth is also the transition from prospective parenthood to real parenthood. For parents, the newborn period is one of vast changes and adjustments. As we shall discuss at the close of this chapter, parents can enjoy this time if they:

• Plan carefully.
• Accept the responsibility.
• Love and communicate with each other.
• Live one day at a time.
• Realize that in time, many frustrations such as sleepless nights will decrease and the joys of parenthood will increase.

INITIAL MEDICAL CARE AND TESTING

Good prenatal care gives the baby the best chance for a healthy start. For healthy development, all newborns need continued medical care. Of course, medical care is a "must" for a sick or very small newborn. But even healthy newborns should be supported by a few simple medical procedures. In hospitals, care is given to the baby from the moment of birth until the baby leaves.

Care during delivery

After delivery of the entire body, the baby is often held head downward. Then suction is applied to nostrils and mouth with a bulb syringe. The baby may be placed on the mother's abdomen as the cord is clamped and cut. The nurse then takes the baby to a table. (There is a special heater above the table.) The newborn is quickly dried with warm towels. This prevents heat loss due to the evaporation of the amniotic fluid. See 5-1.

In most hospitals, the physical condition of the newborn is checked using a procedure developed in the 1950s by Virginia Apgar. The *Apgar test* is used to determine the newborn's

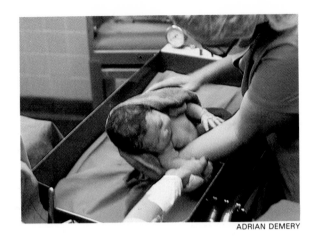
ADRIAN DEMERY

5-1 This healthy newborn is being dried.

chance for survival. A nurse or *pediatrician* gives the test. (A pediatrician is a physician who specializes in the treatment of infants and children.) In the Apgar test the baby is scored as zero, one, or two in each of five areas. See 5-2. The best total score possible on the test is 10. The heart rate and respiratory (breathing) effort are the most important signs of condition. Skin color (a sign of circulation) is the least important sign. The test is given at one minute and five minutes after delivery. (Usually the cord has not been clamped and cut for the first scoring but it has before the second scoring.) At one minute after birth, the baby should receive its lowest score. The five-minute score should be higher. This second score can be used to predict whether the baby will be normal at one year of age.

Most normal babies score six or seven at one minute and eight to 10 at five minutes. If a score of seven or less is assigned at five minutes, the test is repeated at 10 minutes after birth. Following the first scoring time, a score of zero, one, or two requires resuscitation efforts. The baby is given assistance in breathing. A score between three and six requires careful watching and possibly assistance in breathing. If scores are low at the five (and 10) minute time, then intensive care must be given to determine and treat the cause and to provide respiration, temperature, and nutritional support.

APGAR TEST

Sign	SCORES		
	0	1	2
Heart rate	Absent.	Slow; fewer than 100 beats per minute.	More than 100 beats per minute.
Respiratory effort	Absent.	Weak cry; hypoventilation.	Good; strong cry.
Muscle tone	Limp.	Some flexing and bending of extremities.	Well flexed.
*Reflex irritability	No response.	Some motion.	Cry.
Color	Blue; pale.	Body pink; extremities blue.	Completely pink.

*Test for reflex irritability may be done with a nasal catheter causing the newborn to sneeze. The sneezing reflex is not satisfactory if the baby is crying loudly or if the cord has not been clamped. Stimulation of the skin of the feet is more satisfactory for testing reflex irritability.

5-2 A newborn's condition may be quickly determined by the Apgar test.

After the first checking, the baby is weighed and measured. Silver nitrate is used in the eyes to prevent infection. And, before the baby is taken from the delivery room, footprinting is done. See 5-3. Also, identifying bands are placed around the wrists or ankles.

OTHER HOSPITAL CARE

Pediatricians run other tests to determine the newborn's health. Blood tests are run to rule out *anemia* and the presence of *PKU*. Anemia is a low level of oxygen-carrying substances in the blood. PKU or phenylketonuria is a disease which, if left untreated by diet, causes mental retardation.

Before the newborn leaves the hospital, physicians do more checks. If the mother uses an obstetrician for her care and a pediatrician for the baby's care, a second family health history is taken. (The first health history should have been taken during prenatal care.) The pediatrician needs information about only situations that might affect the baby. The baby's reflexes are also checked.

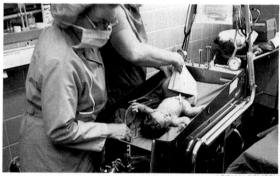
ADRIAN DEMERY

5-3 A newborn is footprinted for identification.

Some pediatricians use the *Neonatal Behavioral Assessment Scales* developed by T. Berry Brazelton. This test is commonly called the *Brazelton scale*. The Brazelton scale is used to determine whether the baby is normal in four behavioral areas. This differs from the Apgar test which is used to predict chances of survival and help newborns with low scores.

One area of the test concerns the newborn's *interaction with the environment*. This portion observes the baby's alertness; attention to sound, light, and other factors; and cuddliness. The *motor processes* are also checked. These include general activity level and reflex behavior. A third area, *control of physical state,* includes self-quieting behaviors and levels of excitement and irritability. The last area is a test of the newborn's *response to stress*. Responses may include startle reactions and trembling.

The Brazelton scale is very detailed in each area. For instance, to check the newborn's attention to sound, the baby's reaction to the human voice is scored on a nine-point scale. Reactions may range from no reaction to turning and reacting to the voice each time words are spoken on both sides of the baby. The same test is then repeated with a bell and a rattle. Because an attempt is made to get the baby's best effort for each item, 30 to 90 minutes may be needed to check all items. (Such a long test for a baby is spread out over several days.)

The Brazelton scale helps to spot any problems as early as possible. For instance, hearing loss is suspected if the baby does not startle to loud sounds and always shows no reaction to the tests with the human voice, bell, and rattle. If a problem is suspected, further tests can be used to confirm or find the exact problem. Parents also find out more about their newborn's personality. They know whether their baby is more likely to be fussy or calm; cuddly or more distant; a self-quieter or one who must be soothed by others; and an active or sleepy baby.

Some babies are born too small or too soon. Some are born with problems like heart, digestive tract, spine, or brain defects. These babies need immediate, intensive care. They are often placed in an *intensive care nursery* (ICN). The lifesaving supports of the ICN can save these newborns from further damage or death. Newborns live in *isolettes*. These heated, completely enclosed beds have two slightly larger than arm-sized doors that open and close to permit care. See 5-4. Isolettes are equipped with devices for giving oxygen and instruments for monitoring breathing and heart rate. The doctors and nurses who work in ICN's have special training in *neonatology*. Neonatology is a branch of pediatrics concerned with newborns.

PHYSICAL CHARACTERISTICS OF NEWBORNS

The song writer who wrote, "You must have been a beautiful baby," was not talking about newborns. The plump, beautiful babies seen in advertisements are usually several months old.

The appearance of newborns is described in 5-5. Newborns possess other physical characteristics that are of concern to parents. Newborns cough and sneeze to clear their air passages and lungs of mucus. They breathe unevenly about 46 times per minute from the diaphragm in the abdominal area. (In contrast, adults breathe about 18 times per minute, usually from the chest.) Newborns' heart rates are often between 120 and 150 beats per minute. (Adults' heart rates are about 70 beats per minute.)

5-4 The isolette provides protection for a baby who was born too soon.

FEATURE	DESCRIPTION
Size	Most full-term babies weigh slightly over seven pounds and are about 20 inches long. Boys are slightly larger than girls. Newborns will lose weight, but will regain birth weight within 10 days. They will grow about one and one-half pounds and one inch during the first month. Newborns look thin because they have little body fat.
Body Proportions	Newborns look out of proportion. Their heads are 1/4 of total length instead of the adults' proportion of 1/10 of total length. Their chests are rounded, stomachs protrude, and pelvis and hips are narrow. Their legs are drawn up and appear to bow; this is due to the pre-birth position. The legs are short in comparison with arms. They have almost no neck.
Face	Newborns have a broad, flat nose and tiny jaw and chin which help them suck more easily.
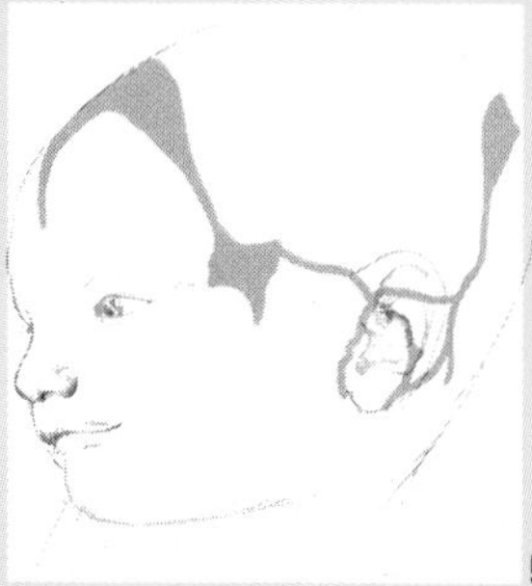 Cranium	Newborns have fontanels (commonly called soft spots) where the skull is not closed, 5-5a. These fontanels allow the skull and brain to grow. The fontanels are filled with bone as the skull grows. The skull completely closes between one and two years of age when brain growth has greatly slowed. You may see the membrane covering the fontanels moving in and out as a newborn breathes. The bones of the skull are soft and may be molded into an egg shape during birth. This is good because it makes the birth easier. The molding will disappear in a couple of weeks. The head may be slightly flattened if the baby always sleeps in the same position. This is not harmful to the brain, but the flattening can be permanent. Hair will cover the flattened area.

5-5a

FEATURE	DESCRIPTION
Skin	Newborns have thin, dry skin. The skin may take on a blotchy, rudy appearance, 5-5b. You may see the blood vessels. The skin of the feet is loose and wrinkly, and the wrists have deep, bracelet-like creases. The scalp skin is also loose. At birth, newborns have protective cheese-like coverings (vernix caseosa), 5-5c. Down (lanugo) on the ears, shoulders, back, forehead, and cheeks is

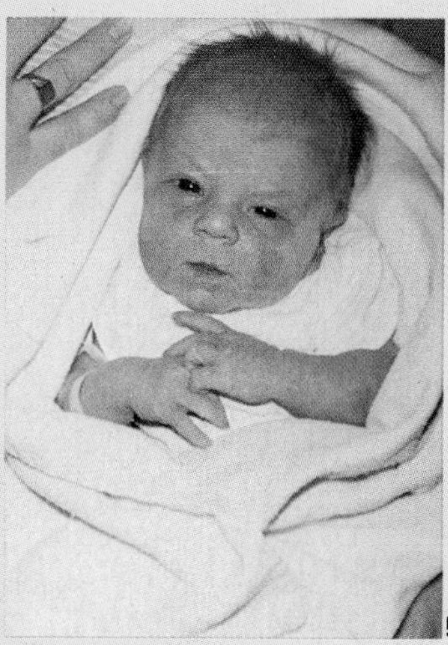

STEPHEN WICKS

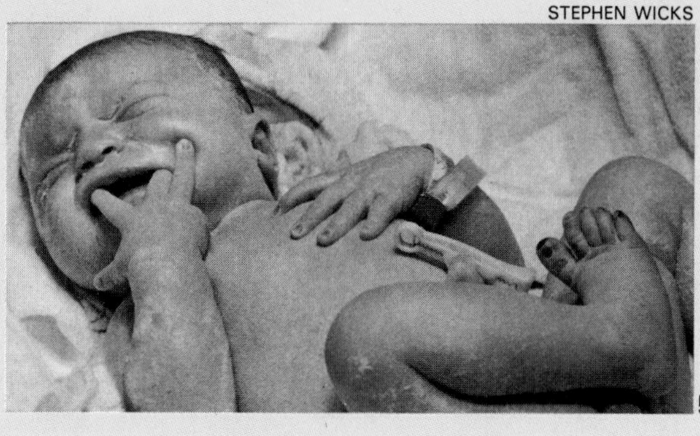

5-5b

5-5c

Continued.

5-5 A newborn has an appearance that is very different from that of older children and adults.

FEATURE	DESCRIPTION
 5-5d	frequently seen in premature babies. Babies often develop a rash one or two days after birth which disappears in a week. Some newborns have a pinkish area on the forehead, eyelids, and back of neck called "stork bites" which fade within a year, 5-5d. The name is derived from the mythical stork who delivered babies, but the pink blotches are due to a collection of small blood vessels. Newborns of black, Mediterranean, and Asian races may have irregular greenish-blue spots (called "Mongolian" spots) on the back. Many newborns have a yellowish discoloration which is due to jaundice.
Eyes	Newborns' eyes appear small. Eyes are a dull gray-blue due to lack of pigmentation. (Eye color is developed around six months.) Red spots may appear in the white of the eyes. Babies do not tear until three months, but drainage from the eyes may be a side effect of silver nitrate. The newborns' eyes may cross at times. (Eyes should work together at six months.)
Mouth	Newborns' cheeks appear swollen due to sucking pads on inside of cheek. The tongue is short and cannot be extended beyond the gums. The lining of the lips will peel. Most newborns are toothless, but some are born with one or more teeth.

5-5 Continued.

All newborns have sticky, tar-colored stools for about two days. If the baby is bottle-fed, the stools turn green and are seedy looking for about a day. Then they turn yellow and are rather loose. Breast-fed babies have orange, loose stools after the initial dark ones. Bottle-fed babies have more bowel movements per day than breast-fed babies.

BONDING

Bonding, or developing an attachment (feeling of affection) is important for parents and their baby. The first hour after birth is perhaps the most sensitive time for bonding. The newborn will watch, hear, and respond to the body movements, voice, and touch of the mother and father. Bonding continues during the next few weeks as mothers and fathers become more and more attached to their babies. See 5-6 and 5-7.

Bonding helps both infants and parents as shown in 5-8. Because bonding is so helpful,

JOHN SHAW

5-6 Bonding occurs as a mother cuddles and looks at her newborn.

JOHN SHAW

5-7 Fathers need to bond with their newborns, too.

BENEFITS OF BONDING

To Infant	To Parents
Increased chance of survival.	Less incidence of child abuse.
Better weight gain.	Faster recovery from delivery.
Less crying; more smiles and laughter.	Longer breast-feeding.
Fewer infections.	More self-confidence as a parent.
Possibly higher IQ.	Less "depression" after delivery.
Better language development.	

5-8 Bonding aids both infants and parents. It is the first step toward a healthy parent-child relationship.

many hospitals have changed their rules regarding premature or ill infants. These new policies allow mothers and fathers to visit the intensive care nursery and feed, touch, talk to, and sing to babies.

EARLY ADAPTIVE BEHAVIOR

All people have built-in behaviors that they did not learn. For instance, your knee jerks when tapped with a mallet. The pupils of your eyes change size when levels of light change. These automatic, unlearned behaviors are called *reflexes*. Newborns enter the world with many reflexes. Some of these are triggered by a specific stimuli from the environment (light, touch, sound) directed to a specific body area (hands, feet, cheeks, eyes, and ears).

Reflexes are very important to newborns for these reasons:

1. Pediatricians can check reflexes to determine the health of the nervous system. The absence or weakness of a reflex may mean prematurity or a birth defect. For instance, newborns jerk or withdraw their legs when the soles of their feet are pricked. This reaction is called the withdrawal reflex, 5-9. The

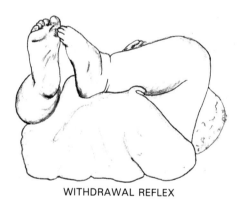

WITHDRAWAL REFLEX

5-9 The withdrawal reflex is one way to tell whether newborns are normal.

reflex continues throughout life, and its absence may be a sign of brain damage. On the other hand, some reflexes should disappear within their given time frames. If these reflexes are present too long, it may be a sign of brain damage. Normal reflexes indicate a normal newborn. But they are not clues as to whether the "normal" baby will be average or superior.

The newborn 93

2. Some reflexes are needed for survival. For instance, when you touch a newborn's cheeks or the skin around the mouth, the head turns and the mouth searches for food. This is called the rooting reflex, 5-10. After finding an object with the mouth, sucking begins. This reflex should vanish in three to four months.
3. Some reflexes lead to voluntary, learned behaviors. The knee jerk does not lead to a learned behavior. It always remains the same. On the other hand, the sucking reflex leads to learned sucking. The newborn learns to vary sucking strength with the softness of the object.
4. Using reflexes may give the newborn the practice needed for developing voluntary behaviors such as sitting, walking, and climbing. Voluntary behaviors are essential for continued development.

There are many reflexes, and researchers are observing and describing more. A few other ones that you may observe in newborns are illustrated in 5-11.

The *grasping or Palmar reflex* is seen at birth and disappears in 3 or 4 months. Newborns will grasp fingers or any object after their hands are stroked. Although newborns do not use their thumbs in the grasping reflex, their grasp is strong enough to lift them into a sitting position. Premature newborns grasp more firmly and longer than do full-term infants.

The *Plantar reflex* happens when the ball of the foot is stroked. The baby's toes curl around an object such as an adult's fingers. The reflex is strong enough to lift the baby's legs off the mattress. The Plantar reflex is seen at birth and disappears between eight and 15 months of age.

The *Babinski reflex* causes babies to spread their toes instead of curling them. To cause the Babinski reflex, the baby's feet must be stroked on the outside of the sole from the heel to the toes. The Babinski reflex begins at birth and ends at one year of age.

The *Moro reflex* occurs from birth until about six months of age. If babies hear a loud noise, see a bright light, feel a change in position, cough, or sneeze, they arch their backs, throw their heads back, and fling out their arms

and legs. Then they rapidly bring their arms and legs toward the centers of their bodies.

The *walking reflex* is first seen in two-week-old infants. If they are held upright and their feet are placed on a hard surface, these infants will appear to walk. Although they lift each leg, their arms do not swing. The walking reflex disappears in 3 or 4 months, several months before walking really occurs.

LEARNING OF NEWBORNS

For years people thought newborns were sleepy, helpless, and unable to understand the world around them. The more people study children's learning, the more they realize that learning begins right after birth. In fact, the brain and some of the senses are active before birth. Because learning begins so early, parents are the first teachers.

The sense organs (eyes, ears, nose, skin, tongue) transmit information from the environment to the brain. All of our sense organs are functioning at birth. (In contrast, dogs and cats are born "blind"!) Thus, newborns have a great ability for learning.

Newborns can tell the difference between human speech and other sounds. Some studies

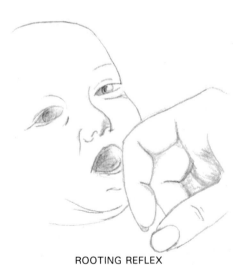

ROOTING REFLEX

5-10 The rooting reflex is used by newborns to help them find a breast or bottle.

found that babies in the delivery room responded to human speech by looking in the direction of the sound. The same babies ignored other sounds. Babies between 12 and 24 hours old can move arms and legs rhythmically to human speech.

During the first few hours after birth, babies can tell the difference between a click and a tone sound. They know whether to turn their heads right or left for a reward of sugar water. Within a week, newborns become even better at distinguishing sounds. For example, newborns will cry in response to another baby's cry, but not to a synthetic cry. By three weeks, babies can distinguish between a parent's and a stranger's voice.

During the first few weeks of life, babies begin to learn about space. If babies see a mov-

Palmar (grasping) Reflex
Newborn's fingers tighten around any object placed in the palm.

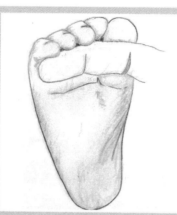

Plantar (grasping) Reflex
Newborn's toes tighten around any object if the ball of the foot is stroked.

Babinski Reflex
Newborn's toes fan out if the outside of the sole is stroked from heels to toes.

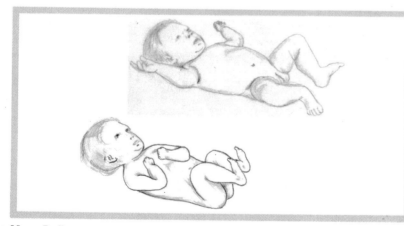

Moro Reflex
This reflex consists of two basic movements. Newborns fling arms and legs out (a) and pull them back again (b) when startled.

Walking Reflex
When babies' feet touch a solid surface, alternating steps are taken as in walking.

5-11 Some major reflexes help infants survive and learn.

ing object approaching them on a collision course, they will turn their heads or pull away as much as possible. If the object is not on a collision course, babies will not defend themselves.

Imitation is a common way of learning for humans. Until recently, experts thought babies didn't imitate until they were at least eight months of age. Now they know newborns can imitate adults' facial and hand gestures. The ability to imitate develops at a fast rate. Within a year, infants can imitate some child-care tasks such as giving a doll or stuffed animal a bottle!

Newborns show that they're learning by their behavior. When presented with a stimulus such as your face, an object, or a sound, they respond by becoming quiet and looking. Their heart rate increases. Newborns also show learning because they can remember for a short period of time. If you show newborns a stuffed dog a few times and then show them the same stuffed dog and a stuffed duck, they will look

ADVANTAGES OF BREAST-FEEDING AND BOTTLE-FEEDING

Breast-Feeding	Bottle-Feeding
Breast milk contains the right proportions of proteins, carbohydrates, fats, vitamins, minerals, and water.	Formulas are similar to breast milk.
Breast milk is easy to digest.	Formulas have iron; breast milk is low in iron. Iron-fortified foods must be added to a breast-fed baby's diet after the baby triples his or her birth weight.
Breast milk is ready immediately. (No mixing, sterilizing, or warming.)	Bottle-feeding makes it easier to be away from home.
Mother does not over-feed. (Over-feeding results in abdominal cramps and loose stools and may set the stage for obesity.)	Because non-nursing mothers do not need as many calories, it is quicker for them to return to a pre-pregnancy size.
Babies fed entirely on breast milk are seldom constipated.	No nursing pads or brassieres are needed.
Breast-fed babies have fewer digestive upsets and disorders, skin disorders, and respiratory infections as compared with formula-fed babies.	There are no worries about an inadequate supply of milk.
Vigorous sucking required for breast-feeding usually satisfies the need for sucking and promotes good development of facial structures.	Formula is not affected by the mother's diet, illnesses, or medications.
Mother's immunities to certain diseases are passed to the baby through the colostrum (a liquid which comes from the breasts for two or three days after delivery).	Anyone can help feed the baby. Feeding may help fathers and others develop a good relationship with the baby.
Nursing stimulates hormones to be released that help the uterus to contract to normal size.	
A warm relationship is easily developed due to touch and eye contact between mother and newborn.	

5-12 Breast-feeding or bottle-feeding is a personal choice, but it should be based on knowledge of the advantages of each.

at the duck. Thus you know they remembered the older stimulus (the dog) and were more interested in the newer stimulus (the duck).

MEETING THE NEWBORN'S NEEDS

All people have needs. We have physical needs—needs for food, clothing, and shelter. We have intellectual needs—needs to learn about our world. We also have social-emotional needs—needs to care for others and have others care for us. Newborns have needs much like our own with one major difference. Newborns are totally dependent on parents and other caring people to help them meet their needs. This section will give you some clues about how to observe and meet the needs of newborns.

Physical needs

Newborns are completely helpless and dependent on adults for meeting their physical needs. They look so small and so helpless, too. Because newborns are so dependent and fragile-looking, it's no wonder that people taking care of them for the first time are a little nervous.

Feeding. People need nutrients to promote growth and maintain good health. Since newborns grow at a very fast rate, their nutritional needs are especially important. These needs can be met by either breast-feeding or bottle-feeding with a formula. The choice is a personal one. The mother and father should compare the advantages of breast-feeding and bottle-feeding their baby. They are described in 5-12. Once a decision is made, they should feel good (never guilty) about their choice.

If the newborn is to be breast-fed, here are some things the mother should do:
- Eat a well-balanced diet. The quality of breast milk varies only slightly from mother to mother. Even malnourished women provide high quality milk but to the detriment of their own bodies. Mothers who breastfeed need a balanced diet with plenty of liquids. See 5-13.
- Consult her physician about a diet suited to their own special needs. As a general rule, nursing mothers should eat 350 to 500 calories more than women who are not

nursing. They should choose foods found in a well-balanced diet to meet the added needs of baby and mother.
- Check with her pediatrician about giving the baby a supplementary source of iron and vitamin D.
- Realize that certain foods may cause reactions. These include coffee, tea, chocolate, cola, cocoa, herbal teas, and artificial sweeteners. The baby's intestinal tract may be irritated by certain foods the mother has eaten such as broccoli, asparagus, eggplant, onions, tomatoes, garlic, and spices. The

BASIC DIET FOR NURSING MOTHERS

Milk 4 servings Typical servings: One cup whole milk, skim milk, buttermilk, or yogurt. Two one-inch cubes of hard cheese.
Protein foods 2 or more servings Typical servings: three oz. of cooked lean solid meat, poultry, or fish. Three-fourths cup cooked dry beans, peas, or lentils; 1/4 cup peanut butter. One oz. nuts. One egg.
Fruits and Vegetables **Vitamin C Foods** 2 servings Typical servings: 3/4 cup to 1 cup oranges, grapefruit, tomatoes, strawberries, cantaloupe, or raw cabbage. **Dark green or deep yellow vegetables** 2 servings Typical servings: 3/4 cup to 1 cup spinach, collard, kale, broccoli, carrots, winter squash, sweet potatoes, or pumpkin. **Other fruits and vegetables** 2 servings Typical servings: 3/4 cup to 1 cup fruits and vegetables including potatoes.
Grain Products, Whole or Enriched 4 or more servings Typical servings: One slice of bread; 1/2 cup rice, hot cereal, or cooked pasta, 2 corn tortillas; 1 muffin; 1 biscuit, dumpling, pancake, or waffle. Two-inch square of cornbread; 3/4 cup of ready-to-eat cereal (not sugared kind).
Liquids, including milk 8 cups

5-13 A nursing mother should consult her physician about a diet suited to her own needs.

mother may need to eliminate some of these foods from her diet while she is nursing.

- Always inform physicians and dentists that she is nursing. Also, the mother should talk to her physician before taking over-the-counter drugs. (Any drug could affect milk and the baby.)
- Rest and avoid stress. Milk can "dry up" when mothers are tired or under stress.
- Consult with her physician, a nurse, or a La Leche (lay chay) League member for help with breast-feeding.
- Use breast-feeding time to build bonding. Mothers should smile at, sing to, talk with, and cuddle their newborns, 5-14.

If bottle-feeding is preferred, here are some things parents should do:

- Consult with their physician about the type of formula to use. Most parents purchase commercially-prepared formula in powdered, concentrated liquid, or ready-to-feed form. Or they may make their own formula with evaporated milk, water, and corn syrup.
- Remember that whole milk is not recommended before the baby is 6 months old. Cow's milk has too much salt and protein for newborns. It may cause irritation, bleeding, pain, and eventually anemia.
- Give newborns the amount of milk they need (about two to two and one-half oz. per pound of body weight in a 24-hour period). Babies do not always finish their bottles.
- Refrigerate ingredients used in making formula. Keep utensils, bottles, and nipples completely clean. Check nipples. (Large holes or clogged holes cause feeding problems. Pieces may be bitten off of worn nipples resulting in possible choking.) Throw away all unfinished formula.
- Cuddle the baby during feeding. Parents may want to take turns feeding the baby. This would give both of them a chance to establish a warm relationship with the baby, 5-15.
- Avoid propping the bottle. Babies can choke while feeding. (When choking occurs, they need to be turned to their side or abdomen and patted on the back.)

Whether breast-fed or bottle-fed, the baby must be burped. Burp the baby to get rid of air that is swallowed while sucking or crying. To burp a newborn, place the baby in a sitting position with a hand on the collar bone and under the chin, or lay the baby face down across your legs. You may burp a newborn on your shoulder, but the shoulder position is easier when the baby is larger. After the baby is in position, pat the baby's back below the ribs for 2 or 3 minutes, unless the baby burps sooner. Burping is often done before, midway, and after feeding.

Clothing and dressing. If you were a newborn, you'd want your clothes to be comfortable, easy to put on and take off, warm but not hot, and safe. Rather loose-fitting clothes for easy movement and clothes without too many ties, buttons, or snaps to lie on are comfortable. Comfortable clothes are often easy to put on and take off, too. Because babies kick off their blankets, warm clothes are needed. Overdressing babies should be avoided because it makes them hot. Newborn's clothes are safe if they are flame retardant and if fasteners and decorative items are secure.

GERBER PRODUCTS

5-14 Breast-feeding helps bonding develop between a mother and her baby.

Besides meeting the baby's needs, parents need to be good consumers of time, energy, and money. Because baby clothes are so cute, it is easy to make unwise choices! The number of clothes should be limited because babies outgrow their clothes quickly. Many parents stay within their clothing budget by watching for sales. Borrowing baby clothes from friends and relatives, choosing clothes suitable for either boys or girls (and storing for the next child), and buying or making clothes for the baby to "grow into" are other ways to save money. Clothes should be easy to launder, also. Clothes which must be hand washed or washed with like colors are not practical. Some basic clothing needs for the newborn include the following:

- 3-4 cotton knit nightgowns or kimonos.
- 3-4 cotton knit shirts.
- 2-3 sweaters.
- 1 knit cap.
- 3-6 dozen diapers (This number is given because babies wear diapers for two or more years, and diapers are also used for protection of bedding, for burping, and as "bibs.")
- 3 plastic pants.
- 3-4 pairs of socks.
- 4-6 bibs

Of course, most parents want at least one dressy outfit for outings and pictures.

Dressing time is a chance to talk with newborns. Newborns talk with their body movements, eyes, and sounds. Tell babies what you're doing as you dress them. ("I'm snapping your shirt . . . snap . . . snap . . . snap.")

Newborns are easy to dress, because they do not squirm a lot. These suggestions should make dressing easy and safe.

- Get the needed clothes and undo any fasteners before you get the baby.
- Support the head when lifting.
- Pull arms and legs through openings because newborns can't push.
- Cuddle fretful babies before continuing to dress.

Diapering. Parents have several options regarding diapers. Cloth diapers can be used with or without *diaper liners.* (Diaper liners are thin sheets of a disposable material laid on the cloth diaper as an inner layer. They help prevent soiling and staining the diaper.) Plastic pants may be worn over the diaper to make them water-proof. A second option is to use disposable diapers. These have waterproof outer layers. In some places, a parent has the option of using a diaper service which picks up soiled diapers and delivers sterilized cloth ones. Parents should consider the cost (including time involved) for each option. Many babies wear cloth diapers most of the time. But they may wear disposable ones when traveling or during emergencies like when the washing machine is out-of-order.

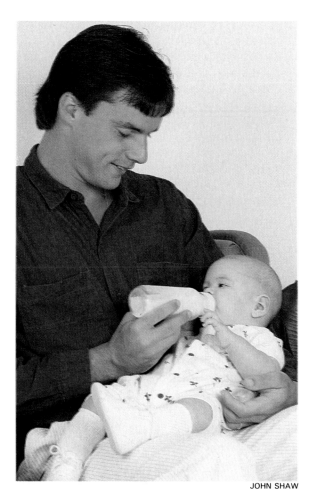

JOHN SHAW

5-15 Bottle-feeding helps the father develop a good relationship with his baby.

To diaper a baby, place the baby on a firm surface. Unfasten and remove the soiled diaper. Thoroughly cleanse the diaper region. With one hand, grasp the baby's ankles and slide the fresh diaper under the baby. (The back of diaper should be at the baby's back.) Pull the front of the diaper up between the baby's legs. Tuck in extra fabric. As you pin the diaper, protect the baby from the pin by slipping two of your fingers between the baby and the diaper. (Diaper pins that have been pushed into a bar of soap will glide easily through a cloth diaper.)

If using disposable diapers, make sure plastic liner is tucked in after pulling diaper to the front. The tape fastens from the front to the back. (Lotion or oil on fingers will prevent tape from sticking.) If you unfasten a disposable diaper and find the baby does not need changing, re-fasten with a household tape or with diaper pins.

Proper laundering is essential for cloth diapers. Keep a diaper pail half-filled with a sudsy or a borax solution. Wet diapers go directly into the pail. Soiled diapers should be rinsed in toilet first. (Hold the diaper firmly while flushing a bowel movement.) Then place the diaper in the pail. Launder diapers daily in hot water and laundry products designed for diapers. Use one or two extra rinses (cold water is fine) to remove soap and detergent traces.

Parents can prevent most diaper rashes by changing the baby's diapers regularly. But diaper rashes may develop from the constant use of plastic pants or from the outer layer of disposable diapers. Bacteria builds up on the warm, moist, and air-free skin causing diaper rash. Most babies develop diaper rashes at one time or another. The most common treatment is to wash the region with soap and water after each change, expose the area without ointment to air, and use petroleum jelly or a rash ointment when diapering. If the rash persists following several days of treatment, you should consult a pediatrician.

Bathing. Newborns don't get very dirty except for their faces, necks, and diaper regions. These areas must be kept clean. The first step in bathing is to collect all supplies, 5-16. Place them within the adult's reach but out of the baby's reach. Never leave a baby unattended—even for a second—on a cabinet or a table!

Because newborns have sensitive, dry skin, daily baby oil baths are suggested for the first 10 days. Clean the eyes, ears, and nose with fresh cotton balls that have been dipped in clear water and squeezed out. Clean the diaper region with soap and water. Except for the eyes, ears, and nose, gently stroke baby oil on the entire baby (including the scalp). Gently brush and comb the baby's hair after dressing.

Sponge baths are used for nearly the remainder of the newborn stage. Generally speaking, the entire body including the scalp must be cleaned once or twice a week. Sponge baths are recommended until the navel has completely healed—up to three weeks after birth. (Leave the cord alone until it becomes wet and loose. Then wipe with a cotton swab dipped in 70 percent rubbing alcohol four or five times per day.) To sponge bathe, follow these directions:

- Place the baby on a towel or a baby-sized sponge placed on a cabinet or on a bathing table. See 5-17.
- Wash face with a washcloth dipped in clear water and squeezed out.
- Clean eyes, ears, and nose with fresh cotton balls dipped in clear water and squeezed out.

OIL AND SPONGE BATH SUPPLIES

Towel or sponge for baby to lie on

Baby soap

Cotton balls

Washcloth, towel, and wrapper (a hooded cape or a hooded front-opening "robe" to wrap around baby)

Baby oil and lotion

Baby powder

Manicure scissors (made for babies)

Hair brush and comb (made for babies)

5-16 Gather and organize all bath supplies before getting the baby.

- Lightly soap rest of the body and rinse with a wet washcloth. Pat the baby dry as you wash each area. Keep the baby covered with a wrapper or an extra towel.
- Restore moisture with baby oil or lotion.
- Shampoo the scalp once or twice a week with soap to prevent scaling called *cradle cap*. Use oil (*not* lotion) on scalp.
- Brush and comb hair after you have dressed the baby.
- Cut the baby's nails when necessary.

Powders are often used on newborns. Don't let powder get in nose or eyes or accumulate in folds of the skin. Caldescene powder is less irritating than talcum powders.

Sleeping. Newborns average about 17 hours of sleep per day, but the range is from 11 to 23 hours. There is no relationship between sleep requirements and good health.

Newborns do not sleep quietly between feedings. They usually take seven or eight naps in which they suck, wheeze, and gurgle. This pattern of "light" sleep continues for the first half-year. Newborns adjust to regular household sounds, so it isn't necessary to whisper or tiptoe while they are sleeping.

Babies should be placed on a firm mattress in a bed that has sides to prevent them from falling. Pillows and stuffed toys should only be used after the baby is six months of age. Until babies can readily rotate their sleep positions, a pillow or stuffed toy could hamper their breathing. Pillows and stuffed toys are probably best never used in a baby bed, because

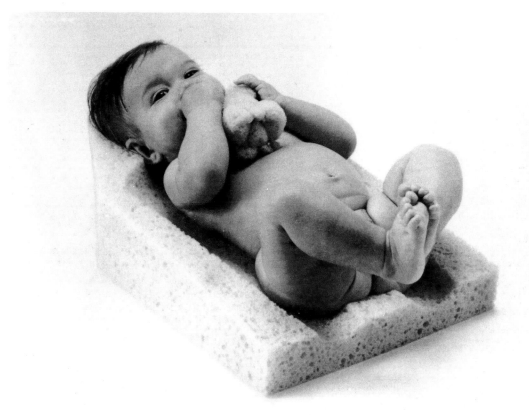

5-17 This type of sponge cradles a baby during sponge baths.

once a baby can stand these items can be used as "helps" in climbing over the railing.

Until babies can roll over, rotate their sleep positions. Changing the sleeping position makes the baby more comfortable. Special care in rotating the sleep positions should be given to the few babies who "insist" on sleeping in one position. Because babies' skulls are soft, their heads may be slightly but permanently flattened in one place. If this occurs, it is not serious. The flat spot does not affect the brain, and hair will make the flattened area unnoticeable.

Bedding equipment and supplies are very simple for newborns. The basic items needed are listed in 5-18.

Exercising. Movement is a large part of life even before birth and in the newborn stage. Watch the constant movement of newborns lying awake on their backs. Exercise is important for muscle development, coordination, and even relaxation. Exercising newborns will not cause them to crawl or walk sooner. But exercise may help the general development of the muscles. To help the baby exercise, follow these hints:

- Babies should be placed on a foam pad or bed where they are comfortable and safe.
- Babies should wear non-restrictive clothing while exercising to allow maximum ability to move.
- Select a good 10 or 15 minute time period. Babies should be in an alert but not in a fussy state. Watch a baby's schedule for several days before selecting a time. (Just before or after a feeding time is not a good time.) The time should be convenient for the adult, too.
- Move gently. If the baby shows resistance, stop.
- Talk or sing to the baby during the exercises. Try some of these exercises for a newborn. Be creative and use some others, too.
  1. With baby on back, lift arms above the head, straight out from the shoulders (in the form of a cross), and down to the sides.
  2. Draw the palms of the hands together as in clapping.
  3. Alternately move one knee up to the chest

and then the other.
  4. Straighten the knees by holding the legs together with one hand under the calves and the other hand gently pushing the knees flat.

Exercising a baby results in added bonuses. Daily exercising, if started early in life, may become a daily, life long habit. Exercise is also a way of having fun with babies and developing a warm relationship. Many families find activities which involve exercise to be great family fun for years.

Scheduling. Babies don't come into the world knowing anything about a schedule. The age-old questions are:

- Should parents try to figure out when their baby is "telling" them that he or she is hungry or sleepy? (Self-demand.)
- Should parents try to teach babies to adopt a schedule of eating or sleeping? (Scheduled.)

One answer that works well for many parents is to watch their baby for a few days. Then they can try to work out a schedule based on their baby's needs as well as their own needs. They should try to keep within a few minutes of the schedule.

In time, babies will adopt the schedule as long as it closely parallels their needs. There is evidence that scheduled-fed babies are less fussy. Parents should keep in mind that their baby's needs change. For instance, three-hour feedings eventually change to four-hour feedings. Also, parents may need to change the schedule occasionally for their own convenience. But parents need to remember that scheduling is one way to show consistency. Babies learn to trust the world (and show less fear and anxiety) when their environment is consistent.

Medical attention. Before the newborn leaves the hospital, the pediatrician will ask the parents to make an appointment for what is called a well-baby checkup. The checkup will be within a month or even less if the baby is small or has special needs. It's a good idea for parents to jot down questions about the care and development of the baby as they occur to them. Then the list will be ready on the day of the appointment.

A family health history will be taken if one has not already been taken. Then the baby is undressed. Babies often start crying, but they are not afraid of the doctor! (The crying appears to be because of temperature changes including cold scales and medical instruments. Crying may also be caused by the lack of support provided by clothing and blankets.) The nurse will weigh and measure the length, head, and chest of the baby.

BEDDING EQUIPMENT AND SUPPLIES

Bed.
Bassinets, cradles, baby beds, or dresser drawers with a pad are all fine "beds." (The bed should be high and stable enough to prevent younger children or pets from tipping it over.) If a cradle or bed with slats is used, the slats should be no further apart than two and three-eighths inches. This prevents babies from wiggling feet first through the slats until their heads are caught, causing serious injury or even death.

Bumper pads.
If babies are placed in cradles or beds with slats, bumper pads should be included. Bumper pads are not used until babies can lift their heads to prevent suffocation. (Most babies can turn and lift their heads at birth or within a few days after birth.) Bumper pads are removed when babies can stand because standing babies can use these as climbing devices.

Large pieces of flannelette sheeting.
2 or 3 pieces of 25 by 35 inch waterproof flannelette sheeting are needed to cover the mattress or pad. This item goes under the sheet. These large pieces are essential once the baby begins to scoot or wiggle around in bed. (Most parents use the sheeting until the child is toilet trained at night.)

Small pieces of flannelette sheeting.
Four to six 18 inch squares of waterproof flannelette sheeting (to catch overflows from diaper or from spitting up) are placed on top of the sheet for newborns who can't scoot much. These small "sheets" are also convenient to put on the lap when holding a baby or on a large bed when changing, dressing, or exercising a baby.

Sheets.
3 or 4 sheets are needed, and fitted bottom sheets are the easiest to use. Sheets come in varous sizes to fit bassinets, standard-size cribs, and cradles. (King-sized pillow cases are the perfect size for many cradle pads.)

Receiving blankets.
3 or 4 cotton flannel blankets may be needed. Receiving blankets, about 30 by 40 inches, are often used. Crib blankets (36 by 50 inches) are perhaps more economical because babies soon outgrow the smaller "receiving blankets." Regardless of the size of the blanket, babies seem to kick off blankets. Thus, sleepwear that keeps baby warm without having to use many blankets is essential. The sleepwear includes drawstring-bottom gowns and sleep-and-play suits. This sleepwear is made to be "roomy" (with raglan-sleeve construction and stretch fabric) and warm (with drawstring bottoms or tube feet and cuffs that convert into mittens).

5-18 The bedding needs of newborns are quite simple.

The pediatrician will examine the baby, answer questions, and make recommendations, 5-19. Parents may ask the nurse or pediatrician to write the recommendations. Parents are told when their baby's next checkup should be.

Intellectual needs

As we have discussed, newborns are learners. Just as parents need to meet the newborn's physical needs, they need to meet the newborn's intellectual needs, too.

Parents need to stimulate newborns. Newborns do not need elaborate stimulation, because their major developmental task is to adjust to their new world. Most infants adapt to their environment, provided that it is consistent and not too startling.

Most parents ask, "When and how do I stimulate my newborn?" Babies learn in their waking, alert state. Their eyes are open and shiny, and they look around. When they are over-stimulated or bored, they either become more active and fretful or go to sleep. (Adults behave in much the same way.)

Because newborns can't walk or crawl, experiences must be taken to them. Newborns learn through their senses.

Most of the stimulation comes from being near parents and other caregivers. Newborns are fascinated at seeing faces, hearing sounds, and feeling warm and loved when cuddled, 5-20. Warm and expressive talk stimulates newborns. Newborns love to hear singing (and they are an uncritical audience).

Newborns enjoy looking at objects. Because their distance vision is very limited for three or four weeks, mobiles hung above the beds are almost useless for the newborn.

Objects can be hung from sturdy ribbon (satin or grosgrain rather than package-wrapping ribbon) or elastic and hung over the bed railing close to corner, 5-21. Objects should be about 12 inches from the newborn's face and almost touching the mattress. Newborns are often placed on their stomachs, and they can see objects in the corners of their bed as they turn their heads left and right. (Because newborns tilt their heads back, they see objects placed in the corners of the bed more easily

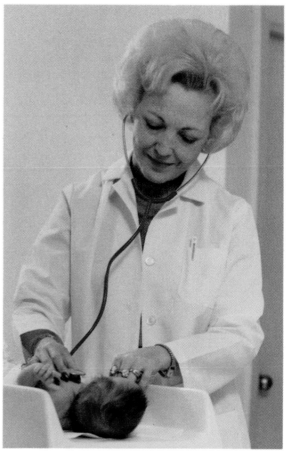

JOHN GUILLET

5-19 This pediatrician enjoys examining the newborn in a well-baby checkup.

than objects placed on the sides.) Objects should be changed frequently. Newborns get bored, too.

Grasping objects during the newborn stage is a reflex action, but for added safety objects should be securely fastened, non-toxic and too large to swallow. Once a baby can move around in the bed or grasp at will, any object that cannot be safely mouthed must be removed.

Other ways to stimulate the newborn include using colorful bed bumper pads. Fabric in bright colors and patterns can be laid over the bumper pads near the corners of the bed to add interest. A wind chime, a music box, or some lullabies or other soothing music recorded on

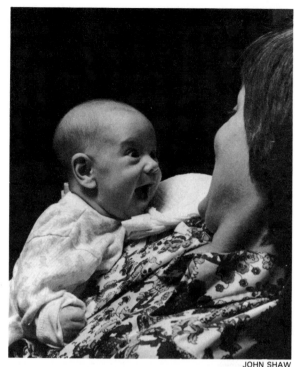

JOHN SHAW

5-20 This four-week-old is beginning to show much excitement over playing with her mother.

tape are other good sensory experiences for newborns.

Social-emotional needs

Each baby is born with an individuality. Some babies are more active than others. Some like to be cuddled a lot and others don't. Some cry a lot and others seem happier. This individuality influences the parents' response to the baby in much the same way another person's personality affects the way you respond. In this section, you will examine the individuality of babies and ways parents can meet their babies' social-emotional needs.

Alertness of newborns. As we have discussed, babies seem to learn best when they are in the *alert inactive* state (quiet but alert). Not only do babies learn best in this state, but they seem to develop warm relationships with others at this time. Newborns are not much fun if they are always asleep or fussy. Parents often refer to alert-inactive babies as "good" babies and fussy babies as "difficult" ones.

Babies differ in alertness because of their individuality and their "age" when they were born. (Premature babies are often not as alert.)

NEWBORN TOYS

Designs and Patterns	Objects that Move	Circular-Shaped Objects	Other Objects
Newborns like bold, black and white patterns. They prefer horizontal and diagonal designs to vertical ones. Babies like spiral patterns and concentric circles more than solid-colored circles.	Balloons and plastic lids with designs painted on them flutter with the bed's movement.	Newborns enjoy balls made from aluminum-foil and bright-colored yarn. Rings are also a favorite.	Pictures of faces are favorites. Newborns also enjoy bright-colored bows and ribbons, artificial flowers and mirrors.

5-21 Newborns' first toys are things to see, and they already show preferences!

Babies differ in the amount of time they are alert. But there seems to be a general pattern in the development of alertness. Unless affected by the drugs used in delivery, newborns are usually alert for a while after their birth. (Remember bonding right after birth gets the parent-child relationship off to a good start.) Then newborns tend to sleep a lot during the next few days. With each passing week, newborns spend more time in the alert inactive stage. They average 11 hours the first week and 22 hours the fourth week.

Parents can establish a good relationship early in the newborn's life, even if the baby is sleepy or fussy most of the time. Time takes care of the sleepiness of healthy newborns. Parents should take advantage of their alert states by cuddling and playing with them. Parents can enjoy fussy newborns in their alert quiet times and attempt to soothe them when fussy.

Soothing a fussy baby. All newborns cry. Some babies cry one-sixth to one-fourth of each 24-hour day, and yet nothing is wrong. Parents need to understand that crying is not related to their parenting abilities. Some babies just cry more and are harder to soothe than others.

Newborns cry for almost any reason because crying is the way they "talk." They may cry because they are tired, hungry, lonely, or uncomfortable. Or they may cry to relax from tension. Colic is a major cause of crying especially during the first three months. *Colic* is a condition (not a disease) in which the baby has intense abdominal pain. There are many causes of colic such as allergies (often to milk or vitamins), tensions, swallowing air when sucking, and hunger. Medication may be prescribed in severe cases, but soothing often works.

Parents should try to soothe newborns. Tiny babies (especially those under 6 months) cannot be spoiled because they don't understand that they can bend others to their will. To soothe a newborn, try to interpret the cry and then respond. Chart 5-22 describes three distinct cries and how to respond to them. Some ways to soothe a baby are listed below.

• Rock the baby in a vertical (over your shoulder) position. Put your hand behind the baby's head and rock fast.
• Carry baby around the house or yard.
• Sing and play music. Babies like the quiet tones of lullabies or even a steady tone. Dr. Hajime Murooka developed a recording of the sounds a baby hears before birth—mother's breathing and heartbeat—and found that these sounds soothe the newborn. (The recording is now sold as *Lullaby from the Womb*.)
• Take the baby for a car ride.

Crying causes tension in parents. Relief from tension is good for family relationships. Using a baby-sitter for an hour or so each day or even an entire afternoon each week may help reduce tensions.

MEETING THE PARENTS' NEEDS

Parenting skills do not come automatically with the birth of a baby; parenting skills are learned. Because learning takes time, the first few weeks are especially difficult ones. Each parent learns to cope in a different way. Even experienced, skilled parents find that they must learn new things with each child. Parents shouldn't forget about their own needs while learning to care for their new child.

Getting enough rest is always important, and it is even more important when parents have a newborn. Newborns cause quick and continuous fatigue. Fatigue is hard on physical health. It can lead to irritability and depression. Thus, it is important for parents to rest when possible. Parents of newborns need to put off unnecessary chores such as cooking difficult dishes or window washing. If possible, they should reschedule their day so that they can sleep or rest while the baby is sleeping. Parents who bottle-feed their baby can take turns feeding so that both parents can get more rest.

Parents need to learn the nitty-gritty of child care rather than think about the more distant future. For instance, during the first four weeks it is more important for parents to learn how to bathe a baby than to plan a playroom. Often new parents feel unsure and clumsy in doing many tasks. With knowledge and practice, speed and efficiency quickly increase. (That is why parents usually say the first child is the hardest.) After basic child care tasks are learned, there will still be enough time to dream and plan for the future!

Parents need to organize their households. Speed and efficiency in child care tasks are increased with organization. Valuable time is wasted in looking for misplaced items. New parents need to find a place for the baby's things. Baby supplies are likely to be kept in several rooms—the kitchen, bathroom, bedroom, and perhaps the living room or den. If parents travel with the baby, additional places such as the car have to be organized for baby's things. Parents need to be mentally organized, too. A bulletin board for pinning physicians' recommendations, appointments, shopping lists, and other reminders may help.

Parents need to have time to spend with other adults—especially with each other. Babies don't need all the attention; mothers and fathers need attention, too. Spending some time with adults each day restores energy. Parents should plan for extra time to be with each other and other adults. Parents who help each other with child care and other tasks have more time for each other. Again, parents have more leisure time if they do the essential chores first. They can put off unessential jobs if time doesn't permit.

Parents need to get out of the house with and without the new baby, 5-23. Spending too much time in the house often gives parents the feeling that they are living in a baby's world. "Getting out," even for a short walk, restores physical and mental energy. Baby's and parents'

JOHN SHAW

5-23 New parents need to spend time away from their baby to help restore mental energy.

THE MEANINGS OF CRIES

Cause	Sound of Cry	Way to Respond
Pain	Cycle begins with shrill scream, followed by silience, and ends with short gasps. Cycle is repeated.	Ease pain if possible. Cuddle baby to calm.
Hunger or Boredom	Slow cries that become louder and rhythmic.	Feed if near feeding time. or Entertain by giving baby a tour of the house or yard.
Upset	Fussy, rather quiet cry. Cry sounds a little forced.	Cuddle or entertain.

5-22 Newborns communicate with their cries.

moods can be improved with an outing. Parents also need to obtain competent baby-sitting services for some outings without the baby. It's fun to be with other adults, and newborns never protest their parents leaving them in good hands!

Married couples usually enjoy having married couples for friends. This is also true for new parents. New parents can learn a lot from and share a lot with other parents. Many first-time parents find it most helpful to have special friends to call on for a little advice. In fact, studies show that many parents who found having children an unhappy experience were isolated from family or friends.

The successful development of newborns is most dependent on the parent-child relationship. When parents have their needs met, newborns have a good chance of having their physical, intellectual, and social-emotional needs met. Babies whose needs are met by loving parents are off to a good start.

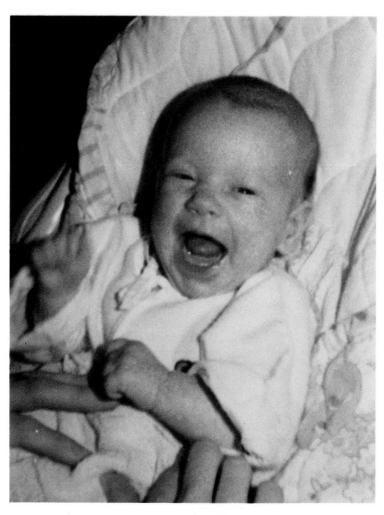

When parents provide loving care, they can have many happy times with infants.

to Know

anemia . . . Apgar test . . . bonding . . .
Brazelton scale . . . colic . . . cradle cap . . .
diaper liner . . . intensive care nursery . . .
isolettes . . . neonate . . . neonatology . . .
PKU . . .pediatrician . . . reflexes

to Review

Write your answers on a separate sheet of
paper.

1. Which of the following is *not* included in
the Apgar test?
   a. Breathing effort.
   b. Heart rate.
   c. Muscle tone.
   d. Eye movements.
   e. Skin color.
   f. Reflex irritability.
2. Explain the difference between reflexes and
voluntary movements. Describe two reflexes
seen in the newborn.
3. Match the following descriptions of a
newborn's appearance with their definitions.

   _____ vernix caseosa
   _____ fontaneles
   _____ lanugo
   _____ "stork bites"

   a. Soft, downy hair on ears, shoulders,
   back, and face.
   b. Whitish, cheese-like covering on skin.
   c. "Soft spots" on skull.
   d. Pink blotches on forehead, eyelids, and
   back of neck.
4. List 3 advantages of breast-feeding and 3
advantages of bottle-feeding.
5. Chris is a 10 lb. newborn who is bottle-fed
every four hours during a 24-hour period.
Calculate the *minimum* ounces of formula
needed for each of Chris' feedings. (Of course,
a little extra is actually added, because Chris
may want more or less than the minimum at
any feeding.)

6. True or false. Newborns who cry a lot are
just spoiled; therefore, the way to stop the
crying is to let them cry it out.
7. Explain how parents may meet their own
needs for:
   a. Rest.
   b. Time spent with each other.
   c. Learning child-care techniques.
   d. Organizing their own household.
   e. "Getting out" of the house.

to Do

1. Look through current magazines and find
pictures of infants. Explain how you can tell
whether or not the baby is a newborn.
2. Divide the class into groups. Make a
shopping list of items needed for clothing and
diapering, bottle-feeding (bottles, nipples,
sterilizer, formula, etc.), bedding, and bathing.
Do some comparison shopping to find the range
of prices for each item. Design a bulletin board
entitled "Big Needs for the Little One."
3. Make some objects to dangle in the bed.
(See 5-17.)
4. Assist a mother of a newborn with the
routine tasks of feeding, bathing, diapering, and
dressing.
5. Ask a pediatrician to talk with your class
about the care of a newborn and the
importance of well-baby checkups.
6. Make arrangements to tour a local hospital.
The focus of the tour should be:
   a. Appearance and activity of newborns.
   b. Nurses' care of newborns.
   c. Pediatricians checking newborns.
   d. Facilities for care of newborns.
   e. Arrangements for mothers and fathers to
   spend time with their newborns.
7. Write a paragraph on the importance of
bonding for both the infant and the parents.

LEVER BROTHERS CO.

Having fun with big sister

part three

Infants

JOHN SHAW

At seven months - sitting up

JOHN SHAW

Hey... I can make things happen

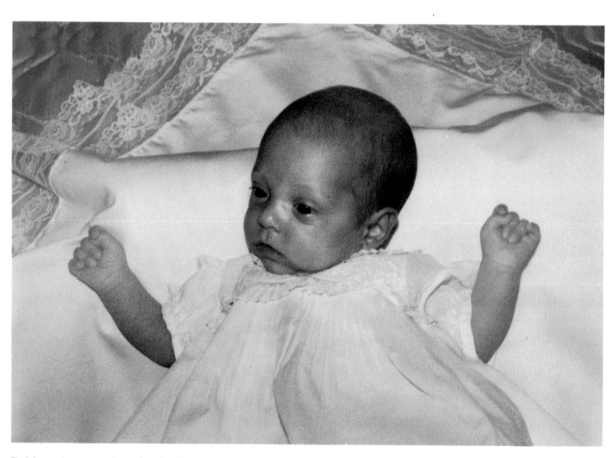

Babies change a lot physically in their first year.

6

Physical development of the infant

After studying this chapter, you will be able to:
- ☐ Describe the changes that occur in the various body systems during the first year.
- ☐ Sequence the development of infant's motor skills.

Babies are able to develop physically, but only with the care of others. The human's physical growth is completed at 20 or 21 years. This growth period is longer than that of any other living creature. Adults must provide for care throughout a good part of this time. Just as physical growth was rapid during the prenatal and neonatal stages, it continues to be rapid during the entire first year of life.

You need to understand the milestones of physical development for these reasons. First, physical development is a good indication of a baby's ability to *thrive* (stay healthy and keep growing and developing). Second, physical development has an important impact on a baby's mental and social-emotional development. For instance, physical development aids mental development. With increased development of the *sensory organs* (eyes, ears, nose, taste buds, and skin) and of *motor skills* (crawling, walking, and grasping objects), babies are able to learn about their world. Physical development also affects social-emotional development. As babies gain motor skills, the feeling of "I can do it" begins. This, in turn, fosters a healthy *self-concept* (self-concept is the way people feel about themselves.)

Physical development of the infant 113

SKELETAL GROWTH

The *skeletal system* is made up of bones and teeth. Most people think of skeletal growth in terms of changes in height and weight and the appearance of teeth. Those involved in health care (such as physicians and nurses) think about skeletal growth in these ways. But they also think of other body changes such as:

- Measurement of the head and thorax (chest).
- Mineral content of bones (this affects their firmness).
- Space between various bones to permit continued growth.
- The number of bones and teeth.

Length and weight

Length and weight changes during the first year are very rapid. (The term length is used for the first year because the baby does not stand. After the first year, the term height is used.) Changes are so quick that even parents and others who see the baby daily are amazed. Usually parents talk about how long and heavy their baby is getting and how fast the baby is outgrowing clothing.

All children have their own rate of growth. But most normal infants grow one-half (9 or 10 inches) of their birth length (20 to 21 inches) during the first year. They double their birth weight in four or five months and triple their birth weight in one year.

The rate of growth is more important than total length and weight increase. As seen in 6-1, the baby's length increases about 20 percent in the first three months. It increases about 50 percent in the first year. Weight, which is doubled by five months, increases about one pound per month for the last six months of the first year. On the average, boys are slightly longer and heavier than girls (by about three-fourths of an inch and one and one-half pounds).

Neonates are born looking very slender. But by nine months, they often turn into chubby babies. The change is due to fat tissues under the skin which increase until nine months. After that fat tissues begin to decrease. Even during these early months, boys have more muscle

length and thickness and girls have more fat. The total weight composition (make-up) for the infant is very different from the adult's. See 6-2.

Body proportions

Infants are not miniature (small) adults in any way. Even their *body proportions* (relative size of body parts) are different. For instance, the head is about one-fourth of the infant's total length. It is one-tenth of the adult's height. Unlike the adult, an infant's forehead is wider than the chin and the jaw is smaller and receding (slopes backward). This is the "baby look" as it is commonly called.

The infant's head is larger than the thorax (chest) from birth until six months. In normal, six-month-old children, the thorax becomes larger. The difference in *circumference* (the distance around) continues to increase with age.

Besides having a large head, an infant has a long trunk, a "pot-bellied" abdomen, and short legs. Thus, the center of gravity is high in the baby's trunk. No wonder babies "toddle" rather than walk as adults! Increases in length are a result of trunk rather than leg growth during the first year.

Bones and teeth

Instead of a sturdy skeletal frame of rigid bones that comprise the adult frame, the infant skeleton is mainly *cartilage* (soft, gristle-like tissue). Infants have large spaces between their "bones" to give the joints great flexibility

AVERAGE LENGTH AND WEIGHT
DURING FIRST YEAR

AGE IN MONTHS	LENGTH IN INCHES	WEIGHT IN POUNDS
Birth	20	7 1/2
3	23 3/4	12 1/2
6	26	16 3/4
9	28	20
12	29 1/2	22 1/4

6-1 The length and weight of a baby increases very rapidly during the first year.

WEIGHT COMPOSITION OF INFANTS AND ADULTS

TOTAL WEIGHT	INFANT	ADULT
Muscle	20%	45%
Internal Organs	15%	10%
Nervous system	15%	3%
Water	75%	60%

6-2 The make-up of weight is most different in infants and adults.

(so they bend without breaking). Infants can suck their toes without any trouble, but sitting or standing are made impossible! It is true that the infant's bones do not fracture (break) easily. But their bones may become deformed more easily than adult bones due to their softness.

Three changes occur in the bones. First, there is an increase in the length of the bones. This is not completed in all parts of the body until about 20 years of age.

Second, *ossification* (the depositing of the minerals calcium and phosphorus) begins to occur. Ossification helps the skeletal frame become sturdy, enabling the infant to sit and eventually to walk. Ossification is also involved in bone length. Once it is completed, the bones cannot lengthen any more. Ossification occurs earlier in the head, hands, and wrists. The long bones of the legs are the last to ossify.

Third, there is a change in the number of bones. In some areas of the body, ossification causes a decrease in the number of bones. For instance, in the chapter on the newborn, you read that the skull bones were separated by fontanels. Ossification in the skull, completed in about two years, results in one skull bone. But in other parts of the body, extra bones develop. For instance, the hand and wrist of a one-year-old infant has only three bones, but there are 28 bones in the adult's hand and wrist.

Teeth, a part of the skeletal system, begin forming in the sixth week of fetal life. By birth, all 20 *deciduous teeth* (also called non-permanent, baby, and milk teeth) and a few permanent teeth are developing deep in the jaw. Usually several deciduous teeth appear during the second half of the first year. See 6-3. The appearance of teeth is often called *teething* or

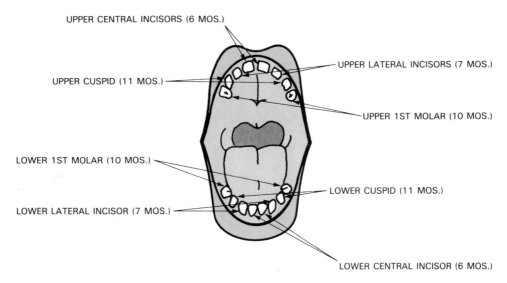

UPPER CENTRAL INCISORS (6 MOS.)

UPPER LATERAL INCISORS (7 MOS.)

UPPER CUSPID (11 MOS.)

UPPER 1ST MOLAR (10 MOS.)

LOWER 1ST MOLAR (10 MOS.)

LOWER CUSPID (11 MOS.)

LOWER LATERAL INCISOR (7 MOS.)

LOWER CENTRAL INCISOR (6 MOS.)

6-3 There is a predictable pattern in the appearance of deciduous teeth.

cutting teeth. The *sequence,* or order, of appearance is more predictable than the time of appearance. In fact, a few babies are born with one or more teeth. And there are some children who do not get any teeth until after the first year.

CHANGES IN OTHER BODY SYSTEMS

The *circulatory* or *cardiovascular system* (heart and blood vessels) grows as the infant grows but at a slower rate. At birth, the heart is .75 percent of the baby's weight, but is .4 percent of the adult's body weight. As the heart grows in size and breathing becomes deeper, the heart rate slows. (Heart rate changes from about 150 beats per minute at one month to about 135 beats per minute at 12 months.) The heart rate during the first year is almost twice as fast as that of an adult.

The *respiratory system* ("windpipe" and lungs) also increases in weight with increased total body weight. Lungs increase in capacity as breathing begins. But babies have weaker lung muscles and smaller chest and abdominal spaces to house body organs than adults. They cannot breathe as deeply as adults. Yet babies have a high demand for oxygen compared to their body size. To meet their needs, babies breathe faster. With increasing age, breathing is deeper and less frequent. During the first week after birth, babies breathe about 46 times per minute, but at one year they breathe 26 to 28 times per minute.

The *digestive system* (esophagus, stomach, intestines, and glands that aid digestion) greatly matures during the first year of life. The small stomach capacity expands rapidly. (Capacity is 30 to 90 cc at birth, 90 to 150 cc at one month, and 210 to 360 cc at one year.) When the stomach capacity is smaller, more frequent feedings are needed. Babies are fed every 2 to 3 hours around the clock at birth, then the feedings are spaced every 4 hours, and so on. The liver and other organs which aid digestion are still immature at birth. Thus, babies can properly digest only breast milk or formula for about six months. Then they can very gradually be fed more complex foods.

The *excretory system* (intestine, kidneys, and bladder) are also immature at birth. Babies have more *extracellular fluid* (fluid outside the cells) per pound of body weight than adults. (Extracellular fluid makes up 43 percent of the newborn's body weight as compared with 25 percent of an adult's weight.) Babies excrete half of this fluid daily in urine and stools. No wonder there are so many diapers! Babies cannot control water exchange very well during infancy. Thus, babies need to be offered fluids frequently. Vomiting, diarrhea, and fever must be treated quickly to prevent too much fluid loss. Swelling, a symptom that too much fluid is being kept in the body, needs quick treatment also. The ability to control the timing of excretion is not developed for almost two years.

NEURAL GROWTH

Although the brain develops rapidly in the unborn baby, *neural growth* (brain and nerve growth) is not finished at birth. At birth the midbrain is the most fully developed part of the brain. The midbrain is located in the lower part of the skull. See 6-4. It controls sleeping, waking, elimination, and the newborn's reflexes such as sucking, swallowing, and coughing.

Two changes occur after birth. One change is that the part of the brain called the *cortex* develops more completely. As you can see in 6-4, the cortex is the *convoluted* (coiled or twisted) gray matter surrounding the midbrain. After birth, new cortex cells are added, cells become larger, and connecting lengths which carry "messages" to the cells are built up. The cortex is about 50 percent complete at six months of age. The cortex is involved in *perception* (seeing, hearing, and other senses), body movement, thinking, and language. Physicians check for the Babinski reflex (see Chapter 5), because this reflex drops out around six months when the cortex takes over many brain functions. The prolonged presence of the Babinski reflex suggests brain damage.

The other major change in neural development is that a sheath (covering) of *myelin* (white, fatty substance) forms around individual nerves. This *insulates* (separates) them from one another. The myelin sheath helps messages pass down the nerves more quickly.

MOTOR DEVELOPMENT

Babies come into the world capable of many reflex movements. During the last 11 months of the first year, most of the reflex movements disappear. These reflexes are replaced by learned or *voluntary movements*. The sequence (order) of motor development is built upon the sequence of brain development. There are three main patterns in the infant's motor development:

1. Movements are slow because babies must think as they move.
2. At first babies show general reactions to things in their world. Later in the first year, babies give more specific reactions to things they see or hear. For instance, if babies are shown something they want, young infants wiggle all over, but older infants smile and reach for the object.
3. Motor development occurs in two directions—head-to-foot and center-to-extremities (trunk outward).

Head-to-foot development

The technical term for head-to-foot development is *cephalocaudal development* (*cephalo* means "head" and *caudal* means "tail"). Head-to-foot development begins before birth. The fetus develops a head, then arm buds, then leg buds. At birth, babies have developed facial muscles but not leg muscles. This enables babies to suck but not to walk.

Drawing 6-5 shows the sequence in which babies gain control of their head, neck, and trunk muscles. Although the order was first described in this way by Mary Shirley in 1933, this order is still used to describe milestones in the infant's motor development. As with all *age*

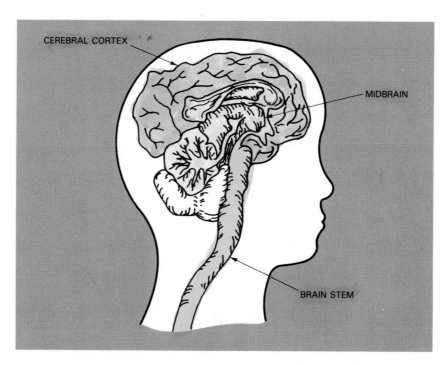

6-4 Each part of our brain controls certain functions— the midbrain helps the person survive and the cortex helps the person think.

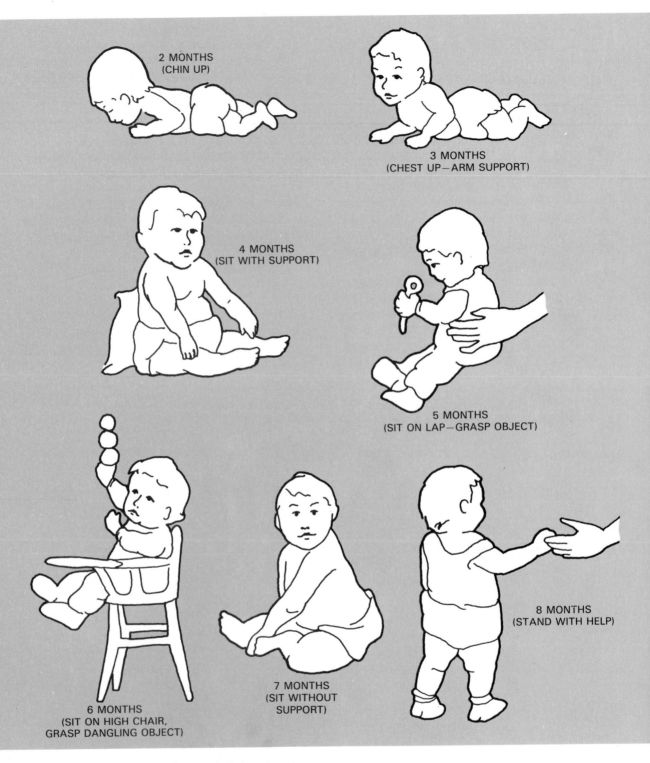

2 MONTHS
(CHIN UP)

3 MONTHS
(CHEST UP—ARM SUPPORT)

4 MONTHS
(SIT WITH SUPPORT)

5 MONTHS
(SIT ON LAP—GRASP OBJECT)

6 MONTHS
(SIT ON HIGH CHAIR,
GRASP DANGLING OBJECT)

7 MONTHS
(SIT WITHOUT
SUPPORT)

8 MONTHS
(STAND WITH HELP)

6-5 Babies gain control over their head and
neck, then their leg muscles.

9 MONTHS
(STAND HOLDING FURNITURE)

10 MONTHS
(CREEP)

11 MONTHS
(WALK WHEN LED)

12 MONTHS
(PULL TO STAND BY
FURNITURE)

14 MONTHS
(STAND ALONE)

15 MONTHS
(WALK ALONE)

6-5 Continued.

Physical development of the infant   119

norms (age averages), they are calculated from a range of ages (some older and some younger). Thus, it is best to think of the order rather than the rate (speed) of development.

Head and neck control. At birth some babies can raise their unsteady heads briefly when lying on their stomachs. By two months most babies spend a great deal of time viewing their world with their heads and chests raised. Between three and four months, eye muscles are well developed. This permits babies to focus on objects in any direction. Their lip muscles are also developed enough to enable them to smile at will and make some sounds with the lips. Head control is almost complete when babies are about six-months-old, 6-6. At this time, babies can raise their heads while lying on their backs and can hold their heads while sitting.

Trunk control. Control over the trunk develops more slowly than head control. As you noted in 6-5, babies placed on their abdomens lift their heads before they can lift both head and chest. Trunk control permits babies to achieve two major landmarks in motor control — rolling over and sitting.

Often between the second and fifth month, babies learn to *roll over*. Usually they will roll from front to back a month before they roll from back to front. This is because it is easier to lift head and trunk when on the abdomen than when on the back. To roll over, the baby must raise the head and one shoulder, arch the back, twist, and give a push with the legs. Sometimes adults see the baby's first roll-over. More often they discover the baby in a different position. They may not remember with certainty the position in which they placed the

6-6 These babies can raise their heads and chests high for rather long periods of time as they view their worlds.

baby. Thus, it may be several days before they know for sure that the baby can really roll-over.

Learning to *sit* takes several months, because the baby must gain strength in the neck and back and gain control over the head. Babies can sit for about one minute with support (being held or with pillows or other soft objects placed at their backs) at three or four months of age. But another three or four months pass before they can sit for a short time without support. Older infants often lean forward and support themselves with their arms and legs, 6-7. They may even topple over if distracted. Progress in sitting is rapid in the next few months. By nine months, most babies can sit 10 minutes or longer without support. They may use their hands for holding objects rather than for support.

Leg Control. Cephalocaudal development ends with leg control. With leg control, *locomotion* (the ability to move from place to place) really begins. Babies usually go through the stages of crawling, creeping, standing, and walking although some babies skip one or more of these stages.

Crawling is one of the first steps toward walking. Hand and foot *coordination* (the smooth working together of many muscles), which is achieved when babies play with their own feet and toes, is often used as the land-

6-7 Until back muscles are strong, leaning forward helps the baby to sit unaided.

AMERICAN GUIDANCE SERVICE, INC.

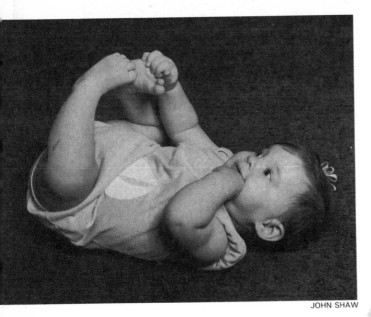

6-8 Playing with toes is a sign of the leg control needed for crawling.

mark for beginning leg control. See 6-8. Babies often play with their own feet and toes at seven months and begin crawling at the same time. A baby crawls by pulling with the arms, but the abdomen is not lifted from the floor.

Babies may begin *creeping* between six and eight months. Babies begin by lifting their abdomens and hips off the floor alternately. The movement may become a rhythmical, rocking motion. Within a couple of months, many babies can move forward or backward on hands and knees or on hands and feet with abdomen off of the floor, 6-9. Babies usually begin creeping by moving one limb at a time. For example, right arm, left leg, left arm, right leg, and repeat. Later they can move opposite side limbs in the same direction at the same time such as right arm and left leg at the same time and then left arm and right leg at the same time. A few babies skip creeping and scoot in a sitting position instead. Once babies can creep or scoot they will try stairs as well as level surfaces.

Six-month-old babies enjoy *standing* when supported under the arms. They push with their feet and bounce on adults' laps. A few months later, babies can pull up into a standing position. But they cannot sit down without help or without "falling" on their hips. Many babies cry for the adult to help them into a sitting position, only to pull into a standing position again right away! At first babies stand with support, holding onto a stable object. As development continues, babies stand further away from objects and use them for balancing by holding on with one hand. Most babies stand alone between 12 and 14 months. They also take a few cautious steps between objects and people, 6-10. When babies stand alone, they often enjoy *cruising* or walking with the support of an adult. This is the time when babies perfect walking skills. They gain confidence before walking alone a few weeks later.

Center-to-extremities development

The technical term for center-to-extremities development is *proximodistal development* (*proximo* means "near" and *distal* means "far"). In center-to-extremities development, the infant is able to control the trunk, then arms, the hands, and the fingers. The infant also is able to control the hips, then legs, feet, and toes.

6-9 Creeping requires being able to raise the trunk of one's body and skilled movements of arms and legs.

6-10 With adults ready to "catch," a baby who is almost ready to walk will take a few steps.

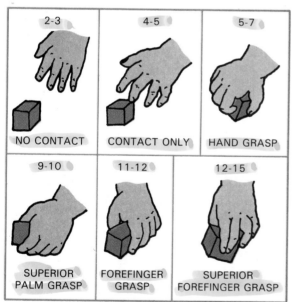

AGE IN MONTHS (APPROXIMATE)

6-11 Grasping ability goes through stages from a rather clumsy grasp in which the fingers press an object in the palm to a precise grasp using the index finger and thumb.

The baby comes into the world with a grasp reflex (Palmar reflex) which disappears around four months of age. The grasp reflex is replaced by voluntary grasping. Voluntary grasping works well by five or six months. Drawing 6-11 shows the grasping development of the infant as it was first described by H.M. Halverson in 1931. The drawing shows that the infant grasps first with fingers pressed against the palm. The thumb is not used much at all. Then the thumb and the four fingers together press against each other to hold the object. This type of grasping is called *prehension*. Finally the infant uses the thumb against the forefinger, permitting the baby to grasp small objects. Chart 6-12 describes the arm and hand control of the infant.

Signs of *hand preference* (ease in using either one's right or left hand) are rarely seen before four months. Hand preference is not often fixed before four or five years of age. Hand preference seems to be determined by heredity and environment. For instance, when both parents are left-handed, about 45 percent of all their children are left-handed, but when both

Physical development of the infant 123

ARM AND HAND CONTROL

Approximate Age in Months	
2	Babies can swipe at objects with either hand.
4 to 5	Babies can reach and grasp a stationary object. There is much body-sway so babies may need support to be successful in grasping.
5 to 6	Babies accept one object handed to them and can reach for and grasp dangling objects.
6 to 7	Babies carry objects grasped to mouth.
7	Babies accept two objects handed to them.
8 to 9	Babies pick up objects with thumb used in opposition to fingers.
10	Babies accept three objects handed to them.

6-12 Complex grasping skills are developed during the first year.

parents are right-handed, only two percent of all their children are left-handed. Two factors in the environment aid hand preference. First, parents model their hand preference. Second, objects—many of which are designed for right-handed people—aid hand preference. Today some parents and schools provide objects for left-hand use such as left-hand scissors.

DIFFERENCES IN PHYSICAL DEVELOPMENT

With few exceptions, the order of physical development is the same for every child. But every child has his or her own rate of development. The rate is affected by heredity, nutrition, illnesses, and activity. Some infants develop quickly; others lag behind. Some infants develop quickly in one area, but they may be slow in another. One infant may develop rapidly in the beginning. But another may start development slowly and pass the other infant later.

If development seems to be much slower than the norms, a physician or child development professional should be consulted. Regular medical care of infants is the best way of finding and treating problems. And, for most of the cases where infants are normal, hearing this report from an expert is comforting.

to Know

age norms . . . body proportions . . . cartilage . . . cephalocaudal development . . . circulatory (or cardiovascular) system . . . cortex . . . crawling . . .creeping . . . cruising . . . deciduous teeth . . . digestive system . . . excetory system . . .hand preference . . . locomotion . . . midbrain . . . motor skills . . . myelin . . . neural growth . . . ossification . . . prehension . . . proximodistal development . . . respiratory system . . . self-concept . . . sensory organs . . . sequence . . . skeletal system . . . teething . . . thrive . . . voluntary movements

to Review

Write your answers on a separate sheet of paper.
1. True or false. Physical growth and development affect mental and emotional aspects of development.
2. Babies _____ (add one-half, double, triple) their birth weight during the first year; they _____ (add one-half, double, triple) their birth length during the first year.
3. True or false. The rate of growth over the months is more important than total growth.
4. What are three changes which occur in the bones during development?
5. True or false. In the first year, total length

is mainly due to increase in leg length.

6. The baby is physically very different from an adult. In comparison to an adult, the baby's:

    a. Heart rate is _____ (slower, faster).

    b. Breathing rate is _____ (slower, faster).

    c. Breathing is _____ (deeper, shallower).

    d. Stomach capacity is _____ (greater, lesser).

    e. Extracellular fluid is _____ (greater, lesser).

    f. Amount of fat per pound of weight is _____ (greater, lesser).

    g. Head length in proportion to total length is _____ (greater, lesser).

7. Reflexes are _____ (learned, unlearned), and voluntary movements are _____ (learned, unlearned).

8. The baby gains body control in a certain order. Number the following motor skills in order of occurance.

    __4__ Sit without support with back straight.

    __1__ Raise head while on abdomen.

    __5__ Creep.

    __7__ Totally develop hand preference.

    __6__ Walk.

    __2__ Roll over from front to back.

    __6__ Stand without help.

    __3__ Pick up object with thumb used in opposition to finger.

9. Which of the following best describes motor skill development of infants?

    a. They learn the same motor skills at the same time.

    b. They develop very rapidly in the same areas and very slowly in the same areas.

    c. They learn at the same rate but the sequence of skills varies.

    d. They learn in the same sequence but rate varies.

to Do

1. Observe a physician giving a well-baby exam. Ask the physician to explain each procedure including weight and length measurements, measurements of head and thorax, measurements of heart and breathing rates, and noting of reflexive and voluntary movement. Also ask how progress is noted such as comparing to age norms and checking progress made by that baby since the last check-up.

2. Ask 4 or 5 mothers who have infants to bring them to class. Or visit an infant day care program to watch infants there. (The infants should be of different ages such as two, four, six, eight, and 11 months.) Compare the babies' abilities to sit, move about, and grasp objects.

3. As a group or class project, write a one-or-two-page brochure that explains what parents can expect in terms of the order (and approximate age) when certain motor skills are learned. Drawings would be nice. The brochure could be checked by a physician before making copies. Find out if copies could be given to new parents at the hospital, posted in medical offices serving children, or printed in a local paper.

4. Observe two or three infants who are between six and 12 months perform motor skills. For example, usually a baby gets into crawling position by pushing up from the abdomen or tilting forward from a sitting position. Observe these motor skills: crawling and creeping; getting into a sitting position; pulling up to a standing position and returning to a sitting position; walking while "holding on;" and other skills.

Babies learn much about the world around
them in their first year of life.

7

Intellectual development of the infant

After studying this chapter, you will be able to:
- ☐ Describe how and what infants learn.
- ☐ Explain how infants express what they know through language.
- ☐ Identify the sequence of the infant's learnings.

Intellectual development (also called mental and cognitive development) is an important aspect of development. Intellectual development consists of *how* you learn, *what* you learn, and *how you express* what you know through language. Intellectual development is as rapid during the baby's first year as physical development. Babies come into the world using all of their sense organs. They react to stimuli (sound, light, and others) with certain reflexes. Within twelve months infants have highly developed sense organs and motor skills. They have used these to learn about many people, objects, places, and events in their world. At birth the main sound babies make is crying. By the end of the first year, they know many words. Some can even say a few words.

HOW INFANTS LEARN

For many years, people have wondered how infants learn. The brain and sense organs mature greatly during the first year. This makes them more helpful for learning. Also, as motor skills develop, infants are able to move toward many sights, sounds, and other learning experiences.

Learning involves more than physical development. Most researchers in child

Intellectual development of the infant 127

development believe that babies want to learn. Each month, infants exert more and more effort to explore their world. Instead of just seeing, hearing, and touching a parade of people, objects, sounds, and events, babies try to make sense of their world. Repeated or similar experiences help babies figure out their world. New experiences help expand their world.

Babies don't just try to figure out what is happening. They also try to cause things to happen, like making their cradle gym bounce or making a ball roll. Babies like to repeat and vary these events, too. Many adults can tell you about picking up a toy thrown from a high chair countless numbers of times. The baby repeats such an action to learn if that is the way something always works. The baby also wants to find out what happens when changes are made such as throwing the object further or in a different direction!

In the process of learning about their world, humans develop specific ways of learning. The ways in which humans learn can be called stages in mental development. The sequence of the stages is very similar for all people. On the other hand, the rate can vary a great deal from person to person. Two factors seem to affect the rate: (1) physical development, mainly brain growth; and (2) the environment.

Just as an infant needs good nutrition for physical growth, the infant also needs a good mental diet. Interesting things to see, hear, and touch provide the needed "food for thought." Because the world is brand new to the infant, common objects and experiences around the house provide a rich mental diet. The adult's face, a cardboard box, some old pots and pans, or a trip in the yard can provide good learning experiences, 7-1.

Perception

Perceptual development is a major step in learning. *Perception* involves organizing information that comes through your senses. For instance, you perceive by noting how things are alike and different in size, color, shape, and texture. Perception also involves the speed in which you organize the information. For instance, a mature reader can not only tell the difference between a "b" and a "d" but can do it with greater speed than a child who is just learning to read. Finally, perception involves the way you select from among many sensory experiences. For instance, a child in a room crowded with strangers may run to his or her mother. But if the child is alone with the mother, he or she may play with a toy and ignore her.

The process of developing perception is called *perceptual learning*. Perceptual learning occurs because the sense organs mature and preferences for certain stimuli change.

Maturing of sense organs. As the sense organs mature, perception improves. Vision becomes much better when the pupil of the eye can widen and narrow with changes in the amount of light (called *pupillary reflex)*. This happens at four to eight weeks of age. Vision also improves as the eye muscles become strong

JOHN SHAW

7-1 Common experiences—even a trip to the back yard—provide a rich mental diet for the infant.

enough to turn the eyes in the direction of an object (called *visual coordination*). Visual coordination improves a few weeks after birth. The visual image must be focused sharply on the retina (called *accommodation of lens*) for good vision. Accommodation of the lens is greatly improved in four months but not fully developed for 11 or 12 years. Finally, for clear vision, both eyes must focus on a single image (called *convergence*). Convergence is developed by the third month.

The other sense organs develop at rapid rates, also. At birth, infants can hear differences between high-pitched and low-pitched sounds. They can move their bodies to the rhythm of adult speech. By three months, babies can tell differences in the sounds of words such as pa and ma. Experts do not know as much about the development of touch, taste, and smell, but these senses also improve as children grow.

Changes in preferences. From the time of birth, babies are bombarded with all types of stimuli. In order to learn, infants must choose among stimuli. Researchers feel that infants have inborn abilities to choose the stimuli most helpful for future learning. Studies show these changes in preferences:

1. Preferences change from parts of objects to complete objects. At first, infants react to (study) parts of objects. later they pay more attention to the entire object. For instance, when babies were shown parts of faces and the entire face at the same time, they reacted in different ways. At two months, they smiled at eyes drawn on a blank background. At three months, they studied the mask with eyes and nose. By five months, they smiled only at the full face.

2. Preferences change from simple to complex objects. Studies have been done on the length of time babies look at an object. Until babies are almost two months old, they do not prefer one object over another. After two months, babies prefer more complex objects. For example, babies show preferences for 3-D objects over 2-D pictures. They prefer patterned or textured cards over plain-white or solid-colored cards. Babies also prefer a drawn human face over any other drawn pattern or solid-colored card. See 7-2. Other preferences shown include slow-moving objects over stable objects and curved lines over straight lines, 7-3. Some

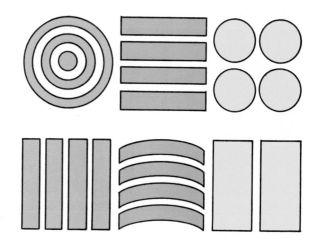

7-2 When shown each of these figures, babies' preferences from least to most liked were: white circle, yellow circle, red circle, concentric circles, circle with words, and circle with face. (Fantz's study.)

7-3 When shown each of these pairs of lines, infants liked the curved lines more than the straight lines. (Fantz's study.)

INFANTS' PREFERENCES FOR EXPERIENCES

APPROXIMATE AGE	SEEING	HEARING	TOUCHING
Birth to 3 months	• Tracks (follows with eyes) slow moving objects. • Looks when held to shoulder. • Looks at hairline part of face at 1 month and at eyes, nose, and mouth at 2 months (often smiles). • Prefers patterns to solids. • Follows the gaze of an adult to look where the adult is looking at 2 months.	• Reacts physically to sounds such as opening eyes widely or startling. • Calmed by gentle speech. • Associates voices with faces at 1 month.	• Reflexive grasping diminishes between 6 weeks and 3 months. • Holds objects less than 1 minute. • At 2 to 3 months swipes at objects suspended overhead.
3 to 6 months	• Prefers red and blue to green and yellow. • Enjoys mirrors but does not know its own image until after 1 year of age. • Grasps what is seen. • Enjoys small objects. • Imitates facial expressions.	• Learns the meaning of familiar sounds such as preparing food and approaching parent. • Reacts to differences in tone of voices • Tries to locate source of sounds. • Repeats own sounds. • Tells differences in sounds such as ''ba'' and ''pa.''	• Grasps with both hands and often clasps hands when object is out of reach at 3-4 months. • Takes 1 object at a time. • Plays with hands at 4 months. • Plays with toes at 5 or 6 months. • Mouths all objects; opens mouth well in advance of approaching objects. • Opens hands wider for larger objects than for smaller objects. • Uses arms and hands like hammers to strike objects.
6 to 9 months	• Examines objects with eyes and hands. • Recognizes drop-offs (but *not* safe from falls). • Looks for hidden (covered) toys.	• Learns noises made by different toys. • Notes differences between questions and statements by the change in the pitch. • Enjoys hearing singing and tries to sing along.	• Manipulates objects by turning, shaking, etc. • Enjoys toys with moving parts such as dials and wheels. • Holds own bottle. • Uses 1 object to work another such as hitting a xylophone with a mallet. • Transfers objects from 1 hand to the other.
9 to 12 months	• Shows less interest in faces except to quickly identify the familiar face and the strange face. • Looks where crawling. • Watches dropped objects with interest to see whether they roll, break, etc. • Enjoys hiding games such as a simple hide and seek.	• Imitates sounds. • Enjoys hearing own name. • Makes sounds of some animals. • Knows meaning of many words and may respond to requests.	• Predicts weight of object with correct arm tension. • Enjoys self-feeding. • Shows held objects to others. • Enjoys dropping objects into pails and boxes. • Enjoys stacking blocks and knocking them down. • Takes lids off of objects. • Pulls and pushes roll toys. • Turns knobs and switches. • Nests (puts smaller into larger) objects.

7-4 Babies change their seeing, hearing, and touching preferences as they try to learn about their worlds.

studies have shown that infants do not react to *very* complex stimuli. Experts think that infants lose interest in very complex stimuli because such objects are beyond their understanding.

3. Preferences change from familiar to novel objects. After two months of age, babies begin to explore things that are somewhat novel (new). Like very complex objects, objects that are too novel are ignored. Chart 7-4 shows some of the changes in seeing, hearing, and touching experiences that most babies prefer during the first year.

Cognition

Cognition means knowing or understanding. Your brain takes the puzzling array of your perceptions and begins to piece together a picture of your world. Cognition gives meaning to perceptions. Thus, perception is important to cognition.

Jean Piaget (pya-zhā), the Swiss psychologist, described how humans learn. He believed people learn by exploring their world. Because of inborn reflexes such as sucking and grasping, people begin to explore the world from birth. As reflexes disappear, voluntary movement and sense perceptions help infants explore.

When babies come upon something new in their world, they react with a behavior (like sucking or grasping) they already know. If the new object is not too different, the known behavior does not have to change. For instance, most rattles are held with one hand and shaken. Once a baby learns to hold and shake a rattle, other rattles can be held and played with in the same way. Piaget called this *assimilation*. In some cases, known behaviors do not work on a new object. The behavior must be changed. A baby who can easily grasp any rattle must change grasping behavior when holding a cup of milk. The baby learns that milk spills from a cup unless both hands are used. Piaget called this *accommodation*. See 7-5. Both assimilation and accommodation help infants learn. When infants do not need to change a behavior

7-5 A baby changes grasping (accommodates) to hold different-shaped objects.

JOHN SHAW

Intellectual development of the infant 131

(assimilation), they practice what they already know. Practice makes the learning more lasting and easier to do. And, when infants need to change their known behavior to make something work (accommodation), they learn new behaviors. These can be used in the future.

As babies explore their world, their thinking changes from pre-logical (like "magic") to logical (able to give objective reasons). For instance, adults smile at a young child who believes there is more ice cream in the parfait glass than a large bowl. The child may believe this even though mother just removed the "not enough" ice cream from the bowl and put it in the parfait glass as the child watched. See 7-6. Normal, older children would be more logical. They understand that as long as nothing is added or taken away the amount remains the same although it may *look* different.

Piaget described how thinking changes from pre-logical to logical in four stages. They are outlined in 7-7. All people go through the stages in order. And stages are never skipped, because learnings in any stage are based on learnings in the stages which come before. For instance, stage 3 learnings are based on learnings in stages 1 and 2.

People who near the end of one stage and the beginning of the next stage are in a transition time. At a transition time, a person may be in the more advanced stage in one area (like math or language) and in the less advanced stage in another area. Learnings achieved in one stage are never forgotten although they may not be used again. For example, you could still give directions by pointing, but you now use words to direct.

The ages given for the stages are approximate. The rate of development depends on brain growth and experiences. To Piaget, adults should provide a good environment and let children learn at their own rates.

Because infants explore their world with their senses and their motor actions, Piaget called the first stage the *sensorimotor stage*. The stage begins at birth and is completed in about two years by most children. During this stage, infants use their senses and motor skills to learn and to communicate with others. Although learning in this stage seems simple to the adult, it takes time. Babies must learn as their senses mature and their motor skills develop. Learning in this stage is very important because it is the basis for all future mental growth.

Piaget described the learnings of the sensorimotor stage in a series of substages. During the first year, most babies go through four substages.

The first substage is practicing reflexes (birth to 1 month). Babies exercise the inborn reflex skills such as sucking, grasping, and crying. With each passing day, the reflexes are used in more skillful ways.

The second substage is repeating new learnings (1 to 4 months). Babies begin to change some of their reflex skills. Before babies sucked and grasped only when stimulated. In this stage, babies do such things as suck their thumbs or open and close their hands. These actions are not planned, but they bring pleasure. Babies repeat the actions often. Piaget

JOHN SHAW

7-6 Although the bowl and the parfait glass hold the same amount of ice cream, pre-logical children will say there is more ice cream in the taller parfait glass.

132

called the main learnings in this stage *primary circular reactions*. They are called "primary" because the actions involve the baby's own body and "circular" because the actions are repeated again and again.

Toward the end of this stage, babies also begin to know what will happen in some of their child care routines. For instance, babies may start sucking as soon as they are picked up to be fed. In a very small way, babies are anticipating the future. In this way, routines help mental growth!

In the third substage, babies begin to control their world (4 to 8 months). The numbers and types of actions increase at a rapid rate throughout this substage. Many new actions—such as kicking—do not have their roots in the reflexes. These new actions aid infants as they explore their worlds.

As babies move about and play or cry, things happen. For instance, the baby may kick and the cradle gym moves. For the first time, babies see a connection between what they did and what happened. Not only do they see a connection, but they remember what they did.

(This is not to say that babies have well-developed memories.) Because of the baby's pleasure in the first event and interest in the "cause and effect," the baby repeats the action. The baby kicks and stops; the cradle gym moves and slows or stops; and the cycle is repeated. Piaget called these learnings *secondary circular reactions*. They are called "secondary" because the actions affect objects outside the baby's own body such as the cradle gym.

During this time, infants also begin looking for objects. This means that they realize objects exist even when they can't see them.

In the fourth substage, babies begin to apply learnings to solve complex problems (8 to 12 months). Babies try to discover an object's purpose. They examine an object very carefully with all their senses, 7-8. Then they experiment with the object. The object may be mouthed like a teething ring, squeezed like a rubber duck, or swung like an object on a mobile.

During this substage, babies combine two or more actions to achieve a goal. For instance, to get a toy that is behind a box, the baby first *pushes* the box aside (first action) and then

PIAGET'S STAGES OF COGNITIVE DEVELOPMENT

Stage 1: Sensorimotor Stage (Birth to 2 years)

Substage i: Practicing Reflexes (Birth to 1 month)

Substage ii: Repeating New Learnings (1 to 4 months)

Substage iii: Beginning to Control Their World (4 to 8 months)

Substage iv: Applying Learnings to Solve Complex Problems (8 to 12 months)

Substage v: Discovering New Ways to Solve Problems (12 to 18 months)

Substage vi: Beginning of Thought (18 months to 2 years)

Stage 2: Preoperational Stage (2 to 7 years)

Stage 3: Concrete Operations Stage (7 to 11 years)

Stage 4: Formal Operations Stage (11 years on)

7-7 Piaget described how thinking changes from pre-logical to logical in four main stages. Infants are in the sensorimotor stage.

LOUIS J. BREAUX, JR.

7-8 A baby studies a new object in detail by touching and looking.

Intellectual development of the infant 133

grasps the toy (second action). Combining actions helps the baby to achieve many more goals than would be possible if a new action had to be learned for each goal. (This is like using four or five letters to make several different words.)

Imitating others, a major way in which we learn, is used much more in the fourth stage. Imitating is copying someone else. Before this stage, babies could imitate simple things that they could see themselves doing. For instance, they might bang their hands on a table after seeing an adult do this action. In this stage they can imitate more complex actions that they cannot see themselves do such as "making faces."

WHAT INFANTS LEARN

As babies explore their world, they learn many concepts. A *concept* is an idea formed by combining what you know about one person, object, place, quality (love, honesty), or event. Thinking is organized through concepts. For instance, if you see an animal you believe to be a dog, you immediately think of all you know about dogs. As you view this animal, you notice how it is like or different from other dogs you recall.

Concepts change as the child's brain matures and experiences increase. Concepts change from simple to complex. A child understands the word chair before knowing about the many types of chairs. Concepts also change from concrete to abstract. Children can draw themselves and their parents before they can draw younger and older people. At first, people think of separate identities, then their concepts broaden to include classes. Children understand dog, then animals, and finally living things. As children grow, their concepts change from incorrect to more accurate. First, a child may call all men "daddy." Later, they understand the correct concept of "men." Concepts are different for each person, too. No two people have exactly the same experiences. And, not only do experiences differ, but many concepts involve our emotions. For example, the concept of "school" may be pleasant for one person but not for another person.

During the first year, infants form many concepts. These concepts help infants make sense out of their worlds. The concepts learned aid further mental development.

Perceptual concepts

As information comes to infants through their sense organs, they begin to develop some rules about their perceptions. These rules may be called perceptual concepts.

Object constancy (sameness). Object constancy is the concept that objects remain the same even if they appear a different size (due to their distance from you), a different shape (due to viewing it from different angles), or a different color (due to amount, source, or direction of light). See 7-9. Object constancy begins during the first year, but it is not fully developed until the second or third year.

Object concept. Object concept has two parts: *object identity* and *object permanence.* Object identity begins to develop around five months. A child who has object identity knows that an object stays the same from one time to the next. For example, a toy bear is the same toy bear each time the child sees it.

Object permanence begins to develop after two months. The child understands that people, objects, and places still exist even when they are no longer seen, felt, or heard. As is true of all concepts, object permanence develops slowly. Two-month-olds show some surprise when toys are suddenly hidden or dropped, but they never search for the object. At six months, babies look for toys they have dropped, and they will search for a partially hidden toy. Between the eighth and twelfth months, they will search for a totally hidden toy.

Object concept is required before infants can care about those who take care of and play with them. Thus parents are often the first "objects" on which babies learn object concept.

To babies, people have permanence before objects. Known people and known objects have permanence before the concept is generalized to all people and objects.

Depth perception. Depth perception is the ability to tell how far away something is. It is

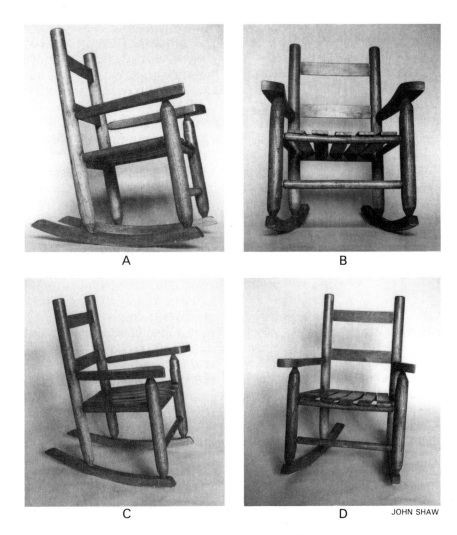

A   B

C   D   JOHN SHAW

7-9 Seeing a chair from different views while crawling (A and B) and later while walking (C and D) helps a baby learn object constancy.

needed for safety purposes to keep you from stepping off of a cliff or other object far from the ground. It is also used to judge how far something is from you so that you can reach it.

The ability of babies to perceive depth has been tested using a *visual cliff*. The visual cliff is made by placing a sheet of heavy plate glass over fabric with a checkerboard design. On one side, the fabric is directly under the glass. On the other side, the fabric is placed several feet below the glass. A plank is laid over the glass at the edge of the "cliff."

Crawling babies are placed on the plank and coaxed to crawl to their mothers who are standing on the far side of the deep end. But the babies will not come, 7-10. When fabric on the deep end is raised within a few inches of the glass, the babies will crawl across. This test shows that depth perception is rather well developed by seven to nine months of age. These studies do not mean that babies are safe from falls.

Intellectual development of the infant 135

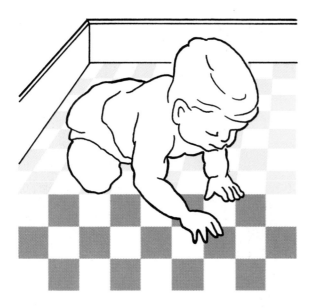

7-10 A baby with depth perception will not crawl to the deep end of the "visual cliff."

Identity and class concepts

As babies explore their world, they learn identity and class concepts. Unlike perceptual concepts which are rather fully developed within a few years, identity and class concepts develop throughout a person's life.

An *identity concept* is a concept of the particular people or objects that are part of a baby's world. Identity concepts are unique to a particular child. Each child has his or her own parents, pet, and toys.

Identity concepts are slow to develop, because even the familiar may look different at times. For instance, a baby may enjoy playing with father until he puts on a hat. Suddenly the baby looks sober or even begins to cry. Soon the baby comes to know father with or without a hat. At this point, the baby has developed an identity concept of "my daddy."

A *class concept* is a concept of a group of people, objects, events, or places that have something in common. When babies talk, you can easily hear them deal with class concepts. A baby who has a pet dog may readily call a dog of a different breed "dog." (The baby saw some common characteristic of dogs.) But words can't be used as the only guide for noting development of class concepts. Babies may refer to a class by using an identity word. For instance, a baby may call all men "daddy." The baby sees a common characteristic, but doesn't know the class word "men." The reverse also may be true. For instance, a baby may call *only* roses in the backyard "flowers." The baby, in this case, is using a class word (flower) to refer to an identity concept (roses in the back yard).

BEGINNINGS OF LANGUAGE DEVELOPMENT

Language is closely related to mental development. As people undestand more concepts, their *vocabularies* tend to grow. (Your vocabulary includes the words you understand and use.) Because language and mental growth are related, vocabulary words are often used to test mental growth. But language does not exactly mirror one's mental growth. One reason is that people can do and understand some things that they can't explain. This is especially true for infants. Their vocabularies lag well behind the concepts they understand. A second reason language is not a perfect sign of mental growth is that people sometimes use words they don't understand.

Language also helps future mental growth. As a person's vocabulary grows, they understand more of what is said. This makes them able to learn more. Also, people often have to explain what they are saying in order that others understand. In trying to explain a concept, the *speaker* may gain a better understanding, too.

Language is related to social and emotional growth, too. You use language to show feelings to others. Before infants develop language, they express their feelings by crying, laughing, clinging, and other physical signs. Even young children express more of their feelings physically (temper tantrums, snatching a toy from another child, hitting) than do older children. As people grow older, they learn to express more of their feelings in words.

Infants "talk"

Infants communicate, even though they don't always speak your language. Infant speech goes through several stages. Again the stages are about the same for all infants, but the rate is very different.

Crying and cooing. Newborns do not have control over their sound-making. They make many sounds during eating and sleeping such as swallowing noisly, smacking, burping, yawning, and sighing. During the first month, babies communicate by crying. Parents can quickly learn what their baby's cries mean.

Between the sixth and eighth week, most babies begin to *coo* (make a light, happy sound). Babies coo more when others talk to, smile at, and touch them. Babies are very polite, for they stop cooing when you begin to talk! When you "talk" to cooing babies, you should wait until they have finished. Then you should respond with sounds. Soon babies will take turns "talking" with you.

Babbling. Between the fourth and fifth month, babies begin to *babble*. Babies babble by making a series of vowel sounds with consonant sounds slowly added to form syllables such as be, da, gi. Early babbling seems to be inborn, because deaf children babble until the sixth month. After six months, babbling depends on hearing.

Babbling is a very important pre-talking skill. In babbling, babies practice all the sounds of all the languages of the world. Babies are ready to learn any language, 7-11. Around one year, they can make only the sounds needed to speak the language they hear.

Babbling is not *monotone* (at a single pitch). Babies babble with *inflections* (changes of pitch) to express happiness, requests, commands, and questions. Often there is so much feeling with the babbling, you can almost guess what the baby is saying!

First words. Babies may begin talking during the last three months of the first year. But many start talking later. Most experts state that in order to count sounds as a word, the same sounds must be used each time to refer to a specific person, object, place, or event. Before talking, babies must:

1. Understand object permanence.
2. Understand that people, objects, places, and events have names.

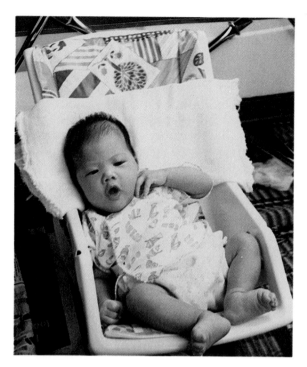

7-11 A young baby babbles all the sounds of all languages.

3. Remember words that go with people, objects, places, and events.
4. Have the ability to make the sounds.
5. Realize that talking is important.

No wonder many babies do not talk during the first year!

Often, first words come from babbling. Babies do what is called *reduplication babbling.* They repeat the same syllable over and over such as da-da-da. An adult that hears da-da-da or ma-ma-ma may say, "That's right, 'da-da' (daddy)." The adult may point to daddy. Or the daddy may pick up the baby, smiles and nods, and call himself "da-da." After a time, the baby makes the connection between the sound (which was already mastered) and the person.

The number of words that babies learn varies a great deal. Most studies show that babies only say around three words by the end of the first year. Spoken vocabulary does not begin to increase rapidly until later in the second year.

Intellectual development of the infant 137

Infants listen

From birth, newborns seem to know human speech from other sounds. Babies move their arms and legs in rhythm to human talk.

Babies can tell differences in spoken sounds after three months. In one test, a sound was played over and over again such as pa-pa-pa. Babies who were nursing sucked very fast at first and then slowed their sucking as the sound was repeated many times. Once the sucking slowed, a new sound was made such as ga-ga-ga. Babies began rapid sucking. They had noticed the change in these very similar sounds!

Babies imitate sounds made by the adults. All imitation requires listening. Babies learn spoken language through imitation. At 12 weeks, the baby makes a sound, the adult repeats the baby's sound, and the baby repeats after the adult. Around nine months, babies can repeat the sounds that adults make first.

During the last three or four months of the first year, babies begin to understand many words. The words people understand but don't say are called their *passive vocabulary*. *Active vocabulary* includes the words used in talking or writing. The passive vocabulary of babies far exceeds their active vocabulary. Once babies get the idea that the objects in their world have names, they learn these names rapidly. They even understand sentences that refer to part of their daily routine such as, "Time for breakfast." Soon their favorite spoken word may be "whaddat" or "What zat" as they begin the complex task of learning language.

to Know

accommodation . . . active vocabulary . . . assimilation . . . babble . . . class concept . . . cognition . . . concept . . . coo . . . depth perception . . . identity concept . . . imitating . . . inflections . . . intellectual development . . . object concept . . . object constancy . . . object identity . . . object permanence . . . passive vocabulary . . . perception . . . perceptual learning . . . primary circular reactions . . . reduplication babbling . . . secondary circular reactions . . . sensorimotor stage . . . visual cliff

to Review

Write your answers on a separate sheet of paper.

1. True or false. A baby's intellectual development is very slow compared with physical development during the first year.

2. What are the two factors which affect the rate of intellectual development?

3. Which of the following is an example of perception?
   a. Tasting a sugar cube.
   b. Telling the difference in mother's face from the faces of other women.
   c. Calling mother "mama."

4. Which member of the following pairs do infants like better?
   a. 2-D pictures — 3-D objects.
   b. Plain white cards — solid-colored cards.
   c. Patterned cards — solid-colored cards.
   d. Human face — other patterns.
   e. Straight lines — curved lines.
   f. Novel objects — familiar objects.

5. Danielle has ridden a tricycle for three years. Now she has a new bicycle. In learning to ride the new bicycle, pedaling would be an example of _____ (assimilation, accommodation) and balancing would be an example of _____ (assimilation, accommodation).

6. Many children stand on a chair or other raised platforms and tell the adult, "I'm taller than you." This is an example of _____ (pre-logical, logical) thought.

7. Which statement would Piaget support?

    a. Children learn more by exploring on their own in a stimulating environment.

    b. Children learn more when adults sit down and teach them.

    c. Children learn the same amount whether they explore on their own or are taught by adults.

8. The baby gains knowledge in a certain order according to Piaget. Place the following intellectual skills in the proper order of occurance.

    ____ Babies change some of their reflex skills such as opening and closing their hands.

    ____ Babies hit their hands on the high chair tray and realize they made the sound.

    ____ Babies exercise inborn reflexes.

    ____ Babies can pick up a rubber duck, place it in the water, and give it a big push.

    ____ Babies look for objects they have dropped.

9. Match the following incidents with the perceptual concepts.

    a. Depth perception.

    b. Object permanence.

    c. Object constancy.

    ____ Sally is looking from a second story window and sees her mother in the garden. She happily exclaims, "Mamma."

    ____ Joe is being carried in a department store by his father who is shopping. When the father stops at one counter, Joe quickly picks up a toy car without knocking over a sign in front of the toys for sale.

    ____ Tyrone awakens and looks around. His mother is not in the room. He begins to cry loudly so his mother will know that he is awake.

10. Pre-talking skills begin at birth. Place the following skills in their proper order of occurance.

    ____ Cooing.

    ____ Crying.

    ____ Reduplication babbling.

    ____ Babbling.

    ____ First words.

to Do

1. Keep a record of an infant exploring his or her world for 30 minutes per day for one week. What senses were used at the time? What were some of the possible learnings?

2. Have your teacher or one student give a common word such as *blue, school, music,* or *food.* Each student should write a few phrases about what they think when they hear the word. Compare the perceptions of class members. Discuss your experiences and emotions associated with your perceptions of that word.

3. Make a poster using words and/or drawings to describe the baby's learnings during the first year as stated by Piaget.

4. Try an object permanence experiment on babies that four, six, and eight months old. To do the experiment follow these steps:

    a. Place a toy in front of the baby. Let the baby play with the object.

    b. Take the toy and use a small baby blanket or towel to partly cover the toy. If the baby gets the toy, continue to step c.

    c. Take the toy and completely cover with blanket or towel. If the baby gets the toy, continue to d.

    d. Take toy and cover with a box. If the baby gets toy, continue to e.

    e. Take the toy, place it in a small box, and place that box in a large box.

Note the ages of the babies and the number of steps they can do.

5. Listen to a recording of the sounds of babies that are two, four, six, eight, ten, and twelve months old. Try to distinguish cooing from babbling. Listen for babbling sounds that are similar to words.

6. Interview the parents of young children about the first words their babies said and age of their babies when talking began. Share your findings with the class, and compare them. Note the similarities and differences in the beginning spoken language.

Each infant has a unique temperament and level of emotions. These affect the infant's social-emotional development.

8

Social-emotional development of the infant

After studying this chapter, you will be able to:
- ☐ Identify temperamental differences in babies.
- ☐ Describe the infant's major first-year social tasks.
- ☐ Explain the roots of four emotions: love, fear, anxiety, and anger.

Social-emotional development (also called affective development) is an important aspect of development. Social-emotional development has three main parts. The first part is a person's *disposition* or mood. Some people have a more cheerful disposition, and others are more grumpy. The second part is learning to interact with people and social groups. These may include family members, schools, and clubs. Finally, social-emotional development includes the ways people show feelings through emotions of love, fear, anxiety, and anger.

Social-emotional development is as rapid during the first year as physical and mental development. Babies enter the world with some individuality. This is the root of their later personality. By the end of the first year, this individuality shows even more. As a baby's social world expands throughout the first year, he or she forms some ideas about whether the world is a friendly place. And, the baby expresses feelings with different emotions.

TEMPERAMENTAL DIFFERENCES IN INFANTS

Temperament is the tendency to react in a certain way such as cheery or grumpy. Some-

TEMPERAMENTAL DIFFERENCES

TEMPERAMENTAL QUALITY	TYPE OF CHILD		
	EASY	SLOW TO WARM UP	DIFFICULT
Activity level—the amount of time the baby is active to the amount of time the baby is inactive. An active baby seems to be always moving. On the other hand, an inactive baby may watch others more than getting involved. An active baby even moves more in his or her sleep than an inactive one.	Varies	Slow to moderate	Varies
Rhythmicity—regularity of hunger, excretion, sleep, and wakefulness. Some babies are very regular in their eating, bowel movements, and sleep patterns. Others are irregular in these areas and thus hard to schedule.	Very regular	Varies	Irregular
Distractibility—the degree to which other stimuli can alter behavior. A distractible baby will stop crying for food if rocked. He or she will stop fussing when given a pacifier or when a parent sings. A baby who is not distractible will continue to cry when hungry even if rocked. Such babies often cry even after eating. A baby who is not distractible will continue to reach for the same object time after time even if other objects are given as a substitute.	Varies	Varies	Varies
Approach/withdrawal—the response to a new person or object. A baby with a positive approach tries new foods, sleeps well in new places, and is more apt to enjoy being held by strangers. A baby who withdraws (negative approach) rejects new foods, stiffens when put in or on something new such as a baby's car seat, and howls in the arms of a stranger.	Positive approach	Initial withdrawal but is positive later	Withdrawal
Adaptibility—the ease with which a baby adapts to any change. An adaptible baby soon accepts food or baths not enjoyed the first time. A baby who is slowly adaptable easily startles, and continues to resist repeated events such as diapering, dressing, or staying with a regularly used sitter.	Very adaptable	Slowly adaptable	Slowly adaptable
Intensity of reaction—the strength of response. A baby with intense reactions rejects food or toys not wanted with great vigor, cries loudly at sounds, and laughs hard during rough play. A baby with a mild reaction tends to whimper more than cry when hungry, does not fuss when clothing is pulled on or off over the head, and does not smile or laugh often.	Low or mild	Mild	Intense

Continued.

8-1 Babies vary in nine temperamental characteristics. Five of these characteristics seem to separate babies into one of three goups—easy, slow to warm up, and difficult.

TEMPERAMENTAL QUALITY	TYPE OF CHILD		
	EASY	SLOW TO WARM UP	DIFFICULT
Threshold of responsiveness—the intensity of stimulation needed to get response. A baby with a high threshold of responsiveness takes a bottle or breast equally well, does not object to wet or soiled diapers, and eats liked and disliked foods. A baby with a low threshold of responsiveness covers ears upon hearing a loud sound, spits food out, and stops activity if someone approaches.	High or low	High or low	High or low
Quality of mood—the amount of pleasant and friendly behavior as compared with unpleasant and unfriendly behavior. A baby with a positive quality of mood plays in bath, smiles at everyone, and laughs loudly during play with others. A baby with a negative quality of mood is not easily satisfied and cries when left alone to play.	Positive	Slightly negative	Negative
Attention span and persistance—the degree to which a baby will continue with the same behavior. A baby with a high attention span will keep doing an action such as crying or playing even if distracted. A baby with a low attention span can be easily distracted by rocking or seeing a new toy.	High or low	High or low	High or low

8-1 Continued.

times the word disposition is also used to define the way people react to themselves, others, and their environment. Experts think temperament is partly inherited. It also may be affected by prenatal conditions and ease of birth. These factors, joined with environment, shape personality. A baby's temperament often shows by two or three months. In many children, but not all, temperament stays the same for years.

Some experts rate characteristics of a baby's temperament. These ratings seem to place most babies in one of three groups. These groups are called *easy, slow to warm up,* and *difficult.* See 8-1. Easy babies have regular habits (eating, sleeping, and others). They respond quickly to a new situation, and they are cheerful. Slow to warm up babies take more time to adapt to new situations. Difficult babies are irregular in their habits. They often withdraw or protest—even with screams—when faced with new situa-

tions. Researchers found that four in ten babies could be called easy. One in ten babies are slow to warm up. And one in ten babies are difficult. A few babies could not be classified in one of these groups, because their temperaments varied so much from day to day.

Babies who are easy usually get off to a good start with their parents. Babies who are difficult often get off to a rough start, because many parents feel that they are doing something wrong. If the parents are stressed, they may increase stress in their child. Good, constant care often pays off even with the most difficult babies. Humans have *self-righting tendencies*—they tend to become closer to normal with time. This causes the difficult baby to become easier with time. Good care of difficult babies including extra holding, cuddling, and soothing, may result in an all-around developmental boost.

Social-emotional development of the infant 143

THE INFANT'S GROWING SOCIAL WORLD

Infants are not truly social at birth. *Social* refers to a relationship between two or more people. Social development is shaped by how other people affect the baby and how the baby affects other people. By the end of the first year, social development is well underway. This section will focus on three aspects of social development in the first year. These are (a) interacting with others; (b) learning to trust; and (c) showing attachment.

Interacting with others

Babies are born with tools for social development. At birth, babies can turn in the direction of the human voice. They move their bodies in rhythm with human speech. And they like to look at other people's faces.

Babies understand social messages by the way others talk to, look at, or hold them. Babies send signals to others through their cries, coos, and smiles. These begin as early as two weeks after birth. Smiles with expressive eyes begin around the fifth or sixth week. See 8-2.

From the third to the sixth month, babies become even better at understanding and sending social signals. They also begin to distinguish people who are often near them from strangers.

Once babies are able to creep easily and have better arm and hand control, they *initiate* (begin) social contact. For instance, they may follow others around the house. Or they reach with their arms to signal, "pick me up."

Interacting with adults. Many studies have shown that parents who kiss, hold, and comfort their babies often have happier, more cuddly babies. Newborn babies who are quickly soothed when they cry seem to cry less than other babies over the months. Talking and playing with babies tends to help their mental development as well as their social development.

Until a few years ago, the mother was thought to be the most important person in the baby's life. Experts felt that the father's role was mainly to give emotional support to his wife's efforts. New findings are changing the old ideas of the father's role. Babies can have good relationships with fathers, too. Fathers who are involved with their children from birth become as close to them as mothers do. Babies respond by becoming close to their fathers.

Mothers and fathers may play very different roles with their children. Research shows that for playtime, babies often prefer fathers over the mothers. See 8-3. Fathers engage in more rough-and-tumble play. They also make up more new games or play known games in different ways. Fathers also permit their babies to explore more. When babies are stressed, they prefer their mothers more often than their fathers. Stress for babies can include fatigue (being tired or sleepy) or illness. It can also include being around an adult stranger or being in situations which cause fear. Babies are helped by being close to both parents.

Other adults (grandparents, friends, and babysitters) are helpful to babies' total develop-

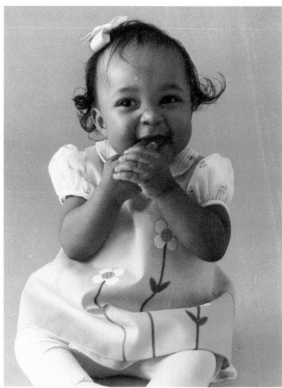

MEAD JOHNSON NUTRITIONAL DIVISION

8-2 Babies communicate happiness and love with their smiles.

144

8-3 Babies often prefer playing with their fathers.

ment. When they care for babies, the babies learn to understand and trust other adults. This helps expand babies' social world.

Interacting with other children. Babies enjoy being around *siblings* (brothers and sisters) and other children. Babies tend to watch and follow children. They like to play with toys that older children have laid down. Infants and older children are both aided by becoming close. Infants learn from older children, and older children learn lessons in loving and caring for others. See 8-4.

Learning to trust

Trust is an important part of social development. The amount a person trusts (or doesn't trust) others affects how he or she interacts with others.

One psychologist, Erik Erikson, thinks that learning to trust others is the first, most basic stage of social-emotional development. He believes personality develops all through life in

8-4 Babies and their older brothers and sisters learn from each other.

Social-emotional development of the infant   145

eight stages. (This book discusses only the first four stages, 8-5). At each stage, a person must complete certain tasks (called by Erikson *psychosocial crises*).

During each stage, a person adjusts well socially if good conditions exist for completing the social-emotional task. If certain harmful conditions exist, there will be problems in social development. Social development is better if a person has positive conditions at each stage. But Erikson believes a person can overcome problems that were caused by earlier, harmful conditions. The title of each stage shows the results of good or poor achievement by using the format, "something versus something else."

The first stage is called "Basic trust versus basic mistrust." Babies have physical needs (food, cleansing, warmth, and sleep) and psychological needs (cuddling, communicating with others, and play). Erikson feels that if these needs are met, babies feel that the world is good and pleasant. This helps them learn to trust others and adapt to their world. If needs are not met or are only met in part, babies feel helpless and confused and they develop mistrust. Feelings of trust or mistrust are the basis for later positive or negative feelings about others.

Consistency (sameness) in babies' worlds help them learn trust. Adults can make babies' lives more consistent in the following ways:

- Meet babies' needs without too much delay. Of course, no one can meet a baby's every need instantly, but the delay should not be too long. (Babies and young children do not understand time.)
- Meet babies' needs each time. Babies need hour to hour and day to day care for their fullest development.
- Keep babies' environments somewhat the same. Having the same caregivers, routines in child care, and surroundings keep the environment the same. Change should be gradual. For instance, some "old" toys and furniture should be left as new items are added.

Babies not only know whether or not their needs are being met, but they sense whether or not their parents enjoy meeting their needs.

ERIKSON'S FIRST FOUR STAGES OF SOCIAL-EMOTIONAL DEVELOPMENT

BASIC TRUST versus BASIC MISTRUST
(First year of life)

Consistency in having needs met and sameness in the environment lead to a feeling that the world is reliable. The baby develops a sense of basic trust. If the world is not seen as a reliable place, basic mustrust develops.

AUTONOMY versus SHAME AND DOUBT
(Second year of life)

INITIATIVE versus GUILT
(Preschool years)

INDUSTRY versus INFERIORITY
(Middle childhood)

8-5 Erikson described personality as the result of either coping or not coping with eight psychological crises of life. (Only the first four crises are given.)

Parents show their feelings while feeding, diapering, and meeting other needs by their movements and voices. Jerky, quick movements and harsh or loud voices say, "let's get through with this job." Cuddling and slower movements and quiet, pleasant voices say, "I like helping you."

When adults meet babies' needs, a relationship of trust develops. But if needs are not met, the babies develop mistrust for others. Figure 8-6 shows the cycle of how parents affect babies and babies, in turn, affect parents. The cycle shows that meeting a baby's needs is helpful to adults as well as babies.

All people must deal with problems which cannot be helped such as handicaps, illness and pain, death of a loved one, and accidents. A person who trusts others can better handle these problems. Babies who trust can more readily develop a full range of emotions from happy to unhappy feelings. Mistrust keeps emotions in a narrow range. People who do not trust others are often distressed (unhappy and confused). Many of them withdraw from other people.

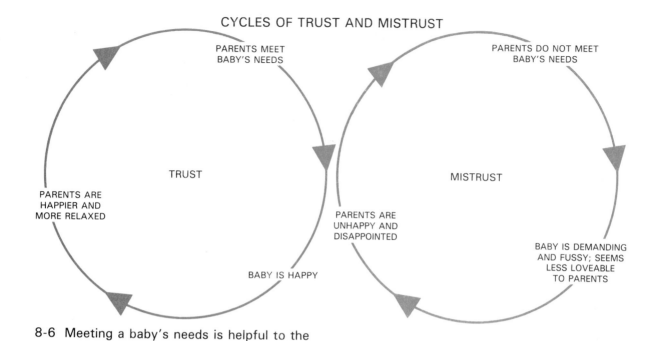

CYCLES OF TRUST AND MISTRUST

PARENTS MEET
BABY'S NEEDS

PARENTS DO NOT MEET
BABY'S NEEDS

TRUST

MISTRUST

PARENTS ARE
HAPPIER AND
MORE RELAXED

PARENTS ARE
UNHAPPY AND
DISAPPOINTED

BABY IS DEMANDING
AND FUSSY; SEEMS
LESS LOVEABLE
TO PARENTS

BABY IS HAPPY

8-6 Meeting a baby's needs is helpful to the parents' happiness as well as the baby's.

Showing attachment

Attachment can be defined as closeness between people that endures over a period of time. Chapter 5, "The newborn," discusses a special type of attachment called bonding. Bonding is the feeling of love parents have for their baby which often begins shortly after birth. During the first year, babies come to care for their parents, too. This is referred to as *attachment*. Some writers do not use the term bonding. They use the word attachment to describe the feelings parents have for their babies and the feelings babies have for parents. In this book, the terms bonding and attachment are used as shown in 8-7 to prevent confusion.

The seeds of attachment—meeting babies' needs—begin at birth. As babies develop mentally, they become attached to those who care for them. If only one person cares for a baby, the baby will form a single attachment. But if several people meet the baby's needs (even the need for play), the baby will form multiple attachments. Some studies show that babies may be just as attached to fathers as mothers even if they spend less time with their fathers.

Because babies cannot say, "I love you," they show attachment in other ways. *Attachment behaviors* include active contact. Trying to stay close to the adult, following, or clinging to the adult are examples of active contact. Other attachment behaviors are signals such as smiling,

AFFECTIONAL TIES TO OTHERS

RELATIONSHIP	TERM USED
Parents come to love their babies often soon after baby's birth. Parents ⟶ Baby	Bonding
Babies come to care for parents due to having their needs met. Tie is realized after 6 months of age. Baby ⟶ Parents	Attachment

8-7 Bonding and attachment are terms used for two loving relationships between parents and babies.

crying, or calling. The strength of attachment cannot be assumed from the strength of the attachment behaviors. For instance, the strongly attached baby who is sure of the parent's return may not cry loudly when left in the care of another person.

The development of attachment often follows the sequence shown in 8-8. Attachment is closely related to fear of strangers and fear of being left alone. These emotions are described in the next section.

Attachment is important for healthy social-emotional development. We all need to be loved and to love. Attachment is also an aid in mental development. Attached babies tend to explore their worlds through play more than babies who are not attached to others.

INFANTS EXPRESS EMOTIONS

Babies begin to express emotions during the first year of life. Emotions continue to be important throughout their lives. Emotions are tied to the physical and mental aspects of a person. *Emotions* are thoughts and feelings which cause changes in the body. For instance, if you are angry (a feeling), you are angry at someone or something (a thought) and you may have an increased heart rate (change in your body). In emotions, thoughts cause the feelings.

Because thinking changes, the situations that cause emotions change over the years. Four-year-olds may fear monsters in their bedrooms at night, but older children do not. Older children *know* monsters are not in their bedrooms. Even the way people respond because of emotions changes as people mature. For instance, a two-year-old may throw a temper tantrum when angry. But adults show their anger in more mature ways. When people act their age, they use *age-appropriate behaviors.* These are proper or normal ways to express emotions at certain ages.

During the first three or four months, babies have two basic responses to their worlds. The first is general distress, shown by crying and muscle tension. The second is general excitement, shown by smiling, cooing, and total body wiggling. By the middle of the first year, babies

are developing some specific emotions. Healthy development is shown by babies who express a range of emotions from happy to unhappy. People develop love, fear, anxiety, and anger during their first year of life.

Love

In the first few months, babies do not know that they depend on others to meet their needs. They do get hungry, wet, soiled, and lonely, and they cry. After their needs are met, they feel full, clean, and comforted. But it takes time for babies to know that other people are meeting these needs. As babies come to know who helps them, they feel close (attached) to them. In this way, love begins around six-months of age, 8-9. Not only do babies show love to important adults, but to children who keep them company as well.

Besides loving people, babies become attached to objects including pacifiers, stuffed toys,

DEVELOPMENT OF ATTACHMENT BEHAVIORS

APPROXIMATE AGE	ATTACHMENT BEHAVIORS
1 month	Baby can tell the differences among familiar (known) and unfamiliar (unknown) voices.
2 weeks to 2 months	Baby smiles.
5 months	Baby gives joyful movements such as kicks, coos, and gurgles. Baby may even laugh.
4 to 5 months	Baby becomes very still and breathing becomes shallow when unknown people are close.
7 to 8 months	Baby cries when a stranger is nearby or when the baby is left alone.

8-8 Attachment behaviors are closely related to the baby's mental development.

JOHN SHAW

8-9 Babies come to love those who care for them.

and even blankets. They are called *transitional objects*. Babies seem to need these objects when they are upset or afraid. They also seem to need them when routines are changed such as during vacation times. A few babies have these objects with them at all times. Sometimes adults worry about children's love for these objects, but such attachments are healthy. Children will give up these objects in time—often before they enter school.

Fear

At birth, babies startle (jerk or show the Moro reflex) when they hear loud sounds or do not have support for their bodies. By four or five months, babies begin to look soberly at strange adults. They may even show fear of known adults in new hairdos, hats, or sunglasses. Babies do not seem to fear strange young children or unknown adults who have their backs to them. Babies seem to fear only the strange adult's face or a change in a known adult's face.

Fear as an emotion occurs around six months. To be fearful, babies must know that

ADRIAN DEMERY

8-10 The unknown, such as these pine needles, causes fear.

they can be hurt. There are two kinds of fears:
1. Fears of the unknown. See 8-10. Infants fear adult strangers, a new bed, or a sudden movement such as an umbrella popping open or a jack-in-the-box toy. They

Social-emotional development of the infant 149

also fear different sounds such as thunder or a low-flying jet.

2. Fears that are learned from direct experiences or taught to the infant. These include soap in the eyes, doctor's offices, or a snapping dog. Fears that are taught include mother saying, "hot stove," when the baby is near the stove. (These fears may be different for each child, because experiences and teachings differ.)

Some babies are more fearful than others. The amount of fearfulness may be due to inborn *sensitivity*. Sensitivity is the ability to notice and react to your own environment.

Fear is also affected by what adults say and how they act in certain events. For instance, adults who tell their babies that many things can hurt ("hot stoves," "fast cars," "bad dog") teach their children to fear. Adults who act or look fearful in events such as a storm also will cause children to be more fearful. Some fear is good, of course, because fear keeps us safer. But too much fear is not emotionally healthy. Fear affects motor and mental growth because fearful babies often will not try new things.

Anxiety

Anxiety is closely related to fear. It is fear of a possible event. On the other hand, people are fearful during an event. For instance, you would be anxious (have anxiety) about possible flooding if the river is near flooding. But you would be fearful if you were being swept away by flood waters. (We sometimes use the terms *worry* or *concern* to mean anxiety.)

For babies to have anxiety, they must be able to think about the future—the very near future, of course. Anxiety is seen most often between the tenth and twelfth month. Anxiety shown by young babies is called *separation anxiety*. See 8-11. Babies become anxious when those adults whom they love leave them (to shop, to work, or for other reasons). The anxiety is more intense when strangers are present such as babysitters.

Separation anxiety can be seen when the parent leaves an almost one-year-old baby with a regular babysitter. The baby may have been content staying with others many times before,

but may now scream when left. Most two-year-olds do not show as much separation anxiety as younger babies do. Studies show that one or more of the following points may explain separation anxiety in babies younger than two years:

- Babies younger than two years old cannot understand why parents must leave them.
- Two-year-olds often have had many experiences with parents returning. They can trust that parents will return.
- *Dependence* (needing or wanting others to fulfill one's needs) is strong during the first year. Two-year-olds are seeking more *independence* (wanting to do things for oneself).
- Young babies cannot talk and express their needs to others very well, especially to those who are not known adults. Two-year-olds can express their needs better.

Anger

Almost from birth, babies seem to be angry at times. Very young babies flail (swing arms

8-11 Even when parents are out of sight for even a moment, babies who are nearing their first birthday looked distressed due to separation anxiety.

and legs in a thrashing motion), turn red, and cry loudly. These actions are like those used to throw a tantrum.

Anger becomes more directed toward a certain person or object by eight to ten months. Babies express anger in physical (not verbal) ways. They may try to get away from a person holding them, or they may grab, shake, or hit an object. Babies seem to show anger under three conditions:

1. Babies seem to show anger when restrained (held against their wills). They may be angered by being held when they want down, by being diapered or dressed when they don't want to be, or by being left in a playpen when they want out. See 8-12.
2. Babies show anger when toys are taken away. Babies also show anger when they cannot reach a toy that they want.
3. Babies who want their needs met may show anger when the adult tries to distract them. For example, showing a crying, hungry baby a toy may result in louder crying and pushing the toy away.

Babies vary in their amount and strength of anger. Some babies whose dispositions are calm seem to show very little anger during the first year. Babies whose moods are more negative may show much more anger. Parents can reduce anger in the baby by restraining only when needed and for short periods of time. Meeting the baby's needs quickly often prevents anger. And, modeling calmness (talking in a quiet voice and not looking upset) when babies are angry helps children see how to control their own anger.

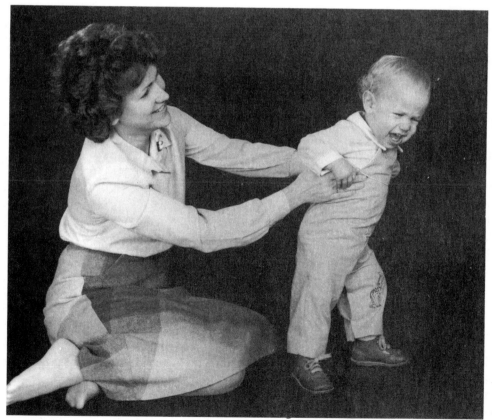

JOHN SHAW

8-12 A baby becomes angry at being restrained.

to Know

age-appropriate behaviors . . . anxiety . . .
attachment . . . attachment behaviors . . .
dependence . . . disposition . . . emotions . . .
independence . . . psychosocial crises . . .
self-righting tendencies . . . sensitivity . . .
siblings . . . separation anxiety . . . social . . .
social-emotional development . . .
temperament . . . transitional objects

to Review

Write your answers on a separate sheet of
paper.

1. True or false. Babies enter the world with
individuality.

2. Name two factors that affect a baby's
temperament.

3. What are three pre-talking social signals
babies can send to the parents?

4. True or false. Interacting with others
depends on motor and mental ability.

5. Babies seem to prefer fathers
for _____ (comfort, play) and mothers
for _____ (comfort, play).

6. True or false. Soothing crying babies spoils
them which, in turn, results in more crying.

7. Adults can help a baby develop trust by:
   a. Meeting the baby's needs as soon as
   possible.
   b. Changing all of the baby's toys once a
   week so the baby doesn't get bored.
   c. Providing for needs with a cheery, loving
   attitude.
   d. Both a and c.

8. Give two examples of attachment behaviors.

9. True or false. Babies who cry loudly when
parents leave them are more strongly attached
to their parents than babies who do not cry
loudly.

10. Which of the following statements about
emotions are true?
   a. Feelings occur before thoughts.
   b. Body (physical) responses are part of
   emotions.
   c. Over the years, the situations which
   cause emotions remain the same.

d. Over the years, the ways a person
expresses emotions remain the same.
   e. Over the years, the situations which
   cause emotions and the ways one expresses
   emotions both change.

11. Identify the emotion which completes each
sentence.
   a. Love
   b. Fear
   c. Anxiety
   d. Anger

_____ comes from good physical care.

_____ is often taught by hearing adults say
"no" and is also modeled.

_____ is seen as a reaction to being held
against one's will.

_____ is similar to attachment.

_____ is seen in the need for transitional
objects.

_____ in its early form may be the startle
reflex.

_____ is not seen as a response to
unknown children.

_____ is closely related to fear.

_____ may be a reaction to an adult trying
to distract a hungry or tired baby.

to Do

1. As a group or class project, write a one-
page or two-page brochure about the
importance of trust in the infant's life and how
adults can help promote trust in the infant.

2. Interview one or more parents about the
expanding social world of their baby. Plan
interview questions before the interview. These
questions are given for starters:
   a. Who were the first people (not including
   hospital staff) to: see your baby; hold your
   baby; and, care for (feed, dress, and
   change) your baby?
   b. Besides the baby's parents, who were
   other important people in your baby's life?
   c. How did your baby react to siblings and
   other children? How did siblings and other
   children react to your baby?
   d. Did your baby become attached to an
   object? What object?

3. Try this experiment in attachment. Have the mother or father of a three-month-old, six-month-old, nine-month-old, and twelve-month-old visit the classroom. Follow this procedure with each baby:

    a. Hand the baby to two different students. Have each hold the baby for two or three minutes unless the baby protests. Then hand the baby back to the parent. (The parent should be seen by the baby at all times.)

    b. Hand the baby to another student. After student holds the baby for two or three minutes, the parent should leave the room so the baby cannot see the parent.

Record each baby's reaction. Did babies over six months react more than the baby under six months? What types of reactions did the babies show? Discuss attachment with the parents. Perhaps the parents can talk about attachment behaviors seen in their babies at other times.

4. Have a class discussion on how emotions are useful and give richness to one's actions. Compare this to how emotions can hinder one's ability to work and play to the fullest.

5. The expression of emotions should change as people mature. Each stage of life has age-appropriate behaviors and immature behaviors. List behaviors that would be considered emotionally immature for a high school student. Compare your list with other lists in your class.

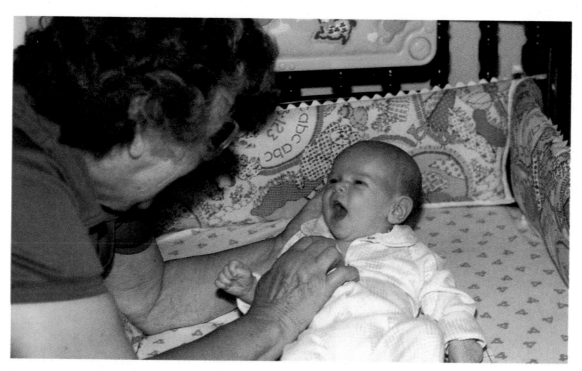

Interacting with adults helps infants begin language learnings early.

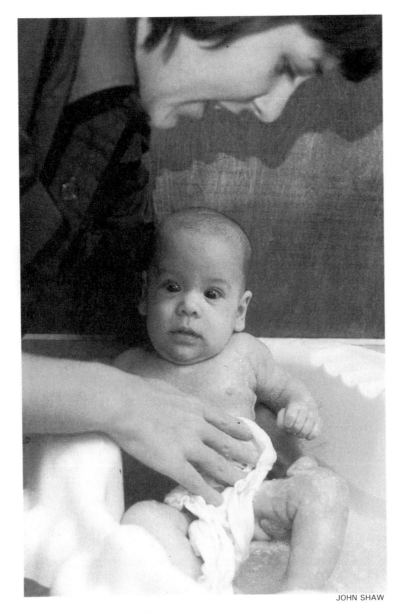

As the infant grows, adults must provide for
many needs.

9

Providing for the infant's developmental needs

After studying this chapter, you will be able to:
- Plan ways to meet the developmental needs of babies in their first year.
- Care for babies' physical needs.
- Stimulate babies' mental development.
- Enhance babies' growing awareness of themselves.

Because development is so rapid during the first year, the baby has many needs. In order to meet physical needs, adults must understand and respond to the baby's signals. Babies also have social and mental needs that must be met. Physical contact while meeting needs helps the baby mentally and socially. Adults also must provide an environment that meets the baby's mental needs.

Feelings of love and joy between the baby and caregivers help the baby develop. Adults need to focus on helping a baby develop trust that all needs will be met promptly. And, out of learning to trust others, the baby becomes more aware of his or her own abilities.

Many of the infant's needs can be met by providing activities. Several games and activities for infants are listed at the end of this chapter.

PHYSICAL NEEDS

Physical needs are the most basic needs of humans. When people are hungry, tired, too hot or cold, ill, or just not comfortable, they suffer physically, mentally, socially, and emotionally. For instance, a baby who is just a little late in getting fed may not want to play and explore. The baby also may be fussy. And babies, unlike other people, require others to meet their every physical need.

Feeding and weaning

Food is the most basic physical need of the baby. Body growth is the most rapid during the first year—often three times greater than in the second or third year. Babies are active, too, as they develop motor skills and explore their worlds. A proper diet provides needed *nutrients*. Nutrients are the substances in food that give the baby energy and aid in growth.

Food isn't just a source of *nourishment* (food which aids growth and development). It provides comfort for the baby as well. As adults care for the baby's food needs, the caregiver should communicate warmth and concern, 9-1. Babies who are fed by gentle, loving adults are more likely to learn what Erikson calls "basic trust."

First-year feeding plan. Babies differ in their food needs. A baby's size, growth rate, activity rate, health, and heredity affect the amount and types of foods needed. A physician or *nutritionist* (a person who studies food needs of people) can provide feeding guidelines for a baby's own needs.

Most babies begin with an all-liquid diet of milk (breast milk or formula). Usually between six months and one year the baby's diet comes to include a variety of foods from the basic four food groups. (The basic four food groups are the milk group, breads and cereals group, fruits and vegetables group, and meat group.) See 9-2 for the general feeding plan of the first year. Most physicians recommend that babies wait until at least six months before beginning foods other than breast milk or formula. Foods other than breast milk (that may or may not be solid in form) are called *solids*. Most physicians do not recommend solids for the first six months

COSCO PETERSON

9-1 Parents can use feeding time as a time for building babies' trust.

BASIC FEEDING PLAN FOR FIRST YEAR

Step 1	Mother's milk or formula (often for the first half year or longer).
Step 2	Mother's milk or formula, plus infant dry cereals mixed with strained juice, mother's milk, or formula.
Step 3	Mother's milk or formula, cereals, and strained single ingredient fruits, vegetables, and meats. (These are added very gradually with the baby's physician often making suggestions about which foods to try first, second, and so on.) When the baby can eat a variety of cereals, fruits, vegetables, and meats, the breast milk or formula is cut to between a 16-ounce (480 ml) minimum and a 25-ounce to 30-ounce (750 to 900 ml) maximum per day. Babies should take one-half of their calories from milk and one-half from solid food.
Step 4	Mother's milk or formula, cereals, and foods with two or more ingredients combined such as apple-banana juice or chicken and noodles.
Step 5	Mother's milk or formula, cereals and foods with some texture. Foods have very small pieces rather than being strained (called "Junior" foods by some commercial companies).

9-2 Babies begin with a milk diet and very gradually add other foods.

for the following reasons:

- A baby cannot properly digest complex nutrients found in solids. Starting solids too early may lead to allergy problems.
- Too much sodium is added to some solids. This may increase the risk of adult *hypertension* (high blood pressure).
- Solids may provide too many calories, causing the baby to gain weight too rapidly.
- Babies are born with a sucking reflex, but they are not born ready to swallow solid food. Jaw and throat muscles must develop before swallowing solids is easy and safe.
- Holding a baby close while breast or bottle feeding provides a young baby with needed physical warmth. Spoon feeding does not permit the same physical closeness.

- There are no nutritional reasons to introduce solids in the first half year.

When babies are old enough to have solids, new foods should be introduced one at a time in small amounts (a bite or two). Once a new food is added, the next one should not be started for four or five days. This gives the adult time to see whether the baby has an *intolerance* to the food. Intolerance to a food often shows in one to four days. It may cause fussiness, rash, or an upset stomach. Although these symptoms may mean other things as well, many physicians recommend waiting until after the first birthday to try these foods again. If babies react to many foods, physicians can test the baby and provide a special diet if needed.

Several foods should not be given to babies, 9-3. Some of these cause choking. Others are

FOODS BABIES SHOULD NOT BE GIVEN

FOOD	REASON
Berries Candy, small Carrot, raw Corn, whole kernel Nuts Popcorn	Choking.
Cake, in excess Candy, in excess Cookies, in excess	Too much sugar.
Crackers, in excess	Too much sodium.
Fruit drinks, artifically flavored Soft drinks	Too much sugar, artificial flavors and colors, and little to no nutritional value. May be high in calories, also.
Yeast or unpasturized yogurt	Difficult to digest.
Coffee Tea Soft drinks with caffeine Cocoa	Stimulants.
Alcohol	Depressant.

9-3 Some foods are not good for a baby's health.

foods with too much sugar or sodium (salt). Some of them have artificial flavors. Unpasteurized yogurt and foods that contain yeast are hard for babies to digest. (Pasteurization, a heating process, kills harmful bacteria.) Also, *stimulants* (substances which speed up functions of vital organs and nervous system such as increasing heart rate) and *depressants* (substances which slow down functions of vital organs and nervous system) are harmful to babies. The stimulant caffeine is found in many colas, coffee, tea, and chocolate. Alcohol is a common depressant.

The daily feeding schedule should fit the needs of the baby. Some babies seem to like smaller, more frequent meals. Other babies take more food but eat less often. Babies will eat less as growth slows during the later part of the first year. And like adults, babies have days when they want more or less food than their usual pattern. Chart 9-4 gives a general feeding schedule for many babies.

Baby foods. Parents today can choose between homemade and commercially prepared baby foods. During the first half of the twentieth century, commercially-prepared baby foods became common. Many parents used them because they saved time and effort. Most parents were aware of the advantages of commercially-prepared foods. See 9-5. Some parents continued to prepare foods in the home for economic or other reasons.

Preparing baby foods in the home has become common again. Parents who prepare their own foods may be concerned about possible harmful effects of additives such as sugar and sodium, preservatives, and color and flavor boosters. Also, kitchen appliances such as the food processor and blender have made baby food preparation easier. Baby food recipe books are now available. Many commercial food companies have reduced the amount or totally removed many of the additives in baby foods. But some parents still prefer preparing their own baby foods in part or in total. See 9-6.

When buying commercially-prepared baby food, check the pull date on the cap or the side of the container to find the last date the product can be sold. (The foods can still be used

for a few days after this date.) Most stores remove older foods from their shelves, but foods on sale may be near the pull date. The containers should be properly sealed. The caps on jars should be concave to show that the jar is still vacuum-sealed. Boxes of foods should not be opened.

Unopened jars of baby food and juices should be stored in a dry, cool place. Never freeze these foods, because the jars might explode. Keep boxed foods away from heat, moisture, and non-food items such as soaps and cleaners. Boxes of foods should be kept on very clean shelves to prevent insect problems.

After baby food jars have been opened, they should be stored in the refrigerator. Jars contain one or two servings. They should be used within two or three days after being opened. Opened boxes of food can be placed inside closed plastic food bags for more protection.

Just before serving, the jar or box should be checked. When removing the cap of a sealed jar, there will be a "pop" sound. If you do not hear a "pop," it means the jar was not properly sealed and you should not use it. Remove the amount of food needed from the jar. Do not feed the baby straight from the jar, since saliva

FIRST YEAR DAILY FEEDING SCHEDULE

MONTHS	HOURS BETWEEN FEEDINGS
1 to 3 *	3 to 4
3-5	5 * *
6	6 * *

* Often sleeps through the night in about 3 months. Babies are given a late evening feeding (about 11:00 p.m.) and they sleep until early morning (5:30 or 6:00 a.m.).
* * Nutritious snacks of their regular baby food (fruit juice, fruit, etc.) or milk and water should be offered about half way between feedings (2 1/2 to 3 hours after each feeding) if the baby is awake.

9-4 A baby's feeding schedule changes during the first year.

from the baby's spoon can harm the food. After removing a serving of food from a refrigerated jar, heat it in an electric or hot water baby dish. Or use a small, sectioned container such as an egg poacher. Before heating baby foods in microwave ovens, read the jar labels. (Some foods explode when heated in microwave ovens.) Most babies like foods at room-temperature. They will eat foods taken from a jar that was just opened without heating. The temperature of heated foods must be tested (by putting a small drop on the wrist) before serving.

Weaning. For bottle-fed babies, *weaning* is the process of taking a baby off the bottle to a cup. For breast-fed babies, weaning is the process of taking the baby off the breast to a bottle or cup. This can be a two-stage process —from breast to bottle and from bottle to cup. Once a baby is fully weaned, he or she takes all liquids from a cup.

The process of weaning should be gradual for two reasons. First, babies must learn a new way to get liquids. If weaning is done too quickly, the baby may not get the needed amount of food. Second, babies need a consistent world to develop trust. Quick changes can cause a seed of mistrust to be planted.

The age to start weaning is not the same for every baby. Many adults do not begin weaning until about nine months. Often they have the baby completely weaned by 18 months. Older babies who drink milk and eat very small amounts of solids can become *anemic* (not have enough iron).

The baby's physician can advise parents about the best time for weaning their baby. Babies also show caregivers they are ready to be weaned, especially from the bottle. Ready-to-wean babies play with their bottles. They may even remove the nipple unit. They are also

ADVANTAGES OF COMMERCIALLY-PREPARED BABY FOOD

Easy to obtain and use. In fact, commercially-prepared foods were first introduced as "convenience foods."

May be more economical than homemade food if one considers cost of ingredients, gas or electricity used to prepare the food, and time.

A variety of foods is available in all four seasons. (Some fruits and vegetables may not be available year-round for preparing home-made foods.)

Foods can be purchased with the right texture for the age of the baby.

Foods are sterile until opened.

Unopened foods can be stored without refrigeration for a long time before they lose quality. (A date is given on the package to tell the period of best quality.)

Foods except dry cereals are packaged in small amounts for one or two servings.

Many additives thought to be harmful have been removed or reduced.

9-5 Commercially-prepared baby foods have many advantages.

ADVANTAGES OF HOMEMADE BABY FOOD

Possibly harmful additives are not used.

Usually less expensive to prepare.

Can be prepared while preparing foods for other members of the family. For instance, a small amount of a cooked vegetable may be removed (before seasoning is added for other family members) and pureed for the baby.

No special appliances are needed to prepare baby food.

Saves storage space required for baby food products.

May be necessary to prepare special food if the baby has allergies.

Recipe books are available with many tasty recipes.

A creative cook is not limited to those commercially-prepared foods that are available.

Brings a sense of satisfaction to those who like to cook.

9-6 Parents may choose to make their own baby food for many reasons.

willing to take a few sips from a cup before their main feeding or as a between meal snack.

Weaning from the breast. When a nursing mother decides to wean her baby, she must reduce her fluid intake. The mother should nurse her baby only when she feels uncomfortable. Mothers often go through the following steps:

- Begin offering formula *as part* of one feeding. (The 6:00 p.m. feeding is usually best, because there is less breast milk then.)
- Increase the amount of formula at this feeding until the baby has taken an entire feeding by bottle for several days.
- Apply the same steps to another feeding until the baby is weaned. (The early morning breast feeding is often the last one to stop.)

Weaning to a cup. Some babies begin to learn drinking from a cup by imitating others. Often, breast-fed babies accept a cup before bottle-fed babies will. Parents often wean to a cup with the following practices:

- Provide their baby with a special baby cup. The cup may have two handles and be weighted to prevent tipping, 9-7.
- Praise their baby for any attempt to handle the cup. Parents should not expect this to be an easy task until about 18 months. Even after that age, many accidents will occur.
- Give the baby a few sips (1 tablespoon in the bottom of a cup) of a liked juice around six months of age. The small amount is less scary if it splashes against the baby's nose and less messy if spilled.
- Once the physician believes the baby is ready for a little milk, let the baby drink small amounts at one feeding. Choose a feeding in which the baby already drinks small amounts of juice or water. A baby should work up to at least four ounces of milk at one feeding.
- Gradually replace other bottle feedings in the same way. The night bottle is often the last to be stopped.

Spoon feeding. Spoon feeding begins when solids are given to the baby. Solid food should not be mixed with liquids and fed from a bottle, because babies may choke. When babies are ready to use their throat and tongue muscles to eat, they are ready to eat solids.

During the first few spoon feedings, babies often push the spoon and the food out of their mouths. This is a natural response to strange contents in the mouth. (Even adults press their tongues against dental tools.)

For the first spoon feedings, the baby should be held in the adult's lap in an almost upright position. A small spoon with a long handle (ice teaspoon) makes feeding easier. Only a small amount of food should be placed on the tip of the spoon. Two or three bites is enough for first feedings. Later, babies can be fed from high chairs or baby feeding tables.

Self-feeding with a spoon begins in the second year. Younger babies may want to help adults by grabbing the spoon. Adults can often solve this problem by giving the baby a spoon to hold (even one for each hand) while they feed. Some parents let the baby try the spoon on the last few bites. The spoon rarely gets in the mouth, but this is good practice for later self-feeding.

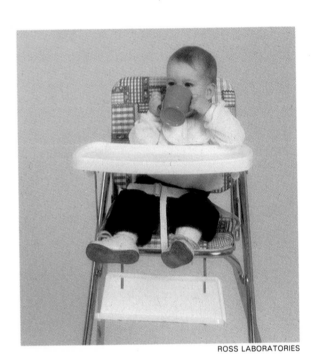

ROSS LABORATORIES

9-7 Cups designed for babies make weaning easier.

Mealtimes should be pleasant for the baby. Caregivers should always be calm regardless of what or how much the baby accepts or rejects. If the adult is unpleasant when the baby rejects a food, the baby is more likely to refuse the same food the next time. Kindness, the psychological "spoonful of sugar," makes foods easier to accept.

Clothing

Infants grow rapidly during the first year. Clothing that fits snugly during the first few weeks or months cannot be worn later in the first year. Because babies grow at different rates, infant clothing must be bought by size, not age. (Sewing patterns should be selected by size and not age, also.) Chart 9-8 is the common sizing used for infants.

From three months to the end of the first year, babies move more with each passing week. Clothing should meet these movement needs. The basic points given in 9-9 can be used in selecting baby clothing.

The style and color of clothing chosen for the baby is a personal choice. Many parents select a variety of styles. Almost any style has its advantages and disadvantages. For instance, two-piece outfits (tops and slacks or shorts) can often be worn longer because they do not get as tight in the crotch as one-piece outfits. Two-piece outfits make changing the diaper easy, too. One-piece outfits such as jumpsuits, rompers (a short, one-piece outfit which resembles a loose T-shirt but with leg openings), and overalls look neater on crawlers. Two-piece outfits separate. One-piece outfits are warmer, too.

Good consumer practices. Because babies quickly outgrow clothing, good consumer practices are important. Adults who shop for infant clothing should follow general good consumer practices such as shopping for quality and comparing prices. But there are other good consumer practices that apply to infant clothing. Some of these practices include the following:

- Buy garments a size or two larger than the infant. These may be worn longer as the baby quickly grows.
- Look for built-in growth features. These

TYPICAL FIRST YEAR CLOTHING SIZES

SIZES FOR CLOTHES OTHER THAN SLEEPWEAR			
	Newborn	**Small**	**Medium**
Length	to 24 in. (to 60 cm)	24 1/2-28 in. (61-70 cm)	28 1/2-32 in. (71-80 cm)
Weight	to 14 lbs. (to 6 kg)	15-20 lbs. (7-9 kg)	21-26 lbs. (9.5-12 kg)
SIZES FOR SLEEPWEAR			
	NB	**1B**	**2B**	**3B**
Length	to 23 in. (to 58 cm)	23 1/2-26 in. (59-65 cm)	26 1/2-29 in. (66-73 cm)	29 1/2-32 in. (74-80 cm)
Weight	to 13 lbs. (to 5.8 kg)	14-17 lbs. (6-7.6 kg)	18-22 lbs. (8-10 kg)	23-26 lbs. (10.3-11.7 kg)

9-8 Baby clothes should be purchased by size, not age.

BASIC POINTS TO CONSIDER IN CHOOSING INFANT CLOTHES

FEATURE	EXAMPLES
Safety	Fire retardant. Not tight or binding. No loose buttons or other fasteners. No loose trim Antibacterial (labeled *Sani-guard* or *Sanitized*).
Comfortable	Soft (made of knitted fabrics). Non-irritating (flat seams, flat as possible fasteners, and garments not so large that the baby rests on the bulk). No fuzzy trims that tickle. Neck openings large enough for easy dressing. Not tight or binding. Right weight for needed warmth. (Several layers of lightweight clothes such as undershirt, T-shirt, and sweater are warmer and more comfortable in cold weather than one heavy garment.) Roomy for active body movements. Anti-static. Absorbent (manufactured fabrics such as polyester or nylon should be blended with cotton to increase absorbency).
Easy care	Machine washable and can be washed with other colors. Soil release finish (makes stain removal easier). Shrinkage control (labeled *Sanforized*). Little or no ironing needed. Easy to mend.

9-9 Babies need clothes that meet their special needs.

include a double row of snaps or buttons at the waistline to lengthen the garment from shoulder to crotch; two buttons on straps used for lengthening; stretch waists; and stretch leg and arm openings.

- Choose more stretch knit garments than woven garments. Stretch knits can be worn longer.
- Keep in mind that two piece garments and clothes with tucks, pleats, and yokes can extend wearing time.

Caring for infant clothes. The most common problem in caring for infant clothes is to protect flame retardant and anti-static fabric finishes and to remove food stains. Proper care of infant clothes include the same steps used in care of any garments.

Before laundering clothes, read labels and hang tags. Follow these directions carefully.

Pretreat stains before washing. This prevents stains from setting in. Also, mend tears before washing to prevent them from becoming larger.

Infants' and young children's clothing often go through more rinses than other clothing. Extra rinses help remove soap residue from clothes. Babies have more sensitive skin than adults, and residue from washing products may cause skin rashes.

Many parents store baby clothes for future children or as keepsakes. Before storing, clothes should be completely clean. Soiled spots change over time, and then stains cannot be removed. When clothes are clean and dry, they are ready to be stored. To prevent yellowing, white clothes should be wrapped in blue tissue paper or blue plastic bags. Vinyl, plastic, leather, or suede should not be stored in plastic bags. These fabrics need air to maintain their strength and oils. Light and dark clothes should be stored in separate boxes to prevent transfer of dyes. All clothing should be stored away from damp areas. Dampness promotes mildew and insect damage.

Shoes are not needed until a baby begins to walk outdoors. Shoes protect and cushion feet from outside hazards. But indoors, babies should walk without shoes to prevent flat-footed walking. Most shoes worn in the first year are for decoration. These should have soft, cloth soles. Socks or footed clothing are needed in cool weather to keep babies' feet from getting cold.

Diapering

The diapering procedure remains the same as described in Chapter 5, "The Newborn." However, older babies do wiggle more and may even protest being diapered. Adults may find the task more challenging. Since diapering requires a few minutes several times a day, it is a good time for social interaction. Babies need to be talked to and played with while they are changed. In such a setting, babies rarely protest the change.

In older babies, there is a reaction between urine and bacteria on diapers and on the baby's skin. The reaction causes an ammonia odor. The problem occurs most often in night diapers. Because of this reaction, babies may develop a diaper rash. To prevent the rash, babies need extra soap and water washing as part of diapering. Also, night diapers need to be washed in a diaper antiseptic.

Adults need to keep areas where the baby is diapered abolutely clean. Most babies mouth everything including the diapering area and equipment. The following steps help to keep the diapering area clean:

- Place a disposable surface, such as a wax paper square, under the diaper. (Wax paper helps prevent leakage.) The paper can be used to handle the diaper until it is thrown away or placed in the diaper pail.
- Check the surface of the changing area for cracks. Cracks cannot be cleaned.
- Scrub the changing table or counter with soap and water, rinse, and treat with a disinfectant daily and after each time a diaper leaks. A solution of one tablespoon chlorine bleach to one gallon water can be used as a disinfectant. The bleach solution may be sprayed on the surface from a spray bottle. Store the solution safely.
- Clean any diaper pails and wastecans used in diapering in the same way that you clean the changing table. These pails and wastecans must be kept away from babies and young children at all times.
- Wash your hands after putting the baby in a safe place.

Tub bathing

Tub bathing can begin as soon as the baby's navel has healed. In preparing for tub bathing, the steps are the same as those used for sponge bathing (see Chapter 5, "The Newborn"). The only difference is that a small tub (or bath table) is filled with about three inches of water. The water should be comfortably warm to the wrist or elbow. The steps for tub bathing are shown in 9-10.

Bathing, like diapering, is a good time in adults' busy days for playing with babies. As babies are bathed, they enjoy parents who talk, sing, cuddle, and smile. Babies often respond well because warm water is relaxing. As babies get older, they enjoy kicking in the water as their parents hold them. Kicking in the water is good for baby's motor skills and fun.

Providing rest and sleep time

Rest and sleep are important to one's health. Babies, like older people, vary in the amount of rest and sleep they need.

Many babies begin sleeping through the night at six weeks of age, but some are night owls for many months. Adults may get some relief by attempting to rearrange babies' schedules. They may awaken babies after four hours of sleep in the morning or afternoon to help the baby sleep at night. (Don't awaken a good daytime sleeper who sleeps at night.)

Some babies who have slept through the night for many weeks may begin to awaken and cry during the night. This often happens between five and eight months. Hunger is not the usual reason for crying. Sleep is lonely. These babies awaken, know parents are nearby, and signal to them. The best things parents can do is check their babies, comfort them for a couple of minutes, and put them down again.

Playing with a baby during the night is not a good habit to form.

Many babies take both long morning and long afternoon naps until five or six months. At this age babies often take a short morning

TUB BATH

Usually recommended as soon as navel and circumcision are healed. Fill the tub—often a large dishpan—with about 3 inches of comfortably warm water. You can test it with your elbow or wrist. A towel on the bottom of the tub will help keep baby from slipping.

1: ON TABLE

Undress baby except for diaper. Cleanse eyes, nose, ears, and face as in sponge bath. Apply Liquid Baby Bath to head with hand, or use washcloth after about first two months. Note: when baby is older and has more hair, use a liquid Baby Shampoo that will not irritate eyes.

2: INTO TUB

After removing baby's diaper, you can place him in the tub. Use a safety hold: Slip right hand under baby's houlders with thumb over right shoulder and fingers under right armpit. Support buttocks with left hand, grasping right thigh with thumb and fingers. Lower baby into tub feet first, keeping head out of water. With left hand rinse head, letting water run well back.

3: BATHING BODY

Soap the front of baby's body, being careful to wash inside all skin folds and creases, then rinse. Reverse your hold to soap and rinse baby's back. It's not necessary to turn him over. The genital area should be cleansed during the bath, just like the rest of baby. In the external folds of a baby girl, a white substance may gather. If it remains after bathing—as it may sometimes do—gently wipe it away with a washcloth or with a cotton ball dipped in oil. Be sure to wipe from front to back. When cleansing a baby boy who has not been circumcised, do not push back the foreskin unless your physician advises you to do so, if your baby has been circumcised, he may be immersed in a tub as soon as the area has healed, or sooner, on your physician's advice.

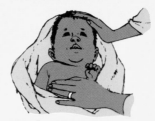

4: OUT OF TUB

Use the same safety hold to lift baby onto a warm, dry surface. Cover baby with a towel and pat dry, paying special attention to folds and creases.

5: DIAPER-AREA CARE

To keep the diaper area dry, use Baby Cornstarch to help prevent chaffing, irritation, and redness.

6: GENERAL SKIN CARE

Moisten fingers on cotton ball dipped in Baby Oil or Baby Lotion. Apply to all tiny creases—around neck, armpits, arms, hands, legs, feet. Use a little Baby Oil on a cotton ball to help remove "cradle cap." Apply Baby Cream to any irritated part. Sprinkle Baby Powder on your hand and pat lightly over large areas of body.

JOHNSON & JOHNSON BABY PRODUCTS CO.

9-10 Tub bathing should be done carefully and quickly for the baby's comfort and safety.

nap and a long afternoon nap. Most babies drop their morning nap between nine and fifteen months. But they will continue to take an afternoon nap until 36 to 60 months.

Establishing routines

Routines help children feel secure because they learn what to expect. Although babies do not know clock time, they do develop a sense of rhythm in their lives from scheduled care. Schedules also help adults get their baby-care tasks done with greater ease.

Routines should fit babies' and adults' needs. In the beginning, there will probably be some trial-and-error attempts to schedule. Schedules also change as babies mature. Feedings are more widely spaced, daytime naps grow shorter, and more playtime is needed.

A question that is often asked is, "Does a person have to follow a schedule closely?" Following a rigid schedule allows for no changes to meet babies' or adults' needs. On the other hand, there is no point to making a schedule if it is not followed. The most sensible approach is to follow a schedule but adjust it when necessary.

Providing sleep and play spaces

Planning for sleep and play spaces for a baby is based on a family's life-style and housing facilities. However, families may follow some general guidelines.

Babies need a place to sleep away from major household activities. Some parents screen off a small section in their bedroom or plan for the baby to share a bedroom with another child. Other parents provide their baby with a separate bedroom or bedroom/playroom combination.

The floor space for sleeping should be large enough for a full-size crib (about 53 by 31 inches). Babies need this much space by three months of age for safety purposes, and children often sleep in a crib until four years of age. Many parents like to have space for a dressing table. Dressing tables can be purchased or made by attaching a vinyl-covered pad and safety belt to a dresser. An adult-sized rocker nearby is also popular. Parents also need space for

clothing and baby products.

Babies shadow adults during their waking hours. Thus, adults should not equip a playroom area and expect a baby to be happy staying there. Playrooms are great for toddlers and older children. But they can only be used by infants as *one* place to play. During the first year, babies need places to play and toys in several rooms where household activities take place. A portable play pen may be used for short periods of time, especially when babies need a safer place to play. Toys should always be placed in the play pen.

In choosing play spaces for babies, adults should keep these points in mind:

- Babies are messy—at least by adult standards. Spaces for children should be scrubbable.
- All spaces for babies and young children must be made safe. A house must be child-proofed by the time a baby can crawl or scoot around. (This is discussed in Chapter 25, "Protecting Children's Health and Safety.")
- Planning special rooms or decorating for children should be done with children in mind. Rooms should be bright and cheerful. Low windows, pictures and wall hangings at the baby's eye level, and floor coverings which permit playing with blocks and wheel toys make spaces better for babies.
- Babies do grow quickly. Spaces should be planned for easy and economic changes as babies' needs change.

INTELLECTUAL NEEDS

Not so long ago, adults thought that they were doing their best when they met the physical needs of babies. But babies need more than good physical care to make good progress. Researchers now know that babies are born with the ability to learn many things. They also know that babies need an environment that gives them a chance to learn, or an *enriched environment,* 9-11. One study found that babies whose caregivers expected them to learn at a very early age developed more quickly than babies of whom less was expected. It is likely that adults who expect more provide more activities that aid learning.

Adults can begin to provide learning experiences for babies soon after birth. In fact, the sooner adults provide activities, the more babies want to learn. But adults shouldn't forget that babies learn at different rates. The rate of learning cannot be increased by providing an excess of activities and toys. Babies can only take in a limited amount at one time. Too many activities can result in confusion or boredom.

Activities are best woven into the routines of the day, such as feeding, bathing, and diapering. Adults do not need to have a set schedule of daily games. The number and types of games are not as important as the warmth and caring that adults show for babies.

Babies each have different likes and dislikes for activities or toys. If a baby enjoys an activity, the adult should not stop it to play something the adult has planned. Adults can try planned games when the baby is not involved with something else.

A skillful caregiver knows how to use activities to meet babies' intellectual needs. Adults can use the following methods:

- Watch for signs of the baby's interest in certain experiences. To check for interest, demonstrate a game or a way to use a toy, and then give the baby a turn. If the baby doesn't begin to play in some way, repeat the demonstration a couple of times. If the baby shows little or no interest, repeat the procedure over a period of two or three days. If there is still no interest, the toy or game is probably too advanced for the baby. It can be tried again in a few weeks.
- Let the baby begin most activities, and then expand on those activities. For instance, the baby may be patting a high chair tray. Expand the activity by patting a different object (that makes a different sound) or by patting the tray harder, softer, faster, or slower than the baby.
- Repeat games many times. Using the games over many months helps the baby retain the skills that are helped by each game.
- Allow the baby to try things on his or her

HEDSTROM

9-11 Babies can learn about the world around them when taken on a trip in a stroller.

own. Letting babies try something on their own or play alone for awhile aids problem solving skills.

Sensory stimulation activities

Sensory stimulation involves learning to notice and find out more about the environment through the five senses. According to Piaget, babies use their senses as a major way of learning. Babies use their senses to learn not only from toys made for them such as a crib mobile, but also from the contents of a drawer or a trip outside.

All the senses—seeing, hearing, touching, tasting, and smelling—need to be stimulated for full development.

Problem solving activities

As babies use their senses to observe their worlds, they try to make sense of what they see, hear, feel, touch, and taste. In an enriched environment, babies learn how their worlds work as they explore on their own.

A few games can help babies begin to think about how their world works. Most of these games are not begun before babies are six months old. Many are continued after the first birthday. Babies need to repeat these kinds of games with many objects and with some changes in order to be sure that this is the way something really works. Problem-solving activities for babies may involve *spatial* (space) concepts, 9-12, the object permanence concept, and using objects as tools.

Motor activities

Movement is important for infants. Even before birth babies move. Although motor nerves are not fully developed for four or five years, *coordination* (the working together of muscles in movements such as walking) improve quickly from birth. As infants explore, motor activity aids mental development as well as coordination. As motor skills improve, babies feel better about their abilities.

Babies will engage in many motor activities on their own if they are given freedom to move. But babies also need to be encouraged to do motor activities.

Games can be used to improve the baby's large and small muscles. *Gross-motor games* exercise large muscles through such activities as rolling over, sitting, crawling, standing, and walking, 9-13. *Fine-motor games* improve coordination in the small muscles, especially those in the fingers and hands, 9-14. Babies exercise small muscles through grasping.

Language activities

Hearing language becomes important after babies are six months old. From this age until

A   JOHN SHAW   B   JOHN SHAW

9-12 Stacking and nesting objects helps babies learn spatial concepts. Hollow blocks or cans can be both stacked (A) and nested (B).

9-13 Splashing in a pool with an adult helps a baby improve large muscle strength.

a child learns to read, language is learned through hearing people talk. Since adults spend more of their time with the baby taking care of physical needs, they should use these times to talk with babies.

Adults can talk about the foods, toys, people, and routines that are part of the baby's world. Exact words are not as important to the infant as hearing language. While dressing a baby, for instance, the adult could make any of the following statements:

- "I'm putting on your green shirt."
- "Isn't this a pretty shirt?"
- "Are you ready for the shirt to go over your head?"
- "Here's a button, here's a button, and here's one."
- "Do you like green?"

Although exact words aren't important, words should be pronounced correctly. Adults can clown with language by stressing certain syllables such as, "Hello-o-o Amee-ee-ee." Changing pitch or singing also varies the sound.

Adults can encourage babies to talk, too. They can ask questions, then pause. Often, the baby will babble in response. If the baby babbles, encouragement should be given such as, "That's right . . ."

Language games can be worked into daily routines. They also can be used during special, fun times shared by babies and adults, 9-15.

SOCIAL-EMOTIONAL NEEDS

Babies have needs which must be met for proper social-emotional development. During the first year, social and emotional development seems to center around the baby-adult interaction, the baby's developing self-awareness, and adults' ways of handling special problems.

Baby-adult interaction

Each baby comes into the world with a unique temperament. Adults may respond positively or negatively toward the baby's temperament. The adult's feelings are conveyed

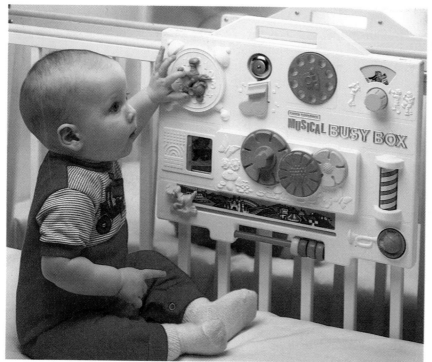

9-14 A baby can improve fine-motor skills using an activity board.

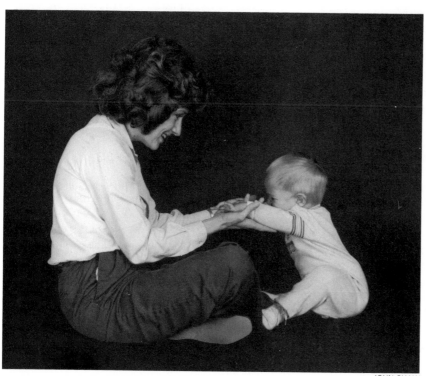

9-15 Language games can be part of fun times shared by babies and adults.

mainly through the way they hold, touch, and look at the baby. In turn, the baby is tuned to the adult's feelings and actions. For instance, if adults are tense or the baby's needs are not met, the baby becomes fussy and difficult. But when adults are relaxed and baby's needs are promptly met, the baby is usually quiet and cooperative.

Adults who have good relationships with babies seem to understand that the baby's temperament must be respected. For instance, active babies will get into more places they don't belong. They require more watching and following than less active children.

Babies feel loved because of physical contact with the adult, 9-16. They do not feel loved because adults go to work and give them objects and toys. Such messages of love are too complex for babies to understand.

Physical messages shape feelings between adults and babies. But a single or seldom sent message does not determine the relationship. Even the most loving adults are at times hurried and tense. What makes the relationship is the total number of messages and the strength of the messages. The balance must be on the positive side for a good relationship.

Adults should realize that relationships with children are rather one-sided for many years. They may get some smiles and hugs from babies, but adults must do most of the giving. This giving is important, though, because the feelings adults show for babies help to shape babies' self-concepts. Fostering good feelings in babies seems to increase the joy and love between babies and their caregivers.

Developing the baby's self-awareness

Babies begin to develop self-awareness as they achieve goals. For instance, when a baby scoots across the floor to get a toy, the baby begins to realize that he or she can make things happen. But babies do not see themselves as separate individuals until eight or nine months of age.

Adults can help self-awareness by using the baby's name as much as possible. Using the baby's name during happy times gives the baby positive feelings about his or her name. Happy times include reunions between adult and baby, such as after a nap or when the adult returns from work. The name also can be used during child care tasks or games like peek-a-boo.

Looking in mirrors also increases self-awareness. Babies enjoy seeing themselves in mirrors even before they know the images they see are their own. Calling the baby's image by name is helpful. Adults may also place babies in front of mirrors so they can watch themselves being fed, dressed, and so on. Babies also enjoy having metal play mirrors as toys, 9-17.

Babies like to point to their own eyes, ears, nose, mouth, and toes. They also enjoy finding these body parts in the mirror.

Toward the end of the first year, babies become possessive about some objects. This

9-16 The mutual feelings of love and joy between a baby and adult can be shared through physical contact.

9-17 A metal baby mirror helps babies see themselves and begin to learn self-awareness.

should be encouraged, because babies' understanding that some objects belong to them is part of self-awareness. Also, one must possess before one can share. Adults can help teach possession by making statements like "Here's Barbara's dress" or "Where are Keith's blocks?"

Handling special problems

All babies have some problems. These may include feeding and sleeping problems, intense fear of strangers, or excessive crying. Adults should be able to recognize and deal with special problems. When they arise, these suggestions may be helpful:

- Determine whether or not the problem is temporary. Wait a few days unless the baby seems ill. Babies do have mood changes. Also, the problem may be a result of the caregiver being hurried or tense. In these cases, the problem will likely end as soon as the adult slows down or relaxes.
- If the problem continues, present it to someone who specializes in child growth and development. One of the best starting places is a pediatrician or a family physician.
- Get help when needed. For instance, parents who have a fussy baby or a "howling night owl" may need to use babysitting services in order to get needed rest or to get away from home for a few hours.
- Give in to a baby's demands sometimes if the results are not serious. Even babies have wills of their own, and letting them have their way sometimes isn't going to spoil or harm them. For instance, if a baby refuses to eat peas, try other vegetables with almost the same vitamins.
- Remain calm. This helps the baby and the adult.

Experienced caregivers seem to almost ignore many common, not too serious problems. Experience teaches that all babies are different and that most problems are resolved in time.

ACTIVITY	SENSE

From ages one to three months

MOBILES ——————————————— Sight

Place mobiles on crib and playpen. Vary the objects on the mobile often. When babies can reach the mobiles, hang them from the ceiling. Most purchased mobiles are strung in such a way that babies can see only the edge of the mobile. These should be restrung so the baby can see whole objects.

JOHN SHAW

TRACKING OBJECTS ——————————————— Sight

Hold an object such as a yarn ball, a small flashlight, or a rattle about 12 inches from the baby's eyes. Move it in a short arc and gradually extend the arc to a half-circle. The baby's eyes should track or follow the object.

HANGING RING ——————————————— Sight

Suspend a colorful ring over the crib or playpen. Move the ring in different directions and spin the ring so the baby sees it in different positions.

TALKING ——————————————— Sight and hearing

Talk to the baby during all routine tasks. Babies tend to respond more when the voice is pitched a littler higher.

WINDCHIME ——————————————— Hearing

Hang a windchime during waking hours.

JOHN SHAW

MUSIC ——————————————— Hearing

Sing and play music from a radio or record player.

Continued.

172

From ages three to six months

DECORATED WRIST BAND AND SOCK ——————————————— Sight

For wrist bands, cut the top off of a child's sock. Use a striped sock band or sew on some fabric decorations. The wrist band helps the baby to discover the hands. A decorated sock helps the baby discover the feet.

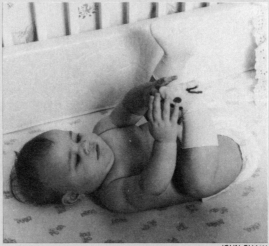

JOHN SHAW

FACE HOOP ————————————————————————————— Sight

Make a face by decorating fabric with fabric scraps or paint. Insert the fabric between round embroidery hoops. Hang face down or hold for the baby to see. (The face hoop is not safe for mouthing.)

JOHN SHAW

PLAY QUILTS ——————————————————————————— Sight and touch

When babies start playing with their blankets, make a play quilt. Use many fabrics with different patterns, colors, and textures.

FIND THE BELL ——————————————————————————— Hearing

Ring a bell while the baby is not watching. When the baby looks in the correct direction, show him or her the bell while ringing it again.

SOUND TOUR ———————————————————————————— Hearing

Carry the baby on a sound tour of the house. Do not make loud sounds like turning on a vacuum cleaner. Instead, use sounds like a note or two on the piano, wind chimes, a music box, light switch clocks, cabinet door closing, fan over range, and door bells.

Continued.
The infant's developmental needs   173

ACTIVITY	SENSE

From ages six to twelve months

CRIB WINDOW — Sight

Using an 18-inch to 20-inch (45 to 50 cm) square piece of heavy gauge clear vinyl, sew two four-foot (120 cm) pieces of 1/2-inch (1.25 cm) wide elastic to the vinyl centered on the elastic strips. Tie to the crib sides. Place any lightweight object on the window for the baby to see. (Remove window when baby is not being watched.)

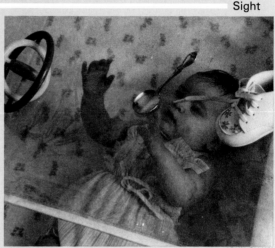

JOHN SHAW

FLOATING TOYS — Sight

Babies enjoy watching toys in the bath. Use clean, empty plastic detergent or shampoo bottles as well as toys made for the bathtub.

SOUND CAN — Hearing

Place some large wooden beads or large thread spools in a juice can. Tape on the lid. Other baby-safe objects can be used.

FEELING TOUR — Touch

Take a tour of the house or yard and touch objects with different textures.

FOOD — Sight, touch, smell, and taste

As babies begin to eat solids, four senses are used at one time.

PROBLEM SOLVING ACTIVITIES

Spatial Relationship Activities

GET THE TOY

Place a toy between two objects such as two chairs or a chair and a wall. Then have the baby get the toy. Each time the game is played, the space between the two objects should be changed. The baby should learn when there is enough space to crawl between two objects and when there is only enough space to reach for the toy.

RIGHT SIDE UP

Show the baby a known object—such as a doll or picture—that is upside down. See whether the baby will turn the object or picture right side up.

STACKING AND NESTING

Find three cans or boxes that are very different in size and that fit inside each other. These can be stacked by placing one on top of the other, or they can be nested by placing one inside the other. (Differences in size should be large for young babies, so if a stacking/nesting

Continued.

174

set with many pieces is purchased, start with only the smallest, the largest, and one middle-sized piece. After the baby can work with three pieces, others may be added one at a time.) Show the baby how to stack the pieces. Then let the baby try. The baby will make mistakes, because stacking is not self-correcting. In other words, the baby can stack the objects in more than one way, because sometimes a larger object can balance on a smaller one. After stacking for several days, try nesting, showing the baby how to nest first. (Nesting is self-correcting.)

UP, DOWN, AND AROUND

Lift the baby up and say, "Up *(baby's name)* goes." As you lower the baby, say, "Down *(baby's name)* comes." Repeat several times. (Never toss and catch a baby.) Next, hold the baby close to your body and as you turn around say, "Around and around *(baby's name)* goes."

FAR AND NEAR

Hold a toy close to the baby's eyes. Move it back slowly and say, "There it goes." Move it forward slowly and say, "Here it comes." (The game helps babies see size differences in near and far objects.)

Object permanence activities

WHERE'S THE OBJECT?

Hide a favorite toy, starting with simple ways of hiding and moving to more complex ways as the baby masters each. 1. Place the toy so that it is partially hidden under a small blanket. 2. Place the toy so that it is totally hidden under the blanket. 3. Wrap the toy in paper so that the shape of the object shows through the paper. 4. Place the toy in or under a box or behind a screen. 5. Place the toy in a box that's in another box. In each game, hide the toy as the baby watches.

PEEK-A-BOO

Cover your eyes and say, "Where did *(baby's name)* go?" Uncover eyes and say, "Peek-a-boo, I see you!" Repeat several times. Then cover the baby's eyes lightly with your hand or a small cloth that is draped over the baby's head and eyes. Say, "Where did *(given name such as Daddy)* go?" Then uncover the baby's eyes and say, "Peek-a-boo, here I am." After a few times, the baby will remove the eye cover.

HIDE-AND-SEEK

Hide from the baby leaving some part of yourself visible. Let the baby find you. Once found, make the reunion happy, with lots of hugs and kisses. (This helps babies overcome their anxiety when left with others.) After many games of being partly hidden, hide your body completely. (But choose a hiding place where the baby can easily find you.)

Using objects as tools

PULLING STRINGS

Babies can learn to get an object by pulling a string using several methods. String-pulled toys can be purchased, or you can attach any toy or safe household object to a string for the baby to pull. Another game is to tie a balloon to a piece of yarn and tie the other end to the baby's wrist. Then show the baby how to get the balloon by pulling the string.

MAKING SOUNDS WITH OBJECTS

By hitting objects together, babies can learn to make different sounds. They will learn to vary the sounds by hitting softer or harder or by changing the objects. Different objects to use include a pan with a spoon, a box with a spoon, a xylophone with a mallet, and a block with a block.

Continued.

The infant's developmental needs   175

Gross-motor games

GETTING OBJECTS

While the baby is watching, roll or move any toy or safe object out of the baby's reach. Encourage the baby to get the object. As the baby's motor skills improve, increase the distance between the baby and the object.

KNOCK THE TOY OFF

When a baby can stand by holding on to a play pen or crib railing, place a stuffed toy on the railing. Encourage the baby to hold on to the railing with one hand and knock the toy off with the other.

SPLASHING IN WATER

Splashing in a tub or pool helps the baby improve motor skills. Babies should be supervised by an adult at all times when in or near water. The adult can hold the baby and encourage the baby to splash and kick.

CARTONS

Place a large carton on its side so that the baby can crawl into it. Let the baby crawl in and out of the carton.

Fine-motor games

CRIB GYM

Adults can buy a commercial crib gym or make one using safe objects such as squeeze toys or rattles. Objects can be changed to keep the baby's interest.

CUPS

A baby can improve fine-motor skills by playing with a plastic infant cup. When the baby can handle the hand-to-mouth movement, add a teaspoon (5 ml) of water to the cup. As the baby becomes more skillful, more water may be added.

BLOCKS

Show the baby how to use blocks in different ways and then let the baby try. Blocks can be stacked, hit together, or placed in a line and moved by pushing the last block.

LANGUAGE GAMES

Verbal imitation

Imitation of verbal (and even non-verbal) signals helps language development. Two stages are used during the baby's first year.

STAGE 1: 0-6 months. Imitate the baby's gestures and babbling. If you see a gesture or hear a sound, repeat it with a smile or laugh. See if the baby repeats. If the baby has not repeated the gesture or sound in 15 seconds, repeat the sound. Once the baby catches on, the baby will imitate sounds in return.

STAGE 2: 6-12 months. In this stage, you can begin by making a gesture or sound. See if the baby imitates. If the baby has not repeated the gesture or sound in 15 seconds, make the same gesture or sound again. The baby should catch on quickly.

Continued.

Books

Look at books as soon as the baby shows interest. Talk about the pictures, but do not read yet. As you talk, point to the picture. Talk as long as the baby looks. As soon as the baby looks away or tries to turn the page, go on to the next picture. Between nine and 12 months, babies can be asked to find certain pictures or parts of pictures such as cars, pets, or people.

Puppets

You can make or purchase a puppet to talk to the baby. First, babies will just look and listen, then later they will talk to the puppet.

Action rhymes

Action rhymes can be used toward the end of the first year. They combine the rhythm of the language with a few motor actions. Any of the following rhymes (or others) can be used:

Jack Be Nimble
Jack be nimble,
Jack be quick,
Jack jump over
    (Lift baby to imitate a jump on the word, "jump.")
The candlestick.

Humpty Dumpty
Humpty Dumpty sat on a wall;
Humpty Dumpty had a great fall.
    (Lower baby from lap as word, "fall," is said.)
All the king's horses and all the king's men
Couldn't put Humpty Dumpty together again.

Pat-A-Cake
Pat-a-cake, pat-a-cake, baker's man,
    (Help baby clap hands on words "pat-a-cake.")
Bake me a cake as fast as you can;
Pat it and roll it, and mark it with B,
    (Help baby roll hands on word, "roll.")
Put in the oven for baby and me.

Pop Goes the Weasel
All around the carpenter's bench
The monkey chased the weasel,
The monkey thought 'twas all in fun,
Then POP, goes the weasel.
    (Lift baby up high or clap on word, "POP.")

to Know

coordination . . . depressants . . .
enriched environment . . . fine-motor games . . .
gross-motor games . . . nourishment . . .
nutrients . . . nutritionist . . .
sensory stimulation . . . solids . . .
stimulants . . . weaning

to Review

Write your answers on a separate sheet of paper.

1. The statement below is followed by three pairs of phrases. From each pair, choose the phrase that best completes the statement. Place an a or b in the blank to show your choice.

Skillful caregivers help babies' learning by:

_____ a. Checking age-charts and doing an activity when it's time.

b. Watching for signs of each baby's interest in certain experiences.

_____ a. Often repeating games many times over several months.

b. Not repeating games because babies get bored with them.

_____ a. Showing babies exactly how to do activities so that the babies will not become confused.

b. Letting babies try things for themselves.

2. Babies most basic needs are in the _____ (physical, intellectual, social) area.

3. Give three reasons for not starting solids before babies are six months of age unless advised by a baby's physician.

4. Which of the following statements about the weaning process are true?

a. Weaning is best done gradually.

b. Weaning from the bottle is often done when the baby is younger than weaning from the breast.

c. Complete weaning prior to nine months has no harmful effects on the baby.

d. Late weaning (after two years) has no harmful effects on the baby.

e. Weaning is a physical and social-emotional process.

5. True or false. Activities and games should be woven into child care routines.

6. Activities that babies play on their own are _____ _____ (more important, less important) than those activities suggested in books and pamphlets.

7. True or false. Language is learned through the day-to-day hearing of the spoken word.

8. List two or three ways to help baby learn to talk and understand words.

to Do

1. Examine ready-made garments or patterns for babies. Note built-in growth features.

2. Examine infant's clothing for good features. Make a list of these good features. Compare your list with others in your class. Attach a hang tag to each clothing item listing its best features.

3. Observe a demonstration of tub bathing a baby and practice the steps with a doll. (Remember to talk and play with the baby as you give the bath.)

4. As an individual or small group project make the materials for one or more "games" such as the crib window, a mobile or gym, face hoop, decorated wrist band or sock, play quilt, sound cans, stacking/nesting toy, and string-pulled toy. If the completed projects are not wanted by the individuals or group, add instructions (and safety rules) and donate to an infant program or hospital.

5. Try as many suggested activities as you can in a babysitting job or as a helper in a group-care program for infants. Discuss with class members what did or did not work and possible "whys."

6. Through a group discussion, make a chalkboard list of all the ways people make you feel valued and loved. Take each way listed and discuss whether a baby could or could not feel loved in this way.

Infants grow physically, mentally, socially, and emotionally as their needs are met.

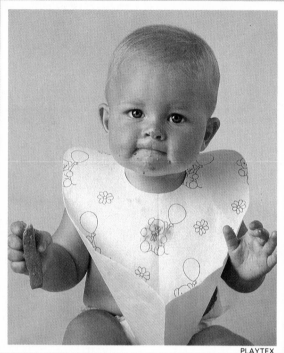

Using silverware is just around the corner

The quiet toddler

Getting ready for a stroll

Kitchen helpers

part four

Toddlers

So much to learn and talk about

JOHN SHAW

Discovering the park together

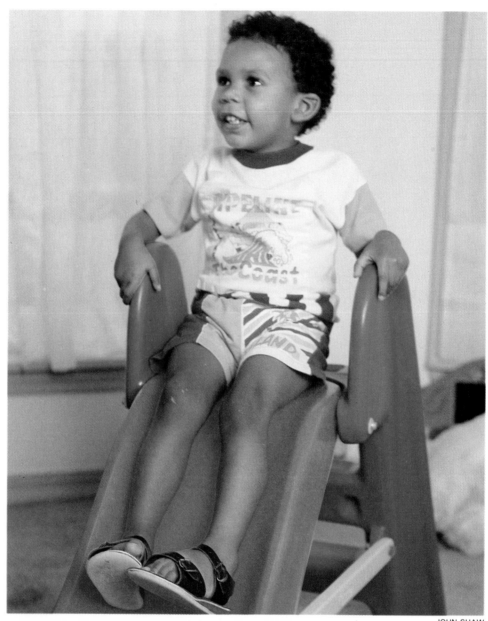

During the toddler years, changes in the body
make many new skills possible.

10

Physical development of the toddler

Physical development in toddlers helps the body mature so that they can handle more complex tasks. Although toddlers do not grow in size as quickly as infants, they go through many important physical changes.

Babies do not have much control over their muscles when they are first born. By the end of their first year, infants are just learning to control voluntary muscle movements. Toddlers improve in both gross-motor and fine-motor skills. By the end of their second year, toddlers have learned many new movements such as running, jumping, throwing, and feeding themselves.

BODY GROWTH AND DEVELOPMENT

After the first year, babies continue to grow rapidly. But they do not grow as rapidly as during the first year. Organ systems continue to mature, too.

Height and weight

Due to environment and heredity, toddlers grow at different rates. Height and the rate of increase in height are controlled mostly by heredity. Weight is influenced more by environment than heredity. Genes influence weight mostly because they determine height. (Taller people usually weigh more than shorter people.) But the environment—foods consumed, exercise, illnesses, and even emotions—plays the major role in weight. Because of these factors, the growth of a toddler is not always the same as norms given for their age.

Body growth begins to slow after the first year. Babies gain about twice as much height in their first year than in their second year. Most babies triple birth weight during the first year, and then gain one-fourth of that during the second. An example is shown in 10-1. Some babies grow a little faster than these norms in their second year. They may be just catching up to norms after a premature birth or illnesses during the first year. Most girls reach 53 percent of their adult height by age two. Boys reach 50 percent of their adult height by age two. And although this is an average, it often is true that a tall two-year-old will be a tall adult and a short two-year-old will be a short adult.

After 24 months, children grow at an even slower but steady rate. They tend to gain two to three inches and about six pounds per year throughout childhood. (This rate of growth stops at about 11 years for girls and 13 years for boys.) Chart 10-2 shows the height and weight norms from 12 to 36 months.

Other body changes

The body proportions of a two-year-old are still different from those of an adult. At 24 months, the head is one-fourth of total length. This is very different from an adult, whose head is one-tenth of his or her height. A 24-month old's chest and abdomen are about the same size. By 30 months, the chest is larger than the abdomen. As the child matures, the difference between chest and abdomen size will become even greater.

As toddlers grow, their bones continue to become harder. But the toddler still has a larger proportion of cartilage than hard bone. This gives toddlers more flexible bones that are less likely to break than those of an adult. On the other hand, the softer bones are more subject to disease or deformation than adult bones. The fontanelles, or gaps between skull bones, are closed or almost closed by the toddler stage. The toddler's spine become S-shaped rather than C-shaped, making standing and walking easier. Shortly after two years, babies have their full sets of deciduous teeth (often called baby teeth). See 10-3.

By the end of the second year, the brain is four-fifths of its adult weight. At this stage, the brain is closer to maturity than any other

GROWTH FROM BIRTH TO AGE TWO YEARS

Let's suppose Sarah was 20.5 inches (51 cm) and weighed seven pounds (3 kg) at birth, and was growing exactly by the norms. Based on her birth length and weight, we would calculate her two year growth in this way:

	FIRST YEAR	SECOND YEAR

Length/Height	Birth.............20.5'' (51 cm)
	Add 9'' (23 cm)-based on
	  norms..........+ 9.0'' (23 cm)
		12 months........29.5'' (74 cm)
		Add 1/2 of 9''
		  (23 cm)........+ 4.5'' (11 cm)

	Total length.......29.5'' (74 cm) a 9'' (23 cm) increase	Total height.......34.0'' (85 cm) a 4.5'' (11 cm) increase
Weight	Birth.............7 lbs. (3 kg) Triple birth weight.....× 3	12 months........21 lbs. (9.5 kg) Add 1/4 of total weight at 12 months...+ 5.25 lbs. (2 kg)
	Total...........21 lbs. (9.5 kg) a 14 lb. (6 kg) gain	Total weight.....26.25 lbs. (12 kg) a 5 lb. (2 kg) gain

10-1 Growth slows after the first year.

AVERAGE LENGTH AND WEIGHT FROM ONE TO THREE YEARS		
AGE IN MONTHS	HEIGHT	WEIGHT
12	30″ (75 cm)	21 lbs. (9.5 kg)
18	32″ (80 cm)	24.5 lbs. (11 kg)
24	34″ (85 cm)	27 lbs. (12 kg)
30	36″ (90 cm)	30 lbs. (13.5 kg)
36	38″ (95 cm)	32 lbs. (14 kg)

10-2 The height and weight of children from one to three years increases rather steadily.

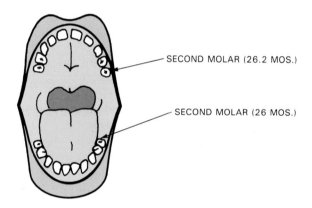

10-3 Soon after their second birthday, toddlers have their full set of deciduous teeth.

organ. Other body organs are continuing to mature, but they mature at a slower rate than the brain. (This is an example of the cephalocaudal principle—development is completed from the brain down the spine.)

Fat tissues under the skin decrease rapidly between nine and 30 months. The chubby baby becomes a slender child, 10-4. *Muscle development* (lengthening and thickening of muscles) is very slow during the toddler stage.

MOTOR DEVELOPMENT

Toddlers refine the motor skills they developed as infants. But they also learn many new skills. Motor skills develop as the child grows and develops. The child's own practice also aids motor development.

Large-muscle development

Large-muscle development refers to the development of the muscles of the trunk, arms, and legs. Movements such as crawling, walking, jumping, and running (gross-motor skills) depend mainly on these large muscles. During the first year, most babies developed these muscles at least to the point of standing and walking with some support. After one year, walking is mastered and children begin many other motor skills. Children of this age love to spend their time running, jumping, and using other large muscles. When they are held in one place too long, they begin squirming (a large-muscle movement) to say, "I want down now!"

Walking. Walking without support may occur two or three months before or after the first birthday. Many people wonder why babies

JOHN SHAW

10-4 The toddler will slowly become slender because fat tissues under the skin are decreasing.

begin walking at different times. Some children are not physically ready to walk but want to so much that they simply fall as they try. Other children who creep with ease and speed may not begin walking early because creeping gets them where the "action is." When one is busy exploring, who has time to learn to walk? Often girls begin to walk before boys. Also, lighter babies are likely to start walking before obese babies.

Some people believe children are beginning to walk sooner than babies have in the past. They think that this is true because babies are better nourished and have fewer illnesses. If children are walking sooner, earlier walking may be due more to the carpeted floors of today (compared to the hardwood floors of the past) than to children's health status. Carpet makes falling less painful.

Although some conditions are helpful, walking is learned in one's own time and way. Only warm adult support—including a positive reaction to the baby's attempts—and a safe area are needed for learning to walk. Pushing a baby to walk early will not help. It may even delay walking and will surely cause frustration for baby and adult.

Regardless of the age of walking, all beginning walkers share some common characteristics. They stand with their feet wide apart for a wider base of support, feet turned outward, and knees slightly flexed. See 10-5. Some children walk on their tiptoes. This is not because they rise to their tiptoes (as one learns to do). It is because they have not learned to lower their heels yet. The first steps often appear to be staggers—with side-steps, backward steps, irregular steps, lurching forward, and weaving. Babies seem to have difficulty balancing their large heads, making falls common.

As the toddler grows, the walking posture changes. See 10-6. A flat spine causes the toddler to tilt forward slightly when walking. As the lower back curve takes on the S-shape, the walk becomes more upright. This, plus improved ability to balance, helps the toddler's walking become more steady. With improved skills, the toddler's stance becomes narrower, the feet straighter, and the knees less flexed.

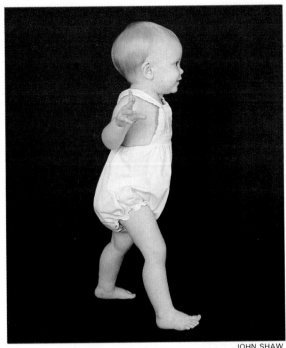

JOHN SHAW

10-5 To maintain balance toddlers first walk with a wide stance and knees flexed.

At two years, a child's walk may look like a run, but it is not a run. Toddlers take about 170 steps per minute and their stride is one-half the length of that of the adult. Can you imagine a shopping trip or a hike, doubling your steps, taking 170 steps per minute, and having someone hold your hands above your head? No wonder young children tire from walking long before adults.

Children must watch their foot placement while walking until almost three years of age. In other words, they must watch each step in the same way you would walk an unknown, sharply winding path or stepping stones across a creek.

After learning to walk, children develop many gross motor skills such as running, jumping, and climbing. The motor skills are combined with objects such as balls and pedalled toys. All of these skills are learned in a setting of experimentation and with a feeling of joy. Toddlers may try bending over to

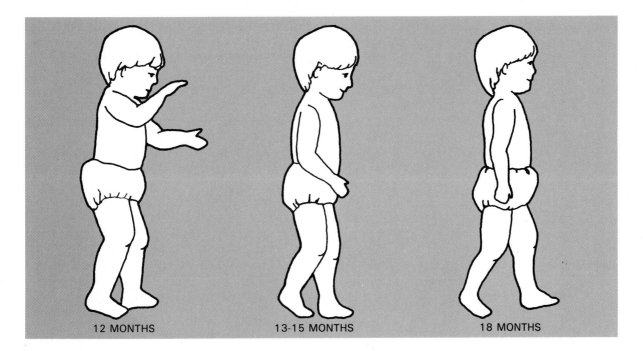

12 MONTHS   13-15 MONTHS   18 MONTHS

10-6 Toddlers walk in a more upright fashion between 12 and 18 months of age.

JOHN SHAW

10-7 Toddlers learn and have fun as they try new motor skills.

watch the world upside down through their legs, 10-7, walking as a tin soldier, doing a new dance step, or running and falling into a heap.

Running. True running, not just a hurried walk, begins around two years of age. Two-year-olds are not skillful runners due to improper arm action. They tend to hold their arms up or out. Running is also awkward because they cannot start or stop quickly.

Jumping. Stepping off of low objects at about 18 months is the way children begin to learn how to jump. Before two years of age, children may step off a low object and remain suspended in air for a brief moment. At two years, children can jump off of low objects with two feet, but they move their arms back instead of helping the jump by swinging their arms forward. See 10-8.

Climbing. Climbing may begin as soon as a baby can crawl or creep. Between 15 and 18 months, babies will climb onto furniture. They will walk up and down stairs with help. For toddlers, going up stairs is easier than coming

Physical development of the toddler 187

hearing the sound it makes when it lands, babies begin to throw on purpose. Planned throwing begins around one year of age.

Year-old babies usually throw from a sitting position such as from their high chair. After babies feel secure in standing or walking, they throw from standing positions. Children under three years of age are not skillful throwers. These children usually use a rigid throw with little or no weight shift. And, their inability to release the ball at the proper time in the throw sends the ball in almost any direction.

For almost a year after a child begins to walk, "catching" a ball or other object is done by squatting down and picking it up, 10-9. Around two years of age, the child will bend at the waist and pick up the thrown object. Children two to three years old may try to catch

10-8 At first toddlers "jump" by stepping off of low objects. Then they jump with both feet while retracting their arms to the rear instead of swinging them forward.

down. Toddlers do not change feet while climbing until after the second birthday.

There does not seem to be a set time when climbing begins. Climbing ability is related to the kinds of stairs the baby has nearby. Babies can climb more easily if the stairs are not too steep. Climbing is also related to courage. A courageous baby is likely to try climbing sooner than a more timid baby.

Throwing and catching. Infants begin throwing accidentally. They simply forget to hold onto an object while swinging their arms. Because they enjoy seeing the object move and

10-9 Toddlers squat to pick up thrown objects until they are about two years old.

by standing in one position with arms extended and elbows stiff. The ball must be exactly on target if the child is to catch it, because the child does not move toward the ball. In fact, many young children close their eyes as the ball comes toward them.

Small-muscle development

Small-muscle development refers to the development of small muscles, especially those of the hands and fingers. Sometimes the voluntary movements that depend mainly on these muscles are called fine motor skills. Fine motor skills also depend on a child's level of *eye-hand coordination*. In other words, children must be able to coordinate what they see with the way they move their hands. As eye-hand coordination and small muscles improve, toddlers can handle more complex fine motor skills.

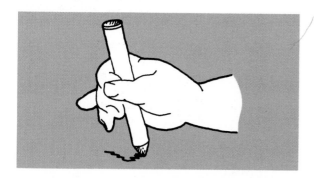

10-10 Toddlers can hold crayons with thumb and fingers, but the grasp is much more awkward than in the mature grasp.

By the end of the first year, babies can hold objects between the thumb and index finger. This makes many new fine motor activities possible. Between 12 and 18 months, toddlers can hold spoons in their fists. They can feed themselves and drink from cups. They may miss their mouths by a little and drop or spill food at first. But with practice and improved eye-hand coordination, toddlers become better at feeding themselves. They also can make marks on paper by holding pencil or crayon in fist. Other skills of the toddler at this age include removing hat and shoes, inserting rather large objects into holes, and turning pages of a book several at a time.

Between 18 months and two years, fine motor skills become even better. By this stage, toddlers can string large beads on cords. They can turn the pages of books one at a time. And they can open doors by turning knobs. Most two-year-olds can hit pegs with a hammer.

After two years, many children hold crayons or pencils with thumb on one side and finger or fingers on the other side. See 10-10. But they still cannot hold or write with a crayon or pencil the way that an adult can.

By two years, most children show a definite hand preference. But they still switch hands alot. They tend to use the right hand for drawing or throwing a ball and the left hand for holding a cup and eating. With each passing year until ages seven or eight, more and more children use the right hand for most activities. At that time 95 percent of all children are right-handed. (This is the same percentage as found among adults.)

to Know

eye-hand coordination . . .
large-muscle development . . .
muscle development . . .
small-muscle development

to Review

Write your answer on a separate sheet of paper.

1. A person's height and the rate of increase in height is mainly due to _____ (heredity, environment). A person's weight and the rate of increase in weight is mainly due to _____ (heredity, environment).

2. True or false. The rate of growth slows after 12 months and the rate remains the same from that time until 35 months.

3. The fastest organ to develop is the:
   a. Heart.
   b. Brain.
   c. Liver.
   d. Lungs.

4. Give three possible reasons why babies might start walking after their first birthdays instead of before their first birthdays.

5. Explain why toddlers may fall if they do not think about what they are doing as they walk. _Because of the unknown + insecurity._

6. Match the toddler's motor action to the skills by putting the correct letter before the skill.

   Skills
   _f_ Walking.
   _b_ Running.
   _a_ Jumping.
   _d_ Climbing.
   _e_ Throwing.
   _c_ Catching.

   Motor Actions
   a. Moves arms toward the back.
   b. Uses improper arm actions and cannot stop or start quickly.
   c. Stands without moving with arms extended in a stiff fashion.
   d. Begins each movement with the same foot rather than changing feet.
   e. Shows little or no weight shift.
   f. Steps forward, backward, and to either side.

7. True or false. Because year-old babies can grasp objects between the thumb and index finger, they hold flatware and crayons the same way that adults hold them.

to Do

1. As a group or class project, write a one-page or two-page brochure explaining motor skills of the toddler. Include information on the order (and approximate age) when motor skills are learned. Also explain the motor actions seen in walking, running, jumping, climbing, throwing, and catching. Illustrations may help. The brochure should be checked by your teacher before making copies. Copies could be given to a local program serving toddlers such as a day care program or nursery school for parents' and other adults' use.

2. Observe the motor skills (both large-muscle and small-muscle) of toddlers between 12 and 35 months of age. Make notes on the kinds of movements they make and how they compare to adult movements. Share your findings with the class.

3. Play catch with a toddler. Use a soft rubber, foam, or cloth ball about six inches in diameter. Notice the skills that the toddler uses. How far can the toddler throw a ball? How straight is the aim? Does the toddler use an over-hand or under-hand throw? Is there a weight shift? How does the toddler stand to catch the ball? Does the toddler move toward the ball if the ball is a little off target? Does the toddler drop the ball? Describe your findings in class.

not ready
physical
handicap
no need

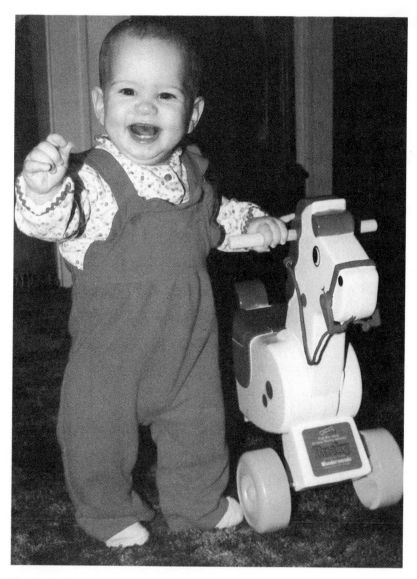

Physical changes make walking and pulling
objects possible for toddlers.

JOHN SHAW

Toddlers love to learn about the world around them.

11

Intellectual development of the toddler

After studying this chapter, you will be able to:
- Describe how and what toddlers learn.
- Sequence milestones in toddlers learning the spoken language.

In past chapters, you have read about the many learnings of babies. Many of these learnings begin during the newborn stage and become much more advanced by one year of age. Along with mental development, motor skills improve greatly as babies enter the toddler stage. As toddlers begin to walk, their physical and mental worlds expand as they roam and explore much more on their own.

Past learning combined with advanced motor skills seem to make toddlers eager learners. Toddlers have uninhibited curiosity about anyone or anything, 11-1. They may not always work hardest to learn what adults want them to learn. But once they decide to solve a problem, they will stay at the task through many tries until they find a solution. Some writers call children this age "scientists" because of their desire to find answers and all-out effort to solve problems.

HOW AND WHAT TODDLERS LEARN

As you read in Chapter 7, Piaget has described how the way that children think changes as they mature. The first stage, which includes children from birth until around two years of age, is called the sensorimotor stage. In this

11-1 Toddlers explore everything including waste cans.

stage, children learn through their senses and motor actions. After one year of age, most toddlers are in the last two substages of sensorimotor intelligence, 11-2. Toward the end of the second year, toddlers may move into the next major stage of intelligence, the *preoperational stage.* (Because children are in the preoperational stage for about five years, this stage is discussed in Chapter 15.)

Substage v: discovering new ways to solve problems (12 to 18 months)

Substage v is seen when very young children actively seek *new* things and *new* ways to explore. Piaget called the main learnings in this substage *tertiary circular reactions.* Tertiary refers to the third level of actions. At this level, the child shows interest in the newness of actions. Circular means that the actions are repeated.

Unlike the earlier behaviors seen in primary circular reactions (substage ii) and in secondary circular reactions (substage iii), tertiary circular reactions differ in two main ways.

First, tertiary circular reactions involve a goal. Before this stage, the baby behaved just

to be behaving. For instance, the baby would swing a toy by its string back and forth many times without any goal in mind. In substage v, the child has a goal in mind. The goal may be very obvious to the adult. For instance, the child may pull an object by its string in order to grasp the object. Or the goal may not be so obvious at first. It may seem like the child is just playing with or even throwing objects. But even in playing with objects, the child is trying to see how they "work," 11-3. They want to know what happens to objects when they are rolled, shaken, thrown, or moved in other ways.

Second, tertiary circular reactions involve looking for the best ways of attaining goals. Thus, each time circular reactions are repeated, they are changed in some way.

Substage vi: beginning of thought (18 months to two years)

Around 18 months to two years of age, most children make the transition from *motoric* (action) intelligence to thinking behaviors. In other words, they think about what they do before they actually do it. These young children are

PIAGET'S STAGES OF COGNITIVE DEVELOPMENT

Stage 1: Sensorimotor Stage (Birth to 2 years)
Substage i: Practicing Reflexes (Birth to 1 month)
Substage ii: Repeating New Learnings (1 to 4 months)
Substage iii: Beginning to Control Their World (4 to 8 months)
Substage iv: Applying Learnings to Solve Complex Problems (8 to 12 months)
Substage v: Discovering New Ways to Solve Problems (12 to 18 months)
Substage vi: Beginning of Thought (18 months to 2 years)
Stage 2: Preoperational Stage (2 to 7 years)
Stage 3: Concrete Operations Stage (7 to 11 years)
Stage 4: Formal Operations Stage (11 years on)

11-2 The toddler completes the sensorimotor stage.

11-3 Children learn by playing with different objects.

not mature thinkers during this transitional period. Although children think, they think mainly in terms of actions. For instance, if you were to ask a 30-month-old child, "What is a ball?" the answer would likely be "to play with," or "to roll."

Piaget gave a good example of how adults can tell that a child is thinking. He described how he had given his daughter a matchbox with a small object inside of it. Piaget's daughter had not played with a matchbox before this time. The matchbox was opened a little. Piaget's daughter first tried to grasp the object. Then she tried to dump it out, but she saw that the object was larger than the opening. She stopped, looked at the box, opened her mouth a little and then opened her mouth wider. She then pushed open the matchbox.

While she was hesitating before acting, she was thinking about how to get the object out of the matchbox. Because thinking at this substage is still based on actions, opening and closing her mouth helped Piaget's daughter imagine what would happen if the matchbox opening were made larger.

Children also show they can think by imitating a model after the model has completed a behavior. The ability to recall a prior behavior of a model and imitate it at a later date is called *deferred imitation.* (Deferred means postponed.) Piaget described how a friend of his child had a temper tantrum at their house. The next day, his child acted out a temper tantrum. Much of a child's play at this stage is deferred imitation, 11-4.

Thinking can also be seen in the child's separation of means and ends. For instance, a child may want to reach a toy on a high shelf (end or goal) in the playroom. The child may have used a step stool in the bathroom, but not in the playroom. The child thinks about the step stool and how it works in the bathroom. The child gets the step stool and reaches the object. If the child cannot bring the step stool into the playroom, the child may use another object as a step stool. The child is thinking about the means, or ways, of achieving an end, or goal.

Thinking can be seen in hiding games, too. Children at this stage will search for objects that

11-4 Feeding one's doll the way adults feed babies is an example of deferred imitation.

Intellectual development of the toddler 195

they have not actually seen hidden. This might happen when the adult pretends to hide a toy in one place but really hides it in another. The child knows the object still exists (object permanence) and thinks about all the places where the adult could have hidden it.

Finally, adults observe the way children think when children use language. Language requires rather high level thinking skills. *Language* is a symbol system in which words are used as labels for people, objects, and ideas. But unlike other symbol systems such as pictures and gestures, words do not sound or look like the people and objects they represent.

In order to learn language, two thinking skills are used. First, children must "catch" the association between the word and the person or object. For instance, toddlers must understand that the word *milk* refers to only one of several liquids drunk from a cup. Second, children must use their memories to recall the word and its meaning when they hear the word or want to say it. The mental skill needed to understand words and to talk separates the state of infancy from early childhood. In fact, the word, "infant," comes from the Latin word *infans,* which means without speech. Language is discussed in more detail later in this chapter.

What toddlers learn is based on the major learnings of their first year. They begin to have a clearer, more complete understanding of their discoveries as infants.

Toddlers learn more about the *properties* of objects such as their color, shape, size, and texture. For instance, they begin to understand that the color red is different from the color blue. Although they may confuse colors, they can tell when two objects are the same color even if they are different shapes.

Toddlers also learn more about what will happen as they *manipulate* objects by throwing, rolling, shaking, or moving them in other ways. See 11-5. They learn that round objects will roll with a push, but flat objects will slide. They also learn that more noise is made by hitting hard objects together than by hitting soft objects together.

As toddlers learn more about objects and gain new thinking skills, they can solve every-day problems for themselves. Toddlers learn how to feed and dress themselves. They know how to open doors. They can put objects in boxes and pails. And they can find many ways to get out-of-reach objects. They may not always solve problems the way an adult would, but toddlers get the job done the best way they know how. For instance, to get a cookie on the kitchen table, toddlers may climb on a chair and reach for the cookie, or they may pull on the tablecloth until the cookie falls to them.

LANGUAGE ABILITIES

As you read in Chapter 7, learning language begins during infancy. Newborns will turn toward someone talking (while not paying special attention to other sounds) minutes after delivery. Babies react to differences in sounds during the first couple of months, and then begin babbling these sounds around six months. They understand many words and even a few sentences and may say a few words toward the end of the first year.

Learning spoken language

Spoken language develops at a faster rate between one and three years than at any other time in a person's life. Adults who are parents or who work with young children need to realize that spoken language is not easy for toddlers to learn. This is because spoken language involves *articulation* (making the sounds) and learning meanings.

Learning to articulate. Babies begin learning how to speak by crying and cooing in vowel sounds which are made with the mouth open. Although there are many more consonant sounds, the number of different consonant sounds made does not exceed the number of vowel sounds until the baby is about a year old.

Children have a more difficult time making consonant sounds than making vowel sounds. They must use more than one different action for each consonant sound they make. Each sound is formed with the lips or teeth in different parts of the mouth. Some consonants are *voiced,* or formed with the mouth and vocal chords. Other consonants are *voiceless,* or

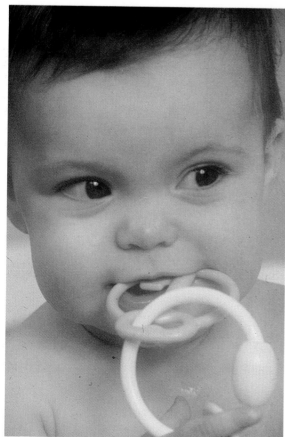

11-5 Mouthing is a major way that toddlers manipulate objects to learn about them.

CONSONANT SOUNDS ARE FORMED IN DIFFERENT WAYS

Consonants	Where/How Formed
k, g	Back of throat.
p, b, t, d	Front and top of mouth.
m, n, f, v	Lower, back part of mouth.
b	Voiced.
v	Voiceless.
ch, sh, th	Consonant combinations.
th (as in those)	Voiced consonant combination.
th (as in think)	Voiceless consonant combination.

11-6 Articulation of consonant sounds is difficult for the young child.

formed with the mouth and breath. Still others are made by combining consonant sounds. The ways in which consonant sounds are formed are shown in 11-6.

Children who cannot make a sound will use a *sound substitution*. They will replace one sound with another such as "t" for a "k." By substituting, the toddler may pronounce the word kite, "tite." Often children can articulate the right sound in one position in a word but not in another position. For instance, a toddler may have no problem pronouncing "m" at the beginning of a word such as "milk." But the toddler may have trouble making the "m" sound in the middle of a word such as "hammer" or at the end of a word such as "broom."

A few children articulate most, if not all, sounds correctly from the beginning. But most children make some substitutions. They tend to correct themselves in time. A few children require help from a trained person. (According to the norms, mastery of speech articulation occurs between the ages of three and eight years, and is thus discussed in Chapter 15.) Toddlers not only substitute a single sound, they may change the sound order of a word. For instance they may say, "perslip," to mean slipper. Toddlers may even change an entire word such as saying, "basket," to mean balcony.

Learning meanings. Without meanings attached to spoken sounds, there would be no language. Meanings attached to spoken sounds give the individual two new tools: communication and a new way to think.

Communication is the skill needed to understand others and to be understood by others. Babies begin communication by understanding a few words such as their name and the names of other special people and objects. They may even know the meanings of a few simple sentences. Babies also try to "talk to" others through crying and babbling. When they begin to say words, they want to be understood, 11-7.

Language is also a tool because it becomes part of the thinking process. In other words, people learn to think in words. As the child

Intellectual development of the toddler   197

learns to talk, words go with actions. For instance, the toddler will say "bye-bye" while waving. Later, children talk to themselves *(self-talk)* while they play or while they are in bed. Self talk often becomes whispered. And, finally, words are just thought without speaking.

Meanings are attached to words *(vocabulary or semantics)* and to the order of words *(grammar or syntax).* Young children develop both vocabulary and grammar.

The baby first uses single words before joining them into "sentences." Sometimes children hear a new word, and then try to find its meaning. But for the most part, children use the words that stand for the people and objects they know and the actions they see. Thus, children's first words are usually nouns and simple action verbs. Nouns may include words like mama, daddy, doggies, and baby. Action verbs may include hi, bye-bye, and words that describe human and animal movements, such as run and fly. The next words learned are descriptive words (adjectives and adverbs) such as big, tiny, hot, pretty, loud, and fast. Young children quickly learn words for affection, too, such as kiss or love (meaning to hold me, hug me, or kiss me).

Learning the meanings of words is not an easy task. To learn the meaning the child must see what features are associated with a name. Seeing the special features is difficult, because many objects with different names share common features. For instance, all farm animals have legs. Children may be confused about the meanings of words that they hear others say. This may cause the child to use a wrong name for an object. They may call a cow a "moo-moo" or a stove "hot." Some common problems for toddlers are *overextending* meanings, *overrestricting* meanings, and *substituting* meanings. These problems are explained in 11-8.

The norms on the number of vocabulary words a child knows at different ages vary a great deal. Different norms are used depending on whether all spoken words are counted or whether only words used with their correct meanings are counted. Children will often use words for awhile, drop them, and pick them up again months later. Regardless of the norms, the size of the vocabulary can be very different among children by three years of age. Most children's vocabularies grow very slowly until 18 months to two years of age. The fastest growth occurs around 30 months of age.

Learning meanings of word order or grammar is more difficult than learning meanings of single words. In all cultures, children learn the rules of word order long before they can explain the rules. For instance, children can use the possessive case (Jane's books) before they know that using an apostrophe with nouns and some pronouns indicates the possessive case.

THE TOOL OF COMMUNICATION

Purposes of Communication	Examples
Desire to achieve a goal.	"Want cookie." (I want a cookie.) "Go bye-bye." (I want to ride in the car.) "No!" (I don't want _____ .)
Identify object.	"See doggie." (I see a dog.) "Big!" (That is big.) "Whatdat?" or "What zat?" (What is that?)
Create a bond with another.	"Mommy?" (Where are you, Mommy? I want you.) "Kiss." (I love you.) "Hurt." (Please help me or please feel sorry for me.)

11-7 Young children communicate to meet their needs.

From one year until 18 months of age, babies use one-word "sentences" called *holophrases*. A single word is often used by the toddler to mean different ideas at different times. For instance, the word bye-bye may be used to identify a moving object (a car), to make a request ("Let's go!"), and to show rejection ("I don't want _____!"). To understand the meanings of holophrases, the adult must note the way the word is said, gestures that accompany the word, and what is happening at the time.

After 18 months, many children begin combining two or more words to form sentences. At the early stage of combining words, toddlers use *telegraphic sentences*. Children use only the most necessary words (just as in a telegram) to form this kind of sentence. Telegraphic sentences begin with the *duo sentence* (two-word sentence) often used by 18-month-old toddlers. By 24 to 30 months, many toddlers begin to speak in *multiple-word sentences* (sentences with three or more words). When the child begins to use multiple-word sentences, the words that are added fill in the gaps of the telegraphic sentence. "Allgone milk" becomes "Milk is gone" or "My milk is gone." By the time the child is using three-word sentences, the word-order of very simple statements is often correct such as "Bird is flying" rather than "Fly bird."

Different rates of learning to talk

As is true of other areas of development, the rate of language development varies more than the sequence of skills among toddlers. Many adults fret about a "slow" talker only to see an almost non-stop talker a few months later. These toddlers were hearing the sounds and learning the meanings all along. When they begin talking they seemed to progress quickly.

Differences in rates of learning to talk can vary by more than a few months. Experts do not have all the answers to explain the reasons for such great differences in rates. They have found some conditions that affect the rate of learning. Talking depends on such factors as:
- Hearing. Clearly hearing human speech is needed for learning to talk without special training. Even ear infections can delay speech in toddlers.
- Interest. Some active toddlers are more interested in motor skills than talking. (They often "catch-up" with earlier talkers quickly.)
- Mental abilities. Because language is so closely related to thinking, a mentally handicapped child is often slower to talk. On the other hand, early talking does not mean that a child is bright. Children of average and even below average mental abilities may begin speech at an early age simply by repeating what they hear.

COMMON VOCABULARY PROBLEMS OF YOUNG CHILDREN

Problems	Examples
Overextending Referring to different objects by the same name if the features are the same or almost the same.	Call all round or roundish objects, "ball." Use words, "all gone" for food that has been eaten, people or objects not seen, or someone who has left the house.
Overrestricting Using a general term to mean a specific person or object.	Use the term, "dog," for their own pet dog, not for the class of dogs.
Substituting Using a known word in the wrong way because they cannot recall or say the correct word.	May say, "cow," to refer to all farm animals, but when asked, can point to the "cow," "horse," "sheep," and "pig."

11-8 Learning the meanings of words is difficult, and all children have problems.

• Need for speech. Some children get what they need without speech. For instance, if a toddler gets milk by pointing, getting a cup, or crying, there is no need to learn the word "milk" or the sentence "I want milk."
• Interesting environment. Just as adults have more to say when they have new experiences, so do toddlers. See 11-9. (See Chapter 12 for some ideas to aid language growth.)
• Sex of toddler. From the first year of life, girls tend to excel in verbal skills more than boys. Researchers do not know whether this is true because of genetic or environmental reasons. (For instance, adults may talk to girl toddlers more than to boys.)

The rate of language development may lag far behind the norms in some cases. In these situations, adults should get professional help. Each child needs the best opportunity possible to develop language, because language is important to mental development and social-emotional development.

11-9 Toddlers talk about their world of toys and activities.

to Know

articulation . . . communication . . .
deferred imitation . . . duo sentence . . .
grammar . . . holophrase . . . language . . .
manipulate . . . multiple-word sentence . . .
properties . . . overextending . . . overrestricting . . .
self-talk . . . sound substitution . . .
substituting . . . telegraphic sentence . . .
tertiary circular reaction . . . vocabulary . . .
voiced . . . voiceless

to Review

Write your answers on a separate sheet of paper.

1. Which of the following statements describes toddlers' learnings?
   a. Toddlers have a real desire to learn about their world.
   b. Toddlers prefer to solve their own tasks, not the tasks adults plan for them.
   c. Toddlers will often try many times to solve their tasks.
   d. Toddlers learn using their past learnings and their increased motor skills.
   e. All of the above statements are true.

2. True or false. Toddlers think of several possible ways to solve a problem when using "tertiary circular reactions" as described by Piaget.

3. In the transition between Piaget's sensorimotor and preoperational stages, problem solving is achieved by:
   a. Thinking on an abstract level.
   b. Trying out all possible answers physically.
   c. Thinking in terms of physical actions.
   d. Watching an adult and copying the adult's action.

4. True or false. Toddlers use their thinking skills to solve many practical problems in their world.

5. Replacing one sound with another sound such as saying "wed wabbit" instead of "red rabbit" is _____ (common, not common) among toddlers.

6. Name the two new tools that a toddler has once meanings are attached to spoken sounds.

vocabulary + grammar

7. In the following pairs of words, which would the toddler probably learn to say first?
   a. Happy.   a. Bye-bye.   a. Kitty.
   b. Daddy.   b. Empty.   b. Pretty.

8. Most toddlers follow the same order in learning grammar. Number the following types of sentences in the order that toddlers use them.
   _2_ Telegraphic sentence.
   _1_ Holophrase.
   _3_ Multiple-word sentence.

9. When toddlers use telegraphic sentences, they leave out the _____ (most, least) important words.

10. Describe three reasons why children may be late talkers.

No need. Physical +/or mental handicap Not ready

to Do

1. Choose one student to read H.A. Rey's *Curious George* (Scholastic Book Services) to the class. (*Curious George* can be found in most libraries containing children's books.) Discuss how curiosity is a motivator and how curiosity can lead to "trouble."

2. Keep a record of a toddler exploring his or her world 30 minutes per day for one week. While observing, note answers to the following questions: What senses were used? What were some of the possible learnings? How do toddlers act around objects that most adults find boring (such as an empty box)?

3. Make a poster describing in words and/or drawings the toddler's learnings between 12 and 24 months as stated by Piaget.

4. Try Piaget's matchbox experiment on a toddler who is between 12 and 17 months and another toddler who is between 18 and 24 months. Test each toddler separately. Place an object inside of a matchbox. leave the matchbox open just a little, but do not open the matchbox wide enough to permit the object to fall through the box. How do the toddlers solve the problem? For instance, did the younger toddler shake the box or tip it from side to side? Did the older toddler try to remove the object through the narrow opening, and then push the box open further?

JOHN SHAW

Many new emotions and interactions with
people are part of the toddler stage.

12

Social-emotional development of the toddler

After studying this chapter, you will be able to:
- Describe how toddlers achieve a self-will.
- Explain the way that toddlers extend their social relationships with others.
- Describe how toddlers develop a sense of importance.
- Identify how toddlers reveal their emotions.

Most babies begin life surrounded by a few people and objects that seem to meet all their needs. Because babies' needs are rather simple at this time, most are quickly met. And, when their needs are met, babies become very attached to their caregivers and learn to trust their world.

As babies move toward toddlerhood two changes happen. First, toddlers begin to express a need to find out more about their worlds and about themselves as distinct individuals. Second, as toddlers find out more about their world, they find that it is not solely devoted to meeting their needs. Toddlers learn that caregivers cannot always be there when toddlers want something, 12-1. But if love and trust are deeply rooted by the end of the first year, toddlers will reach out in their new world. They will learn much about themselves and others. Toddlers will begin to meet some of their needs without always depending on caregivers. And they will show emotions to others and learn how people respond to those emotions.

SELF-AWARENESS

By the time babies have had their first birthday, they have rather highly developed physical and mental skills. They are no longer totally dependent on adults to carry them or push them in a stroller. They can move around by themselves and get objects that they want. They are also developing language. Language is a powerful tool for getting what they want from adults. These fast-paced and ever-growing skills influence the toddlers' relationships with others. In turn, the ways in which others react to them affects how toddlers feel about themselves.

Autonomy

As you read in Chapter 8, Erikson has described social-emotional development in terms of stages in which each person must complete certain tasks. If a person completes the tasks in a healthy way, the person becomes even better able to cope with present and future conflicts. But if hurtful conditions arise in any of these stages, there will be problems in present and future stages.

Erikson stated that the roots of all social-emotional development begin in infancy when the baby learns to trust or mistrust. Those babies whose needs are met develop a sense of trust. This sense of trust aids them as they enter the second period, "autonomy versus shame and doubt." See 12-2.

Autonomy is a form of self-control in which a toddler seeks to develop his or her own will. Autonomy does not mean total freedom. (Even adults do not have total freedom.) Erikson used the term autonomy to mean a child's feeling that he or she can do some things without the help of others. For most toddlers, this stage begins sometime between the twelfth and eighteenth month. The stage is not completed until about three years of age. It often begins so gradually that adults may not see what is happening. They may not know that the child is gaining autonomy until the child yells "No!" or perhaps rebels physically to an adult's request. The adult may wonder why the child who behaved so well suddenly yells or kicks when told what to do.

The reason for the change is rather simple. Toddlers have developed many new skills. They want to test those skills to the limit and to do so by themselves. While trying new ways to use

JOHN SHAW

12-1 Toddlers often feel that they should receive most, if not all, the attention of their caregivers.

skills and exploring new places, they get into everything. Adults may see problems or even danger, but the toddler doesn't always understand. The toddler with a sense of autonomy tries to tell adults, "I want to do this on my own." More importantly, they feel, "I want to do it in my own way and when I choose to do it." Because much of the toddlers world centers around routines, there are many conflicts over eating, sleeping, toileting, and dressing, 12-3.

The toddlers' desires to do activities for themselves are often greater than their abilities. Some of the activities that toddlers want to do are unsafe. Other desires of the toddler are not within reason (by adult standards) at a given time. For example, a working mother may not be able to wait for a toddler to decide how shoes go on toe first. Even when allowed to try on their own, toddlers want quick results—which they rarely get. Defeat from any source—adult's will or toddlers' lack of skill—

Basic Trust versus Basic Mistrust (First Year of Life)
Autonomy versus Shame and Doubt (Second Year of Life) Toddlers seek some self-control (autonomy) using their increasing skills and knowledge. They seek control over whether or not to rely on others as they see fit. Autonomy learned at this stage leads to pride in one's self. Failure to achieve autonomy leads to feelings of shame in front of others and doubts about oneself.
Initiative versus Guilt (Preschool Years)
Industry versus Inferiority (Middle Childhood)

12-2 Seeking autonomy while avoiding shame and doubt is a major social-emotional task for the toddler.

JOHN SHAW

12-3 A conflict of wills between toddler and adult often occurs during daily routines such as eating.

brings negative outbursts from the toddler.

Adults may find it hard to help the toddler achieve autonomy while keeping the toddler safe and preventing conflicts. Erikson feels that adults should be firmly reassuring to the toddler. Adults do not need to give in to the child's will all the time. But when they confront a child, they should keep calm and assure the child that they still love him or her. This way, adults can protect the child from harm without making the child feel shameful or guilty. Chart 12-4 gives some example do's and don'ts for helping the toddler in this stage.

Extending social relations

The motor and mental abilities of one-year-olds increase their chances to interact with others. By two years of age, toddlers spend one-fifth of their waking time in social activities. Through children's interactions with others, they gain skills, knowledge, tastes, and goals. They learn many other skills that help them get along with family members and other social groups, such as self-control and concern for others. In turn, children affect adults and other children as they interact. The process of learning all these skills and attitudes is called *socialization*.

Babies begin their socialization with the main caregivers, who are usually the parents. But for healthy socialization, children need to interact with others. About the time toddlers are securely attached to their main caregivers, toddlers must take the first steps toward separation.

In one way, separation is a rather natural process. As toddlers explore their worlds alone,

Social-emotional development of the toddler 205

DOs	DON'Ts
• Make sure toddler areas for play and care are safe. (See Chapter 24.)	• Don't warn or threaten the toddler constantly.
• Decide on some limits for the toddler. Consistently follow through on the limits by seeing that the toddler does as told in these areas every time.	• Don't make everything off limits for the toddler.
• Permit the toddler to make a few decisions such as whether to have a second helping of peas, whether to play with a truck or paint, or whether to go with Daddy on errands or stay home with Mommy.	• Don't punish the toddler for something one time, but not another. Rather than setting no limits and then punishing when accidents occur, let the toddler know what is off limits.
• Allow the toddler to make mistakes without scolding or criticizing. Toddlers will break things, have toileting accidents, and clutter the house even when trying to cooperate.	• Don't make all decisions for the toddler. • Don't make demands that are too rigid for a toddler to follow or scold and criticize every time the toddler makes a mistake.
• Let the child play in safe places with safe toys in his own way. Erikson sees play as the "safe island" or the "harbor" where children develop autonomy.	• Don't tell the child exactly how to play such as "build your castle in the middle of your sand box" or "put this block on top of this one."
• Praise the toddler for progress toward autonomy.	• Don't couple praise with criticism such as, "You put your shoes on; that's good, but they're on the wrong feet."

12-4 Adults should permit the toddler to explore and make mistakes within adult-set limits.

they choose to spend more time away from their caregivers. Toddlers have a better grasp of the concept of object permanence than they did as infants. This helps assure toddlers that their parents are not gone forever when their parents are out of sight. Increased verbal skill also helps toddlers when parents leave, because parents can explain with words that they will return.

Although many factors reduce separation anxiety in toddlers, leaving parents is still difficult at times. Toddlers continue to be dependent on their main caregivers for social interaction. But toddlers who have a healthy attachment to caregivers have a safe base from which to meet people, 12-5.

As toddlers spend more time away from main caregivers, they learn how to interact with other adults. These may include babysitters, relatives, and neighbors. Parents can help toddlers by not rushing them to meet new adults. They can also help by sharing caregiving tasks. Toddlers who have had more than one main caregiver sometimes find it easier being with other adults than toddlers who are cared for almost exclusively by one adult, such as the mother. When both father and mother have shared in caregiving, toddlers have a wider span of trust in adults, 12-6. They also see and learn to expect differences among people.

Other children are also important to a child's socialization. Babies usually show interest in other children before their first birthday. When babies see each other, they often smile and wave

12-5 Mothers often serve as the security base from which toddlers explore new experiences and new people.

COSCO/PETERSEN

12-6 Fathers widen the span of trust and security toddlers find in caring adults.

their arms. But infants still prefer adults.

During the second year, toddlers tend to separate more from adults and interact with other children. Toddlers' first interactions are brief. They often involve imitating each other's actions with a toy. Later, talking becomes part of the interaction.

Toddlers are possessive about their toys and other belongings when they play. They simply have not learned how to share, 12-7. Between the ages of 30 and 36 months, toddlers become very skillful in keeping their possessions.

Some recent studies show that toddlers are not as *egocentric,* or self-centered, as experts once thought. Toddlers are known to share sometimes. They may return a snatched toy if the owner cries. They praise other children. And they show much concern for the feelings of someone who is hurt. When toddlers have loving relations with their caregivers, they seem better able to extend concern for other children.

Self-esteem

As you read in Chapter 8, young babies seem to sense how others feel about them by the way

COMMUNITY PLAYTHINGS, RIFTIN, NY

12-7 Until the rules of sharing are learned, toddlers fight to keep possession of their toys.

they are spoken to and held. Babies become more aware of themselves as they approach their first birthday. They enjoy hearing their names and looking at themselves in the mirror.

When toddlers begin to strive for autonomy, they want others to accept the fact that they are individuals, 12-8. This is the stage in which children really start to learn about themselves. They begin to learn who they are and what they are able to do. When adults accept the stubborn feelings of toddlers and meet these feelings with kind firmness, toddlers develop *self-esteem.* Self-esteem is the belief that one is worthwhile as a person. However, if adults always scold toddlers, then toddlers will think of their desires to be themselves as getting them into trouble. Constant shaming may make toddlers feel that they are beyond being loved. Toddlers must feel loved even when they make mistakes if they are to have good mental health.

When toddlers feel good about themselves, they seem to admire themselves and their growing control over their bodies. They may even spend much time in front of the mirror admir-

JOHN SHAW

12-8 This toddler is building her self-esteem by carrying her own lunchbox.

208

12-9 Touching a mirror image is one way toddlers say to themselves, "I'm special."

ing themselves, 12-9. They like to show off their physical feats for others. They will often clap for themselves and laugh with glee at their new skills.

Toddlers learn a great deal about their bodies and what their bodies can do. Some concepts are still hard for many toddlers to understand. They can name some body parts. They also know that they can see, hear, touch, taste, and smell. But they may not know the sensory organ that controls each sense (such as eyes for seeing). Toddlers seem to have little awareness of their own weight. They will throw themselves at other people and pets or even try to walk a cardboard plank! Toddlers feel body pain. But unless they can see the cause of pain such as a cut, scrape, or burn, they cannot tell someone what hurts. A toddler with a throat infection may even deny having a sore throat! More advanced body concepts develop in later stages.

EMOTIONS

Very young babies seem to have mainly two emotional states: general excitement and general stress. After six months, babies express the emotions of love, fear, anxiety, and anger. Toddlers' growing mental abilities seem to result in these four general changes in emotions:

1. Toddlers react to a wider range of stimuli than infants. They know about more people to love and more things and people to fear.
2. Toddlers can better sense emotions in others. A newborn cries upon hearing the cry of another baby. Older babies respond to crying and smiling. Toddlers can detect fear in adults. They may even sense that something is wrong when adults are anxious. Toddlers respond to emotions in other children, 12-10. Toddlers can imitate emotions in others, too.

Social-emotional development of the toddler 209

3. Toddlers have a wider range of responses to feeling. A young baby develops many types of cries as signals of stress. Older babies not only cry, but smile, laugh, hug, and cling as ways of showing their feelings. Toddlers' motor skills allow them more physical responses. They can run or hide when fearful, hit or kick when angry, and so on. The toddler's ability to talk allows a verbal response. Even the single word "No!" shows feelings.

4. Toddlers' abilities to imagine increase the number of hard to deal with emotions such as fear of the dark and fear of monsters. Toddlers cannot totally separate the real from the pretend world. But emotions caused by imagination are just as real as the feelings they may have when a prized toy is broken.

Affection

Toddlers are still very attached to the adults who care for them. They express affection for their caregivers by wanting to be near them. They seek caregivers when faced with a strange situation. Attachment to adults seems to aid other aspects of social-emotional development. Toddlers' affection for loving caregivers seem to extend to other adults, children, and pets. See 12-11.

Fears

Many fears which began during infancy are seen well after the first birthday. (A few fears which began early in life are seen in normal adults such as jerking upon hearing a loud noise.) Fears increase very quickly after two years of age. This is because toddlers know about more things to fear than babies. Tod-

ELAINE WOOD/SACUS

12-10 Toddlers sense and respond to emotions in other children.

JOHN SHAW

12-11 Hugging a pet helps toddlers learn to love and care for others.

dlers know of more objects and situations that can hurt them. They also can imagine things that do not exist such as monsters. Before children begin to outgrow fears of imagined creatures, one-fifth of all fears tend to be of this kind. See 12-12. Toddlers may also be afraid of animals, darkness, nightmares, "bad people," injury, and gestures or noises made to frighten them.

Instead of talking about their fears, toddlers tend to act them out in play. It is common to see a 30-month-old child who is afraid of a dog barking and growling in play. Toddlers may imitate "bad people" seen on television or in books, too.

For the most part, fears should be handled in a rather matter-of-fact way by the adult. Toddlers should never be teased about their fears or pushed into frightening situations. Adults may want to keep toddlers from some frightening activities such as watching scary movies.

Anxiety

As you have read in Chapter 8, anxiety begins around eight months as babies show separation anxiety. Separation anxiety continues into the toddler stage and sometimes beyond, 12-13. For instance, toddlers and even older children may cry when left at a day care program or at school. Many toddlers will begin to overcome some of their separation anxieties if they feel certain their caregivers love them

12-12 Toddlers are fearful of monsters and other unnatural creatures that exist in their minds.

Social-emotional development of the toddler 211

12-13 Being separated from caring adults still causes anxiety in the toddler stage.

Anger

Babies show some anger around ten months of age. Anger increases during the toddler years. Sudden emotional outbursts of anger, called *temper tantrums,* often appear during the second year of life. Tantrums tend to happen when things don't go according to toddlers' plans. Since this is often the case, temper tantrums and toddlers seem to go together. Temper tantrums are done mainly to get attention. Often they are not directed at anyone. The child may lie down in the middle of the floor or on the sidewalk and kick and scream. Because temper tantrums are done for attention, ignoring the toddler may get him or her to stop. The toddler does need reassurance and love after the tantrum is over, 12-14. There is not much planned anger directed toward others until the child is three years of age.

and will return. Parents can help by telling toddlers about each separation shortly before it occurs and assuring them of their return. They can also make sure their toddler receives good and loving care during separations.

Nightmares may begin around two years of age. These are displays of other kinds of anxiety. Nightmares may stem from anxieties due to fear of being left alone, of getting hurt, or of causing the anger of adults. The details of the nightmare are very unreal. Unknown lands and monsters are often included. For toddlers who are content during the day, nightmares do not reveal a problem. In fact, nightmares are a way of dealing with anxieties. For most people, nightmares decrease in time.

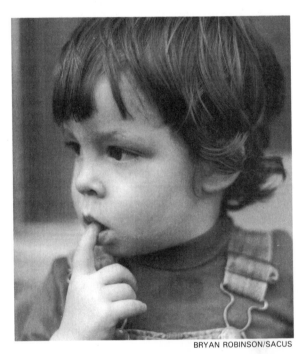

BRYAN ROBINSON/SACUS

12-14 Toddlers often feel alone and perhaps unloved after a temper tantrum.

to Know

autonomy . . . egocentric . . . self-esteem . . .
socialization . . . temper tantrum

to Review

Write your answers on a separate sheet of paper.

1. True or false. Toddlers find their world almost solely devoted to meeting their needs the way toddlers want them met.

2. True or false. Adults' reactions to toddlers' explorations affect how toddlers feel about themselves.

3. Feelings of love and trust between adults and toddlers make toddlers _____ (more, less) likely to explore and get into things.

4. Which of the following pairs are true about autonomy? Autonomy:

a. begins gradually or begins suddenly.

b. is expressed only physically or is expressed physically and verbally.

c. often happens during new activities or often happens during routines.

d. often involves working at their ability level or often involves trying to work beyond their ability level.

5. List three "do's" for adults that will help the toddler develop autonomy rather than shame and doubt.

6. Separation from main caregivers is not aided by:

a. Natural exploration of the toddler.

b. Sharing in caregiving and showing affection to the toddler.

c. Insisting the toddler play alone much more often.

d. Letting other children play with the toddler.

7. Shaming toddlers for their mistakes _____ (is, is not) harmful to the self-esteem.

8. Toddlers' sense of self-esteem is mainly centered around their awareness of their _____ (physical, mental) abilities.

9. What four general changes in emotion occur during the toddler stage?

10. List three fears that are common to toddlers.

11. How should adults react to toddlers' temper tantrums?

to Do

1. Interview one or more parents about ways that their toddlers showed autonomy. (Most parents have amusing stories.) Ask how they gave their toddlers some freedom with some control.

2. We know that toddlers admire themselves in mirrors and clap about their new abilities. Have a class discussion on how adults admire themselves and whether or not self admiration is good.

3. A few writers have referred to toddlers as "terrible twos." Write an essay explaining the following two points: (a) Why would people use this term to describe toddlers? (b) Why is this term not accurate?

4. Observe toddlers in a group care situation. Make notes on how toddlers show autonomy. Under what conditions did adults prevent toddlers from carrying through with their goals? What were the toddlers' reactions?

5. Role play a situation in which a toddler fears the dark and unseen things that loom in the closet and behind the dresser. Have one student play the toddler and one or two students play the parent or parents trying to cope with the toddler's fears.

Although toddlers still need care, they are
beginning to learn to be independent.

13

Providing for the toddler's developmental needs

After studying this chapter, you will be able to:

▢ Plan special ways to meet the developmental needs of toddlers.

▢ Care for toddlers' physical needs.

▢ Stimulate toddlers' growing mental abilities.

▢ Aid toddlers as they begin to adjust to their first social controls.

Toddlers continue to develop at a rapid rate during the years between their first and third birthdays. Toddlers are still dependent on adults to provide for their needs. During these years, toddlers begin learning some self-care skills such as self-feeding, self-dressing, and toileting. They will even help with washing their hands and bathing.

Intellectual abilities seem to blossom at this age. Toddlers learn to use language as a way of talking with others and as an aid to thinking. Toddlers' growing concepts are mainly learned through daily routines in the home. The concepts are then practiced in play.

Toddlers have many social-emotional needs. They are often trying to cope with the desire to do things on their own only to find some things are just too difficult for little bodies and immature minds. Toddlers need loving adults who understand their wills. Adults need to allow some freedoms. They need to praise toddlers when skills are achieved. And they need to "pick up the pieces" when toddlers can't manage.

Many needs can be met by providing activities. Activities and games that meet toddlers' specific needs are listed at the end of this chapter.

PHYSICAL NEEDS

Physical needs must be met so that toddlers will be healthy and safe. Meeting physical needs also helps keep toddlers mentally and socially fit. Providing for physical needs during the toddler years includes seeing that toddlers are fed, clothed, rested, and clean. But it also includes guiding some self-care skills involved in self-feeding, self-cleaning, and toileting. As toddlers learn self-care skills they begin to meet their own physical needs. Self-care skills also help toddlers advance in mental and social-emotional development.

Feeding

Many changes take place in the child's food and eating experiences during the toddler years. Toddlers graduate from the bottle and baby foods to table foods. Adult feeding is stopped in favor of self-feeding. Also, toddlers often join the family for meals rather than being fed at other times.

Eating style of toddlers. A toddler tends to eat less food than a baby nearing the first birthday. Between 12 and 18 months, the toddler's *appetite* (desire for food) decreases because the rate of growth slows down. Toddlers gain only six to eight pounds between the ages of 12 and 30 months.

The eating style of toddlers also comes to include self-feeding, 13-1. Toddlers want to control their own eating. Self-feeding is made possible because the child can learn to pick up food with the fingers or spoons. However, the fine motor skills are not mature. Playing with food—including smearing it on the face, table, and wall or dropping it on the floor—is also part of self-feeding. See 13-2. The toddler is not being naughty. He or she is learning about the texture, color, ability to spread, and other qualities of food. (We will return to this topic under "Preventing feeding problems.") Self-feeding is also a way of showing independence. The self-concept at the toddler stage is mainly rooted in self-care. Thus, self-feeding aids the toddler's growing self-concept.

Meeting nutritional needs. Food intake should always meet the nutritional needs of the

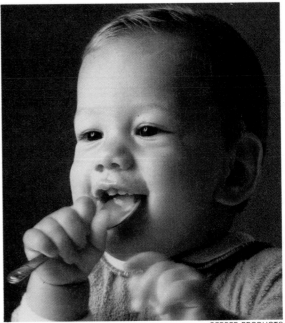

GERBER PRODUCTS

13-1 Toddlers handle spoons with an overhand palm grasp rather than the thumb and finger grasp of the adult.

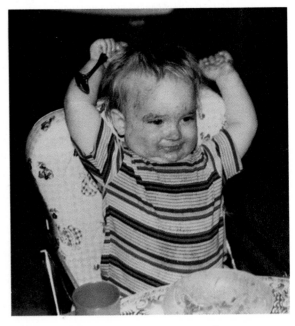

13-2 Toddlers are messy eaters because they are learning about food.

person. Toddlers eat a smaller amount of food than infants or adults. So adults need to take care that foods given toddlers are of high *nutrient density*. High nutrient density foods are high in vitamins and minerals needed for growth and repair of the body. Foods of low nutrient density provide mainly energy, not vitamins and minerals. These foods are sometimes called empty calories. Foods of low nutrient density often prevent children from eating nutritious foods by reducing appetite. Such foods also increase the chance of gaining too much weight.

Chart 13-3 gives the basic recommended food intake of toddlers. Because toddlers often have high activity levels, they may need to eat more than the amounts shown in 13-3. Some toddlers have special food needs. A physician or *registered dietitian* should plan the diets for special cases. (Registered dietitians have special training in nutrition and diet. They meet the qualifications of the American Dietetic Association.) A few foods such as popcorn, nuts, and small, hard foods should not be given to toddlers. These foods may cause choking.

Toddlers often have odd food habits. They may settle on a diet of only a few foods for days or even a few weeks. Or they may skip a meal or two and then eat as though starved a few hours later. Although these habits may concern the adult, the habits should not harm the child. Most toddlers who are provided good diets for

DAILY BASIC DIET FOR TODDLERS

Milk (4 servings)
Typical serving: 3/4 cup (180 mL) whole, reconstituted evaporated, skim, reconstituted dry, buttermilk, or yogurt;* two 3/4 inch (1.9 cm) cubes or 1 oz. (30 g) hard cheese. Part can be in cream soups, custards, or puddings.

Protein Foods (4 servings)
Typical serving: 1 oz. (30 g) cooked lean solid meat, poultry, fish; 1 egg; 1 oz. (30 g) cheese; 1/4 cup (60 mL) cottage cheese; 1 frankfurter; 1/2 cup (120 mL) cooked dry beans, peas, lentils.

Vitamin A-Rich Fruits and Vegetables (1 serving)
Typical serving: 3 tablespoons (45 g) cooked or 1/4 cooked or 1/4 cup (60 mL) raw spinach, kale, collard and other greens, broccoli, sweet potatoes, carrots, tomato, dried apricots.

Vitamin C-Rich Fruits and Vegetables (1 serving)
Typical serving: 1/4 cup (60 mL) fruit juice; 1/4 cup (60 mL) cooked or 1/3 cup (80 mL) raw oranges or grapefruit, pineapple, tangerines, papaya, strawberries, brussel sprouts, broccoli, cauliflower, collard and other greens.

Other Fruits and Vegetables (2 servings)
Typical serving: 3 tablespoons (45 g) cooked or 1/4 cup (60 mL) raw asparagus, bean sprouts, beets, cabbage, celery, cucumbers, green peppers, okra, mushrooms, string beans, squash, apples, fresh apricots, bananas, berries, grapes, watermelon, pears, figs, dates, prunes, raisins.

Cereals, whole or enriched, Potatoes, Legumes (5 servings)
Typical serving: 3/4 slice bread; 1/3 cup (80 mL) cooked rice, hot cereal, pasta, corn; 1/2 muffin, biscuit, pancake, waffle; 1-inch (2.5 cm) square cornbread; 1/2 cup (120 mL) ready-to-eat cereal; 3 tablespoons (45 g) potato; 1/3 cup (80 mL) dried beans or dried peas.

*Whole milk fortified with Vitamin D preferred

13-3 A well-balanced diet is needed to meet toddlers' growth and energy needs.

FEEDING PROBLEMS OF TODDLERS

PROBLEM:
Refuses to eat a meal or just takes a few bites.

POSSIBLE SOLUTIONS:
- Keep records of all the foods the toddler eats during the week. (The toddler may be getting enough of the needed foods.)
- Break meals up by offering part of the meal early and the rest of the meal in two or three hours.
- Make snacks high in nutritional quality.
- Eat foods of high nutritional quality. Toddlers imitate adult food habits.
- Serve small portions and let the toddler ask for seconds. Too much food can be discouraging.
- Make mealtime pleasant even when the toddler refuses to eat.

PROBLEM:
Refuses new foods.

POSSIBLE SOLUTIONS:
- Offer a taste or two of new foods on a regular basis to help the toddler to accept them over time.
- Offer only one new food at a time.
- Serve a taste or two of a new food on a plate that also has favorite foods.
- Model proper food attitudes for toddlers. For instance, saying, "Eat your spinach, it's good for you," may give the toddler the idea that spinach is a "must" but that it is not good tasting.
- Try a new way of preparing foods. For example, toddlers usually like simple foods more than mixtures (casseroles). They like raw vegetables such as raw carrots more than cooked carrots. Toddlers prefer finger foods (foods picked up with the fingers) to foods eaten with flatware. And they like less salty and spicy foods more than highly seasoned foods.
- Remain pleasant with the toddler; force feeding and anger do not work.

PROBLEM:
Shows lack of skill in self-feeding and plays with food.

POSSIBLE SOLUTIONS:
- Give the toddler time to learn how to feed. (Most children cannot hold flatware in the mature way until five years of age or older.)
- Provide a comfortable setting for eating. The correct chair provides support (so that the child is not sliding down), is the correct height, and has a place for feet to touch rather than dangle.
- Provide suitable eating equipment such as small plates (especially those with sides), small cups with handles and weighted bottoms, and baby or junior flatware (or small spoons and salad forks).
- Use a high chair or table and chair that can be easily cleaned. (Nearby floor and walls should also be easily cleaned.)
- Keep cleaning supplies handy during the meal.
- When possible, prepare foods in easy to manage form such as finger foods. ("Runny" foods, foods which must be cut, and foods which are difficult to pick up such as peas or spaghetti will be messy for the toddler.)
- Praise the toddler for successes. Never laugh at mishaps.
- Prevent playing with food by staying near the toddler during eating time and removing food once the toddler is playing more than eating.
- Be firm in saying "no" when the toddler goes too far with playing. For instance, you may say, "Balls are for throwing; food is for eating" or "I want the kitchen to stay clean; food on the floor is messy." If the toddler does not control the play, remove the food or the toddler. (Toddlers learn quickly when "eating rules" are fair and enforced.)

13-4 Feeding problems are common for toddlers.

meals and snacks will have their food needs met on a long-term basis.

Preventing feeding problems. Eating right at the toddler stage is needed for present health. But it is also important for forming life-long eating habits. Toddlers seem to have some feeding problems. Most of these stem from their stage of development—the slowing growth, the growing motor and learning skills, and the changing social needs. Some common feeding problems and suggestions for helping solve them are shown in 13-4. Most feeding problems are worked out in time by patient adults.

Clothing

Choosing the right clothes and shoes for toddlers is important. Proper clothing helps toddlers be active without being uncomfortable or unsafe. Proper clothing stands up under the strain of constant movement and sometimes messy play. Clothing gives a sense of "mine," too. And, some toddlers express personal taste through clothing. They may prefer to wear a certain color, fabric, or style of clothing. Or they may even want to wear the same garment day after day.

Choosing garments. Although toddlers grow more slowly than do infants, toddlers do outgrow their clothes rather quickly. Fit is highly important for the on-the-go toddler. Clothes that are too tight will bind and restrict movement. Clothes that are too loose are uncomfortable and perhaps unsafe. To check for fit, it is best for toddlers to try on garments. When it is not possible for the toddler to try on the garment, clothing should be chosen by measurement, not by age. Chart 13-5 shows the common sizing used for toddlers.

Quality features include safety, comfortable fabric and construction, growth features, durability, attractive style, and easy care. See Chart 13-6 for some examples of each of these features.

Toddlers enjoy clothes with cute fabric designs and other details such as buttons, zippers, pockets, and bows. Toddlers often show and tell you about these features. Adults can offer a toddler a choice between a couple of garments. (Even limited choosing gives the child practice in decision-making.)

Some adults consider *self-dressing* features in choosing clothing for the toddler. Such features make dressing and undressing without help easier. However, the toddler's interest and skill seems to be in taking clothes off, not in dressing. By eighteen months, toddlers will help by extending arms and legs while being dressed. They will also unzip zippers and remove mittens, hats, socks, and untied shoes, 13-7. A few items are designed to teach self-dressing to children under three years of age, 13-8. Adults should accept any self-dressing tried by a toddler even if it means that clothes are on backwards or fastened incorrectly. Because self-dressing becomes a more common activity from three years of age, self-dressing is covered in more detail in Chapter 17.

TYPICAL TODDLER CLOTHING SIZES

Sizes for Clothing	1T	2T	3T	4T
Height	29"-32" (72.5-80 cm)	32 1/2"-35" (81-87.5 cm)	35 1/2"-38" (89-95 cm)	38 1/2"-41" (96-102.5 cm)
Weight	23-27 lbs. (10-12 kg)	28-31 lbs. (12.6-14 kg)	32-36 lbs. (14-16 kg)	37-40 lbs. (17-18 kg)

13-5 Toddler clothes, like all clothing, should be purchased by size, not age.

IMPORTANT FEATURES IN TODDLER CLOTHES

SAFETY	COMFORT	GROWTH FEATURES	QUALITY CONSTRUCTION	EASY CARE
Fire retardant (will burn, but smolders slowly rather than flames up when on fire). No loose buttons, fasteners, or trim. Belts, ties, sashes, and drawstrings fastened to the garment securely. (Toddlers can trip, choke, or cut off circulation if these items are misused.) Bright clothing (increases ability to see toddlers).	Made of light weight and absorbent fabrics. Made of fabrics with stretch or ease qualities. Elastic encased or nonbinding. Fullness in pant legs to permit knee bending and stooping with ease. Collars and sleeves that do not rub or bind. Coats, sweaters, and jackets that can fit over clothes without binding. Underwear that is not binding. Neck openings large enough for ease of dressing.	Made of stretch fabrics. Dresses without definite waist-lines. Pants and skirts with elastic or adjustable waistbands. Adjustable shoulder straps. Clothes with deep hems, large seams, and pleats or tucks that can be easily let out. Two-piece outfits.	Reinforcement at points of strain such as seams, knees, plackets, and pocket edges. Stitches that are even and not too long. Seams that are flat, smooth, and finished. Securely attached fasteners and trims. Built-in growth features such as deep hems. Plaids, stripes, and checks matched.	Washable (especially machine washable with other colors). Little or no ironing needed. Easy to mend.

13-6 Toddlers' clothes need to have certain features.

Fitting shoes. Because the bones and muscles of the foot are developing, shoe fit is important not only for comfort but also for proper development. Permanent damage can happen when children's shoes do not fit properly. Toddlers often outgrow their shoes before they wear them out. The average rate of foot growth for two-year-olds is one change in size every three months. For children between the ages of two and three years, the rate is one change in size every four months.

The feet of the toddler are flat because the arch is relaxed. The flat-footed look disappears around three years of age. Going barefooted or wearing cozy socks without shoes is good for the development of the arch. Shoes, even high-top shoes, do not provide support. High top shoes are used because they are more difficult for the toddler to remove.

Shoes are needed to protect the walking toddler against outdoor cold and dampness and objects that can hurt the feet. Shoes that fit properly have one-half inch of space between the large toe and shoe when the toddler stands. They also have a flexible sole and a snug-fitting heel.

Rest and sleep

Toddlers' rest and sleep habits may change after infancy. Toddlers often sleep fewer hours and have fewer sleep times than babies. Chart 13-9 shows the general trend in sleep patterns.

JOHN SHAW

13-7 Removing shoes and other clothing is mastered months before learning to dress oneself.

Sleep needs of all toddlers vary some from time to time. For instance, toddlers may sleep less when under some types of stress and more than average when recovering from an illness.

AVERAGE SLEEP OF TODDLERS

Age	Night	Naps
(9 to 12 months)	(12 to 14 hours)	(1 to 4 hours, morning and afternoon)
13 to 18 months	10 to 12 hours	1 to 3 hours, afternoon
19 to 30 months	10 to 12 hours	1 to 3 hours, afternoon
31 to 36 months	10 to 15 hours	Naps beginning to disappear*

*Two-thirds of two-year-olds take a nap; 10 percent of three-year-olds take a nap.

13-9 The sleep needs of toddlers change over time.

JOHN SHAW

13-8 Simple dressing aids such as a mitten and zipper sewn in a cloth book help teach toddlers self-dressing skills.

The toddler's developmental needs 221

Age should not be used to figure how much sleep a toddler needs. Rather toddlers should be awakened at the same time each morning for about a week, and then watched to note when they become sleepy. The amount of time between the average "sleepy time" and the same "getting up" time is close to the amount of sleep needed.

Toddlers are more likely than babies to resist rest and sleep even when tired and unhappy. Bedtime problems stem partly from the toddlers' struggle for autonomy. Often adults become physically tired in trying to cope with the "night owls." Adults may even feel stress if bedtime becomes a battle of wills. These ideas may help solve problems:

- Accept the fact that adults cannot force toddlers to sleep. Resistance often disappears after the toddler years.
- Have a definite hour for bedtime. Use a neutral sign such as a clock (not a person) to signal the hour.
- Set up a nighttime (and even naptime) *ritual* (pattern). The ritual should not be hurried or drug out — perhaps an hour at night. The ritual should include only restful activities such as warm bath, a drink of water, a story, song, a bedtime prayer, and/or a hug.
- Provide a comfortable place for sleep.

- Tell toddlers who do not want to sleep that they do not have to sleep, only stay in bed. Toddlers usually accept this.
- Comfort fearful toddlers. Tell them where you'll be while they sleep. Provide a nightlight or other soft light in their room. Place a beloved stuffed animal or doll in their bed. Tell fearful toddlers that you are there to keep them safe and will check on them every 10 to 15 minutes. (Toddlers are often asleep after two or three check times, 13-10.)
- Comfort toddlers who awaken with nightmares. Do not ask them to tell you about their nightmares, because it is best to forget them. (If they want to tell you about their nightmares, listen. But assure them that these are just bad dreams.)
- Return children who get out of their beds to their beds. Meet any real needs such as a drink for a child who is thirsty, but turn down unnecessary requests or demands. Be firm, but calm. Keep the child away from where the "action is" such as where others are watching television, reading, or doing housework.

Adults' actions will determine whether toddlers learn the tricks to get what they want or learn that adults will insist on their staying in bed.

13-10 Checking on toddlers helps them feel secure enough to get needed rest and sleep.

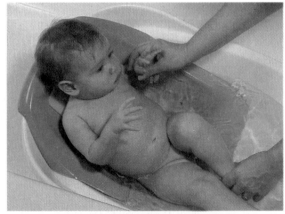

13-11 A toddler tub placed in a regular bathtub can be easily filled and drained. It is a good place for toddlers to splash.

Hygiene

One of the most important parts of hygiene for toddlers is bathing. Bathing is fun for most toddlers. Although toddlers can sit and stand easily, toddlers are not safe when left alone while bathing. Toddlers seem to feel more secure being bathed in a child's tub. The tub can be placed inside of a regular tub for easy bathing and less messy splashing, 13-11.

Toddlers may want to help a little with their bathing. A mitt-type wipe is easy for toddlers to use. It can be made by sewing three edges of two washcloths together. Most toddlers have fun trying to hold slippery soap. Some toddlers enjoy rinsing themselves with a hand held shower.

Toddlers also need some time for water play during the bath, 13-12. Toddlers not only have fun playing in water, but they learn a great deal, too. They learn that some toys float and some sink; water power can push toys; water can be held for a brief time in the cupped hand; water makes all things wet; "I" can make water splash, squirt, and drip; the bottom of the tub can be seen through the water; and soap makes bubbles. Many bath toys are sold for toddlers. Toys can also be made easily from household objects, 13-13.

Dental care is also important for toddlers. Proper diet helps teeth stay healthy. And dental checkups should begin at two years of age. But cleaning teeth regularly is also needed for dental health. In the United States, five percent of all one-year-olds and 10 percent of all two-year-olds have cavities. Around 18 months of age, toothbrushing with a child-sized brush can replace tooth wiping. Adults must brush the toddlers' teeth, 13-14. However, the toddler may "help" around 30 months of age. (Adults should supervise brushing throughout the preschool years.)

Toilet training

Toilet training is one of the most discussed aspects of toddler training. *Toilet training* is the process by which adults help children achieve control over the excretory systems, namely bowel movements and urination. Over the years adults have shifted in their timing for training. Adults have tried very early training

JOHN SHAW

13-12 Water play during the bath is fun.

13-13 Many bath toys can be made from household items.

muscles which are low in the body are among the last to develop (a good example of the cephalocaudal or head-to-tail development principle). Nerves can control these muscles around 18 months of age. (Children tend to learn to control bowel movements before they learn to control their bladders.)

4. Ability to walk (or often run) to the potty.
5. Ability to remove or push down clothes. Several layers of clothes or a one-piece jumpsuit are often hard for the toddler to manage. Some fasteners can make the task impossible.

Emotional readiness must occur at the same time the child is physically developed if toilet training is to work. Toddlers must see the need to use the potty. "On-the-go" toddlers often do not want to sit the needed time. And, saying "no" to toilet training is part of the self will which toddlers want to express. Toddlers may also need to master fears of falling in, of the flushing water, and even of the stools passed.

Procedure for toilet training. Many methods have been tried for toilet training. Although many ways can work, certain ideas are known to help the toilet training process.

(before the child is a year of age). They have permitted the child to become self-trained (the time of the child's own choosing). And they have tried every time between these extremes. Two things are certain in toilet training. First, the timing of training varies from toddler to toddler. And second, for many toddlers, total training is not completed quickly. Training may take most of the toddler years and perhaps even more time to complete.

Physical and emotional factors. Many things are involved in toilet training including physical development, motor skills, and emotional readiness. The physical and motor skills involved are these:

1. Ability to feel the sensation of a full bladder or bowel. Until about 15 months, children move their bowels and pass urine without knowing in advance or without realizing they have done so.
2. Ability to know what the sensation of needing to eliminate means in time to get to the potty.
3. Ability to control muscles used for "holding in" or "letting go." These

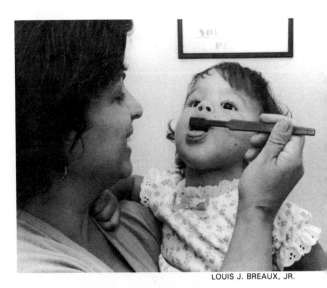

13-14 The adult must brush the toddler's teeth.

First, adults should realize that toilet training is not a one-way street. Adults cannot do toilet training to or for the toddler. Toddlers must be ready and help with their own training. Adults should also accept the fact that toddlers vary in age of complete control. The average age for complete day control is 28 months, but the normal range is very wide. There is no relationship between being a big or smart girl or boy and age of training. A rule of thumb is that a child must be able to stay dry two or more hours before the child can begin to learn.

Even before toddlers are ready for training, adults can help them see what is expected. For instance, if an adult notes the child is eliminating, he or she should say something to make the child aware of it. When a diaper gets wet or soiled, the adult should say to the child as he or she changes the diaper, "Try to tell me next time, that way we can use the toilet."

When the toddler is ready, the needed toilet training equipment should be obtained. Regular toilets are hard to use and sometimes scary. A toilet training chair designed for toddlers is the easiest to use, 13-15. There are also "chairs" which fit on standard commode seats which are made for toddlers. When standard commodes are used with or without toddler seats, a sturdy and stable platform in front of the stool is needed. (Getting on a high stool is hard and having one's legs dangle for a few minutes hurts.) Show the child the potty that will be used. Some toddlers will sit on it with their clothes on as a way of checking it out. Bathroom light switches should be within easy reach or night lights should be used.

Easy to manage clothing is a must. Many adults wait until warm weather for training because toddlers can wear fewer clothes. They can also wear easy to manage elastic-waist shorts or pants.

13-15 Toilet training chairs are easy for toddlers to use.

JOHN SHAW

The toddler's developmental needs 225

Once training begins, adults should encourage the toddler to use the toilet. But they should not put requests in moral terms such as, "Be a good boy (or girl) and use the potty." Toddlers should be taken to the toilet at set times until they go on their own. Before and after meals, before and after sleep times, and every two hours are recommended. Children will need to be reminded to use the toilet for many years after they are trained.

Adults need to accept success and failure in a matter-of-fact way. Some praise is needed, but too much praise adds to the pressure to achieve the next time. Adults should not let failures make children feel bad or little. They should stop training during illness or if a child shows signs of stress. Using diapers during sleep times or when away from home for long periods of time makes training less stressful.

No matter how much care is taken, there will be accidents. Being prepared helps prevent accidents from causing too much stress for toddlers or adults. *Training pants* (pants which have a multi-layered cotton fabric crotch) help lessen the mess of accidents. Household cleaning products should be ready for cleaning accidents.

The point of toilet training is to help children handle their elimination needs in the way our society expects—cleanly, without help, and without fuss. Complete training is a long process.

Indoor and outdoor spaces

Toddlers still enjoy being near adults and other children for most of their waking hours. But between the second and third birthday, many toddlers begin playing more and more on their own. They begin to play with more toys. And they need a place where they can rest and sleep without being disturbed. Thus, many families plan indoor and outdoor play spaces and bedrooms for their toddlers.

Bedrooms and play spaces must be safe. (See Chapter 24 for safety tips.) And, if possible, these areas should fit toddlers' needs for play, rest, and learning self-help skills. Open floor and yard space helps active play. A cozy chair, a fuzzy throw rug, a corner area, and a bed of

one's own are examples of quiet places. Self-help features include low shelves for toys, low hooks for a coat or sweater, a sturdy footstool for climbing one step, and light switches within reach.

Special furniture and room decorations are nice for toddlers, too. Furniture designed for toddlers is often made smaller than other furniture. It also may be brightly painted. Bedspreads, window coverings, wallpaper, floor coverings, lamps, and night lights can have designs that the toddler will like. Wall hangings and pictures can be chosen with the toddler in mind, 13-16. Even a few of the toddler's toys or books on display can make the room or area special.

INTELLECTUAL NEEDS

For the most part, toddlers learn as they are involved in daily activities. They learn as they are eating, bathing, dressing, "helping" with household tasks, and going on errands with adults. Adults should take advantage of everyday activities to help toddlers learn. For instance, during meals alone toddlers can learn much. They can talk with others at the table (language learnings). They can see, taste, smell, and feel foods with their many colors, shapes, sizes, textures, and odors (sensory learnings). They can make some choices about the foods and amounts of each that they want (decision-making). Toddlers can handle finger foods and flatware (motor skills). They hear comments such as "food helps us grow and become strong" (a nutrition lesson). And they join others in celebrations involving food such as eating birthday cake (a social time).

Many other activities help toddlers learn, 13-17. Bathing and dressing provide the means for language, sensory, health, and motor learnings. "Helping" with household tasks develops spatial concepts as toddlers put items in drawers or laundry in a basket. Vocabulary increases as toddlers learn the names of common objects found in the home and yard. Science becomes a part of everyday life as toddlers see how the vacuum cleaner picks up dirt and little objects, how air dries clothes, and how heat makes cookies "get bigger."

13-16 Bedroom furniture and decorations should be chosen with the toddler in mind.

keep ideas in minds and use them only to enrich toddlers' own learnings. This method is the best way to meet toddlers' intellectual needs.

Sensory stimulation activities

As you read in Chapter 11, toddlers use all their senses as they explore. Toddlers learn about the qualities of objects through the senses. Through sight, they learn about the colors and the darkness or lightness of objects. Touch teaches them whether objects are rough or smooth. Toddlers use hearing and touch to find out how hard or soft objects are. They use taste to learn about sweet and sour. Through all of the senses, toddlers form concepts of objects. For instance, they learn that an orange is round, smooth, orange colored, sweet-smelling, sweet-tasting, fairly hard on the outside, and soft and juicy on the inside.

Games can be used to enrich what toddlers are learning on their own. As toddlers play games, talking should be part of the activity.

Problem-solving activities

Toddlers can solve many problems. They can solve problems only by trying out their ideas.

Toddlers also learn as they play in a safe environment with many objects to explore. Play provides the chance to check and recheck learnings. For instance, a toddler may fill a plastic pail with the same toys many times as a way of checking the amount of space the toys need. Adults may play with toddlers some of the time such as in a chase game or in catch the ball. For the most part, however, adults let toddlers play on their own. Adults should intervene only when help is needed. For instance, they may show a toddler how to put a piece in a difficult puzzle or introduce new objects or ideas to play that has become boring.

Adults may need a few ideas for games to enrich toddlers learnings. Adult-planned games should be used when they seem to fit the toddler's own interest and skills. These planned games should never be used at a given time each day or in a drill fashion. Adults should try to

13-17 Helping bring in the garden harvest helps toddlers learn about their world.

The toddler's developmental needs   227

They are not ready to solve problems just by thinking through likely answers. Many of the best problem-solving games involve motor actions such as opening and closing containers, finding hidden objects, and watching how things move. See 13-18.

Motor activities

As you read in Chapter 10, toddlers are developing motor skills at a very rapid rate. Because most toddlers are always on the go, they need very few planned motor activities, 13-19. Some games can be used to improve gross-motor skills, while others improve fine-motor skills. See 13-20.

Language activities

As you read in Chapter 11, language is often used as the landmark that separates toddlers from babies. Language learning is very important to mental and social development.

There are ways to enhance the toddler's use of language. Well organized homes and early childhood programs that provide opportunities to explore and play help language learning. Good feelings between the child and caregivers also seem to increase the child's verbal skills.

JOHN SHAW

13-19 The toddler develops most gross-motor skills in play.

The toddler's world of action needs a background of language. Talking should go with many of the games played to improve other skills. Adult and child talk should be part of the daily routines, too. As adults do things, they talk about what they are doing and what the toddler is doing.

Adults should begin talking in a conversational manner even before the child can take part. They should pause as though the child will answer. Here is an example:

Adult: "Aren't you hungry?"
Pause: (About half a second)
Imagined response from toddler: "Yes"
Pause: (About half a second)
Adult: "You surely are." Lunch smells good, doesn't it?"

As adults speak to toddlers, they should use all types of sentences. Using statements, questions, and exclamations helps the toddler hear the rise and fall of the voice. Adults can also help toddlers learn to make different sounds. For instance, they can make sounds that go with toys such as "rrr" for a siren.

JOHN SHAW

13-18 Shaking sound "cans" help toddlers hear differences in sounds.

Speech should be clear and simple. Most adults match their sentences to the child's level. For instance, new words are explained using words that the child already knows. ("A *bus* is like a big *car.*") However, mispronouncing words is harmful. Talking beneath the child's level is not helpful. There should be a slight reach if development is to occur.

Adults should model language for toddlers. But they should be relaxed about the toddler's language errors. These examples show ways to model:

Toddler: "My *wed* (red) *sooes* (shoes)."
Adult: "Yes, these are your pretty *red shoes.*"
(Purpose: to correct pronounciation.)
Toddler: "I *singed* a song."
Adult: "You *sang* a song about a rainy day."
(Purpose: to correct grammar.)
Toddler: "See the plane *go.*"
Adult: "The plane *flies* very fast."
(Purpose: to give a new word.)
Toddler: "See the *smoke.*"
Adult: "It does look like smoke." Sniff loudly. "But it doesn't smell like smoke." "We see fog." "Fog is a cloud near the ground." "Can you say, *fog*?"
(Purpose: to correct meaning.)

In each case the adult corrects by expanding the sentence. Toddlers (and even older children) often feel defeated when adults only correct errors.

"Reading" books and saying poems and

JOHN SHAW

13-20 Hitting a peg with a hammer develops fine-motor skills and teaches cause and effect. Toddlers learn that the force and speed of the pounding affects the peg's descent.

rhymes help language development. These activities should begin early in the toddler years. There are several features to look for in choosing books:

1. Colorful and simple pictures are a must. Young children's books are called *picture books,* because pictures carry the theme or the story rather than words. (Picture books may not even have words.)

2. The theme or story should be about toddlers' favorite subjects. Subjects may include animals, toys, fun places to visit, cars and trucks, or home and family.

3. Books should be durable. They should be sturdy and washable (or wipeable). Thus, books made of cloth, vinyl, and heavy cardboard with a plastic coating are best, 13-21. You can make books by sewing a few plastic kitchen storage bags together. Then you can slip pictures mounted on heavy paper or cardboard into the bags. (These books have the added bonus of having pictures which can be changed.)

4. Pages should be easy for the toddler to turn and keep open.

Toddlers will not sit still and look at books for a long time. Young toddlers may just enjoy glancing at a page and then turning it. (Using the motor skill of turning the page is more fun than looking at the pictures.) Later, toddlers look at the pictures for a little longer time, but they often still do not want the book read. Adults can name one object and point to it. Then they can ask toddlers to point to the objects named. As language develops, toddlers can name objects in the pictures and even make some sounds of animals or other objects. The two-year-old often enjoys hearing the whole story as long as it contains a short sentence or two for each picture page.

Many older toddlers (and even older preschool children) insist on hearing the same story over and over again. The same story is often requested at bedtime. Routines that stay the same, including favorite, often-repeated stories, add security to the toddler's life. The child knows what will happen first, in the middle, and at the end of the story. Sometimes children will insist that not even a word be changed. The loving adult who reads daily to a child is likely to bring more security than the story itself.

SOCIAL-EMOTIONAL NEEDS

Toddlerhood is a little like the teenage years in that the toddler is in a *transition stage* (passing from one stage to another). Adults cannot handle toddlers as babies *or* as five-year-olds. Toddlers are somewhere in-between.

JOHN SHAW

13-21 Toddler books need to be sturdy and easy to clean.

13-22 In wanting to gain independence, toddlers often pull away from adults.

own special needs, there are some common needs of toddlers.

First, toddlers need to feel loved. They need to feel loved by caring adults. They seem to sense love that is physically and directly shown to them. For instance, most toddlers respond to cuddling, loving words, and special times each day when attention is focused on them, 13-23. Toddlers do not seem to sense love shown in more indirect ways such as preparing meals, washing clothes, or saving money in an account with their names.

Toddlers also want to feel lovable. When toddlers are always made to feel that they are "bad," they may grow to dislike themselves. Behavior that is not acceptable should only be labeled as a mistake. Adults should not call the child bad, selfish, naughty, mean, or other negative names. Harsh punishment may cause

Toddlers want to do things for themselves, but their desire is greater than their ability. Toddlers are trying to become persons in their own right, 13-22. They go back and forth between wanting to be totally independent and wanting to be totally dependent.

These changes in toddlers' wills are confusing to adults. Most adults find that working with toddlers is similar to kite-flying — letting out and pulling in the strings with changes in the wind. That is, they have to give toddlers some freedom at times and firmness at other times depending on toddlers' needs.

Discipline: balancing the toddler's needs for self-assertion and obedience

Toddlers do not have *self-restraint*. In other words, they cannot always control themselves. They also do not know all the rules of acceptable behavior. Limits must be set for toddlers. Safety is the main reason for setting limits. Limits also show toddlers how to become more socially acceptable.

Adults must help toddlers find the balance between *self-assertion* (doing as one chooses) and *obedience* (acting within the limits set by others). The best way to do this seems to be to meet their needs rather than punish their "crimes." Although each toddler has his or her

COSCO/PETERSON

13-23 Special times spent with loving adults help toddlers feel loved.

The toddler's developmental needs 231

toddlers to feel that they are "bad," too.

Toddlers need respect. Toddlers are people who are worthy of the same respect shown to others. Toddlers' mistakes should not be met with hurtful teasing or adult "temper tantrums." Respect fosters self-esteem. It also serves as the model for the growing child's relationships with others.

Toddlers need understanding and patient guidance. Adults need to understand that toddlers need a degree of freedom. Giving toddlers some choices allows a toddler to express his or her tastes. For instance, adults can let toddlers choose between two green vegetables for lunch. Sometimes a toddler may choose between self-control and adult-control. The adult may say, "You may color on the paper, or I'll have to put the crayons away." Toddlers seem to be more willing to accept firm "no's" when needed if choices are given at other times. Patience must be paired with understanding the toddler. Limits that are given in one situation will seldom carry over to similar cases. For instance, a toddler pulling books from a bookcase may be told "no" as the adult removes the hand from the books. The toddler may pause only a moment and reach for the books with the other hand. Thus, needed limits must be given for each case. Limits must also be repeated again and again before they become part of the toddler's life.

Toddlers need consistency in discipline. But they also need some flexibility in discipline at times. Consistency helps a person to feel secure. However, flexibility may be needed when toddlers are ill or when other problems occur. Once the situation is back to normal, consistency takes over. Of course, discipline changes as children grow. As they grow, children are often allowed more freedom.

Toddlers have their good days and their problem days just as adults do. When limits are set and discipline is firm but kind, the balance will slowly swing in favor of the good days. Good days are a sign that toddlers are growing in their ability to find the balance between self-assertion and the need to obey. And finding that balance is a skill that is needed throughout life.

Guidance: helping toddlers control their emotions

Understanding toddlers' emotions is the first step in helping toddlers control their emotions. Helping toddlers control their emotions is also a matter of controlling one's own emotions while dealing with the toddler. Problems with toddlers often include contrariness, temper tantrums, and fears and anxieties.

Contrariness. By 18 months many toddlers show definite signs of *contrariness.* In other words, toddlers tend to oppose adults and even other toddlers. "Yes" is replaced by "no" even when "yes" is what the toddler really wants. "Me want" is replaced with "Don't want."

Certain methods often work to reduce contrariness. The simplest is to allow the toddler to make some choices. As long as results are not harmful, allowing toddlers some freedom makes obeying less difficult.

Telling the toddler about changes five minutes in advance also helps reduce contrariness. This time allows the toddler to be emotionally prepared for the change of activities, 13-24. "No's" are often toddlers' responses to sudden changes in activities, and backing down is more difficult once "no's" are said. If "no" is said to the advance announcement, it should be ignored until time for the event to occur. If "no" is repeated, verbalize the toddles feelings. For instance, the adult can say, "I know you are really having fun in the sandbox, but we must eat now." If the toddler still resists, use calm actions such as picking up the toddler.

Another way to reduce contrariness is to play a pretend game of obedience. The adult might try saying, "I'm going to get my hands washed before you do." (Of course, after much scrubbing, the toddler wins.) Sometimes these pretend games of obedience become rituals such as a "chase" to the bedroom at naptime.

Temper tantrums. As toddlers discover powers of self-assertion, temper tantrums may occur. Many two-year-olds have temper tantrums, but some do not. Lively toddlers, toddlers under stress (even a little hungry), and toddlers who have not learned to talk (and thus express needs in words) are more prone to tantrums than other toddlers. The number and frequency of temper tantrums may be reduced by trying these ideas:

- Reduce or avoid demands when the toddler is tired, hungry, or ill.
- Make requests in a pleasant tone of voice.
- Remove difficult toys or play equipment which seems to frustrate. (Some toddlers can take challenge more than do others.)
- Have enough toys or ideas to prevent boredom.
- Offer help when the toddler seems to need it. (Waiting until the child shows frustration is often too late.)
- Give in on small demands. (Toddlers need to "get their way" sometimes.)
- Praise the toddler for signs of control.

Once a temper tantrum is underway, the adult should allow the tantrum to continue. The tantrum is a form of release for the child.

Leaving the child alone (if at home or in a preschool program) often helps, because tantrums are often performed for the audience. Toddlers have been known to follow adults from room to room resuming the tantrum display each time. If a tantrum occurs in public, the adult and child should go to a quiet place for the toddler to "cool off."

Adults should acknowledge the feelings of toddlers and show comfort. For instance, the adult may say, "I know you really wanted to stay outside. I'm sorry you are so upset about coming inside." After the tantrum, hugs are often helpful. When comfort is withheld, toddlers may feel unlovable.

Spankings should not be used as punishment for tantrums. If the adult expresses displeasure (or even anger) in a physical way, he or she is modeling that behavior for the toddler.

13-24 Telling toddlers what will happen next prepares them for a change of events.

COSCO/PETERSON

Tantrums, when handled calmly, often decrease during the preschool years. Adult calmness also serves as a model of non-physical ways of dealing with anger.

Fears and anxieties. As you read in Chapter 10, fears and anxieties should not be dismissed as "silly" by the adult. Children should not be teased about fears and anxieties. Such feelings should be handled in a matter-of-fact way.

Adults should show differences between real and pretend things in the toddler's world. For instance, adults should explain that dreams are not real. This will help reduce toddlers' fears of pretend things. Toddlers will often ask whether something is real or pretend. Toddlers will even ask about the same thing many times just to be certain.

Giving toddlers security also reduces fear. Night lights, toys in bed, and familiar babysitters add security.

Situations that cause very high fear or anxiety should be avoided. However some situations, such as going to the doctor, cannot be avoided. These should be explained in a simple, honest way. As they are explained, only fears that the toddler has already shown should be mentioned.

If toddlers are to overcome fears and anxieties, they need to see and talk about what they fear in safe ways. Telling a toddler that other children have the same fear may be a comfort. Gradual exposure to a feared subject may also help. See 13-25. For instance, if the toddler is afraid of dogs, the adult may talk about dogs. Later, the adult may read the child a book about dogs or give the child a toy dog. After some time the toddler may stand near a friendly dog behind a fence. This method is better for the toddler than suddenly exposing the child to fearful situations.

Toddlers should be praised for small steps toward overcoming fears. For instance, toddlers can be praised for "only crying a little"

JOHN SHAW

13-25 Toddlers are helped when books deal with their feelings such as separation anxiety.

or for not running from the puppy behind the fence.

Most of the toddler's present fears and anxieties will disappear with age. If fears and anxieties are handled in understanding ways, toddlers will be better able to cope with present and future fears and anxieties.

Planning self-awareness activities

A person's self-awareness begins at birth and continues throughout life. The roots of self-awareness seem to be formed in the toddler years. Self-awareness grows mainly out of the toddler's daily contact with his or her world. See 13-26. A few planned activities may enhance self-awareness.

With help from loving adults and the increasing mental ability to know what one can and cannot do, toddlers can smoothly leave the baby years behind. And they emerge as happy, confident young children, 13-27.

13-27 As toddlers begin to understand their abilities, they become more confident and content.

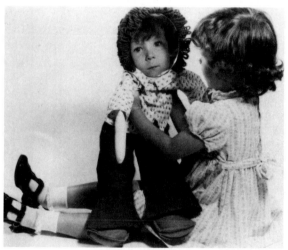

13-26 A ''Me Doll'' helps toddlers understand that they are seeing themselves in the mirror.

The toddler's developmental needs   235

ACTIVITY	SENSE

Looking at objects — Sight

Ask the child to look in a certain area (such as out of a window) and name something that he or she sees. When the child points to or names an object, say, "That's right, it's a _____." Then talk about the qualities of the object. You may include color, size, sound it makes, and what it does. Talk about other times when the toddler has seen the object. Three or four objects at one time are enough for most toddlers.

Dark and light — Sight

Use a shoe box or other small box with a lid. Cut a nickel-sized hole in the center of the lid. Put a small toy in the box and put a lid on the box. Tell the child to look through the hole and ask him or her what is seen. Explain that it is dark when the lid is on the box. Tell the child to take the lid off the box and look through the hole again. Ask the child if the object can be seen. Explain that it is light when the lid is off. Try looking at other objects in the same way. Leave the box for the toddler's own play.

Matching colors — Sight

Place four or five red objects and three or four non-red objects in front of the child. The objects should be of interest to the toddler. Help the child identify all of the objects. Then pick up one red object and ask the name of the object. After the child has named the object, say, "Right. It is a _____. It is a red _____. Can you say red?" Show the child another red object and call it red. Then show the child two objects—one that is red and one that is not. Ask which one is red. Continue until the child has found all the red objects. When the toddler is correct, say, "that's good. You found the red _____." When a mistake is made, say, "No, that's not red. It has to look like this _____ (point to object)."

Variations: After the toddler can quickly find red objects, these variations can be used on other days. 1. Find red objects in the house and outside. 2. "Hide" ribbons of different colors and have the child bring you the red ones. 3. Show the toddler three crayons of different colors (one of which is red), and have the toddler make red marks on paper. 4. Go through the entire procedure with other colors.

(Note that the tasks are to help toddlers to *match* colors. Naming all the colors is a skill more often seen in the later preschool years or even in the early school years.)

Photo album — Sight

Look at recent pictures in the family photo album. The toddler can point to (and perhaps name) members of the family, pets, toys, and other familiar items.

Naming sounds — Hearing

When you notice that a toddler hears a sound, stop briefly and listen. Then say, "Do you hear that? I hear a _____. Do you hear it too?" Point in the direction of the sound.

Continued.

Sound cans — Hearing

Place some objects such as paper clips, beads, rice, or sand into separate containers. Glue or tape the containers so that the toddler cannot open them. Have the toddler shake the sound cans to hear the difference between loud and soft sounds.

Which soundmaker? — Hearing

Play with a toddler using a bell, a whistle, and a drum (or a pan or box used like a drum). Then cover the toddler's eyes while you make one of the sounds. Ask the toddler which soundmaker was used to make the noise.

Variation: Sounds can be tape recorded. After playing each sound, have the toddler point to the soundmaker.

Animal sounds — Hearing

Sing ''Old MacDonald had a Farm,'' and point to pictures of each animal as you sing. Start with a few of the toddler's favorite animals and gradually add others.

Recognizing objects by touch — Touch

Put three or four familiar objects in a paper bag or pillowcase. Pull an object out of the bag. Ask the toddler to name it. Then show the toddler how to feel the object using the fingers. As the toddler feels the object, the adult should describe the texture. For instance, a ball may feel ''round and soft.'' Continue in the same way with the other objects. After feeling all the objects, put them back into the bag. Have the child identify each one by feeling without peeking.

Variations: 1. Place pictures or identical objects outside the bag. Then have the toddler feel an object in the bag and point to the object or picture outside of the bag. 2. Describe and name an object and have the toddler find it. For instance, say, ''Put your hand in the bag and see if you can find the comb with all the points.''

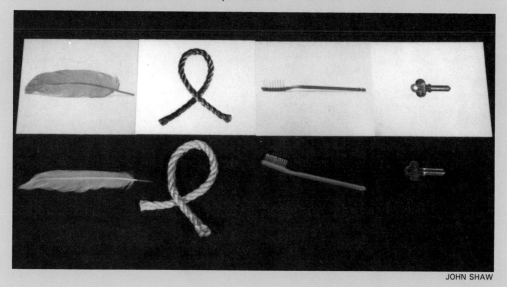

JOHN SHAW

Continued.

The toddler's developmental needs 237

Feeling boards
Touch

Make three to five matching pairs of boards by gluing materials to small blocks of wood. Materials may include felt, sandpaper, a smooth plastic sheet, fur, and others. (The materials chosen should have very different textures.) First, have the toddler look at and feel each surface as you describe the texture. Then put one member of each pair into a bag. One by one, the toddler should match each block in the bag with the same block outside of the bag. Praise good matches. If the toddler does not get a match, encourage him or her to try again.

Feeling tour of the yard
Touch

Help the toddler find rough and smooth objects in the yard. Some textures to feel might include rough and smooth rocks, rough bark, a smooth blade of grass, and a smooth rose petal. A sample of each can be brought inside for more feeling and describing.

Recognizing objects by smell
Smell

Select three or four familiar objects that have distinct odors. Show the toddler how to smell by sniffing loudly. First, smell and talk about each object's odor. Then have the toddler close his or her eyes and identify each object by smelling it. If the toddler needs help, name two objects from which the toddler can choose. For instance, say, ''Is this soap or a banana?''

What's cooking?
Smell

When cooking a food with a distinct odor, sniff loudly and tell the toddler what you smell. For instance, say, ''I smell chicken frying,'' or ''I smell a cake baking.'' Later, ask the toddler, ''What's cooking? What smells so good?''

Variation: Smell and talk about the other odors of the toddler's world such as flowers, burning leaves, an outdoor barbecue, or the rain.

Sweet and sour
Taste

Give the toddler a sugar cube and refer to it as *sweet*. Then have the toddler taste lemon juice mixed with water. Refer to it as *sour*. (Use equal parts of lemon juice and water. Pure lemon juice is too sour and can be hard on the teeth.) Sweeten the lemon juice and water with sugar and serve as lemonade. Although the toddler may not understand, explain, ''I am making this sour lemon juice sweeter with this sweet sugar. Now we have lemonade. It is sweet.''

Variation: Give the toddler a small amount of salt to taste. Then give the toddler a bite of a salty food such as a salty cracker. Use the term *salty* to describe both flavors.

Continued.

What's In the Box?

Place a small toy inside a box (shoebox or box with a lid and simple closure) and close the lid. Sit with the toddler on the floor and say, "Look at the box." Shake it and say, "Listen, there is something inside." Have the toddler open the box. If the toddler cannot open the box in a couple of minutes, show how the box is opened. Close the box, and ask the toddler to try again.

Variations: 1. Try different boxes with different openings. 2. Ask the toddler to hide the toy in the box and close it. Then you open the box.

Opening lids

Place a small object in a container with a snap-on lid. Show the toddler how it works. Then let the toddler try to open it. When the toddler has mastered one type of lid, try another. For instance, use screw-on lids and plugs. (Do *not* show toddlers or even older preschool children how safety caps work.)

JOHN SHAW

Drop-in toys

Cut a circle large enough for a ball to be dropped through, in the bottom of a box. Show the toddler how to drop balls or other small objects through the hole and get the objects.

Variation: Simple sorting boxes can be purchased. These have holes to fit the shapes of objects, such as round, square, and star-shaped.

Puzzles

Very simple puzzles are fun for toddlers. Begin with one-piece puzzles and work up to puzzle with five or six pieces during the toddler years. For toddlers, each puzzle piece should be an entire object or picture of an object and not a "jigsaw" piece. A knob on the puzzle piece helps fine motor control.

JOHN SHAW

Continued.

The toddler's developmental needs 239

Stacking and nesting

If the toddler can nest and stack two or three objects as described in Chapter 9, add a few more pieces for nesting and stacking. Rings can be sequenced also. The toddler should start with two or three rings and slowly add the other rings as the toddler masters the game. (If there is only a very little difference in the size of the objects, the task becomes much more difficult. These objects can be saved for children who are a little older.)

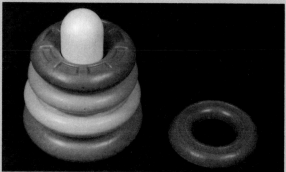
JOHN SHAW

Where am I?

Hide from the toddler who is involved in another activity. Call out. The toddler will look for you. Praise the child for finding you. (Of course, you do not hide behind locked doors or other places where toddlers cannot search.)

Where is the toy?

Hide a toy wrapped in newspaper and placed in a box. Or hide a toy in a box and place this box inside another box or boxes. Then ask the child to find the toy.

Rolling cars

Place small cars or trucks on a board that is flat on the floor. Chair cushions, sturdy cardboard lids, or trays can be used as the board. Say, "The cars do not go." As you slowly raise the board on one end say, "Here they go." After the toddler has played with the cars in this way many times, ask, "Can you make the car go down the hill fast (slow)?" See whether the toddler increases (decreases) the slope of the board.

JOHN SHAW

Through the tunnel

Using a mailing tube with both ends removed, show the toddler how to roll objects through it. Toddlers will learn how objects can go in one open end and come out the other open end. After much play, some toddlers may learn to vary the slope of the tube to control the speed of the object's roll.

JOHN SHAW

Continued.

GROSS-MOTOR GAMES

Pick up the ball

As the toddler stands, roll the ball and say, ''Pick up the ball.'' Model bending at the waist. The child must bend at the waist before playing this game.

Variation: Pick up toys or books in the play area by bending at the waist.

Climb and sit

Place the toddler facing the front of a chair or sofa. The toddler's hands should be on the seat. Raise that toddler's knee to chair or sofa, and give a slight boost. Turn the toddler, if needed. Aid should be reduced after a few tries. (If the chair or sofa seems too high, the seat cushion can often be removed. This way, the toddler has less distance to climb.)

Push and pull

Push and pull toys aid motor skills of walking and crawling. Push toys seem to be easier since the toddler can see the toy's action without walking backward or looking back over the shoulder.

JOHN SHAW

Riding toys

Toys that the toddler pushes with the feet or toys that are mounted and ridden such as bouncing horses are good for developing gross-motor skills.

FINE MOTOR GAMES

Pounding pegs

A hammer and peg set can help the child coordinate what is seen with the action. Toddlers should use both hands on the hammer to prevent getting the fingers hit.

Pop beads

Unsnapping (and later, snapping) pop beads helps fine motor control. Toddlers love to wear pop beads as a necklace. (These make a safe necklace, too, because they pop open if they are caught on another object.)

Continued.

The toddler's developmental needs 241

Blocks

Building a tower with three to five blocks and knocking it down is fun for toddlers. As toddlers grow, they will build taller towers. Balancing the blocks in towers requires good fine-motor control.

Variation: Push three or four blocks in a "train" while saying "choo-choo." Pushing blocks in a train requires much fine-motor control.

JOHN SHAW

Scribbling

Tape paper (even newspaper will do) to a table or high chair tray. Give the toddler a crayon. Show the toddler how to make marks. (Remember, the toddler cannot yet hold a crayon in a mature way.)

Getting dressed

Toddlers can learn to put on mittens and zip zippers. (They cannot start jacket zippers.) Special items, such as dressing dolls and books, can make this learning even more fun.

Make a face

Putting the eyes, nose, and mouth on a felt face can be much fun. The parts of the face are made out of felt with a hook-and-loop tape backing, such as Velcro. Because the pieces are rather small, the toddler should be supervised during play.

Variation: Many other "pictures" can be made using felt pieces. For instance, the toddler can put wheels on cars or trains. Or they can put flowers on stems.

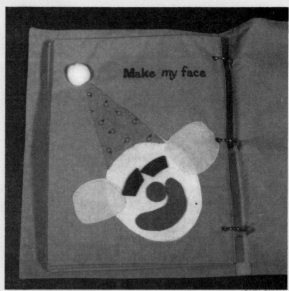

JOHN SHAW

Continued.

LANGUAGE GAMES

Show me

Young toddlers enjoy the action of running around and pointing to objects. When an adult names objects for the toddler to touch, toddlers improve language skills as well. To help toddlers, make statements such as, "Show me the door." As the toddler touches the door, praise with a statement such as, "You're right. That's the door."

Variation: Have the toddler hunt for a partially hidden object such as a toy.

Follow directions

Give the toddler simple directions using familiar objects. For instance, say to the toddler, "Bring me the ball." Praise the toddler for following directions properly.

Variation: Play "Follow the leader" with simple verbal action commands such as, "Clap your hands," or, "Pat your head."

Telephones

Listening to voices on a phone and talking into a phone can aid language development. Toddlers enjoy play phones. Some types have recorded voices that "talk" with the toddler. Talking on a real phone with adult supervision is also good language practice.

"Here we go 'Round the Mulberry Bush"

Acting out meanings of words is most helpful to the toddler. This song allows you to sing and act out such lines as, "This is the way we eat our soup," and, "This is the way we wash our hands." Many other verses can be used.

SELF-AWARENESS ACTIVITIES

Name the parts of the face

Place the toddler's hands on your face. Name aloud each part of your face as the child feels it. Then have the toddler name the parts.

Mirrors

With the toddler on your lap, hold a mirror to reflect the toddler's face. Say, "Who is that?" If the toddler doesn't answer, say, "That's you." Say the toddler's name.

Variations: 1. Name the toddler's face parts while looking into a mirror. Touch and name the toddler's part of the face and the reflected image of the same part. 2. Make or purchase a special doll with a mirror for the face. 3. Provide a low mirror for the toddler to watch during play. This gives the toddler a chance to see the entire body and to watch motor skills.

Dress-up

For children under three years of age, dressing up with old purses, hats, necklaces, and large, flat shoes is liked. To help the toddler play dress-up, start with one object, such as a hat. Show the toddler and say, "Look at this pretty hat. I'm going to wear it." Put it on and talk about how pretty it is. Then say, "Do you want to wear a hat?" Put it on the toddler's head, saying how nice it looks. If the toddler enjoys this, try other items.

Pretend

Have a pretend tea party with a toddler. Talk about the pretend foods in much the same way that you would talk about real food. If the toddler looks confused, say, "How funny! We can pretend to have a party!"

Variation: Pretend to be an animal, a bus driver, or anything the child knows about.

A book about me

Photograph the toddlers daily activities. Place the pictures in a photo album or in plastic bags that are fastened together with string.

to Know

appetite . . . contrariness . . . nutrient density . . .
obedience . . . picture books . . .
registered dietitian . . . ritual . . .
self-assertion . . . self-dressing . . .
self-restraint . . . toilet training . . .
training pants . . . transition stage

to Review

Write your answers on a separate sheet of paper.

1. True or false. Besides meeting food, clothing, rest, sleep, and hygiene needs, teaching self-care skills is part of meeting the physical needs of toddlers.

2. Which of the following statements about feeding toddlers are true?
   a. Because toddlers are larger, their appetites increase.
   b. Toddlers want to feed themselves.
   c. Toddlers who play with their food are being naughty.
   d. Empty calorie foods, which provide energy, are all right for toddlers due to their high energy demands.
   e. Many of the toddler's feeding problems are worked out in time.

3. Toddlers' self-dressing involves more _____ (putting on, taking off) clothes.

4. True or false. Shoes aid toddlers' walking by providing good support.

5. Give four suggestions that may help toddlers cope with unwanted bedtime.

6. Toddlers feel the sensation of a full bladder or bowel at:
   a. 9 months.
   b. 15 months.
   c. 18 months.
   d. 24 months.

7. True or false. Toilet training chairs do not make toilet training easier.

8. Intellectual needs are best met:
   a. Through planned activities.
   b. When toddlers are involved with household activities on a day-to-day basis.
   c. When needed concepts and skills are taught in a drill fashion.
   d. When language is not part of most activities.

9. Give two ways to reduce contrariness in toddlers.

10. Give three ways to reduce the number of temper tantrums in toddlers.

11. True or false. Toddlers become less fearful when quickly exposed to the feared situation again.

to Do

1. Prepare one week's menus for a toddler. Use Chart 13-4, "Daily Basic Diet for Toddlers," as a guide.

2. Prepare a poster or mobile of good finger foods for toddlers.

3. Borrow some toddler clothes from department stores or from parents. Examine each garment for the features listed on Chart 13-6, "Basic Points to Consider in Choosing Toddler Clothes." Make a list of the good features included. Compare your list with others in the class. Attach a hang tag for each clothing item listing its best features.

4. Invite two or three successful caregivers to share with the class hints that have helped them solve some toddler problems. The guests may include feeding problems, bathing and toothbrushing problems, toilet training, contrariness, temper tantrums, and fears/anxieties.

5. As an individual or small group project, gather or make the materials for some of the planned activities listed for toddlers. Then make a display, adding cards that explain how the materials are used.

6. Try some planned activities while babysitting or as a helper in a group-care program for toddlers. Discuss with your class what did or did not work and possible reasons.

Eating without help is one step that toddlers take toward caring for themselves.

A special treat

Conquering the park

part five

Preschoolers

JOHN SHAW

The birthday party

JOHN SHAW

Helping Dad with shopping

Preschoolers change physically to look more
like adults and less like babies.

14

Physical development of the preschooler

After studying this chapter, you will be able to:
- ☐ Describe physical development occuring in preschool children.
- ☐ Describe the landmarks of preschool children in gross-motor and fine-motor skills.

The bodies of preschoolers continue to mature so that more complex tasks can be mastered. Preschool children grow even more slowly than toddlers. But they change in many ways to become more like adults and less like babies.

Toddlers have gained many gross-motor and fine-motor skills. But toddlers do not always have as much control over their movements as they would like. In the preschool years, children improve on skills such as walking, running, balancing, and self-dressing.

BODY GROWTH AND DEVELOPMENT

Compared with the toddler years, the growth rate slows even more for *preschool children* (children between the ages of three and five years). If the growth rate did not slow, we would be a species of giants! The growth rate slows almost equally for all preschool children. This means that children who are larger than their age mates at three years of age likely will be larger than their age mates at the end of the preschool years. Instead of growing much larger, the preschooler's body proportions change and organ systems continue to mature.

Height and weight

About half as much growth in height occurs in the preschool stage as occurs in the toddler stage. Most preschool children grow about two and one-half inches to three inches each year. On the average, girls are shorter than boys but the difference is one-half inch or less. See 14-1.

The rate of weight gain also slows during the preschool years. However, there is a slight increase in the rate of weight gain between four years and five and one-half years. Preschoolers gain about three to five pounds per year. Seventy-five percent of the weight gained during the preschool ages is due to muscle development. Because boys have greater muscle development even during the preschool years, they average a pound heavier than girls in this age-group. See Chart 14-2.

Other body changes

Babyish features disappear during the preschool years. Body proportions begin to look more like those of an adult, 14-3. The head will be close to one-eighth of body size by five and one-half years. (At birth, the head is one-fourth of body size. It is one-fifth of body size at two years. Adults' heads are one-tenth of their body size.) The lower face of the preschooler grows more rapidly than the head. This growth pattern helps the preschooler's face

AVERAGE HEIGHT FROM THREE TO FIVE YEARS

AGE IN YEARS	BOYS	GIRLS
3	38'' (95 cm)	37.25'' (93 cm)
3 1/2	39.25'' (98 cm)	39.25'' (98 cm)
4	40.75'' (102 cm)	40.50'' (101 cm)
4 1/2	42'' (105 cm)	42'' (105 cm)
5	43.25'' (108 cm)	43'' (107.5 cm)
5 1/2	45'' (112.5 cm)	44.50'' (111 cm)

14-1 The height of children from three to five years increases rather steadily. Boys tend to be slightly taller than girls.

AVERAGE WEIGHT FROM THREE TO FIVE YEARS

AGE IN YEARS	BOYS	GIRLS
3	32.25 lbs. (14.5 kg)	31.75 lbs. (14.3 kg)
3 1/2	34.25 lbs. (15.4 kg)	34 lbs. (15.3 kg)
4	36.50 lbs. (16.4 kg)	36.25 lbs. (16.3 kg)
4 1/2	38.50 lbs. (17.3 kg)	38.50 lbs. (17.3 kg)
5	41.50 lbs. (18.7 kg)	41 lbs. (18.4 kg)
5 1/2	45.50 lbs. (20.5 kg)	44 lbs. (20 kg)

14-2 The weight of children from three to five years increases rather steadily. Boys tend to be slightly heavier than girls.

JOHN SHAW

14-3 The preschool girl has body proportions more like those of an adult than does her toddler-aged brother.

The preschooler's brain continues to grow, but it grows at a slower rate. The brain is about 75 to 80 percent of its adult size by age three and 90 percent of its adult size by age four. The brain becomes more *convoluted,* or more wrinkled and thicker. There are more connections between parts of the brain. These connections help voluntary movements such as walking, running, and drawing. They also increase *alertness* (ability to respond quickly), *attention* (ability to apply oneself to a task), and *memory* (ability to retain and recall).

Other organs are continuing to mature, also. The heart rate slows and becomes steady. Blood pressure increases. Breathing slows and is deeper. Although the digestive tract is maturing, it lags behind the maturity of other organs. Therefore, the preschooler's digestive tract is more irritated by high fiber foods and seasonings than the adult's.

look more like the adult face. Until 30 months of age, the waist, hips, and chest measure almost the same. This gives a "squat" look to toddlers. By five years of age, the waist is smaller in girth than the shoulders and hips. The trunk grows to allow more space for internal organs (heart, lungs, liver, and others). As the trunk grows, the abdomen protrudes less. The legs grow rapidly, too. By five and one-half years, most children's legs are about one-half the length of the body—the same as the adult leg to body proportions.

The bones continue to ossify (harden) and grow larger and longer. Deciduous ("baby") teeth begin to fall out between four and five years of age, 14-4. Although permanent teeth may not erupt until the early school years, they are developing rapidly under the gums. Bone and teeth development can be damaged by malnutrition and other health problems during the preschool years. Bones, muscles, and joints are more prone to injury in preschool children than in older children.

JOHN SHAW

14-4 Toward the end of the preschool years, many children lose their first deciduous teeth.

Physical development of the preschooler 251

Fat tissues continue to lessen slowly. At five and one-half years, the fat tissues are less than half as thick as they were at age one.

MOTOR DEVELOPMENT

The motor development of preschoolers improves with body growth and development and with physical play. Preschoolers have an increase in muscle development. Their eye-hand coordination (relationship between what one sees and the hand action in a task) becomes more refined. And their *reaction time* (time required to react to a sight, sound, etc.) becomes shorter. Preschool children are thus able to engage in many types of physical activities. And, through play, preschool children's motor skills develop at a rapid rate, 14-5.

Large-muscle development

As preschool children's large muscles develop, the children improve in strength and coordination. Compared with the toddler, the large-muscle movements of the preschool child are much more smooth and much less awkward.

Walking. Preschool children lose their wide-footed stance. And, because their balance becomes better, they can hold their hands close to their bodies. Preschoolers loose the toddler appearance of a tightrope walker. By three years of age, toddlers do not need to monitor their feet as they walk. As balance becomes better over the preschool years, the arms will swing in the alternate rhythm of foot placement. (They move the right arm and left foot forward, then the left arm and right foot.) Preschoolers have stronger legs and can lock their knees (knees are straight, not bent) during the support phase of each step. This aids walking ability and gives a graceful look to the child's walk.

Preschool children will try different ways to walk—sideways, backwards, and on tiptoes. By three years of age, most children spin around

JOHN SHAW

14-5 Strength, coordination, and motor skills are developed through play.

and around to *seek vertigo* (try to become dizzy). This activity also aids balance, 14-6.

Running. Unlike toddlers, three-year-olds can run with sudden stops and starts. They can turn corners quickly. Running with alternate rhythm of the arms and legs is also learned in the preschool years. Speed in running increases throughout these years. Faster speed is most noticeable in five-year-olds.

Jumping. Jumping with a forward arm action is often seen in four-year-old children. This helps preschoolers increase their broad-jump distance and the hurdle-height clearance. Stronger muscles and better balance also help. Often girls lag slightly behind the boys in the broad jump but equal the boys in the hurdle jump during the preschool years.

Climbing. The major change in climbing from the toddler to the preschool years is the ability to alternate steps. Most three-year-olds will alternate steps while climbing up stairs or ladders. But they will not alternate steps while climbing down until four years of age. Longer legs, better balance, and increased courage aid climbing skills.

Throwing and catching. Two new actions in preschoolers help their throwing ability. One is *body rotation,* and the other is *weight shift.* Body rotation is the action of turning the trunk of the body to the left when the right hand is used to throw (or turning to the right when the left hand is used). Weight shift is the change of weight from the back foot to the front foot. Body rotation and weight shift may begin during the third year. They become much more refined by the end of the preschool period, 14-7. These two changes — plus increased strength, balance, and coordination — improve

JOHN SHAW

14-6 Whirling about and getting dizzy is a fun walking movement that helps develop balance.

JOHN SHAW

14-7 Some body rotation and weight shift can be seen as preschool children throw balls.

Physical development of the preschooler   253

the preschooler's throwing distance, speed, and accuracy.

Catching a ball with the arms to one's side until the ball approaches is most often seen by four or five years of age. However, preschool children have a hard time predicting the pathway of balls thrown from a distance. (Difficulty is further increased when small balls, such as tennis-ball size, are thrown.) Preschool children can catch balls that they bounce better than balls thrown by others.

Balancing. Preschool children can do both *dynamic balance tasks* and *static balance tasks*. Dynamic balance tasks involve balancing while moving such as walking on a line or balance beam, 14-8. Static balance tasks involve holding one position such as standing on one foot.

Around three years of age, children can walk heel-toe on a straight, one-inch-wide line without "falling off." It takes almost one more year before children can walk a circular, one-inch-wide line. One study had children walk on a balance beam 8.25 yards long, 2.4 inches wide, and 4 inches high. Children under three years of age could not walk on the beam. Three-year-olds could walk part of the way, and four-year-olds could walk the entire length without falling.

Test scores from various studies showed wide differences in the static balance skills of children of the same ages. (These differences in scores may be due to problems in getting accurate scores.) Three-year-olds can balance for a few seconds on one foot. But static balance is not too well developed until four or five years of age.

Hopping and skipping. Preschool children often begin hopping on their preferred foot around three years of age. By four and five years of age, children can hop longer distances and faster. Rhythmic hopping (hopping on one foot and then the other without breaking the rhythmic pattern) and precision hopping (following a certain pathway) is difficult for most five-year-olds.

Skipping skills are often seen between four and six years of age. Skipping is a type of rhythmic hopping—step-hop (on one foot) and step-hop (on the other foot). Early attempts to skip often involve a step-hop on the preferred foot, then a step (minus the hop) on the other foot.

Small-muscle development

As children move into the preschool stage, their ability to *manipulate,* or work with the hands, is still clumsy. But as preschoolers play with small objects, their small muscles develop and fine-motor skills improve. Improved eye-hand coordination also helps fine-motor skills. Chart 14-9 outlines what to expect in the fine-motor skills of preschool children. (Remember that in development, the ages may vary. But the order of development is almost the same for all children.)

JOHN SHAW

14-8 Walking on a line in a heel-toe fashion is fun and shows good balance.

SEQUENCE OF THE DEVELOPMENT OF FINE MOTOR SKILLS

AGE	SKILLS	
Three Years	Builds uneven tower of blocks. Pours water from a small pitcher.	
	Copies a circle (with some skill).	◯
	Draws a straight line.	——
Four Years	Cuts on line with scissors. Washes hands.	
	Copies a "t."	✝
	Makes a few letters.	
Five Years	Folds paper along the diagonal.	▱
	Copies a square and a triangle.	▢ △
	Traces a diamond shape.	◇
	Laces shoes and may tie them. Copies most letters.	

14-9 Fine motor skills develop in a certain order.

At age three, most children can feed themselves using a spoon and fork, but they are still rather messy. They can build towers from blocks, but the towers are crooked. Three-year-olds can draw straight lines and copy circles. They can unbutton buttons and pull up large zippers.

By four years, movements are more steady. Four-year-olds may try to use a knife when they feed themselves. They are able to build straight towers and place blocks with steady hands. Four-year-olds begin to cut along lines with scissors. (Scissors used at this age should have rounded tips.) These children can brush their teeth, comb their hair, and wash their hands. They can also begin to lace, but probably not tie, their shoes.

At five years of age, eye-hand coordination is greatly improved. Right or left hand preference is definite by this age. Five-year-olds use spoon, fork, and knife to feed themselves. They can build towers and place other small toys with skill. They can make simple drawings freehand. Five-year-olds can fasten large buttons and work large zippers. They may even be able to tie shoe laces.

to Know

alertness . . . attention . . . body rotation . . .
dynamic balance tasks . . . memory . . .
preschool children . . . reaction time . . .
seek vertigo . . . static balance tasks . . .
weight shift

to Review

Write your answers on a separate sheet of paper.

1. True or false. As compared with the toddler years, the rate of growth speeds up during the preschool years.

2. Preschool children's weight increase is mainly due to:
   a. Increase in fat.
   b. Head (brain) growth.
   c. Muscle development.

3. True or false. The preschool child's legs are about half of the total body length near the end of the preschool years.

4. True or false. Connections between parts of the brain increase both motor and mental abilities.

5. One of the slowest maturing organs is the:
   a. Brain.
   b. Digestive tract.
   c. Heart.

6. Match the preschool child's motor action to the skills by putting the letter (or letters) before the skill.

   Skills
   _c_ Walking.
   _d_ Running.
   _a_ Jumping.
   _b_ Throwing.

   Motor actions
   a. Uses forward action of arms.
   b. Shows some body rotation and weight shift.
   c. Locks knees during support phase of movement.
   d. Swings arms in alternate rhythm of feet placement.

7. List four fine motor skills developed in the preschool period.
   building z blocks
   lacing shoes
   using a spoon, fork + knife
   cutting z sizzors

to Do

1. As a group or class project, write a one-page or two-page brochure about what adults can expect in terms of the motor skills of preschool children. Illustrations may help. (The brochure should be checked by your teacher before making copies.) Copies could be given to local programs serving preschool children for parents' and other adults' use.

2. Observe the motor skills (both large-muscle and small-muscle) of children ages three, four, and five. Make a chart to record the advancing skills. The chart might look like this:

MOTOR SKILLS

Age of child _____
Male/Female _____

Motor skill

Hopping
   Can hop _____
   Distance hopped _____
   Can hop rhythmically _____
   Can hop with precision _____

Jumping
   Length of broad jump _____
   Height of hurdle jump _____
   Forward movement of arms seen _____

Compare the skills of each age by using the average for each skill.

3. On 3 by 5 inch cards, draw a circle, a square, a rectangle, an equilateral triangle (one with all three sides the same length), and a diamond. Have children ages three, four, and five draw each of these shapes on a piece of paper. (Children should use a crayon or pencil.) Make a bulletin board of these drawings with age-labels. Compare the drawings by age-group.

4. Informally compare the skills of three-year-olds and five-year-olds in handling scissors, pencils or crayons, and a paint brush. What changes happen in the two-year period? Describe your findings in class.

JOHN SHAW

As preschoolers grow, they become more coordinated and gain confidence doing new activities.

REBECCA LAWRENCE

Preschool children are just beginning to think
as adults do. There are still many problems
with the ways that they think.

15

Intellectual development of the preschooler

After studying this chapter, you will be able to:
- Tell how new thinking skills emerge in preschool children.
- Explain why children think and say things that seem rather absurd to adults.
- Identify the major concepts learned at this stage of mental development.
- Chart the increasing language skills of preschoolers.

In earlier chapters, you read about the many learnings of infants and toddlers. These learnings greatly expand during the next three years. The increased motor coordination of preschoolers leads to a more careful and detailed look at objects, people, and events. The further maturing of the brain permits preschool children to attend to their world for longer periods of time. It also allows preschoolers to think and recall more.

Infants and toddlers express their knowledge of objects in their sensory motor contact with objects. These very young children learn about objects as they see, smell, hear, and taste them. The image of the object is probably only there when the child is in contact with the object and fades as soon as contact is broken.

Piaget has described the second major stage of mental development as the *preoperational stage.* (*Pre* means before and *operations* — as defined by Piaget — means mental actions.) This stage happens before the point when children acquire what Piaget calls operations. Three standards must be met before operations truly exist.

1. Operations must be mental rather than dependent on the senses and motor actions as was true in the sensorimotor

stage. The preschool child achieves this standard.

2. Operations must be what most people consider *logical thinking*. Logical thinking includes combining ideas or objects (adding), placing things in order (sequencing), or doing "if-then" thinking. Preschool children can not carry out logical thinking.

3. Operations must be seen as reversible. To reverse, the person must be able to retrace the steps to the start of the task and "undo" the task. For instance, if you add two to three and obtain five, then you can reverse by subtracting two from five and obtaining three. Preschool children do not see operations as reversible.

The transition between the sensorimotor and preoperational stages is very gradual. Some actions to help thinking will still be needed in the preoperational stage and even later. Even some adults move their fingers while adding or explaining ideas!

HOW PRESCHOOL CHILDREN LEARN

The preoperational stage occurs during the preschool years and may include the first year or two of school. Chart 15-1 shows that there are two substages of the preoperational stage — the preconceptual and the intuitive substages. In the *preconceptual substage,* children ages two to four are developing some concepts. But many of these concepts are incomplete or are not logical. For instance, the preconceptual child may see different members of the same class as identical. Because of the lack of logic, the child may insist that every Santa seen is the "same real" Santa, not one of Santa's helpers. They may believe this even though the Santas may look different.

By the *intuitive substage,* children solve many problems correctly. But they base their solutions on "feeling" their way through a problem rather than logic. Piaget gives this example of intuitive thinking:

A child is shown three beads (red, yellow, and blue) strung on a wire and inserted into a hollow cardboard tube so that the child cannot see the beads. See 15-2. The child watches the beads inserted in the tube. The tube is held vertically in front of the child. Then the child draws with colors or tells the color order of the beads in the tube. The tube is turned in a half rotation (180 degrees) and the child is asked which color bead is now on top. The tube is then turned one full rotation, one and one-half turns, two turns, and so on. Intuitive thinking children can answer correctly as long as they can imagine the position of the beads inside the tube. But they cannot arrive at a rule about the relationship between the number of turns or half turns and the color of the top bead. Such thinking is logic in the true sense.

PIAGET'S STAGES OF COGNITIVE DEVELOPMENT		
Stage 1:	Sensorimotor Stage (Birth to 2 years)	
Stage 2:	Preoperational Stage (2 to 7 years)	
	Substage i : Preconceptual (2 to 4 years)	
	Substage ii: Intuitive (4 to 7 years)	
Stage 3:	Concrete Operations Stage (7 to 11 years)	
Stage 4:	Formal Operations Stage (11 years on)	

15-1 The preschool child functions in the preoperational stage.

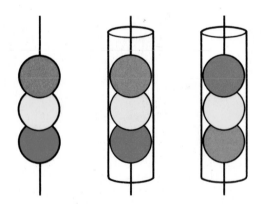

15-2 Some preschool children can mentally keep track of the beads with one or two turns of the tube. But they cannot count the rotations and explain the order of the beads.

New abilities emerge

Preschool children become better able to think in their heads. They are much less dependent on actions. But their mental images are limited to what they have experienced in a sensory or motor way. The preoperational child's thought is characterized by five new abilities.

Deferred imitation. *Deferred imitation* is the imitation of behaviors that have not been seen for some time. This type of action is first seen at the end of the sensorimotor stage. For instance, the child may imitate the game of peek-a-boo played with adults earlier in the day. The imitation is as exact as the child can make it. Deferred imitation happens before the child is able to create symbols of his or her own.

Symbolic play. Preschool children play many games of pretend. In play, something from the child's real world (including dreams) is changed in some ways. The ideas in the pretend games may represent anything the preschool child wishes. Symbols of the child's own choosing are used to represent the pretend world and the child's role in it. See 15-3. Because children make up their own symbols, pretend play is a mental step beyond imitation.

Drawing. Preschool children have left the scribbling stage. They no longer make marks without any attempt to make "something." Now they attempt to represent their world through drawings. Preschool drawings are realistic in intent. But children draw what they think, not what is visually accurate. A side view of a goldfish may show both eyes and even a smiling mouth! Drawing is thought of as a step midway between symbolic play and mental image. This is because preschool children often draw first and then decide what their pictures represent.

15-3 A crate may be anything that a young child imagines.

Mental images. *Mental images* are symbols of objects and past experiences which are stored in the mind. Like all symbols, they are not exact copies of real objects and experiences. However, mental images do have a relationship to the "real" world. Unlike imitation, symbolic play, and drawings, mental images are private and *internalized* (thought about only). Mental images are the "pictures" you have in your mind when words or experiences trigger the image. You learn about the mental images of others when they are able and willing to share what is on their minds.

Language. Spoken words are symbols in place of objects. Piaget calls words or other symbols given by society *signs.* (Although signs are symbols, Piaget uses the term *symbols* to mean symbols of one's own choosing such as in play or drawing.) The symbols used in language are the most abstract of all symbols.

This is because words bear no relationship to what they represent. For instance, the word *car* does not look, sound, or move like a car. Although words are very abstract, they do aid thinking. Once language abilities emerge, thinking is helped because the child can exchange ideas with others and think in terms of words.

Obstacles to complete logical thought

Preschool children are mentally advanced compared to children in the sensorimotor stage. And yet, they are not yet logical. There are several roadblocks to complete logical thought.

Egocentrism. *Egocentrism* is seen in preschool children, especially those under four years of age. Children who are egocentric believe that everyone thinks in the same way and thinks the same things as they do. See 15-4. Even when shown evidence that their ideas are wrong, they conclude that the evidence must

JOHN SHAW

15-4 The three-year-old (left) is asked to describe what she believes is the older girl's view of the bear. She describes the bear's face—the view from her side of the table.

262

be wrong. Egocentrism does not mean that children are selfish or overly concerned with themselves.

There are many examples of egocentric thought. These examples may help make the meaning clearer.

- Children offer candy from their mouths. Because they are enjoying it, they think that you would, too!
- Children tell about events from the middle instead of the beginning. They think that others know the beginning.
- If children say they think the slide is tall, they think you see it as tall. (They do not see that the adult's size might even make the slide look small.)

Centration. Because the child is egocentric, centration happens in the thinking. *Centration* is centering attention on just one aspect of an object or event instead of looking at all aspects at the same time. Children thus lose important information. A good example of centration can be seen in Piaget's liquid task, 15-5. The preoperational child centers on the tall beaker (or the wide beaker), and simply translate tall (or wide) into "more." The other dimension — taller *but thinner* (or wider *but shorter*) — is not judged. To think of both height and width at the same time requires *decentering,* or looking at two or more aspects at one time.

Focus on states, not on transformations. When a series of steps or events occur to bring about a change, preoperational children seem to focus on each step or event (*a state*). They do not look at the sequence of changes by which one state is changed to another (*a transformation*). Preoperational children can see each link in the chain of events. They can even describe the series of steps or events. But they do not mentally join the series. The questions of how something occurred or of what something was like before some change took place do not enter their minds. Piaget uses the example of the mind working in the same way as watching a film and seeing each frame as a separate and unrelated picture rather than a continuous story.

The pencil task can be used to study whether children focus on states or transformations. As shown in 15-6, if a pencil is held upright and

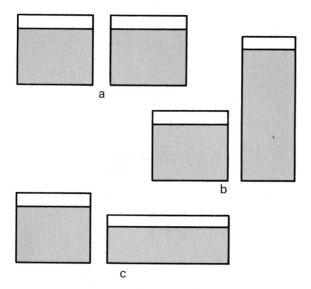

15-5 Preschool children know that the amount of liquid in the two equal-sized glasses is the same (a). But when the liquid of one container is poured into a tall tube (b) or a wider bowl (c), preschool children say the amount of liquid has changed.

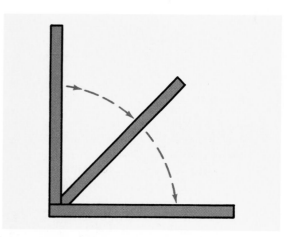

15-6 When preschool children are asked to watch as a rod is dropped and then draw what they have seen, they draw only the first state or the last state. They do not draw any of the in-between states.

Intellectual development of the preschooler 263

allowed to fall, it passes from an original (vertical) to a final (horizontal) state through a series of angled states. Preoperational children, after watching the pencil fall, draw only the initial or the final state.

Lack of reversibility. As you have already read, adult logic requires that mental actions be seen as reversible. *Reversibility* is the ability to follow a line of reasoning back to where it started. People who can subtract what they have added or can divide what they have multiplied see operations as reversible. Preschool children do not think of "undoing" what was done.

Reversibility is difficult because children in the sensorimotor stage do not see actions as reversible. Perception can be a roadblock to reversibility. Preoperational children allow the perception of length to outweight the logic that "as long as nothing is added and nothing is taken away, it is the same." This is shown in the button task, 15-7. Mathematics and other tasks requiring logic will help children form the concept of reversibility during the school years.

Transductive reasoning. Preschool age children do *transductive reasoning*. This type of thinking involves associating actions or objects without using logic. Reasoning in this fashion causes logic problems such as these:

1. Preschoolers may relate events which occur close together in time. Mother may make coffee just before Dad comes home from work each day. The child may conclude, "Coffee brings Dad home."
2. Preschool children may use different arguments to explain similar cause-and-effect relationships. A child may say, "Large boats float because they are large. Small leaves float because they are small."
3. A child can be given information from which to draw a conclusion, but does not draw any conclusion. Tell a preoperational child that all living things with four legs are called animals and that a tiger is a living thing with four legs. Then ask what the child knows about tigers. The child will likely never conclude that the tiger is an animal. He or she will name other characteristics such as stripes.

WHAT PRESCHOOL CHILDREN LEARN

Preschool children have much more advanced concepts than do infants and toddlers. Yet preschool children do not think in a logical way. Thus, there are many errors and gaps in preschool children's concepts.

Physical knowledge concepts

Physical knowledge includes concepts about size, shape, color, texture, and other qualities of objects and people. People develop physical knowledge concepts through sensory contacts.

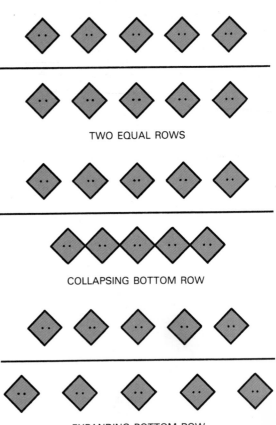

TWO EQUAL ROWS

COLLAPSING BOTTOM ROW

EXPANDING BOTTOM ROW

15-7 Preschool children judge the number of buttons in paired-rows to be the "same" only if their endpoints (called frontiers) match. Thus the collapsed row is seen as having fewer buttons and the expanded row is seen as having more buttons than each of their paired rows.

Perception is important in the development of correct physical concepts. People must be able to detect differences in size, shape, color, texture, and other features of objects or people in order to develop concepts. Preschool children become much better at noting differences in objects. However, preschool children are limited in two ways.

First, preschool children may not note the feature which is the most important in an object. For instance, the child must be able to note the stripes of a zebra to distinguish it from animals similar in form such as horses. No wonder young children may have problems in learning to read. Even after a child learns that the color and the size of the print are not the key features, the child must learn the arrangements of the lines that make up letters. They may find it especially difficult in noting differences among *b, d, g,* and *p* and in *Z* and *N*. Finally, after letters are learned, children must learn how words differ due to the order of the letters in the words *was* and *saw*.

Second, preschoolers also have a tendency to note parts, not wholes. Preschool children were shown drawings such as those in 15-8. Preschool children recognized the parts but not the whole. (Nine-year-olds could see both.) The ability to see both parts and the total figure are important to accurate perception.

Logical knowledge concepts

Logical knowledge concepts are concepts not directly experienced through the senses. Rather they are understood only mentally. Logical knowledge concepts include classification, seriation, number, space, and time concepts. These concepts are most difficult for preschool children because their thinking lacks logic.

Classification. *Classification* is mentally grouping objects by the ways they are similar. When asked to put objects that are alike together, preschool children can see likenesses in objects. But they find what is similar between two objects, and then change the standard for the third object. For instance, a child puts together a red square and a blue square (both squares). Then the child may add a blue circle to the blue square (both blue). The child ignores the differences in the objects. Toward the end of the preschool period, some children can group according to one property at a time such as color or shape.

Seriation. *Seriation* is the ability to mentally order a set of objects according to increasing or decreasing size, weight, or volume. Piaget checked the ability to do a length seriation task by giving a child a series of 10 sticks that varied in length. (The sticks varied in length by 1/4 inch.) The adult begins by showing the sticks in the proper order. Three ability levels are

15-8 Most preschool children will see only the parts of these drawings. They do not see the faces in the whole drawings.

often noted in preschool children.

1. In level 1, the youngest children place the sticks with no order seen, 15-9(a).

2. In level 2, children four to five years old place pairs comprised of a small stick and a large stick, 15-9(b). They do not see the order between more than two objects at once.

3. In level 3, children five to seven years old align the tops of the sticks in a stair-step way which shows an orderly change in height. But they do not pay attention to the alignment of the bottoms of the sticks, 15-9(c). A few children at this level can align four or five sticks but have trouble with the entire set.

Number. Many preschool children can count, but counting does not show a mature concept of number. As you read, conservation of quantity is difficult for preschool children. (See the task done with buttons.) By five or six years of age, some ability to conserve quantity begins. Number concepts are perhaps made more difficult for the child because people use many indefinite terms such as *less, few, many,* and *same.*

Space. Preschool children have some knowledge of words such as *up, down, left, right,* *under, over, here,* and *there.* But they have many problems with spatial (space) concepts. There are many examples of these problems. For instance, until they are almost five years old, children have problems telling you what is on the other side of walls which separate rooms in their home.

Preschool children think of an object's or person's location in relation to themselves. Thus, learning left and right from another's perspective is very hard — especially if the person is facing them.

Preschool children draw what they think about space and not what they see. For instance, preschool children draw objects at right angles to the side of a hill. See 15-10.

Time. Time concepts are difficult for preschool children. Preschoolers can only recall a recent past. Thus, "today" and "tomorrow" mean more than "yesterday." In a way, these children are gripped by the moment. They fail to see the lapse of time. Thus preschoolers feel as if they can make a long trip but can instantly return to get something.

Time concepts are difficult in themselves. There is no physical change in the days of the week. Morning and afternoon and seasonal changes are gradual. Children link time to

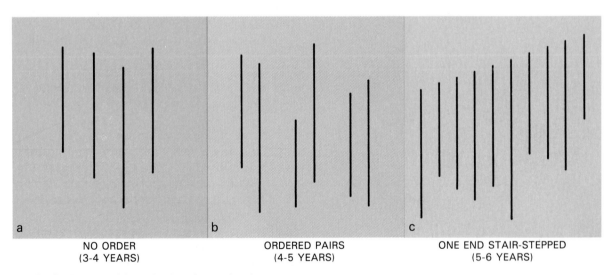

a — NO ORDER (3-4 YEARS)

b — ORDERED PAIRS (4-5 YEARS)

c — ONE END STAIR-STEPPED (5-6 YEARS)

15-9 Seriation of length develops slowly through a series of stages.

events. No wonder they are confused when the timing of an event is changed. There are different ways to designate time which adds to the confusion. For instance, someone may say it is 20 minutes until 3:00, 40 minutes after 2:00, or two-forty (2:40). An adult may tell a child that his or her birthday is "in two weeks" or is "week after next." People refer to the "days" of the week and the "days" of the month. One young child asked about the "nights." For these reasons, time concepts are among the last concepts to develop.

Causality concepts

Preschool children try to deal with *causality concepts*—the interrelationship of cause and effect. Many cause and effect questions deal with natural happenings which may be too difficult for these young children to understand. Children ask such questions as these: "What causes the rain?" "What will happen to my dead fish?" "How can a 'shot' make my throat better?"

Although scientific answers may be given to preschool children, these young children seem to settle on their own ideas. Their ideas can be called beliefs in artificalism and animism. *Artificialism* is the belief that humans or human-like things, including giants, cause all things. *Animism* is giving life and human qualities to nonhumans including plants, animals, and nonliving objects. For instance, a preschooler may say, "Mommy, make it stop raining," (artificialism). Or preschoolers may make statements such as, "The tree likes my book," (animism). These beliefs will be replaced with correct ideas of casuality as the child leaves the preoperational stage.

LANGUAGE ABILITIES INCREASE

As you read in Chapter 11, the use of language marks the transition from infancy to the early childhood years. Toddlers use language for both communication and as part of the thinking process. By the end of the toddler period, most children are ready to talk. Some are talking rather well.

The age of three years seems to be an important time for language use. Preschool children need language to express their needs and feelings to others. But their speech is as egocentric as their thinking. In other words, they talk but often do not communicate. Egocentric speech includes telling a story from the middle rather than the beginning. Another example is using pronouns without saying who is meant such as, "She is eating," leaving "she" to be guessed by the adult. Three types of egocentric speech have been noted:

1. Repeating words with no thought of talking to anyone.
2. Giving a *monologue* (talking to himself or herself) as though thinking aloud.
3. Engaging in a *collective monologue* (talking to another person, but not listening to what the other person has said).

At this time, the "why" behind egocentric speech is not fully understood. Perhaps the speech is due to egocentric thinking. Or it could be due to children's thinking aloud. Regardless of the reason(s) for egocentric speech, all children go through this stage of language development. Egocentric speech disappears in time, making communication easier.

Preschool children's communication is also made easier by other factors. They have bet-

15-10 A preschool child draws trees and other objects at right angles to the hill.

ter articulation, or ability to make the sounds of words. Their vocabulary is increased. And preschoolers have more advanced grammar. The advances in these areas of language during the preschool years are helpful.

Articulation of preschool children

In Chapter 11, you read that most toddlers have some problems making all the sounds in their spoken language. Most children substitute one sound for another (sound substitution) for a period of time. In English, mastering sounds occurs between three and eight years. Preschool children vary in the rate in which they learn to master the various sounds. But the order of mastery is about the same for most children. Total mastery means that the child can articulate the sound in different positions within words. (Most sounds, but not all, can be found in the beginning, middle, and end of words.) Chart 15-11 shows the sounds that most preschool children have mastered.

Vocabulary of preschool children

The norms for vocabulary vary due to ways vocabulary is measured. (See Chapter 11 for a more complete discussion.) From several studies, vocabulary growth is given as 900 words at age three, 1500 words at age four, and 2000 words at age five. No matter what the number of words, experts agree that words for concrete things (such as names for objects and people) are learned before words for abstract ideas (such as names for emotions). They also know that young preschool children often give their own meanings to words. For instance, a child three or four years old may use the terms *less* and *more* to mean more. The child may use *same* to mean same or different.

Grammar of preschool children

Sentence structure becomes much more complex during the preschool period. During the beginning of this stage, preschool children do not seem to notice word order. These young children will respond to "Give doll the Mommy" as quickly as they do to "Give Mommy the doll." By five-years of age, children will not respond to "Give doll the Mommy." In like manner, preschool children's speaking grammar matures a great deal between three and five years of age.

Three-year-olds' grammer. Three-year-olds begin using sentences where the actor appears before the action, and the object of the action appears after the action. (This type of sentence is called active voice.) An example of the "actor-action-object" type of sentence is, "The dog bit the boy." Three-year-olds do not understand the passive voice. Passive voice reverses the "actor-action-object" format as in, "The boy was bitten by the dog." It seems as though the three-year-old does not notice such words as *by* or *was* which signal the passive voice. The three-year-old treats the passive voice equal to the active voice and uses word order to decide meaning. Thus, in the example of the passive voice, the child would picture the boy biting the dog.

Questions are difficult, too, because word order is switched. Three-year-olds use question words such as why to ask questions. But they do not switch word order. For example, a three-year-old may ask, "When Mary will come?"

Negatives are most difficult. Once the child has an idea about negatives other than "no,"

ARTICULATION MASTERY OF PRESCHOOL CHILDREN

Age	Sound	Word Examples
3 years	m	monkey, hammer, broom
	n	nails, penny, lion
	p	pig, happy, cup
	h	hand, doghouse, —
	w	window, bowl, —
4 years	b	boat, baby, tub
	k	cat, chicken, book
	g	girl, wagon, pig
	f	fork, telephone, knife
5 years	y	yellow, onion, —
	ng	—, fingers, ring
	d	dog, ladder, bed

15-11 Ninety percent of all preschool children master these sounds by the given age.

extra negatives are added. Sentences such as, "I don't never want no more spinach," are common at this age.

As shown in Chart 15-12, three-year-olds begin to have some ideas about the rules of grammar. Once they learn the rules, they tend to apply the rule even to the exceptions. For instance, three-year-olds get the idea that "ed" means past tense. Once they know the rule, they tend to make all irregular verb forms regular such as "I eated" instead of "I ate." Children often use irregular words such as see/saw, am/was, come/came, and go/went. Many adults are concerned, because the child used the irregular form before this age. Adding "ed" to all verbs simply shows that the child has learned that there are rules. In time, the child will learn the exceptions to the rules.

Four- and five-year-olds' grammar. Older preschool children can understand the passive voice. However, the passive voice is more difficult. It can even cause problems during the school years.

These children can also ask questions by switching the word order. They no longer simply put the question word at the beginning of the sentence. ("What the dog is eating?") Instead, they move the helping verb to a position just after the question word. ("What is the dog eating?") By five years of age many children can ask *tag questions*—questions which ask for a yes or no answer. An example of a tag question is, "The baby is small, isn't he?"

Four- and five-year olds speak in longer sentences. Longer sentences are made by using clauses, conjunctions, and prepositions. Instead of saying, "We played games. I had fun," the older preschool child says, "I had fun, because we played games."

GRAMMAR OF THREE-YEAR-OLDS

Form Used in Speech	Examples
The *ing* verb ending used.	rolling, falling
Past tense for regular verbs (ed) used.	rolled, walked
Past tense for some irregular verbs used.	sank, ate
Verb "to be" used to link noun to adjective.	Truck is red; I am good.
The *s* for making plural used.	cars, dolls
The *s* for possessive used.	Bob's, daddy's
Articles used.	a, the
Prepositions referring to space used.	on, in

15-12 Three-year-olds are learning many of the rules of grammar.

Older preschool children seem to have two problems with grammar. First, they have trouble with pronouns. The objective case pronouns are used where subjective case pronouns should be used. For instance, the child may say, "Him and me went to town" instead of "He and I went to town." Pronouns seem to cause problems for children into the school years. Second, children continue to apply grammar rules to every case. "Eated" may be used instead of "ate." Even "ated" is heard once the child learns the irregular form. A five-year-old may learn to use the plural form "feet" only to ask, "May I go barefeeted?" The many irregular forms in the English language will cause problems for years.

to Know

animism . . . artificialism . . . classification . . . casuality concepts . . . centration . . . decentering . . . deferred imitation . . . egocentrism . . . intuitive substage . . . logical knowledge concepts . . . mental images . . . physical knowledge concepts . . . preconceptual substage . . . preoperational stage . . . reversibility . . . seriation . . . signs . . . symbols . . . states . . . transductive reasoning . . . transformation

to Review

Write your answers on a separate sheet of paper

1. True or false. There is a clean break (with no overlapping) between the sensorimotor and preoperational stages of development.

2. Complete each of the following sentences by placing the correct terms in the blanks.

Terms
a. Deferred imitation.
b. Symbolic play.
c. Drawing.
d. Mental images.
e. Language.

Sentences
1. ___C___ is a step between symbolic play and mental images.
2. ___E___ is made up of the most abstract symbols.
3. ___A___ is seen as a step before using symbols of one's own.
4. ___D___ are symbols stored in the mind.
5. In ___B___, children use ideas from their real world, dreams, and imagination.

3. A four-year-old begins a seven-hour car trip to his grandparents' home. Many times during the first hour, the child asks, "When will we get there?" The parents respond, "We will be there soon after lunchtime," thinking that the statement will help their child understand. A few minutes later, the child says, "Let's eat lunch." This is an example of _____ (lack of reversibility, transductive reasoning).

4. Two children are playing together. They want to play different games. Each insists that their game is the best. This is an example of _____ (egocentrism, centration).

5. Briefly describe the preschooler's ability to understand the following logical knowledge concepts:
a. Classification.
b. Seriation.
c. Space.
d. Time.

6. True or false. Children who are given scientific answers for natural happenings will not use artificialism and animism as answers.

7. True or false. Preschool children often seem to be talking to themselves.

8. Of the following sentence pairs, choose the sentence that a three-year-old is most likely to say.
a. "Mommy fixed my toy."
b. "My toy was fixed by mommy."

a. "Why are we going home?"
b. "Why we are going home?"

a. "I like food. I like apples best."
b. "I like food, and I like apples best."

9. True or false. Hearing correct grammar from older children and adults insures that the preschool child will use correct grammar, too.

to Do

1. Watch a group of preschool children play a pretend game. What symbols were used? Examples are material symbols such as a block for a boat, sound symbols such as sirens, noises, and action symbols such as pretending to eat. In what ways were the symbols like reality? Discuss your findings with the class.

2. Draw or collect pictures of purchased and household items that can be used in pretend play. Sort items into two groups. One group is items that often stand for one thing in play such as a baby doll. Another group is items that can be many things in play such as a box. Mount each group of pictures on a separate poster. Discuss with the class these two questions:

a. Are purchased items or household items more apt to be used in one way? Which are more likely to be used in many ways?

b. From which type of items do you think children mentally profit more—items that are often used in one way or items that are used in many ways?

3. Ask a preschool center director for permission to visit with the children about their drawings. (Secure permission to borrow some of the drawings after the visit or to take Polaroid pictures of them.) Ask the children to tell you about the drawings. (Say, "Tell me about your picture" rather than, "What is this?") Take notes on their responses. Using the borrowed drawings or the photos and your notes, share with the class the symbols used in the drawings. Look for ways in which the drawings were an attempt to show reality but were not visually accurate. Such ways might include being able to see four wheels as complete circles on a car.

4. Try Piaget's liquid task (as described in 15-5) with a three-year-old and a five-year-old. Discuss how people's eyes trick them. Can problems with perception arise in storing food left-overs, in packing luggage, and in other tasks? Can you think of examples where items are commercially packaged in ways to make customers believe they are getting more (although the amount is correctly given)? Why do some weight-loss diet ideas suggest that dieters eat more meals on smaller plates (such as pie plates rather than dinner plates)?

5. Try two of Piaget's logical concept tasks.

a. Obtain a set of attribute or parquetry blocks (flat blocks in various colors and geometric shapes often made of wood or plastic). The blocks may be borrowed from a preschool center or purchased. Ask a three-year-old to put the ones that are alike in some way together. Repeat the task with a five-year-old. Were there differences in the ability of the children to classify blocks?

b. Make or borrow a set of seriation rods. (Pencil-size diameter dowels can be cut into 10 different lengths. The lengths should vary at least 1/4 inch). Ask children ages three, four, and five to put the sticks in order from the longest to the shortest. (You may show them one time.) Compare your results with those shown in 15-9.

6. Record the speech of preschool children in play. Listen to the tape and try to answer these questions:

a. What sound substitutions did you hear?

b. Did you hear complex sentences—both statements and questions? Give examples.

c. What incorrect grammar did you hear?

d. What concepts seemed to be correctly understood by the children? What, if any, misconceptions (incorrect ideas) were expressed?

Preschool children leave behind much of the temper tantrums of the toddler stage. They become happier and more confident, and they increase their circle of friends.

16

Social-emotional development of the preschooler

After studying this chapter, you will be able to:

☐ Describe Erikson's stage of "initiative versus guilt."

☐ Explain the adult and child roles in learning to show responsibility.

☐ Trace how preschool children learn gender role.

☐ Discuss the growing importance of friends.

☐ Show how feelings and emotions change during the prechool years.

As you read earlier, toddlers begin to separate from parents and move toward more contacts with others. Preschool children continue to extend their social relations beyond the family circle. In the process of reaching out, they learn more about themselves as distinct individuals within adult and child social groups.

Preschoolers are more able than toddlers to balance between self will and adult will. As preschoolers begin to take initiative and show responsibility, they also begin to learn to control their emotions. They start to understand that temper tantrums and some other ways of showing feelings are not acceptable to adults. The preschoolers' emotions also become more complex as they understand more about their world.

DEVELOPS SOCIAL AWARENESS

Social awareness of children grows during the preschool years. Preschool children continue to learn about themselves. And they will greatly extend their social relations within and outside of the family circle.

Taking the initiative

As you read in Chapter 12, Erikson described the toddler's desire for autonomy (will to determine the kind and amount of adult aid needed) which must be met if shame and doubt are to be prevented. Feelings of self-control aid the preschool child in dealing with Erikson's third stage, "initiative versus guilt." See 16-1.

Between three and six years of age, children become even less dependent on adults (more autonomous). Because preschool children have improving abilities and limitless energy, they seek many new goals. Children who are allowed to ask questions, experiment, and explore develop *initiative*. Initiative is the ability to think or act without being urged. Children of this age want to wholly experience many things. For instance, a preschool child cannot learn about water without becoming completely wet! See 16-2. Because preschool children have such a strong desire to make things happen, Erikson refers to children of this age as *intrusive*. Intrusive children intrude or force themselves on another person or at a project. They may show a never-ending curiosity, talk alot and loudly, move all the time, and even attack others to achieve a goal.

Initiative is highly important. It later leads to ambition and finding a career. Yet initiative also leads to failures. Preschool children's ideas of what to do may go beyond their abilities. Some activities may not be allowed by adults.

Limits are needed by children because they must learn self-control. (Even adults must show initiative within a limited framework.) However, the preschool child's social-emotional hazard is *guilt* (feeling blame for a "wrong"). Guilt comes quickly to these young children because they tend to judge an act as completely right or completely wrong. Thus, when mistakes are made, the preschool child may translate this as, "I am bad." When children judge themselves harshly, they develop a sense of guilt. When children feel too guilty, obedience becomes so important that children are fearful of trying new things. This fear and guilt stifles initiative. To prevent too much guilt, children must know that it's all right to make mistakes. (We will return to this point in the next chapter.)

Showing responsibility

During the preschool years, children often take the first steps toward becoming a depend-

ERIKSON'S STAGE
OF INITIATIVE VERSUS GUILT

Basic Trust versus Basic Mistrust
(First Year of Life)

Autonomy versus Shame and Doubt
(Second Year of Life)

Initiative versus Guilt (Preschool Years)
Preschool children have growing abilities, much energy, and desire to engage in activities.
They begin trying things on their own (initiative).
The sense of initiative learned at this stage leads to ambition and purpose. Too many failures and too many no's from adults lead to guilt and fear of trying new things.

Industry versus Inferiority (Middle Childhood)

16-1 Showing initiative while avoiding guilt is a major social-emotional task of childhood.

COMMUNITY PLAYTHINGS

16-2 As long as safety is not a problem, children should be allowed to experience many things freely.

able person. People are seen as dependable when they show *responsibility* (do what is required or expected on their own). Like many learnings, learning to show responsibility takes many years and requires experience. People have many successes and failures before they learn responsibility. Adults help children to show responsibility by their examples and by giving children chances to learn.

In order to learn to show responsibility, tasks must be selected that the child can do. The child should have both the ability and the time to do each task. The child must be shown how to do tasks and any requirements must be made clear. Adults need to follow through with praise or

JOHN SHAW

16-3 Children learn to be dependable when they can help with real tasks in their world.

other rewards for successes and help after failures. For preschool children, household tasks are often chosen such as helping in the kitchen, putting toys away, and folding laundry. In preschool programs, children are often required to put away toys, books, and other materials, to help distribute snacks, and to help care for plants and animals in the classroom. Erikson believes that children should take part in the routines of their world in real and important ways. See 16-3.

Learning gender roles

Learning about yourself is an important aspect of social awareness, because you learn how to fit into certain social groups (family, school, clubs, and others). In order to fit into any social group, you learn what is expected. *Gender role learning* is knowing what is expected of a male or a female. Expectations must be learned in terms of physical behaviors such as the way a person dresses, talks, sits, and walks. Expectations must also be learned in terms of priorities and attitudes. For instance, people must learn accepted ways to treat members of the same and opposite sex. Also, they must learn the roles males and females play in the family, workplace, and community.

Gender role is a major concept that is learned in the preschool years. Most children cannot identify whether they are a boy or girl until age two. By three years of age, gender role learning, mainly physical expectations, is beginning. By five years of age, children realize some physical differences in the sexes. Five-year-olds also know that sex does not change and that they will always be male or female. By the end of the preschool years, children often overdo the gender roles they are learning. For instance, a boy may not touch a doll—if other boys are nearby. (But he may play dolls with a sister in the home although he may deny it!) At five or six years of age, children also see their sex as positive and the opposite sex as negative. Specific attitudes about gender roles are developed more slowly and are rather set by the end of the elementary school years.

Experts do not know exactly how gender role is learned, but it is probably due to several factors. Although each factor alone helps gender-role learning, the way each factor works with another seems to be very important, too.

The biological factor. As you learned in Chapter 4, at the moment the egg and sperm are united, the sex of the child is determined. From this point on, there are differences in the levels of hormones found in the developing baby. These hormones do cause physical differences and may influence mental and personality traits, too. (Experts do not yet know exactly what non-physical traits are inborn and what are learned.)

The social factors. From the moment of birth, *sex typing* begins. Sex typing is treating boys and girls differently. Some adults sex type rigidly, treating boys and girls very differently. Other adults sex type more broadly, 16-4. There are many examples of sex typing. There are "boy" names and "girl" names. In nursery decorations and clothing, blue means "It's a boy," and pink means "It's a girl." Adults may say things such as "He's all boy," or "She's a doll." Some studies show that boys are handled in rougher ways than girls even in the first few months of life. By age three, sex-typing may be more pronounced. Toys given to boys are often objects that foster gross-motor activities (balls and bats) and aggressive behaviors (toy weapons). Girls may receive toys that symbolize home and child rearing (dolls and tea sets). Behaviors may be treated in different ways, too. For instance, parents may be more negative when boys cry or ask for help than when girls do the same.

Identification and modeling factors. Children also learn their gender roles through *identification and modeling*. Identification and modeling is the process by which a person begins to think and behave as though the characteristics of another person belong to him or her. The person may see the similarities ("I have blue eyes like my father"), have the similarities pointed out ("You enjoy reading like your Aunt Sue"), or even belong to a group whose similarities are mentioned ("The whole family is musical"). The identification is strengthened if the person sees the model as good. For example, the child who loves Aunt Sue is glad about liking to read. That child will try to take on other characteristics of the aunt. Naturally, children see more similarity in the same-sex model. Thus, children learn more about their gender role in this way.

Children do not just identify with and model after family members who often have many similarities. They may learn gender role by modeling many others. Other models may include teachers and television, movie, and storybook characters.

Cultural factors. Different cultures or groups have differing beliefs about gender roles. (The group may be a nation, a region, a socio-economic group, a religious group, or another group.) Some groups stress differences between male roles and female roles. Other groups stress

16-4 Clothing and games permit many girls today to be sex-typed in a broader sense than they were in the past.

similarities between male and female roles.

In the United States and in many other countries, traditional gender roles were most common until rather recently. These traditional gender roles see the male as more aggressive and as the economic head of the family. The traditional gender role sees the female as soft-hearted and as the wife and mother who stays home. But there has been an increase in the number of women employed outside the home. Also, more men have been sharing household and child care duties. With these changes, there has been some change toward broader gender role typing and modeling. Some people believe that in order to thrive within today's life-style, boys and girls need to learn male and female roles and how to use them at different times, 16-5. For instance, both men and women may want to show assertive traits (such as willingness to express opinions) on the job. But they both may want to show loving, gentle traits with their children. This dual gender role is called *androgyny*. Other people prefer to retain the more traditional gender roles. When options are available, the choice is personal.

Within the cultural framework, children choose which roles they use for modeling. Their options can affect the gender role that they adopt. If the culture shows few options such as stating that girls must wear dresses, gender role is learned rather quickly. However, when a culture has more options for gender role, the child sees differences in same-sex models and must make choices. In these cultures, gender role learning is a little slower.

Extending social relations

Preschool children are very sociable. Over 30 percent of the child's waking hours are spent in social activities. Preschool children not only improve motor skills and knowledge through social activities, but they also increase their social learnings. These social learnings include sharing, controlling aggression, thinking of other's feelings, and joint efforts.

Adults are still important. Preschool children are still highly dependent on adults for meeting many of their needs. Adults also serve as social models. They teach children by example.

ELAINE M. WARD, SOUTHERN ASSOCIATION ON CHILDREN UNDER SIX

16-5 Playing dress-up helps young children learn the roles of both men and women.

Teachings include gender roles, friendships, morals, self-control, manners, responsibility, and much more.

Other children become more important. *Siblings* (brothers and sisters) and *peers* are more important to preschool children than to toddlers. (Peers are children near the same age. The term does not usually refer to brothers and sisters.) Preschool children's reactions to other children at this age are very different. Some preschoolers have fun playing with other children; others do not. The ease of making friends depends on a child's friendliness, ability to follow group "rules," and lack of dependence on adults. Friends of the same sex are also preferred, 16-6.

Social-emotional development of the preschooler   277

CARTER'S

16-6 Most preschool children enjoy having friends with same-sex friends preferred.

Preschool children have a rather egocentric (self-centered) view about friendships. They see friends (and nice siblings) as people who "play with you," "help you," and "share their toys and candy." Because of this self-centered view, usually only two or three preschool children form a closed circle of friends. After all, if there are too many friends, a child may not get enough from a friend. (For instance, a toy may be shared with another child.) To protect their interests, preschool children will often call out, "You can't play with us." When a friend does not do as the child desires, feelings quickly change. Someone else becomes the child's best friend—at least for the moment.

There are many learnings in the peer group. As preschoolers play together, play experiences become richer. Children get new ideas and can play games needing more than one child. Children are taught how to behave with peers through group play. Peers are a society of "equals." Children can simply reject (refuse to play with) a child who "doesn't play fair." Children become less egocentric in peer groups. They hear other children's points of view. Sometimes, children are even physically forced to see from another's point of view. Finally, children learn that friends are fun. A child can play with friends, sit and talk with friends, and celebrate with friends, 16-7.

FEELING AND CONTROLLING EMOTIONS

By the toddler years, children feel many emotions and express these emotions in very

16-7 Children enjoy having a birthday party with their friends.

intense ways. Preschool children will continue to react to the more common child-like stresses such as adult "no's," short separations from caring adults, and fear of "monsters." Besides these *stressors* (things that cause stress), preschool children will react to many more long-lasting and serious stressors. These may include illness, moving, death, adult quarrels, and divorce.

Preschool children not only feel many emotions, but they are expected to control many of their intense feelings. Controlling outward signs of emotions (crying, screaming, hitting, etc.) is important if children are to become socially acceptable. But if children control emotions without admitting underlying feelings to self and even to others, the child may become emotionally troubled. Children need to express feelings such as "I'm angry" or "I'm afraid you'll leave me the way you left Daddy."

Dependency

Preschool children often feel a conflict between their dependency needs and the need to become more independent. (Need to become independent comes from the child's desire as well as the adult's insistence.) Like toddlers, three-year-olds most often show their dependency in emotional ways. *Emotional dependency* is seeking attention, approval, comfort, and contact. In emotional dependency, the child is often dependent only on one person. Unlike toddlers, a three-year-old is more apt to accept comfort from a stranger. But three-year-olds still prefer a loved adult or a peer. By five years of age, children express more *instrumental dependency,* or need for help in achieveing a goal, than emotional dependency. For instance, older preschool children may ask the adult to button their coat or get a toy off a high shelf, 16-8. In most cases, the child really

JOHN SHAW

16-8 Preschool children show instrumental dependency by asking adults to help them learn new skills.

does need help. But sometimes the child asks for help that is not needed as a way of checking the adult's love or concern. In other words, emotional dependency is sometimes disguised as instrumental dependency.

Even as adults, people can show both emotional and instrumental dependency. But adults are expected to be more independent than dependent. It takes many years to learn the fine balance.

Fear and anxiety

Many of the toddler's fears disappear by the preschool years. New fears and anxieties replace older ones. Boys often report a greater variety of fears as they grow older. Girls report more intense reactions to fears. Although fears are very personal, there are some common features of preschool fears.

- Fear of the known such as vacuum cleaners, disappears. But fear of the imagined, such as monsters and robbers, is intense. Often these fears are associated with the dark.
- Fears of physical injuries; death in fires, auto accidents, or drowning; or bites and stings of animals and insects become more common. These fears emerge as children know they can be hurt. See 16-9.
- Fear of pain caused by medical and dental work is often shown.
- Fears often spread from specific to general. For instance, fear of a tornado may spread to general fear of a thunderstorm or even a good breeze.

As you can see, these fears are due to the growing mind. Many new concepts are understood only a little. This creates fears and anxieties that would not exist in adults. For instance, a preschool child would not understand that only certain weather conditions cause tornadoes. On the positive side, some fears may help protect children from trying unsafe activities.

Anger and aggression

Anger and aggression begin around 10 months of age and peak with displays of temper in the toddler years. Anger and aggression continue in the preschool years. However, many changes do occur during these years.

Anger and aggression are more general (not as directed toward oneself, others, or at something) in the toddler years. During the preschool years, anger and aggression become more specific. Three types of aggression are often seen in preschool children:

1. Aggression may be a sign of affection. For instance, a little shove may be given in a greeting. Of course, the child receiving such a greeting may not recognize it as such. Fights can start from innocent behaviors.
2. Anger and aggression may be *instrumental* (goal seeking) *aggression.* Examples of goals would be getting a toy or trying to be first in line.

REBECCA LAWRENCE

16-9 The fear of being hurt is a common emotion in the preschool years.

Anger and aggression may be called *hostile aggression* — aggression intending to hurt another. For instance, the hostile child may continue to fight after getting a toy back. Or the child may pick a fight or destroy property "for no reason." (Of course, there is a reason although it may not be known.)

Anger in the preschool years is directed at objects. For instance the child may blame the bike for the fall rather than the child's lack of skill. (Such thinking comes from animistic thinking as you read in Chapter 15.)

Children tend to hit or bite less, and threaten or yell more, in the preschool years. Increased language skills cause this change. However, boys tend to be more physical than girls. (Girls tend to be more verbal.) Perhaps boys are more physical because of delayed development in language as compared to girls. But it seems more likely that aggression is an inborn male trait. American culture seems to support more aggression in boys than in girls, too.

Anger and aggression seem to be directed more toward siblings and peers than toward adults. Preschool children seem to have learned that aggression toward adults, especially the physical type, is not acceptable. Also, anger and aggression are directed more at siblings and close friends than at casual peers.

Several conditions cause, or at least strengthen, anger and aggression. Having one's goals blocked can cause anger, 16-10. One study showed that preschool children have 90 of their goals blocked per day. The preschool child who likes to take charge is affected most by not getting what is wanted when it is wanted. The more care-free child is not often unhappy when goals are blocked. This type of child simply changes the goal. For instance, if a toy is taken by another child, another toy is simply found.

Studies show that punishment by aggression (spanking), especially for a child's aggressive act, increases aggression in preschool children.

16-10 Not getting one's way can trigger an angry response by young children.

JOHN SHAW

Spanking increases the child's anger. This produces a negative, aggressive response from the child. Furthermore, adults are serving as models of aggression—the exact behavior they wish to stop.

Not stopping a child's aggression in non-aggressive ways increases aggression. Even letting a child hit a pillow or kick a tree trunk is saying aggression is all right. Instead, children need to be taught that it is all right to feel angry, but acts of anger must be controlled.

Children see aggression modeled in many ways, including adults acts, peer acts, and the television. All studies show that one learns to be more aggressive by examples.

Society tries to teach an attitude of being assertive (speaking out, standing up for one's rights, and defending oneself), but not being hurtful to others. Trying to find this line between assertiveness and aggression can be most difficult for preschool children. (It can even be difficult for adults at times.) Because of this, preschoolers may act aggressive when they are trying to be assertive.

The amount of aggression in a child is stable from three to five years of age. And the amount of aggression seen in preschool boys is somewhat the same into the teen and adult years. The even amount is probably due to two main factors. First, the conditions that cause aggression tend to stay the same. Second, children tend to learn a response to those conditions. For instance, a bigger and older sibling may take toys away from a younger sibling for years (same condition). The younger child may learn that fighting sometimes gets the toy back.

There are ways of helping children deal with their angry feelings. You will read a few ideas on this topic in the next chapter.

Jealousy

Jealousy begins when people realize that they must share with others the love, attention, possessions, and time once given only to them. Jealousy is often a product of changes in the members of the family. You read in the chapter on the newborn that fathers are sometimes jealous of their babies. They feel jealous because babies take away wives in many ways. Mothers, too, are often jealous when children turn to their fathers. A mother may feel jealousy especially after a day in which her total energy seemed to be spent on the children.

In like manner, sibling jealousy begins when the bond between older children and their parents seems to be changed. The most common time is when a new sibling is born. Now children must share their parents' love. Babies take alot of time and energy which children translate as love. Children may feel there is "more love for baby and less for me."

Toddlers seem to have an especially hard time accepting new babies. Toddlers still need a great deal of adults' time. They are often negative and defiant because they do not have a sense of balance between self-control and adult control. The expressions of their emotions are crude. Toddlers tend to use physical expressions such as hitting which are more apt to be punished. All these factors make toddlers open to the feeling that they are losing love and attention.

Preschool children show fewer attachment behaviors than do toddlers, but attachment has not disappeared. In times of stress, including when a new sibling is present, preschool children may try to recapture the early attachment feelings. They may cry, cling, and show other signs of emotional dependence, and use other behaviors such as toileting accidents. Behaviors which are outgrown, but return in time of stress, are called *regression behaviors*. See 16-11.

Some preschool children may feel jealousy but ignore the feeling. *Repressed jealousy* is jealousy not directly expressed and even denied. It may be shown in nightmares, physical problems (upset stomachs, headaches, fever, change in appetite), and regression behaviors.

Unlike toddlers, preschool children are better able to understand when parents explain why the baby gets so much attention. Preschoolers are able to talk about some of their feelings. They can feel important by helping with a new baby. And preschoolers have contacts outside of the family—friends and people in preschool programs—to give to them when parents cannot. Thus, they can often adjust to a new baby better than can toddlers.

Jealousy over a new sibling is best handled in open, honest ways. (Some specific suggestions will be given in the next chapter.) And, jealousy does not end with the new baby. As siblings age, jealousy and rivalry may continue. (You will learn more about older siblings in Chapter 22, "Children are Members of Families.")

Grief

Death is a basic part of life, and even young children need to learn to come to terms with it. One-fifth of all children lose a parent before they finish elementary school. Many more face the death of a close friend or relative or of pets during childhood.

An understanding of death develops gradually. Around six or seven months, the baby has separations from caring adults. These

JOHN SHAW

16-11 Sucking on a bottle is an often seen regression behavior of preschool children. These children are trying to regain for themselves the baby status in their families.

separations, most of which are brief, are the earliest times of loss in a child's life. Early separation may set the stage for later responses to separation, loss, and even death. Until age three or four, children have little, if any, understanding of death. Preschool children's concepts of death are limited. They try to learn the physical facts of death. They find many facts difficult to believe, and thus they question the facts. Some concepts that give children trouble include the following:

- Life can stop.
- Death is forever (a most difficult time concept).
- People and pets cannot come back to life, even if they really want to. (Children have trouble with this concept because of artificialism—the belief that people are all powerful, even over death.)

Religious and other beliefs about death are not often explored by preschool children. However, preschoolers may repeat statements that they have heard dealing with belief.

Children must learn to express grief, 16-12. Toddlers and even preschool children may act in what may seem to be inappropriate ways to death and its rituals. This is because they have not learned adult ways of expressing grief. Those who have studied people's reactions to death have found that the feelings of preschool children and adults are very much alike. Both have feelings of anger, protest, sadness, and loneliness. And both desire to be in close contact with others. Adults need to be honest about the loss and their feelings. And they need to allow children to talk about death and grieve in their own ways—even through pretend play. In time, most children come to terms with their loss and stress lessens. And, through their experiences, they learn more about death and grief. (A few suggestions are given in the next chapter on helping children cope with grief.)

JOHN SHAW

16-12 When preschool children lose a loved one—even a pet—they must find ways to express their grief.

to Know

androgyny . . . emotional dependency . . . gender role learning . . . guilt . . . hostile . . . identification and modeling . . . initiative . . . instrumental aggression . . . instrumental dependency . . . intrusive . . . peers . . . regression behaviors . . . repressed jealousy . . . responsibility . . . sex typing . . . siblings . . . stressors

to Review

Write your answers on a separate sheet of paper.

1. True or false. When limits are given to preschool children, they will quit showing initiative and feel guilty.

2. Adults help children learn to show responsibility by _example_ and _giving chances_

3. In gender role learning, _____ (physical, attitude) expectations are learned first.

4. A preschool child identifies with and imitates models of the _____ (same sex, opposite sex).

5. Preschool children tend to have a closed circle of friends because:
   a. Too many friends overwhelm the child.
   b. Children's games are usually played with only two or three children.
   c. Children have an egocentric view of friendships.

*6. List four reasons why peers are important to preschool children.

7. Which of these fears are most common to preschool children? (You may list more than one.)
   a. Loud sounds.
   b. Monsters.
   c. Physical injury.
   d. Flushing toilets and vacuum cleaners.
   e. Being teased by other children.

8. True or false. Anger in the preschool years is always a sign of frustration.

9. Preschool children direct their anger more at _____ (known, unknown) children and adults.

10. True or false. Jealousy over a new baby is common.

11. What are three physical concepts about death that children must learn?

permanence   nothing lasts forever   the concept of afterlife does not exist

to Do

1. Interview teachers of preschool children about how the indoor and outdoor space, equipment, and materials found in their programs do the following:
   a. Encourage children to take the initiative for their own learnings.
   b. Minimize feelings of guilt about mistakes made when the initiative exceeds the child's skill.
   c. Give children a way to show responsibility.

2. Find some examples of sexual stereotyping in our society. (Sexual stereotyping is a statement or even a hint that men _always_ do or should do certain things or women _always_ do or should do certain things.) Discuss how sexual stereotyping affects gender role learning.

3. Watch nursery school children at play. List some of the sex differences you noted in their play activities, what they talked about, and other interactions.

4. Draw a cartoon which shows preschool children's ideas of friendship.

5. Have a classroom discussion on how adults show both emotional and instrumental dependency at times.

6. Interview preschool children about something scary that happened to them. Have them draw a picture. Display these on a bulletin board.

7. Discuss the pros and cons of adults using fears for discipline purposes. How can adults teach dangers without starting fears in children?

8. Read about the development of phobias. Write a short report on your findings.

9. Discuss some statements made about death that may confuse preschool children about the physical reality of death. Look up the term _euphemism_ in the dictionary. Are many of our culture's statements about death euphemisms? Explain.

1. find out that friends
2. Social equality
3. Richer play experiences
4. They learn how to behave peers.

JOHN SHAW

As preschoolers grow, their physical, intellectual, and social-emotional needs change.

17

Providing for the preschooler's developmental needs

After studying this chapter, you will be able to:
- ☐ Plan ways to meet the developmental needs of preschool children.
- ☐ Help preschool children care for their own physical needs.
- ☐ Stimulate preschool children's mental thinking.
- ☐ Assist preschool children as they expand their social world and gain control over the expression of their feelings.

Preschool children's motor, mental, and social skills develop at a rapid rate. These skills make preschoolers better able than infants and toddlers to meet their own needs. Not only are preschool children rather skillful, but they want to do things for themselves and for others. For instance, they like to use their motor skills to feed and dress themselves and help with everyday tasks.

Mental thinking (as opposed to physical thinking) gets well underway during the preschool years. Preschoolers can mentally see objects and actions. They can even solve problems in mental ways. Concepts become more accurate. Language helps preschoolers expand concepts. Language is also a sign of preschoolers' progress in learning concepts.

Social skills also develop in the preschool years. Preschool children's social world grows to include many new adults, close friends, peers, and perhaps younger siblings. Adults expect preschool children to become more independent, show more responsibility, and control their feelings more. Peers and siblings treat children more as equals. Peers do not treat each other as children who are due the special favors often given by adults. For instance, peers do not always let the child have the biggest piece of dessert or the first turn.

Preschool children are learning a whole way of life where needs in one area of development affect needs in other areas of development. Thus, preschool children's changing physical, mental, and social needs demand a great deal of support and much time from caring adults.

PHYSICAL NEEDS

Preschool children are no longer completely dependent on adults to meet their every physical need. As the body matures, motor skills are refined, and the mind grows, these children are better able to help in their own care. At this age, children want to help meet their own needs. For instance, they want to help with meal preparation and learn to dress themselves. See 17-1.

Children will take the initiative in learning how to meet their physical needs. But adults must be there to help. In a sense, this is the first real chance for the child and adult to work as a team in meeting the child's physical needs.

Meeting nutrition needs

Nutrition that meets the preschool child's needs must be carefully planned. Children at this age vary in their growth and energy output from month to month. And, for preschool children, eating junk foods (foods low in nutritional quality) may become more of a problem.

You are what you eat. The slogan, "You are what you eat," is correct. Diet affects growth. Growth slows during the preschool years as compared with the first three years of life. But a preschooler's growth is not at all complete. In the three preschool years (ages three through five), height increases about seven inches and weight increases about 13 pounds. Other body systems must keep pace with skeletal growth. If the diet is not adequate, the body may conserve fuel needed for its own upkeep. These conditions may cause the rate of growth to slow. Children are also more prone to diseases—and recovery time is slower—when nutrition needs are not met.

The preschool child is an active child. Watch preschool children at play. Their bodies twist, turn, and bounce as they "walk." Preschool children don't even sit still. Thus, their energy needs are very high. Their energy must come from their diet.

Proper diet is needed for brain growth, too. General alertness is affected by a person's daily diet. Diet also seems to affect emotions. When daily food needs are met, the child seems less irritable and restless.

The daily basic diet needs for most prechool children are given in 17-2. The diet plan may need to be adapted to a child's own needs. Some changes may be needed for growth rate which varies from month to month, for energy output differences, for current health status, and for ethnic diets such as Chinese or Mexican. When a child needs a special diet for health reasons, a physician or registered dietitian should be consulted.

Snacks should be nutritious as well as provide calories. Health experts state that children (and adults) should lessen their intake of sugar, salt, and animal fats. Sugar can lead to tooth decay, obesity, and other health problems. Animal fats and high salt intakes, even in early

JOHN SHAW

17-1 Children like to help make their own food and do other self-care tasks.

DAILY BASIC DIET FOR PRESCHOOL CHILDREN

Milk (3 servings)
Typical serving: 1 cup (240 mL) whole, reconstituted evaporated, skim, reconstituted dry, buttermilk, or yogurt;* two 1-inch (2.5 cm) cubes or 1.5 oz. (45 g) hard cheese. Part can be in cream soups, custards, or pudding.

Protein Foods (6 exchanges)**
One exchange: 1 oz. (30 g) cooked lean solid meat, poultry, fish; 1/2 cup (120 mL) cooked dry beans, peas, lentils; 1 oz. (30 g) cheese; 1/4 cup (60 mL) cottage cheese; 2 tablespoons (30 g) peanut butter; 1 egg; 1 frankfurter.

Vitamin A-Rich Fruits and Vegetables (1 serving)
Typical serving: 1/2 cup (120 mL) cooked or 2/3 cup (160 mL) raw spinach, kale, collard and other greens, broccoli, sweet potatoes, yellow squash, carrots, tomato, apricots.

Vitamin C-Rich Fruits and Vegetables (1 serving)
Typical serving: 1/2 cup (120 mL) juice or cooked; 1 piece, or 2/3 cup (160 mL); raw oranges, grapefruit, pineapple, tangerine, papaya, strawberries, brussel sprouts, broccoli, cauliflower, collard and other greens.

Other Fruits and Vegetables (2 servings)
Typical serving: 1/2 cup (120 mL) cooked or 2/3 cup (160 mL) raw asparagus, bean sprouts, beets, cabbage, celery, cucumbers, green peppers, okra, mushrooms, string beans, non-yellow squash, apples, bananas, berries, grapes, watermelon, pears, figs, dates, prunes, raisins.

Cereals (whole or enriched), Potatoes, Legumes (5 servings)
Typical serving: 1 slice bread; 1/2 cup (120 mL) cooked rice, corn, hot cereal, cooked pasta; 1 muffin, biscuit, pancake, or waffle; 2-inch (5 cm) square of cornbread; 3/4 cup (180 mL) ready-to-eat cereal; 2 corn tortillas; 1 large flour tortilla; 1 small or 1/2 cup (120 mL) dried beans or peas.

*Whole milk fortified with Vitamin D preferred.

**The term *food exchange* implies that any item within a given food group has about the same food value as any other food item for that food group. To use the exchange system, select foods in the given amount for each allowed exchange. For instance, six exchanges can be six different food choices. Or, the same food can be eaten for more than one exchange. For example, if one ounce (30 g) cheese equals one exchange, then one and one-half ounces (45 g) equals one and one-half exchanges and two ounces (60 g) equals two exchanges.

17-2 A well-balanced diet is needed to meet preschool children's growth and energy needs.

life, may increase the chances of high blood pressure later on in life. The concern is especially high if a high blood pressure problem exists in the family's health history. Snack foods are often high in sugar, salt, and animal fats.

Food attitudes are learned. The food attitudes formed in the preschool years may last a lifetime. Offering a variety of foods in a pleasant atmosphere helps preschoolers form good food attitudes.

For the most part, humans like variety in their lives. This includes what they eat. Of course, children—and even adults—may go through phases where they want the same food(s) day after day for a time. And many people eat or drink a few of the same foods daily but vary other foods.

As you can see in 17-2, a child can have many options within any food grouping (such as protein or milk). Children should be able to eat foods they like and still have their nutritional needs met. Forcing a child to eat things they don't like can cause negative feelings toward good diets. See 17-3. Using food to reward or

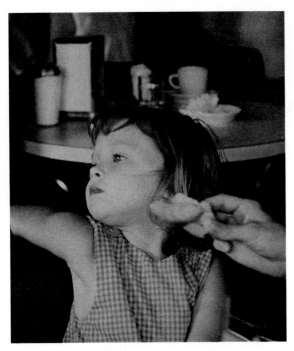

17-3 Preschool children often reject foods if they feel that they are being forced to try them.

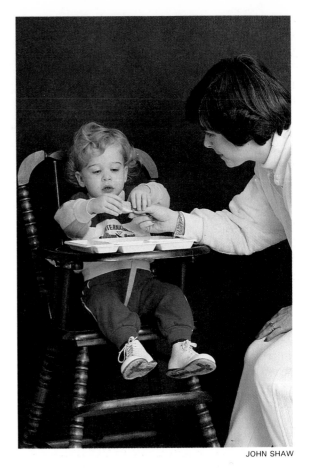

JOHN SHAW

17-4 Taking one bite seems to be much better than having to eat the whole thing.

punish (Adult: "You can't have your dessert until you eat your peas!") can also have a bad effect. Children who are rewarded and punished with food may learn to eat as a way of blackmail. (Child: "How many cookies do I get if I eat my peas?")

Adults can prevent some eating problems in preschool children. Many suggestions can help. Adults need to know that children and adults have different senses of taste (and smell). For instance, many adults wonder why some children do not like spinach. There is an acid in spinach (oxalic acid) that leaves a bitter aftertaste in children but not in adults. Children often prefer mild flavors and odors over strong flavors and odors. They do not tend to like foods that are very spicy, either.

Foods that can be eaten separately rather than in combinations are often better liked by children. If children taste one food they do not like in a casserole, soup, or salad, they may reject the entire dish. Mixtures of fruits are accepted more easily than mixtures of vegetables. Children may eat what they have chosen to mix rather than adult-chosen mixtures. For instance, children may mix their own salads from several bowls of pre-cut vegetables. This way they can choose to have carrots but leave out celery. Or perhaps they will try one piece of celery.

Children often prefer foods nearer room temperature to foods that are too hot or too cold. Most children do not care for hot drinks. They will accept soup cooled with an ice cube or two over a steaming bowl. Cold foods are eaten very slowly. There may be more of an ice cream cone on the outside than on the inside of a preschool child!

Children show likes and dislikes for methods of food preparation. A child who turns down cooked carrots may eat a crisp, raw carrot. (Vitamins are saved in raw foods, too.) A salad dressing, not too tangy, may make almost any vegetable or fruit easier to eat.

Children will often take one bite or a small amount of a food just to see whether they like it. See 17-4. New foods should be given in small amounts (one slice or a tablespoon) with more ample portions of known, liked foods served at the same time.

Foods should be easy for preschoolers to eat. Bite-sized and finger foods are preferred over foods that are harder to eat. Most children at this age cannot cut food. And spoons and forks may not be held in mature ways. These problems make eating messier for preschoolers than it is for older children and adults. See 17-5.

Children like attractive-looking foods. Foods of different sizes, shapes, colors, textures, and temperatures look better than foods that look the same. Plates should have some empty space, too. Full plates can give a feeling of too much even before one bite is taken. (Seconds can be made available.) Children also enjoy foods prepared especially for them, 17-6. Special dishes, napkins, or centerpieces may make a good meal or snack even more special.

JOHN SHAW

JOHN SHAW

JOHN SHAW

17-6 Foods that look fun to eat also seem to taste better.

JOHN SHAW

17-5 Preschool children still cannot hold a spoon or fork in an adult way.

Children enjoy helping with food preparation. Children learn about colors, shapes, tastes, odors, textures, and appliance names (blender, oven). They learn food preparation terms (cut, boil, poach, bake) and names of foods. Cooking teaches math concepts (measurement, numbers on blenders, temperature, time, shape of pans). It also introduces children to science as they see changes in foods (rising, baking, freezing, boiling, and others). (We will return to cooking experiences in Chapter 24.) And, as an added bonus, children often eat what they help prepare!

Eating with others should be pleasant for children. Meals should be times for relaxing, sharing, and fun. There should be a quiet time before and after meals. Enough time should be given for the meal itself, because eating with children takes time.

Setting an example of taking turns talking and other table manners allow good learning at meal time. However, discipline (especially punishment and scoldings) should not take place at the table. All talk should be pleasant.

An attractive room for eating helps, too. Dishes and flatware suited to the child's hands make mealtime more comfortable. They also lessen the chance of accidents. Preschool children may want to help make the table attractive by choosing the napkins, picking a flower from the garden for the table, or helping set the table.

Food becomes a part of many celebrations. Preschool children may look forward to helping prepare a special holiday dish or choosing their birthday menu. Trying different eating styles is fun, too. A restaurant, a cafeteria, a picnic, a clam bake, or a covered dish get together provides children with more food experiences. See 17-7.

Selecting the right clothes

Selecting the right clothes for preschool children is important. Clothes protect the child's body from harsh weather conditions and from bumps, scrapes, and cuts. Clothes are also important to the growing self-concept.

Fit. Fit is a most important feature of preschool children's clothes. Clothes must give the active child complete freedom to move. Children are best fitted by size, not age. Sizes for children's clothes are often given as 1 through 6x. Hang tags and charts on children's sizes often give several measurements (chest, waist, hip, inseam, and others) rather than just height and weight. You may note some overlap of sizes such as "Toddler Size 4" (4T) and "Children Size 4" (4). Often the chest and waist measurements are the same in "Toddler" and "Children" sizes. However, "Children" sizes are often longer, and both the shoulders and back are wider than "Toddler" sizes. In addition to regular sizes, some clothes for children can be bought in sizes to fit the slender child (called by names such as "Slims" and "Superslims") and the heavier child (called by names such as "Chubbies" and "Huskies").

Fabric and construction features. Preschool children's clothes must have most of the same quality fabric and construction features as toddler clothes. (Review the clothing section in Chapter 13, especially Chart 13-6.) Two other points need to be made about preschool clothing construction features. First, because preschool children grow mainly in the length of the arms and legs and the width of the shoulders, these growth features should be considered:

- Wide hems that can be let out as arms and legs grow.
- Kimono or raglan sleeves that allow for increase in the width of the shoulders.
- Adjustable shoulder straps and waistbands that allow for both length and width increases.

Second, because preschool children explore more of their indoor and outdoor world, more safety features need to be included. Outdoor clothing worn after dark should have a trim of reflective tape or ribbon. The tape or ribbon will reflect the light of cars or other vehicles. Hoods attached to coats and rainwear should easily detach if caught on large objects. Children have suffered neck and back injuries from nondetachable hoods. Floppy headwear can prevent children from seeing traffic or other hazards. Floppy or wide pantlegs and extra long shoelaces can cause tripping. Long,

OSCAR MAYER AND COMPANY

17-7 Special places to eat seem to increase young children's appetites.

wide sleeves that are not gathered into a cuff, drawstring ties, long sashes and scarves, and too large of clothes are also dangerous.

Self-dressing features. By the end of the preschool years, many children can dress themselves with only a little help from adults. Of course, adults should always be nearby to help the child and to check the child's attempts. Chart 17-8 shows the features that aid self-dressing. In addition to self-dressing features in garments, special learning aids are available,

SELF-DRESSING FEATURES

Feature	Reason for Feature
Large openings, especially for slipover garments.	Children are not skilled in pulling clothes just right to squeeze through small openings. Children do not like (and may fear) tight neck openings pulled over their face and ears.
Easy to recognize fronts and backs of garments such as labels, threads, or tape sewn in the back of garments.	Children cannot easily hold a garment by the shoulder seams or waist to determine back from front. Children can be taught to place slipover garments with the label face down before putting arms in sleeve openings and to place the label of step-in clothes (pants and skirts) next to the body before stepping in to the garment. Children may need help with wrap dresses, skirts, and jumpsuits.
Front rather than back openings such as front buttons and attached belts which hook in front.	Back closures are not easy for children to reach and cannot be seen.
Elastic in waists of pants, shorts, and skirts, and in sleeve (at wrist).	Elastic is easier to manage than are buttons, hooks, snaps, and zippers.
Easy to work fasteners such as the following: a. Zippers with large pull tabs. b. Smooth, flat buttons, at least the size of a nickel. c. Shank or sew-through buttons sewn with elastic thread for a little give. d. Gripper snaps the size of a dime that do not fit too tightly together. e. Velcro instead of other fasteners.	Children do not have the small-muscle skills needed to work small, tight-fitting fasteners.

17-8 Self-dressing features encourage learning how to dress oneself.

The preschooler's developmental needs 293

17-9. These give children extra dressing practice.

Shoes and socks. Most preschool children grow one shoe size every four months. By the preschool years, children may have more than one style of shoe. Along with size, certain features should be checked for in each style. See 17-10. When you buy bigger shoes, you may also need to buy bigger socks. Socks sizes correspond to shoe size. Socks should be one-half inch longer than the longest toe.

Clothes and the self-concept. Preschool children are well on their way to developing a unique personality. Clothes are one way to express personality. Preschool children show off their clothes and talk about clothes worn by others. For instance, children may make comments about pockets or trim.

Preschool children should make a few choices about their clothes. Perhaps they can choose the color they want from otherwise identical outfits. If the outfit is to be sewn, a choice could be made between two pattern views or among a few trims. Not only will children enjoy clothes that they have chosen more, but they are also learning how to make decisions.

Handling sleep and toileting problems

The routines of meeting sleep and toileting needs are often well established by the end of the toddler years. Some children are still having problems in these areas. Most children will have a few problems from time to time.

Sleep needs are individual. They will even vary for an individual from time to time. Most children give up all daytime naps during the

JOHN SHAW

JOHN SHAW

17-9 Many toys make learning to dress oneself more fun.

STYLE AND FIT FOR CHILDREN'S SHOES

Style	Fitting Features
Activity shoes	Flexible soles that are 1/4 inch (.63 cm) to 3/8 inch (.94 cm) thick to absorb the pounding of walking, running, and jumping.
Sneakers and athletic shoes	Arch support in correct position. Check fit with the socks to be worn with the shoes. The socks are often bulky, requiring larger shoes.
Sandals	Adjustable straps and buckles that do not press into foot.
Dress shoes	As flexible a sole as possible. (Thin soles of dress shoes do not absorb pounding. Therefore dress shoes should be worn for short periods of time.)

17-10 Shoe fit includes more than the right length and width.

preschool years. But they will continue to need 10 or more hours of sleep at night. If bedtime rules have been enforced in the toddler years, most preschool children accept them. However, the bedtime ritual is still wanted (and needed). Fears of the dark and monsters are still there, but many preschool children develop little rituals (locking windows or having a doll watch over their sleep) that help ease such stress.

Toileting accidents occur once in a while with most preschool children. During these years, daytime accidents are most often caused by waiting too long to take care of one's needs. Children of this age, and even early school age children, may need to be reminded to go to the bathroom. Reminders should be given after awakening in the morning or from naps, before going outside to play, before and after meals, and before leaving the house. Only older children think to take care of future needs to lessen the chances of emergencies. Time seems to be the major cure for bedtime accidents. Most children are not night trained until at least three years of age. Causes of bedtime accidents in the later part of the preschool years (and even in the school years) may be many. Some problems include deep sleeping, fear of getting up in a dark house, too much liquid prior to bedtime, and physical problems (only in a few

cases). Most children outgrow these problems within a few years. For those who do not, medical or other trained help may be needed.

Providing needed space and furnishings

Unlike babies and toddlers who want to be in the almost steady company of adults, preschool children want to be on their own more. These children want some space to call their own. Often preschool children have more toys and belongings than do younger children. They need to be able to safely get and return many of their own things. Thus, careful planning for space and furnishings is needed.

Plans for children's areas are personal choices. Adults must consider the house size and the amount of space that could be used for children. The general decor of the house should also be considered. Other factors that affect plans include budget and whether one wants to buy something that can be used for many years or something suitable for a more limited time. Thus, only a few very general suggestions can be made.

Preschool children want a little space to call their own. This may be anything from one or more rooms to a chest or drawer. Even when a bedroom is shared with another child, a screen, a storage cabinet, or a curtain can serve

The preschooler's developmental needs 295

as a room divider. This allows some private space for times when children want or need to be alone.

Preschool children can learn self-help and responsibility for the care of their belongings. However, they need some storage space that is easy for them to use. See 17-11. For instance, a pegboard wall with holders for equipment allows toys to be stored neatly, but in sight. A window can be flanked with storage shelves and a window seat or desk can be used in front of the window. Strips of hook and loop tape tacked to a wall of the closet or other places can hold lightweight toys. Storage ideas are limited only to one's imagination.

Storage needs to be planned in such a way that preschool children can help themselves more. For instance, clothes hooks and rods need to be lowered for a child's use. Often-used toys and items need to be placed near where they are to be used and within the child's reach. And toys and clothes need to be arranged in ways that the child understands.

INTELLECTUAL NEEDS

Adults have the task of helping preschool children meet their intellectual needs. As in the toddler years, adults continue to direct children's attention to things to do and problems to solve. Preschool children may be enrolled in special programs. But the home and neighborhood play groups can remain the most important places for learning. Preschool children's mental abilities can and do develop any time and any place. Think about the learning that comes from a simple shopping trip, 17-12. In shopping, these intellectual skills are used: Observing properties of items (finding an item by its shape, color, size, texture, or sound). Classifying items (an item is found in certain types of stores such as food in grocery stores and in certain places in a store such as fresh fruits in the produce section). Number skills (one buys a certain number of items). Language skills are learned, too, as items are named.

Some adults suggest that formal instruction (mainly reading and math) should begin in the preschool years. But many other adults who

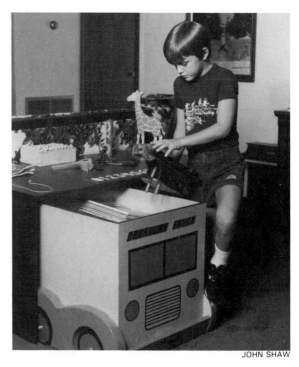

JOHN SHAW

17-11 Storage space helps when adults try to teach children how to care for their own things.

have studied and worked with young children question this point of view for these reasons:

1. Young children must arrive at their own meanings and develop their own skills. Repeating without meaning is not real learning. Adults need to become "tour guides" who provide materials, who ask questions, and who present problems for children to solve.

2. Problem-solving in the real world gives a practical reason for learning. For instance, in setting the table, the child may see the need for counting forks. But the child may not see the need to count objects in a picture shown by an adult.

3. *Divergent thinking* (coming up with different possible ideas) is more often developed through rich, everyday experiences. On the other hand, *convergent thinking* (coming up with only one right

answer or way) is more often seen in formal lessons. Answers to many of life's problems require divergent minds.

4. Some children feel stress as a result of formal lessons. If young children see learning as fun, this attitude may carry over to the years ahead.

As you read in Chapter 15, many learnings occur during the preschool years. The activities which are suggested at the end of this chapter are given as ways of enriching learnings when the child seems eager to develop a new meaning or skill.

Learning through observing

Children must learn to really observe by seeing, hearing, touching, smelling, and tasting.

THE FIRST YEARS

17-12 Many learnings come from everyday tasks such as shopping.

During the preschool years, children should be able to see details and *compare* (see how things are alike) and *contrast* (see how things are not alike). Games can be used to improve these skills.

Television viewing. Children also observe by watching television. Attractive characters, animation, movement, repetition, and many sounds used on children's television programs and many commercials cause children to observe. However, *passive observing* (attending without responding) is not the same as learning. Most television shows do not require responses from children. Even if a show encourages a child to respond, the child may simply watch without responding.

Children need more time to digest an idea than the few seconds a television image may provide. Caring and teaching adults are more important to children's learning than any television program. Thus, television should not be used as a babysitter. However, when a quality program is viewed with a sharing adult who builds on the concepts, then a learning boost will likely occur. More tips on television viewing are found in Chapter 21.

Learning through problem solving

Problem solving is a rather broad term. It most often includes noting a problem, observing and questioning what one sees, and solving the problem. Almost from birth, babies are action problem solvers as they physically try to make things work. By the preschool years, mental and action problem solving skills are used. Mental problem solving depends on basic skills in classification, seriation, transformation, and reversals.

Classification. *Classification* is grouping things by kind such as saying that a poodle and a German shepherd are both dogs. The ability to classify grows out of the ability to compare (and contrast). People group by likenesses in *properties*. Properties are any qualities which can be used in comparing. There are perceptual properties—size, color, shape, texture, and others. Other types of properties include ways in which things are used (art tools, cars, food). The things that are alike in some property are called *class*. All of those things that do not belong to the class are called the *complement*. For instance, if the class is dogs, then people, other animals, cars—everything except dogs— would make up the complement.

Preschool children, especially three- and four-year-olds, have three main problems when they try to classify. First, the child may see how things are alike. But they change properties as they classify. As you read in Chapter 15, they may begin to classify by color and then get shape involved. Second, the child may sort more than classify. They get the class, but they sort the complement rather than treating it as a whole group. See 17-13. Third, the child finds it difficult to classify items one way and then classify the same items another way. For instance, they have trouble classifying blocks by color and then by shape. Some sorting and classifying activities can help children overcome these problems. Sorting games should be tried first. When they are mastered, classifying games can be tried.

Seriation. Seriation is putting objects or events in a series or order. For instance, children may line up from shortest to tallest or from tallest to shortest. The keys on the piano are ordered in a pitch series from high to low or from low to high. In retelling a story, events must be put in order. The number system is a series.

As you read in Chapter 15, preschool children have problems putting things in an order. Adults can help learning with games, but they should keep two points in mind. First, restrict the number of items to five or fewer. Second, make the differences in the items easy to notice.

Transformations. The changes that have occurred between one state and another are called *transformations*. A caterpillar is transformed to a butterfly. Heat transforms ice to water. Understanding transformation is logically very difficult for preschool children. They need to observe and experience transformations. Some activities can help.

Reversals. Before the child can mentally handle *reversals* (mentally do and undo an action), they need to perform some physical reversals. Like transformations, reversals must be experienced—not taught. Activities can be used to help the child see how reversals happen.

Learning through symbolizing

Intellectual needs are also met as the child begins to think in terms of symbols. Symbols have differing degrees of abstractness—from a little abstract to highly abstract.

Enactive representation. Enactive representation is using one's own body, including the sounds one can make, to represent another person or an object. Often enactive representation is the least abstract of all symbols.

Children need many chances to pretend to be other people and other things. For the most part, children need only a little help in pre-

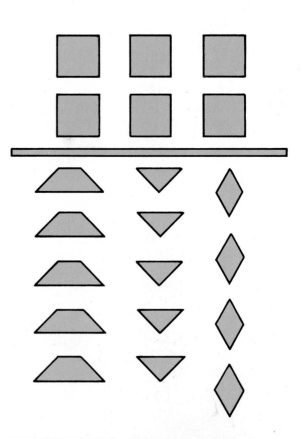

17-13 Preschool children can group things that are alike—the squares. But they also sort the complement (other shapes) rather than placing them in a random way.

298

tending. Many children begin pretending around their first birthday, but pretending does not reach a peak until the preschool years.

Concrete, three-dimensional representation. We live in a three-dimensional (3-D) world. Using objects such as building blocks, clay pieces, dolls, and many other objects to represent the real world is called *concrete, 3-D representation*. See 17-14.

Children think using 3-D objects as they pretend. Children usually supply the ideas with little help. In fact, adults need to be careful not show or tell too much about how to pretend or the value of pretend play is lost. (In Chapter 24, you will read more about pretend play.)

JOHN SHAW

17-14 One of the best ways to symbolize the real world is through 3-D objects.

Two-dimensional (2-D) representation. Two-dimensional (2-D) representation is symbolizing one's world through flat art media—paints, crayons, pencils, and other media. Younger children make their art products first and then sometimes decide what they represent. As children mature, the idea comes before the product is made. As is true of all representations, the child decides on the symbol, not the adult. (Chapter 24 deals further with art.)

Abstract symbolic representation. Signs (such as traffic signs and signals), words, numbers, graphs, music notation, and scientific notation are some forms of *abstract symbolic representation*. (Piaget called these symbols, "signs," because they are developed and agreed upon by a group of people.) Because these signs (symbols) are not at all like the real thing, they are highly abstract.

In the preschool years, the spoken language is the main type of abstract symbolic representation that the child begins to learn. One of the main issues in early childhood education is whether young children should be taught to read (and perhaps do formal math problems). Many experts feel that most preschool children need more time to deal with their real world. They think children should deal with less abstract forms of symbols. Unless the child sees the mental link between the real thing and its symbol (such as a real cat and the word *cat*), the symbol means nothing. And, when learning is meaningless (and too difficult) it is not fun, but stressful!

Learning through motor skills

As children move and act upon objects, they not only become more skillful in physical ways, but in mental ways. Children learn as they move their bodies in space. They learn as they do things with their hands.

Because preschool children are in almost constant motion, many gross-motor skills are learned as preschool children just play. However, a few planned activities may be fun and help mental development as well.

Fine-motor skills should be enjoyed, too. Some of the best items are art materials, puzzles, 17-15, small wooden beads to string,

The preschooler's developmental needs   299

pegboards, lacing cards, small construction toys such as Lego Blocks and Tinker Toys, and self-dressing aids.

Learning through language

Preschool children learn language from what they hear—articulation of sounds, vocabulary, and grammar. Thus, adults must be the best language models they can be.

Preschool children need many daily chances to talk with adults and older children. The old saying, "Children should be seen and not heard" hurts language learning. When pre-school children play only with age mates or younger children, language is not learned as quickly as it is when children talk with adults. For this reason, only and first-born children are often better in language than are younger siblings.

Talk needs to be a part of all activities. When talk is only to give orders, language learnings are not expanded. But when activities and talk are combined, children's concepts and skills grow broad and deep.

Television viewing should be limited. Although talk occurs on television programs, the talk is one-way. The child hears but does not respond. Even in children's shows that ask children to respond, the responses are wanted in one or two words. Studies show that children who watch less than five hours of TV per week do much better in school. (Some children watch five or more hours per day!)

Reading to children every day increases language learnings. Books take us beyond the day-to-day world. Reading helps to expand concepts. But it also helps children see books and reading as important. They may model this behavior. (You will read about how to choose books and use them in Chapter 24.)

SOCIAL-EMOTIONAL NEEDS

The toddler years are testing years. Toddlers ask "Who am I?" and "What can I do on my own?" Although toddlers get some answers to these questions, the questions are more fully answered in the preschool years. It is during these years that children's personalities seem to

JOHN SHAW

17-15 Puzzles and other small objects help children develop fine-motor skills.

blossom and become more stable.

Preschool children learn more about themselves. They test their skills with successes and mistakes. They begin to see themselves as boys or girls with role differences.

Adults are needed if the social-emotional needs of preschool children are to be properly met. Lots of reasons for limits or requirements must be given and often repeated. Firmness and fairness must be the adult's rule if the child's self-concept is to remain healthy.

Discipline: helping with initiative and mistakes

Preschool children define themselves in terms of what they can do. In order to find out what they can do, almost all children try many activities. (In other words, they show initiative.) The very active preschool children are very curious. They do many things on impulse. And they don't think about the results of their actions. In trying new things, preschool children go beyond their abilities and make mistakes. These mistakes are very self-defeating, because preschool children see almost everything as within their control. Too many mistakes may bring on guilt.

When children are successful, they need to hear positive statements from adults. Children need adults to tell them what they are like. This gives children a feeling of self-worth.

Children learn more by their own attempts than by having adults do for them or tell them what to do. Preschoolers learn from both successes and mistakes. Thus children must be given some freedom to try. Adults must accept the fact that children will try things even when told no. Some preschool children decide that the pleasure of doing something is worth the punishment. Children can even dream up new activities not presently covered by the rules.

Preschool children should be given reasonable limits. Limits are needed for safety purposes and as a preparation for adjusting to the real world. These rules should be spelled out. When children fail to obey, reasonable punishment should be given by a loving, but firm adult.

Honest communication. Parents and other adults need to communicate honestly when guiding and disciplining children. Being honest helps children build trusting relationships. It also helps children realize that they should be truthful.

Children need to see adults admit mistakes — from cooking to discipline practices. Children learn when they hear adults say, "I goofed!" or "I'm sorry." They begin to understand that all people make mistakes. They also start to see that making mistakes doesn't make them bad.

Sharing responsibility

Preschool children see tasks as new skills to learn, as fun, and as a way to please others. See 17-16.

17-16 Helping others is a fun way to learn and to please.

JOHN SHAW

The preschooler's developmental needs   301

Some adults offer few, if any, opportunities for children to help. These adults may see preschool children as not having the desire to help. For instance, the child may have stopped in the middle of the task to play. Or these adults may think children lack the ability. For instance, the child may have broken a dish. A few adults think of children as servants who should perform tasks upon demand and to adult standards. Most adults believe, and professionals agree, that family life and school life are made better when both adults and children help each other. A partnership is formed. However, the adult cannot expect preschool children to be equal partners in performing tasks.

These suggestions will help children share responsibility:

- Children may suggest tasks. But adults must decide which tasks are within their grasp and safe, 17-17.
- The physical space should aid children in performing tasks. Low hooks or clothes rods, a place for each item, and a sturdy stool for reaching a cabinet are examples of helps.
- Adults can talk about the tasks planned for the day, and they can tell children exactly what they are to do. Young preschoolers often help the adult do a task, but five-year-olds can work alone on some tasks.
- Adults should not expect perfection. The finished task should remain as it is, or the task can be explained again for the child to do over. (When adults redo tasks, children feel failure.)
- Adults can make some tasks seem more fun by creating a game. For instance, blocks can be hauled to the "lumber yard" (the shelf).
- At times, adults should respect children's priorities. There may be no harm in letting a child do a job ten minutes later.

Children need to be rewarded for tasks completed. Adults must decide whether work is done for love only (and thus should not involve pay) or work should have pay (with money or other wants fulfilled). Some adults compromise on this issue. They expect certain jobs to be done without pay. But they may consider other jobs—those elected by the child—to be beyond the call of duty. The extra jobs may involve pay. Whether adults pay or do not pay, children need to be thanked and skills need to be praised.

Aiding gender role learning

Due to changes in our society today, many parents and other adults are questioning the more rigid gender roles of the past. As is true with all personal priorities, parents need to be informed about the issues and make decisions. How adults feel about gender roles are made known to children in many ways. How adults sex-type, the roles adults allow or encourage their children to try, and most importantly, the day-to-day attitudes adults convey, all affect children.

Preschool children learn their gender-roles mainly through observing adults of the same sex. They learn as they help the same-sex parent in the home with household tasks and with errands. Seeing parents and other adults at work also shows children adult gender roles.

JOHN SHAW

17-17 A child should only be given a pet to care for if the parent thinks the child can handle the responsibility.

See 17-18. Toys and books related to jobs allow children to learn about many gender roles, 17-19.

Providing time for friendships

Living in a social world involves balancing between self-assertion (insisting on one's rights) and cooperation (joint effort). Because preschool children must learn to see from another person's point of view, the balance between "my will" and the wills of others takes a long time— often years.

Seeing differences in people helps children learn to see from another's point of view. The process begins in the infant and toddler years when children expand their social world beyond parents to include other family members. Friendships with peers help children see even more differences in people. Friction, which almost always occurs in play groups, shows children in a very direct way that others see things in a different way. In peer groups, children also witness *altruistic behavior* (concern for others). This helps children learn that others are important, too.

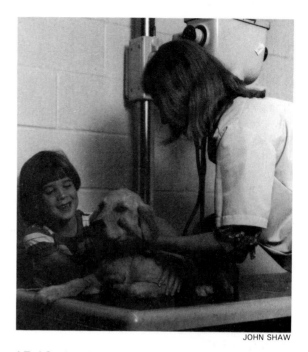

JOHN SHAW

17-18 As she watches her mother work, this preschool girl is learning that women too can work outside the home as well as in the home.

JOHN SHAW

17-19 Books on occupations allow children to think about what they want to be when they grow up.

Friendship is a way to learn from others. Preschool children's ideas are expanded through play. Play groups also mean fun times which are an important part of children's lives. See 17-20.

Adults can aid children's social relations by providing time for children to have friends. These friends may be neighborhood play groups or other children's groups. Church groups, preschool programs, or special interest groups (swimming or dance class) may be offered. Adults should allow children to interact with each other and not interfere with little conflicts (except for safety reasons).

Conflicts can be reduced in the following ways:

- Teach children that they *do not* always have to share, any more than adults do. (Sometimes adults expect children to share all their toys, even with casual friends. Adults are not expected to share all their belongings with even close friends.)
- Model concern for the hurt rather than shame the aggressor. (Children learn more when adults show real concern for the hurt or wronged child while ignoring the child who was in the wrong. They see that care is given to children who are harmed. And aggressive children do not see adults model aggressive behavior.)
- Explain feelings of both children wanting the same toy or wanting to do the same thing. (Often toys are given up rather quickly when the adult says, "Pat needs to play with the car for a little while, but when she's ready to give it up she'll let you know.")

Helping children with emotional control

Emotions are intense in the preschool years. The growing minds of preschool children broaden their emotions. For instance, a young infant who has no concept of property will not react when a grasped object is taken. In like manner, most children under three years of age do not grieve because they have little concept of death.

The growing minds of children not only broaden their emotions, but help them to control how their emotions are expressed.

17-20 Through play these children are expanding their ideas about Mardi Gras celebration.

People cannot control feelings. But they must learn to control how feelings are expressed. Better control of the expression of feelings is a major task of the preschool years.

Children can be helped to control the expression of their feelings. Adults can help by setting an example of control. Children imitate control, or the lack of control, seen in adults. They also imitate other children and television and movie roles.

Adults need to explain to children that it is all right to feel sad, angry, hurt, and happy. They should also tell children it is all right to express some emotions. ("It is all right to cry when we feel very sad," "We laugh when we're happy," and "You should tell another child, 'It makes me mad when you take my toys. Give them back'." But children need to hear that people must not hurt others even when they are wronged. ("Hitting hurts" or "You make others feel so unhappy when you call them names.") Adults should talk about how the control of feelings is a problem for all people. There are many books on this topic, 17-21.

Dependency. Preschool children need to become more independent. But sometimes they do not want to l ˉo of h lp from adults. Other times, they are n   handle tasks on their own. And there are   es when adults want to help, but preschoolers do not need or want to

304

17-21 Preschool children can get ideas from books about how to express their feelings in more positive ways.

be helped. Knowing when and in what ways to assist preschoolers is difficult at times.

Adults can help by showing love to children. This gives children a secure base from which to try things on their own. When children ask for help, adults should be willing to help. But they need to judge how much help is needed. (Adults need to avoid being too helpful or overprotective.) Housing should be arranged with low hooks, stools, and other helps that make tasks more manageable for children. And adults should plan tasks for preschoolers that are within their abilities. Adults need to praise children when they try tasks on their own.

Fear and anxiety. Some fear and anxiety help protect people. But too much fear and anxiety may be harmful. These ideas may help keep children's fears and anxieties in check.
- Accept the expressed fears and anxieties of children. (Never make fun of them.)
- Assure children that you will help keep them safe. (Never threaten to leave a child—even in a playful way.)
- Model courage. Children learn fears from adults.
- Handle one fear at a time. Reasons why children should not be afraid have to be repeated often. Small steps taken slowly in dealing with fears and anxieties may help.
- Consult a physician if fears seem too prolonged or too intense.

Anger. Handling children's anger is not only draining, but often stirs up angry feelings in adults. Adults should note the difference in anger (a feeling) and aggression (an attempt to hurt or an act of hurting someone). They should not try to stop anger in children. Instead they need to help children to try to manage anger in ways other than aggression. Looking for reasons why the child feels angry—wants attention, frustrated in reaching goal, or revenge—is helpful. Understanding motives makes finding ways to manage anger easier.

Competitive situations between peers should be reduced. For instance, enough toys should be supplied so that children do not have to wait

The preschooler's developmental needs 305

too long for a turn. Play should be de-escalated. Some games that begin on a rather low key become aggressive. Other types of games can calm children or encourage cooperation. Close supervision of peer playgroups is needed. That way adults can stop aggression before the act occurs (and the child gets some satisfaction from the act). If punishment is needed, non-physical forms of punishment should be used. However, a child should know when adults disapprove of aggressive acts. Likewise, adults need to praise cooperation.

Jealousy over a new baby. Preschool children need help in accepting a new baby. Parents should tell the child about the new baby before the event. They should sound pleased but not overly excited because children may think new babies are more important than they are.

The new baby should be described in realistic ways in terms of the work involved and other facts. Some preschool children are led to believe that the new baby will be an instant, able playmate. If possible, seeing a friend's new baby can help. The child should be involved in plans for the new baby.

Preschool children seem to be happier when they can stay in their own home or near their own home and visit their mother in the hospital (even by telephone or closed circuit television). They do not prefer to be sent to stay with friends or relatives for several days. (A preschool child can imagine so much, and separations from loved ones are always difficult.)

Older children need time alone with parents after the new baby arrives, 17-22. A little time spent with a preschool child says, "I love you, too." But showering an older child with gifts does not make up for time and may be seen as a bribe.

Older children should be allowed to help with the new baby. Adults should sincerely thank those extra feet and hands which help so much, 17-23. But adults should avoid talking about how grown up older children are. Older children may want to be babies at times. Preschoolers enjoy being told or shown with photos how they were once cared for in the same ways. Some children enjoy pretending to care for a baby with a doll.

Grief. As you read in Chapter 16, grief is a new emotion for preschool children. This is because preschoolers are just starting to understand the concept of death. Adults need to help children understand and deal with death and grief.

Usually, death is not discussed unless someone (or a pet) that is close to the child has died or is dying. But if a child asks about death, any questions should be answered honestly. Many books are available to help adults explain death. See 17-24.

If a family member or close friend is terminally ill, the preschool child should be prepared. Simple, truthful statements are best,

COVER GIRL

17-22 Time with mother helps a preschool child feel special, even when there is a new baby.

such as "You know that Grandma is very sick. The nurses and doctors are trying to help. But Grandma is getting sicker and may soon die." Children should not be told that the sick person is on vacation.

When death occurs, adults should explain what has happened at the child's level. Adults should be truthful and explain what they believe to be true about death. Children become worried if they feel that adults are keeping facts from them or avoiding their questions. The physical facts of death should be explained so that children do not expect the person (or pet) to return. ("Father is dead. This means that he doesn't move or breathe any more.") Religious beliefs about death also should be explained simply. Children also need to know that they have not caused the death. (Since preschoolers still believe in artificialism, they may think that they caused the death by being angry at a person.)

Adults should be prepared to answer questions and repeat facts for a long time following a death. A child may seem to understand that Mother has died when it is first explained. But a week later, the child may ask, "When is Mommy coming home?"

As children begin to understand death, they may become afraid that a parent or other loved one will die. Parents can reassure their children that they will probably live a long time. But they should never promise children that they won't die. If a parent should die after such a promise, the child may feel betrayed and develop a lack of trust in others.

Adults should also help children express their grief over a death. They should let children know that it is all right to be sad and even cry. Adults should set an example by not trying to hide their own sad feelings. Children should be given time to experience sadness and loss. (For this reason, a pet that has died should not be replaced too soon.)

Parents need to make a decision about whether the child should be included in rituals such as the funeral. The decision depends on the age of the child, the child's wishes, and the beliefs of the family. Some feel that seeing open coffins or coffins being lowered into the ground makes death more real. Others feel that this is too much for the child. (In some cases, families elect that the memory for adults and children alike be a living one.) If the child is to attend any rituals for the deceased, these should be explained in advance.

JOHN SHAW

17-23 There are many ways in which an older child can help with a new baby.

JOHN SHAW

17-24 Carefully chosen books may help answer some questions children have about death.

The preschooler's developmental needs 307

Magnifying objects

Show the child a simple magnifying glass. Help the child look at a leaf, penny, fingernail, design, piece of food, or other small object. Use a pencil to point to details that you want the child to see. Later, ask the child to describe the objects shown.

Little bits of big objects

Give the child a paper towel tube or small mailing tube to use as a telescope. Show the child how to look through the tube with one eye while the other eye is closed. (You might explain that a real telescope helps people see things far away.) Point to a rather large object such as a chair. Ask the child to look at it through the tube. Help the child move the tube until the object is found. Then ask, "Which part of the chair (or other object) do you see?" Name parts for the child to find, and ask questions about each part such as its color or shape.

Guess what it is

Gather some of the child's toys. Have the child name and point to important parts of each toy. For instance the parts of a plane would include the wings, the tail, and the cockpit ("place where the pilot sits"). After looking at several objects, begin the guessing game. Have the child close his or her eyes. Place an object in front of the child, covering all but one part with a cloth. Then ask the child to identify the object. Let the child check by taking the cloth away.

Variations: 1. Identify objects in the child's closet or toy chest, in the refrigerator, or on any shelf by the part seen. 2. Identify objects in picture books by their parts. Pictures from magazines, family photo albums, and children's jigsaw puzzles can also be used. 3. When children have mastered the simpler versions, try having them identify the parts not seen.

Alike and different

Gather pairs of objects or pictures that are exactly alike. Mix up the objects and have the child put the ones that are alike together. Books can be made where detachable pieces can be matched to those that are attached to the page.

Variation: Have the child explain how some items are the same in some ways and different in others. Examples of objects to compare include a fork and a spoon, a poodle and a collie, an apple and an orange, two different hats, or two different coins.

JOHN SHAW

Continued.

SORTING ACTIVITIES

Red here, blue there

Gather red and blue objects (beads, small blocks, marbles, and others) and two pieces of paper (one red and one blue). (Or two boxes—one with a red label and one with a blue label—can be used.) Begin by placing a red object on the red paper. Say, "I am putting the red block on the red paper." Repeat with a blue item. Then pick up a red or a blue object and ask, "Where does this blue block (or red block) go?" If the child understands, give the object to the child to put on the paper. The child may continue until all objects are sorted. (If the child does not understand, repeat the first step.)

Variation: Use other properties such as size, shape, and texture. After the child can easily sort by perceptual properties, try usability properties such as toys and clothes.

Button sort

Use an egg carton or other sectioned container, and sort buttons into three or more groups. You may have the child sort according to color, size, way sewn on, or shape. (Buttons can be sorted using pieces of paper or boxes if sectioned containers are not handy.)

Variation: Sort many other objects for fun and even as a household task. Flatware, laundry, toys, and groceries can all be sorted.

Make a book

Children can cut or tear pictures from newspapers, catalogs, and magazines. The pictures can be mounted by groups such as fruits, cars, dogs, and toys. (The child should decide on the groups.)

CLASSIFYING ACTIVITIES

Two houses

Show the child a group of small blocks or beads that may be classified by color or shape. Ask, "Are any of these alike in some way?" The child may respond by saying that some of the objects are blue. Or the child may say some are red, some are blue, some ar round. If the child does not single out a property, say, "Would you like to find all the red or all the blue or all the round ones?" (The child should make one choice.) Then, get out a shoebox or other small box and say, "Let's put all the blue blocks (or whatever the child has chosen) in here. We will put all the blocks that are not blue in this other box." After the child has grouped the blocks correctly, say, "This is the house for blue things. We have so many colors in here (point to other box). Let's call it the house for things that are not blue."

Variation: Classify any other objects. (Remember that in classification, there are only two groups—the class and the complement.)

Does it belong?

After the child can easily classify, bring out another object and put it with the class. Ask the child, "Does this belong?" The child should explain why it does or does not belong.

Continued.

SERIATION ACTIVITIES

Make yourself little

Help the child act out different sizes with the body. Show how to make yourself little (crouch down), bigger (stand), and biggest (stretch).

Little, bigger, biggest

Gather three boxes—one very small, one larger, and one even larger. (Nesting blocks, discussed in Chapter 9, could be used.) Set the boxes in front of the child so that the smallest box is to the child's left, the medium one is in front of the child, and the largest one is to the right. Ask the child to find the little box, then the bigger box, then the biggest box. If the child makes a mistake and does not correct it, try nesting to correct.

Variations: 1. Reverse the order by starting with the biggest on the child's left. 2. Use four or five boxes that vary in size.

The Three Billy Goats Gruff

Read this story to the child. (A copy with illustrations will help the child see the sizes of the goats better.) After reading the story, talk about the sizes of the goats that crossed the bridge.

Ordering blocks

Cover three blocks of wood with different grades of sandpaper. Have the child order them from least rough to roughest by touching the blocks. Then have the child order them using only sight. (Blocks can also be painted shades and tints of colors such as pink, red, and maroon.)

Variations: 1. Use three objects that have different weights for ordering by weight. 2. Use different geometric shapes and have the child order them by the number of sides. An example would be triangle, square, pentagon. (This is the most difficult variation.)

TRANSFORMATION ACTIVITIES

Growing plants

Help the child plant a fast-growing seed such as a bean or put a sweet potato in water. Observe it daily and talk about the changes taking place. (Taking polaroid pictures can help the child recall past states.)

I am growing

Look at the family photo album or other pictures of the child. Point out changes in size, hair length, and motor skill abilities (for instance, lying, sitting, and standing).

Cooking

Have the child help with cooking. Point out changes that happen. For instance, baked goods rise or get bigger. Liquids freeze to make ice and ice cream. Gelatin liquids become firm. Sugar dissolves. Eggs boil and get firm. Fried foods become brown. Many other changes can be observed.

Continued.

Making new colors

Gather paints, crayons, or colored water. Show the child how to make new colors by combining two colors. Let the child do his or her own combinations.

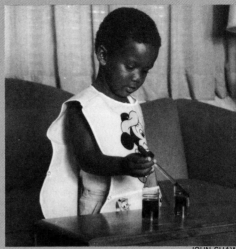

JOHN SHAW

REVERSAL ACTIVITIES

Tower of blocks

Help the child use building blocks to build a tower. Have the child knock it down and build it again.

Lacing cards

Lacing cards can be purchased. Or you can make your own by drawing a picture on cardboard and punching holes in the cardboard. A shoestring can be used for the lace. Children can lace, undo, and relace the cards many times.

Water and sand play

Gather two containers of different sizes and put some water in one. Let the child pour the water from one container into the other and then back. A similar reversal can be done with sand.

JOHN SHAW

Continued.

The preschooler's developmental needs 311

ENACTIVE REPRESENTATION ACTIVITIES

I'm a monster!

Begin by asking the child, "How do you think monsters look? How do you think they move? What sounds do you think they make? Show me." (Pretending to be a monster may help children overcome fears of monsters.)

Variation: Have the child pretend to be any person or thing.

Pantomime

Have the child act out an action. The adult may suggest one, or the child may choose one. Have others try to guess what the action is.

Ballet

Ballet is acting out a story or idea through dance. Play some music and let the child act out something in the form of dance. The child can choose what to be and how to dance it. You may need to give a few ideas to get the child started.

GROSS-MOTOR SKILL GAMES

Jumping

Have the child try these jumping skills: 1. Jump over a rope or stick with both feet. 2. Jump over an object with one foot. 3. Jump from one marked spot to another. (Mark the spots with tape.) 4. Jump down from a four-inch height, landing on both feet. (Gradually increase the height to as much as 12 inches, as the child seems ready.) 5. Jump up and down in place. (Start by having the child stay in a three-foot circle as he or she jumps. Gradually decrease to a one-foot circle.)

Skipping

Teach the child to skip by doing a step-hop on one foot and then a step-hop on the other. After the step-hop is mastered, add music or a rhythmic beat. The pattern of the sound should help the child skip with the beat.

Hopping

Teach hopping in the following progression: 1. Hop on the balls of both feet and land lightly. (This is a little jump, not hopping.) 2. Hop on one foot without letting the heel touch the ground. 3. Hop high like a bouncing ball. 4. Hop as far as possible in two hops.

Continued.

312

Sliding

Teach the child to slide by moving one foot to the side and bringing the other foot up to it. Do not let the body bounce. Once the step is mastered, have the child slide through narrow spaces. Or have the child slide to music.

Galloping

For galloping, have the child slide one foot forward and bring the other foot up to it. The body can bounce some. Once the child has mastered the step, have the child change the lead foot.

Variations: 1. Gallop with large steps and small steps. 2. Gallop lightly (quietly) and heavily (with more noise).

Balancing

Use tape or two ropes to mark a curving path. Have the child walk between the tape markers or ropes. Once the child shows good balance, these more difficult steps can be tried: 1. Walk a straight line, heel to toe, with arms out. (Later, have arms to the side of the body.) 2. Walk a curved line, heel to toe, with arms out. (Later, have arms to the side of the body.) 3. Walk backwards on a straight line with arms out. (Later, have arms to the side of the body.) 4. Walk a low, four-inch wide balance beam, a raised board, or a curb.

Obstacle course

Make an obstacle course of tables, chairs, and sturdy boxes. Or use some outdoor play equipment. Have the child go under, around, through, and/or on top of the obstacles.

Bending, twisting, and swaying

Have the child try movements with feet in place, such as bending, twisting, and swaying. Use such movements to pretend to be the wind, a rocking boat, a swaying tree, or any other object. Or move to music.

Throw and catch

For throwing, have the child throw beanbags or balls at targets. Have the child catch thrown beanbags or balls and bounced balls.

Variation: Ball catching is made more difficult by using a greater distance of throw; slightly high, low, or off to the side throws; throws without a bounce; and smaller balls.

to Know

abstract symbolic representation . . .
authoritative adult . . . class . . .
class complement . . . classification . . .
compare . . . concrete, 3-D representation . . .
contrast . . . convergent thinking . . .
divergent thinking . . . enactive representation . . .
problem solving . . . properties . . . reversals . . .
seriation . . . transformation . . .
2-D representation

to Review

Write your answers on a separate sheet of paper.

1. Which of the following statements are true about preschool children's diet? (You may choose more than one.)

    a. A preschool child has a steady growth pattern that results in the same food needs from month to month.

    b. Food is needed to meet the high energy output of preschool children.

    c. Diet can affect a preschool child's emotions.

    d. Eating junk food can be more of a problem for preschool children than for toddlers.

    e. Preschool children should be told to eat their vegetables or give up their dessert because vegetables are good for them.

    f. Preschool children and adults like foods prepared and served in the same way.

2. True or false. By the end of the preschool years, children have learned enough self-dressing skills that they can dress themselves with very little help from adults.

3. Preschool children grow mainly in _____arms_____ and _____legs_____ which must be considered in clothing fit.

4. Preschool children have toileting accidents. Name the major reason for daytime accidents. Name two or three reasons for bedtime accidents.

5. True or false. Preschool children learn best when enrolled in preschool programs with well-trained teachers.

6. From the list below, which is the least abstract item? Which is the most abstract item?

    a. A stuffed, toy duck.

    b. A real duck.

    c. A picture of a duck.

    d. Pretending to be a duck by waddling and saying, "quack, quack."

    e. The word, *duck*.

7. True or false. Because preschool children are no longer in the sensorimotor stage, they no longer learn through motor games.

8. _____ (Adults, Other children) are the best resource for preschoolers as they are learning language skills.

9. Discuss two things that adults can do to make children's mistakes less self-defeating.

10. Preschool children begin to learn how to help by working _____ (with adults, alone).

11. Adults _____ (should, should not) redo tasks that preschool children have done below standards.

12. True or false. Gender roles are learned mainly by example.

13. Describe two ways to reduce conflict among preschoolers.

14. True or false. The way adults control their emotions does not affect children's emotional control.

to Do

1. Discuss some examples of junk foods. (Read the ingredients listed.) Why are they called junk foods? Using Chart 17-1 as a guide, plan several nutritious snacks.

2. Borrow some clothes designed for preschool children from department stores or from parents. Examine each garment for self-help features listed in 17-8.

3. Visit some homes which have bedrooms and/or playrooms designed for preschool children. (Or look at rooms in furniture stores or magazines.) How was storage planned? How was the child's desire to be more independent through self-help met in the design?

4. Make or gather the materials for one or more of the examples of planned activities for preschool children. Use the planned activity while babysitting or as a helper in a group-care program. Discuss with your class what did or did not work and possible whys.

5. List some ordinary events or objects such as Halloween costumes, a tall slide, and a large playful dog. Describe how the situation may appear to a preschool child.

6. Read about phobias and discuss the readings. How can adults teach dangers without instilling fears?

7. Role play a situation where a child is angry and hits a friend. Have one person be an adult who is supervising the children. Discuss some good discipline methods.

8. Interview several parents about how their older children showed jealousy toward a new sibling and how they handled it.

9. Discuss how an older child must feel when a parent makes these types of statements about a new baby.

    a. "We got this baby just for you."

    b. "You'll have so much fun with your brother (or sister)."

    c. "Look, _____ (name of baby) loves you."

    d. "_____ (name of baby) brought you this gift."

    e. "We expect you to be our big boy (or girl) now."

Many of preschoolers' physical, mental, and social-emotional needs are met in play.

JOHN SHAW

School days

Girls!

JOHN SHAW

Sharing secrets with a friend

316

part six

School-age children

THE TRAVELERS INSURANCE COMPANIES

Going to the zoo with the family

School-age children grow and develop,
becoming more and more like adults.

18

Physical development of the school-age child

After studying this chapter, you will be able to:
- ☐ Describe the physical changes occuring in school-age children.
- ☐ Identify some areas of improvement in motor skills.

Many changes happen in children during the school years. The growth rate remains steady, at about the same rate as that of the preschool years. During the preschool years, the body changes from the babyish look of the toddler to the slender look of a child. School-age children gradually take on even more adult features.

Although changes may seem awkward as they happen, body changes help school-age children become more coordinated. School-age children become even more skilled at running, jumping, climbing, throwing, and catching. Small motor skills also improve. Older school-age children become skillful at such tasks as model building and handicrafts.

BODY GROWTH AND DEVELOPMENT

Compared with the preschool years, the rate of growth stays about the same for *school-age children*. (School-age children are ages six through 12. This period is also called *middle childhood.*) Toward the end of the middle childhood, some children — mainly girls — begin the *growth spurt* and other body changes of the pre-teen and teen years. (A growth spurt is a rapid period of growth, usually associated with adolescence.) Body proportions change some and organ systems mature more during these years.

Height and weight

Growth rate is slow during middle childhood. Height increases more steadily than weight. This is because height is mainly determined by one's genes. (Height is not easily affected by the environment except for long-term conditions such as malnutrition or certain illnesses.) Between six and eight years, children grow two to three inches per year. From nine to 11 years, boys add about one inch and girls add about two inches per year. See Chart 18-1.

Weight somewhat parallels height. Taller children tend to be heavier and shorter children tend to be lighter. Weight is also influenced by the environment. The main factors in the environment which affect weight are nutrition, illness, activity, and stress. Between six and eight years, children add three to six pounds per year. From nine to 11 years, boys add four pounds and girls add five pounds per year. See Chart 18-2.

Boys are taller and heavier than females until 10 or 11 years of age. At this time, most females enter a growth spurt. Many girls find themselves taller than boys at this age. Children are often sensitive to the size difference, especially if they are getting interested in the opposite sex. In reality, the average difference is small—about one inch at age 12. The difference shows up mainly in a slow-maturing boy and a fast-maturing girl. Girls are closer to body maturity than boys. For instance, 75 percent of adult height is attained by seven years of age for girls and by nine years of age for boys. However, growth spurts tend to be individual. Some children grow very quickly at age 10 while others grow more slowly until age 11. Most boys catch up in growth during the early teen years.

Body proportions

During middle childhood, body proportions become even more like those of an adult. A child's waist and head begin to look smaller. This is because the ratio of both the head and waist circumference (distance around) to total height decreases. School-age children also have longer arms and legs that increase their reach. The ratio of leg length to height increases. The change in ratio makes for a lower center of gravity and better balance. See 18-3. During these years, the trunk grows until it is two times as long and two times as wide as it was at birth. The abdomen protrudes even less than it did in the preschool years. The ribs become less horizontal and more oblique (slanting) in position.

The face changes a great deal in middle childhood. In earlier stages, the upper half of the head grew very fast due to brain development. In the school years, the lower half of the

AVERAGE HEIGHT FROM SIX TO TWELVE YEARS

AGE IN YEARS	BOYS	GIRLS
6	46.5" (116 cm)	46.5" (116 cm)
7	49" (122.5 cm)	49" (122.5 cm)
8	51.5" (129 cm)	50.5" (126 cm)
9	53" (132.5 cm)	53" (132.5 cm)
10	55" (137.5 cm)	56" (140 cm)
11	57.5" (144 cm)	58.5" (146 cm)
12	59.5" (149 cm)	60.5" (151 cm)

18-1 The height of children from six to twelve years increases rather steadily. Boys are equal to or taller than girls until 10 years of age.

AGE IN YEARS	BOYS	GIRLS
6	48.5 lbs. (21.8 kg)	46.5 lbs. (20.9 kg)
7	54 lbs. (24.3 kg)	51.5 lbs. (23.1 kg)
8	61 lbs. (27.5 kg)	57.5 lbs. (23.8 kg)
9	66 lbs. (29.7 kg)	64 lbs. (28.8 kg)
10	72.5 lbs. (32.6 kg)	74 lbs. (33.3 kg)
11	80.5 lbs. (36.2 kg)	88.5 lbs. (39.8 kg)
12	92 lbs. (41.4 kg)	97 lbs. (43.6 kg)

18-2 The weight of children from six to twelve years increases rather steadily. Boys are slightly heavier than girls until 10 years of age.

SPIEGEL, INC.

18-3 School-age children develop more adult-like proportions. These new proportions make many tasks easier than they were in the preschool years.

face catches up. The forehead is not so high. Facial features become more prominent. For instance, the nose is not as flat as it was in the preschool years.

Bone growth

The bones continue to ossify (harden) and grow larger and longer. The most significant bone growth is in the teeth. Middle childhood is a time of constantly losing teeth and growing *permanent teeth*. Unlike baby teeth, permanent teeth are intended to last a lifetime. The permanent teeth are harder and less sharp than baby teeth. Girls often lose and replace teeth before boys do. The first two teeth, often the bottom front teeth, fall out during the late preschool years. The last of the 20 baby teeth, the cuspids (shown in Chapter 6) fall out around age 12. The Tooth Fairy is kept busy during these years! The first set of permanent teeth to erupt may not be seen by the adult, because they do not replace lost teeth. The teeth are called six-year molars because of their average age of eruption. They are found behind the second set of deciduous (baby) molars. See 18-4. The next permanent teeth replace lost baby teeth. The permanent teeth change the look of the lower part of the face, 18-5.

Muscle growth

Muscles grow and become more firmly attached to bones during middle childhood.

Physical development of the school-age child 321

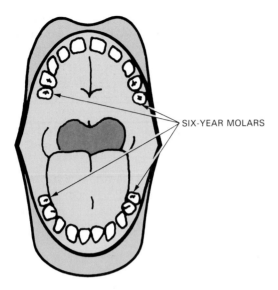

SIX-YEAR MOLARS

18-4 Six-year molars are the child's first permanent teeth.

However, the muscles are not mature and are easily injured. (Orthopedic [bone and muscle] defects are the most common defect of this age.) The growth of the skeleton is more rapid than the growth of the muscles. The lag in muscle growth gives a loose-jointed, somewhat awkward look. Children of this age cannot completely prevent movement of their muscles. This makes sitting still almost impossible! And, they may complain of aches and pains. These muscle aches are called *growth pains.* Growth pains are caused by muscles trying to catch up with skeleton size.

Organ growth

Brain growth slows during middle childhood. The brain reaches 90 percent of adult weight by age five and 95 percent of adult weight by age 10. More connections are made between

LOUIS J. BREAUX, JR.

8-5 Permanent teeth, which almost look large for the child's face for a time, the look of the lower jaw line.

nerve cells. The parts of the brain become more specialized. For instance, one part of the brain becomes the speech center. Another part becomes the visual center.

Other organs continue to mature, also. The heart grows slowly. The heart beat is between 70 and 100 beats per minute. Because the heart is small in relationship to the rest of the body, too much strain is dangerous.

Respiration (breathing) rate slows from 20 to 30 inhalations (breaths taken in) per minute in the preschool years to 17 to 25 in middle childhood. School-age children are less prone to respiratory illnesses than are younger children.

The eyeball begins to mature during the school years. After age seven, *visual acuity* (ability to see a sharply focused image) can be near the 20/20 adult norm. *Binocular vision* (seeing an object with both eyes at the same time) becomes fully developed at this time, also.

Hearing improves in the preschool years. *Auditory acuity* (keen hearing of sounds) is mature at age seven. At this age, children can hear small differences in some words such as *pin, pen,* and *pan.* This is a skill needed in learning to read.

Other changes in middle childhood include a decrease in fat tissues. Skin becomes less delicate or fine in texture. Often, light hair becomes darker during these years.

MOTOR DEVELOPMENT

Motor skills improve during middle childhood. But the improvement is not as great as the improvement between the ages of one and five. School-age children seem to have a surplus of energy. They seem to enjoy almost all large motor activities. This is especially true of children ages six, seven, and eight. These children are more developed in large-muscle coordination than in small-muscle coordination. They enjoy running, jumping, climbing, and playing simple games such as tag and catch. Children ages nine through 12 begin to develop interests in more specific motor skills. They tend to prefer organized sports, skating, or bicycling over just running or jumping. See 18-6. (This is due to increased mental ability as well as improved large-muscle coordination.)

Motor skills become better in middle childhood for several reasons. The first is a faster *reaction time.* Reaction time is the time required to respond to a stimulus such as a thrown ball. Another help is an improvement in *precision.* Precision includes balance, steadiness, and skill in aiming at a target. Greater speed and improved strength also improve motor skills. Finally, school-age children have improved *flexibility.* Flexibility is the ability to move, bend, and stretch easily.

In the early part of middle childhood, boys perform better than girls in tasks requiring power, force, and speed. After girls begin their growth spurt, they often equal or excel boys

18-6 Older school-age children enjoy organized sports such as baseball.

Physical development of the school-age child   323

of the same age in these tasks. Girls of all school ages tend to perform better than boys in tasks requiring flexibility or rhythm. Experts do not know whether these motor differences in the sexes are due to genes or environment. (Environment would include such factors as whether or not a child is encouraged to practice certain motor skills.) Studies do show that a girl or boy highly skilled in one motor activity is likely to excel in others.

School-age children also have highly developed fine motor skills. Improved skill helps them with art activities, craft work, writing, playing musical instruments, self-dressing, and many other tasks needing small muscle precision. These skills seem to increase steadily during the school years. Improvement in writing ability is shown in 18-7.

Laterality

Laterality is the ability to tell the difference between the left and right sides of the body and to prefer one side to another. Laterality seems to develop fully during the school years. For instance, five-year-old children have trouble knowing the left and right hands of others although they know their own left and right. By six years of age, 75 percent of all children know the left and right hands of others. And, by seven years of age, this number has increased to 95 percent.

Laterality seems to develop more fully as a result of motor activities. For instance, a child will say, "I write with my right (or left) hand." In turn, laterality aids motor skills. Even the cognitive skill of knowing the difference between *b* and *d* depends on laterality. When laterality is not developed, the child may write

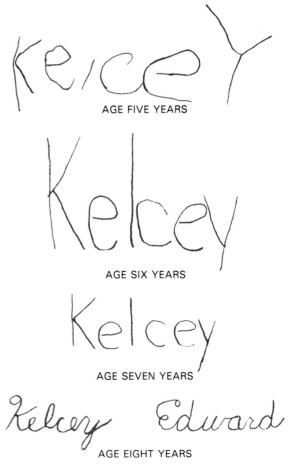

AGE FIVE YEARS

AGE SIX YEARS

AGE SEVEN YEARS

AGE EIGHT YEARS

18-7 Fine motor skills increase with each year as seen in writing attempts.

b for *d*. This error is referred to as a *letter reversal*. Children without developed laterality may even reverse an entire word such as *was* for *saw*. This type of error is called a *word reversal*.

to Know

auditory acuity . . . binocular vision . . .
flexibility . . . growth pains . . . laterality . . .
letter reversal . . . middle childhood . . .
permanent teeth . . . precision . . .
reaction time . . . school-age children . . .
visual acuity . . . word reversal

to Review

Write your answers on a separate sheet of paper.
1. As compared with the preschool years,
growth rate during the school years is:
    a. Faster.
    b. Slower.
    c. About the same.
2. True or false. Boys are taller and heavier
than girls throughout all of middle childhood.
3. School-age children's:
    a. arms and legs are rather short.
    b. upper half of the face grows more than
    the lower half.
    c. facial features sharpen.
    d. waist begins to look larger in comparison
    to the trunk of the body.
4. True or false. The first permanent teeth to
erupt replace lost baby teeth.
5. Match the parts of the body to the changes
that are occurring in middle childhood.
    a. Bones.
    b. Muscles.
    c. Brain.
    d. Heart.
    e. Eyes and ears.
    f. Light hair.
___ 1. Darkening.
___ 2. Becoming more specialized.
___ 3. Remaining small in relation to rest of
body.
___ 4. Becoming more firmly attached to bones.
___ 5. Reaching adult maturity.
___ 6. Growing larger and longer.

6. Quality of gross motor skills increases due
to _____, _____, _____,
_____, and _____.
7. True or false. Fine motor skills do not
improve in middle childhood, because children
prefer large-muscle to small-muscle activities.

to Do

1. Make a collage of pictures of children from
ages six through twelve years. What physical
changes do you notice?
2. Observe the play of six- and seven-year-olds
and of eleven- and twelve-year-olds. How does
their play differ in terms of motor skills?
3. Make a poster called "Qualities Needed In
Motor Skills." Divide the poster into five areas
and label the qualities: reaction time, precision,
speed, strength, and flexibility. Find pictures or
draw sketches of activities that fit each quality.
For example, basketball requires precision.
4. Make a list of gross-motor and fine-motor
activities. Ask a class of fourth or fifth grade
students to check their three favorite activities.
Tabulate the results. Were gross motor or fine
motor activities chosen most often?
5. Make a continuous spiral on an eight by 10
inch sheet of paper. Duplicate copies for three
classes. Have one class each of first, third, and
fifth grade students cut on the line. Ask the
teacher to record the time it took most of the
children to cut the spiral. Compare the ability
to cut.
6. Devise a game that will test children's
knowledge of their right and left and others'
right and left. Try the game with children ages
six through eight.

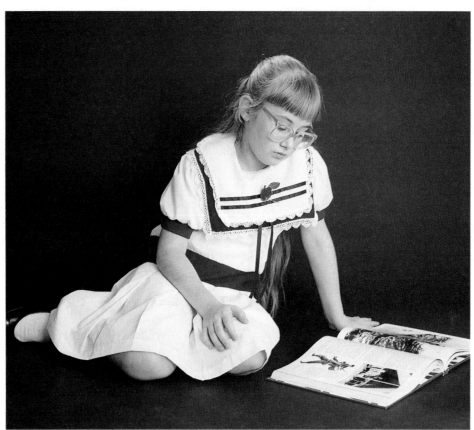

Intellectual ability becomes complex during
middle childhood.

19

Intellectual development of the school-age child

After studying this chapter, you will be able to:

- ☐ Explain how logic skills emerge in school-age children.
- ☐ Identify the major logical knowledge concepts of middle childhood.
- ☐ Describe school-age children's language skills.

In Chapter 15 you read about preschool children's ability to think mentally. Such thinking goes beyond infants' ways of thinking through the senses and body actions. Thinking mentally involves thinking with symbols rather than having contact with the real object or event. Some of these symbols are very close to the real thing such as toy trucks or dolls, while others are very abstract such as words. School-age children can think using even more abstract symbols than preschoolers.

Although preschool children think about real objects in symbolic ways, they are not always logical in a true sense of the word. Many of their perceptions are flawed. And since preschool thinking is based on perception, logic is also flawed. In middle childhood, perception becomes more accurate. During this stage, children begin to rely on logical thinking rather than perception.

As children approach school age, they begin to notice some problems in their thinking. Around seven years of age, children become less dependent on perception as they think. Logic slowly begins to replace perception. Piaget has called this third stage of mental abilities the *concrete operational stage.* See 19-1. *Operations* are thought processes that are

PIAGET'S STAGES OF COGNITIVE DEVELOPMENT

Stage 1: Sensorimotor Stage (Birth to 2 years)

Stage 2: Preoperational Stage (2 to 7 years)

Stage 3: Concrete Operations Stage (7 to 11 years)

Stage 4: Formal Operations Stage (11 years on)

19-1 The school-age child functions in the concrete operational stage.

based on logic more than perception. When there is a conflict between thought and perception, the child makes the logical decision. For instance, the child in this stage thinks "the tall glass looks as if it has more liquid. But it could not really have more because I saw the liquid poured from the shorter glass." The term *concrete* means that logic is based on what the child has at some time experienced. People in the stage of concrete operations are not ready to use logic based on problems. The last stage of mental abilities is called *formal operations* (ages 11 and older). In formal operations, a person can reason more abstractly.

The difference between concrete and formal operations can be seen in how a child plays a checker or chess game. A child at the concrete operations level can play checkers or chess by the rules. But the child makes each move in terms of what is on the board at that time. The child does not think in terms of the next three to five moves. Older players in the formal operations stage can think ahead and plan strategies. A person in formal operations plans game strategy by thinking, "What if my opponent does such and such, then what will be my options?"

HOW SCHOOL-AGE CHILDREN THINK

The concrete operational stage is a bridge between preoperational (before logic) thought and formal operations. In Chapter 15 you read about the obstacles to complete logical thought seen in preschool children—egocentrism, centration, focus on states, lack of reversibility,

and transductive reasoning. School-age children slowly become free from these problems, and thus become logical.

Seeing from the viewpoint of others

School-age children are unlike preschool children who are egocentric (think others see the way they do). In middle childhood, children begin to see that others have ideas that are different from their own. Realizing that others have different ideas leads to doubt and the need to find the right answer. School-age children work to prove or deny answers by using logic.

Piaget believed that contact with peers is the greatest help in freeing children from egocentric thinking. For real communication with others, the person must recognize the point of view of others and notice how it compares with their own ideas.

Knowing whether a child is or is not egocentric can be somewhat difficult. When children stop using collective monologues (talking at others more than with others), they have become less egocentric. Piaget did design a task for checking egocentrism or the lack of egocentrism. See 19-2.

Decentering perception

During the school years, the child *decenters perception*. In other words, the child comes to focus on more than one aspect of something at one time. This means that the child can see more than one change in an object at one time. In Piaget's water task with a tall, thin glass and a short, wide glass, the child now sees that the greater width in the first glass makes up for the greater height in the other glass. Because the child can note both width and height changes at the same time, it is easier to understand how the same amount of liquid looks taller in a thinner glass.

Noting transformations

Remember that preschoolers do not note transformations. Instead, they note each change (state) when it happens as though it were a separate event. School-age children mentally put together changes in an object. They can join a series of events to see a transformation. For instance, when they watch a liquid being poured from one glass to another, they see the liquid in the first glass, then going through the air to the second glass, then in the second glass. Once the transformation is noted, children know that the liquid in the second glass is the same as the liquid in the first glass. They know that the liquid is the same even if the glasses are different shapes. (Preschool children see the liquid in the first glass. But even if they watch some-

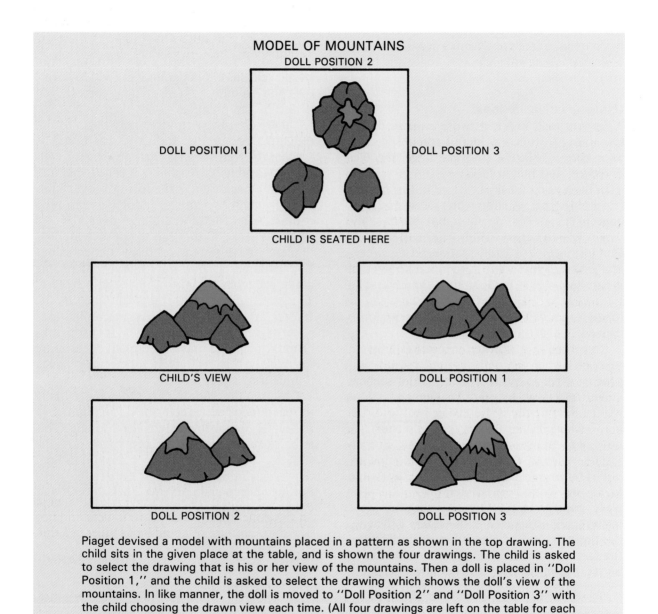

Piaget devised a model with mountains placed in a pattern as shown in the top drawing. The child sits in the given place at the table, and is shown the four drawings. The child is asked to select the drawing that is his or her view of the mountains. Then a doll is placed in "Doll Position 1," and the child is asked to select the drawing which shows the doll's view of the mountains. In like manner, the doll is moved to "Doll Position 2" and "Doll Position 3" with the child choosing the drawn view each time. (All four drawings are left on the table for each choice). A child who can correctly choose each drawing from the four views is learning to see from the viewpoint of others.

19-2 This task helps adults detect whether children are still egocentric.

one pour it, they do not recall the transformation. They see the liquid in the second glass. But they don't have any reason to believe it is the same liquid that was in the first glass.)

Being able to note transformations helps children understand other concepts. For instance, school-age children can accept the fact that their parents were once babies. They can believe that a tree grew from a seed. And they understand that water can turn to ice and other science principles.

Using reversibility logic

As you read in Chapter 15, reversibility is the ability to follow a line of reasoning back to where it started. Reversibility involves *inversion* and *reciprocity*.

In inversion, a task is carried out in reverse (inverted) order. A child who understands this concept thinks, "If you put something back the way it was to begin with, it will be the same." For instance, if a child sees someone take a straight string and curve it, the child knows that it can be made straight again. The child who flattens a clay ball knows that the clay can be made into a ball again. (In math, inversion is carried out in subtraction.)

Reciprocity is another important part of reversibility. When children understand reciprocity, they know that one change such as height makes up for another change such as width. Reciprocity is closely tied to decentering, because in both cases the child must see how two changes affect each other. For instance, when a string is curved, the ends are not as far away from each other as they would be if the string was straight. A child who understands reciprocity knows that the curve in the string brings the ends closer. Likewise, the flattened ball of clay is bigger in diameter than a sphere. The child knows the clay can be bigger in diameter because it is flatter. (In math, reciprocity is carried out in division.)

Using deductive and inductive reasoning

Preschool children reason from particular to particular (transductive reasoning). However, the school-age child uses *deductive reasoning*. Deductive reasoning is reasoning from the general to the specific. For instance, it is a general statement that all fish live in water. One specific type of fish is a guppy. If a child knows both of these facts, he or she can use deductive reasoning to conclude that guppies live in the water. See 19-3.

Deductive reasoning can only be accurate if the statements used (called premises) are true. For instance, if the child is told that all birds can fly and that a penguin is a bird, the child would reason that penguins can fly. However, the child's method of reasoning is correct even if one of the premises is not true.

Older school-age children may begin to use *inductive reasoning*. Inductive reasoning is reasoning from specific facts to general conclusions. Inductive reasoning is called scientific reasoning because it is the form of logic commonly used by scientists. Inductive reasoning is most often found in children over 11 years of age. These children can weigh several ideas that they have tested and draw a conclusion. For instance, a child may know that people make ice cubes by putting water in a freezer. The child may try putting fruit juice in the freezer and find that it becomes solid, too. After trying other liquids, such as soft drinks or milk, the child may use inductive reasoning to conclude that very cold temperatures change liquids into solids.

Children (and adults) are much more likely to reach incorrect conclusions using inductive reasoning than using deductive reasoning. This is because people seldom test every possible situation before drawing a conclusion. (Sometimes, it is impossible to test every situation.) For instance, a child may see ducks, geese, and swans swimming in a pond and conclude that all birds can swim.

WHAT SCHOOL-AGE CHILDREN LEARN

Because school-age children use logic in their thought processes, they are able to learn many new things. Logic aids the learning of school subjects such as language arts, reading, math, geography, science, and the arts. School-age children's concepts are clearly more advanced than preschool children's concepts. But they

19-3 School-age children begin to use deductive reasoning to form their own concepts about the world around them.

still have trouble grasping some concepts such as events in history, scientific logic, and value systems.

Physical knowledge concepts

School-age children build on the physical knowledge concepts that they began to form in the preschool years. Physical knowledge concepts include the properties of objects and the actions of objects or the actions performed on objects. Physical knowledge concepts become more advanced because perception matures. The eyes and ears mature making what one sees and hears very accurate (exact). The brain, too, processes what is seen and heard in more defined ways.

Perception changes in many ways. First, school-age children become more careful in learning about their world. For instance, by nine years of age, the child uses the eyes or fingertips to trace the outline of an object rather

than giving the object a quick glance. Second, school-age children learn what to attend to and what to ignore as they examine an object. The child simply ignores unneeded information. For instance, if the child is identifying geometric shapes, the color of the shapes is ignored. Third, school-age children correctly pair visual (seen) and auditory (heard) stimuli such as the written letters and their sounds or written music notes and their pitches.

Improved memory also helps improve physical knowledge concepts. Memory is aided because school-age children see the need for remembering. Also, children develop methods to help them remember. Such methods include singing their ABC's or learning a rhyme about the number of days in the months of a year.

Logic allows school-age children to form better, more accurate physical knowledge concepts. Logic is used over perception when a conflict between the two occurs. The ability to

a
CONSERVATION OF LENGTH

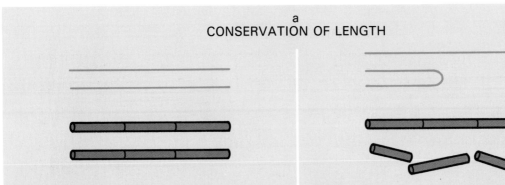

Step 1. The child is shown two pieces of string (or two rods) which are the same length. The child is asked, "Are the two strings (rods) the same length or are they different?" Once the child agrees that they are equal in length, begin Step 2.

Step 2. With the child watching, the string is curved (or the rod is broken into three pieces). The child is asked, "Are the two strings (all three pieces of the rod together) the same length or are they different?" "Why?" (Or "How do you know?")

b
CONSERVATION OF LIQUID

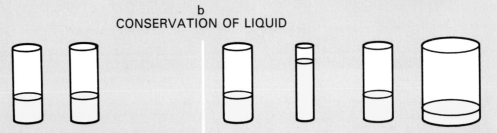

Step 1. The child is shown two glasses which are exactly the same and which are filled with the same amount of water (colored with food coloring). The child is asked, "Is there the same amount of water in both glasses or are they different?" Once the child agrees that they are equal in amount, begin Step 2.

Step 2. With the child watching, water from one glass is poured into a taller but thinner glass or into a shorter but wider glass. The child is asked, "Do the glasses have the same amount of water or are they different?" "Why?" (Or "How do you know?")

c
CONSERVATION OF MASS

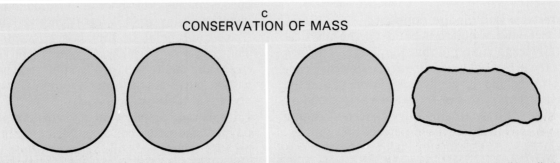

Step 1. The child is shown two clay balls of equal size and shape. The child is asked, "Do the balls have the same amount of clay or are they different?" Once the child agrees that they are equal in amount, begin Step 2.

Step 2. With the child watching, one clay ball is rolled into a sausage shape. The child is asked, "Do the sausage-shaped clay and the ball of clay have the same amount of clay or are they different?" "Why?" (Or "How do you know?")

Continued.

19-4 Conservation of various changes occurs at different ages. Conservation of length, liquid, and mass occurs around six or seven years of age. Conservation of area occurs around nine or 10 years of age. Conservation of volume occurs around 11 years of age.

CONSERVATION OF AREA
d

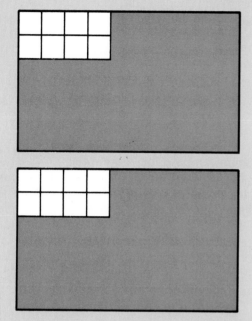

Step 1. The child is shown two sheets of cardboard with the same number of white blocks on each sheet placed in exactly the same way. The child is asked, ''Are the amounts of uncovered space (red) the same or are they different?'' Once the child agrees that the uncovered space is equal, begin Step 2.

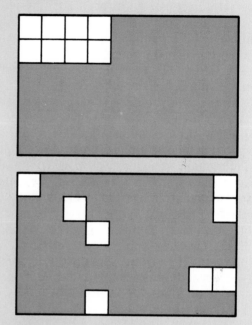

Step 2. With the child watching, the blocks on one sheet are moved apart. The child is asked, ''Are the amounts of uncovered space (red) the same or are they different?'' ''Why?'' (Or, ''How do you know?'')

CONSERVATION OF VOLUME
e

Step 1. The child is shown two clay balls of equal size and shape. The balls are placed in two glasses of water. (The glasses are exactly the same and are filled with the same amount of water.) The water level in the glasses rise to the same level. The child is asked, ''Do the balls displace the same amount of water (cause the water to rise to the same level) or are the amounts different?'' Once the child agrees that both balls displace the same amount of water, begin Step 2.

Step 2. With the child watching, one clay ball is rolled into a sausage shape. The child is asked, ''Will the 'Sausage' shaped clay displace the same amount of water (cause the water to rise to the same level) as the clay ball?'' ''Why?'' (Or ''How do you know?'')

19-4 Continued.

Intellectual development of the school-age child 333

use logic helps children master the concept of *conservation*. This concept must be understood before children can form accurate physical knowledge concepts. Conservation means that changing an object's shape, direction, or position does not alter the quantities of the object. Conservation applies to various quantities such as length, mass, weight, or volume.

Children's ability to understand conservation can be measured by their answers to questions about various conservation tasks. For instance, a person may pour a liquid from a short, wide glass into a tall, thin glass. When asked about the amount of water in both glasses, the child who understands conservation will say that the amounts are the same. Other types of conservation tasks include flattening a ball of clay and bending a rope.

Understanding various types of conservation tasks occurs at different times for a child. Some knowledge of conservation begins around six years of age. But other conservation tasks cannot be solved until 11 years of age or even older. See 19-4.

Children go through three stages in learning any type of conservation concept. First, they do not understand conservation. Next, they go back and forth between understanding conservation and thinking quantities change. Finally, they always understand that quantities do not change and can give reasons why. In the last stage, children truly understand conservation.

Perception, memory, and logic work together to help the child's development of physical knowledge concepts. With increased physical knowledge, the child is better able to give more meaning to words, drawings, and other symbols.

Logical knowledge concepts

Logical knowledge concepts are understandings of relationships which occur in the mind. These concepts become well developed in the middle childhood years. School-age children deepen their concepts of classification, seriation, number, space, distance, time, and speed. These concepts become more accurate as children replace perceptual thinking with logic.

Classification. As you read in Chapter 15, classification is the grouping of objects into a class and its complement. During the preschool years, children often sort objects. Some preschoolers can classify by one quality at a time such as color. Many advanced skills emerge in

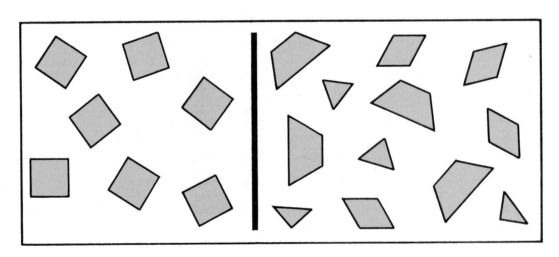

19-5 School-age children group things that are alike—the class of squares. They also place the complement (other shapes) in a random way.

the middle childhood years.

As school-age children classify, the quality (shape, color, way used) that defines the class remains stable. School-age children do not group by shape and switch to color in the process. School-age children also include all objects that meet the quality for that class. Children quit sorting the complement and place objects in a random way, 19-5. By middle childhood, children fully understand the class and the complement. (A photo of the often seen sorting method of the preschool child is shown in Chapter 17.)

School-age children learn hierarchial classification. Hierarchial classification is having classes within other classes. Hierarchies imply that you can break large classes down to form smaller subgroups and that you can build larger classes from several subgroups. For instance, the large class of animals can be broken down into subgroup classes such as birds and fish. Or the smaller classes of birds, fish, and others can be put together to form the large class of animals. (The idea of reversibility must be present in hierarchial classification.) Being able to mentally see both large classes and subgroups at the same time is called class inclusion. Many children over ages seven or eight answer questions correctly on class inclusion, 19-6.

Multiple classification is also grasped during the school years. Multiple classification involves classifying by two or more qualities at the same time. For instance, the florist may tell you, "We have roses and tulips and both can bought in red and yellow." You would then know that there are four types of flowers — red roses, yellow roses, red tulips, and yellow tulips. Knowing this involves classifying by color and by type of flower at the same time. Multiple classification tasks can be solved around eight years of age. See 19-7.

Seriation. School-age children can show relationship among objects by putting them in order. As you read in Chapter 15, this task is called seriation. Seriation involves ordering a chain of differences. There are many types of differences such as those seen (color, shape, size), heard (pitch, loudness), and felt (texture and temperature). Other differences involve time or order of events. Series are used in daily

JOHN SHAW

19-6 One way Piaget tested hierarchial classification was to ask a question such as, "Are there more suckers or candy?" School-age children who understand class inclusion will say, "Candy."

Intellectual development of the school-age child 335

19-7 To test multiple classification, Piaget used a board divided into squares (called cells). Objects are drawn in all but one cell. Cards from which to choose the correct picture for the empty cell are shown to the child. In order to solve the problem, the child must see the pattern. In the four-cell card shown, the rows (across) have the same color. (In Row 1 are solid objects and in Row 2 is a light colored, dotted object.) The columns (down) have the same objects. (In Column 1 are flowers and in Column 2 is an apple.) Thus, the correct object for the empty cell is the light colored, dotted apple.

life such as in calendars and the chemical elements.

Seriation tasks vary in their difficulty. For instance, quite a few preschool children can order objects by length. But children may be nine years old or older before they can order objects by weight or volume. School-age children develop many new seriation skills.

School-age children can seriate a group of objects by one variable (length, color, weight) easily. They do not have to do as much trial and error as preschool children. And they can seriate faster than preschool children.

School-age children can run two series of objects so that they are in correspondence with each other. For instance, they may have two different sets of colors ranging from dark to light. The children place both sets so that the darkest of each is next to each other and so on. See 19-8.

Double seriation is arranging objects while keeping in mind two variables at the same time. For instance, a calendar has the days of the month written from left to right with the dates falling on a certain day of the week written from top to bottom. Double seriation is a more difficult seriation task often not understood until middle childhood. See 19-9.

School-age children can handle word problems such as: If Jim is faster than Robert, and

JOHN SHAW

19-8 In running the two size series shown, the child places the largest umbrella under the largest doll and the next to the largest umbrella under the next to the largest doll and so on.

Robert is faster than Juan, who is the fastest? This problem requires a special type of seriation called transitivity. *Transitivity* is the ability to recognize a relationship between two objects or events by knowing the relationship between each of them and a third. For instance, a child can find the relationship between Jim's speed and Juan's speed by knowing the relationship between Jim's speed and Robert's speed and between Juan's speed and Robert's speed.

Number. During the last part of the preschool stage and the early part of middle childhood, children learn many basic concepts about number. Some of these basic ideas must be grasped before children can understand math.

School-age children learn the concept of *one-to-one matching* (also called *one-to-one correspondence*). One-to-one matching involves knowing that if objects in two sets are matched and no objects are left over in one of the sets, the sets are equal. Children begin to learn this concept by pairing objects from each group by placing them close to each other — even touch-

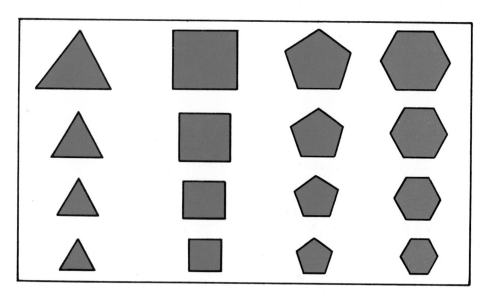

19-9 Shapes in four sizes were used to create this double seriation pattern. The shapes in the rows (across) increase in the number of sides (triangle has three sides, square has four sides). The like shapes in the columns (from top to bottom) decrease in size.

Intellectual development of the school-age child   337

ing each other. See 19-10. In later years, children can mentally see that the groups are the same or different in number. These children do not have to pair objects physically.

After one-to-one matching is grasped, children can compare two sets of objects. They can detect whether one set is greater than, less than, or equal to the other set. (Children may use other words to explain such as most instead of greater than.)

Seeing the relationship between ordinal (first, second) and cardinal (one object, two objects) numbers is the next step in learning number concepts. Children start by counting while touching or pointing to each object (which is one-to-one matching between number name and object). Then children must learn that the last object counted in a group tells how many objects there are. Class inclusion is involved for the child must see that one is included in two, two in three, and so on.

Children also learn that groups are changed in number if more objects are put with the group (adding). They also learn that the number changes if objects are taken away from the group (subtracting).

Space. School-age children have many correct ideas about space. They can tell whether objects are *open* or *closed* and whether they are *far away* or *near*. They also can see the relationship of two or more objects. They understand such concepts as *close to, connected, behind* or *in front of, above,* or *below,* and *left* or *right*. They know, too, that distant objects such as the flying jet do not get smaller.

However, school-age children may have problems with the relationship between horizontal and vertical. See 19-11. They also have problems with *projective spatial concepts*—the ability to describe a familiar pathway.

Distance, time, and speed. Children who are younger than eight years of age have problems grasping distance, time, and speed. They mainly have trouble understanding the ways these concepts are related. Time and distance are often confused. For instance, the young, school-age child may say that walking some place "is far," but that running makes it "near."

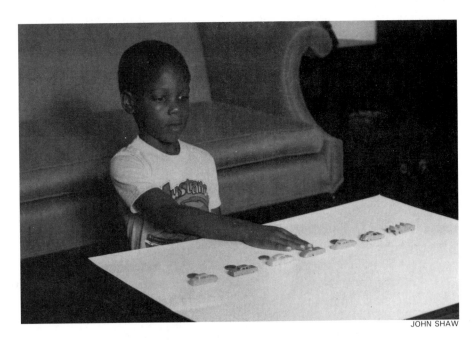

JOHN SHAW

19-10 The younger school-age child places the coins next to the cars for one-to-one matching.

338

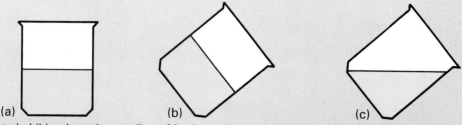

(a)   (b)   (c)

Piaget tested children's understanding of horizontal and vertical by showing them a drawing of a beaker of water as shown in "a." In the second step, the child is given an outline drawing of the same beaker in a tipped position (without water drawn). The child is asked to draw how the water would look in the tipped beaker. Most school-age children still have problems with the horizontal and vertical and draw the water as shown in "b" rather than in the correct way as shown in "c."

19-11 Most school-age children still have problems with the horizontal and vertical.

Children under age eight rarely consider different lengths of paths. Instead, they only consider the starting and ending times of traveling. See 19-12.

Speed can be correctly judged by these young school-age children only if two people or objects are going the same direction on the same path and one overtakes the other. Speed is not judged correctly when travel of people or objects is toward one another.

Clock time and calendar time are often learned when children are in the first or second grade. However, time and age are not well understood until children are around 10 or 11 years of age. The time of historical events seems difficult to grasp until the teen years. Stories written for children often reflect their understandings of time. For instance, stories for the

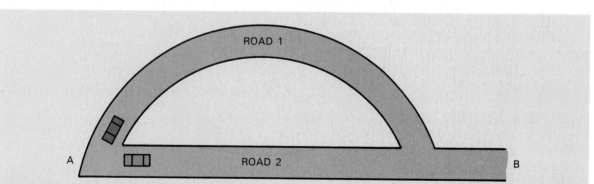

To test the child's concept of the relationship between time and speed, Piaget showed the child two roads and two cars. Both cars leave point A at the same time and arrive at point B at the same time, but travel different road, Road 1 and Road 2. Children younger than eight years of age often say that the cars move at the same speed because they both start at the same time at point A and arrive at the same time at point B. Older children often note than Road 1 is longer which requires the car on this road to move faster in order to arrive at point B at the same time as the other car (velocity = speed/time).

19-12 Children under eight often have trouble with time and distance concepts.

very young child often begin "Once upon a time . . .". Stories for young school-age children give hints as to seasons or years. Books for the late childhood years such as *Gulliver's Travels* mention exact times.

Causality concepts. School-age children begin to resolve many cause and effect or causality relationships. As children become more logical, cause and effect relationships become more exact. When children lose much of their own egocentrism, they begin to understand that natural happenings are not caused by humans. Thus, artificialism as a way of thinking is replaced with more of a scientific approach.

Animism, or the belief that non-living things have life-like qualities, is often given up for scientific answers. However, natural things which are thought of as powerful (sun and stars, oceans, mountains) may be seen as having life by older children.

LANGUAGE IS MASTERED

Around six or seven years of age children's speech becomes more social. These children give up egocentric speech (more or less talking to themselves). Instead, they want to talk with their friends and with adults. However, the speech of school-age children is not as involved or intellectual as many adult conversations.

Speaking vocabulary continues to grow in middle childhood. Children of this age give more exact definitions than do younger children. For instance, if you asked children to define the word *orange,* preschool children would often say, "You eat it." School-age children would give a more exact definition such as, "It is a color or a fruit." Definitions of words are often used as part of tests given to children during the school years. See 19-13. A *reading vocabulary* (words one can read) develops during these years. A *spelling/writing vocabulary* (words one can spell orally or in writing) also develops. Reading helps the growth of the speaking vocabulary.

Articulation of all English sounds is often mastered by eight years of age. See 19-14. Children who have the most articulation prob-

TEACHING RESOURCES

19-13 Defining words is part of many tests for school-age children.

ARTICULATION MASTERY OF SCHOOL-AGE CHILDREN

Age	Sound	Word Examples
6 years	l r t sh ch Blends	lamp, balloon, ball rabbit, barn, car table, potatoes, coat shoe, dishes, fish chair, matches, watch *dr*um, *cl*ock, *bl*ocks, *gl*asses, *cr*ayons
7 years	v th (voiceless) j s z Blends	vacuum, television, stove thumb, toothbrush, teeth jump, magic, orange sun, pencil, bus zebra, razor, feathers *tr*ain, *st*ar, *sl*ide, *sw*ing, *sp*oon
8 years	th (voiced) Blends	that, feathers, — *sc*ooter, *sn*owman, de*sk*, ne*st*

19-14 Ninety percent of all school-age children have mastered these sounds by the given age.

lems at the end of the preschool years often continue to have speech handicaps in the school years. Speech problems are also related to reading problems. This is because children need to say sounds in exact ways in order to understand and pronounce what they read.

Syntax (sentence structure) becomes more complex until about age nine. At this age, children have mastered a grammar. They use a set of rules to govern sentence structure such as using pronouns, making plurals, and showing tense. These rules may or may not be "Standard English" or the English accepted by grammar experts. Changing one's grammar after this age requires a relearning effort.

Middle childhood is also the age of playing with words. Chants are learned such as jump-rope rhymes. See 19-15. Sometimes chants seem to be used as a means of power or luck over reality. Name calling can even become a word contest which may turn a fight into laughter. Humor is expressed more in words during the middle childhood years. Children come to enjoy many kinds of jokes and simpler puns.

SPIEGEL, INC.

19-15 Saying jump-rope rhymes is one way school-age children play with words.

to Know

class inclusion . . . concrete . . .
concrete operational stage . . . conservation . . .
decentering perception . . .
deductive reasoning . . . double seriation . . .
formal operations . . .
hierarchial classification . . .
inductive reasoning . . . inversion . . .
multiple classification . . .
one-to-one matching . . .
projective spatial concepts . . .
reading vocabulary . . . reciprocity . . .
spelling/writing vocabulary . . . transitivity

to Review

Write your answers on a separate sheet of paper.
1. Upon hearing another person's point of view, a child in the concrete operational stage thinks that their own ideas are _____ (right, possibly wrong).
2. True or false. When noting a change in an object, school-age children begin to take into account more than one aspect of the change at the same time.
3. Give two examples of deductive reasoning.
4. Classification skills develop in a given order according to Piaget. List the following classification skills in the order that they happen.
 a. Break large classes down into subclasses and combine smaller subclasses into large classes.
 b. Sort objects.
 c. Classify using two or more qualities (color, shape, size, or other) at the same time.
 d. Classify, keeping the quality that defines the class stable. (For instance, if the child starts with squares, only squares are used for the class.)

5. Seriation skills develop in a given order according to Piaget. List the following seriation skills in the order that they happen.
 a. Run two series that are alike in some way (length, shade, or other) in correspondence with each other.
 b. Order objects by one variable using a trial-and-error method.
 c. Do a double seriation.
 d. Solve transitivity problems.
 e. Order objects by one variable without using a trial-and-error method.
6. Before children can compare the quantities of two groups of objects in terms of one group having more objects than the other group, they must be able to _____ (count, do one-to-one matching).
7. True or false. Spatial and speed concepts are mastered early in the school years.
8. True or false. When school-age children become logical, all causality concepts are mastered at the same time.
9. _____ and _____ vocabularies develop in middle childhood.
10. Norms show that the articulation of English sounds is mastered around _____ years of age, and the complexity of sentence structure increases until _____ years of age.

to Do

1. In a class or panel discussion, consider these questions:
 a. What are some words that describe adults who readily see from the viewpoint of others? (For instance, one term could be open minded.) What are some words that describe those adults who have problems in seeing from the viewpoint of others?

b. What skills are needed to see from the viewpoint of others? What are the reasons school-age children can only begin to develop the skill of seeing from the viewpoint of others?

c. Give some incidents where not seeing from the viewpoint of others had led to serious situations and where it has led to funny situations.

2. Select one of Piaget's tasks shown in 19-4. Make or gather the equipment needed and test a four-, six-, and eight-year-old individually. After asking whether the first and second objects are the same or are different, ask "Why?" Record each child's reason(s).

3. Make a list of all the ways you could classify students in your class.

4. Make a bulletin board depicting objects that come in a series such as measuring cups.

5. Ask an elementary school librarian or town librarian to show you some school-age children's books whose authors use puns and word play effectively. You might start by reading through the writings of Dr. Seuss and Shel Silverstein. After selecting a book, do one of the following:

a. Share some examples of the author's plays on words with your class.

b. Read the book to school-age children (or one child) and share their reactions to the story with your class.

School-age children learn by asking such questions as, "What makes soap bubbles float through the air?"

Peer groups play an important role in middle childhood.

20

Social-emotional development of the school-age child

After studying this chapter, you will be able to:
- Explain how Erikson's stage of "industry versus inferiority" establishes adult work patterns.
- Relate how adult and peer relationships assist school-age children's social development.
- Explain how school-age children's emotions approach their mature form.

During the preschool years, children enter the world of friendships with other children. Although preschool children learn much about getting along with peers, adults are often ready to help and encourage them when needed. Middle childhood begins a whole new social experience. Even children who have gotten off to a good start in the years before school have many adjustments to make. School-age children have to be much more independent. They need to get along with age mates. And they should master skills needed in order to fit into society.

SELF-CONCEPT

As you have read, the self-concept begins in infancy. Children come to middle childhood with an approach to life from the framework of self-confidence (feeling sure of one's own self) or the opposite, self-doubt (having a lack of sureness in one's own self). Self-confidence comes from achieving something one feels is important. It also comes from being included in family and peer groups and from feeling loved.

School-age children take a very close look at themselves, 20-1. They become keenly aware of their own shortcomings (areas where a per-

JOHN SHAW

20-1 School-age children often spend much time alone thinking about themselves.

son wants or needs to improve) and failures. *Self-evaluation,* or judging oneself, becomes more complex for several reasons.

Egocentric thought (where one does not see the point of view of others) does a flipflop during middle childhood. In this stage, children become almost totally concerned with what others think of them.

Reading, mathematics, music, computer literacy, and other skills that school-age children are learning to handle are abstract. Because of this, they are harder to evaluate than many of the motor skills learned in the preschool years. For instance, a child finds it much more difficult to say, "I'm a good reader" than, "I can walk."

Toddlers and preschool children are often evaluated in comparison to their own earlier skills. For the most part, school-age children are evaluated in comparison to other children's skills. For instance, school grades are earned more in comparison to other children's work than in comparison to the child's own previous work.

In the middle childhood years, the peer group joins the adult world as a source of evaluation. Peers can evaluate harshly. Adults cannot often change the ways peers judge each other. In fact,

when an adult steps in to protect or defend a child, peer judgment can become more harsh.

In the next chapter, you will read about how to help the school-age child's self-esteem.

SHOWING SOCIAL AWARENESS

During middle childhood, children begin to show much greater social awareness. School-age children develop a sense of industry as they learn some of the skills needed in the adult's world of work. They also deepen their social relationships with adults and peers.

Sense of industry

As you read in Chapter 16, Erikson described the preschool child's sense of initiative (thinking or acting without being urged). The preschool child's ability to experience many things brings the school-age child to Erikson's fourth stage of development, "industry versus inferiority." See 20-2.

In the school years, children want to satisfy themselves while being acceptable to society. The almost constant play of the preschool child is replaced with more and more meaningful work—at least by adult standards. (In no way

ERIKSON'S STAGE OF INDUSTRY
VERSUS INFERIORITY

Basic Trust versus Basic Mistrust (First Year of Life)

Autonomy versus Shame and Doubt (Second Year of Life)

Initiative versus Guilt (Preschool Years)

Industry versus Inferiority (Middle Childhood)
Middle childhood is the time for developing the tools of society in preparation for adult work. If children are encouraged to use these tools, they develop a sense of industry. If too little is expected or if they are cricitized for their efforts, a sense of inferiority develops. Inferiority results in poor work habits, avoidance of competition, and the inability to cope with later tasks.

20-2 Showing industry while avoiding inferiority is a major social-emotional task of school-age children.

20-3 Youth organizations such as scout troops encourage and recognize children who learn useful skills.

does this mean that play is not important even in the middle childhood years.) If children are successful in gaining industry in this fourth stage, several goals are met.

The proper attitude toward work is learned at this time. Children with a sense of industry see work as the way to learn new ideas and skills and to perform in worthwhile ways. These children also see work as a way to win approval from others. Parents, teachers, and peers encourage the learning of skills. Even social organizations such as 4-H, Boy Scouts, or Girl Scouts make the learning of skills the route to success and higher status. See 20-3.

The skills learned in this stage help the child become ready for adult life. Each society has its skills which are important in adult life. In the United States today, the tools of literacy are becoming more and more important to success. See 20-4.

Children learn to do things with and for others in this stage. The initiative stage of the preschool years was more of an, "I want to do things on my own and for myself," stage. In the industry stage, children want to work with and for others. Cooperation can be truly learned and practiced.

The sense of industry heightens children's responsibility. It also gives them more independence.

20-4 In our high tech society, the tools of literacy include computer skills.

Social-emotional development of the school-age child   347

Two main problems may develop in this stage. First, some children come to place too much importance on work. These children begin to see work as the only way to measure their own worth. To these children, work becomes the most important aspect of their life. They neglect their relationships with others. Erikson refers to these children as "slaves of their technology."

Second, children may develop feelings of inferiority. Inferiority may be the root of poor work habits, feelings of uselessness, fear of competition, and imitative rather than creative attempts. Inferiority may be the result of a handicap. But inferiority can also be present in normal children. All children have areas where they lack knowledge or skills. They also have success areas. If one's success areas do not relate to what one's culture values, then those successes are seen as less important. When children's efforts are not praised, they lose even more confidence in their ability to produce. Inferiority seems to be even more harmful to the self-concept than either doubt (seen in the toddler years) or guilt (seen in the preschool years).

Adults model and guide

Although the peer group becomes a more major part of school-age children's social lives, adults are still important. Adults serve very special purposes in the lives of school-age children. Adults need to encourage children as they test their abilities. For instance, children do better in school when they have loving, caring parents than when parents show little or no concern. See 20-5. Adults encourage children in many ways. They may provide the

JOHN SHAW

20-5 A parent's contact with the school principal is one way to show concern.

needed time to help children in their activities. Adults often help meet the costs of children's training or participation. They make arrangements for children to get safely to and from the site of activities. Adults may even sponsor and supervise group activities for children.

School-age children often question adults' wisdom. And yet, school-age children need adults to listen to them and, at times, to advise and set limits. Adults must learn the balance between letting go and being there for children.

LOUIS J. BREAUX, JR.

20-6 A warm and helpful father helps a girl learn her feminine role.

In a similar manner, adults model values and attitudes about almost all aspects of life. The saying, "actions speak louder than words," is true. School-age children watch and listen to important adults in their lives. They pattern many of their thoughts and actions after these adults.

Adults must be careful not to label personality. Labeling includes thinking of or calling a child a baby, shy, or other similar descriptions. Such labeling is called *character definition*. When children are labeled, they often behave as they are labeled even if they could behave in other ways. Adults and others may even help children practice their labeled roles. For example, family members think of Karen as a "baby." Susie, who is Karen's friend, becomes a "little mother" to Karen. Because Karen soon thinks of herself as a "baby," she allows others to make decisions for her. Not only is Karen labeled, but Susie is soon labeled a "little mother" to people other than Karen. These labels may be reinforced for the rest of their lives and cause great harm.

Adults also help extend the gender role development in the school years. Mothers and other female adults close to school-age girls affect girls' feminine gender role learnings. These learnings include goals in the world of work. Fathers and other male adults close to school-age boys affect boys' masculine gender role learnings. Fathers and other adult males who model warmth and sureness in their masculine roles directly affect feminity in girls. See 20-6. Warm, masculine-type models also help girls in their teens relate well to males in their age group. The same is true for female adults and their affect on school-age boys' learning.

School-age children enjoy just being with adults. Elementary school children are still interested in doing things with and for their families, 20-7. These children also enjoy being with other adults such as their teachers and youth leaders.

Peers become important

As you read in previous chapters on social development, children of all ages like other

JOHN SHAW

20-7 Doing things with one's family is still important to school-age children.

children—both siblings and peers. However, peers become even more important in middle childhood. The elementary school years are often called the *gang years,* because peers become important. On the other hand, adults become less important as children spend more time with peers. In mobile societies such as the United States, friendships often replace close relationships to relatives.

Stages of friendships. Friendships are developmental. This means that the nature of friendships change as children mature. Preschool children refer to nearby children who play with them as friends. The preschool stage of these very informal friendships can be called playmateship, 20-8.

At ages six through eight years, meaningful relationships are not in full bloom. The number of friends children have does increase throughout these years. Also, there is more separation of sexes by age eight. The peer groups are informal and are made up of children who live near each other. Groups are often within walking or cycling distance. The membership of these groups changes as families move in and out of the neighborhood. Egocentrism, still present in children's thinking in these early school years, affects friendships. In this stage, a child often sees a friend as someone who "helps me" (and seldom in terms of how the child can help the friend). For this reason, the stage may be called the *stage of one-way assistance.* Give and take does occur, but it serves the separate rather than the mutual interest of friends.

Between the ages of nine and 11 years, more close friendships are formed. Boys choose boys for friends, and girls choose girls for friends. Showing of dislike between the sexes occurs. However, girls may become interested in opposite sex around age 11. See 20-9. Simliar interests and tastes determine friendships more often than physical nearness. Some formal groups such as team sport groups are formed at this time, also. The nature of friendships becomes one of helping each other. This stage is often called the *stage of reciprocity.* This stage occurs at the same time as Erikson's stage of industry where cooperation is needed to achieve group goals.

Purposes of peer groups. Peer groups serve many purposes. First, close friendships are formed from peer groups. Middle childhood is the age for exploring the nature of friendships such as sharing with friends and loyalty.

20-9 Toward the end of the elementary school years, girls show more interest in boys than boys do in girls.

20-8 In the preschool years, children form informal friendship groups.

Second, friendships with peers provide school-age children the chance to join rather formal groups such as 4-H or scouts. Even the earlier play groups become more organized as children participate in games with rules. These groups teach children that social relationships involve rules and that rules help groups work as teams. See 20-10. Peer group codes contain more rules about what not to do than what should be done. Children learn that *ostracism* (removal from the group) can occur if rules are broken.

With each passing year, children desire to become more self-controlling. A third purpose of peers is to help children become less dependent on adults. The peer group serves as a sifter for thinking through adult-taught priorities. Peers help children decide what priorities to keep and what priorities to throw away. As children consider priorities, they learn to conform to others at times and to stand firm in their own beliefs at other times.

Fourth, peers provide emotional support. There is a comfort that adults cannot provide when peers realize that other age mates share similar feelings. Peers have similar interests, fears, angers, and anxieties. Special friends may huddle, talk, giggle, argue, and fight as they share secrets.

Peers share information with each other as a fifth function. Children learn from their peers as they do group projects. Not only being a part of the group but being the best in the group makes children want to learn all they can from their peers.

Finally, peers affect each child's self-concept. Once egocentrism disappears, self-judgment is always tempered by judgments of others. As Robert Burns said, "we see ourselves as others see us." School-age children are highly concerned about how they appear to others. In peer groups, children are given rather stable roles such as "captain of the team" or the "last one chosen." This makes children well aware of how others feel toward them. Once peer attitudes are absorbed, children react to themselves as others have reacted to them.

Popular and unpopular children. Forming relationships with others is a vital part of the

JOHN SHAW

20-10 Rule games such as softball help children learn that social relationships are governed by rules.

growing process of school-age children. Friendships are thus a necessity, not a luxury. About 10 percent of all school-age children could be thought of as friendless. About half of these children experience active rejection such as being bullied by others and being the subjects of name calling. The other half of the friendless children are ignored.

Certain qualities seem to make children likeable by peer standards. These qualities change somewhat during the school years. For instance, first graders say they like tough children. But in later grades, children see nice

TRAITS OF POPULAR AND UNPOPULAR CHILDREN

Traits of Popular Children	Traits of Unpopular Children
Healthy.	Aggressive or hostile.
Vigorous (have much energy).	Thinks of the world as unfair.
Poised.	Anxious.
Adaptable.	Quarrelsome.
Considerate (thinks of others).	Not a good sport.
Self-assured.	Uncertain about oneself.
Creative.	Unattractive.
Self-controlling (rather than too dependent on others).	
Attractive.	

20-11 Certain traits are related to children's popularity and unpopularity in the school years.

and smart children as popular. Skills that are desirable in a culture, such as athletic ability, affect popularity. Certain general traits seem to be related to popularity and unpopularity during the elementary years. See 20-11. The traits may affect popularity for many years to come—even into the adult years.

CONTROLLING EMOTIONS

As you read in Chapter 16, emotional development gets well under way during the preschool years. By school entrance, the major emotions have not only appeared but are fairly established in behavior patterns. In middle childhood, emotional development and personality continue to merge. Thus, the emotions felt by school-age children affect all of their behavior.

Love

All school-age children need love just as they did during their infant, toddler, and preschool years. They show love to adults and age mates who care for them and accept them as they are. School-age children do not seek relationships where they must give too much in return. They do care for others who share common interests.

The need for love is shown in school-age children's great desire to be accepted by others—adults and especially peers. These children, however, do not express their love as openly (with hugs and kisses) as do younger children. In middle childhood love for adults is shown more by wanting to be with adults and by doing things for and with them. Affection for peers is shown by wanting to be with them, by sharing secrets, by staying in touch through telephone and notes, and by giving small presents. See 20-12.

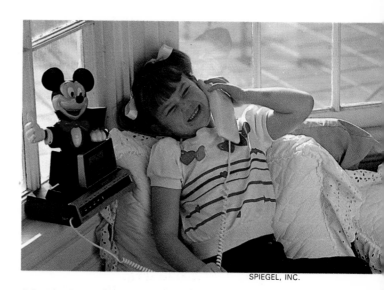

SPIEGEL, INC.

20-12 Spending hours on the telephone is one way that peers stay close.

Social-emotional development of the school-age child 353

School-age children who do not feel loved have a narrowed emotional range. They experience little or no joy, grief, or guilt. Thinking abilities are hurt because these unloved children cannot concentrate. And, these children often turn to anti-social behavior such as hostile acts.

Fear and anxiety

Fear and anxiety continues in middle childhood. But some of the earlier preschool fears and worries become less threatening. There is a greater separation of fantasy and reality. Thus, fear of the dark disappears after age seven. Fear of the supernatural declines by ages nine or 10. Fears of physical harm such as disease, injury, and death continue from the preschool years into the school years. School-age children's fears and worries also center around people and their actions, possible embarrassment, and the future. See 20-13.

Fears and worries of middle childhood often do not disappear with age. Some studies report that over half of the school-age children's fears and worries persist into adult years. And, these fears and worries change from specific fears to more generalized forms. An example would be when a person says "I'm worried, but I don't know why." General worries are often more difficult to overcome than specific fears.

Anger and aggression

Preschool children express anger physically. School-age children have more ability to control their bodies and to use words. They also know what is and is not acceptable. Therefore, children in middle childhood express their anger in less direct ways. Anger may be shown in the forms of *impertinence* (not showing respect), *sulkiness,* and *scapegoating* (blaming others for one's own mistakes). See 20-14. School-age children also show anger by gossiping, plotting,

FEARS AND ANXIETIES IN MIDDLE CHILDHOOD

Types of Fears/Anxieties	Examples
People and Their Actions	Family quarrels. Divorce/disagreement of parents. Fear that custodial parent may leave (for children who have single parents). Kidnappers and child enticers. Abuse. Unfriendly school gangs.
Embarrassment	School failure. Not being chosen for a team sport, part in a play, or other event. Making a mistake in a game, recital, or other performance. Poor personal appearance. Physical examinations and changing clothes in a gym locker room or other public place. Personal handicaps.
The Future	Any new situation such as a new school or new neighborhood. The world in general such as pollution, war, economic changes.

20-13 People and their actions, embarrassment, and the future comprise the major fears and worries of middle childhood.

and even imagining the downfall of their enemies. Withdrawal from a situation such as quitting or doing less than one's best may be another sign of anger.

The form of anger and aggression changes with age. Likewise, as people grow older, they become angry about different things. Like preschool children, school-age children are angered when their wants are denied and their possessions are threatened. But unlike preschool children, school-age children are also angered by what they see as wrongs to others. In later years, anger at social wrongs may be turned into positive social action.

MELODY HOUSE

20-14 School-age children often express their anger by becoming sullen rather than by a show of temper.

Social-emotional development of the school-age child   355

to Know

character definition . . . gang years . . .
self-evaluation . . . stage of one-way assistance . . .
stage of reciprocity

to Review

Write your answers on a separate sheet of paper.
1. List three reasons why self-evaluation is difficult in middle childhood.
2. _____ (Play, Meaningful work) is the root of Erikson's stage of industry.
3. True or false. School-age children learn skills for feelings of self-worth.
4. Which of the following statements are true? (You may choose more than one.)
    a. School-age children need adults to make most decisions for them.
    b. Adults need to encourage children to be independent.
    c. Adults affect the gender role learnings of children even in the school years.
    d. Because peer influence is so great during the school years, it matters little what attitudes or priorities adults convey by their actions or words.
    e. Family activities such as vacations should stop during middle childhood, because children need and want to be with their peers.
5. True or false. Fathers and other adult males affect boys' but not girls' gender role learnings.
6. Peers are _____ (more, less) important in mobile societies.
7. List the six purposes of the peer group.
8. Match the statements about friendships with the stages. (Note that some of the statements may be used to describe more than one stage of friendship.)
    Stages:
    ___ Playmateship
    ___ Stage of one-way assistance
    ___ Stage of reciprocity
    Statements:
    a. Friendships change often.
    b. Friendships are stable.

c. Friends have like interests.
d. Friends are neighborhood children.
e. Friends are mixed-sex groups.
f. Friends are like-sex groups.
g. Friends are people who help me.
i. Friends are people who share and meet each other's needs.
j. Friends are sought for playing informal games such as chase or biking.
k. Friends are sought for group projects.

to Do

1. Discuss how the world of work and home care tasks have changed during the last two or three decades. Your high school counselor and a home economics teacher are good resource people. Discuss how these jobs have changed the skills important in the adult years. How have the needed adult skills changed the knowledge and skills needed by school-age children? What courses have been added to the school curriculum in the last thirty years?
2. Discuss how adults who are labeled "workaholics" may have developed this pattern in middle childhood. What are the problems of workaholics in terms of personal sacrifices and in terms of their relationships with their families, friends, and co-workers? How can a person achieve a balance between work and leisure times?
3. Interview several four- and five-year-olds, seven- and eight-year-olds, and ten- and eleven-year-olds on friendship. Make up your own questions, but remain flexible in your questions as you interview. How did the children's comments follow the stages of friendships as given in this chapter?
4. Make a bulletin board of magazine or drawn pictures showing the purposes of friendships.
5. Develop a chart of traits you feel add to popularity or unpopularity in the teen and young adult years. How do these traits compare with those given in Chart 20-12?
6. Defend the statement, "Friendships are a necessity, not a luxury."

School-age children spend more time with
their peers than younger children do, but
family is still important.

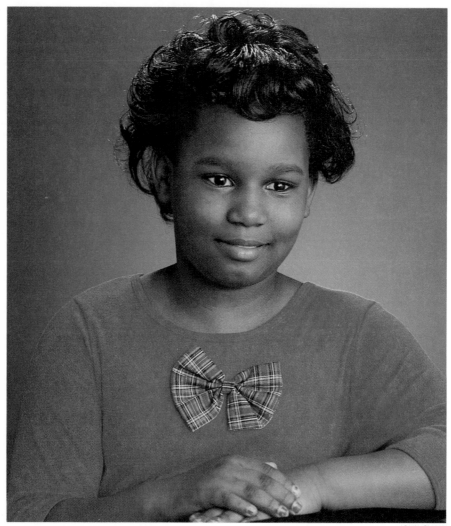

JOHN SHAW

Although school-age children do not need adults for much direct physical care, they still need much guidance and support.

21

Providing for the school-age child's developmental needs

After studying this chapter, you will be able to:
- ☐ Plan ways to meet the developmental needs of school-age children.
- ☐ Guide school-age children in meeting their physical needs.
- ☐ Help school-age children select activities that aid their growing mental skills both in and out of school.
- ☐ Encourage children as they try to meet their budding social needs.

The motor, mental, and social skills of school-age children develop at a very rapid rate. During these years between six and 12, children should progress from the dependent first-grader to the almost independent teen. Many developmental needs must be met.

The middle childhood years require more exchanges of ideas between children and adults than actual physical help. During these years children develop life-long habits such as eating and grooming habits. They also develop work habits such as task persistence (staying at a task until it .is completed or progress is made). Adults can help children develop these habits by giving reasons for good habits, by setting examples, and by providing chances to practice. See 21-1.

Preschool children learn mainly through their motor actions and perceptions. By the school years, children are expected to think in a mental way. They need to handle abstract symbol systems such as words, mathematics, and computer languages. Adults are needed to help encourage children as they learn new methods of problem-solving and become *literate* (able to handle symbol systems).

The middle childhood years are also years of venturing into the peer world. Children need

JOHN SHAW

21-1 Parents can encourage children to develop good work habits.

guidance in meeting this new challenge. School-age children must learn how to cooperate and compete with their peers. All of these changes are filled with intense feelings. These feelings need to be controlled or put to use in ways that are acceptable to society.

PHYSICAL NEEDS

Most school-age children quickly outgrow the need for direct physical care. But they still have many physical needs that must be met with the help of adults. As these children begin to think for themselves and as peers become more important, meeting needs becomes more com-

plex. Personal tastes and wanting peer acceptance may limit methods of meeting needs. For instance, having a warm coat is not as important to school-age children as having a coat that peers will like.

Encouraging health and safety practices

The school-age child is still growing, but not at the rate seen in infancy. Between the ages of six and 12 years, boys gain a total of about 43.5 pounds. Girls gain 50.5 pounds. An adequate diet is needed to meet growth needs. Foods are also needed to meet the great energy demands stemming from school-age children's physical activities. Proper diets help these

DAILY BASIC DIET FOR SCHOOL-AGE CHILDREN

Milk (4 servings)
Typical serving: 1 cup (240 mL) whole, reconstituted evaporated, skim, reconstituted dry, buttermilk, or yogurt;* two 1-inch (2.5 cm) cubes or 1.5 oz. (45 g) hard cheese. Part can be in cream soups, custards, or puddings.

Protein Foods (7-8 exchanges)**
1 exchange: 1 oz. (30 g) cooked lean solid meat, poultry, fish; 1/2 cup (120 mL) dry beans, peas, lentils; 1 oz. (30 g) cheese; 1/4 cup (60 mL) cottage cheese; 2 tablespoons (30 g) peanut butter; 1 egg; 1 frankfurter.

Vitamin A-Rich Fruits and Vegetables (1 serving)
Typical serving: 1/2 cup (120 mL) cooked or 2/3 cups (160 mL) raw spinach, kale, collard and other greens, broccoli, sweet potatoes, yellow squash, carrots, tomato, apricots.

Vitamin C-Rich Fruits and Vegetables (1 serving minimum)
Typical serving: 1/2 cup (120 mL) juice, 1/2 cup (120 mL) cooked, or 2/3 cup (160 mL) raw oranges, grapefruit, pineapple, tangerines, papaya, strawberries, broccoli, brussel sprouts, cauliflower, collard and other greens.

Other Fruits and Vegetables (2-3 servings minimum)
Typical serving: 1/2 cup (120 mL) cooked or 2/3 cup (160 mL) raw asparagus, bean sprouts, beets, cabbage, celery, cucumbers, green peppers, okra, mushrooms, string beans, non-yellow squash, apples, bananas, berries, grapes, watermelon, pears, figs, dates, prunes, raisins.

Cereals, whole or enriched, Potatoes, Legumes (5 servings)
Typical serving: 1 slice bread; 1/2 cup (120 mL) cooked rice, corn, hot cereal, pasta; 1 muffin, biscuit, pancake, or waffle; 2-inch (5 cm) square of cornbread; 2 corn tortillas; 1 large flour tortilla; 1 small or 1/2 cup (120 mL) cooked potato; 3/4 cup (180 mL) ready-to-eat cereal; 3/4 cup (180 mL) dried beans or dried peas.

*Whole milk fortified with Vitamin D preferred.
**The term *food exchange* implies that any item within a given food group has about the same food value as any other food item for that food group. To use the exchange system, select foods in the given amount for each allowed exchange. For instance, six exchanges can be six different food choices. Or, the same food can be eaten for more than one exchange. For example, if one ounce (30 g) cheese equals one exchange, then one and one-half ounces (45 g) equals one and one-half exchanges and two ounces (60 g) equals two exchanges.

21-2 A well-balanced diet is needed to meet school-age children's growth and energy needs.

children resist infections. The school-age child also needs to store some nutrients for the rapid growth of the teen years. Chart 21-2 gives the daily basic diet for school-age children. The diet plan should be adjusted to meet a child's own needs.

When children go to school, adults can no longer supervise all of children's eating habits. For instance, children often eat their lunches at school (or other places) on school days. Some schools publish their weekly menus to help parents plan the other meals and snacks of the day. However, at times children may not eat what is on their school lunch plate. Even children who carry their lunches to school may give away or throw away some of their food. Parents and school staff need to encourage children to eat a proper diet while away from home. School lunch supervisors, in turn, need to consider children's likes as well as meet dietary needs within cost, equipment, staff, and time constraints.

School-age children's snacks are often not supervised. By this age, children often use their spending money for snacks of their choice. These snacks are often junk foods (foods of low nutritional quality). Children often eat junk foods in the home, too. Children who eat too many junk foods can lose their appetite for nourishing foods. Too many junk foods can also increase tooth decay and cause obesity. (Obese children can have profound social adjustment problems by nine years of age.)

Adults can encourage healthy snacking by keeping nutritious, ready-to-eat snacks on hand. See 21-3. Examples would be cheese cubes, fresh fruit, and carrot or celery sticks. Adults can encourage children to prepare their own nutritious snacks, too. Because school-age children enjoy eating, they often enjoy cooking. Many good cookbooks are written for the school-age child. They contain simple recipes that children can prepare on their own.

Middle childhood is the healthiest time of life. Vaccines have protected many children from such childhood illnesses as measles and mumps. The common cold is the most common contagious illness for this age group. Tooth decay is also a major problem. One-eighth of all six-year-olds and three-fourths of all eleven-year-olds have decay in their permanent teeth.

Accidents happen often in middle childhood because these children are active and daring. Some injuries are due to sports. For instance, bruises, sprains, or broken bones may result from contact sports such as football. Foot damage can occur in girls who toe dance prior to the teen years. Children of this age are victims of car, bicycle, and water accidents. Common-sense safety rules need to be taught and modeled.

Selecting the right clothing
Like children of all ages, school-age children need clothing that fits and has quality construction features. School-age children are very active. Clothing should have growth features

PHOTO: NANCY BROWN, MODEL: MICHAEL PHILLIPS, SENECA FOODS

21-3 When tasty, nutritious foods are provided, school-age children will prefer them over junk foods.

LOUIS J. BREAUX, JR.

21-4 The skills needed for tying shoes are often mastered in the early school years.

and should withstand stress and strain. Most school-age children have developed self-dressing skills except for a hard-to-reach button or a specially-tied bow. See 21-4. Younger school-age children may still need to have some self-dressing features. Shoe and sock size will change on the average of every six months for six- to 12-year-olds.

More important than for younger children, school-age children need to make decisions about their own clothing and shoes. Children of this age develop their own preferences for color and style. These children are also very concerned about how peers view them. The right clothing and shoes help make children feel part of the group, 21-5. If clothing and shoes are too different from what others are wearing, children may feel rejected. Compliments on clothing help boost children's morale.

Providing needed space and furnishings

School-age children are unlike babies and toddlers who do not especially want a room of their own. School-age children need and want an area of their own. Certain features should be considered in planning a space for school-age children:

- Space that can be used for many purposes—playing, working on hobbies, studying, daydreaming, sleeping, resting, and dressing—is best. Children often want space for their friends to visit for the afternoon or even overnight.
- Storage space is needed for clothes and shoes, play and hobby equipment, and books. Display areas for photos, pennants, collections, hobbies, and keepsakes are often prized.
- Attractive space is important to school-age

SPIEGEL, INC.

21-5 School-age children want to dress in much the same way as their peers.

children. They like to choose their own color schemes and accessories. See 21-6.
- Easy-to-clean rooms help children who are just learning home care skills.

In addition to these features, parents may want to invest in furniture and accessories that the child can use as a teen and young adult.

INTELLECTUAL NEEDS

School-age children have intellectual needs that must be met with the help of adults. Some children's intellectual needs are not met. This may be because adults feel that they do not know how to help or because they feel that these mental needs are met by the school. On the other hand, another major problem is that some parents and other adults are too concerned with turning out smart children. These adults may educate children to the point that children cannot enjoy their youth. Adults' good intentions may burden children. School-age children need time to play, to engage in hobbies, to be with peers, and to daydream. In fact, the effort to produce children who are good at many things may spread their time and effort so that they cannot excel at anything.

Adults can help their school-age children meet their intellectual needs in many ways. First, adults need to provide chances for children to do activities which require effort over longer and longer periods of time as children mature. Such activities would include learning to play an instrument or working on crafts. Second, adults need to allow children to choose the activities that they themselves find most rewarding. Third, adults need to encourage children but limit the overuse of rewards and praise. Too many rewards suggest that the activity itself is not satisfying. Studies show that successful people are willing to work hard for the enjoyment of mastering the activity rather than for a reward. Finally, as in all areas, adults need to be honest models. Adults who show interest in their own activities and whose skills and satisfactions grew over long periods of time are the best models for children.

The school does meet many specific mental needs of children. But there are many activities that can be done out of school to help children grow mentally. Parents and other adults responsible for children need to prepare children for school. They also need to support the school's program for best results.

Providing activities that help intellectual growth

As you read in Chapter 19, perception matures, thinking becomes logical, and language continues to develop during middle childhood. The school provides much training in perception, logic, and language during

LIS KING

21-6 School-age children prefer bedrooms planned with their tastes in mind.

school hours. Even during non-school hours, the school provides homework and extra-curricular activities. However, other enrichment activities are fun and help mental development.

Children need a rich out-of-school world, a world of things to do and see. Even day-to-day activities are often rich in learning materials. For instance, children may learn about conservation by finding the right-sized container to serve or store food. Seriation ideas are used in selecting a grade of sandpaper or nails for a project.

There are games, too, that are designed to aid perception, logic, and language. These games should always be done in the spirit of fun. Some ideas are given at the end of the chapter.

Perception. Games from many sources are available to help children with visual and spatial (space) perception. Children's magazines, books, and computer programs are filled with puzzles such as mazes, word finds, and hidden pictures (objects hidden in a large picture). Some school-age children enjoy making their own puzzles. Jigsaw puzzles of varying difficulty levels are also fun to do and aid perception.

Art and craft projects help develop perception of color, form, and texture. Music helps rhythmic and pitch perception. And, gross-motor and fine-motor activities aid touch and movement perception.

Perceptions need to be remembered. Memory is used when children represent the real world in symbol form—art works and words. Some table games have been designed to directly aid memory, 21-7.

Logic. Although daily activities aid the growth of logic in school-age children, planned activities can help. For instance, children need many experiences with single classification and multiple classification. They need experiences with seriation. They need to experience *spatial rotations* (turns in space), which are basic for reading maps and diagrams. See 21-8. Some

JOHN SHAW

21-7 Some commercial games are designed to help memory.

21-8 Setting a table helps young school-age children understand spatial rotations. Children see that objects placed to the right or left of a plate appear to be on opposite sides when the plates are across the table from each other.

educators even favor teaching Piaget's conservation tasks although they were planned by him for testing children's mental development.

Games of logic are available from the same sources as games that aid perception—children's magazines, books, and computer games. Games of logic seem to span the generations. You may see school-age children, their parents, and even grandparents liking these games and playing them together. Games of logic are provided for many levels of ability. For children to enjoy these games, the games must match their thinking levels. Otherwise, these games are meaningless.

Language. Children learn the language they hear, speak, and read. Adults can enrich children's language learnings in many ways. Adults can share ideas and experiences with children. They can read to children and listen to their oral reading. And adults can encourage children to express themselves correctly.

Schools send home many materials which aid language development. These include books to read, words to spell, and reports to write. Adults should be sure that children follow through with these activities.

There are many language games that are fun as well as helpful. Games such as "Scrabble" and "Password" are popular games. Individual word puzzles of all types are available, too. These include crossword puzzles, word finds, and scrambled words.

Preparing the child to enter school

Between late August and September each year, several million five- and six-year-olds enter school. Many older children also enter new schools at this time because their families have moved. Starting school is exciting and perhaps scary for these children.

Entering school is a developmental task to be mastered. Children must deal with new people—both children and adults. They also must deal with new concepts and skills and with a different daily structure. See 21-9. School-age children spend 44 percent of their waking hours at school.

Success with the school-entrance task is a step forward. Most children are able to master the task with few problems. A few children have severe problems. If the problems persist, the beginning crisis can become a chronic problem called *school avoidance* (or *school phobia*). Children who have school avoidance are afraid of school.

Because entering school is a developmental task, adults are needed to help children make the transition from home to school. In order to help children, adults need to understand the nature of the task. Kindergarten and first grade are not a repeat of the preschool program. Elementary schools have different goals. Elementary schools teach children to learn without much help, follow directions, stay with a task, and put the teacher's desires ahead of one's own wishes. The building blocks for these goals should begin in the preschool years. One building block is a secure and trusting relationship between adult and child. Another is the adult's ability to let go to some extent to help

21-9 The people, concepts, and schedules of elementary school are very different from those of the preschooler's world.

the child become more independent. In this way, the child is better prepared to become part of the group in the school setting. A third building block is helping the child overcome separation anxiety. Teaching children to accept the authority of adults other than parents is a fourth building block. Children who have occasional babysitters or who have been in a preschool program also have an easier time meeting the new goals.

In elementary school, there is a switch away from the home and preschool program of learning about real objects through direct experiences and some symbolic play. School programs stress learning abstract symbol systems, 21-10. Before school, children are encouraged to interact in action ways with their world. Schools require children to listen, look, and give verbal and written responses. In many schools, the period of transition between preschool level and school level learning methods is not long. Stress may accompany the change. Adults need to realize that children may manage anxiety at school, but they may show anxiety outside of school in non-school tasks. Adults need to practice extra patience during the adjustment time. This is a poor time to add new learnings or tasks to a child's life such as music lessons or a new pet.

School also means getting along with peers for many hours. Children sit next to, line up by, work with, eat with, and share with other children. Unlike the preschool play groups, where children choose their own friends and play when they want, school relationships are more teacher directed. Children who are adaptable and who have had contacts with others find it easier to adjust to other children than children who have not had such contacts before the school years.

As school time nears, adults need to prepare children. They should answer any questions children may have about school. Knowing the details can help children overcome their anxiety. Adults need to respond to children's negative statements such as, "I won't go." Adults should let children know that they understand their concerns but that school is a must. For instance, a parent may say, "I know that you are scared, but all boys and girls must go to school." Then the subject should be dropped. Adults cannot expect to make such a child happy about school.

Adults should caution older children not to frighten or tease younger children about school. Older children enjoy helping adults prevent fears in younger children.

The topic of school should be treated rather casually. School should be viewed as a normal course of events. Children can become more anxious when parents are overexcited.

School entrance requirements should be fulfilled early. Such requirements as medical check-ups and vaccinations are stressful in

RADIO SHACK, A DIV. OF TANDY CORP.

21-10 Computer languages use abstract symbols in the forms of words, numbers, and graphs.

themselves. They may add to the child's concerns about starting school if the events are too close.

Children should be included in shopping trips for school clothes and supplies. Young children feel grown-up when they can help select school needs. See 21-11.

Some schools will provide lists of suggested activities to help prepare children for school. Adults can use these, but they should not try to cram in too many new activities. For instance, adults cannot make up for years of not reading stories to children in a two-week period before school starts. Trying to give the child a crash course will do little good in preparing the child. It will frustrate adult and child. And it may add to the child's anxiety about starting school.

Adults need to make transportation plans clear to children. Younger children who walk or catch a bus need practice. Some adults include nearby, older children who attend the same school in their practice sessions. (These older children often keep a watchful eye on younger school-age children.) Children should be reminded not to talk to or go with strangers. They should know their full name, parent's names, address, and phone number.

Adults should create a normal routine for the first few days of school. Overdoing photos, sounding anxious, getting the child ready too early (or too late), or doing a special breakfast are not ways to make school a matter-of-fact experience. Adults' moods are caught by children.

Goodbyes should be said at the bus stop, on the school yard, or at the classroom door. These goodbyes should be warm but not clingy. The teary-eyed child often regains control soon after the adult is out of sight. See 21-12.

21-11 Children enjoy choosing some of their own school supplies.

JOHN SHAW

The school-age child's developmental needs 369

21-12 Children with warm, loving parents often get over their goodbye tears as soon as they enter the classroom.

Teachers are experienced in handling the tears that come with starting school.

If the first days are successful, children often begin to look forward to school. Likewise, they look forward to the end of the school day and vacation times.

Reinforcing school tasks

No matter how much help parents and other adults have given babies and young children, adults must continue working with their children. School children need daily encouragement and help. Help is not effective if given only a few days after school reports (report cards, check sheets, parent-teacher meetings) are given to parents. The schools and parents and other adults close to children have the same goal. They all want to give children the best possible education. When those concerned work as a team, children are helped.

Adults need to see that children attend school regularly and follow the rules. They also need to take an interest in what children are learning. Talking daily with children about school work, looking at their papers, and staying in close contact with the school helps.

Adults and children need to plan a quiet place for work. Children need a desk for some of their work such as writing. But many children also enjoy a place to stretch out while reading. See 21-13.

Adults and children also need to plan a given time for doing homework. The amount of time set aside varies with the age needs of the child. However, adults should remember that 30 to 60 minutes well spent is better than longer times spent unwisely. Elementary school children need time to play and perhaps have a snack or evening meal before doing homework. Homework should not be done after hours of television viewing or other activities. School-age children who do not have homework can use the set time for reading or being read to, drawing, or doing other activities that complement school tasks. For instance, adults may supervise a cooking project to reinforce fractions.

Adults need to supervise but not *do* children's homework for them. In the elementary school, homework is most often assigned to reinforce skills learned in class. Doing children's homework makes them reliant on adults for solving their own tasks. It also prevents the child from getting the needed practice. (If homework is often too difficult, adults should talk to the teacher.)

Adults need to limit TV viewing and leisure activities on school nights. Several studies show that as hours of TV viewing increase, grades drop at the same rate. Children who do not watch as much TV tend to concentrate better and use their imaginations more. Also, school-age children who learn to budget their work and leisure times develop proper life long work and play habits.

LOUIS J. BREAUX, JR.

21-13 Some school-age children enjoy stretching out to read.

Guiding television viewing

Television may have changed people's lives more than any other invention of the twentieth century. Over 99 percent of American families have one set and over 70 percent have more than one set. The average set runs more than six hours each day. In fact, many families alter their sleeping habits and plan their meals and leisure times around television programs.

Preschool and school-age children watch television an average of four hours a day. By age 18 years, most children will have spent more time watching television than any other activity except sleeping. Thus, television has become many children's babysitters or friends and has replaced many other activities.

There are both good and bad effects to viewing programs. As you read in Chapter 17, children may learn useful information from many programs especially if there is adult aid. Thus, television can be a positive tool for learning and entertainment. On the other hand, there are two negative effects. First, television replaces many other worthwhile activities, especially involvement with others and hands-on activities. The best way to overcome this negative effect is for adults to limit the number of hours the set runs while children are in the home. Instead of television, adults should plan other interesting activities for them. The second negative effect of television is that the content of some programs may lead to serious problems. Adults need to be prepared to handle these problems, 21-14.

SOCIAL NEEDS

In many ways, social development becomes the most important aspect of development in middle childhood. The peer group becomes more and more important as children progress through the school years. Relationships with peers affect all aspects of development. For instance, school-age children's physical skills are often judged by whether they have the skills needed for playing sports and games with peers. In middle childhood, children attend school with peers. These children make daily judgments of their own learnings compared with

Problems in Content	Ways to Handle
Violence Violence is shown frequently. Ninety-eight percent of all cartoons contain violence, and 80 percent of all prime time shows contain at least one act of physical violence.	Adults can prevent children from watching violent shows. In order to know which shows contain violence, adults can write to Action for Children's Television (ACT) for a list of programs the experts feel are too violent for children, or they can preview shows before allowing children to watch.
Children report being frightened or having nightmares after viewing violence.	Since preschool children have problems in seeing differences in fantasy and reality, programs should be selected with care and, if violence is seen, an adult should be there to discuss it.
For some children, watching violence (even aggression which was in self-defense or done in the act of bringing the "bad person" to justice) has resulted in increased aggression toward others; slow reactions to the real troubles of others; belief that aggression has no lasting harm and that it is the way to cope; and a desire to watch more violent programs.	Adults need to watch for any signs of increased aggression toward others after a child views violence. (Adults need to know that the cyclic effect of aggression occurs more in the pre-teen years, especially before the age of 8 and in those who are mentally handicapped.) When pre-teens do watch violent acts, adults need to point out motives and unpleasant results and to clarify other issues.
Showing Groups of People in Unfavorable Ways Minority groups may be given minor roles or be shown as poor or involved in illegal acts. Females may be shown as less competent (not as smart or as skilled) than males.	Adults may select programs showing minority groups and females in positive ways. Educational television programs have made efforts in overcoming these problems. Adults are also needed to reinforce positive messages.
Television Commercials Some advertised non-food products are unsafe and many advertised food products are of poor nutritional quality.	Adults need to discuss the content of commercials, pointing out risk factors in some products. Adults can also select quality programs on Public Broadcasting Stations (PBS) which do not have commercials.

Continued.

21-14 Caring adults can lessen the negative effects of television contact.

Problems in Content	Ways to Handle
Several studies note that children often become angry at adults and some feel rejected by adults when these adults do not buy the advertised products.	Adults must remain firm on not buying when they see risks in certain products or when purchases do not fit their budgets. It does help children to understand if reasons are given for saying no. Also, the values of products should be discussed during commercials or soon after rather than during a shopping trip.
Educational Programs Although programs are often planned to aid both mental and social development, programs are also a one-way medium in which the child simply receives information at one set pace.	Adults need to explain and extend concepts. Adults also need to limit the hours of viewing in order that children may talk, play, and read.
Some educational programs are planned as a way of helping children from poor and less educated families keep up with other children. However, some reports show that these poorer children watch less often than the more advantaged children.	Adults who work with children and their families need to encourage family viewing of good programs as well as share ideas for other worthwhile family activities.

21-14 Continued.

those of their peers. Peer groups also act as a source of socialization. Each group teaches their own rules of conduct needed for acceptance.

Adults are needed in a guidance role in helping children meet their social needs. This role is not always easy. Adults often find themselves not knowing whether it is best to step in to protect children from heartbreak or to step back to allow children to cope on their own. Adults may also feel torn between trying to enforce the priorities they have taught and allowing children to make some of their own decisions.

Encouraging industry

As you read in Chapter 20, middle childhood is the time when children develop attitudes which prepare them for adult work. See 21-15.

LOUISIANA DEPARTMENT OF WILDLIFE AND FISHERIES

21-15 Becoming involved in such activities as camping during middle childhood helps prepare children for the adult world of work.

The school-age child's developmental needs 373

Erikson called this stage the stage of "industry versus inferiority." The attitudes children must learn help children become a part of the peer group. They also lead children to become productive members of society in the young adult years. Failure in this stage leads to feelings of inferiority with social problems in middle childhood and even in the future.

Adults can help children achieve industry by focusing on what children can do rather than on children's faults. When standards are too high, children feel that their work is not worthwhile. Even small successes help children's self-esteem. This is because unlike adults, school-age children feel that they have an unlimited amount of time to attain their goals.

Adults can also help by encouraging children to succeed in school. When adults insist that children do the best that they can, most children do.

Adults should plan activities where children can develop physical, mental, and social skills. By the school years, children begin to develop more unevenly. For instance, a child who has developed advanced reading skills may lag in motor skills. Children still have a wide range of talents, so they could achieve in many fields. A child should not be expected to excel in all areas. But equal care must be given to keep options open.

Adults can suggest hobbies where children can succeed. See 21-16. Children enjoy the processes involved in hobbies such as making and finding objects. They also enjoy the products such as the coins or the learned music. Products are treasured by children and are displayed or performed for all to see.

Keeping open family communication

Establishing good communication lines during the school years is important. As children grow older, communication allows parents to offer support and help children grow socially. Also, studies show that parent influence is highest among teens whose parents were involved with them and who tried to understand them during middle childhood.

Young school-age children view their parents as the greatest in every way. By nine or 10 years

JOHN SHAW

21-16 Hobbies such as photography can be fun learning experiences.

of age, children begin to see their parents' mistakes. Feelings between parents and children become somewhat strained. Throughout this stage, good communication can help ease the strain.

To communicate clearly, adults need to be honest and open. They need to explain why they feel a certain way and show willingness to listen to their children's feelings. For instance, parents may be upset because their child went to a friend's home after school without telling them first. They should explain that they get worried and concerned when they do not know where their child is. They should also allow the child to give input on how they can avoid the problem in the future.

Adults need to take care so they do not allow stress to interfere with open communication. For instance, an adult may say, "Get down from there. Do you want to fall and break your neck?" Or a mother may ask, "Do you enjoy making your mother miserable?" Such unfair questions are often asked out of frustration, but they hamper clear communication.

Parents sometimes find themselves talking about side issues when they become angry. They must take care not to harm a child's self-concept because of their anger. Instead, they should stick to the issues. For instance, a parent may want to discuss why swearing is not allowed at home. Statements such as, "You have a filthy mouth," do not allow open communication on the real issue. Such statements can also make the child believe that he or she is a bad person.

Listening is another important part of communication. Parents may pick up on children's emotions by listening to their comments. For instance, a child may say, "You *always* pick on me!" Parents can use such comments as a chance to ask children what is on their mind. They may learn that certain actions of theirs bother their children. Parents may also clear up misunderstandings at these times.

When children realize that their parents will listen, they are more likely to come to their parents with problems. For instance, children may be having problems with friendships or school work. Children often look to parents in these situations. Giving advice and assuring children helps them bounce back from problems. Children see their parents as people who weathered some of the same problems.

Throughout the school years, parents are still admired. This is true even though children feel that parents create many of their problems. Open communication allows children to build strong bonds with their parents that will last into adulthood.

Enjoying family ties

School-age children think of their families as home base. They not only think of home as a place for food, clothing, and shelter but also for *psychological security*. Psychological security is a feeling that someone cares and will help when needed.

The family provides a balance between letting go and holding on in the school years. In this role, the family provides security for trying new skills. If children are to become in-dependent, adults need to step back and let children feel the results of their own mistakes. But they also need to be available for support when children need it.

Parents are in a good position to help children learn some of the skills needed for self-growth and *peer acceptance*. (Peer acceptance is approval from one's age-mates.) Most parents enjoy helping their children grow as a result of shared learnings. The basics of some needed skills can be taught in the preschool or early school years. See 21-17.

Family activities can extend the skills being learned in school-age peer groups. In addition to direct help, parents can help by organizing the child's schedule, seeing that needed equip-

JOHN SHAW

21-17 Even in the preschool years, children need to begin learning some of the skills involved with organized peer games.

The school-age child's developmental needs **375**

ment is ready (washing uniforms, buying ballet slippers), and being the chauffeur to and from activities.

School-age children enjoy just being with their family. They want to learn home care skills. Children are pleased when they are old enough and skilled enough to do many things that were not allowed in the preschool years. Children also enjoy family times. They enjoy family meals, weekend outings, yearly vacations, and family celebrations. Celebrations, 21-18, are much fun. The special plans and the surprises are all a part of taking a major role in *family rituals* (customs that the family shares). School-age children may even think about how they will continue these rituals when they are adults.

Providing time for friendships

As you read in Chapter 20, friendships are needed in middle childhood. The peer group serves many functions. It is a means for forming close friendships, joining formal groups, re-thinking adult priorities, providing emotional help, and sharing learnings. And perhaps most importantly, the peer group serves as the basis for self-esteem.

Adults can help school-age children with their ventures into friendships. They can let go by encouraging children to take part in peer activities. Some adults have so many other plans that children do not have the chance to form friendships. Children need time to be with friends, 21-19. Letting go also means accepting the fact that children will like best friends almost as much as the family. Children will ask to include these friends in family activities.

Because the peer group is so important, fears of being rejected are real in middle childhood. Every child at one time or another is made to feel rejected by peers. See 21-20. You often hear school-age children make remarks such as, "Nobody likes me," or, "All I do is goof!" Such statements from a child who is usually accepted are best ignored. But adults do need to help when children experience general rejection, especially if the rejection lasts over a week. How to help depends on the child, but these ideas often work:

THE LANE COMPANY, INC.

21-18 Family celebrations such as Father's Day are very special to school-age children.

REBECCA LAWRENCE

21-19 School-age children need to have fun times with friends.

- Try to discover the problem behind the rejection. The problem may be the child's physical appearance such as being obese or sloppy. The problem may be the lack of certain skills—physical or athletic skills, academic skills, or social skills (being too shy or aggressive).
- Give children direct help in overcoming the problem. The child may need a weight-loss diet, grooming tools and lessons, coaching in a new skill, or suggestions (even role play) on how to make friends.
- Plan games and activities where there is not so much pressure on a child's own skills. For instance, play dodge ball rather than softball.

Children also need help when they lose their best friends through conflict, new interest, or moving away. School-age children can suffer great pain, even *depression,* when there is a

JOHN SHAW

21-20 Being left out of a game—even for a few minutes—can make children feel unhappy.

break-up. Depression is a mental state where the person feels down and shows a decrease in many activities such as eating, sleeping, working, or playing.

Adults can help in many cases. Children may talk to adults about the loss of a friend. Adults should choose words carefully when they discuss the break-up. For instance, they should not say, "It's not as bad as you think. You'll feel better soon." Many children will tune out well-meaning adults at this point. Instead, adults should try to talk about the emotions felt without mention of getting over them.

Adults need to stay neutral if the break-up was due to conflict. Joining a child's anger or hurt places all the blame for the break-up on the former friend. It may also say to the child, "You made a poor friendship choice."

Adults can prepare children in advance for breaks in friendships. Preparation should begin in the preschool or early school years. It can include talking about why people become friends and sometimes end friendships. Adults can also tell children about some of their friendships and break-ups (or read stories about loss of friends and the hurt it causes). Preparation can also include encouraging children to play with more than one child so that the loss of one friend will not be too crushing.

Adults need to be patient with children who grieve over their loss. But they should seek professional help through a physician or school guidance counselor if signs of depression are noted.

Helping children control their emotions

School-age children are expected to learn to control their emotions. Controlling emotions means expressing emotions at the proper times and in proper ways. Controlling emotions may be different from culture to culture. For instance, grief may be expressed with little or no crying to wailing (long, loud cries). Most cultures allow for differences in control between boys and girls. For instance, in the United States, boys are usually allowed to show more aggression than girls are.

As you read in Chapter 20, the major emotions are fairly set in school-age children's behavior; thus, adult help is needed long before the school years. This guidance and help should be continued in middle childhood.

Adults should explain that all people have strong feelings. Parents and other adults should talk about some of their emotions. School-age children may also be helped when they read about the struggles of other children and of adults to control their feelings. Adults can also point out that a person controls his or her emotions out of respect for others.

Children need to see a model of control. For instance, adults should model *psychological discipline.* Using psychological discipline involves using discussions and other non-physical means to let children know they have done wrong. This method is better than *physical control* (spankings and other physical punishment) for school-age children. See 21-21.

Control of emotions can be helped in indirect ways, too. Physical exercise and creative tasks help children control their anger. Children show less fear of the physical world as they gain skills and knowledge. For instance, fear of water is overcome when a person learns to swim well. And, as children improve skills, they develop healthy self-concepts. Having healthy self-concepts helps children overcome many social fears because children are not as worried about being embarrassed.

JOHN SHAW

21-21 Discussing problems helps children learn self-control.

PERCEPTION ACTIVITIES

Parquetry blocks ————————

Parquetry blocks can be purchased or made. They are in the shapes of square, triangle, and trapezoid, as shown. Show children cards with pictures of various arrangements of the blocks. Have them arrange the blocks to match the cards.

JOHN SHAW

Design cubes ————————

Design cubes, like parquetry blocks, can be purchased or made. Children can arrange these blocks to match pictures also.

Memory chain ————————

Memory chain games can be played as seated games or to jump rope or other active routines. People start by choosing a category. Then one person says a word in the category. The next person names this word and adds another word to the chain. Words are added until a person cannot repeat the entire chain.

LOGIC ACTIVITIES

Ordered question games ————————

Twenty questions and similar games are games in which problems are solved in an ordered series of questions. People can only ask questions that can be answered with yes or no. They must use logic to decide on questions that will give the most information and then put together the answers to reach a conclusion.

Games of strategy ————————

In order to play tic-tac-toe, dominoes, chess, checkers, or card games effectively, a person must know the strategies of play and the logic behind them. Team sports, too, use strategy which can be discussed by players and observers.

Problems of relationships ————————

Figuring relationships is difficult for many people. Logic problems can help children understand relationships better. An example of this type of problem would be, ''My father is the brother of your sister. What relative am I of yours?''

Continued.

The school-age child's developmental needs   379

Number series

Number series require the person to find a pattern in a series of numbers. A simple number series would be 2, 4, 6, 8. In this series, 2 is added to the previous number to get the next number in the series. A more complex series question would be, "What is the next number in the series 12, 11, 9, 6?"

Math logic

Many logic problems are math problems. An example of such a problem is, "A rabbit raiser leaves his 17 rabbits to his three sons. The will states that the first son is to receive one-half of the rabbits. The second son is to receive one third of the rabbits. The third son is to receive one-ninth of the rabbits. How can the rabbits be divided among the heirs?"

Verbal logic problems

Most problems of this type are stories with a problem to solve. For instance, "A man must cross a river with a bucket of grain, a goose, and a fox. He can only take one with him in the boat for each crossing, but he can make more than one crossing. He cannot, however, leave an animal with something it will eat. How can he get all three to the other side of the river in the boat?"

Object manipulation problems

These problems ask how to get objects from one state or design to another in a certain number of moves. The "Rubik's Cube" is a famous puzzle of this type. Another problem is, "Arrange 12 toothpicks as in the drawing. Change the design to two squares by removing two toothpicks. No toothpicks can be moved. Each toothpick that remains must be a part of the square."

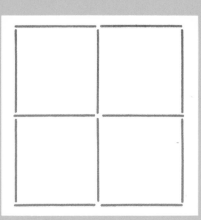

LANGUAGE ACTIVITIES

Anagrams

In anagrams, the letters in words are rearranged to form other words. For instance, *won* can be arranged to form *now*. Another example is rearranging *odor* to form *door*. An adult can write a coded message using anagrams for a child to decode. For instance, the anagrams can be decoded in this nonsense phrase: *"Pots the looped form braking."* The result is, *"Stop the poodle from barking."*

Deriving words

Children have much fun finding little words in bigger words. For instance, the word *grandmother* contains *ran, an, and, grand, mother, other, moth, her,* and *the.* Even more words can be formed if children are allowed to rearrange the letters.

to Know

depression . . . family rituals . . . literate . . .
peer acceptance . . . physical control . . .
psychological discipline . . .
psychological security . . . school avoidance . . .
spatial rotations

to Review

Write your answers on a separate sheet of paper.
1. True or false. During the school-age years, children still need much help with self-care tasks.
2. List four reasons why school-age children need an adequate diet.
3. True or false. Middle childhood is the healthiest time of life.
4. Children become _____ (more, less) conscious of clothing styles in the school years.
5. True or false. Play is not important in the school years.
6. List three reasons why entering school for the first time or as a transfer students is stressful.
7. Children are *not* best prepared for school life by:
   a. Having a secure relationship with an adult such as a parent.
   b. Being dependent on adults.
   c. Being left with babysitters or enrolled in a preschool program.
   d. Learning that authority may come from adults other than parents.
8. True or false. There are no negative effects to watching worthwhile television programs.
9. _____ (Physical, Mental, Social) development is the most critical aspect of development in middle childhood.
10. Children can be helped to achieve industry when adults encourage children _____ (to just get by, to do their best) in everything.
11. True or false. In order for children to become independent, parents should allow children to learn from their own mistakes.
12. List three ways that adults can help children deal with losing a best friend.

to Do

1. As a class or group project, prepare one recipe for school-age children. Serve it as a mid-morning or afternoon snack. Ask the children why they did or did not like the snack.
2. Interview a few school-age boys and/or girls. Ask them some of the features they'd like in a bedroom of their own. Combining as many of the common features as possible, prepare sketches or models of some good bedrooms for school-age children. As a follow-up, seek comments on the sketches or models from several school-age children.
3. Make posters that show reading or spelling words for first, third, and sixth grade levels. (An elementary school principal or teachers can give you these lists.) Discuss how the words differ on these levels.
4. Visit a preschool classroom and an elementary classroom. Discuss what differences you saw in the ways children were being taught.
5. Make a bulletin board display of the ways adults can reinforce school tasks.
6. Discuss why all people get depressed when they lose a friend. How can a person overcome these sad feelings?
7. Discuss the statement from the chapter, "A person controls his or her emotions out of respect for others."

JOHN SHAW

Playing with Dad

The family historian

JOHN SHAW

Looking after sis

382

part seven

Special considerations

JOHN SHAW

Children with special needs are a lot like other children

Families are the main force in shaping a child's physical, intellectual, and social-emotional growth.

22

Children are members of families

After studying this chapter, you will be able to:
- Explain the major roles of parents in today's society.
- Name the main advantages and disadvantages of living in different types of families.
- Describe four sibling relationships and explain how a child's birth order affects development.
- Explain how stress hurts children and the ways stress and its effects may be lessened.

The family is the oldest known social group. But experts do not know exactly why family life came into being. Most people believe that people began living in families mainly for children's well-being. Families have had different ideas about children's needs throughout history. Changing ideas about the needs of children have caused changes in the roles of parents, in family structure, and in relationships among brothers and sisters. The nature of stress in families is mirrored in society's many changes, too.

PARENT-CHILD RELATIONSHIPS

Parent-child relationships have always been important. But until the 1700s, parents mainly met the physical needs of children—food, clothing, shelter, and safety needs. Because adults did not know that children had so many other needs, children were expected to take on major tasks by four to seven years of age.

As adults learned more about children's needs, parent-child relationships changed. People still see physical needs as important. But they also see childhood as a special time in each person's life. They consider childhood a time for learning about the world and for coming to know what is expected from society. People today also feel that as children learn, they should be happy and as free from anxiety as possible. And most people believe that children's needs are best met first in a loving family and later by other social groups.

Roles of parents

In American society today, parents' roles mainly involve nurturance and control. *Nurturance,* in a narrow sense, includes the physical aspects of child care such as feeding, dressing, and bathing children. In a broad sense, nurturance also includes meeting emotional and social needs such as helping children feel secure and loved. Studies in child development show that physical care, love, and concern are very important for children's healthy growth.

Control refers to the parents' practice of authority and responsibility for the welfare of children. Parents use control to socialize children. In other words, through control children take on the behavior patterns, personal priorities, and attitudes desired by a society. In the United States, the law requires that parents control their children. For instance, the law requires parents to see that their children attend school.

Until very recently in many families, mothers more often performed the nurturance role and fathers exercised control. Today, there is a trend toward the blurring of these roles. Mothers and fathers may take on both roles. See 22-1. Many changes in society have prompted this trend. Some changes include the higher status of women, the known importance of fathers in the care of children, and the growth of single-parent families.

Family types

There are many family types in the world today. Family types result from the way or ways that people's needs and problems are best solved in a society. In turn, family types which fit the norm for a society receive more support from society. In the United States, children are members of many types of families. The main types are extended, two parent, single parent, and blended families, and families with adopted children.

Extended families. The *extended family* is a complex family type in which blood relationships hold the family together. In the past, the extended family was most often composed of an older couple with their sons, daughters-in-law, and grandchildren. Today, many other kin groupings may form an extended family.

Sometimes the extended family lives in one home. Each family unit (husband, wife, and their children) have some private space. But cooking and eating are done together. Besides living under one roof, smaller family units may build their houses near each other—often on land owned by the family.

In extended families, family members often work together in a family-owned business. They also share in housework and child care. Each family member has a certain task to do. Family members do not often change roles with others. For instance, cooking is done by the same person or persons each day.

PLAYSKOOL, INC., CHICAGO, IL

22-1 Fathers are now seen as highly important in the nurturance of their children.

In the United States, extended families are not as common as they once were. Fewer family businesses and less economic need for large families are reasons for the decline in the numbers of extended families.

Extended families have many advantages. Children learn to interact with many people of all ages in extended families. The young and the old are in daily contact. This daily contact fosters knowledge of and respect for each other. Extended families are good at handing down *family culture* (what a family believes and does) and *family history* (the family's past). See 22-2. Due to the number of members, extended families can perform more duties than small family groups. For instance, children of working parents can be cared for within the family. Also, when stress-causing events such as death happen in extended families, many others are there to help both children and adults.

There are some problems that are felt more often in extended families than in other families. Sometimes children and even adults find that they must deal with too many people. Also, decisions are made with the good of the entire family in mind rather than the special needs of each person.

Two parent families. A father, a mother, and their biological children make up a *two parent family*. This type of family is found in most societies. In two parent families, grown children leave home when they become adults. When these children are married, they begin their own families away from their parents.

Many people think of the typical American family as a two parent type. Many people see this family as the "Norman Rockwell" type in which the father goes to work and the mother stays home to care for children. But the fact is that 16 percent (less than one in five) of all American families are the two-parent type. Even fewer families have mothers who are not employed outside the home. But during the course of a lifetime, many more people than those now living in two parent families have lived in or will live in this type of family. For instance, a child may live in a two parent family and then in a single parent family.

JOHN SHAW

22-2 Grandfathers often take pride in handing down their families' cultures and histories.

Two parent families have some advantages compared with other family types. The small size of the family allows parents and children to feel a great closeness. Needs may also be more easily met because there are few family members. Children are also more apt to learn more flexible housework and childcare roles in the two parent family than in the extended family. Because the blurring of these roles is a trend, children who see role sharing may be better prepared for the future. On the other hand, two parent families do not have some

Children are members of families 387

of the advantages found in the extended family. For instance, children may not learn to get along with many types of people including the elderly. Also, the large pool of kin for learning many skills and priorities may not be present. Finally, relatives may not be near enough for support and caring in times of stress.

Single parent families. *Single parent families* are defined as families headed by one adult. Single parent families result from death of one parent, divorce (and separation and desertion), births outside of marriage, and adoption of children by single persons. The statistics show these facts:

1. One out of every five children is being raised in single parent families. The numbers are growing, too, due to more divorces and more births outside of marriage.

2. Women head 90 percent of the single parent families. The number of men who are single parents is 10 percent, but that number is increasing.

3. Single parenting is, in many cases, a transition between divorce and remarriage. Within five years of being divorced, three-fourths of all divorced people are remarried. Many widowed parents remarry, and parents who have not been married may marry, too.

Single parents and their children face many problems that are the same as those of other families. But some problems are unique to the single parent family or are felt more keenly by them. See 22-3.

Financial problems are often cited as the greatest problem faced by the single parent. Two out of every five single parent families have incomes below the poverty level as compared with one out of 16 two parent families. Mothers have more financial problems than fathers in single parent families. The average income of single mothers is about one-third of that of two parent families. Single fathers have incomes that are close to three-fourths of that of two parent families.

Men and women report different types of

22-3 Single parent families have some special problems.

problems as single parents. Fathers report more problems with housework and the physical aspects of child care such as cooking and clothes buying. Mothers report discipline of children and not enough income as their major problems.

Emotional problems can be very real for single parent families, too. In cases where two parent families become single parent families, family life is disrupted. Anger and grief are present in both divorce and death situations. Single parents also feel more *social isolation—* feelings of being alone. There may be no one to talk to about problems and feelings. When a person feels alone, poor health, depression, and fears may result.

Besides coping with their own feelings, single parents must deal with their children's problems. Parents are the base from which children grow. When death or divorce end a two parent family, children feel the loss of a relationship and a role model. In cases of divorce, children may feel that they caused the problems or that their parents may "divorce" them too. Children's daily life patterns also change as one parent takes over duties of both parents.

Children react to changes. The problems in children's behavior are not caused by the number of parents but by stress. The way a child reacts depends on age and personality. See 22-4. Although most single parent homes become stable in two years, a few long term effects may continue. For instance, in father-absent homes, boys may rebel or do poorly in their school work. Teenage girls may become over aggressive or shy around boys.

Single parent families need support. They may need outside help with some problems.

CHILDREN'S REACTIONS TO LOSS OF A PARENT THROUGH DEATH OR DIVORCE·

Two- and Three-Year-Olds

Whine.
Cry.
Cling.
Have sleep problems.
Have bed accidents.
May regress (act younger). This occurs most often at a time of day when the absent parent was often with the child.

Four-Year-Olds

Whine.
Cry.
Hit others.
Feel they caused the divorce (and sometimes the death).

Five-Year-Olds

Feel anxious.
Act aggressively.
Want physical contact with others.
Feel abandoned.
Deny loss and even pretend parents will be together again.
Have problems in creative play.

School-Age Children

Deny loss.
Feel bitter (blames parent whom they think is responsible).
Feel angry.
Feel deprived.
Fear future.
Feel lonely.
Show antisocial behavior such as lying or stealing.
Have more headaches and stomachaches.
Have school problems such as cannot pay attention.
Show premature (early) detachment—reject parent who is gone and those qualities they shared with that parent. (For instance, if the father has athletic ability, the child rejects sports.)
Daydreams more.

22-4 The way children react to divorce or death often depends on their age.

These might include finances, child care, and housework. Adults may need to talk about their feelings and reactions with other adults. Some single parents find special groups such as Parents Without Partners very helpful. See 22-5. Parents should not use children as their sole source of friendship.

Single parent families need to look at the positive side of their situation. Children in a well-adjusted single parent home are more stable than children whose two parent homes are unhappy.

Children in single parent families need special care and support. They need time to work out their feelings. Adults should allow children to express their feelings through actions and words. (Books on the topic may be helpful.) However, a parent should be careful not to express hostile feelings about the other parent to children. Children should not be asked to choose sides or to carry messages back and forth between divorced parents.

Children need to know that their parents still love them. Parents should explain that the divorce is not a child's fault. They should not expect children to handle the divorce in an adult way. Children may feel stress if they are expected to act too mature for their ages. On the other hand, these children still need consistent, firm discipline.

When possible, both parents should still take part in child rearing. *Joint custody,* or co-parenting, in which both parents are involved in decisions affecting children's lives, is becoming more common. Children seem to adjust better when both parents spend some time with them.

When the family structure changes, teachers and other adults who work with children should be informed. These adults can be more helpful to children if they are aware of the home situation.

Blended families. *Blended families* are families that come from the marriage of a single parent and a single person (never before married or married before but without children) or the marriage of two single parents. Blended families are also called *stepfamilies.* Between eight and 10 million children live in blended families. Many other children have stepfamilies with whom they do not live. These numbers continue to rise.

Living in a blended family is different from moving from a two parent family to a single parent family. Studies show that family members in blended families face different types of problems.

All family members are involved in instant relationships — the stepparents and stepchildren and the stepchildren with each other. And, as in all marriages, the husband-wife role must be worked out. In addition, relationships with family members from the previous marriage(s) must be worked out.

In most cases, one stepparent enters a single parent family which has been working together as a family. (In more than half the cases, step-fathers enter into a single parent family headed by the mother.) All daily living patterns from eating to child care have to be reset. Single parents often take pride in the fact that they can run a single household. Thus, they may have problems in sharing their roles in a blended family.

Disciplining stepchildren is more difficult than disciplining biological children. Step-parents are often afraid to punish because they want to be liked by their stepchildren.

Children have problems in adjusting to a new family. Many children are asked to adjust to two sets of priorities or rules. The problem can be a major one for school-age children. This is because school-age children are trying to weigh family and peer priorities in the search for more self-identity. Dealing with two families may further confuse their own identity.

One study reported that although blended families do face problems almost two-thirds of these families do have good relationsips. For instance, both mothers and children tended to rate stepfathers as just as good of parents as biological fathers. But some special effort is needed to help families blend smoothly.

Parents need to have some remarriage preparation sessions. Counselors or clergy may conduct such sessions. Older children need to be a part of some of the sessions.

All children (beyond infancy) need to be

22-5 Discussion meetings and social affairs are two important functions of Parents Without Partners, Inc.

prepared for the new marriage and family life to follow. Children should be told by their parent that the parent and new spouse love each other, and that they hope the marriage is going to work out well for everyone. Telling children that the new marriage *will* work, or that it's going to be much better or fun is not the honest approach.

Children also need to know that other children face similar problems. For instance, stepchildren often have problems in knowing what to call their new stepparents. They have a hard time deciding who to invite to school or other special functions. Books on blended families may help children, 22-6.

Families with adopted children. *Adoption* means that a child of one pair of parents (or parent) legally becomes the child of other parents (or parent). Adoption is the legal way in which the rights and responsibilities between a child and the natural parents (or parent) are ended and then transferred to the adoptive parents (or parent). The idea behind adoption is to give the child a new lifetime family and home.

JOHN SHAW

22-6 Books on blended families help children realize that others are having similar problems.

TYPES OF ADOPTIONS

Type	Pros	Cons
Agency	Legal aspects are handled in a correct manner.	Concern for children is put over concern for those wanting children. Thus, when there is a shortage of children, many suitable homes may be turned down for homes that seem better in some ways to the agency.
	Matching of children with adoptive parents can be done on basis of physical appearance and educational level.	
	Natural parents can request certain types of families for their children in terms of such factors as religious background and certain interests.	Often many requirements must be met by the adopting families such as age, years of marriage, religious beliefs, income, type of housing (apartments, houses, etc.), and residence.
	Adopting parents can make certain choices such as sex of child, age of child, and family background.	
	Information on children is given to adopting parents. (Information does not identify natural parents.)	Study on adopting families is very detailed and goes into all aspects of each person's personal and married life.
	Information on adopting parents may be given to natural parents. (Information does not identify adopting parents.)	Long waiting periods are common when children for adoption are on a decline.
	Social workers provide counsel to both natural parents and adopting parents.	
	Adopting families are supervised from time of placement of children until adoption is final.	
	Adoption is less expensive as compared with independent adoptions. A sliding scale may be used—adopting parents who have more income pay more; adopting parents who have less income pay somewhat less.	
Independent	There are no stated qualifications for adopting parents. Thus older persons, single persons, remarried couples, and couples married less than three to five years may get a child.	Legal safeguards may or may not be met. (Lawyers who handle adoption cases should be hired.)
	Natural parents who want to know the adopting families use this type of adoption.	Records of the natural parents and the adopting parents may not be kept confidential (secret).
	Waiting lists are not as long as those of an agency.	The child may not receive careful medical checks.
		Matching of child with adopting family is seldom done.
		Adopting parents may know little of the child's background.
		The child may be placed in an unsuitable home because the child is placed prior to a study of the adopting family. (Some study is done before adoption becomes final.)
		Payment may be higher than that asked by an agency. (Some adopting couples may find themselves involved in a black market adoption without knowing it.)

22-7 Both types of legal adoptions have some advantages and disadvantages which adopting families should consider.

More couples are seeking to have children by adoption than ever before. People want to adopt for these reasons:

- The couple cannot give birth to children or can give birth only with great difficulty.
- The couple may want to add to their own family.
- The couple knows a child who needs a home.
- A single person wants children.

There is not a surplus of children—especially babies—waiting to be adopted. For this reason, couples and single people are adopting more foreign-born children, older children, handicapped children, and biracial children (children whose natural parents are of two different races).

Most parents who have adopted children have put much effort into finding children. By law there are two ways to receive an adopted child—through an adoption agency and through an independent source. An *adoption agency* is a state-funded or a private (church, organization) agency licensed by the state to handle adoptions. The agency works out the details between the natural parents and the adopting parents. The final, legal aspects of the adoption are handled in the state courts. In an *independent adoption,* a person such as a lawyer, physician, or clergyman works out details. In a few independent adoptions, no one works between the natural and adopting parents. Such cases include adoption of relatives or stepchildren. Independent adoptions must follow state laws and are handled in the state courts, also. Foreign adoptions can be either agency or independent adoptions. Chart 22-7 gives the pros and cons of each type of adoption.

When payments are made beyond medical and legal costs to the agency, independent source, or natural parents, the child is said to be bought. Adoption in this way is not legal and is called a *black market adoption.*

Children who are adopted often have very stable and happy home lives. This is because their adopted families wanted them very much, 22-8. Some problems can exist, however.

Parents who do not experience nine months of pregnancy may not make as smooth a transition to parenthood as natural parents do. Persons wanting to adopt may be on a waiting list for years. But they may be called one day and told that a child will be ready for them the next day! Also, adopting parents may not have all the needed facts on the child they adopt such as medical records.

Other problems may rise related to natural parents. Natural parents may want to regain the child. Or they may want to become part of the child's life. Children who are adopted as babies or very young children often question the reasons for their adoption. They may want to know facts about—or even to meet—their natural parents. Older children who have lived with their natural parents need to make changes to adjust to their new parents.

Some adopted children come from group homes (a children's home) or *foster homes.* Foster homes are families who take care of, but do not adopt, children who cannot live with their natural parents. These children must make changes much like those children who live in blended families.

JOHN SHAW

22-8 Adoption is often a happy situation for both parents and children.

When adoptive parents are loving and answer their children's questions in direct and honest ways, stress may not develop. Most parents are able to create a loving family life which overcomes stress that adopted children may feel.

SIBLING RELATIONSHIPS

In most families, children grow up with *siblings*—brothers and sisters. In the United States, only about one in 10 couples have only children. The average number of children per family is two, but more parents in the 1980s seem to be electing to have three children.

Sibling interactions

Siblings have a major influence on each other's lives. Siblings are playmates, teachers and learners, protectors, and rivals. Children learn much about social give and take through sibling relationships.

Playmates. Brothers and sisters are built-in playmates for each other. In play, siblings learn to set goals and cooperate. Siblings also share hours of fun, 22-9. These fun times are often remembered and re-lived in adult years.

Teachers and learners. Older children often act as teachers while younger siblings are eager learners. In teaching, siblings explain, define, describe, show, and select examples. Whether they are the older or younger siblings, most brothers and sisters show interest in and aid the efforts their siblings make toward reaching goals.

Older siblings model social skills, too. These social skills include gender role learnings. Gender roles are learned faster by younger siblings than by firstborns and only children. Having a sibling also helps children decide what is good and bad behavior with others. Children often define good behavior in terms such as "plays with me," "helps with chores," and "doesn't tattle." They define bad behavior as being "bossy" or a "pest."

Protectors. Siblings protect each other, too. The protector role is most often seen in these situations: 1. When there is a sibling age gap of three or more years. 2. When siblings come from large families. 3. When adults are not close enough to supervise such as outside, on the way to and from school, or while parents work outside the home. 4. When a younger sibling is attacked in a physical or verbal way by peers.

Of course, children should never be solely in charge of other children. However, older children can help adults watch after younger brothers and sisters. As a bonus, older children who help parents in the care of younger siblings are better prepared for parenthood and careers that involve young children. See 22-10.

Rivals. When there are two or more children in a family, children compete. Rivalry is expressed in both physical and verbal ways. Younger children and boys engage in physical battle more than older children and girls. They also plead, whine, and sulk. Older children more often command, boss, and engage in name-calling.

There are many reasons why rivalry occurs. Children may compete for the love and attention of shared parents and even shared friends. Children may also be jealous of siblings who

JOHN SHAW

22-9 Celebrations are often shared with siblings.

seem more capable than they are. Rivalry, too, is caused by not being able to see from another's point of view. To young children, fair means equal rather than meeting another child's special needs.

Adults cannot prevent rivalry, but they can lessen it. They need to give all of their children lots of love. Each child also needs positive feedback without being compared to other children. Children are different. Making comparisons only triggers resentment toward the child being praised and anger toward the adult.

Parents need to use space control. Children need space for their own things. High shelves keep toddlers out of older children's toys and books. Sometimes children should not be expected to share any more than adults share all their things. Likewise, children should have some time to play alone or with their own friends. Siblings, especially younger children, who are always around do become pests.

Fights should be ignored unless children are in physical danger or property could be damaged. Children may feel rewarded for fighting if adults are there to settle each dispute. Fighting often gets the adult attention children wanted! If the fight must be stopped, adults should simply tell children to stop. No threat should be added. If the command does not work, the children should be separated.

At times, family togetherness and support should be stressed. For instance, families should take part in some activities that all enjoy. Children should be taught to take pleasure in another's good fortune. See 22-11. (An identical twin who lost in a round of an all-school spelling bee told his brother, "Now you have to bring home the trophy for us.") Adults should explain that although family members get angry at each other, they still love each other. And, above all, adults should praise loving behavior.

Birth order and development

To some degree, social roles and personalities of children are affected by their order at birth. Findings on birth order, however, cannot be applied to any one child. Personality is also

JOHN SHAW

22-10 Caring for a brother or sister prepares children for future parenthood.

CONGOLEUM CORPORATION

22-11 Brothers can be supportive of sisters who are trying to meet goals.

Children are members of families 395

affected by the sex of the siblings, the number of older and younger siblings, and the attitudes of the parents and the culture. For instance, findings on intelligence and birth order are consistent for middle-class families. But they are not for lower-class families who may not give firstborns more attention. Also, the effects of birth order seem to be reduced with larger age-gaps between a child and the next older sibling.

Only children. As you read in an earlier section of this chapter, 10 percent of married couples have only one child. This figure has doubled since the 1950s. The increase is partly because more women are in the world of work and because women are having children later in life.

Myth surrounds only children. Some believe that only children are lonely, spoiled, selfish, not as bright as other children, dependent, and just plain different. Like all children, only children are distinct persons with their own personalities. As a whole, however, only children do well. They are not lonely if playmates are provided. In fact, they learn to spend time alone as well as spending time in the company of others. Only children are not often as selfish or jealous as other children. This is because they are not constantly threatened with the loss of attention or possessions. Only children are known for their high intelligence quotients (IQ's). All but one of the first astronauts were only children. A listing of some of the traits of only children is given in 22-12.

Firstborns. You will see in 22-12 that firstborns have many of the same traits as only children. This is partly because most firstborns (except multiple birth siblings) are only children for a period of time. Like only children, firstborns are often very bright. Firstborns often become the teachers of their younger siblings, and teaching benefits the intellect. Firstborns are also mentally creative, because siblings look to them for ideas.

Like only children, firstborns are often called *experimental children.* In other words, parents must try new, untested ideas on them. Because they are experimental children, they are not always treated the same way in similar situations. Also, they are both punished more severely and rewarded more than children born later. New parents are often more anxious and not as sure of themselves in childrearing than are parents of more than one child.

Firstborns are often not as popular with other children as are only and laterborn children. Firstborns tend to use high-power social tactics—bossing, threats, and physical force—as they serve as protectors to and teachers of younger siblings. High-power social tactics do not make for popularity in the peer culture.

Middleborns. Birth order findings seem to best fit families with four or fewer children. For this reason, *middleborns* in this text refers to the second child in a family of three siblings and both the second and third children in families of four siblings. Findings on middleborns, shown in 22-12, do not fit large families (five or more siblings) or families who have multiple birth siblings such as twins.

Middleborns seem to have IQ's that are not as high as those of only and firstborn children but are higher than those of lastborns. There is some decrease in adult time if children are spaced closer than three years. There is little decrease in adult time when the age gap is three or more years—especially if the second child is a boy and the first is a girl. Adult time seems to affect intelligence mainly in middle-class families.

In social development, middleborns seem to be adaptable (able to adjust to the new). Middleborns do not seem to feel as displaced as firstborns when other children are born. They have always shared their parents with others. They also receive many hand-me-down clothes and toys. On the negative side, they may feel caught in the middle. Some middleborns feel that they must constantly compete with the older sibling. The middleborn may also feel that the lastborn steals attention as the family baby.

Lastborns. As shown in Chart 22-12, lastborns do better socially than mentally. Their intelligence quotients are usually less than those of their siblings. This may be because they rarely have a teacher role.

Lastborns are often described as relaxed and cheerful. Parents are not often anxious about

Only Children

High intelligence quotient (IQ).
Achiever.
Perfectionist.
High self-esteem.
Self-confident.
Relaxed.
Not jealous.
Unselfish.
Socially outgoing.
Assumes leadership role as an adult.

Firstborn Children

Highest intelligence quotient (IQ).
Achiever (stays in school more years).
Creative.
Lots of zeal and drive.
Ambitious.
Anxious.
Conservative.
Mature acting.
Conforms to rules.
Wants company in times of stress.
Tendency to be angry and irritable.
Not popular.
Assumes leadership role as an adult.

Middleborns

Slightly lower intelligence quotient than only children and firstborns.
Less highly driven.
Turns to the nonacademic areas such as sports or the arts.
Cheerful.
Easy going.
Relaxed.
Patient.
Adaptable.
Gentle.
Tactful.
Outgoing.
Popular.
Charming.
See themselves as less skillful than older siblings if compared in such a manner.
Feels lost in the middle at times.

Lastborns

Lowest intelligence quotient as compared with only children and older siblings.
May underachieve (does not do as well as he or she could).
Seeks pleasure.
Relaxed.
Secure.
Calm.
Kindhearted.
Popular.
Negotiates (work out terms with others) well.
Good companion.
Needs to feel loved and cherished as an adult.

22-12 Birth order can affect mental and social-emotional development.

childrearing by this child. Lastborns deal with more personalities from the time they are infants than do older siblings. And they are used to receiving attention and care from older siblings, 22-13.

On the negative side, parents may baby lastborns because they know he or she is their last child. Siblings tend to do things for lasborns, too. These factors may cause lastborns to be more dependent and less mature. Lastborns are more likely to resort to sulking, tattling, teasing, and counter-aggression (fighting back).

A child's own identity. Birth order alone need not affect a child's later success. Adults can avoid the pitfalls of birth order by using comments that focus on the child rather than the child's birth order. Comments referring to birth order can create bad side effects such as dependency. ("She's just a baby.") Other comments may cause anxiety. ("You're the oldest; so you should know better.")

Adults also need to treat each child fairly. Unfair treatment includes showing favoritism

Children are members of families 397

LOUIS J. BREAUX, JR.

22-13 Lastborns get plenty of attention from older siblings.

to the firstborns and forgetting to praise the middleborns. Spoiling the lastborns and expecting too much from firstborns and only children is also unfair treatment. Adults need to promote the best traits of their children. Adults also need to help children overcome the negative effects of birth order. If adults treat children as individuals, children, in turn, will develop their own identities.

Children of multiple births

As you read in Chapter 3, multiple births are two or more identical or fraternal children born at the same time. Many people ask whether multiple birth children are different from *singletons* (children born one at a time). In many ways, they are.

For parents, at least twice as many needs must be met at once. In meeting these needs, tasks, time, and costs are often doubled or tripled. Most parents soon realize that extra help is needed especially in the first few months after birth.

Multiple birth children react to their world differently than many other children. This is because there is always another person (or persons) at the same age, who may be doing the same thing at the same time, and who may even be a look-alike in most ways. For these

reasons, multiple births are perhaps the closest of all human relationships. These relationships may be even closer than that of parent and child, 22-14. These special siblings have few problems in remaining close. Rather their problems are in developing *separate identities* — feelings of being a distinct person. The multiple-birth siblings who have the most problems in becoming distinct persons are identical children and same-sex, look-alike fraternal children. If multiple birth siblings are thought of as distinct children rather than treated as a unit, their identity problem will be made small.

As adults foster separate identities in multiple-birth siblings, they need to be careful not to destroy the special bond. Even singletons who are close in age share many of the same experiences and often become close even as adults. Identical children share more than the same birthday. They share a common gene make-up. There are many stories of how identical children even when reared apart had many of the same health problems, interests, and careers. To be more alike than different may be normal for them. Adults should allow children to choose how much alike or different they wish to be. In this way, separateness and closeness will be worked out by these special brothers and sisters just as it is by all other siblings.

STRESS IN FAMILIES

A child's well-being is closely tied to the state of the family. Pressures on families seem more intense than ever before. American society has changed rapidly. With changes in societies have come changes in families. These changes can cause stress. For instance, stress can come with loss of kin support networks when families move. Losing a full-time mother when she enters the job market can also cause stress.

Pressures have affected parents, too. Many parents are confused about their role in helping their children become the best they can be. Some parents may develop problem attitudes. These attitudes, in turn, can leave emotional scars on their children that last a lifetime.

22-14 Twins and other multiple-birth children are often very close to each other.

Mobile families

The United States is a *mobile* society. In other words, families move alot. Earlier in history, more people lived in extended family types. Today, more than one-fifth of the population moves each year. Six million people live in mobile homes. And on the average, each person moves 14 times in a lifetime.

Although a few people enjoy moving, most feel some stress. The stress is often short-lived (a few weeks or months). But for others it may last a couple of years. The following situations help to lessen stress from moving:

* Moves do not occur too often.
* No added stress is present such as death or divorce.
* Parents are pleased about the move.
* Children have siblings who can act as playmates until new friends are found.
* School-age children move at the beginning or end of a school term.
* School-age children have good grades.
* Children have special skills or interests (sports, hobbies) that help provide some stability.

Stress occurs because moving is a change. There must be time to get used to a new town or city, a new school, a new job, and new people. To children, one's house and yard are symbols of where one belongs. (The young and the elderly cling more to physical things than do persons in other age groups.) Moving can cause feelings of loneliness. It takes time to form close family and friend ties. And, children may become unsure about the past with many moves. For instance, children may ask the following questions: "Did this happen, or did I dream it?" "Did I know this person when we lived in this town or that town?" "Where was my bedroom when we lived in that town?"

Adults can help take the edge off the stress of moving for children. They can start by pointing out the positive side of moving for the family. They may let children know that the family will have a better income and better schools. Children can widen their interests, make more friends, and learn more about different people. However, adults need to be honest about the move. They need to mention the bad as well as the good. For instance, the family will miss old friends and the house. Adults should also explain each step that will be happening as they move. Children will ask many questions. They may even want to act out certain events, 22-15.

If possible, parents should take children with them to see the new home and school before the move. Otherwise, a few pictures of the new area may help make the change easier.

JOHN SHAW

22-15 Young children may need to act out moving as a way to prepare for the real move.

Children should be able to help with the packing. It is often best to pack preschool children's things last. A few favorite toys should be placed in the car or in luggage carried with the family.

Adults need to plan more time to be with children both before and after the move. A few special treats and family times are needed. This may mean getting extra help in packing and unpacking. Or the family may need to let some housework slide.

Working mothers

Mothers have always worked hard at home. But the term *working mothers* (or women) refers to mothers (or women) who are paid for work beyond homemaking tasks. Most of these mothers are employed outside of their homes. See 22-16. However, some have careers that permit them to work in their own houses.

Since 1940, the number of working women has increased ten-fold. Over half of the mothers of this country work outside the home during some or all of their children's childhood years. And, almost three-fourths of these women have full-time careers. The number of working mothers will likely increase. There are many reasons for this trend. Many two parent families need or desire two incomes due to higher standards of living and rising costs. More single parent families are headed by women than by men. Also, many women see careers outside of homemaking as rewarding.

Many people ask, "How do working mothers affect their children's development?" There have been many studies on this question. First, research seems to show that babies have fewer adjustment problems if mothers return to work before babies are three months old or after babies near their second birthdays. As you recall from Chapter 6, babies develop strong attachments to their caregivers at this time. Changing this tie may not be best for babies. Another awkward time to enter the work force is when children are ages 11 through 13. These children are trying to cope with many new ideas. They may have difficulty dealing with other changes in their lives such as mothers who return to work after years of being home.

Some studies show that today's children receive as much attention from their working mothers as yesterday's children did from their full-time mothers. This may be true because working mothers may use more labor-saving devices in the home. Also, working mothers may try to make up for the time away from home by planning to spend time with their children each day.

Children of working mothers seem to have some advantages over those mothers who do not work. For instance, children with working mothers tend to miss fewer days of school. Working mothers need to organize their free time. They also need to have children help with housework. Therefore, their children may live in more structured homes with more clearly stated rules. Children also learn to do more home care tasks. As children learn to do more, they may show more self-esteem. Another advantage of having a working mother is that children interact more with others. They spend

JOHN SHAW

22-16 Many mothers work outside of the home.

400

more time with fathers, neighbors, and other adults and with other children. See 22-17.

Working mothers help to broaden gender-role concepts for children. Children who grow up in these homes do not think of women only as homemakers and men only as wage earners. (One exception reported in studies is in lower-class homes. Sons in these families tend to view the mother's job as meaning that the father is a failure as the wage earner.)

Working does affect the emotional state of women. Sometimes working brings happiness. Sometimes it brings *role strain*—a feeling of having too many jobs in a given time. And sometimes it brings *role guilt*—a feeling of not doing one's best at work or at home due to role strain. When mothers and their families are happy with employment or with full-time homemaking, then children seem to adjust well. But, when mothers or their families are unhappy about mother's working or not working, there is more family stress. Most women do have some problems as a result of their work. For instance, they cannot always find time to

ADRIAN DEMERY

22-17 Spending more time with a father can be a positive aspect of having a working mother.

relax. They may have trouble making childcare arrangements (which is more difficult when children are sick). Some mothers end up spoiling children as a result of trying to make up for time away from home. And mothers often feel guilty for not being able to attend some of the children's school and other activities during work hours.

If care is taken, the stress caused by a mother's working can be kept low. First, if a mother has a choice, she should be sure about her decision to work. Each mother needs to think about working or not working in terms of her family's needs and wishes. But she should also consider her own needs and wishes.

Working mothers need to carefully budget their time. Mothers should let non-essentials go if need be. Family time is needed and should be planned. Parents need to give their children some *quality time*—a time when parents are totally there for their children—each day. Also, mothers need to check on needed clothes, lunch, and homework before children go to bed. This helps avoid stressful morning panic before leaving for work.

Mothers should plan housework tasks that involve other members of the family as much as possible. Some families have a housework time (often on a weekend) in which every member helps. Housework may be made more fun with music and topped off with a special snack.

Quality childcare services are needed for young children whose parents work. Parents need to plan what is to be done in case the child is sick, sitter is ill, or center is closed. If a child is to be alone after school, safety measures and what to do if a problem arises need to be discussed.

Working mothers should meet and talk with teachers. They should attend events important to their children. Or they should carefully explain why they can't come this time. Likewise, mothers should include their children in their worklife. They can set up a work visit, explain their job, and share good stories about their job.

Working mothers still need to set limits for their children. A mother cannot make up for time away from her family by letting children do what they want to do. As with other children, children of working mothers want and need guidance.

Mothers need to recognize and accept the feelings of their children. Feelings are shown in many ways. For instance, two- through four-year-olds may regress (act less mature than before) for a few weeks after mothers return to work. Sick children may want their mothers to stay home. Feelings are most often expressed during the early evening hours when all family members are tired and hungry. Children often want to share their entire day at this time. But parents want to relax a few minutes after long hours at work. Some mothers insist on a few minutes alone. Then they can devote their complete attention to their families.

Children in self-care or latchkey children

In the 1800s, society began to recognize the problems of children of working parents. These children often wore their house keys around their necks. During WWII, the term *latchkey* was coined. Today a more preferred term is *children in self-care.* Mainly school-age children are left in self-care after school, but some preschool children stay home alone all day.

It is estimated that between 25 and 33 percent of all children below the teen years are in self-care. The numbers increase if teenagers are included. The problem is increasing due to: a) more working mothers; b) the high costs of child care; c) the decrease in the number of families who have grandparents or other adults in the home; d) the decrease in family size resulting in fewer older children caring for younger ones; and 3) the lack of after-school programs designed for the school-age child.

Children, their parents, and the community are all affected by self-care. Some of these effects are positive and some are negative as shown in 22-18.

There are ways in which parents can decrease risks and increase the positive effects. First, parents should plan for self-care. The following steps may be taken:
• Establish a routine for children to follow.
• List telephone numbers on or near the phone

and teach younger children how to place calls.
• Give children safety tips such as not telling others that they are alone, locking doors, planning what to do in case strangers call or come to the door, explaining what to do in case of fire or other accidents, and requiring children to receive permission before leaving the house or entertaining anyone at home including school friends.
• Teach children which equipment and appliances they may use and how to use them.

Parents may take other steps as well. They can provide a pet to reduce fear or loneliness. Parents should also determine whether there are community resources available such as a hot line. Parents and children can enroll in programs or read some of the literature from these programs designed for self-care. Such programs include "I Can Do" (Camp Fire), "Prepared for Today" (Boy Scouts), and "I'm in Charge" (The National Committee for the Prevention of Child Abuse).

Parents and others in society can also work for better, lower-cost child care programs. Some such programs are already provided by religious groups. Child-care block grants provide federal monies for school-based child care. More work can be done to provide safe, realistic alternatives to self-care.

Parents with problem attitudes

Parents have great effects—both good and bad—on the behavior of children. Parents with problem attitudes have child-rearing practices that cause stress in children. This stress can result in physical, mental, and emotional hurt to children. And children may model these same behaviors when they are parents. In this way, problem attitudes are often passed down from grandparent to parent, from parent to child, and so on.

Neglect and abuse. Neglect is a failure to properly meet the needs of children. Neglect can be physical, mental, or emotional, but it does not involve violence toward the child. A neglected child may not be provided with enough food, clothing, shelter, protection, guidance, or love.

EFFECTS OF SELF-CARE

POSITIVE EFFECTS	NEGATIVE EFFECTS

ON CHILDREN

Children can show initiative and industry. (This is especially true for 8- through 13-year-old children who are old enough to understand parents' rules and who are less prone to peer pressure than teens.) Provides child care experiences for older siblings.	Minor emergencies can become life threatening. For instance, a young child may open the window "to let the fire out." There is greater risk for sexual abuse from older siblings and non-parent adults. Children may have increased feelings of being separated from or rejected by parents (who are at work) and by peers (with whom they cannot play). This may lead to long-term emotional and social handicaps. Feelings of anxiety may be especially strong for 8- through 13-year-old children who fear house break-ins. Children may be overexposed to TV and have no guidance while watching. Lack of adult guidance may lead to poor food choices and improper nutrition for children. Academic achievement may drop due to excessive TV watching and no help with homework until parents and children are both very tired. Children have increased risks of exposure to alcohol and other drugs.

FOR PARENTS

Child care costs are reduced. With careful planning for the self-care situation, the adult-child relationship may be close and children may more quickly learn self-care and how to be more responsible.	Parents have many feelings of guilt and concern. Loss of work productivity while checking or refereeing children over the telephone. (This becomes especially true for after-school hours).

FOR THE COMMUNITY

Challenges people to consider the needs of children and their families such as low-cost day care programs and after-school programs. Challenges people to provide training for parents and children who must rely on self-care.	Risks of accidents including home fires increase. Rates of vandalism, arson, shoplifting, and vagrancy among older children and teens may rise.

22-18 There are both positive and negative effects to self-care.

Neglect most often occurs when parents do not know how to care for their children. Or neglect may happen when parents are under so much stress themselves that they cannot focus on their children's needs. Some common conditions of neglected children which may help adults spot these children are given in Appendix B.

Abuse, unlike neglect, is intended hurt to a child. *Accidents* are not abuse because the harmful actions were not intended. Abuse includes hurting a child's body, using very harsh language in talking to or about a child, and sexual contact or activities between an adult and child. Appendix B also gives some common signs seen in children who are being abused.

The statistics on abuse are alarming. Almost 85 percent of all abuse is physical. In two-thirds of the cases, abused children are under three years of age. One-half are under six months of age. These children are beaten, bruised, burned, and cut. They may have their bones and teeth broken. Physical abuse is second only to accidents as a killer of children. Verbal abuse probably accompanies almost all cases of physical abuse. And, verbal abuse occurs in other cases where children are not physically abused.

Figures for child sexual abuse are estimates because of the number of unreported cases and because the definition of sexual abuse differs from state to state. It is believed that between 30 and 46 percent of all children are sexually abused before the age of 18. It is also estimated that one-third of all girls and one-sixth of all boys are abused. Sexual abuse is just now being studied. Chart 22-19 explains some of the myths and realities of this form of abuse.

Adults should learn all they can about abuse. They need to be active in the prevention of abuse and care of children and adults involved in abuse. In order to do this, one must be familiar with the signs and realities of abuse. They should also know the answers to these four questions: Who is abused? Who are the adults

MYTHS AND REALITIES OF SEXUAL ABUSE

MYTH	REALITY
Sexual abuse is rare.	Sexual abuse occurs frequently and takes many forms such as pornography and incest.
The offender is an unknown, dangerous person.	In 85 percent of the cases, the offender is a known person such as a relative or friend.
The incident occurs suddenly when the adult was momentarily out of control.	The abuse is often repeated over and over again and may occur over several years.
Child sexual abuse is usually a violent attack.	More often child sexual abuse is subtle "force." The offender may call it a "new game."
Children often make up stories of sexual abuse.	Children rarely make up such stories; in fact, they are often reluctant to tell out of fear of the offender or out of guilt for being involved.
Children who recant stories of sexual abuse were lying about the first report.	Children may have been pressured to change their stories.

22-19 Adults need to know the realities of child sexual abuse in order to prevent and treat this serious problem.

who abuse and neglect? What happens to abused and neglected children? How can adults help protect children from abuse and neglect?

Who is abused? All children in a family may be abused. But in many cases only one child is abused. Some children are more likely to be the victims of abuse. Children who are born too small, have birth defects, or are sickly are more likely to be abused than healthy children. This is because unhealthy children may cry a lot. They also have more needs, require more care over a longer period of time, and develop more slowly than do healthy children. Children who look like or have traits like those of disliked kin may also be abused. And, as children get older, clashes and arguments result in abuse.

Sexual abuse within the home most often occurs in blended families or in families in which parents are not closely supervising the children at home. Although sexual abuse outside the home is a social mental health problem, parents can lessen the chances of their children being abused by using close supervision and communication.

Who are the adults who abuse and neglect? Neglect may result from families who are too poor to care for their children. Abusing parents come from all income levels and all ranges of intelligence and education. All abusing parents do have problem attitudes. But most of these parents do not have obvious signs of problems that can be easily seen by others. For instance, abusing parents may appear very nice, quiet, and kind on the job or around friends. However, a closer look at these parents show that most of them have one or more of these traits:

1. They believe that physical force should be used to punish children. Cultures with strong taboos against striking a child (or other adults) have very few cases of child abuse.
2. They were abused as children.
3. They have low self-images.
4. They may feel alone. In fact, they are often away from kin and do not have close friends.
5. They are under stress. They may have problems at the workplace or may be unhappy in family life. They may also feel helpless in coping with their tasks including child care.
6. They have too high of goals for their children. Even infant motor skills such as walking may be expected too soon.

What happens to neglected and abused children? Physical harm is just one result of abuse and neglect. Some children even die from their injuries. Victims are at a risk for many other long-term problems such as neglect and abuse of others, anxiety, shame, guilt, depression, and a poor self-concept.

How can adults help protect children from neglect and abuse? Some social changes have been discussed at national meetings on the problems of neglect and abuse. These suggested changes include:

• Societal rejections of violence and aggression.
• Better economic security for families.
• Universal education in child development and parenting.
• Efforts to reduce premature births and birth defects.
• Adequate child care facilities.
• Education of children about their rights for care and abuse-free childhood.
• Education of all adults on how to spot child abuse and steps to take when abuse is suspected.

When abuse is about to occur, adults should call a "Child Abuse Hotline." Such hotlines are listed in many local phone directories as well as in national directories of toll free numbers. Also listed in these directories is "Parents Anonymous," a national organization with local chapters who can provide support services any time during the 24-hour day.

Reporting is the first step in helping a family in which one suspects or knows of abuse. In fact, failure to report is a criminal offense in many states. To report, the adult calls the local Office of Youth and Human Resources (Child Welfare Office). Under the state's child abuse law, a case worker checks on the situation. The reporter's name and information are kept confidential. If there is evidence of abuse, the child will be brought to the attention of a protective social agency and/or law enforcement agency. For reporting purposes, adults may also call other groups specializing in families such as family counseling groups or the American Humane Association.

Overprotection. *Overprotection* means preventing or retarding the child's growth toward social maturity. Parents who over-protect have too much contact with the child. They seek to narrow the child's contact with others such as peers. These parents often help the child too much. For instance, they may do the talking for the child, prepare school work, and solve the child's conflicts. Children who are overprotected suffer from what is called "smother love." The amount of love and help that is right for one child can be too much or too little for other children.

Overprotection occurs more often in small families, when the child was long awaited, and when the husband-wife relationship is not close. In many cases, overprotection is the way parents make up for their own feelings of rejection. (The parents may or may not be aware of those feelings.) Overprotection also occurs when parents want to protect their children from the problems of life that they had. Children's illnesses or defects do not cause, but do increase, the degree of overprotection in some parents.

Overprotected children are tense and timid. They become adults who are too dependent on others. They may continue to depend on their parents. Or they may transfer their dependency to a husband or wife, a friend, or an employer or co-worker.

Parents may overcome problems of over-protection as children grow older or when other children are born. Counselors can also help.

Disregarding a child's personality. People who disregard a child's personality do not see the child as a unique person. Parents who have this problem attitude try to mold their children as they see fit. The reasons for disregarding a child's personality include these:

- Parents may see their children as extensions of themselves. This idea is made stronger when parents (and even others) note that the child looks much like a parent or seems to share the same traits.
- Parents may want their children to fulfill their dreams because they themselves were unable to do so. Or they may want the child to share the same career. For instance, the parent may have wanted to become a lawyer but couldn't afford law school. This parent pushes the child toward a law career. Or the parent may be an architect and dream of opening a firm with the child as a partner. The problem arises when children lack either the talent or interest or both to fulfill the parents' plans for them.
- Parents may like to dominate others including their children. Some parents have a controlling role in their jobs and continue in this role at home. On the other hand, parents who must conform to the demands of others on a job may relieve their stress by controlling their children.
- Some parents think respect is doing exactly as the parent wishes.
- A few parents may never realize that others—including their children—have a point of view that is different from their own opinions.

Children whose parents disregard their personality are likely to rebel as teenagers or young adults, if not before this time. Those children who do conform may not be truly happy. Perhaps the most stressful of all outcomes is that children often come to feel that they are only loved when they do as parents wish. The feelings that love has a price tag attached carries over into other relationships. They may feel that teachers, peers, and all other people expect things in return for affection.

to Know

abuse . . . adoption . . . adoption agency . . .
black market adoption . . . blended family . . .
children in self-care . . . experimental children . . .
extended family . . . family culture . . .
family history . . . foster home . . .
independent adoption . . . joint custody . . .
latchkey . . . middleborn . . . mobile . . .
neglect . . . nurturance . . . overprotection . . .
premature detachment . . . quality time . . .
role guilt . . . role strain . . .
separate identities . . . single parent family . . .
singletons . . . social isolation . . .
two parent family . . . working mothers

to Review

Write your answers on a separate sheet of paper.

1. True or false. The years of childhood have always been about 17 years.
2. The role of parents involve _____ and _____.
3. Why has there been more of a blurring of the male and female roles in parenting?
4. Match the following descriptions of family life with the family type which best fits.

Family types
   a. Extended families.
   b. Two parent families.
   c. Single parent families.
   d. Blended families.
   e. Families with adopted children.

Descriptions
___ Also called kin group.
___ Often thought of as the typical family.
___ Social isolation may be a problem.
___ Often work together in business, homecare, and child care tasks.
___ Often feel strain in discipline of children.
___ Transition to parenthood may be too quick.
___ Older family members hand down the family culture and family history to younger family members.
___ Greatest problem of the family seems to be financial.
___ Often father must change all living habits.
___ Children lack one parent gender-role model.

5. List the four main types of sibling interactions.
6. True or false. Only children are spoiled.
7. True or false. A parent should not allow multiple birth children to wear identical outfits.
8. For the child's adjustment, the best time for mothers to begin or return to work is when the child is _____ or _____ in age.
9. True or false. There are positive effects to caring for oneself while parents work.
10. Name four possible advantages that children of working mothers have over those children whose mothers to not work.
11. True or false. An abusing parent often acts mentally ill in other settings such as on the job.
12. Problem attitudes of parents _____ (are, are not) passed down from parent to child and then to grandchild.

to Do

1. Make a bulletin board or poster with names and pictures of high achievers such as political leaders, astronauts, or research experts. Under each name, write the person's birth order. Are most of the people firstborns, only children, or in other places of birth order?
2. Interview teachers in your school to determine whether or not they are firstborn children who taught their younger siblings.
3. Write a fiction story entitled, "The Joys and Trials of . . ." (living in an extended family, living in a single parent family, living in a blended family, being a twin or triplet, being a middleborn child, or moving to a new location).
4. Ask an elementary school librarian for books on children and divorce and/or children in blended families. Give the bibliographical information, the age for which the book was written, and a few statements giving the main ideas the book conveys.
5. Secure literature designed for self-care and report on its contents.
6. Invite a resource person from one of the local social service agencies to speak on available services for children and their parents when parents have problem attitudes.

Children with developmental differences need
some special help.

23

Children with developmental differences

Children whose development differs greatly from other children are called *exceptional children*. Exceptional children's development can differ in one or more of these areas: seeing, hearing, motor skills, speech, thinking, or social behaviors. Exceptional development includes development that is faster and beyond as well as development that is slower or below that of others.

Exceptional development can be described in four ways. First, a child can have one or more than one talent or problem. For instance, a child may be exceptional in art only (a single talent). Or a child may be exceptional in art and many academic subjects, too (a multi-talent). Second, most exceptionalities are measured. A child shows a talent or a shortcoming on a certain test. For instance, vision ability is tested and scored. Third, measurements from the test results are reported in terms of the degree of exceptionality. Often used terms are mild (or borderline) to severe (or profound). Finally, an exceptionality may be chronic (extend over a long period, perhaps a lifetime) or correctable. For instance, a missing hand cannot be replaced, but a speech problem may be overcome.

Knowledge of a child's exceptionality does not always predict how far that child will go in life. Bright persons may go far or waste their talents. Children with chronic problems may or may not learn to *compensate* (make up) for their problems.

One out of every 10 children is exceptional. The percentage of children involved varies with the type of exceptionality. About 3.5 percent of all children have speech problems. But deafness affects far fewer children (about .075 percent of all children). The way exceptional is defined also affects the total number of children involved. Certain types of talents and problems are hard to define. More children are called exceptional when terms are defined broadly than when terms are defined in a more narrow sense. For instance, anywhere from three to 45 percent of all children have learning disabilities depending on the way the term learning disabilities is defined. Because by law exceptional children must have their special needs met, definitions of terms must not be so broad that enough funds could not be provided for children who need help the most.

CHILDREN ARE MORE ALIKE THAN DIFFERENT

Exceptional and non-exceptional children are more alike than different. All children have the same needs. They need physical care, adults to rely on, and love, 23-1. Of course, exceptional children need some special care.

Children are also more alike than different because all children must go through the same stages in their development. For exceptional children, the speed of development is different from that of non-exceptional children. For instance, learning to talk is slower for a deaf child. Very bright children often develop at a fast pace from the start. Mentally slower children develop at a slower rate. Not only is the speed of development different, but the degree of development may also be different from that of other children. For instance, a crippled child may learn to walk but not jump a rope. Bright children often attain very high-level thinking skills. Mentally slower children may not be able to handle abstract symbol systems (words, math symbols, signs) as well as other children.

Exceptional and non-exceptional children are also alike in all ways but the exceptional area(s) of development. For instance, a child with a physical handicap may be average or above average in academic learning. A deaf child may be a good athlete. This point is sometimes hard for the non-exceptional person to see. In order to prove this point, many exceptional children work extra hard to compensate for their differences in areas where they are not different from others.

CHILDREN WHO ARE EXCEPTIONAL

As you have read, the development of exceptional children differs from that of other

JOHN SHAW

23-1 Exceptional children have the same basic needs as other young children.

410

children. When development is faster or beyond average development, the words *gifted* and *talented* are often used. And when development is slower or below average, the term *handicapped* is often used.

A child may be gifted or handicapped in many areas of development. A child may be gifted or handicapped in one area of development and average in other areas of development. Or a child may be handicapped in one area of development and gifted in another area of development.

Gifted and talented children

Almost every child has something that he or she can do better than most children of the same age. For instance, a child might speak, read, sing, or jump rope better than other children. Because all children have gifts, the words gifted and talented are hard to define. Gifted and talented children are often defined as children who can or who do show high performance in one or more of these areas:

- General mental ability (high IQ).
- Specific academic aptitude (very good in one or more subject areas).
- Creative or productive thinking (writer or inventor).
- Leadership ability (planner or organizer).
- Very high skill in visual or performing arts (exceptional in art, music, or dance).
- Very high psychomotor ability (exceptional in sports).

Some children seem to be gifted or talented in almost all areas, 23-2. Others are talented in one or two areas only.

JOHN SHAW

23-2 These bright twins do above average school work and have musical talent.

BASIC TRAITS OF GIFTED AND TALENTED CHILDREN

Traits	Examples
Early use of advanced vocabulary.	At age two, the child says, ''I see a kitten in the backyard and he's climbing our fence'' instead of saying ''There's a kitten.''
Can learn to read without being taught at age three or four.	Most gifted children do not read early perhaps due to the fact that they see no need for reading. However, those who do, learn on their own.
Keen observation and curiosity.	As a toddler, the child remembers where all the toys go on the shelf. At ages two and three, the child begins to ask many what, where, how, and why questions such as ''How does the water get out of the bathtub?'' ''Where does the water go?'' ''Why does water go down?''
Memory for details.	The child recalls many past experiences with details that even adults have forgotten.
Long attention spans.	At one year of age, the child may look at a book for five minutes. Other children may just glance at the book. By school age, the child may spend hours on a project and even be totally unaware of other events.
Understand complex ideas.	A gifted preschool child might note that the window glass is warm on the sunny side of the house but not on the shady side.
Have changing interests.	Gifted children want to learn so much that the topics that interest them change often.
Develop critical thinking skills—make careful judgments.	Gifted children note where things do not add up. For instance, seeing water drops form on the outside of a glass, a gifted child may ask, ''How does water get there? It didn't rain on the glass.'' Older gifted children often note the lack of logic in some statements made by others. Gifted children are more self-critical, too. For instance, they may say, ''I should have done better. That was a silly mistake.''
Show talents early.	In visual arts, a gifted child may show facial expressions (sadness, anger, surprise) while peers are still putting circles for the eyes and nose and a curved line for the mouth.
Do not like repetition.	Gifted children like the new and unsolved. For this reason, a gifted child may become bored when asked to do 50 math problems on an easy level.

23-3 Gifted children are all different, but they do seem to share some of the same traits.

Statistics on gifted and talented children show that about 16 out of every 100 children are above average. About three of the 16 are very gifted. About three to five percent of all school-age children—some two to five million children—qualify for special school programs.

Giftedness and talent seem to be partly due to genes. Certain talents seem to run in families. For instance, musical ability ran in the Bach families. Giftedness and talent also seem to be due to an environment in which the child is encouraged to pursue his or her gifts. Challenge and help may make the difference between a child who is above average and one who is very gifted or talented.

Just as all children are unique, so are the gifted and talented. But, gifted and talented children often have some shared traits that set them apart from their peers. See 23-3. In order to know whether a child is gifted or talented, test scores, art products, or judged performances in music, dance, or sports must be used.

Handicapped children

Many other words besides the term handicap are used to describe a lag in development. Other terms include disability, impairment, disorder, and problem. This section includes a review of some common types of handicaps.

Physical handicaps. There are many types of physical handicaps. Some children have vision handicaps. *Vision handicaps* may range from problems that can be corrected by glasses to such severe problems that the person cannot see at all. Some *legally blind* children do not have any vision. But some may see light, colors, shadow forms, or even large pictures. The most common signs of visual handicaps include squinting, bringing objects close to the face, and rubbing eyes. Poor distance judgments (missing step ups and down, bumping into objects, and knocking into things) are another sign. So is self-stimulation play such as rocking movements or making noises.

Hearing impaired people have hearing loss ranging from hard-of-hearing to deafness. People who are *hard-of-hearing* do not hear well, but they can use the sense of hearing for learning and communication. (Some hard-of-hearing people use hearing aids.) *Deaf* people have such severe hearing loss that they cannot depend on the sense of hearing for learning and communication even with use of hearing aids. Common signs of hearing problems include not responding to sounds, no talking or speech problems, and watching other people's faces and movements closely. Many hearing impaired children use touching behaviors more than other children of the same age.

There are many other kinds of physical handicaps in addition to vision and hearing problems. These include missing limbs; bone, joint, and muscle diseases; and damage to the brain or nervous system. See 23-4. All of these problems cause lags in gross motor development. Of all the many handicaps, these physical handicaps are often the easiest to see.

Speech impairment. People who are *speech impaired* have speech so different from others that it calls attention to itself, cannot be understood by others, or causes the speaker to have a poor self-concept. Speech impaired

JOHN SHAW

23-4 Being crippled is a common physical handicap.

children can have problems in one of these three areas:

- Articulation such as using one sound for another, distorting sounds, or leaving out or adding some sounds in words.
- Voice problems such as being too high or too low in pitch, too loud or too quiet, or nasal or husky.
- Rhythm problems such as repeating sounds or words, being unable to get speech out, or speaking very rapidly.

Mental handicaps. A *mentally handicapped* child is often defined as a child whose intellectual abilities are a year or more behind the norm. See 23-5. There are many causes of mental handicaps. They include defective genes, prenatal and birth problems, injuries and infections to the brain after birth, and lack of basic experiences in the environment.

As is true of all children, mentally handicapped children are all different. Due to their handicap, they often share these signs:

- Delay in motor skills.
- Smaller vocabularies and shorter sentence length.
- A grasp of simple but not highly complex ideas.
- Attempts to avoid tasks that they are able to do.
- Short attention spans.
- Like of repetition.
- Problems in making choices as compared with non-handicapped children.

Mental handicaps may vary from mild to severe. Therefore, signs may not be as noticeable in some children as they are in others.

Learning disabilities. There is a great deal of debate on the term *learning disabilities.* Learning disabilities are often defined as handicaps in one or more areas involved in spoken or written language, mathematics, and *spatial orientation.* (Spatial orientation is the ability to see the relationship of one's body to objects in space.) Some learning disabilities include *dyslexia* (trouble with reading) and *dyscalcula* (trouble with math). Learning disabled children have average and often above-average intelligence. However, they function at lower levels due to their handicaps.

The question is often asked, "What causes a child to be learning disabled?" Studies show that it isn't because the parents haven't tried or do not care. They also show that it isn't because the child is spoiled, lazy, stubborn, or mentally handicapped. Learning disabilities seem to be caused by many things including heredity and problems before birth such as lack of enough oxygen or food for the fetus or a virus during the unborn's early months. Problems in the birth itself may also cause learning disabilities. Other causes are accidents, high fever, and breathing or nutritional problems after birth.

In the past, learning disabilities were rarely noted before the school years. This is because as the term learning implies, the disability shows up when formal learning begins. Very bright learning-disabled children are often able to cover up their handicap even in the lower grades. For instance, children may memorize the words in an easy-level reading text rather than really reading the words. Another reason is because the signs shown in 23-6 seem to be

COMMUNITY PLAYTHINGS OF RIFTON, NEW YORK

23-5 Mental handicaps may result in motor skill problems.

414

Signs	Examples
Brain messages are jumbled although the sense organs are normal.	Reads *on* for *no*. Writes *24* for *42*. Says *hopsitals* and *aminals* for *hospitals* and *animals*. Calls breakfast *lunch*. May stop in the middle of a sentence and start a new idea. May think someone asked, "How old are you?" instead of "How are you?"
Poor spatial orientation.	Has problems in doing tasks that require one to use spatial concepts—up-down, left-right, above-below, top-bottom, in-out, into-out of, under-over, and apart-together. Doesn't see things in front of his or her face. Gets lost. Has problems writing on a line. Has problems with jigsaw puzzles.
Seems awkward or clumsy.	Has trouble tying shoes or buttoning small buttons. Poor at sports. Trips or gets off balance due to misjudging distance. Has poor timing. Is unable to coordinate several things at one time.
Has short attention spans.	Can't listen to the story or finish project.
Hyperactive.	Always moving to the point of bothering others.
Acts disorderly.	Needs more attention than most children of the same age and gets it by misbehaving. May also misbehave to get others to think of the behavior as bad rather than dumb.
Inflexible.	Becomes upset when any routine is changed such as a missed activity. Becomes anxious in new places or around new people. Rejects things that seem different such as a broken cracker that isn't square or round. Demands that others cater to his or her needs even when it is not possible. For instance, insists on having water on a trip when there is no place to get water for miles.

23-6 In general, learning disabled children cannot seem to get their thoughts all together. The exact signs differ from child to child.

common to many young children. The differences are that the learning-disabled child seems to be in a world of mental disorder when peers are ready to begin formal learning. Also, the problems seem to be part of the everyday life of the learning-disabled child. Problems only show up in other children occasionally.

Greater awareness of the handicap, more testing programs, and more preschool programs have made it possible to find and help these children at an earlier age.

Behavior disorders. *Behavior disorders* are emotional problems that surface in a person's behavior. Behavior disorders are often extremes of either outward or withdrawn behaviors. Outward behaviors include *aggressive behaviors* (name-calling, fighting, or bullying without being provoked into such actions) and *hyper-active behaviors* (moving around alot, not paying attention, and acting before thinking). *Withdrawn behaviors* include not relating well to other people, not wanting any changes to occur and panic when they do occur, poor self-concept, and sometimes loss of reality.

As with all other forms of exceptionality, behavior disorders are seen in all degrees of severity. Causes of behavioral disorders are often a puzzle. In some cases, stress seems to be the cause. Stressful situations make all people anxious at times. But when a person's anxiety becomes too severe and constant, the person has a mental health problem. Behavioral disorders may also be due to defects, injuries to the brain, and other physical reasons. Science is only in the early stages of solving the puzzle of behavioral disorders.

JOHN SHAW

23-7 Tests are used to pinpoint the gift or handicap in each child.

EXCEPTIONAL CHILDREN NEED SPECIAL HELP

Family members often feel shock when they learn for the first time that their child is exceptional—especially if their child is handicapped. Sometimes the crises must be faced from birth. For other families, the problem may not be noticed until the child does not make normal progress in motor skills, language, or in school work. And, for still other parents, a tragic accident or illness strikes suddenly leaving a child handicapped. To some extent, even giftedness or talent shocks parents. This is because the active minds or special talents of these children often baffle adults. And when children are not challenged, they may waste their gifts and even become problems.

All exceptional children need special help. Parents generally start to seek help through a pediatrician (physician who specializes in care of children) or their family physician. The physician can refer the child for the many needed tests. See 23-7. Once testing is completed, the strengths and weaknesses of the child are explained to parents. Ways to help the child are also discussed.

Exceptional children between the ages of 3 and 17 can be educated with public funds as required in Public Law 94-142. See 23-8. Of

JOHN SHAW

23-8 Special programs that meet the needs of a child are available through public funds.

JOHN SHAW

Children with developmental differences 417

course, parents may choose private schools or other help.

Once problems are found, a plan for the education of each child is written. This plan is called the *Individual Education Plan* (IEP). The plan consists of what is to be done for the child and how it is to be carried out. The plan is explained to the parent who must sign the IEP. Parents also meet with their child's teachers on a regular basis. See 23-9. The child is also re-tested on a regular basis so that the best plans for the child can be made.

Members of the family often join support groups. Many of these groups are national but also have local chapters. At the national level, these groups provide family members with the latest information on the exceptionality. National groups also seek money for research and assistance to families. For instance, families may need expensive equipment for the care or education of a child. At the local level, groups support the goals of the national groups. They also provide helpful contacts and services among those who have similar needs.

JOHN SHAW

23-9 Parents help in planning for their exceptional children's education.

to Know

aggressive behaviors . . . behavior disorders . . .
deaf . . . exceptional children . . .
gifted children . . . handicapped children . . .
hard-of-hearing . . . hearing impaired . . .
hyperactive behaviors . . .
Individual Education Plan . . .
learning disabilities . . . legally blind . . .
mentally handicapped . . . spatial orientation . . .
speech impaired . . . talented children . . .
vision handicaps . . . withdrawn behaviors

to Review

Write your answers on a separate sheet of paper.
1. True or false. A child may be handicapped in one area and gifted in another area of development.
2. Exceptionalities _____ (are, are not) seen in degrees and _____ (may, may not) last a lifetime.
3. True or false. Some forms of exceptionality are hard to define in exact ways.
4. For exceptional children, the _____ of development and/or the _____ of development will differ from that of other children.
5. Name three types (areas) of gifts and talents.
6. Match the following traits seen in exceptional children with the type of exceptionality which best fits.

Traits
___ Asks many complex questions at a young age.
___ Watches others' faces very closely.
___ Uses one sound for another sound.
___ Shows poor distance judgment.
___ Writes *saw* for *was*.
___ Likes much repetition.
___ Can't identify right and left.
___ Uses a large vocabulary.
___ Hits without being provoked.
___ Never seems to really look at others.
___ Has many, many interests.
___ Has poor self-concept.

___ At an early age, plays a musical instrument with much skill.
___ Has delayed motor skills and finds complex ideas hard to grasp.

Types of Exceptionality
a. Gifted and talented children.
b. Children with vision handicaps.
c. Children with hearing handicaps.
d. Speech impaired children.
e. Mentally handicapped children.
f. Learning disabled children.
g. Children with behavior disorders.

7. Order from 1 to 5 the steps in giving special help to an exceptional child.
___ Testing.
___ Writing an IEP.
___ Referral for testing a child.
___ Finding a suitable program for helping the child.
___ Re-testing and writing a new IEP from time to time.

to Do

1. Invite a resource person from an agency dealing with handicapped children to discuss or bring information on one handicap in depth. For example, cerebral palsy would be good for an in-depth review because it occurs often and affects several areas of development.
2. Invite two or more parents of handicapped children to discuss their children's handicaps, how they help their children, and what support groups are available for help.
3. Read a biography or autobiography of a very gifted or talented person. Report to your class on the traits that were seen at an early age.
4. Read a biography or autobiography of a handicapped person. Report to your class on how this person compensated for the handicap(s).
5. Observe a program serving exceptional children. How does the program differ from a regular classroom in terms of the housing and equipment, class size, staff-child ratio, subjects taught, way teaching is done, and other factors?

JOHN SHAW

Dressing up

DEL MONTE CORP.

The kindergarten play

CLINTON E. FRANK ADVERTISING, INC.

Nursing the boys back to health

part eight

Caring for children

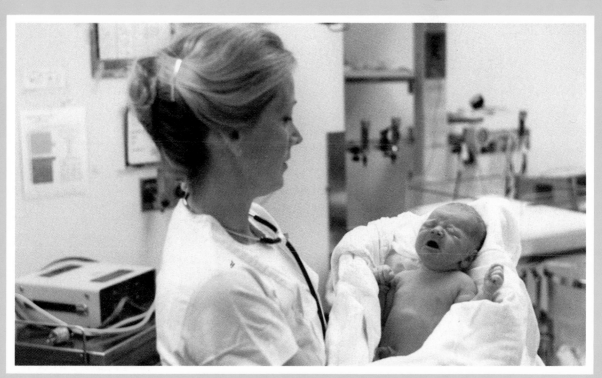

A special kind of career

Important facts and skills needed in later life
are learned in play.

24

Teaching through play activities

After studying this chapter, you will be able to:
- ☐ Describe how children learn from their physical and social worlds and mirror these learnings in play, visual arts, and music.
- ☐ Use activities which encourage learning and expressing by children at different developmental levels.

Children are curious, eager learners. They want to find out about new objects and places. They ask countless questions. And, they strive for self-direction. Children express their learnings in many ways—through play, art, and music.

Learning and expressing are highly linked. Learnings are mirrored in children's expressions. And, children's expressions expand and refine their learnings. See 24-1.

Children need adults to help them learn and to invite self-expression. Adults can see what the child is ready to do. They can provide the time, space, and materials for activities. And they can give children ideas as needed. For the most part, children learn more from all their senses and from their own actions than from being told. Adults need to provide experiences that are important to children—not things which simply amuse them. Many suggestions are given at the end of this chapter.

LANGUAGE

People communicate (give and receive ideas) in many ways such as through art and music, but language is the most direct way. Language involves spoken and written forms. Language may be produced or received, 24-2.

REBECCA LAWRENCE

24-1 While playing in the sand, a child can express what he or she knows as well as learn more about the nature of sand.

Language is made up of abstract symbols. The word cat, whether spoken or read, is not really like the animal in any way. Word orders of sentences also carry meanings. For instance, "Joe hit the car," is very different in meaning from, "The car hit Joe," although the same words were used. Even punctuation marks such as commas can change the meaning of a sentence. For instance, "No price too high," has a different meaning than, "No, price too high." Because language is so abstract, children need help from adults for proper learning.

Nourishing spoken language

As you read in Chapter 7, babbling seems to be inborn. But after one year of age, language must be learned. Adults set the stage for spoken language development.

To help, adults must provide a world of things to see and do. The language of a per-

Form	Spoken	Written
Produced	Speaking (talking)	Writing
Received	Listening (with understanding)	Reading

24-2 A person may produce and receive language in both spoken and written forms.

son clearly reflects his or her experiences. Language blossoms in a special world of many things to see and do, but it never flowers in an empty world. Just as adults have more to share after exciting experiences, so do children. Quality experiences—the right experiences for a child—become the basis of quality language. These experiences often spark creative language use in children as well. For instance, a young child thought of this poem while watching the spectrum of water coming from a water hose:

Water drip; water fall;
Running down my Christmas wall.
(Keith Decker, age 3)

Children need to feel free to talk. Adults need to be aware of chances to expand and strengthen children's language. As a model of the language, the adult needs to use more complete sentences and to use more exact terms. For instance, instead of saying, "Put it over there," and pointing, the adult should say, "Put the book on the bottom shelf." The adult may still point or show if the direction needs to be explained.

Adults need to ask more open-ended questions than questions that can be answered in a word or two. Asking, "What will happen next?" or, "What makes you think that . . . ?" is more helpful in getting a child to talk than saying, "Do you think the dog will get away?" Children can answer the last question with a gesture!

Children enjoy talking with other children. Play and talk go hand in hand. Children's spoken language power increases as they talk with others.

Reading to children is also important to helping children's spoken language. There is a close relationship between children's spoken language development and their being read to. Hearing stories and poems is helpful in two main ways. First, books enrich life and develop appreciation for beauty. Books answer children's endless questions and cause children to want to know even more. Through quality stories and poems children hear the rhythm of language, the rise and fall of the voice, and tongue-tickling phrases.

Second, children who have learned to love books have increased self-expression through dramatic play, art, music, and other experiences. See 24-3. Hearing good literature is also reflected in children's spoken language. Children who are read to may even make up their own poems at an early age.

In order for books to stretch the mind and stir creativity, they must be chosen with care. A children's librarian can help people make good choices.

Books need to be on the child's level. Babies and toddlers enjoy hearing nursery rhymes.

Toddlers and preschool children enjoy picture books with quality pictures. First picture books need only simple captions (or perhaps no caption at all). Later picture books have simple plot lines. In picture books, the pictures tell the story. Books for older children have more involved plots and more word descriptions.

Books should be experienced with delight. Storytime (and poem time) should be a relaxed time. Children should be held or seated near the adult who reads. Adults should read in interesting ways and show the pictures. They can encourage remarks or laughter as the book is read.

Adults can plan some follow-up activities after reading a story or poem. These activities do not have to be done right after the book is read. But they should be done while the book is still fresh in the child's mind. Follow-up activities include talking about the story, finding details in the pictures, and relating the book to the child's own experiences. Other activities include drawing a picture or making a 3-D model. Or children can do activities discussed in the book, such as going to the airport.

24-3 Children have fun drawing their favorite stories.

Nourishing written language

Growth in written language involves gaining skill in handwriting techniques, learning to read, and using writing as a way of sharing. These skills grow slowly over many years. They begin to develop in the preschool years.

Handwriting. Learning to write alphabet letters and numerals grows out of drawing. Some young children cannot tell the difference between drawing and writing. Most children develop a special scribble used for writing which is made up of connected, looping lines. These looping lines are called *linear mock writing* by one researcher. See 24-4. Some children expect adults and older children to be able to read this linear mock writing. Most children read a general message from their own writing. For instance, they will say that their writing is about a dog. A few children, however, will not read their own scribbles for another person because they can't read. When children begin to understand the relationship between written and spoken language, they develop a symbol or a group of symbols to represent a word. See 24-5. It is common to see children alternate between linear mock writing and symbols.

In time, children do mock writing in left to right order from top to bottom of page. To fill the page they may write the same symbols (letters or shapes) over and over again. They may write all the words they know such as names of family members. Or they may copy words seen around them.

When children begin writing, they will sometimes write from right to left. They also will rotate some letters. See 24-6. Children rotate objects in their hands. Thus, they come to see objects from many directions. It takes time for children to mentally see how letters should be turned.

Children who are interested in writing should be encouraged in their efforts. Adults can help by providing writing tools—pencils (and other markers) and paper. They can also show children letters and numerals that are designed for young children. Adults should model correct use of capital and lower case letters. They should also write words on lines so that children can tell that some letters go below the line.

Adults should encourage children to practice writing in meaningful ways. Adults can help children see that the messages people speak can be written. A very meaningful first word to write is the child's own name. Making labels for objects in the home is meaningful, too.

Reading. In recent years, there has been some push to start teaching children to read before they enter the first grade. Some researchers agree with this approach because some children do read on their own before first grade. Also, they feel that early teaching can help identify children who have reading problems before they start school. Such children can be put in special programs early so that poor reading does not cause other learning problems in the school years.

Other experts wonder why people are in such a hurry to teach reading to preschool children. They argue that many children suffer from stress in formal reading programs. They also point out that most early readers do not seem

24-4 A looping line is used by young children to mock real writing.

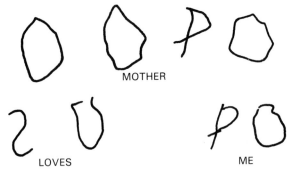

24-5 Before using standard letters, children make up their own symbols for a few words.

to be more skillful than children who begin reading a year or two later. These experts also feel that preschoolers should not be forced to move ahead in mental development while physical and social development lag behind.

Of course, having a good learning environment from birth helps reading ability. In order to learn to read, children need to broaden their spoken language skills. They should hear quality stories and poems daily. Singing and reciting rhymes and poems and telling stories also helps children. Dramatic play is another help. Children also need to observe written words around them and try handwriting.

Writing. Once a child has gained some skill in reading and spelling words and can do handwriting, written communication begins. In the early school years, children often begin to label their drawings. Simple messages are written, too, such as, "I love you." Children who enjoy verbal expression may even try creative writing at early ages as shown in 24-7.

JOHN SHAW

24-6 It takes time for children to learn the way letters are turned in space.

MATH

Children are born into a world where the materials for math thinking surround them. Everywhere babies see different shapes and patterns. They see different numbers and sizes of objects. Within a few months, toddlers see written numerals on many things.

Disappearing Candy on Halloween

Once there was a Jack 'O Lantern who sat in a window sill and thought, "I'll never get to go somewhere. All I do is sit in a dumb window sill on Halloween night while kids get to go trick-or-treating. Then they get candy. All I get is lighted with a match!" But the Jack 'O Lantern was wrong. That night a little girl picked up Jack 'O Lantern and put candy in him. Every once in a while, there would be a "Crunch! Crunch!" Then the neighbors would say, "You are getting sleepy."
When the girl got tired of trick-or-treating, she went home. She decided to eat her candy. Then she reached inside the Jack 'O Lantern and pulled out nothing. She picked up Jack 'O Lantern and stared with her eyes as big as saucers. She asked, "What has happened to my candy?" She began trick-or-treating again. Meanwhile back at the house, Jack 'O Lantern thought, "Well I guess Halloween is not so bad as long as you are patient and have bushels of candy."

Kelcey Decker, age 7

The Sad Pumpkin

Once there was a pumpkin. He hated any pie. One day someone gave him some pie, and he began to cry. The cook asked, "Why are you crying?" He said, "Because I hate this pie." And when the cook heard this, she too began to cry. The maid came in and when she saw the mess, she said, "What's the meaning of this? I really cannot guess." And when the maid heard, she too began to cry. When the wise man came in, he gave a big, long sigh. He said, "This pumpkin hates it, 'cause it's pumpkin pie."

Keith Decker, age 7

24-7 Creative writing is one form of verbal expression.

Children respond to this world of math. One of children's first words is, "more." Even as young as two years of age, children may call curved objects, "round." Slowly other shape names are used in their play. Preschool children begin making shapes with blocks and drawing them although they do not master complex shapes until the school years. And, by two or three years of age, children ask to be first and show how big they are with outstretched arms.

Although children live in a world of math, math concepts are difficult for young children. In children's talk, adults can hear many mistakes in their concepts. They may use such phrases as, "round eggs," "the bigger half," "the walk was a million miles," and the boy at the end of a nursery school line who was the, "last first."

Math is difficult for young minds for two reasons. First, math involves relationships. If a person says that there are five birds, five is not a feature of the birds by itself as the color of each bird would be. Five is the way the birds are related to each other in a person's mind. Second, math always follows laws. For instance, five is always one more than four.

Learning how many

In Chapter 15, you read that most preschool children do not see the sameness in quantity. They do not understand that five is always five. They may think that a spread-out group of five objects is more than a clumped group of five. Until sameness in quantity is seen, addition cannot be learned. For instance, 5 + 0, 4 + 1, and 3 + 2 are simply three ways to arrange five objects into two subgroups. And, until children can reverse, they cannot see how subtraction and addition are related.

Adults often think children understand how many when they hear children count from one to 10 or even further. But often this counting is *rote counting*. Rote counting is counting by repeating the names of numbers in order in much the same way as one learns a rhyme. In rote counting, children may count the same object more than once and may not count every object. Even children who touch (or point to) each object and count correctly may think each

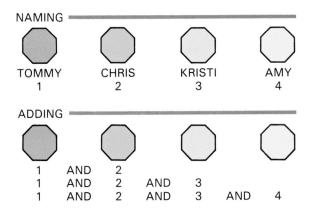

24-8 Young children often see counting as naming rather than as adding.

number refers to only one object, 24-8. These children still may not think of counting as adding. Many activities can be used to help the child develop the concept of how many.

Written names for numbers

Numerals are the written names for numbers such as 4, four, and IV. Numerals are often confusing to children. Numerals are used in at least four ways. They are used to tell how many, such as four balls. Numerals used in this way are called *cardinal numerals*. Numerals can be used to tell order such as the second week. This type is called *ordinal numerals*. Numerals are also used to mark locations such as Room 210. Finally, numerals are used as labels which do not have anything to do with math such as TV channels. For young children, learning to read names for numbers should not be introduced until counting is mastered.

Adults can help prepare children by allowing them to play with numerals. See 24-9. Parents can show children numerals in their home. This helps children to later read and write numerals. Other activities also can be used.

Naming and making shapes

Many books talk about teaching geometry to young children. Of course, children are not ready to deal with geometry proofs. Teaching geometry simply means helping children find and name the shapes of figures. It also means teaching children to make some of them. Adults can help by naming shapes as they talk to children. For instance, they may say, "Look at the round button." Jigsaw puzzles can also be used to teach about shapes. So can other activities.

Learning about size

Size concepts can be difficult because size involves comparing two or more objects. For instance, people often say that one person is taller than another. Even if someone says, "That's a big dog," the person means that the dog is bigger than most other dogs. Size concepts are also hard to learn because people do not always use exact terms. For instance, the word big may refer to the height, width, depth, or weight of an object. Big is even used to describe behavior such as a big boy.

Adults can help children by using exact terms when talking about size. For instance, they should refer to a skyscraper as tall rather than big. A road of blocks in the floor should be called long rather than big. Children love synonyms for size such as wee or tiny for small and giant or huge for large. Adults can also use activities to help children grasp size concepts.

Seeing patterns

Math is made up of many patterns. But most patterns are too hard for young children to grasp. Number patterns are especially hard because numbers are so abstract. However, young children can grasp the idea that patterns have parts that are repeated. Children start by understanding visual patterns. Adults can help with activities. Later, children can apply what they have learned to the more abstract patterns involved with numbers and math.

SCIENCE

Children are born scientists. They wonder, and they seek answers to their wonderings. The raw materials of science surround children — in their homes, in their yards, and in their preschools and schools. Science for young children is catching a cricket, putting it in a jar,

JOHN SHAW

24-9 Playing with numerals is fun even before one can read and write.

and watching it. It is watching water freeze and snow melt. It is asking, "Why do I need to eat my green beans?" And, it is wondering how clouds move. In aiding children's science learnings adults should encourage children to wonder, to appreciate the beauty of their world, and to focus on science in everyday life.

Science is wondering. To wonder, children must first be aware, then focus on an object or happening by ignoring other things, and then observe. See 24-10.

Children usually explore and ask questions without being led by adults. But adults can use some methods to help children explore. They can ask children to name the sense(s) used in learning about many objects—a bell, a rainbow, the rain, foods, a frog, or any other object. Adults can encourage children to classify objects. Adults may ask, "How are these two objects alike? How are they different?" Adults should also ask many questions to encourage children to test ideas. For instance, adults may ask, "What goes through a sifter?" "What do magnets pick up?" "Which objects float?" "What would happen if . . . ?"

Science is appreciating beauty. Most children are awed by the world of living and non-living things. They are eager to share their finds with others. See 24-11.

Adults can encourage the child's enjoyment by being awed, too. Adults can call attention to the beauty of many science concepts. These include light coming through a prism, the colors on butterflies wings, the smell of roses, the songs of birds, and the soft eyes of a deer. Adults can also read books on nature. They can visit zoos, gardens, and forests with children. (Some places have special children's tours.) Adults can also help children make collections of beautiful things—seeds, rocks, and shells.

Science is caring for the world. For the most part, children translate beauty into caring. But because of their young minds, children may not know that living things can be hurt or even killed. They may not understand that resources such as water, land, and air can be damaged

JOHN SHAW

24-10 All scientists—both children and adults—observe in order to learn.

24-11 Children like to share the special things they find in nature.

as a way to learn about the everyday world. For this reason, the topics and their order may differ from child to child. Generally speaking, topics should focus on the natural play and questions of children.

Children should focus on substances (physical matter of things). As children play, they handle liquid, granular, and solid substances. Activities should focus on the properties of substances. For instance, an adult may ask, "What is water like?" See 24-13. Other activities should focus on what objects can be made from (or with) a substance or how the substance is used.

Children should focus on overcoming fears with science facts. For instance, children are often fearful of thunderstorms. By the early

and that beauty can be spoiled when people are not careful.

Lessons on care must begin early. Adults can begin by giving children tasks in caring for living things from the toddler years on. See 24-12. (The task should be matched to the age of the child.) Adults should also model care. This includes practicing energy saving in the home and asking young children to help turn off lights and running water when it is not needed. Families should also help with clean-up work around the home and in their community.

Science is part of everyday life. Science activities should focus on what children see and question around them. Science should never be a magic show. Instead, it should be explained

24-12 Caring for nature must be learned early in life.

Teaching through play activities 431

school years, children begin understanding the causes of thunder and lightning. Adults can use this explanation:

Thunder is a loud noise caused by lightning which rapidly heats the air causing the air to expand. (To demonstrate the sound, blow up a paper bag, hold the neck of the bag tightly, and hit the bag with the other hand. As the air expands and breaks the bag, there is a pop.) Lightning is a flash in the sky caused by energy (electricity) being released. (In a dark room, "lightning" [static electricity] can be created by rubbing two inflated balloons on your clothes and then holding the balloons close to each other. A spark jumps between the two balloons much as lightning does within a cloud or between a cloud and the ground.)

Children should focus on activities that can involve many learnings and are fun. See 24-14. For example, cooking is one of the best ways to learn many science concepts, and both preparing and eating food are fun.

CHILDREN'S SOCIAL WORLD

A child's social world is made up of the child and the people around him or her. Learnings in the social world include self-understandings, awareness of and respect for others, and skills in solving social living problems. And, as in all learnings, children need adults' help. Adults provide valuable help by modeling good social habits. They may also help by providing activities.

Self-understandings include learning that each person is unique and has self-worth. As you read in the chapters on social-emotional development, self-understandings are aided when children grow up in a social world where adults meet their needs with love and concern. Adults also help children gain self-understandings by letting children express their own ideas and try things in their own ways.

As children develop feelings of self-worth, they begin to translate these feelings to others. But as children realize that others have feelings, they may not know how to respond to others.

JOHN SHAW

24-13 Children need to have many first-hand experiences with substances such as water.

Adults can help children learn to respond to others with respect. Children need to learn how to live with others. Getting along depends on being able to see from another's point of view. Mental growth is needed. But practicing and teaching considerate actions is also needed.

PLAY

In *play,* one interacts with the world of people, objects, and even ideas (word play, problem-solving games). Play is a self-chosen activity which is done for its own sake. Most of all, play is fun.

Importance of play

Until recently, play has not been carefully studied in terms of its value. It has not always been given an important place in a person's life. In fact, play—even for children—was not accepted in early history. Children worked! In the more recent past, play was seen as something done by children and by adults in their spare time.

Play and physical development. The most often noted need for play is that it helps physical development. Muscles and nerves are improved. The heart and lung systems are aided. Proper weight is more likely to be maintained. Balance and coordination are improved. All of these happen as a result of play, 24-15. Children and adults who are active tend to feel healthier than those who are not active.

Play and mental development. Children learn through play. In turn, children's learning is mirrored in play. In play, children learn concepts about their physical world. Play brings children in contact with objects. Children can cause objects to do many things. They observe the results of actions. Children soon see how objects differ. They also learn how things are made. For instance, balloons are filled with air to make them fat. And children come to see the physical limits of objects. For instance, a balloon does not bounce in the same way as a rubber ball.

Through play, children learn relationship concepts. Number concepts form as the child sees that more blocks mean a higher tower or a longer train. In filling a sand pail, children see that small objects fit inside but the beach

JOHN SHAW

24-14 Science learnings may be gained from such cooking activities as roasting pumpkin seeds.

TUPPERWARE TOYS

24-15 A toy can help eye-hand coordination.

ball will not fit. In like manner, other relationship concepts develop.

Symbol systems are used in play, too. In symbol-type play, the child selects the most important aspects of an experience. For example, doll play is mostly feeding, bathing, changing clothes, and rocking dolls. In pretending to be a wild animal, the child may make loud sounds and pretend attacks.

Play becomes a way for learning language. For the infant, the sound of peek-a-boo comes to signal the return of a person. The older child learns many words while playing with others. Children also try out new rhythm and sound patterns in language. Infants begin with babbling sounds. Older children try rhymes, jingles, and even Pig Latin.

Humor is also mental play. Humor is the thought that there is a mistake which is not hurtful. (Hurtful mistakes are not humor!) For instance, in play a child may show humor by making a change from the usual — orange milk, flying dogs, and adults playing with toys.

Play also improves creative thinking. Through play, children try new ideas. For this reason, children who play the most are more apt as adults to become artists and scientists.

Finally, in play, children learn they can make mistakes. The pressure is off. Thus, pleasure affects the child's attitude toward learning.

Play and social-emotional development. Children build awareness of others through play. Through greater awareness, trusting relationships develop. Babies play games only with the people they trust such as parents and other caregivers. Parents who play with their children during the childhood years seem to be close to them in later years.

Along with awareness of others comes concepts of rights and properties, sharing, and settling disputes. In play, children learn to detect others' feelings. Good players seem to have the most friends, 24-16.

Children work out many of their problems in play. Children make things happen their own way in play. For instance, preschool children often feel very limited in what they can do or make happen. By playing dinosaurs, they can identify with the dinosaur's size and strength, and thus make up for their own weaknesses.

24-16 Team games help social development.

Stages of play

Play mirrors changes that take place in children's physical, mental, and social-emotional development. In a real way, play pulls together all aspects of development.

Because play changes as children grow older, there are certain stages in play. These stages are hierarchial—that is, one stage builds into the next. Thus, babies do not begin to play in advanced stages. However, once children reach a higher stage of play, they can play in earlier stages. When older children play with younger children, most often the stage of play fits the younger children. When children play with new types of objects, the stage of play is also less advanced.

Stages are most often described in terms of the child's play with objects and with people. Chart 24-17 shows stages of play with objects and with people and how these two areas

STAGES OF PLAY

Age	Play with Objects	Play with People
From a few months to school age.	**Practice Play** Babies explore objects by picking them up and by tracking them with their eyes. Play activities are repeated over and over again.	**Solitary Play** Babies ignore other children who are nearby. Sometimes babies treat others as objects to be pushed or walked on, to be poked in the eyes or nose, or to have hair pulled. **Onlooker Play** Toddlers watch others play but do not join in their play. **Parallel Play** Children play near other children and often play with the same or almost the same toys. They note that others have interests and skills much like their own. However, there is no real interaction among children.
From age 3 years through elementary grades.	**Symbolic Play** Children engage in fantasty play. They pretend they are someone else. Also, they project mental images on objects. For instance, the stick becomes a horse.	**Associative Play** Two or more children play at a common activity. The children share ideas. However, the play is not well-organized. For instance two or more children may play the baby bear of *The Three Bears* at the same time. Or one child may decide to run a food store and another may be a mother—but the mother never shops at the food store.
Peaks at 9 or 10 years.	**Rule Play** Children make rules to govern their games or carefully follow the rules that were already established.	**Cooperative Play** Two or more children share common goals and play complementary roles such as chaser and the chased.

24-17 The stages of play can be described in terms of how children play with objects and how they interact with peers in a play situation.

parallel each other. There is not total agreement as to these stages. Thus, the chart is only one way of viewing the stages of play.

Types of play

There are many types of play. One way to classify play is by the stages of play. Another way to think about play is by the basic skills involved. Skill types include active-physical play, manipulative-constructive play, imitative-imaginative play, and language-logic play.

Active-physical play. *Active-physical play* involves gross-motor skills. Gross-motor skills involve the use of the large muscles in movement. Such movements include walking, running, hopping, jumping, twisting, bending, skipping, galloping, catching, throwing, balancing, pushing, pulling, and rocking.

Through active-physical play, children get to know space and the movement of the body and objects in space. As a bonus, terms for movements and positions in space take on meaning. These terms include forward, backward, big, little, fast, slow, under, over, up, down, behind, in front of, through, beside, and between.

Active-physical play also helps children develop reaction time. Reaction time is a slow to develop skill. Improved reaction time comes as the body matures and the child practices.

Children also improve and test many physical skills. They learn about their own strength. Pushing, pulling, lifting, and carrying give children concepts of how strong they are. Children learn to spring to lift their body and catch it on impact. Upward movement is an often needed skill. Catching oneself in the right way on landing protects the body from injuries. Children improve their balance. Balance is needed for almost every large-muscle movement, 24-18. Children also become more graceful. Grace comes when the large-muscle skills are developed and are coordinated with each other. Grace is pleasing to see. And it permits a person to engage in many fun activities such as roller skating.

Manipulative-constructive play. *Manipulative-constructive play* involves small-muscle skills. Small-muscle skills develop after the basic large-muscle movements. For instance, writing, a fine-motor skill, develops after walking. However, small-muscle skills do develop very early in life. Crawling babies can pick up small objects (gravel, paper) in a carpet and carefully put them in their mouths, ears, and noses. Eye-hand coordination is also involved in manipulative-constructive play.

Many toys and materials aid fine-motor skills. These include jigsaw puzzles, blocks and other construction materials, beads for stringing, pegs and pegboards, art tools, woodworking tools, and cooking tools. Fine-motor skill toys are made for little and unskilled hands as well as for more skilled hands. See 24-19.

JOHN SHAW

24-18 Balance, which is needed for most activities, is developed very slowly.

24-19 Some building toys are made for advanced fine-motor skills.

24-20 Making things with blocks and other building toys helps build the child's mental image of the real thing.

Besides small-muscle skills, manipulative-constructive play helps children's ability to mentally picture objects. It also helps children make abstract models of what they see as shown in 24-20.

Imitative-imaginative play. In *imitative-imaginative play,* children pretend to be persons or objects other than themselves. They carry out this play verbally and/or in actions. There are three stages of imitative-imaginative play. The first stage, imitative play, begins about two years of age — just as children begin to use symbolic thought. Symbolic thought allows the child to let one thing stand for another. For instance, a stack of books becomes a space ship. The second stage, dramatic play, begins around three or four years of age. Dramatic play involves role playing with more than one child. However, each child's role is independent of others. For instance, two children may be space people but each play the game in their own way. In the last stage, socio-dramatic play, a group of five- to seven-year-old children play with a theme. They assign roles to each child. Instead of just being space people, the children are looking for new planets or playing star wars. Each child has a special job in the play, 24-21.

Imitative-imaginative play has great worth. Children learn to imagine or picture themselves as if they are other people and objects. Memory is helped because children must recall events in play. Language is aided because children must listen and speak during play. There is much freedom in expression, too, as children try to bridge the gap between what they know and do not know. Children can use their bodies to extend their language. For example, a child may say, "I'm a barber," while using the fingers to snip.

Children can also try out many roles and even reverse roles in play. In this way, children get some feel for others' real life roles. Children join in holiday and other rituals as they act out roles, 24-22. Children can also express fears, resentments, and even hostile feelings in socially approved ways. *Play therapy,* using play as a way to help children with their problems, is used by trained counselors.

Teaching through play activities   437

24-21 As older children play house, they take on specific roles of adults.

Language-logic play. *Language-logic play* is a form of mental play most often seen in school-age children. There are so many types of games that only a few can be named. Some language games include those in which children use vocabulary skills to compete. See 24-23. Other language games include humor that is based on language such as puns. Logic games require much thought about one's actions. For instance, children must think ahead an plan strategies for sports and table games. Logic games also include object puzzles and word problems.

24-22 The mood and meaning of holidays are captured through role playing.

Adult role in play

Children should be allowed as much freedom as possible during play. Children's play can be restricted by toys which suggest something specific to do such as a jigsaw puzzle. Adults restrict play by setting many rules for play for safety or other reasons. And peers restrict play by telling each other what and how to play. Although play can never be totally free, adults can help keep restrictions to a limit.

Adults need to see the importance of play and express that feeling to children. Think of the attitude an adult expresses to a child when the adult says, "Can't you see I'm busy? Go away and play." Toys need to be seen as important, too. Toys should not be given the dictionary meaning of a bauble — a thing of no real value.

Adults should allow children time to explore materials on their own. Adults should observe some play. At times, adults may add ideas or materials. Children should decide whether to use them. Some examples of how to add ideas and materials include modeling an action such as pretending to eat make-believe food. Adults can increase language by adding to a child's growl by saying, "Growl—I'm a tiger looking at you with my sharp eyes." They can also explain new concepts. For instance, adults can describe airplanes as objects that go very fast down a special road called a runway so they can fly in the air. They can use blocks and a toy plane to explain. And adults should change toys or add new toys from time to time.

Toys should be selected with care. Toys should be safe and fun. (Toy safety is discussed in detail in Chapter 25.) And toys need to be right for the child. Because all children are different, they like different types of toys. Many infants and toddlers like texture toys, squeeze toys, and toys that make sounds. Preschool children like toys for large-muscle play (balls, pedal toys, climbing toys) and small-muscle play (puzzles, beads, pegs). They also like construction toys. Role-playing toys are needed, too. These include floor blocks, dress-up clothes, puppets, toy cars, trucks, planes, animals, and people. *Prop boxes* can also be used for role-playing. A prop box is a collection of real objects placed in a box to fit a certain type of role such as store clerk or nurse. Rule games are popular with school-age children.

Toys should be planned for different play settings such as indoors, outdoors, and travel. Travel toys must be chosen with much thought. These toys must be held in children's hands or laps. They must be safe in a moving car. They cannot make too much noise for a small space or distract the driver. And toys must be able to withstand the heat or cold of a closed car. Some toys and games are designed for travel such as cassette tapes of songs and stories, magnetic game boards, and games where older players spot things such as license plates and road signs while moving.

Children's toy collections need to be balanced. Children need different types of toys to aid all aspects of development. Adults need to avoid providing too many toys that simply perform. These toys do not allow much involvement. They should select toys that can be

24-23 Playing "Scrabble" is a way to increase vocabulary while having fun.

JOHN SHAW

Teaching through play activities 439

used for many things such as building blocks, art supplies, and balls. See 24-24.

As toys are purchased, adults need to be good consumers. Toys are costly. They should also keep in mind that too many toys are often bought. Many learnings come from making toys. Children often spend as much time making toys as they do playing with them. Children often spend hours piling lumber scraps and boxes to make a play house. Making toys also teaches children to save useful items often thrown away.

VISUAL ARTS

The *visual arts* include painting, constructing, and photography. They are highly important in children's lives. The visual arts help development in many ways. Fine motor skills are improved as children handle brushes, scissors, and crayons and as they fold paper.

Intellectual learnings abound in the visual arts, too. Sensory experiences help children refine their concepts of color, line, shape or form, texture, and size. And because children create what they know, visual arts cause children to think about their world. The ideas children have are recorded in their products.

Finally, visual arts help children develop in the social-emotional areas. Children make choices about what they want to do and how they want to do an art activity. They can express their feelings in art, too. Pride in their art products and acceptance of their products by others helps their self-concept. See 24-25.

Stages of development in visual arts

The total development of children determines the ways that they use crayons, paints, clay, and other *visual art media*. Children progress from playing with the art media to using art media as a means of representing objects, experiences, and feelings. Thus, development is divided into the manipulative stage and the representation stage. The stages of children's development are studied by watching children

LANDFIELD CO., RIG-A-JIG™

24-24 This building set can be used to make other toys.

use art media and by looking at children's *art products* (pictures, 3-D structures, and other finished works).

Manipulative stage. In the *manipulative stage,* children play with art media rather than try to create something. Early in this stage, children under two years of age enjoy art for motor reasons. Paper is covered with marks and clay is pinched, patted, and even eaten.

Soon the child begins to see what is happening as a result of certain actions. The child from 24 to 30 months begins the second step in this stage called scribbling. *Scribbling* consists of dots, straight and curved lines, loops, spirals, and imperfect circles. Scribbling is serious business because the child must make eyes and hands work together.

The third step in the manipulative stage occurs from 30 to 42 months. In this step, the child begins to use basic shapes such as crosses, rectangles (including squares), and ovals (including circles). Shapes are combined in drawings, too. Rhoda Kellogg, a noted researcher in children's art, calls a design made up of two shapes a *combine.* She calls a design made up of three or more shapes an *aggregate.* Because motor play is so important, many shapes, combines, and aggregates are lost in the layers and layers of crayon marks and paint.

In the transition step between the manipulative stage and the representation stage, children ages 42 to 60 months create their first symbols. Because the child often decides what the symbol is after it is made, the symbol may or may

24-25 Children express their feelings through art.

not be named. The face is often the first and favorite symbol seen in children's drawings. Even when a body is drawn, it appears to be an afterthought. Lines are added to draw arms, hands, body, and legs, and circles are used for feet or shoes, 24-26. The head remains the largest part of children's drawings for years. Although symbols are used, there are no spatial relations among objects. Symbols seem to just float.

Representation stage. Most five- or six-year-old children have reached the *representation stage.* In this stage, children create symbols that represent objects, experiences, and feelings. Adults can see that a child has entered this stage when the child decides what the symbol is before creating it. ("I'm going to draw a tree.") Another signal is that the child shows spatial relations among objects. In a simple spatial relationship, the child shows what is on the

A

B

C

D

24-26 Human figure drawing begins with the head (A). Later, single lines are added to show trunk, arms, legs, fingers, and feet (B). Next, double lines are used for body thickness (C). Finally, details are added to clothing (D).

ground and what is not on the ground by means of a base line or base lines. A *base line* is a line of grass, dirt, or water drawn near the bottom of paper. Or the base line can be the lower edge of the paper itself. The sky often appears as a strip of color across the top of the paper. "Air" is between the objects on the base line and the sky. See 24-27. Two or more base lines may be drawn which show objects at varying distances. The objects closest to the child are always drawn on the base line closest to the lower edge of the paper.

Other spatial relations in the representative stage include *folding over*. Folding over is showing a spatial idea by drawing objects perpendicular to the base line even when it means drawing objects upside down. See 24-28. Some children draw a mixture of side view and top view in one drawing. For instance, a child may draw a table and chairs with chairs showing from the side view but with the whole top of the table showing.

In an effort to depict what is known about an object rather than what is visually true, the child's symbols often have certain features. Children often exaggerate (or increase) size to show importance. For instance, children tend to exaggerate human figure drawings. Children's symbols are often *transparencies*. Transparencies can be *X-ray* type pictures which show the inside and outside of an object at the same time. For instance, a drawing of a house may have windows on it, but it may show people and furniture inside the house as well. In other types of transparencies, children mix the profile and far-side views of an object. For instance, a profile view of a person may show two eyes.

After age seven or eight, representation becomes more exact. The human face becomes more detailed and shows expression, 24-29. Visual depth also becomes a part of these more advanced drawings, 24-30. And perspective of objects is shown as children see it, not as they

24-27 A base line of ground or water is the first way children show spatial relationships among objects.

24-28 Children often show objects that are across from each other by drawing objects at right angles to a base line. This results in upside down objects.

24-29 School-age children add many details to the human face.

24-30 School-age children begin to include visual depth in their drawings.

think it should look. By nine or ten years of age, children can draw objects from their perspective and from the perspective of others.

Adult role in visual arts

The adult's role is to introduce children to artistic skills and to art activities suited to their stages of development.

To fulfill this role, adults should provide the right environment and supplies for children. See 24-31. They must show children how to use

ENVIRONMENT AND SUPPLIES FOR THE VISUAL ARTS

The Environment	
Space	Find a place to draw, paint, model clay, cut and paste in the kitchen, playroom or outside. The space must be easy to clean.
Storage	Use a large cardboard box to store supplies. The box can be decorated with the child's artwork.
Display	Hang pictures on the refrigerator with magnets, mount on a special bulletin board, hang from an indoor ''clothesline,'' or put in a picture frame. Artwork should be changed frequently.
Keeping artwork	Select a few products and put in scrapbooks or photo albums (laminated pieces stay in better condition.) To reduce the bulk of products, photograph the original.
The Supplies	
Paper	Buy newsprint and construction paper (both in 12'' x 18'' [30 cm x 45 cm] size), shelf paper, and paper bags.

Continued.

24-31 Art learnings are enhanced by the right environment and supplies.

Crayons	Buy large crayons in the eight basic oclors for small hands. (For very young children, non-toxic, washable crayons are best.)
Paint	Buy dry tempera which is mixed with water for brush painting and with liquid starch for finger painting.
	Pudding Finger Paint Prepare instant vanilla pudding to which a few drops of food coloring have been added.
Scissors	Buy quality child-sized scissors. They may be purchased for left-handed and right-handed children. Depending on the child's age, one may select either blunt or pointed styles. The lengths selected is also affected by age.
Paint brushes	Buy three or four brushes with about 1-inch wide bristles and short handles.
Paste	Buy white paste or glue that works on paper and cloth. Make your own paste.
	Flour Paste 1 cup (240 ml) flour 1/2 cup (120 ml) water Combine the flour and water. Mix well until creamy. Store in covered container.
Clay	Buy plasticine (a clay that remains soft due to oil) or play dough. Play dough may also be made.
	Peanut Butter Play Dough 2 cups (480 ml) peanut butter 1 cup (240 ml) flour 1 cup (240 ml) confectioner's sugar Combine and mix.
	Play Dough 2 cups (480 ml) flour 1 cup (240 ml) salt 2 cups (480 ml) water 2 tablespoons (30 g) salad oil 4 teaspoons (20 g) cream of tartar food coloring Combine and cook until mixture thickens into a soft ball. When cool enough to handle, knead. Store in an airtight container.
Collage materials	Collect alphabet cereal, pasta, dried beans or peas, seeds, boxes, cloth, yarn, ribbon, paper of all kinds, flowers, leaves, twigs, straws, and other objects that can be glued to a flat surface.
Art smock and clean-up supplies	Use an old, long-sleeved man's shirt. (Cut sleeves to child's wrist length and put on backward. Button only the top button.) Use a vinyl piece to cover work table. Have sponges and paper towels handy to wipe up spills.

24-31 Continued.

artistic tools such as scissors and paint brushes. Once children understand how to use tools, adults should let children do their own work. They should not make models for children to copy or add to the child's work. Children's work will reflect their skill in handling tools and their way of seeing the world.

Adults should encourage children by showing interest in their artwork. They can help children try new techniques by saying that they have confidence in the children. Adults can also show interest by joining children in art activities. See 24-32. (However, adults should never compete.) And adults can display children's artwork.

MUSIC

Sounds in many pitches, rhythmic patterns, and degrees of loudness are the parts of music. These parts surround people from birth. Not only do children hear sounds, but they respond by quietly attending, moving, and making sounds. Thus, musical development is like all other development. Those children who have had a rich world of sound and movement will have a good background for later learnings and pleasure.

Music for children

Music provides chances for sensory and expressive experiences. Listening to music is the basis of all music learning. As children become more tuned to the sounds around them, they learn to translate the sounds in musical ways. For instance, they may say that sounds have high or low pitch or even or uneven rhythm. Also, listening to the sounds of music can lead to better listening in other areas.

Singing seems to make children feel good. They often sing or chant to tell what they are doing—"Feed . . . ing ba . . . by." The words

JOHN SHAW

24-32 Adults and children can share time during art activities.

used in singing are the same words that are used in talking. Thus, singing helps language learnings. Although young children do enjoy singing, they do not have the ability to sing well by adult standards. Until young children find a singing voice, they simply talk in a sustained hum sound that they call singing. When the singing voice is found, the range is often limited to about six tones (from middle C to A). Preschool children often cannot sing a tune. They are not able to match their voice pitch to the notes of the music. With practice and listening, this skill develops over time. Preschool children may also have problems in singing with other voices or with musical instruments. In order to sing with others, children must hear their own voice, the voices of other singers or instruments, and the unison sound. No wonder a nursery school group sings in parts—20 parts!

Making music is fun, too. Even babies invent ways to make sounds such as shaking or hitting things and making sounds with their voices or hands. When children can care for musical instruments, they should be allowed to use them. Many instruments require more strength and skill of the fingers than young children have. Therefore the first instruments used by children are often *percussion instruments*. The tone from a percussion instrument is produced when some part of the instrument is struck. Percussion instruments without a definite pitch such as a drum are called *rhythm instruments*. Melody percussion instruments such as a xylophone produce various pitches when certain bars are struck. See 24-33. By using these instruments, young children see how sounds are made, play rhythmic patterns, and perhaps play simple melodies.

For young children, there is a oneness between movement and music. Even toddlers move to music without being prompted by adults. Since young children need chances to move, music can be a fun way to support this need.

Adult role in music

The adult's role is to introduce children to music activities suited to their interests in all areas. This includes listening, singing, playing instruments, and moving to music. In addition to providing activities, adults can provide an environment that is rich in sound. They can model enthusiasm in appreciating a variety of music. And, perhaps the most difficult role is listening to and praising children's musical attempts. Children need adult encouragement if they are to practice enough to gain musical ability. Especially during the school years, parents and other adults may listen to many less-than-perfect performances. But with loving acceptance, children can become skilled musicians or at least gain appreciation of music.

JOHN SHAW

24-33 Rhythm instruments are the best instruments for young children.

Counting by touch

Arrange objects on a table in different ways. Begin with three objects and increase to 10 objects as the child masters each step. Ask the child to look at the objects and then touch each one being careful to touch each object once and only once. Children are not ready to count mentally until they can correctly touch ten objects in any way that they are placed.

Counting movable objects

Start with two objects and slowly increase to 10. As you help the child count, move the objects close together and hold your hand over all of the objects counted. This method helps the child see that three is not just the name of the last object counted. Rather it is a quantity that includes objects one and two. For this reason, small movable objects should be used for early counting.

Counting non-movable objects

Preschool children should touch or point to each object as they count. After the last object is counted, ask "How many are there all together?"

Variation: Count objects in pictures or drawings in the same way.

Counting without touching

Have the child count up to five objects by pointing without touching or by nodding. Use cards with objects drawn in random ways and in the same manner used on playing cards and die. Do not use this activity until counting by touching is learned. Five objects is enough. (Even adults see only seven or fewer objects at a time. They must add groupings to mentally count many objects.)

Everyday counting

Ask children to bring enough supplies for an everyday activity. This might be bringing enough napkins for the dinner table or bringing enough scissors for those who are cutting paper. Children need to learn on their own how counting is helpful in daily tasks. The child will go back and forth getting the right number before seeing that counting makes the task easy. (Adults should be aware that showing the child how counting is used seldom helps.)

Names and numerals

Show children how numerals are like their names. Start by having a child count some objects such as buttons. Then say, "We can write how many buttons you counted. You count, then watch me write how many." Write on a piece of paper the Arabic numeral (1, 2, 3, and so on) representing the number of buttons. As you write, say something to the effect of, "This is how we write a 2. This 2 means we counted two objects just like Bobby means you." Place the paper under the group of objects that the child counted.

Pick the right name

Arrange objects into groups of one, two, or three. Place cards with the numerals 1, 2, and 3 written on them on the table. (You may write the numeral on pieces of paper or use purchased cards with numerals.) Ask the child to find the numeral that tells how many is in each group. After the child has mastered three numerals, add another (up to a total of 10). (Adults need to remember that this is a reading activity and some children are not ready to match numerals with groups of objects.)

Continued.

Shape sorting

Shape sorters have holes that fit various shapes, such as square, circle, and pentagon. Have the child match an object with the hole through which it will drop. As children master simple shape sorters, more advanced ones can be used.

TUPPERWARE TOYS

Making shapes

Gather a set of pre-cut shapes made of paper, plastic, or wood. (Parquetry blocks, shown in Chapter 21, can be used.) Have the child arrange them to make other shapes, designs, or pictures. Ask older children what the name of the shape is and why. (For instance, the child made a square. The child knows that it is a square because it has four equal sides.)

Prints

Help the child cut various geometric shapes from one-half-inch thick cleaning sponges. The sponges can be dipped in paint and stamped on paper.

Peg board

Make a peg board by placing evenly spaced rows of nails in a flat piece of wood. Place rubber bands around the nails to make various shapes. You can make shapes and have the child name them. When the child has mastered naming the shapes, you can name a shape and have the child make it.

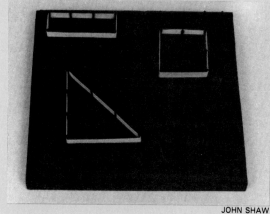

JOHN SHAW

Continued.

Comparing two sizes

Gather two objects that are the same shape but different sizes, such as two balls or two round baking pans. Ask the child to show you the larger (or bigger) object. (Begin with great size differences and then use objects that are closer in size.) Place the larger shape sometimes to the right, to the right, above, or below the smaller shape and ask the child to find the larger object each time. Repeat the same activity, but have the child find the smaller shape. Always model the language used to discuss size. For instance, say, ''This ball (point) is larger than this ball (point),'' or, ''This ball (point) is smaller than this ball (point).''

Comparing three sizes

Gather three objects that are the same shape but different sizes. Ask the child to show you the largest, the smallest, and the middle-sized shape. Be sure to put the shapes in different orders. Middle-sized is often confused with middle-positioned when the object is always placed between the largest and the smallest.

Pattern hunt

Challenge the child to see how many different patterns can be found in one room of the house, such as the kitchen. Patterns might be found in fabric, wallpaper, storage containers, cabinet doors, and other places. Discuss why something is or is not a pattern.

Making patterns

Supply the child with beads, pegs and pegboard, parquetry blocks, or other building kits so that children can make their own patterns.

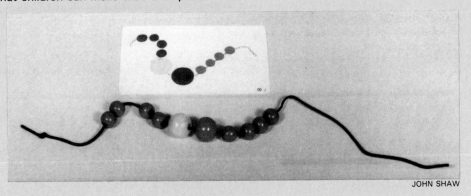

JOHN SHAW

SOCIAL ACTIVITIES

Family talk

Discuss families with a child. Ask the child to name all those who live in their house. (It is alright to include pets.) Ask the child to name those who live in a friend's family. Discuss what the child thinks makes a family. Ask why the child thinks people need families.

Job play

Show the child that all people have certain jobs to do at home, at work, and in other settings such as clubs. Visit places where people work in the community or show the child using books or magazines. Have the child act out various job roles.

Continued.

Culture exchange

Plan ways to learn about people of other cultures. You may look at books or pictures or arrange for the child to meet people from other cultures. Plan a meal based on another culture and have the child help with planning and preparing. Or play games from another culture.

Lazy Day

Have children choose roles within a community. Tell the children that this day, no one will do their job. After role playing for a while, discuss what happened. Help children see that they need to finish their tasks.

VISUAL ARTS ACTIVITIES

Squeeze bag art

Use a self-locking, clear food storage bag. Put a few tablespoons of fingerpaint inside. Smooth the bag until paint covers the inside of the bag with a solid film. Press air out, lock the bag, and seal the bag with tape. Place the bag on a flat surface. The child can draw on it with fingers. To renew drawing surface, rub the bag lightly with your hand.

Deodorant bottle pens

Gather deodorant bottles which have rings and balls. Remove the rings and balls. Fill bottles with tempera paint mixed with water, then replace the rings and balls. (Do not use starch in tempera.) Children can roll paint on paper to make designs.

Gadget painting

Use gadgets such as spools, cookie cutters, hair curlers, wheels from toys, small paint rollers (found where house paints are sold), potato mashers, and bottle caps. Have children dip the gadgets into liquid tempera and stamp or roll them onto the paper.

Sponge painting

Cut sponges into various shapes. Attach a spring-type clothespin to each sponge. Have children dip sponges into tempera and stamp on paper.

Blowing color

Place a drop or two of tempera on edge of paper. Have children use straws to blow runny tempera around.

Blots

Fold a 9 by 12 inch or smaller piece of construction paper in half. Open the paper. Have children drop one color on one side of the paper in blots in several places. The paper is folded and rubbed with the hand. Repeat the process with another color. Do not use too many colors in one design. Using white paint after all other colors have been used makes for a good contrast. (Paint can be dropped from a brush or an eye dropper.)

Color change

Using crayons and construction paper, make new colors. For example, red paper and yellow crayons make marks look orange.

Continued.

Crayon rubbings

Place paper doilies and geometric shapes under typing paper. Have children use peeled crayons and rub lightly over the paper. Children enjoy rubbings with leaves, yarn, and coins.

Collages

A collage is a picture or design made by gluing flat objects on a background. Supply children with paper, small objects, and fabrics. Have children arrange and attach them to a piece of paper or cardboard. A 3-D effect is obtained when one uses objects with some thickness.

Montages

Montages are combinations of pictures or parts of pictures to form a new picture. Have children cut and paste pictures or parts of pictures on stiff paper or cardboard. (Usually a montage covers the entire background and pictures may overlap.) Montages are good for classification skills because they may be done on themes—people, holidays, animals, or the child's favorite things.

Clay work

Have children work with a soft, pliable modeling compound. Plasticine is best for young children. First clay work should be done with hands only. Plastic knives, nails, cookie cutters, and other gadgets should not be used in the beginning.

MUSIC ACTIVITIES

Hearing sounds

Play records or tapes of sounds in nature and sounds that are made from manufactured products. Talk about the tones heard in terms of sound qualities such as high-low, loud-soft, near-far, continuous-discontinuous, and the direction of the sound.

Story sounds

Read stories that mention sounds. Ask children to make the sounds mentioned in the story using their voices, their bodies, or objects.

Matching sounds

Play different tones on the piano or on bells. Ask the child to match his or her voice to the pitch. (Notes should be between middle C and one octave above middle C.)

Find the sound

Have children pretend to be kittens or other animals that make a sound. Have the kittens hide while mother cat (one of the children) pretends to be asleep. After the kittens have hidden, the mother cat awakens and meows a call to her kittens. Kittens meow in response, and the mother cat must find the kittens by following the sounds.

Variations: 1. Have children point in the direction of a sound that is heard. 2. Have children locate a loudly ticking clock or a metronome.

Echoing rhythms

Tap a simple rhythmic pattern using the body or a rhythm instrument. Have the child repeat the pattern. After doing several patterns, have the child start and you can repeat the pattern.

Learning about tones

Use a xylophone or a bell set. Show children that the longest bar or largest tube makes the lowest sound and that the shortest bar or smallest tube makes the highest sound. (Because many instruments are set up with lowest notes to the left of the musician, the lowest tones should be to the child's left as you demonstrate.)

to Know

active-physical play . . .
imitative-imaginative play . .
language-logic play . . . linear mock writing . . .
manipulative stage . . .
manipulative-constructive play . . .
numerals . . . percussion instrument . . . play . . .
play therapy . . . representation stage . . .
rhythm instrument . . . rote counting . . .
scribbling . . . self-understandings . . . visual arts

to Review

Write your answers on a separate sheet of paper.

1. The relationship between learning and expressing can be described as:
    a. Learning leads to expression.
    b. Expression leads to learning.
    c. Learning and expressing are mutually interacting (affect each other in a back and forth way).

2. Which of the following statements are true? (You may choose more than one.) Language develops:
    a. In a world of books.
    b. In a world of quality things to see and do.
    c. In a natural world without any special help.
    d. In a world in which adults explain new words and expand sentence patterns.
    e. In a world where play with others is enjoyed.

3. Handwriting grows out of _____ (reading, drawing).

4. True or false. Reading before first grade seems to be most helpful to children.

5. Give two reasons why mathematics concepts are difficult for young children.

6. Social learnings have their roots in _____ (self-understandings, understandings of others).

7. True or false. Children's science learnings are mainly made up of special activities planned for children.

8. Play helps children with:
    a. Physical development.
    b. Mental development.
    c. Physical and social-emotional development.
    d. All of the above.

9. Match the basic skills with the type of play.
    Types of play:
    ___ Active-physical play.
    ___ Manipulative-constructive play.
    ___ Imitative-imaginative play.
    ___ Language-logic play.
    Skills:
    a. Symbolizing skills.
    b. Small-muscle skills.
    c. Large-muscle skills.
    d. High-level mental skills.

10. True or false. Visual arts are mainly important for social-emotional reasons.

11. _____ is basic to all music learnings.

to Do

1. Select at least two activities which are given as examples of ways to help children learn or express themselves. Try the chosen activities on a child or small group of children. Report to the class on how the children responded.

2. Make a bulletin board on "Science is . . ." (wondering, appreciating beauty, caring for our world, and part of our everyday life).

3. Observe two children of different ages at play. Try to place the children in terms of the stage of play with objects and the stage of play with people. Explain your reasons for placing the child in the stages.

4. Make a display of children's visual arts products. Label the products with the correct stage and any other descriptive term such as "Representation Stage—Transparency."

5. Help an older preschool child or school-age child make a simple musical instrument. One good source is the book, *Music and Instruments for Children to Make* (Book 1 and Book 2), by John and Martha Faulhaber Hawkinson. Your music teacher may have additional resources.

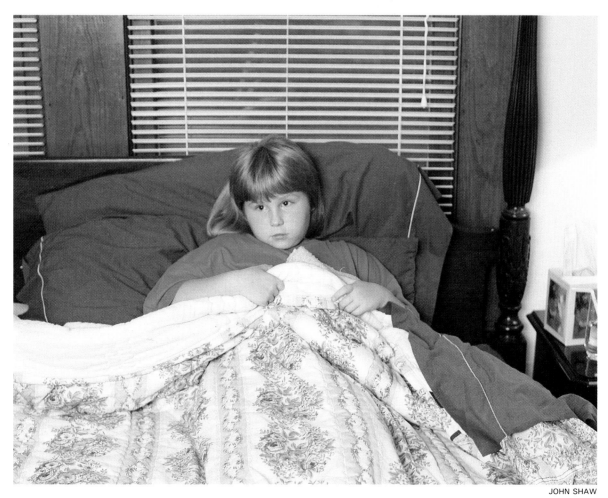

Children need special care to stay healthy
and safe.

454

25

Protecting children's health and safety

After studying this chapter, you will be able to:
- ☐ Explain some of the ways to protect children from diseases and illnesses.
- ☐ Create a safe environment for young children and teach simple safety practices.
- ☐ Discuss the steps in preparing a child for medical care in the physician's office, in the hospital, and at home.

Health and safety advances are greater today than ever before. Yet growing up is still risky business. Each day infants and children face risks of illness, injury, and even death. Although people have varying degrees of control over these risks, many risks can be avoided with proper adult care. The health and safety of children rests more squarely on adult shoulders than almost any other aspect of a child's development.

PROTECTING FROM DISEASES AND ILLNESSES

A disease, an injury, or an abnormal condition may cause pain, damage physical health for life, and hurt the self-concept of a child. Early detection, prevention, and good treatment of health problems increase the chances of a healthy life. And a healthy life permits a child to benefit from all of life's experiences.

Nutrition, rest, cleanliness, and exercise

Adequate nutrition, rest, cleanliness, and exercise are basic physical needs. These needs must be met throughout life for good health. Careful attention to basic health needs may be more important in childhood than at any other time in life.

Basic health care is important because children must grow and develop as well as have energy for daily activities. And when a disease or injury occurs, children who are otherwise healthy have the best chance for rapid and complete recovery. Also, medical science cannot undo the effects of long term neglect of health needs.

Adults need to help children meet basic physical needs early in life and model good health practices. Such actions postively affect the child's present health. But they also help the child develop good life-long care habits.

Medical and dental care

Keeping a child well is a major goal of health care. For this reason, the physician examines a child regularly, not just during sickness. Earlier chapters discuss well-baby checkups—checkups given when a baby or child is not known to be sick. Through such checkups, possible health problems may be noted before they become serious or even prevented. Doctors note the growth and development of the child. They can provide protection against certain diseases (which is the topic of the next section). They also note the child's eating, sleeping, and playing habits. And doctors answer parents' questions about their child's development. Because well-baby checkups are so important, doctors suggest a schedule for regular visits. The schedule varies slightly among physicians, but the following is often used:

- Birth to six months of age—once per month.
- Six months to one year of age—every two months.
- One to two years of age—every three months.
- Two to six years of age—every six months.
- Six to 18 years—once per year.

Dental care should begin after the child has most of the primary teeth. Most children have these teeth between two and three years of age. Dentists clean teeth. They inspect and x-ray teeth for *dental caries* (decayed places in teeth). They repair damaged teeth. And dentists teach dental health and care. A dentist who specializes in general dentistry may refer a child to an *orthodontist*. An orthodontist is a dentist who treats teeth which are not straight. When teeth are straight, a pretty smile is not the only outcome. Straight teeth allow foods to be chewed properly and help lessen the chance of tooth and gum diseases. See 25-1.

Immunization

People who have *immunity* to a disease have or will quickly develop *antibodies* when exposed to the disease. These antibodies are agents which prevent the person from having the disease. (A person does not develop immunity to some diseases.)

The newborn may be immune to several diseases because the mother's antibodies entered the baby's blood through the placenta. (Infants who are breastfed also receive antibodies from the mother through the first few feedings.) This type of immunity is called *passive immunity*.

25-1 Even teeth that look all right at first glance may need straightening for good dental health.

Passive immunity does not last after the first few months of life. Also, passive immunity only provides immunity to diseases for which the mother has antibodies.

Further protection can be given to prevent children from having some diseases. Physicians call this type of protection by all of these terms: *vaccination, inoculation,* and *immunization.* Regardless of the term used, children are given an injection or drops that contain an *antigen.* An antigen is made from the substance that causes a disease. The substance is changed so that the antigen does not cause a reaction as serious as the disease itself. Children react by developing *active immunity*—the person's body produces its own antibodies. Many times, more than one treatment (or *primary dose*) is needed to develop full immunity.

Vaccinations have been developed to prevent some very serious diseases. The diseases were once common causes of serious illness and death among children. They include tetanus, diptheria, pertussis (whooping cough), polio, measles, rubella (German measles), and mumps.

For the most protection, infants should begin receiving immunizations around two months of age. Studies are still being done to find the best timing. The idea is to protect the baby without having immunization compete with antibodies received from the mother. The schedule shown in 25-2 is based on current

COMMON CHILDHOOD IMMUNIZATIONS

DISEASE	IMMUNIZATION SCHEDULE					
	2 months	4 months	6 months	15 months	18 months	4 to 6 years
DTP Diptheria: Hoarseness, sore throat, fever. Tetanus: Tightening of jaw muscles followed by tightening of back muscles. Pertussis: Long coughing spasms which sometimes end in vomiting.	P	P	P		B	B
Polio Fever headache, vomiting, stiff neck and back, in some cases muscle pain and tenderness followed by paralysis.	P	P	P		B	B
Measles High fever, cough, runny nose, light sensitive eyes, blotchy rash.				P		
Rubella Swollen lymph glands, mild fever, headache, sore throat, cough, rash.				P		
Mumps Swollen salivary glands, fever, chills, loss of appetite.				P		

P—primary dose   B—booster

25-2 This schedule comes from the American Academy of Pediatrics for infants who start their immunization program at two months. (Other schedules are available for infants and children beginning their immunizations later.)

knowledge. Immunizations need to start early because children do not become immune until about one month after the last primary dose. Later, children are given boosters for some immunizations. This is because the number of antibodies produced by some vaccinations decreases over time.

Each child's physician or clinic keeps records of immunizations. These records are needed before giving more doses. They are also needed for official records often required by schools and camps. Parents should keep a record, too, for their own information.

Medical attention during illness

There are times when children need special medical attention. Many childhood illnesses are soon over and are no cause for worry. But there are many *symptoms* (signs of an illness or injury) which may indicate need for prompt medical help. Chart 25-3 lists some of the major symptoms which should be brought to a physician's attention. Even if symptoms are vague but the child's behavior seems very different from usual, the physician should be called.

When physicians are called, they need specific information in order to understand the child's condition. The adult should think of questions the physician may ask. The following would most likely be asked:

1. What are *all* the child's symptoms? (Give exact information if possible such as, "temperature of 102°F," or, "vomited five times in the last two hours and each time was about one cup of fluid lost."
2. How long have you noted the symptoms?
3. Has the child been recently exposed to a *contagious disease* (disease which can be caught from another person)?
4. Have you treated the child's illness in any way? When? Have you given food or liquid to the child? When? Does the child take any medicines regularly? What medicines?
5. Do you know whether or not the child is allergic to any medicine? (A new physician will not know about a child's allergies.)
6. What is the name and phone number of your pharmacy? (The physician may phone in a prescription.)

Adults need to write all of this information before calling a physician except in extreme emergencies.

Adults should also take notepaper to the phone to write the physician's instructions. They should ask the physician questions which might include these:

1. Is there anything that I should know about giving medication or other treatments? What other measures should be taken (keep the child lightly covered, warmly covered, in bed)?
2. When may I expect an improvement?
3. What changes would merit another call or office visit?

Instructions should be read back to the doctor to be sure they are correct.

PREVENTING ACCIDENTS

Accidents claim the lives of more children than any of the major killer diseases of childhood. Children depend on adults for their protection. Protection can be provided in two ways. First, adults can create a safe environment by removing dangerous objects, preventing unsafe situations, and taking safety measures. See 25-4. Second, adults can model and teach safety practices.

Several factors lead to an increased accident rate among children. Children have a great amount of energy and curiosity. By toddlerhood, the motor skills and curiosity are geared up to operate in an intense way.

Accidents happen more often when children are not carefully supervised. One example is in large families where younger children are supervised by older ones. Another is when adults are busy with supper and other chores in the late afternoon and early evening hours. When adults are ill or are preoccupied, accidents are also likely.

Accidents happen more often before children learn safety practices. Adults can help prevent many accidents by removing hazards and taking safety measures and by making the child aware of the need for safety.

SYMPTOMS INDICATING POSSIBLE ILLNESS

AREA OF CONCERN	SYMPTOMS
Appetite	More than one feeding refused.
Blood	Large amount lost in bleeding. Bleeding cannot be stopped.
Body movement	Convulsions. Immobility in any part of the body. Shaking. Stiffness of body.
Bones and muscles	Swelling. Pain. Difficulty in movement.
Brain	Dizziness. Visual problems. Acts strange or looks different. Is unconscious.
Breathing	Hoarse or noisy. Difficulty in breathing. Slow or rapid. Continued coughing, sneezing, or wheezing.
Color	Flushed or pale.
Digestive system	Vomits all or large part of feeding. Vomits between feeding. Forceful vomiting as opposed to spitting up foods. Abdominal pain or tenderness. Vomits for several hours with inability to retain fluids. Sudden increase or decrease in number of bowel movements. Stools unusual in color, odor, or consistency.
Eyes	Irritated or red. Sensitive to light. Blurred vision.
Fever	Rectal temperature of 101 °F or above. Mild fever that lasts several days.
General behavior	Unusually quiet, irritable, or drowsy. Looks strange after a fall or other accident. Already ill, there is a rise in fever or new symptoms appear.
Nose	Nasal discharge (note color, amount, and consistency).
Pain	Sharp screaming. Ear rubbing, head rolling, or drawing of legs toward abdomen.
Skin	Dry or hot. Excessive perspiration. Rash or hives.
Throat	Sore. Red. Choking.
Urine	Change in amount. Change in color or odor.

25-3 Medical help is needed when certain symptoms appear.

KINDERGARD

KINDERGARD

25-4 Adults must take such precautions as locking cabinets to help keep the child's environment safe.

25-5 By placing plugs in electrical outlets, adults can help keep children safe from electrical shock.

Creating a safe environment is a must for preschool children. These children often cannot make sound safety judgments. Young children may not understand the reasons for being careful. They may be too involved in reaching their own goals to remember the warnings. Thus, it is urgent that adults do all they can to keep the environment safe for children. In such an environment, accidents are reduced while children can play without too much concern for safety. See 25-5. Later, children are ready to take on the tasks of helping to protect themselves.

Anticipating possible hazards

Creating an environment without any risks is impossible. Even if possible, it would not be wise because children must learn to face and cope with risks. But risks must not be too great for the child or serious accidents are likely. To prevent these serious accidents, adults must anticipate possible hazards.

Children's developmental changes lead to certain types of accidents. Babies face hazards at birth. But these hazards multiply with growing motor skills, curiosity, and independence. Chart 25-6 shows some of the common accidents for each stage of development. Because each child is different, adults need to watch each baby's development carefully. And, as growth stages are seen, the adult must see the need for certain safety measures. For instance, a child who can crawl up one step or any low object can climb (and will climb if given a chance) an entire flight of steep stairs. Falls are common when babies first climb.

Helping children meet goals in a safe way

Adults should help children meet their goals in safe ways. Young children learn about their

460

worlds by climbing, putting everything in their mouth, or other activities. Adults need to provide these children with safe environments as they explore rather than try to change children's goals. For instance, when babies want to climb, it is all right to let them climb up and down on a carpeted step or two or off and on a chair or toy chest (and even take small tumbles). But the steep basement stairs must be blocked off from the toddler. In this way, children can meet

ACCIDENTS CHILDREN ARE LIKELY TO MEET

AGE OF CHILD	CHARACTERISTICS OF CHILD LEADING TO POSSIBLE ACCIDENTS	MAJOR ACCIDENTS
Birth through three months	Skin is much more sensitive to heat than adult's skin. Wiggles and rolls off of flat surfaces but cannot move away from danger. Puts objects into mouth and swallows them.	Bath scalding. Falls. Injuries from swallowing small objects. Drowning. Strangling on cords or smothering from items such as dry cleaning bags or balloons.
Four through six months	Skin is more sensitive to heat than adult's skin. Moves by rolling over and may crawl or creep. Grasping is so improved that any object may be grasped and placed in eyes, ears, nose, or mouth. Hits objects including breakable ones.	Bath scalding and burns from hot water faucet. Falls. Injuries caused by swallowing small objects or putting them into eyes, ears, or nose. Injuries from broken objects such as glass or plastics.
Six through 12 months	Sits alone. Grabs things in sight. Looks for objects put out of sight or fallen out of sight (around 10 months). Puts things in eyes, ears, nose, or mouth. Hits, pokes, and pushes objects. May walk with or without help.	Falls from stairs or high places. Injuries caused by pulling on cords of kitchen appliances such as toaster or coffee maker, by pulling or grasping serving containers, plates, bowls, and cups with hot foods or beverages. Burns from open heaters, registers, and floor furnaces. Injuries caused by swallowing small objects or putting them into ears, eyes, or nose. Injuries from dangerous objects such as knives, sharp-edged furniture, breakable objects, and electrical outlets.
One to two years	Walks. Climbs. Throws objects. Pulls open drawers and doors. Takes things apart. Puts things in mouth.	Falls on stairs, in tubs or pools, and off of high objects such as crib railing or table. Burns from grabbing handles of pots on stove. Poisoning from medicines and cleaning agents. Injuries from dangerous objects such as knives, electrical outlets, breakable objects, toys with small parts, and sharp-edged objects inside and outside. Injuries caused by being on driveways and roads and in outside storage areas.

Continued.

25-6 As children develop, the type of accidents most likely to occur change.

AGE OF CHILD	CHARACTERISTICS OF CHILD LEADING TO POSSIBLE ACCIDENTS	MAJOR ACCIDENTS
Two through three years	Can rotate forearm to turn door knob. Likes to climb on things. Likes to play with and in water. Fascinated by fire. Moves at fast speed. Does not like to be restrained. Likes ride-on toys.	Injuries caused by getting into almost anything that is not locked or equipped with special devices. Injuries caused by falls from high places, jumps onto dangerous surfaces such as concrete or sharp-edged objects, and falls off ride-on toys, swings, and ladders. Drowning. Injuries related to tricycles and other ride-on toys. Burns from cigarette lighters, matches, and open flames. Injuries caused by playing in driveways and roads and darting across streets and roads. Injuries caused by swallowing small objects or putting them into eyes, ears, and nose.
Three to six years	Explores neighborhood. Plays rougher games. Plays with other children. Tries to use tools and equipment of the home.	Poisoning from medicines and household products. Injuries from using home, shop, and garden tools. Injuries related to action games, bicycles, and rough play. Various injuries from interesting hazards such as old refrigerators, deep holes (including wells), trash heaps, and construction sites. Drowning. Burns from electrical outlets and appliances and from open flames. Traffic injuries.
Six to 12 years	Participates in sports. Likely to try stunts on a dare. In traffic as a pedestrian or on bicycle. Interested in firearms and fireworks. Uses tools in home and yard care.	Sports-related injuries. Drowning. Firearm and fireworks accidents. Traffic injuries.

25-6 Continued.

their goals. And they can learn how to cope with possible dangers when the risks are not too great.

Childproofing the environment

Adults must note dangerous things in children's worlds. Moving objects out of a child's reach or preventing a dangerous situation is called *childproofing* the environment.

To childproof, the adult must move around where the child moves. And, the adult must be at least one step ahead of the child's develop-ment. For instance, the child may pull up to standing position the first time by grasping the tablecloth (and pulling off hot soup). Adults must also childproof every part of the environment—indoors, outdoors, and in vehicles. They also need to check items belonging to the child—baby items and toys. Pets must be chosen with care, too.

Indoor safety. The indoor environment is often the greatest hazard to a child. Some unsafe indoor items and situations and suggested childproofing measures are given in 25-7.

INDOOR DANGERS

DANGER	REASON FOR DANGER	CHILDPROOFING MEASURES
Beverages:		
Alcoholic	Alcohol is a drug which acts as a depressant.	Keep locked or out of the reach of children.
Carbonated	Unopened carbonated beverages are under pressure. They can explode, breaking the glass bottle.	Keep glass bottles out of reach or buy soft drinks in plastic bottles or cans.
Cords:		
Drapery and venetian	Double cords can wrap around neck, causing strangulation.	Knot the looped cords to prevent slipping over a child's head.
Small appliance	Child can pull appliance down using cord. Playing with cord can result in electrocution.	Drape cords behind appliances while in use. Put cords away when appliances are not in use. Keep small appliances out of children's reach.
Table lamp	Child can pull lamp down. Playing with cord can result in electrocution.	Wrap the cord around the back table leg. Store lamps that are seldom used.
Curtains	Child can suffocate if curtain is wrapped around head.	Keep out of baby's and young child's reach. If buying window coverings, consider short curtains, blinds, or shutters.
Doors:		
Swinging	Some doors lead to unsafe areas. Others are used often by children and children may accidentally lock themselves in a room.	Keep doors to unsafe areas locked or secured with a safety device. Locks on doors to bathrooms or bedrooms should be removed. Or a key or other unlocking device should be kept nearby.
Sliding glass	Child may walk into or through glass. Fingers can be pinched by door.	Block off door if seldom used or put decals on glass at the child's eye level. Place a door stop high on the door jamb.
Electrical outlets	Child can be electrocuted by putting objects or fingers in outlets.	Unused outlets should be capped with safety devices or sealed with electrical tape. Heavy furniture can also be placed in front of some outlets that are never used or which have cords plugged in them rather permanently.
Fans	Fingers can be cut by twirling fan blades.	Place window screening between fan blades and grills. Keep fans out of the reach of children.
Firearms	Child may decide to play with gun and accidentally fire it.	Lock firearms and ammunition in separate places. Keep key out of reach.
Fireplaces, open heaters, registers, and floor furnaces	Getting too close can cause burns.	Place guards in front of fireplaces and open heaters and around registers and floor furnaces.

Continued.

25-7 There are many dangerous items indoors.

DANGER	REASON FOR DANGER	CHILDPROOFING MEASURES
Furniture	Unstable furniture can fall on child. Furniture with sharp edges can cause cuts and bruises.	Remove when possible unsteady furniture such as plant holders, some lamp tables, and some portable TVs. Pad sharp edges of furniture. Remove or keep out of reach furniture with glass components.
Hot liquids and foods	These can cause burns if spilled on child.	Keep hot liquids and foods out of children's reach. Turn pot handles toward wall. Keep cords behind small appliances being used. Avoid using hanging tablecloths with small children around; they can pull tablecloths down to spill hot liquids and foods.
Insects, spiders, and rodents	These can bite and spread disease.	Have all pests exterminated. (Be careful not to allow children into areas that have been sprayed for pests until sprays have been cleaned off of surfaces. Also keep traps out of the reach of children.)
Matches and lighters	Children like to play with these. They can burn themselves or even start fires.	Keep all matches and cigarette lighters out of sight and reach.
Rugs, area and throw	Children can slip on or trip over loose rugs.	Use non-skid mats or put rubber guards under rugs.
Stairs	Small children may fall down stairs.	Place safety gates at the top and bottom of stairs not to be used by baby or child.
Tools	Many tools are heavy or sharp. Used improperly, they can cause many injuries.	Dangerous tools should be locked out of the child's reach.
Tubs	Child may slip or drown in tub.	Use non-skid mats or apply adhesive rubber appliques on the bottom of the tub. Babies and young children should *never* be left alone in a tub or any other body of water.
Waste baskets and garbage cans	Children can get into garbage and find many harmful objects.	Never place anything in trash or garbage containers within a child's reach that would be harmful to a child. Tie knots in plastic can liners. Put can lids inside cans and stuff papers on top before throwing away. Place broken glass in a sturdy container before throwing away. Do not throw away unused medicines (flush contents).
Water, hot	Water that comes out of the faucet at too high of a temperature can scald child.	Set hot water heaters at no more than 120 °F (49 °C). Paint hot water faucets with a little red fingernail polish to help small children remember which is hot. When bathing a baby or child in a sink or tub, run a little cold water last to cool the faucet.
Windows	Child can fall through or out of windows.	Use tight-fitting screens or locks which cannot be removed by the child. Equip windows above the first floor with locked screens and safety bars.

25-7 Continued.

Poisoning is a major concern with indoor safety. Poisonings of children under five years of age account for more than half of all accidental poisonings in American homes each year. Children in this age range like to examine objects. This means sometimes swallowing attractively packaged household products and medicines which look (or even taste) like candy.

Children need not be victims of poison if safety measures are taken. Adults need to learn which products are dangerous, 25-8. They must read labels on all products and heed warnings. Household products must be stored above floor level (rather than under the kitchen sink and bath lavatories) for crawling babies. They must be locked up when children can walk and climb. (Reach is almost without limits when a child can climb.) When using an unsafe product and called to the door or telephone, adults must take quick action. (Proper actions are discussed later in this chapter.)

Products must be kept in their original containers with label in tact. Never transfer poisons to food or drink containers (box, jar, bottle). Do not put a safe substance in a cleaned container which originally held a poisonous product such as water in a bleach bottle. In this case, a child seeing water used from a bleach bottle may think the contents of bleach bottles are safe. Medicines must be in childproof containers. Household products must be in safety containers. Containers must be checked carefully each time they are used because the container may be difficult to close firmly or may be faulty.

Products which are lethal (deadly) in small amounts should not be kept in the house. The risks are too great. For instance, one teaspoon of oil of wintergreen contains six grams of salicylates. This is equivalent to the amount in 20 adult aspirin.

Medicines are safer when adults take these

POISONS CAUSE ACCIDENTS

CLEANING PRODUCTS	GARAGE AND GARDEN PRODUCTS	MEDICINES	PERSONAL PRODUCTS
Air fresheners	Antifreeze	Amphetamines	After shaves
Ammonia	Caustic lime	Antibiotics	Deodorant
Bleach	Fertilizers	Anticonvulsants	Hair coloring products
Cleaners	Gasoline, kerosene, lighter fluid, oil, and other petroleum products	Antidepressants and tranquilizers	Hair removers
Dishwasher and dishwashing products	Paints	Antidiarrheals	Lotions
Disinfectants	Pesticides	Aspirin and acetraminophen (such as Tylenol)	Mouthwashes
Drain openers	Putty	Camphor	Nail polishes and polish removers
Floor waxes	Strychnine	Cold preparations	Perfume
Furniture polishes	Varnish	Iron, vitamins with iron	Permanent wave solutions
Laundry products	Weed killers	Oil of wintergreen	Powders, talcum (baby and body powders)
Lye		Sleeping pills	Rubbing alcohol
Metal polishes		Vitamins	Shampoos
Oven cleaners			Soaps
Rust removers			
Spot removers			
Toilet bowl cleaners			
Water softeners			

25-8 There are many substances that are poisonous.

safety measures:

- Flush old medicines.
- Replace childproof caps carefully after use.
- Lock medicines in a cabinet or in a small chest or suitcase.
- Never give medicines in the dark.
- Never refer to medicines as candy.
- Do not give medicines in baby bottles or juice glasses.
- Do not take medicines (even vitamins) in front of young children.
- When carrying medicines, put a limited amount of medicine in a purse or pocket in a childproof container.

Outdoor safety. The outdoor area must be checked, too. Common unsafe things in the outdoor area can include rocks, broken glass, ruts, holes, and bumps. Nails and other objects can cause punctures. Otherwise safe areas may turn into slippery areas when wet.

If the outdoor area has pools, ponds, wells, or even deep holes, they should be fenced (without toe holds). They also should be closed and safely locked or covered in a way to provide complete safety. Doors and trunk lids should be removed from old refrigerators, freezers, stoves, and cars if these are near children's playing areas.

The outside area presents a special problem in safety—plant life. There are many plants, flowers, vegetables, shrubs, and trees that are poisonous or have poisonous parts. One of the major problems in plant poisonings is that when children eat a plant leaf it is not always obvious to the adult. Children do not show such sings as holding an empty bottle of medicine or gagging and crying after swallowing drain cleaner. And yet, plants are dangerous. Many eaten plants harm the digestive tract in ways similar to eating ground glass because of the chemical in these plants. Some very beautiful plants are deadly. For instance, one leaf of a poinsettia can kill a child. Chart 25-9 contains a listing of some plants known to be poisonous. Poisonous houseplants should be removed when there are young children around. Young children need close supervision in their outside play areas, especially in wooded areas, gardens, and greenhouses.

Another major problem in outdoor safety is making sure children will not wander out of a given area. Yard areas are best fenced in. Gates should be locked or equipped with childproof safety devices such as a screen door latch on the outside of the gate or a bolt pushed from the inside to the outside of the gate where the nut is attached. Such devices require the adult to reach over the gate to unlock the gate, but they are out of reach for the young child.

When young children are using driveways or carports for pull/push toys or for ride-on toys, they should be closely supervised. An extension ladder laid across the driveway a few feet from the street can help remind the very young child to turn around. The extension ladder can be replaced with a "stop" sign or a "U-turn" sign for older preschoolers. However, ladders and signs are only reminders, not safety devices. Close supervision is a must!

Traffic safety. Auto crashes are the number one cause of death for infants and children. Yet it is estimated that deaths could be reduced 90 percent with the correct use of a proper *restraint system.* Restraint systems include car seats, harnesses, and other devices which hold children safely in place during accidents or sudden stops or turns. Approved restraints have passed crash tests as being suitable for certain size infants and children. A few of these seats have been approved for air travel, too.

Many adults feel that they can hold babies and protect them during an auto crash. Not only do loose objects fly about in a collision or hard stop, but the weight of an object is greatly increased. For instance, in a 30 MPH crash, a ten-pound baby moves forward with a force of 300 pounds. Such force is impossible for an adult to hold. At the same speed, a 125-pound adult is thrown forward with a force of between one and two tons. A baby who is being held by an adult or sharing a seat belt with an adult is apt to be crushed in an auto crash even at a rather slow speed.

Car beds and infant feeding seats offer no crash protection. They should never be used in a moving car. Regular seat belts do not protect children under age five for these reasons:

1. These young children can slip through or

POISONOUS PLANTS

Almond	Cry-baby tree	Lily-of-the-valley	Privet (lingustrum)
Allamanda	Cyclamen	Lobelia	Rain tree
Amaryllis	Daffodil	Love-in-a-mist	Ranunculus
American cherry laurel	Daphne	Mahonia	Rattlebox (wild pea)
Angels trumpet	Datura	Marijuana	Rhododendron
Arbor vitae	Death camas	Mayapple (Mandrake)	Rhubarb
Autumn crocus	Diffenbachia (Dumb cane)	Mango	Rosary pea
Azalea	Dogbane (Indian hemp)	Milkbush	Sago palm
Barbados nut	Elderberry	Milkweed	Sedum
Barberry	Elephant ear	Mimosa	Snowdrop
Bittersweet	False indigo (Coffee weed)	Misson bells	Snowflakes
Black locust	Four-o-clock	Mistletoe	Snow-on-the-mountain
Bloodroot	Foxglobe	Monkshood	Sorghum
Blue bonnet	Golden chain	Moonseed	Spanish dagger
Boxwood	Grape hyacinth	Mushroom (wild)	(Yucca)
Bracken fern	Holly	Narcissus (daffodil)	Star of Bethlehem
Buckeye	Horsetail	Nightblooming cereus	Stinging nettle
Bull nettle	Hyacinth	Night jasmine	Strawberry bush
Buttercup	Hydrangea	Nightshade	(Bursting heart)
Caladium	Iris (Flag lilly)	Oaks	Sudan grass
Camellia	Irish potato	Oleander	Sweet-shrub
Castor bean	Ivy	Pansy	Staggerbush
Century plant	Jack-in-the-pulpit	Pea	Tansy
Cherry tree	Japanese plum	Peach	Tapioca
Chinaberry tree	Japanese yew	Periwinkle	Tobacco
Chinese forget-me-not	Jasmine	Peony	Tomato
Christ thorn	Jequirity bean	Pheasant's eye	Tulip
Cinnamon	Lucky bean)	Pimpernel	Tung nut tree
Clematis	Jerusalem cherry	Poinsettia	Varnish tree
Columbine	Jimpson weed	Poison berry	Wandering jew
Corncockle	Johnson grass	Poison hemlock	Water hemlock
Cowbane (Beaver poison)	Latana (Ham and eggs)	Poison ivy (oak, sumac)	Wormseed (Mexican
Crape jasmine	Larkspur	Pokeberry	tea)
Cotton	Laurels	Poppy	Yellow oleander
Crown imperial	Lilies	Potato	Yew

25-9 These plants, or parts of these plants, are highly poisonous.

tunnel under a regular seat belt because they do not have long, heavy legs to anchor them down.

2. Regular seat belts can ride up where there are no bones to protect the child's abdomen and the standard shoulder harnesses can move across the child's face or neck which is most unsafe.

3. Young children need a harness designed for their size and body proportions to protect their necks. Compared to adults, babies' neck muscles are weak and their heads are heavier in proportion to their total weight.

Protecting children's health and safety 467

For auto safety, certified (tested and approved) restraint systems should be obtained. These are required by law in some states. New ones may be purchased in many stores selling baby items or in car dealerships. In some towns and cities, adults may rent or borrow restraint systems.

Restraint systems must be installed properly to be safe and work properly. For instance, some car seats require a tether to be installed in the rear window shelf or bolted to the floor of the car. If the child often rides in more than one car, these models may present problems. Restraint systems should be approved for the model of car in which it will be used.

The child must be properly buckled into the restraint system before starting the car. Each buckle, strap, and shield is there for a purpose. The child is not protected unless the restraint is used correctly, 25-10. If a child restraint system is not being used, the sitting child must be buckled firmly with the regular seat belt. The child should be in the center back seat. (This is the safest place for a child who is not properly restrained, but *in no way* matches the safety of proper equipment.)

Older children may use a regular car restraint system. But if they are less than 55 inches tall, they should have the harness part tucked behind them. The seat belt should be buckled, however.

Adults should make sure that car doors are locked at all times. They should never allow passengers — especially children — to ride in these ways:

- With any part of the body out of an open window.
- In cargo areas of station wagons or hatchbacks.
- Kneeling on the floor board of the front seat.
- Carried in adult laps in front or back seats.
- Sharing a seat belt with another child or with an adult.

Adults should set an example of always wearing a seat belt and driving safely. They should stop the car for a while when children get tired or need attention. Travel toys and games can be used to make long trips more pleasant. (Some ideas were discussed in Chapter 24.)

Children who have always used restraint systems and have seen adults use them do not refuse to wear them. They do not know there is a choice. Children who have not used these systems must be patiently but firmly taught to stay in them. An infant or young child in no way has the ability to make a reasoned choice about their own safety. Only the adult is responsible. Restraint systems provide added safety. According to several studies, children seem better behaved in cars when restrained than not restrained. Perhaps restraint systems cause children to feel less car motion (which is tiring) and enable them to see out of windows better. Restraint systems also give less freedom to do things which result in adult correction while helping children learn correct car behavior.

Young children on foot or riding tricycles and bicycles are another traffic concern. These children are not able to see ahead or react with caution to moving traffic. Skill in traffic safety is not completely mastered until children are around eleven years old. Such a skill depends on knowing that traffic which is fun to watch can be unsafe. The skill depends on having perceptual judgments of space, speed, direction, distance, and the interaction of these perceptions. And traffic safety skill requires timing one's brain and body to react quickly and correctly. The solution to traffic problems is not in scoldings and warnings. Rather, adults must set limits for play areas, supervise children closely, model safe behavior, and teach safety. Teaching safety is discussed later in the chapter.

Baby item and toy safety. Many injuries each year are related to children's products. The number of injuries could be lowered if adults would take care in choosing baby items and toys. And, adults must realize that even safe items and toys which are misused become dangerous. Supervision and teaching safety is a must!

Selection of baby items and toys is important. Some safety features are now required by law. For instance, the slats in cribs and playpens must be placed no more than 2 3/8 inches apart. Non-toxic paints are required on baby items and toys. However, items and toys purchased prior to the law or homemade items may not meet these standards. Some new toys must carry warnings such as, "Not Intended for Children Under 3 Years of Age." And, some items such as lawn darts cannot be sold in toy departments or toy stores.

In selecting baby items and toys, adults should read labels and carefully examine items for safety features. Safety features are especially important on baby items, 25-11. Toys should be checked for durability. And adults should consider the age and level of skill of the child for whom the toy is chosen, 25-12.

Another consideration is the supervision needed for the item. For instance, can an adult supervise the use of electrical toys until the child knows how to use them properly? Can toys meant for older children be kept away from younger children or siblings?

Adults also need to think about the space needed for use and storage of equipment. For instance, is there a safe place to ride a bicycle? Is there a place to store outdoor toys when not in use? Are there places to store each toy to prevent clutter which may lead to accidents?

Baby items and toys should be checked often, too. A few things to check for are these:
- Sharp points, jagged edges, and loose small parts.
- Rust on outdoor equipment which leads to weakening of the structure.
- Stuffed toys and dolls which need to be repaired and cleaned.
- Electrical parts which need to be replaced. (This is an adult—not a child—task.)

COSCO-PETERSON

25-10 Buckling must be done correctly if a restraint system is to work.

SAFETY STANDARDS FOR BABY ITEMS

ITEM	SAFETY STANDARDS
Baby vehicle (carriage or stroller)	Should be pre-tested for balance and weight distribution. Safety brake can be quickly set. Protective bumpers should pad.
Car seats	Must be listed as meeting Federal Motor Vehicle Standard #213. Should be tested for strength and performance in crashes. Proper installation is needed. (Some car seat models do not fit some cars.)
Crib	Slats no more than 2 3/8 in. (6 cm) apart. Height of crib side from bottom of mattress to top of railing no less than 26 in. (65 cm). Child has outgrown crib when side rail is less than three-fourths of child's height. Children 35 in. (87.5 cm) and taller must be removed from portable cribs. Latch-on drop side(s) should be releasable only on outside and require a double kick. (This prevents young children and large dogs from tripping latch.) Crib side(s) should lock at maximum height. Paints used on cribs should be lead free. Teething rails are desirable. No horizontal bars inside, because these can be used for climbing. Once babies can stand, bumper pads should be removed. Bumper pads are not recommended until babies can raise their heads. Bumper pads with six or more ties are the safest.
Crib mattress	When rail is in lowest position, the top of the mattress support and the top of the rail should be no less than 9 in. (22.5 cm) for standard crib and 5 in. (12.5 cm) for portable crib. Mattress should be covered with durable plastic that has air vents. Torn mattress covers should be discarded. Mattress should fit snugly in crib. (Space between crib and mattress should be smaller than two adult fingers held together.)
High chair	Wide-spread legs improve stability. Tray should lock in place. Crotch snap and wrap-around seat straps are needed. Non-skid rubber mats (available for bath tubs) placed on seat helps prevent baby from sliding.
Playpen	Slats should be no more than 2 3/8 in. (6 cm) apart. If mesh netting is used, the weave should be smaller than tiny baby buttons and pierced earrings. Floor should not collapse. Hinges on folding models should lock tightly.
Vaporizer	Has Underwriters' Laboratories (UL) seal. Cold water models are safer than steam models.
Walker	Round based ones are less likely to tip. Legs on other models should be wide-spread to help prevent tipping. Bumpers on walkers protect furniture.

25-11 Safety features of baby items should be of major concern.

Adults can add a few safety devices to baby items and toys, too. For instance, if a toy chest is not properly ventilated, a few air holes can be drilled. A piece of adhesive tape can be placed around each wheel edge of skates. This slows the wheels down. The tape will be worn off by the time the child is a skillful skater. To remind children not to hold the chains of a swing too low (and thus be thrown off balance), mark with paint or tape the proper holding place.

Pet safety. Because pets can bite, transmit diseases, and cause allergic responses, pets must be chosen carefully. Adults should choose

SAFE TOYS FOR INFANTS, TODDLERS, AND OLDER CHILDREN

SAFETY FEATURE	WHAT TO LOOK FOR
For Infants and Toddlers	
Large size—larger than the child's two fists.	Even large toys can break exposing small parts such as squeakers on squeeze toys. The law bans small parts in new toys intended for children under age three. Toys made before the law and homemade toys may still have small parts.
Non-breakable.	Toys that break may expose small parts or may break into small pieces. Toys made of glass or brittle plastic are the most unsafe.
Has no sharp edges or points.	The law bans new toys with sharp edges or points intended for children under age eight. Broken toys often have sharp edges. Wires with sharp points are often inside stuffed toys.
Non-toxic.	Painted toys should be labeled non-toxic. It is best to avoid all painted toys for children who put playthings in their mouths.
No long cords or strings.	Toys with long strings or cords (such as toy telephones, pull toys, cords used for bead stringing, and long cords used to hang toys from crib or playyard) should not be used with infants and young children who can get them wrapped around their neck.
Non-flammable, flame-retardant, or flame-resistant.	Dolls and stuffed toys should be made of materials not likely to ignite.
Made of washable and hygenic materials.	Dolls and stuffed toys must be clean when bought and must be easy to keep clean.
For Older Children	
Safe electric toys.	Electric toys must meet requirements for maximum (at the most) surface temperatures, electrical wiring, and display of warning labels. Electrical toys which heat are intended for children over age eight.
Noise at acceptable levels.	The law requires a label on toys that produce a noise above a certain level. The label warns: "Do not fire closer than one foot to the ear. Do not use indoors." Toys making sounds which can result in ear damage are banned.
Items used for age intended.	Chemistry sets, hobby sets, balloons, and games and toys with small parts are extremely dangerous if misused or left within the reach of younger children.
Sturdy, safe large equipment.	Space between moving parts is wide enough not to pinch or crush fingers. Bolt ends should be covered with plastic end caps. Swing seats should be lightweight and have smooth rolled edges. All swing sets, gyms, and other large equipment should be anchored firmly to the ground.
Safe tricycles and bicycles.	Tricycles and bicycles should have proper assembly. Seats should be adjusted to rider's height. pedals should have skid resistant surfaces. Reflectors—at least 2 inches (5 cm) in diameter—should be used on bicycles.

25-12 Special safety features should be noted in selecting toys for infants, toddlers, and older children.

Protecting children's health and safety 471

animals or breeds of animals that are less apt to bite. Dogs who are one year and older and cats who are nine months and older have developed immunity to many diseases. These animals make better children's pets than puppies and kittens. If a child shows an allergy to the pet, the animal must be kept away from the child.

KINDERGARD

25-13 Safety devices help protect children from many dangers.

Pets should be seen on a regular basis by a *veterinarian* (animal doctor). The veterinarian will advise on regular care of the animals. A sick pet should be examined at once.

Children should be taught how to treat a pet. Adults should not expect young children to care for a pet. Children in the lower elementary grades can take *some* pet care duties if taught. Adults must also remind children to wash their hands each time after handling a pet.

Using safety devices and taking safety measures

To help prevent possible accidents, adults must be a step ahead of children. Adults cannot wait until they see a child open a door or climb on a chair. Behind the first opened door or the shelf reached with the help of a chair, danger may be present. Adults should never rely on norms or past experiences to tell them when to childproof. One child develops before another even within the same family. Some children explore more than others.

To prevent accidents or make them less serious, safety devices are needed. These include electrical outlet covers, safety latches on cabinets and drawers which can only be released by adult hand pressure, and safety knobs which fit over standard knobs but require adult grip for opening. See 25-13. These devices are helpful but do not take the place of careful watching of children. Fire and smoke detectors need to be installed. And fire extinguishers must be ready for use.

Adults need to keep emergency phone numbers updated and quickly available. See 25-14. First-aid supplies, including a first aid chart or book, should be kept current and nearby as well. See 25-15. Training in first aid is most helpful. (Some states require day care centers to have a staff member on duty at all times who has the American Red Cross Standard First Aid Certificate or its equivalent.)

Teaching safety

Teaching safety is an ongoing process which begins almost at birth and continues for life.

EMERGENCY PHONE NUMBERS

Local emergency number
(if you have one): *555-1234*

Ambulance: *555-7890*

Dentist: *555-6543*

Doctor: *555-7654*

Drugstore: *555-8901*

Fire department: *555-4321*

Hospital: *555-5678*

Neighbors (two nearest)

Name: *Mrs. Rodriguez: 555-3345*

Name: *Mr. Peterson: 555-6767*

Police department: *555-8091*

Poison control center
(if one is nearby): *555-9001*

Relatives

Name: *Grace Brock (Grandma): 555-2323*

Name: *Mr. and Mrs. Mason (Uncle Dave and Aunt Sarah): 555-8776*

Taxi: *555-3645*

25-14 Posting the correct emergency telephone numbers for your area near the telephone saves needed minutes in a crisis.

FIRST AID ITEMS

Adhesive bandages (various sizes).

Adhesive tape.

Antiseptic for cuts and scratches.

Calamine lotion (for insect bites).

Gauze bandages and squares.

Scissors.

Syrup of ipecac (given to induce vomiting for *some but not all* poisonings).

First aid chart or book (for quick reference).

25-15 Minor mishaps can be treated with a few first aid supplies.

Protecting children's health and safety 473

The first lessons occur in the home and yard and expand to include one's total environment such as school safety, water safety, traffic safety, and job safety.

Adults are models for the child. A child will absorb the adult's approach to everyday actions—even safety measures such as buckling car safety belts and looking before crossing streets. Imagine what a child is learning if pulled in haste across a street before oncoming traffic! Adults may even exaggerate behavior to make a model clearer. For instance, they may stop, look, and say, "I don't see a car coming," before walking across a street.

Adults should carefully explain the boundaries of play. Children must be shown as well as told what they can and cannot do.

Warnings are only helpful if they are stated in positive ways. For instance, an adult may say, "Grass is for playing and streets are for cars and trucks." Negatively stated warnings may tempt the child to do something that is unsafe. Also, overly repeated warnings lose their meanings.

All warnings should be coupled with reasons, or the child may think that a given action is all right if the adult is not watching. For instance, adults should explain the importance of safety devices such as seat belts, crash helmets, and life jackets. They should also explain how to use the devices properly, 25-16.

Adults need to insist on obedience. Children want and need to be protected. Parents require obedience when they take action against wrong rather than threatening children. Taking action does not necessarily mean physical punishment. It can mean requiring the child to stay in the bedroom or come inside for a short time. Insisting on obedience is a way of saying, "I care about you."

Adults should practice safety measures with children. These might include a fire drill or a

25-16 Using safety devices makes a person's life safer and more fun.

safe walk to school. Adults can also read books or stories on safety to children. Or they can watch special segments on safety in children's television programs. They can follow up by having children talk about, act out, or draw the safety actions.

PREPARING A CHILD FOR ROUTINE AND HOSPITAL CARE

Medical care is a part of most children's lives either on a routine basis or when problems arise. Going to the doctor or dentist can be a stress-filled situation for both child and adult. There are ways to ease the stress.

Preparing children for routine care

Adults should realize that children react in different ways depending on their age. Children under two years of age often cry and scream while being examined. (They may begin crying when undressed and placed on cold scales.) Two- and three-year-olds often cry. But they may also hide from or kick and push the doctor. (Hiding or kicking and pushing is an attempt to get rid of those who are checking or treating them.) Older children are better able to understand what going to the doctor means. These children are apt to become anxious ahead of time. They become more anxious as time approaches such as in the car or walking in the office. They often react by crying or kicking during routines which are not comfortable such as throat cultures and injections. Many children are more relaxed about procedures which are not seen as painful. Following the visit, older children may react in a rather bossy way. This may be done to reduce feelings of powerlessness that they felt during the visit.

Adults can lessen some of the stress of routine care in several ways. First, they can select a doctor or dentist with care. Belief in the doctor or dentist as capable and caring is most important. Adults should also feel free to ask questions of the doctor and dentist and feel these questions are being answered completely and clearly. The doctor and dentist should appeal to the child, too. Children often like physicians and dentists who greet them in a friendly way and by name. They also like caregivers who notice something personal such as a child's new hair cut or pretty dress. Talking to the child during the check-up and remaining calm even if the child doesn't are other qualities that children like. Children also like waiting rooms and examination rooms which are appealing to them. See 25-17.

When going to appointments, adults should take along books, toys, and clothing changes (if necessary) in case there is a wait. They should ask before giving a child candy or gum which changes color of mouth and throat. This may make *diagnosis* (identifying the disease) more difficult. Some physicians give treats after the examination. Adults should also be prepared with information and questions to save time.

If a child feels sick, adults can reassure the child that it is all right to feel sick. Pain or other sick feelings or reactions are very frightening to a child. Adults can also explain just a little about procedures and relate them as much as possible to everyday life. They may use such phrases as, "x-rays are pictures," and, "the dentist will look at your teeth." Too many

JOHN SHAW

25-17 Waiting rooms which appeal to the child make medical care less stressful.

explanations can add to fear such as, "They'll use *a large machine* to make x-rays."

During the actual examination, these practices with young children are best:

- Stay with the child and be in view. (Dentists usually prefer that the adult stay in waiting room.)
- Use a soft, soothing voice. A child may stop crying to hear an almost whisper.
- Hold the child if the physician requests.
- Do not say, "It will not hurt." Some procedures do hurt. Just tell the child, "It will be all right," or "Soon it will be over." If child cries, reassure child that crying is all right by saying something such as "I know this hurts, but it will stop hurting after awhile."
- Do not distract a baby or child by making noises of any kind such as clucking noises or jingling keys. Such sounds interfere with physicians ability to hear internal sounds. Some babies and children cry louder, too, when the adult tries to district. (Perhaps they feel that the reason for the distraction is that the procedure will be painful.)

Above all, children should never be threatened with a doctor's visit or shot. These threats add to anxiety of a child during a visit. They are also meaningless because shots or other procedures are never given as punishment. Such threats are not fair to the child or to medical caregivers.

Preparing children for hospital care

Hospital care is often a special problem to both parents and child. Hospitals may be seen as a place where people experience separation from loved ones, pain, and even death. Hospitals also may seem large and impersonal (not concerned about the child as a person). Parents tend to feel that they are no longer in charge of the care of their child in hospitals. And they are often asked to assist when painful tests and treatments are given such as an IV (intravenous treatment). To help those causing pain and fear in a young child can be almost unbearable.

Parents or other adults may also feel guilty about the cause for needed hospital care. They may feel that they could have prevented a fall if they had been watching more carefully. Or they may think, "I should have known that cough was bad."

Children also may fear *hospitalization* (being cared for in a hospital). Children from one to four years of age often fear separation from parents. Older children are concerned about what will be done to their bodies. Children react to actual tests and treatments in ways similar to reactions in an office visit. But hospital reactions can be more intense. This is because new people are caring for the child. Also, more frequent, unfamiliar, and probably more painful tests and procedures are used. Hospital stays are longer than office visits. And surroundings in hospitals are unfamiliar. Some children may think of hospital care as punishment.

There are several ways to ease the stress of hospital care for parent and child. Adults should start by finding out as much as possible about the stay. Then they will be better prepared to help the child. If possible, they should tell the child about the stay ahead of time. Good points (such as the child will feel better) should be the focus of the talk. But adults should never say, "It won't hurt." The child will feel that adults can be trusted when they are honest.

A doctor's kit and some books may help children solve some of their fears. See 25-18. Some hospitals have playrooms where children can act out hospital care. (The rooms also provide for art activities, games, and reading.)

A child should be given a tour of the children's area of the hospital or other areas where the child will be. The main nurse or aide to care for the child should take the child on the tour if possible. Children need to develop friendships with those they'll be seeing most often. See 25-19. In these ways, hospitals become less strange.

Parents should plan to room in with babies and young children when possible. Many hospitals help parents by providing a bed or reclining chair, food service, phone, TV, and magazines. Members of service groups may help parents by doing such things as serving snacks throughout the day, shopping for small purchases, and lending books or magazines. They may also give little surprises to children

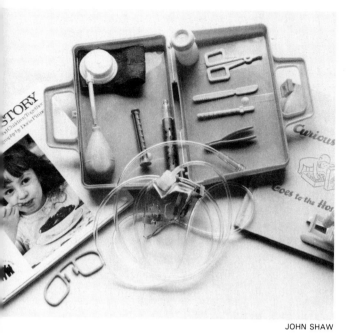

25-18 Play medical kits and books about hospitals may lessen children's fears.

JOHN SHAW

such as a book or toy. Or they may volunteer to sit with the child for a while so the parent can take a break.

While in the hospital, parents can help care for non-medical needs such as feeding, bathing, and toileting. They should go with the child for tests and treatment when permitted. In some hospitals, parents go with the child to surgery and stay with the child until the child is unconscious. Parents may also be present in the recovery room as the child awakens.

Children need things to remind them of home and make them feel comforted during their stay. See 25-20. Adults should bring some of the child's own toys, pajamas, or other items to the hospital. They should check on what types of items the hospital allows to be brought from home. If the child can have visitors or phone calls, adults can arrange for friends, important adults, and siblings to stay in contact.

Older children may want to have a scrapbook or box to help them remember their stay. The book or box might include pictures, hospital bracelets, covers to disposable thermometers,

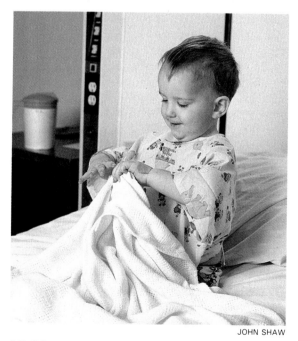

JOHN SHAW

25-19 A warm feeling between a child and a nurse makes hospital care less stressful.

UPJOHN HEALTHCARE SERVICES

25-20 Having items from home can make a hospital stay more comfortable.

Protecting children's health and safety 477

and syringes without needles. Children can use hospital items to show and tell others about their hospital stay. Talking about a hospital stay, like talking about any other experience, is good for children.

CARING FOR AN ILL OR INJURED CHILD

Parents and other adults who work with children need to care for ill or injured children at some time. See 25-21. Children experience many scrapes as they learn what their bodies can and cannot do. Young children, especially those under seven or eight years of age, have many common illnesses such as colds and digestive upsets. Adults often handle such small problems. But physicians also expect adults to follow through with care for more complex problems.

There are several common conditions which adults must frequently treat in children. Practices often recommended by doctors are shown in 25-22. A current first aid chart or book

25-21 If adults know some simple first aid steps, many minor accidents can be treated at home.

should be used to give *first aid* (aid before getting medical help) for major inuries. Some first aid procedures are shown in Appendix A.

For many illnesses, adults are expected to give medications. Accurate measuring devices should be used. See 25-23. For instance, a medically defined teaspoon contains exactly 5cc of liquid, but a household teaspoon varies from 1/2 teaspoon (2.5 cc) to 1 1/2 teaspoons (7.5 cc) of liquid. The amount of liquid given may also depend on who pours the medicine. Incorrect dosages may result in infections that do not clear up (from too little medicine) or in being poisoned (from too much medicine).

Methods of giving medicines can be a problem, too. Babies may suck medicine through a nursing nipple with ring attached. Or they take medicine from a syringe (no needle) inserted far back at the side of the mouth. Medical measuring devices are often used for giving medicines to older children. (The same device is used for measuring and giving medicines.) Before children can swallow tablets, they can be crushed (and mixed with sugar or a bite of food if bitter) and taken from a spoon. An older child can learn to swallow a tablet by tipping the head back. This action causes the tablet to sink in back of throat. Children can also learn to swallow a capsule by bending forward. This causes the light weight capsule to float toward back of throat.

Keeping an active child in bed is a challenge to most parents. As children begin to recover, they often do not want to stay in bed. Quiet games, books, television, records or tapes, paper and pencil or crayons, help children pass the time. Visits from adults (and other children if the illness is not contagious) are also helpful.

When children are ill or injured, they need a little extra attention. Babies and young children often need lots of holding and rocking. Older children may need lots of explanations about their illness or injury and the treatment. Most children enjoy little surprises, too. These might include a little gift, a special dish if food is all right, new bed clothing, or a get well card. Above all, adults should appear cheerful and confident, because anxious parents can cause a child to worry.

PROBLEM	PROCEDURE RECOMMENDED BY DOCTORS
Diarrhea (watery stools)	Dilute milk or formula. Give child electrolyte solutions such as *Pedialyte* or a sugar-water mixture. The first solids given are ripe mashed banana, scrapped apple, and rice cereal. Return to regular diet after 24 hours of normal stools. Call physician if other symptoms appear or if diarrhea does not cease in 24 hours.
Fever—temperature above normal—98.6 °F (37 °C) oral, 99.6 °F (37.5 °C) rectal, 97.6 °F (36 °C) axillary (in the armpit)	Keep child cool with minimum clothing and coverings but do not let child shiver. (Shivering increases temperature.) Give the child cool fluids—the more the better. Give fever reducing drugs as prescribed by the doctor. Sponge bathe by wiping the back, arms, and legs of the child in lukewarm water or equal parts of water and rubbing alcohol. Call physician if fever is high, if other symptoms appear, or if the fever remains (even if mild) after three days.
Runny nose	Use a nasal aspirator (a rubber syringe) and suck mucus out of nose. Place salt-water drops made by combining 1/4 teaspoon (1 mL) salt in four ounces (118 mL) of water in the nose five times per day. Using the drops causes sneezing and clears the passages. Use a cool air humidifier in the child's bedroom. Call the doctor if other symptoms appear.
Scrapes and scratches	Wash with soap and water and rinse well. If desired, apply an antiseptic made for scrapes or cuts. Cover with an adhesive strip bandage or a small piece of gauze held with adhesive tape if the wound is in an area open to dirt or further injury. Consult the doctor if the wound is deep or puncture-like or if the wound does not heal as it should.
Vomiting (does not include spitting up a little breast milk or formula)	Do not feed or even give water for four hours after the last time the child vomited. After four hours offer one ounce (29.5 mL) fluid (except milk) and repeat every four hours. If there is no more vomiting, feed simple foods for the next 48 hours such as crackers, gelatin, broth, rice, and applesauce but no milk or milk products. Call the doctor if other symptoms appear or if vomiting does not cease after four hours.

25-22 Doctors often expect adults to care for these health problems.

CARING FOR A TERMINALLY ILL CHILD

Despite great advances in treatments, medical science cannot cure every illness. Among those who are *terminally ill* (people who have diseases which will result in their deaths) are children. Terminal illness in children include some birth defects such as heart and liver diseases and cystic fibrosis. Other diseases such as AIDS and various types of cancer are also terminal illnesses.

Helping a family who is facing the death of a family member, especially a child, is one of the most profound emotional experiences

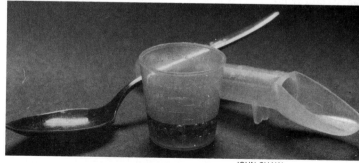
JOHN SHAW

25-23 Medical measuring devices which can be purchased should always be used when giving liquid medicines.

anyone will ever encounter. Often the child's family feels this period more keenly than the ill child. They already feel a sense of loss that the death will bring and they show this by going through the stages of coping with death. Families show denial—"the doctors are wrong." They may try bargaining with God—"Just let my child live, and I will . . ." Families will then feel depression, thinking about the loss and its impact, and finally acceptance. On the other hand, the family wants to appear cheerful for the ill child's sake or for the sake of others and tries to remain hopeful.

Family members need the help of professionals during this time of crisis. Many hospitals which treat terminally ill children have a group of professionals (medical professionals, religious leaders, and social workers) who provide help to the family in both team and individual efforts. Parent support groups for many illnesses are also available and members often provide much comfort because they have gone through or are going through the same problems.

Besides trying to cope with their own feelings, families must help and seek help for the ill child. How a child perceives his or her condition depends to a great extent upon his or her age. Children begin to understand death in the preschool years, but their understandings are rather limited until school age. What and how much to tell a child is a personal decision best made after the family discusses the child's case with professionals and among themselves.

Parents need to be aware of children's feelings and needs to understand their own illnesses. Older children often realize what may happen. They may be fearful of possible tests and treatments, of the separation that death brings, and of being left alone. Ill children are likely to be concerned about their parents' feelings of loss. Ill children need to be allowed to do all they can physically tolerate and to do as much as possible for themselves.

Friends are needed at this time, too. Friends should become informed as much as possible on the disease and its treatments in order that they better understand what they are told. The role of friends can best be described as a listening rather than an advising one. Certainly friends should express their concern and sorrow, but they should carefully think through their words. For example, saying, "I understand how you feel" may cause a hurt response such as "How could you? Your child is healthy!"

If possible, friends should offer their help. They should think through the family's needs and then suggest a concrete way they can help. For instance, a friend may offer, "Let me cook your dinner tonight" or "I can take Cindy (the family's well child) to her ballet lesson." Such offers are more easily accepted than the rather vague offer of help, "Let me know if there is anything I can do." Most of all, friends need to remember that they'll be needed in the weeks and months after the loss.

to Know

active immunity . . . antibodies . . . antigen . . . childproofing . . . contagious disease . . . dental caries . . . diagnosis . . . hospitalization . . . immunity . . . immunization . . . inoculation . . . orthodontist . . . passive immunity . . . restraint system . . . symptoms . . . terminally ill . . . vaccination

to Review

Write your answers on a separate sheet of paper.
1. True or false. Good nutrition serves as a physical support when accident or injury occurs.
2. What are the two best ways that adults can prevent accidents?
    a. Warn or threaten the child.
    b. Create a safe environment.

c. Prevent the child from doing dangerous things such as keeping all objects out of the child's mouth.

d. Let the child learn from experience. (For instance, a child who touches a stove will learn that it is hot.)

e. Teach safety.

f. Remove all unsafe items from home and yard.

3. True or false. The type of accidents common to children change with the child's age.

4. Why does the time of day affect the number of accidents in children?

5. Children under the age of five years account for what percent of all accidents?

a. 10.

b. 25.

c. 50.

d. 75.

e. 85.

6. True or false. Plant poisonings are more difficult to detect than household poisonings.

7. Which of the following is the number one cause of death for infants and children?

a. Plant poisonings.

b. Household poisonings.

c. Household falls such as on stairs.

d. Traffic-related accidents.

e. Diseases.

8. Explain why holding a baby or young child on your lap in a car or sharing your seat belt is unsafe for the child.

9. List four ways an adult can lessen the stress of medical care for a child.

10. Give three reasons why hospitals are stressful for parents.

11. True or false. Teaspoons from household flatware are suitable for measuring liquid medicines.

12. List two guidelines for helping the family of a terminally ill child.

to Do

1. Select a safety book suitable for children ages three to five. Read the book to a child or a small group of children. Do a short follow-up lesson by having the children dramatize a safety practice, draw a safety practice, or do another activity.

2. Go on a shopping trip to purchase the latest inexpensive safety devices or write companies for brochures on their devices. Give a demonstration on how each device works. (Parents of young children could be invited.)

3. If your home economics department has a child development laboratory or if your local school has a kindergarten or pre-kindergarten program, check the toys and outdoor equipment for safety. Make suggestions for discarding, repairing, or recycling (such as using the tires of a broken truck for sand play).

4. Borrow or purchase a few toys often used with children under three years of age. Examine the toys for safety features. Is there anything about the toys that appears to be unsafe?

5. Interview in your classroom a state highway patrol officer or local city police officer concerning restraint systems for children. Some of the questions you might ask are:

a. What are the statistics on traffic injuries to infants and young children in your state or city?

b. What percentage of adults wear safety restraint devices?

c. Why are restraint devices important?

d. What are the local laws regarding the use of restraint systems for children? For adults? (The person to be interviewed should have a list of questions in advance.)

6. Select a way to prevent an accident that can be illustrated on a poster. (Check to prevent duplicate ideas.) Display the posters in the classrooms.

7. Ask a local hospital administrator to take your class on a tour of the children's section of the hospital.

8. Take one or two rooms of your home and list ways to childproof them.

9. Make a list of emergency telephone numbers for your own home. Place a list near each telephone. (Use Chart 25-14 as a guide for the numbers needed.)

10. Invite a support team from a hospital to discuss how they help families cope with the death of children.

Good group settings can enhance physical,
mental, and social-emotional growth.

26

Fostering development in group settings

After studying this chapter, you will be able to:
- ☐ Trace the roots of the major types of group programs for young children.
- ☐ Describe what to look for when choosing a quality program.
- ☐ Discuss the effects of group care on children's development.

Programs for young children have not always been common. Today, the picture has changed. Not only do programs for young children exist, but they do so in great numbers.

Programs for young children have been affected by the way the young child has been seen. Until the middle 1800s, children were seen as miniature adults — adults in every way except size. When children were able to feed and dress themselves and take care of their toileting needs, they began to work at adult tasks. Even child labor laws did not exist.

Not all adults agreed that children were miniature adults. For the most part, these adults were thought of as radicals. Their idea — that young children were living things that need special care — was met with doubt and even scorn. A few early childhood programs based on these ideas began to appear, however.

Not until the 1890s did researchers begin to find facts to support the idea that children were indeed not miniature adults. Many studies of children's development were done. And, educators began to adopt program practices which would support and improve the development of children.

In the last three decades there has been great growth of group programs for young children.

This growth is due to many factors. One factor is growing concern about the lack of quality education for children and youth. Another is knowledge of the harmful effects of poverty. The growing numbers of mothers in the work force have brought about a need for more programs. And the reports of good effects group programs have on young children have been yet another factor. The numbers of young children enrolled in group settings has grown. But the types of group settings available today have also grown. There has been a trend towards programs for younger children which now includes infant/toddler programs. There is also a trend toward reaching children with special needs — young children who are gifted or handicapped.

TYPES OF GROUP PROGRAMS

Group programs for young children vary greatly. See 26-1. Because there are such wide differences in programs, even those having the same name, they may vary from the descriptions in this book.

Day care programs

The term *day care* often refers to programs that operate for extended hours (often nine to 12 hours). These programs offer services for children from babies to preschool age. They may even serve school-age children for after-school hours and during school holidays.

Day care programs are perhaps the oldest type of group programs for young children. In Europe in the late 1700s and early 1800s, day care programs were called *Infant Schools*. In spite of the name, these programs served poor children from the toddler years until the children were five or six years of age and able to enter the work force. By the mid-1800s, day care for children of the poor was found in urban areas in the United States. Many of these day care programs also had parent programs in which home and child care was taught. Federal funds were used to aid day care programs during the Depression and World War II. After World War II, day care programs declined until the 1960s. At this time, women entered the work force in great numbers. Some educators today are fearful that there will not be enough quality day care programs available for children by the 1990s given today's trend of working mothers.

As you read in Chapter 2, there are three types of day care — in-home care, family day care, and group day care. Each type has its merits and drawbacks. Most day-care programs are for-profit, privately owned programs. They may be owned by individuals or family corporations. A few for-profit day care programs have grown into large chains. Other day-care programs are not-for-profit programs. These may be funded by parents' groups as cooperatives, by religious and service groups such as churches, and by businesses for employees such as colleges, industries, hospitals, and all branches of the armed services. Business funded programs are often called *work-related day care programs.*

26-1 Group programs vary from those which only care for basic needs to those which provide reading and other activities to enhance development.

Kindergartens

Kindergartens are publicly and privately operated programs for four- and five-year-old children. In the United States, kindergartens are part of the public education system in every state. As part of the public education system, kindergartens serve as an entrance to school education.

Kindergartens were founded as private programs in Germany. The programs enrolled children from ages three through seven years and provided teaching suggestions for mothers who had younger children. The word kindergarten means "children's garden." The name kindergarten was chosen by Friedrich Froebel, the founder, who thought of young children as tender plants rather than as miniature adults. Froebel felt that a school for young children should be different from a school for older children. See 26-2. He planned many children's activities which we still see in kindergartens as well as other programs for young children. Some examples include block building, bead stringing, art work, sand play, math work, study of animals and plants, *finger plays* (poems and rhymes which were acted out with the hands), stories, and music. These activities were far from the drill methods used in other schools of Froebel's time. In fact, Froebel's statement that "play is the highest level of child development" was held in scorn by many of his time.

26-2 Kindergartens allow more time for play and creativity than school for older children.

JOHN SHAW

Kindergartens came to the United States with the German immigrants in the mid-1800s. Soon English-speaking groups began to adopt the kindergartens. Because so many people began to see the good effects of kindergarten programs on the lives of young children, public schools began to include them as part of public education.

Over the years, kindergartens have changed some in keeping with the needs of children. See 26-3. In the past few years, there has been concern that too much stress is being caused in children by efforts to teach reading and other abstract learnings. The challenge of kindergartens is to fit the needs of children today and lead slowly toward children's next years in school.

Nursery schools

Nursery school is the term which applies to an educational program (not just physical care) planned for children ages two, three, and four. Most nursery schools are privately owned, but a few are in public schools.

Nursery schools were developed in England in the early 1900s. They were designed to help meet the needs of two- to five-year-old children that could not be met by families living in slums. Nursery schools came to the United States at the same time child development was becoming a science. They opened as laboratory schools directed by staff of research and teaching hospitals and colleges. The purposes of the schools were to study children and to train mothers and teachers in caring for and teaching young children.

The program activities of the nursery school are planned to build on life within the family. Thus, most activities are first-hand experiences. There is much play in a setting rich with materials, equipment, other children, and loving and well-trained adults. See 26-4.

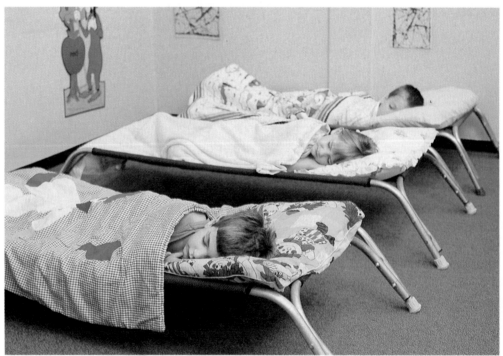

JOHN SHAW

26-3 Kindergarten children have special needs that should be met.

Today some nursery schools are still operated for child study and for career training. These laboratory nursery schools are found in colleges, universities, and some high schools across the nation. However more nursery schools are owned by individuals. Some of these nursery schools have programs very much like those offered in laboratory settings. Others are only called nursery schools while their only concern is to meet the physical needs of the child.

Montessori schools

Montessori schools, named for their founder, Maria Montessori, opened in Rome, Italy, in the early 1900s. Montessori was a medical doctor who had worked with mentally handicapped children. Her success with these exceptional children was so great that she was asked to plan an all-day program for slum children between the ages of two and one-half and seven years. She named her school the *Casa dei Bambini* which means "children's house."

Montessori believed that children are different from adults and that they differ from each other. She also felt that children can absorb and learn from their world as they work at tasks. (Montessori did not like Froebel's ideas about the child's need for play. She said that the child works for work's sake and not to complete a task as does the adult.)

The Montessori classroom is made up of a mix of children from a three-year age span. Children within this span are not separated by grade. Children are free to move about the

26-4 Nursery schools offer many rich play activities.

JOHN SHAW

classroom at will, to work with other children, and to use any materials they understand. See 26-5. Teachers guide the children's use of materials. But they do not teach in the sense of telling children what is right. In this way, Montessori schools strive to make each child more in charge of their own learnings.

Activities center on sensory learnings as children learn to see, hear, touch, taste, and smell the world around them. Daily living activities such as preparing food, ironing, and washing hands are also a major part of the program. Language and many other activities are part of the program, too.

Head Start

In the 1960s, Americans became concerned with the effects of poverty in America. Studies showed how important the early years were to the child's development. *Head Start* was launched in 1965 as a federal program for children from families with low incomes. These children seemed to need more than they were getting from their homes—more food, medical care, and learning help. At first Head Start was much like other programs for young children from middle-class families. Soon new program activities and new ways to teach were planned with these children in mind.

Parents and families are an important part of planning and operating local Head Start programs. Community involvement is also important. Although activities are designed to strengthen learning, they are also designed to meet some special needs of low income children. Activities help children build self-esteem. They focus on helping children and their families work together to solve problems. And they often relate to the child's ethnic background and culture, 26-6.

CHOOSING A GROUP PROGRAM

An early childhood program must be chosen with care. Finding the right program for a child is a major task that should never be taken

AMERICAN MONTESSORI SOCIETY

26-5 Children in Montessori schools are free to work on their own or in groups as they want.

488

CAROL J. PARKER/SACUS

26-6 Children in Head Start programs are encouraged to be proud of their cultural heritage.

lightly. Programs should be chosen in keeping with the needs of each family. Because needs of families differ, a given program may or may not meet those needs. Although there should be a special match between family and program, a few basic guidelines should be considered by all families who are choosing a group program for their young children.

Regulations

Regulations are standards that govern a group program. Regulations cover housing, equipment, staff, services of the program (children's activities, feeding), and business operations (funding, taxes, insurance). Some regulations, such as fire safety, apply to all programs. Some regulations apply only to *private programs*—programs owned by individuals, churches, or other non-government groups. Others apply only to *public programs*—programs funded by federal or state monies such as public schools and Head Start.

Children should only attend programs that meet the regulations. However, three points need to be made clear about regulations. First, regulations are minimum standards. You can compare this idea to passing a test. Some pass with very high grades, others barely pass, and many others are between these two groups. Child programs may meet the regulations and be of rather low quality.

Second, some regulations are easier to check than are others. For instance, if a fence is required around the outside play area, this is very easy to check. On the other hand, a warm and loving staff is much harder to check.

Finally, some regulations are simply on record with little or no enforcement. For instance, there are many regulations that cover family day care. But homes are seldom checked by officials to see if all regulations are met. The main reason that regulations are not enforced is because there are not enough people in state and city offices to check all programs.

Housing and equipment

The type of housing and equipment varies with the program's goals. However, the housing should be healthy and safe. There should be enough space for comfort and activities. Furniture, equipment, and materials should be of the proper size and meet the needs of the children in the program. See 26-7. The housing and equipment should convey the idea, "It's nice here!"

Staff

Young children have so many needs that they must be housed in small groups with enough adults. Regulations that govern a given program state the maximum number of children who may be housed as one group and the number of adults who must be on duty at all times. The numbers of children who can be housed as one group are often between five and eight infants, 12 and 16 two- and three-year-olds, and 16 and 22 four- and five-year-olds. One teacher and one other adult is required for each of these small groups. Other staff are required for preparing meals, cleaning, and special duties.

Children need adults who are in good physical and mental health. Children also need adults who give them a sense of security. Children need to feel loved and wanted. The child must *feel* loved, not just be loved. To feel loved, children must know that what they do matters to others. They need to have others hug them,

26-7 Housing and equipment in a good program provide plenty of space, neat, cheery surroundings, and activities suited to a person's development.

comfort them, and listen to and talk with them. Children even need adults to say no or scold them when needed. See 26-8.

Adults must also provide guidance for children in their care. Children need adults who can help their development during these early years of their lives. In order to meet children's needs at different stages of development, adults need to apply what is known about children's development. For instance, adults who care for infants must cuddle and accept dependent babies. Adults who work with toddlers must encourage them to explore and learn while being ever mindful of their safety. And, adults who serve preschool children must welcome children's curiosity, questions, and energy.

Staff members should also work well with adults. For instance, staff members must work well with each other. And, staff members and parents must really talk and share for the sake of each child.

Program activities

Program activities vary with the goals of a given early childhood program. Generally, a good program helps children grow in all areas and builds confidence. It gives children the feeling that they can do things for themselves.

Good programs use day-to-day routines as a way of helping children learn. For instance, in good programs, eating is more than curbing hunger. Snacks and meals offer a time to learn about foods and styles of eating. They also offer the chance to just talk with others, 26-9. Self-care is also part of daily routines. Children want to become independent by learning to take care of themselves. Many programs encourage self-help skills.

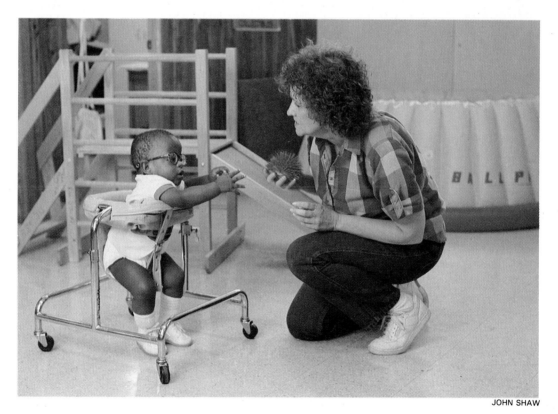

JOHN SHAW

26-8 Staff members must care deeply for the children they teach.

26-9 Snack time is a time for sharing with others.

Special activities are often planned, too, as ways to help children develop. These program activities often include:

- Language learnings. Language skills are improved by talking, listening, and looking at good books.
- Math learnings. Math skills are developed by such activities as counting, matching shapes in puzzles, and seeing who is taller.
- Social learnings. Social learnings are many as children try new roles and help each other. See 26-10. Celebrating holidays and birthdays are fun social events, too.
- Science learnings. Learning about living and non-living worlds is most exciting for young children. Children learn through activities with pets, plants, cooking, and others, 26-11.
- Creative fun. Children enjoy expressing themselves through art, dramatic play, and music.

- Motor skills. Gross-motor skills are developed through active play, especially outdoor play. Fine-motor skills are improved as children play with general materials (art materials, puzzles, and building materials) as well as materials designed for the purpose of helping fine-motor skills.

Many good programs make use of people who are not on their staff and of nearby places as a way to help children learn. Many people in the community (which includes parents!) are often willing to share their careers or personal skills with children. And, when a parent shares skills, both the child's and parent's self-concepts are given a boost. Many communities have places and events which are most helpful to children. *Field trips*—taking children to places off of the program's property—can be used to provide first-hand learnings, 26-12.

Other considerations

Some families have needs that can better be met in programs having some special services. These might include transportation to and from the program, extended hours, or programs for exceptional children. See 26-13. Programs with

26-10 As children help each other, they learn important ways to say, "I care about you."

26-11 Learning about substances such as water is fun and exciting.

26-12 Children always enjoy field trips.

special services are not always found in some communities or are not conveniently located. If several families have the same needs, they may be able to get programs to add these services. Work-related day-care programs are good examples of how businesses have met the special needs of their employees.

Good programs for young children cost money. Costs of programs are rising due to increased costs of staff salaries, buildings, and equipment and supplies. Costs of programs vary with the type of program, days and hours of care, age group served, and location.

Families may or may not have to pay all of a program's costs. *For-profit programs* (programs that are businesses in that they are set up to make money) get most, if not all, of their income from charges to families. These programs are the most costly to families. *Not-for-*

Fostering development in group settings   493

26-13 Programs for exceptional children offer needed services for these children.

profit programs (programs in which income only covers costs) are often mainly funded from non-family sources such as state and federal government, churches, and service groups. Families do not pay any of the costs or pay a small fraction of the total costs. Families do fund not-for-profit programs that are operated as *cooperatives* (co-ops). Through co-ops, parents keep their cash costs down by offering services (work without pay) and donations (gifts such as toys).

Families must decide what they can afford and try to get the best program for their money. See 26-14. How much a family can afford depends on income and expenses. Often families use the figure of 10 percent of the total gross income for the entire family to meet their child care needs. Besides the direct costs, families need to look at the costs in terms of *hidden added costs*. These are costs that add to the direct costs such as costs of transporta-

tion, supplies, and disposable diapers and formula (for babies). Families must also consider *hidden cost credits*. These are credits that lower direct costs of child care. They include money that may be added from a second income. They also include money saved in the cost of utilities and food for at-home care and child care tax credits.

EFFECTS OF GROUP CARE ON CHILDREN'S DEVELOPMENT

The effects of group care depend on the reasons families want their children in programs and the help families give children during the adjustment period. Effects also depend on the quality of the preschool programs.

Reasons families enroll children

Parents give many reasons for placing children in group programs. Many parents feel

26-14 Families must decide whether they can afford programs with such extras as swimming lessons.

HOME LIFE AND GROUP LIFE DIFFER

Home life is . . .	Group life is . . .
Housed mostly in an adult-sized world with many objects off limits.	Housed mostly in a child-sized world with few objects off limits.
Equipped with some toys.	Equipped with many toys.
Contact with one adult in most cases.	Shared time with one or more adults.
Playing alone or with siblings for the most part.	Playing with other age-mates.
Having experiences in many home-care tasks such as cooking, laundry, running errands, and taking care of a new baby.	Having more experiences that are planned for children such as art, music, science, and group games.

26-15 Group life cannot replace the teachings of home life. But when quality group life is used to support and enrich home life, children grow in many ways.

that programs can help their children grow in mental and social ways. Other parents need programs to care for their children while they work. Some parents enroll their children because they need relief from full-time care for health or other reasons. A few parents want their children to attend a program for a few hours a day or one or two days a week. These parents keep their children at home for most of the time.

Families need to understand that group care can enrich—but cannot replace—home life. Group care is not better than a good home life; group care is different. Chart 26-15 contrasts home and group care. Studies have been done on the effects of group programs on children's health, mental development, and social development.

Effects on health

There has been some concern over the health of young children enrolled in group programs. Studies do not agree on the number of common illnesses in enrolled children versus children not enrolled. But there seems to be no increase in serious illness in children who attend programs that follow good health practices. Families should consult their doctors about what is best for their children.

Effects on mental development

Group programs do not seem to have either a positive or negative effect on the mental development of children from middle-class homes. But as a whole, group programs offer more activities in certain areas than do most homes. Programs such as Head Start can help the mental development of children from low-income families. If gains from such programs are to remain stable, however, there must be home and school follow-up for many years.

Effects on social development

Since the early 1900s, there has been concern that group programs weaken bonds between children and their families. Many recent studies do not find the child-family bond hurt due to care in group programs. One example is a recent two-year study (the Harvard Study) that was made of children between the ages of three and one-half months and two and one-half years. The Harvard Study found that even constant day-long separation of these children from their families did not change the importance of the family in the child's life.

Some studies do show that children are more aggressive as a result of group programs. Contacts with peers tend to increase aggression in children because they must stand up for themselves. On the positive side, children may be learning needed coping skills that will help them in the future, 26-16.

JOHN SHAW

26-16 In group programs, children must learn to share with others.

The adjustment period

The change from home care to group care is a time of adjustment for children who are six months of age and older. These children have separation anxiety. Even young school-age children may feel a bit uneasy for the first few days away from home.

Adults need to make the adjustment seem casual. Adults can make a child more anxious by talking too much. Adults can be anxious, too. Adults must do their best to stay calm and confident. Even if adults only look anxious, children tend to cling more. Adults should also show that they are sure of the child's ability to adjust. For instance, they may say, "I know there are many new boys and girls, but you *will* make new friends. Everyone is new for a while."

About a month before enrolling a child in a group program the adult should explain what the new program is like. For instance, he or she may explain that there will be other children, toys, and activities. Adult and child should visit the program if possible.

Some children do not make an adjustment even after a few weeks. In these cases, adults should either try other programs or work with children in making a slower adjustment. For instance, children may need to play with other children in their own homes and in their friend's homes. See 26-17. Later these children may stay in group care for short periods of time. This might include nursery care during religious services or temporary care in group programs while adults do a few errands. Once these adjustments are made, children often adjust to group programs with less stress.

Quality of group programs

Only high quality programs can have good effects. High quality programs have been described earlier in this chapter. But you cannot judge a program by simply meeting the adults, seeing the indoor and outdoor areas, and noting the papers that say that the program is meeting standards. See 26-18. The only way

26-17 Children who have trouble adjusting to group programs may need to spend time with one or two other children as a step in adjusting.

PLAYWORLD SYSTEMS

26-18 Having nice outdoor areas for play is only one quality of good programs.

to be sure of the quality of a program is to get involved. Families need to quickly recognize programs that are not safe for children. These are signs of poor programs:

* Programs that people cannot visit without asking. Programs should welcome parents' visits at any time.
* Programs with staff who are not trained to work with young children.
* Programs that do not take special interests in children's needs. Programs having large groups of children and few adults are more likely to have this problem.
* Programs that push children to perform above their abilities and thus cause stress.

Adults need to remember that children are defenseless clients of programs which they attend. That is, young children cannot measure the quality of a program for themselves or take action if the quality is not good. Children are dependent on families to find quality programs for them. See 26-19.

26-19 Young children need to have adults find the best programs for them.

to Know

Casa dei Bambini . . . day care . . . field trips . . .
finger plays . . . Head Start . . .
hidden added costs . . . hidden cost credits . . .
Infant School . . . kindergarten . . .
Montessori schools . . . nursery schools . . .
private programs . . . public programs . . .
regulations . . . work-related day care programs

to Review

Write your answers on a separate sheet of paper.
1. True or false. Children have always been seen as different from adults in ways other than physical size.
2. Group programs for children are growing both in _____ and _____.
3. Match the names of the types of group programs with their descriptions. (You may use each name more than once.)
  a. Day Care programs.
  b. Kindergartens.
  c. Nursery schools.
  d. Montessori schools.
  e. Head Start programs.
____ Businesses may operate these for their employees' children.
____ Based on the methods used to help mentally handicapped children.
____ The oldest types of group programs.
____ Funded by government monies to help children of the poor overcome some of their problems.
____ Based on the idea, "play is the highest level of child development."
____ Stress that children absorb from their world as they work at tasks.
____ Have served as a laboratory setting for the study of children.
____ Today, most are operated on a for-profit basis.
____ Have a focus on sensory learnings and daily living tasks.
____ Part of the public education system in every state in the United States.
4. List five guidelines to use for choosing a quality day care program.
5. True or false. A tour of a facility (indoor and outdoor) is the best way to find out the quality of a program.
6. True or false. Children seem to be at a higher health risk for serious illnesses than children who stay at home.
7. _____ (Some, All) children who attend quality group programs do better mentally than children who stay at home.
8. Suggest three ways families can help their young children adjust to a group program.

to Do

1. Read a book or article on the life of one of the early pioneers in group programs for young children. Share your reading by preparing an oral report or a group skit.
2. Visit two or three group programs for young children in your area. Have a class discussion on how they differ in their goals.
3. Interview families about the needs of child care services in your area. Share your findings in class.
4. Examine a licensing manual in your state. Review the standards which must be met for family day care and group day care. Also scan the state fire and health department regulations.
5. Make a directory of child care programs in your area. The directory can include the name of program, owner, address, phone number, admission requirements, hours operated, and comments on special services or licensing. Copies of this directory could be placed in physicians' offices, the Chamber of Commerce, and other places where parents may read it.

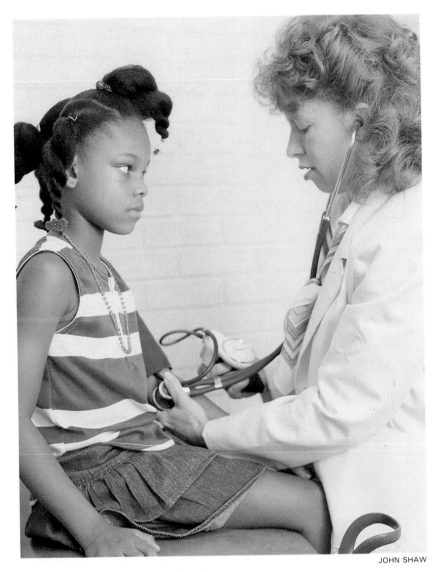

JOHN SHAW

There are many careers related to children.

27

Examining careers in child-related fields

After studying this chapter, you will be able to:
- ☐ Describe some of the careers in child-related fields.
- ☐ Explain how personal and professional qualifications affect your career choice.
- ☐ Describe the processes involved in finding a career.
- ☐ Explain several ways of getting involved in child-related careers.

You live in the midst of change. You cannot be sure of all the concerns people will be facing in the coming years. But there are some trends that you can use as guidelines as you explore career options. It is quite clear that one of these trends is an effort to improve the quality of child life for all children.

In the past, parents, often with the help of members of the extended family, reared their children with little or no outside help. Even agencies such as schools and hospitals were used only to a limited extent. In fact, stepping outside the family for some types of help was sometimes seen as a family failure. Over the years, family life has changed greatly. The support that the extended family provided is not as common. Families move more often, adding to the distance between the family and other relatives. There is a growing trend for mothers of preschool and school-age children to work outside the home.

In addition to these trends, many people now support the belief that a child has the right to a quality life. This has caused an increased demand for child-related services. Careers in child-related fields have grown out of the demands for services. And the demands for services are growing daily.

TYPES OF CAREERS IN CHILD-RELATED FIELDS

Careers in child-related fields may be described in many ways. One way to describe child-related careers is in terms of the amount of contact with children. In some careers, adults are involved in *direct intervention* with children. See 27-1. In other words, these adults work directly with children. People in such careers include elementary school teachers and pediatricians. In other careers, adults serve as *consultants*. These adults share their knowledge about children with other adults. For instance, college professors of child development may serve as consultants to teachers who work with children. Parent educators serve as consultants to parents-to-be and parents. In other careers, professionals are involved in *product development and sales* for children. These adults do not often work directly with children or serve as consultants. They use their knowledge of children to design and sell products such as toys, clothing, furniture, records and films, and educational materials.

Careers in child-related fields may also be described in terms of general career fields. Six areas to consider are health and protective services; care and education; entertainment; design; advertising, marketing, and management; and research and consulting.

Health and protective services

There has been an increased demand for physical and mental health services for children. Adults in these services have a good background in their area of health care. However, they have special knowledge of the health needs of children. Adults may provide health services in these positions:

- Pediatricians—physicians who specialize in the care of children.

JOHN SHAW

27-1 Teaching is one career that involves direct intervention with children.

- Pediatric dentists—dentists who specialize in the care of children. See 27-2.
- Pediatric nurses and school nurses—nurses who specialize in the care of children.
- Child psychologists—professionals who specialize in the emotional and mental health of children.
- Dietitians—specialists in nutrition who may plan the diets of healthy children and of children with special food needs.
- School food service personnel—people who plan school menus and prepare and serve food to meet the needs of children.

Adults who have careers in *protective services* work to find injustices to children. These adults also work to correct poor situations. Positions include juvenile officers and judges, child welfare workers, and *licensing personnel*. (Licensing personnel check the quality of certain services for children such as day care.) Careers in protective services are increasing as society broadens its concerns for the rights and needs of children.

Care and education

As you read in Chapter 26, more young children are enrolled in group settings than ever

27-3 Teachers who have knowledge in special subjects such as computers are needed in education careers.

before. Private programs are growing in number. And government agencies on both the federal and state levels are committed to the education of children. See 27-3. Public support

JOHN SHAW

27-2 Caring for children's teeth and gums is one of the many careers in health and protective services.

Examining careers in child-related fields 503

can be seen in the growth of public school kindergartens and programs for even younger children, in services for exceptional children, and in Head Start and other programs to help the poor.

Care and education careers can be found in both public and private settings. These careers are included:

- Child care personnel—people who care for infants, toddlers, preschool children. They may care for school-age children during after-school hours and holidays.
- Teachers and teacher aides—professionals who teach and assist teachers in public and private school programs serving children of all ages.
- Special education teachers—teachers who work with children who have handicaps or other learning problems. Many specialize in one or two types of learning problems or handicaps.
- Administrators—directors of child care and education programs and principals and supervisors of school programs.
- Children's librarians—specialized librarians who work in school libraries or in children's sections of other libraries. They often read stories to children and design programs to help children learn to read for fun.
- High school teachers and college professors—Professionals who are involved in many fields concerning children's health, education, and welfare.
- Child and youth leaders—people who work with children in religious programs, youth organizations such as scouting groups, recreational programs, and camps.
- Recreational instructors—professionals who guide or teach children in such areas as music, art, dance, and hobbies.

Care and education careers are growing in numbers. Some people predict that there will be a day care crisis before the year 2000 due to the lack of programs and teachers. There seems to be even more of a demand for teachers with special skills. See 27-4.

DILCON SCHOOL, BUREAU OF INDIAN AFFAIRS

27-4 Teachers who can provide instruction in two or more languages are in demand as society seeks to meet the needs of diverse cultural groups.

27-5 Quality entertainment brings joy and laughter to children's lives.

Entertainment

The growth of careers in children's entertainment is rather recent. Entertainment planned for children did not exist until people began to see children as different from adults. Even when children were no longer seen as miniature adults, children's entertainment was limited to plays, books, and a few games.

In recent years entertainment in general has become a big business. As a result, children's entertainment has expanded greatly. Many new children's television programs, movies, and live programs have been produced. A wider variety of children's books and games are available. People in entertainment careers include producers, directors, writers, actors, and musicians. See 27-5.

Design

Design careers have followed a pattern of development similar to the pattern of entertainment careers. As people began to see children as different from adults, they designed items with children in mind. Children's items were designed to better meet children's physical, mental, and social-emotional development. The new concern has affected the design of clothes, buildings, furniture, and toys. See 27-6. Designers of these items need an understanding of child development as well as artistic talent and knowledge of design.

27-6 Children need products such as toys designed just for them.

Examining careers in child-related fields 505

Advertising, marketing, and management

With the number of products for children increasing, people who understand children's needs are becoming an important part of many businesses. Careers in advertising, marketing, and mananging in businesses which produce and sell children's products are growing. As with design careers, sensitivity to children's needs is helpful. Career positions are available in large corporations, agencies, and firms. Positions are also available in smaller, local businesses. See 27-7.

Research and consulting

Research on children is being conducted in all fields such as health, education, entertainment, design, and business. See 27-8. Research studies provide knowledge that people need to serve children in the best ways known. The field of research is growing so rapidly that there is a massive amount of information. For instance, over 100,000 research studies on children's education alone are published each year. The major problem is getting this information to those involved in education careers.

Consultants work as team members with other adults on behalf of children. They are the major knowledge link between researchers and others involved with child-related careers. Consultants relay information to those in careers involving direct intervention with children, product development, and selling. Some adults serve as consultants on a daily basis. Such people include child development experts who provide state and federal lawmakers with needed information. Other adults work as consultants when called upon for written or oral input. With knowledge increasing daily, consultant careers will become more in demand.

Chances for self-employment

The careers just discussed and others related to children offer many chances for self-employment. Businesses that are owned by one person are called *entrepreneurships*. The most common child-related entrepreneurships are in day care. Such businesses are usually in-home day care, but some are day care centers. Many

JOHN SHAW

27-7 In the business world, sales clerks in children's stores or departments have daily contact with children.

EDUCATIONAL TEACHING AIDS

27-8 Researchers are needed in all fields concerned with children and their needs.

other careers work well for self-employment. These include child photography, recreational instruction, and private medical practice.

Self-employed people must have many skills other than those related to their specialty. For instance, owners of day care centers must know much more than how to teach and care for children. They must be able to manage money. They must charge clients enough to pay for supplies, rent, salaries, and other expenses involved in running a day care center. They must find ways to advertise their center. Owners must be sure that their centers comply with any laws that apply to day care centers. And they may serve as managers to day care workers, receptionists, and other workers.

Many people find owning their own businesses rewarding, 27-9. They like having the freedom to run their business the way that they see as best. And they may like the variety of being able to fill different roles—teacher, manager, budget director. But there are drawbacks to consider. Owners of entrepreneurships may be required to use their personal money if the business goes into debt. Although they may ask for advice, business owners must make their own decisions about the business and live with them. And many owners work longer hours than they would if they were employed by others.

If you are prepared to meet the challenges of ownership, the prospects are good. Creativity, knowledge, and hard work can make your business both rewarding and profitable.

If you have the skills, knowledge, and energy, you may enjoy starting and running your own business. Self-employment in child-related fields can be satisfying and profitable.

JOHN SHAW

27-9 Owning a business is hard work, but many people find it rewarding.

HEADING TOWARD A CAREER

There is an increasing interest in children's development and concern about ways to meet children's needs. Adults in both families and child-related careers are most important in the lives of children. If you choose to work with children, you must be qualified to meet children's needs in the best ways. And you must be prepared to find and secure a job.

Personal qualifications

Personal qualifications are all the traits you possess that are not taught as part of the training for a career. These traits are part of your total life—during working and non-working hours. Personal traits are harder to define and measure than learnings which are the result of career training. For this reason, very little research has been done on personal qualifications. Thus, only general traits can be described.

Concern for children. The most important personal qualification is a deep concern for children. See 27-10. Sometimes, in the effort to perform well—for example, to teach the perfect lesson—people lose sight of the most important concern of all, the child. If you work directly or indirectly with children, you must always measure a practice or product in terms of what will be best for the child.

Many qualities go along with being concerned for children. The importance of having the qualities depends on how closely you work with children. You need to be kind and patient with children and their families. You must be able to cope with children's noise and activity.

You should enjoy children's physical, mental, and social worlds. This includes children's games, songs, stories, and even humor. (For instance, children often tell "jokes" with the punch line missing.)

You need to feel comfortable in helping young children with physical needs. This might include helping with toileting or dressing. Or it might mean letting a child show you a sore throat or loose tooth.

Finally, you must be able to accept physical closeness from young children. These children want to touch adults' clothing, jewelry, and hair. Sometimes they may do so with paint, dirt, or food on their hands. And children need adults who will hold their hands, hug them, and let them sit on the adult's lap.

Flexibility. In working with children, it is important to remain open to new ideas. People must perform on much less than complete knowledge about children. Therefore, they must keep seeking new insights.

Adaptability is also important because children can be very unpredictable. Research shows that the constant changes required in working with children often cause *career burnout*. Career burnout is a state in which a person becomes emotionally tired of a career. Career burnout may even lead to health problems from stress.

Leadership skills. No matter what kind of career you choose, you need to be a leader at times. Sometimes people take a *formal leadership* role. Formal leadership is used by elected officials and managers in an organized group. The group might be a club, committee, or business. These people have been chosen by others to lead the group. But often, people need to take an *informal leadership* role. When people are informal leaders, they lead or guide others even though they are not officially chosen to lead. People may be informal leaders within an organized group as well as outside of one.

Leadership involves motivating others to complete tasks or goals. Many qualities are needed to fulfill this role. Leaders must be able to communicate with others. They must have positive attitudes and help others keep a positive attitude. Leaders need to handle responsibility. This means following through to complete what is started, accepting blame for mistakes, and keeping promises. Leaders need to be good decision-makers who are confident in their choices. They should know how to set goals that will help the group fill its purpose. And they must be able to *delegate responsibilities* to others in a group. Delegating means giving responsibilities to others. It also means making sure that the others can handle the responsibility and finish the task.

JOHN SHAW

27-10 People who work with children should be concerned about children's well-being.

skills is through your high school chapter of *Future Homemakers of America—Home Economics Related Occupations (FHA-HERO)*. FHA-HERO has as one of its stated purposes, "to provide opportunities for decision-making and for assuming responsibility." FHA-HERO also encourages students and teachers to use this decision-making guide: a) identify concerns, b) set a goal, c) form a plan, d) act on the plan, and e) follow up on the activity planned.

Professional qualifications

Professional qualifications are all the physical, mental, and social-emotional skills you need to perform in a given career. See 27-11. Unlike personal qualifications, these skills are most often learned in training. Training might include classes in school or

Leadership ability is especially important when working with children. Children look up to all adults. Even if you are a volunteer helper in a day care center, you are a leader to the children there. Therefore you need to be self-confident. Your confidence will help children feel secure. And you need to be able to set limits and be firm with children. Children are not self-disciplined yet and they need your help to meet goals. Being able to listen patiently is important, too. Children may need to try several times before they explain something in a way that adults will understand.

Like other personal qualities, leadership qualities are a part of your total life, not just your working hours. Some people seem to have more natural leadership ability than others. But you can improve your ability through practice. Even babysitting gives you practice at making decisions and being responsible. So does being a member or an officer of a school club. For example, an excellent way to develop leadership

JOHN SHAW

27-11 Professional qualifications help this teacher meet both the regular and special needs of the children she serves.

Examining careers in child-related fields 509

college or on-the-job training. However, you may need an aptitude for learning these skills or certain background training. For instance, before you may study to become a pediatrician, you need a college degree in certain areas (often pre-medicine). You also need to score at a certain level on a test or tests designed to measure background knowledge. You might also need to submit references, be interviewed by faculty at medical school, and have physical examinations.

Child development is the basic science for understanding children. If you want to have a career in a child-related field, you must have a basic knowledge of child development. Because physical, mental, and social-emotional development are related, you cannot study one aspect without the other aspects. But professional training for a given career often stresses one aspect of development more than others. For instance, pediatricians deal more with physical aspects of development. But they still must be aware of how other aspects of development are affecting the child's health.

In addition to knowledge of child development, you need specialized knowledge in your career area. For instance, teachers must have specialized knowledge in these and other areas:
• Ways that children learn.
• What to teach and in what order to teach certain facts and skills.
• The best methods and materials for teaching the facts and skills.
• How to evaluate children's knowledge.

In some careers, there are specialties within a specialty. More in-depth learnings are required in these careers. For instance, there are *pediatric opthamologists*—children's eye physicians. These adults are trained in general medicine. Then they are trained to treat diseases of the eye. Finally, they are trained to care for children's eye problems. Because so few adults have specialties within specialties, these adults often serve as researchers or consultants. They may only directly handle the most difficult cases.

The training needed for a job is affected by the level of a job. For instance, there are many levels of positions within the field of day care.

The career ladder shown in 27-12 shows some of these levels. Day care aides and some day care workers do not need college degrees. They may have had some training in high school, vocational classes, community college, or college. Supervisors generally have at least bachelor's degrees in child development, early childhood education, or a related area. Many supervisors and most directors have master's degrees in a specialized area of child development. Consultants may have more than one master's degree or a doctorate degree.

Training needed is affected by the level of responsibility needed for a career. For instance, teachers have greater professional responsibilities than teacher aides. Some careers

27-12 People are needed at a variety of levels in the field of day care.

require study in schools and colleges and supervised work in the career field. Professional qualifications for other careers, such as entertainment, may be learned through on-the-job training.

In addition to basic career training, adults in child-related careers are expected to keep up with the latest knowledge and practice in their fields. See 27-13. Keeping up in a child-related career may require more classroom study, attending workshops or seminars, or study or practice on one's own. It may also involve on-the-job training in a different setting. Or it may involve exchanging knowledge and practices among those working in the many child-related careers.

Job search skills

Being qualified is one part of finding a child-related career. Another part is looking for and securing a specific job. Finding the job that you want can be hard work. There are many steps involved.

The first step is to determine what kind of job you want. Once you know that, you can find out where to look for jobs in that field. For instance, you may determine that you want to be a summer day camp counselor. You may find ads for such jobs in a local newspaper. Or you may call local park districts, schools, or churches to find out whether they offer such programs. Once you find out where such programs are held, you need to find out who handles hiring counselors and how to apply.

If you determine that you want a higher level job, you will probably need to write a *resume*. A resume is a short, written history of your education, work experience, and other qualifications for employment.

Next, you will need to set up a job interview. Some places allow you to set up an interview over the phone. Others prefer a written letter

BINNEY AND SMITH

27-13 Workshops help professionals keep up-to-date.

requesting an interview. See 27-14.

At some point, often just before the interview, you will fill out a job application. The application asks for such information as your name, address, social security number, educational background, and past jobs. It often asks for *personal references*—people who know you well enough to say whether they think you will make a good worker. Relatives usually can't be used for personal references. But past employers and former teachers can often be used.

At the interview, you need to put your best foot forward. Your personal appearance should be neat. As a rule, jeans do not make a good

```
                              1603 Green Street
                              Southland, Wisconsin  66732
                              April 15, 1990


    Mr. Craig Bear
    Program Director
    Happy Trails Day Camp
    Rural Route 3
    Southland Township, Wisconsin  66732


    Dear Mr. Bear:

    I am interested in working as a counselor-in-training at
    Happy Trails this summer.  My counselor at Southland High
    School, Mr. O'Brien, suggested that I contact you.

    Although I expect this job to be a good learning experience
    for me, I think I have much to offer you as an employee.  I
    have taken three child development classes in high school.
    In two of the classes, I worked for four hours per week in
    the school day care center.  While working there, I have been
    in charge of planning many activities including stories and
    plays, crafts, games, and snacktimes.  I am also a Sunday
    school teacher for a class of four first-graders.  I enjoy
    being with children and helping them.  In fact, I hope to
    open my own day care center after I graduate from college.

    Can we meet some time soon for an interview?  I will call
    your office on April 20 to see if we can schedule an
    appointment.  If you would like to talk to me sooner or if
    you have any questions, feel free to call me at 555-1525.
    Thank you for your time and consideration.


                              Sincerely,

                              Willa Holtz
                              Willa Holtz
```

27-14 Written letters are often used to set up an interview for a job.

impression at interviews. Clean, neat dress pants, dresses, or suits are appropriate (depending on the type of job that you want). Good posture, a pleasant smile, and good eye contact are also important in an interview.

You may want to rehearse the interview with someone before you go. That way you can anticipate some of the questions they will ask and give some thought to your answers. Sometimes you will be interviewed a second or third time before a decision is made.

Unless you are told differently, you will probably be contacted within a week to be told whether or not you are offered the job. If an offer is made, respond promptly and politely as to whether you accept the job. If you are not hired, it is still important to be polite and friendly. They may consider you for a future position.

HOW TO GET INVOLVED

Careers in child-related fields are on the increase. Competent adults will be needed to meet the many needs of children. You can begin thinking about careers and basic preparation in the teen and young adult years. In fact, some adults have stated that they became interested in a career during their elementary school years.

In order to make any wise career choice, you must get involved. There are many ways to get involved in child-related careers. The following ways can be used as starting points.

First, study and observe children's development. Take courses and read books on children's development. Observe children in group programs, with their families, and at play with friends.

Next, get involved with children and children's products. Babysitting is an excellent way to learn about children. See 27-15. Other ways are working as a volunteer assistant in a day care center, Sunday school class, or summer camp. Getting involved with professionals is helpful, too. You may be able to get tours or serve as an assistant in a business. Some teens and young adults may find paid positions which help them learn as well as earn money needed for further training.

Joining organizations which are concerned about children and their families will also help prepare you. You may want to join one or more of these organizations: Future Homemakers of America, The National Association for the Education of Young Children, and the Association for Childhood Education, International. Professional organizations publish journals, or magazines, to keep members informed on current child care issues. They also publish position statements (beliefs supported by research) and other materials to aid understanding of children. Almost all organizations have meetings that provide a means for finding out the latest news and for sharing ideas with others in child care.

Joining professional organizations also helps you show your interest in child care to others. For instance, your membership may help you show school officials the need for high school classes in child development. Organizations may give you the chance to work toward quality day

JOHN SHAW

27-15 Babysitting is one of the best ways to get experience in caring for children.

care programs. Joining a group says to parents and the public in general, "I am joining with others in an effort to provide the best for our children."

As you consider your future, talk with guidance counselors and professionals about the qualifications needed for certain careers. Also ask about the *employment opportunities*—positions presently open or expected to be open in that field. You also need to evaluate your own interests and personal qualifications. And you must consider your ability to acquire the needed professional qualifications.

Finally, begin to work toward entering the career. This may include taking certain background courses and getting better grades or increasing needed skills. It may also mean applying to schools or colleges or to businesses. And you may need to begin saving money needed for training or apply for loans or scholarships.

Choosing a career is serious. Careers are more than what you do for so many hours a day. To a great extent, careers influence many aspects of your *life-style*—the way you live. Careers often affect where you live, who you meet, what your income is, and what you consider to be important.

JOHN SHAW

This dance instructor enjoys working with children. Although mainly concerned with physical ability, knowledge of all aspects of child development is useful in her work.

to Know

career burnout . . . consultants . . . direct intervention . . . entrepreneurship . . . formal leadership . . . informal leadership . . . life-style . . . personal qualifications . . . personal references . . . product development and sales . . . professional qualifications . . . resume

to Review

Write your answers on a separate sheet of paper.

1. In general, careers in child-related fields are _____ (increasing, decreasing) in numbers.

2. True or false. All people involved in careers in child-related fields work directly with children.

3. _____ do not often work directly with children; instead they share their knowledge about children with other adults.

4. Name three items that people can design and sell for children.

5. Match the specific career with the career area by placing a letter or letters in each blank.

Career areas
_____ Health and protective services.
_____ Care and education.
_____ Entertainment.
_____ Design.
_____ Advertising, marketing, and management.
_____ Research and consulting.

Specific careers

a. Child welfare case worker.
b. Music teacher.
c. Speaker at an in-service meeting for teachers.
d. School librarian.
e. Pediatrician.
f. Architect of school buildings.
g. Dietition in a summer camp for overweight children.
h. Director of a children's holiday television special.
i. 4-H sponsor.
j. Juvenile judge.
k. Person who tests children's skills in walking balance beams and writes a report on the findings.
l. Manager in an advertising agency promoting a product for children.

6. True or false. An owner of a day care center must be able to manage money.

7. The most important personal qualification for working in a child-related field is:
a. Patience.
b. High level of intelligence.
c. Good physical health.
d. Deep concern for children.
e. Desire to work hard.

8. List three personal qualities needed by adults working directly with children.

9. Professional qualifications are mainly _____ (taught, not taught).

10. True or false. Professional qualifications for all careers in child-related fields require study in schools and colleges.

11. All adults involved in careers in child-related fields must have a basic knowledge of _____ in order to be effective.

to Do

1. Make a list of careers in child-related fields that are available in your area.

2. As a class or group project, compile a list of questions concerning careers in child related fields which you could use to find out more about a career. For instance, you could ask when the person first became interested in the field, why he or she became interested, and the personal and professional qualifications for those entering the same field. Interview one or more people involved in careers in child-related fields.

3. As an individual project, list some of your pesonal traits. Put them in order from weak to strong traits. Ask yourself how your traits match the desired personal qualifications of those entering careers in child-related fields.

4. Observe an effective teacher working with young children. Which personal qualifications for working with young children did this person exhibit? Discuss examples with your class.

5. Using information given by your school guidance counselor, prepare a chart of child-related occupations. List the occupation, pre-training needed, formal training needed, and on-the-job training needed.

6. Hold some mock interviews for jobs in child-related fields. Invite one or two employers (such as day care director or a toy store owner) to conduct the interviews. A few days before, choose four or five students to be interviewed. (Discuss some general interview procedures and possible questions with these students before the interviews.) After the interviews, have the employers share constructive comments on the strengths and weaknesses of the students during the interviews.

7. As a class, sponsor a babysitting clinic. (Find resources at the library or through government agencies.) Invite other students to attend.

Choking (THE HEIMLICH MANEUVER)

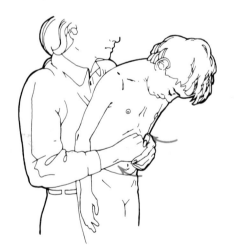

Call for help!

Do not slap child on back.
Do not hold upside down.
Do not probe throat with fingers.

1 Recognize choking.

A child found unconscious and not breathing and not showing signs of other injury is most likely choking. Lips and fingernails bluish. DO NOTHING if child is pink, talking or breathing.

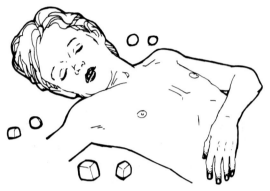

2 Pick child up from rear around the waist.

Place fist of one hand above navel but well below ribcage as pictured. Cover fist with other hand. (For very small children, use two fingers from each hand.)

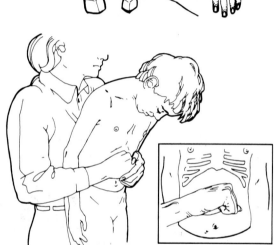

3 Pull upward with both hands quickly but gently three to four times.

Repeat if necessary to dislodge object from windpipe. (For very small children, lessen force of thrusts.)

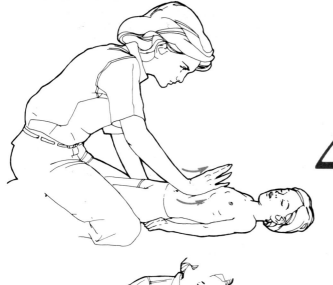

4 If child is too big to pick up, kneel over child as shown.

Place hands above navel, well below ribcage. Press upward into stomach with 3-4 quick thrusts. Repeat if necessary.

5 If all else fails, use back blows.

Drape small child or infant over arm or thigh so head is down. Child's abdomen should be against your arm or thigh. Strike child sharply three to four times between shoulder blades.

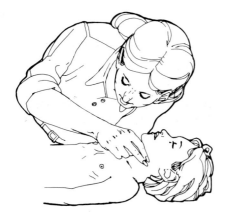

6 Watch breathing and check pulse.

Be prepared to give mouth-to-mouth breathing and chest compressions.

Bleeding

Call for help!

1 **Make sure child is breathing and has a pulse.**
If child is not breathing or does not have pulse in neck, take steps to clear the airway or administer CPR before you stop the bleeding.

2 **Apply direct pressure on bleeding wound with clean cloth.**

3 **Keep pressure on.**
Elevate limb above heart (unless broken limb).

4 **Bandage firmly but not tightly**
when bleeding is controlled.

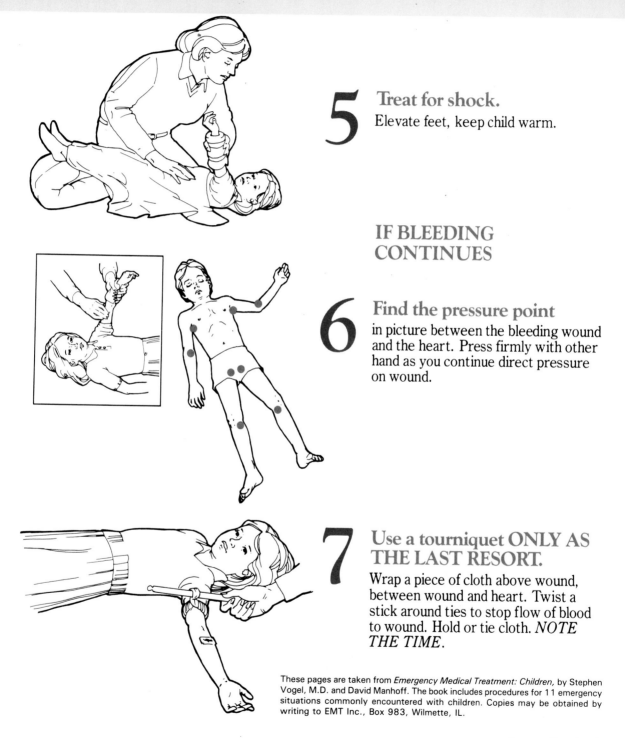

5 Treat for shock.
Elevate feet, keep child warm.

IF BLEEDING CONTINUES

6 Find the pressure point
in picture between the bleeding wound and the heart. Press firmly with other hand as you continue direct pressure on wound.

7 Use a tourniquet ONLY AS THE LAST RESORT.
Wrap a piece of cloth above wound, between wound and heart. Twist a stick around ties to stop flow of blood to wound. Hold or tie cloth. *NOTE THE TIME.*

These pages are taken from *Emergency Medical Treatment: Children,* by Stephen Vogel, M.D. and David Manhoff. The book includes procedures for 11 emergency situations commonly encountered with children. Copies may be obtained by writing to EMT Inc., Box 983, Wilmette, IL.

Appendix B *Signs of Child Abuse and Neglect*

When child abuse or neglect is suspected, it should be reported to the proper authorities so that help can be given. If you work with children, you may notice signs of abuse or neglect that should be reported. In fact, you may be required by law to report suspected abuse or neglect. The following signs will help you identify children who are abused or neglected.

NEGLECT

Physical Neglect Signs

- Is malnourished.
- Fails to receive needed health care without any parental religious objection.
- Fails to receive proper hygiene (not washed; not bathed; poor mouth care; skin, nails, and hair not groomed).
- Has insufficient clothing or clothing which is dirty or in terrible disrepair.
- Lives in filthy living conditions and/or inadequate shelter such as fire hazards.

Mental or Educational Neglect Signs

- Lacks moral training.
- Lacks constructive discipline.
- Fails to receive a good adult example.
- Fails to have adequate supervision.
- Is left alone for hours.
- Fails to attend school regularly due to faults of the parents.
- Fails to receive parent stimulation toward learning or to receive an education in keeping with a child's ability.
- Fails to be provided with wholesome recreational activities.

Emotional Neglect Signs

- Experiences constant friction in the home.
- Is denied normal experiences that produce feelings of being wanted, loved, secure, and worthy.
- Is rejected through indifference.
- Is overtly rejected such as abandoment.

ABUSE

Physical Abuse Signs

- Seems fearful or quiet around parents but has no close feelings for parents.
- Is wary of physical contact initiated by an adult.
- Has little or no reaction to pain and thus seems much less afraid than most children of his/her age.
- Has unexplained injuries or shows evidence of repeated injuries such as many bruises in various stages of healing and repeated fractures.
- Is dressed inappropriately for degree or type of injury such as a child clad in pajamas in an emergency room who was reportedly injured on a bicycle.
- X-rays indicate changes in long bones.
- Has injuries not given on previous health records.
- Has parents who have taken the child to many hospitals and physicians without appropriate explanation.
- Has parents who refuse further diagnostic studies of their child's injuries.
- Has parents who show detachment or see the child as bad or "different" during treatment of the child.
- Has parents who give too many minute details about cause of injury.
- Tries to protect parents during questioning about injuries.

Verbal Abuse Signs

- Has low self-concept.
- Is either too quiet and polite *or* uses harsh and improper language in dealing with others, especially those smaller in size or younger.
- Expresses long-term feelings of damage and isolation.

Sexual Abuse Signs

- Has extreme and sudden changes in behavior such as loss of appetite or sudden drop in grades.
- Has nightmares and other sleep problems.
- Regresses to younger behaviors such as renewed bedwetting or thumb sucking.
- Has torn or stained underwear.
- Has infections (with symptoms such as bleeding or other discharges and kitching) or swollen genitals.
- Fears a person or shows an intense dislike at being left alone with that person.
- Has a sexually transmitted disease or pregnancy.
- Has unusual interest in or knowledge of sexual matters.

Glossary

abstract symbolic representation: using such signs as words, numbers, or musical notation to represent the real world. The signs do not really resemble the things they represent.

abuse: intended physical, mental, or emotional hurt to a child.

accidents: unintentional harms that may happen to an adult or child.

accommodation: changing an old action to make it possible to work with a new object, such as changing the way a rattle was grasped to hold a cup without spilling.

accommodation of lens: the ability to have a visual image focused sharply on the retina.

Acquired Immune Deficiency Syndrome (AIDS): a sexually transmitted disease causing a breakdown of the immune system. AIDS may be transferred from mother to child in the birth process.

active immunity: immunity brought about because the body produces antibodies.

active-physical play: games and activities involving such gross motor skills as walking, running, hopping, jumping, twisting, bending, skipping, galloping, catching, throwing, balancing, pushing, pulling, and rocking.

active vocabulary: the words that a person understands and uses in talking or writing.

adoption: the process by which the child of one pair of parents (or parent) legally becomes the child of other parents (or another parent).

adoption agency: a state-funded or private agency licensed by the state to handle adoptions.

adrenaline: a hormone which prepares the body to cope with stress.

age-appropriate behaviors: expressing emotions in ways that are proper or normal for a person at a certain age.

age norms: average ages for children to reach certain points of development, such as talking, walking, or cutting teeth.

age of viability: the seventh month of pregnancy; the age at which the fetus could survive with special help if it was born.

aggregate: a design made up of three or more shapes.

aggressive behaviors: performing negative actions such as name-calling or fighting without being provoked into such actions.

alert inactive state: the state in which newborns are quiet but alert; the time when newborns learn and interact with people best.

alertness: ability to respond quickly.

altruistic behavior: showing concern for others.

amniocentesis: a test in which a needle is inserted through the woman's abdomen into the amniotic sac and a sample of the fluid is removed for a cell study.

amnion: a fluid filled sac that surrounds the baby in the uterus.

androgyny: having a gender role with qualities of both sexes.

anemia: a condition in which there is a low level of oxygen-carrying substances in the blood.

animism: giving life and human qualities to nonhumans such as plants, animals, and nonliving objects.

antibodies: agents in a person that prevent that

person from having a certain disease.

anti-Rh — immune globuline: a vaccine which prevents Rh − mothers from causing Rh disease in their Rh + babies.

anxiety: fear of a possible or future event.

Apgar test: a test used immediately after delivery to determine a newborn's chance for survival.

appetite: the desire for food.

articulation: making the sounds involved in spoken language.

artificialism: the belief that humans or human-like creatures cause all things.

art products: the finished art pieces that are made from art media.

assimilation: using a new object in the same way that a similar, old object was used, such as shaking a new rattle in the same way that an old rattle was shaken.

attachment: closeness between people that endures over a period of time.

attachment behaviors: showing a person that one feels close to that person through such actions as physical contact.

attention: ability to apply oneself to a task.

auditory acuity: the keen hearing of sounds.

authoritarian: a parenting style in which the main objective is to make children totally obedient.

autonomy: a form of self-control in which a person seeks to do his or her own will.

B

babble: to make a series of vowel sounds with consonant sounds slowly added to form syllables such as be, da, gi.

base line: in a drawing or painting, a line of grass, dirt, or water near the bottom of the paper used as the point on which all other objects in the picture rest.

behavior disorders: emotional problems that surface in a person's behavior.

binocular vision: the ability to see an object with both eyes at the same time.

birth control methods: methods used to prevent conception.

birthing room: a hospital room that is set up like a typical bedroom and is used for labor and delivery. Family members and a few close friends are allowed to stay in the room with the mother-to-be.

black market adoption: an illegal form of adoption in which payments are made beyond medical and legal costs to the agency, independent source, or natural parents.

blended family (stepfamily): a family that comes from the marriage of a single parent and a single person (never before married or married before but without children) or the marriage of two single parents.

body cells: cells which make up bones, nerves, muscles, and organs.

body rotation: the action of turning the trunk of the body to the left when the right hand is used to throw or turning to the right when the left hand is used.

bonding: developing a feeling of affection between parents and their baby.

brazelton scale: a test used to determine whether a baby is normal in these four behavioral areas: interaction with the environment, motor processes, control of physical state, and response to stress.

breech birth: a birth in which the baby comes out in a buttocks first position rather than a head first position.

C

cardinal numerals: numerals used to tell how many, such as four balls.

cartilage: soft, gristle-like tissue that is structural like bones, but more flexible.

Casa dei Bambini: an all-day program for slum children from ages two and one-half to seven that was set up by Maria Montessori in the early 1900s.

causality concepts: concepts that are formed about the interrelationship between cause and effect.

cell: the smallest unit of life that is able to reproduce itself.

centration: centering attention on just one aspect of an object or event instead of looking at all aspects at the same time.

cephalocaudal development: head-to-foot development.

Certified Nurse Midwife: a nurse with special training in delivering babies of normal pregnancies.

Cesarean (C-section) method: a method of delivery in which the mother's abdomen and uterus are surgically opened and the baby is removed.

character: an inward force that guides a person's conduct.

character definition: giving people labels such as shy, baby, or little mother.

child-centered society: a society that sees children as important and that works for the good of children.

child development: the scientific study of children from conception to adolescence.

childproofing: moving dangerous objects out of a child's reach or preventing a dangerous situation.

children in self-care (latchkey children): children who are at home alone after school or for a portion of the day and must care for themselves during that time.

chorion: the membrane that surrounds the baby in the uterus.

chromosomes: chemical compounds which contain all of the information needed to make a living thing look and function the way it does.

circulatory (cardiovascular) system: the heart and blood vessels.

class: a group of things that are alike in some property.

class complement: in classifying, any things that do not belong to the class.

class concept: a concept of a group of people, objects, events, or places that have something in common.

classification: mentally grouping objects by the ways they are similar.

cognition: knowing or understanding.

colic: a condition in which a newborn has intense abdominal pain.

collective monologue: talking to another person, but not listening to what the other person has said.

combine: a design made up of two shapes.

communication: the skill needed to understand others and to be understood by others.

compare: to see how things are alike.

compensate: to make up for a problem by excelling in another area.

concept: an idea formed by combining what a person knows about one person, object, place, quality, or event.

conception: the union of an ovum and a sperm.

concrete: based on actual experience.

concrete operational stage: Piaget's third stage of mental development in which children begin to think logically, but logic is based on what the child has at some time experienced.

concrete, 3-D representation: using three-dimensional objects such as dolls and blocks to represent the real world.

conservation: the concept that changing an object's shape, direction, or position does not alter the quantities of the object.

consultant: one who shares knowledge, such as knowledge about children, with other adults.

contagious disease: a disease which can be caught from another person.

contrariness: the tendency to oppose almost everything that is said by others.

contrast: to see how things are different.

control: the parents' practice of authority and responsibility of the welfare of their children.

convergence: the ability to focus both eyes on a single image.

convergent thinking: coming up with only one right answer or way to do something.

coo: a light, happy sound that babies begin to use for communication between six and eight weeks after birth.

coordination: the smooth working together of many muscles.

cortex: the section of the brain involved in perception, body movement, thinking, and language.

cradle cap: scaling of skin on the newborn's scalp.

crawling: moving by pulling with the arms but not lifting the abdomen from the floor.

creeping: moving by using hands and knees or hands and feet.

crossing over: the action in which a pair of

genes switch from their original chromosome to the one with which they are paired.

cruising: walking with the support of an adult.

culture: the way of life for a group of people; the group's language, attitudes, values, rituals, and skills.

D

day care: programs that operate for extended hours and offer services for children from babies to preschool age.

deaf: having such severe hearing loss that the sense of hearing cannot be used for learning and communication even with the use of hearing aids.

decentering perception: looking at two or more aspects of an object at the same time.

deciduous teeth: the first set of teeth in a person, later replaced by permanent teeth. Also called non-permanent, baby, and milk teeth.

deductive reasoning: reasoning from the general to the specific.

deferred imitation: seeing an action modeled by another person and then imitating that action at a later time.

delegate responsibilities: to give responsibilities to others and to make sure that the others can handle the responsibilities and finish the task.

democratic: a parenting style in which parents set some rules but allow children some freedom.

dental caries: decayed places in the teeth.

dependence: needing or wanting others to fulfill one's needs.

depressants: substances which slow down functions of vital organs and nervous system.

depression: a mental state where a person feels down and shows a decrease in many activities such as eating, sleeping, working, or playing.

depth perception: the ability to tell how far away something is.

development: the process of growth that goes on in a human from conception until death.

developmental tasks: tasks which Havighurst believes should be mastered at a certain stage in a person's life.

diabetes: a condition causing excess sugar in the blood and urine.

diagnosis: identifying the disease that is causing a person's illness.

diaper liners: thin sheets of a disposable material that is laid on a cloth diaper as an inner layer.

digestive system: esophagus, stomach, intestines, and glands that aid digestion.

dilation: the first stage of labor in which the cervix opens wider.

direct intervention: working person-to-person with children.

discipline: using different methods and techniques to help teach children self-control.

disposition: general mood, such as a tendency to be cheerful most of the time or a tendency to be grumpy most of the time.

divergent thinking: coming up with different possible ideas or different possible solutions to a problem.

dizygotic pregnancy: a multiple pregnancy in which children develop from two or more ova.

dominant trait: a trait which shows up in a person even if only one gene in a gene pair is for that trait.

double seriation: arranging objects in a series while keeping in mind two variables at the same time.

duo sentence: a two-word, telegraphic sentence commonly used by children around 18 months old.

dynamic balancing tasks: performing tasks that involve balancing while moving such as walking on a line.

dyscalcula: a learning disability in which people have trouble with math.

dyslexia: a learning disability in which people have trouble with reading.

E

egocentric: self-centered.

egocentrism: the belief that everyone thinks in the same way and thinks the same things as one person.

embryonic stage: the second stage of pregnancy lasting about six weeks.

emotional dependency: seeking attention, approval, comfort, and contact.

emotions: thoughts and feelings that cause changes in a person's body.

employment opportunities: positions presently open or expected to be open within a field of employment.

enactive representation: using one's own body, including the sounds one can make, to represent another person or an object.

enculturation: the process of handing down a culture from one generation to the next.

enriched environment: an environment with many objects, sounds, etc., to give a person a chance to learn.

entrepreneurship: a business that is owned and run by one person.

episiotomy: an incision from the vagina to the anus made to prevent tearing during the delivery of a baby.

erythroblastosis fetalis: a type of anemia which detroys the blood; Rh disease.

excretory system: intestine, kidneys, and bladder.

experimental children: a name sometimes used to describe firstborn children because parents often try new, untested ideas on them.

expulsion: the process of the baby or the placenta moving out of the mother.

extended family: a family of blood kin and spouses that lives in the same house or very close to each other. Generally, one older couple with their sons, daughters-in-law, and grandchildren live together.

extracellular fluid: fluid outside of the cells in the body.

eye-hand coordination: the ability to coordinate what a person sees with the way he or she moves his or her hands.

F

Fallopian tube: a hollow tube connected to the uterus with fingerlike projections that reach toward the ovary.

false labor: irregular contractions that happen in some women before true labor begins.

family culture: the beliefs and traditions of a family.

family day care: care provided for a small number of children in another person's home.

family history: stories of the family's past.

family planning: deciding on the number and spacing of children that a couple will have.

family rituals: customs that the family shares.

fetal stage: the third stage of pregnancy, lasting from about nine weeks after conception until birth.

fetus: a term used to describe a baby in the fetal stage of development.

field trips: trips that children enrolled in a program take that are off of the program's property.

fine-motor games: games which improve coordination in the small muscles, especially those in the fingers and hands.

finger plays: poems and rhymes which are acted out with the hands.

first aid: treatment for an illness or accident that is given immediately, before medical help.

flexibility: the ability to move, bend, and stretch easily.

folding over: in drawing or painting, showing a spatial idea by drawing objects perpendicular to the base line even when it means drawing objects upside down or sideways.

follicle: a small sac inside the ovary which stores an ovum.

forceps: a tool used during delivery to speed up the birth process. The tool is used to grip the baby's head and very gently pull or turn the baby.

foregone income: earnings given up by a parent or parents because a parent stays home to raise a child.

formal leadership: leadership used by elected or appointed officials and managers in organized groups.

for-profit programs: day care programs that are set up as businesses and designed to make a profit for the owners.

foster homes: families who take care of, but do not adopt, children who cannot live with their natural parents.

fraternal: brotherly; children of a dizygotic pregnancy.

G

gang years: a term often used to describe the elementary school years because peers become so important at this time.

gender role learning: knowing what is expected of a male or female in his or her own society.

genes: bead-like structures that are strung together to form chromosomes; they determine the various traits of a person.

germ cells: cells that are the basis for the growth of a person; sperm and ova.

germinal stage: the first stage of pregnancy which lasts about two weeks.

gifted children: children whose development is beyond or faster than average development in one or more areas.

grammar: the meaning given to word order.

gross-motor games: games which exercise the large muscles through such activities as rolling over, sitting, crawling, standing, walking, running, and jumping.

group day care: care provided for a fairly large number of children who are enrolled in a center.

growth pains: muscle pains caused by muscles trying to catch up with skeleton size.

growth spurt: a rapid period of growth, usually associated with adolescence.

guidance: all of a person's actions and words around children, affecting the way children think and act.

guilt: feeling blame for something that a person thinks is wrong.

H

handicapped children: children whose development is below or slower than average in one or more areas.

hand preference: ease in using one's right or left hand.

hard-of-hearing: not being able to hear well, but having the ability to use the sense of hearing for learning and communication. Some hard-of-hearing people use hearing aids.

Head Start: a federally funded program that provides extra medical care, nutrition, and learning help to low-income children who do not get enough care at home.

hearing impaired: having hearing loss ranging from hard-of-hearing to deafness.

heredity: all of the traits from blood relatives that are passed down to a child.

hidden added costs: costs that add to the direct cost of day care such as costs of transportation, supplies, and disposable diapers.

hidden cost credits: savings or earnings that lower the direct costs of child care, such as being able to earn a second income and saving money on the cost of utilities and food for at-home care.

holophrase: a single word used to have the meaning of a sentence, commonly used by children one year to 18 months old.

hospitalization: being cared for in a hospital.

hostile aggression: aggression intending to hurt another.

hyperactive behaviors: moving around much more than average people do, having a short attention span, and acting before thinking.

hypertension: high blood pressure.

I

identical: children of a monozygotic pregnancy.

identification and modeling: the process by which a person begins to think and behave as though the characteristics of another person belong to him or her.

identity concept: a concept of each particular person or object that is part of a baby's world.

imitating: copying the actions of someone else.

imitative-imaginative play: play in which children pretend to be persons or objects other than themselves.

immunity: having agents which prevent a person from developing a disease.

immunization: an injection or drops that are given to a person to provide immunity to a certain disease.

independence: wanting to do things for oneself.

independent adoption: an adoption in which a person such as a lawyer, physician, or clergyman works out the details. In some independent adoptions, no one works between the natural and adopting parents.

indirect costs: resources other than actual expenses spent on something such as child care that could have been used to meet other goals.

Individual Education Plan: an educational plan that is tailored to the special needs of an exceptional child.

inductive reasoning: reasoning from specific facts to general conclusions.

Infant School: a day care program that originated in Europe that provided care for children from the toddler years to age five or six.

inflections: changes in pitch.

informal leadership: the ability to lead or guide others even though a person is not officially chosen to lead.

in-home care: care for children provided by a person who is hired to come into the home to provide care.

initiative: the ability to think or act without being urged.

inoculation: an injection or drops that are given to a person to provide immunity to a certain disease.

instrumental aggression: aggressive acts taken because a person wants to achieve a goal.

instrumental dependency: need for help in achieving a goal.

intellectual development: development of a person's mind including how a person learns, what the person learns, and how he or she expresses what is learned.

intensive care nursery (ICN): a nursery with special lifesaving and support equipment used for newborns with special health problems that require immediate care.

internalized: something that is thought about but is not shared with others.

intolerance: a negative reaction to eating a food, such as a rash or an upset stomach.

intrusive: a type of person who shows persistence in meeting a goal.

intuitive substage: a substage of the preoperational stage in which children can solve many problems correctly, but they rely on imagining how they would act out the solution rather than relying on logic.

inversion: carrying out a task or thought in reverse, or inverted, order.

isolette: a heated, completely enclosed bed with two slightly larger than arm-sized doors that open and close to permit care. The bed is used for an infant who needs intensive care.

J

joint custody: an agreement between divorced parents in which both parents are involved in decisions affecting their children's lives.

K

kindergarten: a publicly or privately funded program for four- and five-year-old children that encourages play and treats children with tender care and nurturance; literally, children's garden.

L

labor: the process by which the baby is moved out of the mother's body.

Lamaze method (psychoprophylactic method): a type of delivery in which the pregnant woman uses breathing patterns to keep her mind off of pain rather than using drugs.

language: a symbol system in which words are used as labels for people, objects, and ideas.

language-logic play: a form of mental play common in school-age children that may involve play with words such as word puzzles or puns, strategies, or problem-solving.

large-muscle development: development of the muscles of the trunk, arms, and legs.

laterality: the ability to tell the difference between the left and right sides of the body and to prefer one side to the other.

learning disabilities: handicaps in one or more areas involved in spoken or written language, mathematics, and spatial orientation.

Leboyer method: a method of delivery which focuses on making the baby as comfortable as possible during and immediately after delivery.

legally blind: having no vision or only having the ability to see light, colors, shadow forms, or outlines of large objects.

letter reversal: writing the mirror image of a letter such as writing "b" for "d."

licensing personnel: people who check the quality of certain services for children such as day care.

life-style: the way a person lives.

lightening: a change in the position of the unborn, most common during the last few weeks of pregnancy.

linear mock writing: a special scribble that young children use to represent writing which is made of connected, looping lines.

literate: able to handle symbol systems such as the English language.

locomotion: the ability to move from place to place.

logical knowledge concepts: concepts not directly experienced through the senses; concepts developed through thought.

logical thinking: thinking that involves combining ideas or objects (adding), placing things in order (sequencing), or doing "if-then" thinking.

M

manipulate: to handle objects in various ways such as rolling, shaking, or bending.

manipulative-constructive play: activities and games that involve fine-motor skills, such as painting and stringing beads.

manipulative stage: a stage in working with art media in which children play with the media rather than trying to create something.

memory: ability to retain and recall information.

mental images: symbols of objects and past experiences which are stored in the mind.

mentally handicapped: having intellectual abilities that are a year or more behind the norm.

middleborns: the second children in families of three siblings and the second and third children in families of four siblings.

middle childhood: the period of development from ages six through 12.

mirror twins: identical twins that look the way a person and that person's mirror image would look.

mobile: in a state of moving or relocating frequently.

monologue: talking to oneself.

monotone: sounds all in the same pitch.

monozygotic pregnancy: a multiple pregnancy in which chilren develop from a single ovum united with a single sperm.

Montessori schools: schools which encourage children to learn as they work at tasks. Children are allowed to roam freely and participate in whatever tasks they wish.

motoric: involving action.

motor skills: skills involving muscle movement, such as crawling, walking, and manipulating objects.

multiple classification: classifying by two or more qualities at one time.

multiple-generation family: a family in which grandparents or other older relatives live with younger family members.

multiple pregnancy: a pregnancy in which two or more babies develop.

multiple-word sentence: a sentence with three or more words.

muscle development: lengthening and thickening of muscles.

myelin: a covering of a white, fatty substance that forms around individual nerves.

N

natural childbirth: a method in delivery in which the pregnant woman has the birth process explained to reduce fear and is taught breathing and relaxation techniques to reduce pain and assist delivery rather than using drugs.

neglect: failure in properly meeting the needs of children.

neonate: the medical term for a baby from birth to the age of one month.

neonatology: a branch of pediatrics concerned with newborns.

neural growth: brain and nerve growth.

not-for-profit programs: day care programs in which the program's income only covers the costs of operating the program.

nourishment: food which aids growth and development.

nucleus: the center of a cell. It contains the hereditary blueprint for that cell.

numerals: the written names for numbers such as four, IV, and 4.

nursery school: an educational program planned for children ages two, three, and four.

nurturance: all aspects of child care including feeding, dressing, bathing, and meeting emotional needs.

nutrient density: the level of nutrients in a food in relationship to the level of calories in the food.

nutrients: the substances in food that give a person energy and aid growth.

nutritionist: a person who studies the food needs of people.

O

obedience: acting within limits set by others.

object concept: gaining an understanding of an object; having object identity and object permanence concepts for that object.

object constancy: the concept that objects remain the same even if they appear slightly different due to changed perception.

object identity: understanding that an object stays the same from one time that it is seen until the next.

object permanence: understanding that people, objects, and places still exist even when they are no longer seen, felt, or heard.

obstetrician: a physician skilled in the medical care of a pregnant woman through the time she gives birth and for the six or more weeks of recovery from the birth.

one-to-one matching (one-to-one correspondence): understanding that if objects in two sets are matched and no objects are left over in either set, the sets are equal.

operations: thought processes that are based on logic more than perception.

ordinal numerals: numerals used to tell order, such as the second week.

orthodontist: a dentist who specializes in treating teeth that are not straight.

ossification: the hardening of bones caused by depositing calcium and phosphorous in them.

ostracism: removal from the group.

overextending: referring to different objects by the same name if the features are the same or almost the same.

overprotection: preventing or retarding a child's growth toward social maturity.

overrestricting: using a general term to mean a specific person or object.

ovum: female sex cell; egg.

P

passive immunity: the newborn's immunity to diseases brought about by antibodies that were passed to the infant from the mother through the placenta.

passive observing: watching another's actions without responding.

passive vocabulary: the words that a person understands, but does not say.

paternity leave: an unpaid, six-month leave of absence for a father after the birth of his child. At the end of six months, the father must be offered a job and salary comparable to the one he left.

pediatrician: a physician skilled in the medical care of children.

peer acceptance: approval from one's age-mates.

peers: children who are around the same age, but not brothers and sisters.

perception: organizing information that comes to a person through the senses.

perceptual learning: the process of developing perception.

percussion instruments: musical instruments that produce a tone when some part of the instrument is struck.

permanent teeth: the teeth that are intended to last a person's lifetime; they are harder and less sharp than baby teeth.

permissive: a parenting style in which parents give children almost no guidelines or rules.

personal qualifications: all the traits that a person possesses that are not taught as part of the training for a career.

personal references: names of people given to a prospective employer by a job applicant. The employer may contact these people to ask questions about the applicant's work habits and qualifications.

physical control: spanking and other physical forms of punishment used for discipline.

physical knowledge concepts: concepts about the size, shape, color, texture, and other qualities of objects and people.

picture books: books in which pictures carry the theme rather than words.

PKU (phenolketonuria): a disease which, if left untreated by diet, causes mental retardation.

placenta: an organ filled with blood vessels which nourishes the baby in the uterus.

play: a self-chosen activity which is done for its own sake.

play therapy: a method used by trained counselors in which play is used as a way to help children with their problems.

positive signs: signs of pregnancy which physicians identify as definitely caused by pregnancy.

postnatal care (postpartum care): care the mother receives in the six to eight weeks following the birth of her baby.

postpartum blues: a down feeling experienced by some women within a few days after pregnancy. The feeling is caused by hormone changes.

potential: the greatest amount or level of something that a person can attain.

precision: ability to perform motor skills accurately; involving balance, steadiness, and skill in aiming at a target.

preconceptual substage: a substage of the preoperational stage in which children are developing some concepts, but many concepts are incomplete or not logical.

prehension: holding an object by pressing the thumb and the four fingers against each other.

prenatal development: the development that takes place between conception and birth.

preoperational stage: the second of Piaget's developmental stages in which children have begun to do some mental thinking rather than solving all problems by acting, but thinking is not yet truly logical.

preschool children: children between the ages of three and five years.

presumptive signs: signs of pregnancy that could be symptoms of something other than pregnancy.

primary circular reactions: learnings that babies have from acting on their own bodies and by repeating the actions often.

primary dose: the main treatment given to provide immunity for a disease.

principles of growth and development: statements of the general patterns in which growth and development take place in people.

private programs: day care programs owned by individuals, churches, or other non-government groups.

problem solving: noting a problem, observing and questioning what one sees, and solving the problem.

product development and sales: an area of business involved with designing usable products and selling them to consumers.

professional qualifications: the physical, mental, and social-emotional skills needed to perform in a given career.

projective spatial concepts: the ability to describe a familiar pathway.

prop box: a collection of real objects that fit a certain role such as nurse or store clerk. The box is used by children as they pretend to take on that role.

properties: qualities of objects that can be evaluated with the senses such as color, size, shape, and texture.

protective services: a career area involved with finding injustices to children and correcting poor situations.

proximodistal development: center-to-extremities development; for instance, ability to control the trunk first, then the arms, then hands, then fingers.

psychosocial crises: stages developed by Erikson in which people must complete certain tasks to adjust well in society.

psychological discipline: correcting or punishing children without using physical punishment; discussing problems with children.

psychological security: a feeling that someone cares and will help a person when needed.

public programs: day care programs funded by

federal or state monies.

pupillary reflex: the tendency of the pupil of the eye to widen and narrow with changes in the amount of light.

Q

quality time: a time when a person is totally available for another person.

R

reaction time: time required for a person to react to a sight, sound, or other stimulus.

reading vocabulary: all the words that one can read.

recessive trait: a trait which does not show in a person if only one gene in the gene pair is for that trait.

reciprocity: understanding that if matter stays the same in quantity, a change in one dimension is made up for in another dimension.

reduplication babbling: repeating the same syllable over and over again such as da-da-da-da.

reflexes: automatic, unlearned behaviors.

registered dietitian: a professional with special training in nutrition and diet who meets the qualifications of the American Dietetics Association.

regression behaviors: behaviors which are outgrown, but are returned to in times of stress.

regulations: standards that govern group programs regarding staff, housing, equipment, services, business operations, and other areas.

representation stage: a stage of working with visual arts in which children create symbols that represent objects, experiences, and feelings.

repressed jealousy: jealousy that is not directly expressed or that may even be denied.

respiratory system: windpipe and lungs.

responsibility: the ability to do what is required or expected on one's own.

restraint system: a car seat, harness, or other device which holds a person safely in place within a car during accidents or sudden stops or turns.

resume: a short, written history of a person's education, work experience, and other qualifications for employment.

reversibility: the ability to follow a line of reasoning back to where it started.

Rh factor: a protein substance found in the red blood cells of about 85 percent of the population.

rhythm instruments: percussion instruments that do not produce a definite pitch, such as drums.

rights: powers or privileges that are enforced by law.

ritual: a pattern of activities repeated at a regular time, such as a bedtime ritual including a bath, a drink of water, a story, and a hug.

role guilt: a feeling of not doing one's best in one role because a person has too many roles at one time. Role guilt is especially common among working mothers.

role strain: a feeling of having too many different jobs at one given time.

rote counting: counting by repeating the names of numbers in order much the same way as one learns a rhyme.

rubella: three-day measles.

S

school-age children: children ages six through twelve.

school avoidance (school phobia): a problem in which children are afraid of school.

secondary circular reactions: learnings that a baby gains from actions done to an object other than the baby itself that are repeated.

seek vertigo: to try to become dizzy.

self-assertion: doing what one chooses rather than doing what others want.

self-concept: the way a person feels about himself or herself.

self-dressing: dressing oneself without help from others. Many clothes include features to make self-dressing easier for young children.

self-esteem: the belief in oneself as a worthwhile person.

self-evaluation: judging oneself in terms of successes and failures.

self-restraint: the ability to control oneself.

self-righting tendencies: the tendency that humans have to become closer to normal with time.

self-talk: talking to oneself.

self-understandings: coming to understand and appreciate oneself as a person, and realizing that each person is unique and has self-worth.

sensitivity: the ability of a person to notice and react to his or her own environment.

sensorimotor stage: the first of Piaget's stages of development. In this stage, children use their senses and motor skills to learn and communicate with others.

sensory organs: organs involved in a person's ability to see, hear, smell, taste, and feel; eyes, ears, nose, taste buds, and skin.

sensory stimulation: providing an environment that encourages people to learn through the five senses.

separate identity: a feeling of being a distinct person.

separation anxiety: anxiety most common in babies caused by the fear that loved ones who leave them will not return.

sequenced steps: steps in growth and development that follow one another in a specific order.

seriation: mentally ordering a set of objects according to increasing or decreasing size, weight, volume, or another quality.

sex chromosome: the chromosome that controls a person's sex. The X chromosome is for female traits and the Y chromosome is for male traits.

sex typing: treating boys and girls differently.

sexually transmitted diseases (STDs): highly contagious diseases passed from one person to another mainly through sexual contact.

Siamese twins: twins that are joined in one or more places.

siblings: brothers and sisters.

signs: symbols that are given meaning by society.

single parent family: a family that is headed by one adult.

singletons: children born one at a time, as opposed to twins or other children of multiple births.

skeletal system: the portion of the body made of hard, structural tissue; the bones and teeth.

small-muscle development: the development of the small muscles, especially those of the hands and fingers.

social: a relationship between two or more people.

social-emotional development: development of a person involving the person's disposition, interaction with other people and social groups, and expression of feelings.

social isolation: feelings of being alone and having no one to talk to about problems and feelings.

socialization: the process of learning the skills and attitudes needed to get along with family members and other social groups.

social policy: action taken throughout a society such as child labor laws, child custody laws, required schooling laws, and standards for day care centers.

sole proprietorship: a business that is owned by one person.

solids: foods other than breast milk which may or may not be in solid form.

sound substitution: replacing one sound for another in speech, such as replacing a "t" for a "k."

spatial orientation: the ability to see the relationship of one's body to objects in space.

spatial rotations: turns of objects in space. These rotations affect a person's ability to picture things from different directions and affect such skills as reading maps.

speech impaired: having speech so different from others that it calls attention to itself, cannot be understood by others, or causes the speaker to have a poor self-concept.

spelling/writing vocabulary: all the words that one can spell orally or in writing.

sperm: male sex cell.

spontaneous abortion: miscarriage; premature termination of a pregnancy.

stage of one-way assistance: a stage of friendship in which give and take occurs, but it serves the separate rather than the mutual interest of friends.

stage of reciprocity: a stage of friendship in which friends help each other and work together to meet mutual goals.

state: one step within a series of steps, such as a ball at the top of the hill is one state in the process of rolling down the hill.

static balancing tasks: tasks involving holding one position while balancing such as standing on one foot.

stimulants: substances which speed up functions of vital organs and nervous system such as increasing heart rate.

stressors: things that cause stress.

substituting: using a known word in the wrong way because a person cannot recall or say the correct word.

symbols: anything used to represent a concrete object or event such as an action or a drawing.

symptoms: signs of an illness or injury.

T

tag question: a question which asks for a yes or no answer.

talented children: children whose development is beyond or faster than average development in one or more areas.

teachable moment: a time when a person can learn a new task because the body is ready, society requires, and the self is ready to master.

teething: the appearance of teeth as they come up through the gums.

telegraphic sentence: a sentence which only uses the most important words, usually used in the toddler years.

temperament: the tendency to react to the environment in a certain way such as cheery or grumpy.

temper tantrum: a sudden outburst of emotional anger.

terminally ill: having a disease which will result in death.

tertiary circular reactions: learnings gained by trying new actions and repeating the new actions.

the show: a small amount of blood in the mucous plug in the cervix. The plug becomes loose within 24 hours of the beginning of labor.

toilet training: the process by which adults help children achieve control over the excretory systems, namely bowel movements and urination.

toxemia: a metabolic disorder that affects blood, causing swelling.

training pants: pants used by children during toilet training to help lessen the mess of accidents. The pants have a multi-layered cotton fabric crotch.

transductive reasoning: a flaw in logic that involves associating actions that may not be related in the way that the person believes they are related.

transformation: a sequence of changes by which one state is changed to another.

transitional objects: objects that babies tend to cling to in times of fear, stress, or changes in routines. Some babies keep such objects with them at all times.

transition stage: a stage of development in which a person is passing from one stage to another.

transition time: a stage of development in which one change in a person triggers the need for many other changes.

transitivity: the ability to recognize a relationship between two objects or events by knowing the relationship between each of them and a third.

transparencies: X-ray type drawings in which the outside and inside of an object are shown at the same time.

2-D representation: symbolizing one's world through flat art media, such as drawing or painting.

two parent family: a family that lives in one household consisting of a father, a mother, and their biological children.

U

umbilical cord: the cord that connects the baby to the placenta.

uterus: the organ in which the baby is developed and protected until birth.

V

vaccination: an injection or drops that are given to a person to provide immunity to a certain disease.

vision handicaps: problems with vision ranging from problems with clear focus that can be corrected with glasses to such severe problems that the person cannot see at all.

visual acuity: ability to see a sharply focused image.

visual art media: materials used to produce visual art, such as crayons, clay, and paints.

visual arts: physical forms of art such as painting, constructing three-dimensional art forms, and photography.

visual cliff: a testing tool made by placing a sheet of heavy plate glass over fabric with a checkerboard design. On one side, the fabric is next to the glass, and on the other side, the fabric is several feet below the glass. The cliff tests the baby's depth perception.

visual coordination: the ability to turn the eyes in the direction of an object.

vocabulary: the words that a person understands and uses.

voiced: consonants formed with the mouth and vocal chords.

voiceless: consonants formed with the mouth and breath.

voluntary movements: movements that are not automatic; movements that are learned.

W

weaning: the process of taking a baby off the bottle to a cup, or the process of taking a breast-fed baby off of the breast to a bottle or cup.

weight shift: the change of weight from the back foot to the front foot.

withdrawn behaviors: behaviors that show a separation from the rest of society such as not relating well to other people, not wanting changes to occur, and poor self-concept.

word reversal: ordering the letters in a word backwards such as writing "was" for "saw."

working mothers (women): mothers (or women) who are paid for work beyond their homemaking tasks.

work-related day care programs: day care programs that are funded by businesses for the use of their employees.

Z

zygote: the fertilized egg.

Index

ACKNOWLEDGEMENTS

The author wishes to thank Thomas J. Roberts for providing the drawings on pages 118, 119, 136, 187, 188, and 189. Thanks are also expressed to Sue Roshto Heck for typing the manuscript.